THE
HISTORICAL
IMPORTANCE

of *Two Treatises of Government* cannot be overestimated. It is the work in which John Locke launched his momentous attack against autocratic monarchy—arguing that earthly rulers derive their rights, not from God, but from contracts made by men, and that the people have a right to rebel against a ruler who betrays that contract. In *Two Treatises* John Locke set forth his ideas on natural law, on the freedom and equality of all men, ideas that were to greatly influence Thomas Jefferson and the American Federalists.

It has been assumed that Locke wrote this volume to justify the Glorious Revolution of 1688 in England. Peter Laslett presents striking evidence that it was written approximately ten years earlier. Through the discovery of a manuscript believed to be Locke's final and perfected version, Laslett concludes that Two Treatises of Government *was a demand for a revolution, a far more radical and significant document than was long thought. This new edition is an important contribution to history; it is the result of painstaking research and inspired interpretation on the part of an outstanding scholar.*

Other Books of Interest

THE UNITED STATES POLITICAL SYSTEM AND HOW IT WORKS *by David Cushman Coyle*

A key to national, state and local politics by an authority in economics and political affairs.

(#MP487—60¢)

THE LIVING U.S. CONSTITUTION *edited by Saul K. Padover*

Complete text of one of the world's greatest documents and the history of its making.

(#MP412—60¢)

AMERICAN DIPLOMACY: 1900–1950 *by George F. Kennan*

A trenchant appraisal of U.S. foreign relations by a distinguished diplomat, former U.S. ambassador to the Soviet Union. (#MP360—60¢)

THE PRINCE *by Niccolò Machiavelli*

The classic work on statesmanship and power, the techniques and strategy of gaining and keeping political control. (#MP417—60¢)

JOHN LOCKE

TWO TREATISES
OF GOVERNMENT

A CRITICAL EDITION
WITH AN INTRODUCTION AND
APPARATUS CRITICUS

By

PETER LASLETT

*Fellow of Trinity College and Lecturer
in History in the
University of Cambridge*

REVISED EDITION

A MENTOR BOOK

PUBLISHED BY

THE NEW AMERICAN LIBRARY,
NEW YORK AND TORONTO

THE NEW ENGLISH LIBRARY LIMITED, LONDON

Attention is drawn to the note made to the original title-page (see page 170 of this volume), which shows that such titles as *Two Treatises of Civil Government,* or *The Second Treatise of Civil Government* are solecisms.

AMICIS SUIS

A.A.S.	A.S.
J.P.C.	N.J.M.
W.G.R.	W.J.L.P.

MAII MCMLVIII
IN STATU PUPILLARI

CONTENTS

Foreword

INTRODUCTION

  I   The Book   15

  II   Locke the man and Locke the writer   28

  III   *Two Treatises of Government* and the
        Revolution of 1688   58

  IV   Locke and Hobbes   80

  V   The social and political theory of *Two
      Treatises of Government*   106

Appendix A: Check-list of printings, 1689–1960   136

Appendix B: Sources of *Two Treatises of
          Government* in Locke's reading   146

Editorial note   162

THE TEXT

Preface   171

First Treatise   175

Second Treatise   299

Collation of First Treatise   479

Collation of Second Treatise   507

Bibliography   543

Index   557

FOREWORD

Locke's *Two Treatises of Government* has been a set text at Cambridge for many years. At the time of shortage even this was a difficult book to get: the bookshops were all out of stock. So it was that a member of Christ's found himself in the college library in 1944 or 1945, reading the work in an eighteenth-century volume, wonderfully decorated in the best style. It was Locke's own copy, corrected for posterity.

Scholarship owes a debt to this conscientious reader which is here gratefully acknowledged. Examination of the volume which he brought again to notice after 180 years soon made two things apparent. One was drearily to be expected; the reprints in circulation were for the most part worthless imitations. The other was exciting but discouraging. This was not the only corrected copy which Locke had left behind him; the other copy, referred to in this one (see below, page 164), was perhaps the more authentic. Where was it? Did it contain the missing continuation of the *First Treatise,* a continuation which was longer than the whole book?

This other copy has never been found and Locke's continuation seems to be lost for ever. But the search did lead to the recovery for scholars of Locke's personal library, that very considerable and important part of it which still survives as a collection. To the present Earl of Lovelace who owns this inheritance from Peter King, his ancestor and Locke's cousin, the editor expresses his very grateful thanks: to him and to his family, to his grandfather, William 1st Earl of Lovelace who sited and designed the lovely house at Ben Damph Forest where the library now stands.

The evidence from this unexpected source and the evidence from the great Lovelace collection of Locke papers which is now in the Bodleian Library soon made it evident that to establish a true text of Locke *on Government* would have to be a considerable undertaking. A critical edition of the type which is now presented became an inescapable duty.

It has taken a number of people a great deal of time, energy and skill to bring the job to this conclusion. I should like to record my deep gratitude to Mr Hanson, Keeper of Printed Books at the Bodleian Library, and to Professor Fredson Bowers of the University of Virginia, bibliographical lecturer both at Oxford and Cambridge. But once entered upon, I find that the list of my debts to fellow members of the *republic of letters,* as John Locke would have called it, becomes unmanageable. I have named some of them in the appended list of acknowledgements. I can only hope that the friends, acquaintances, correspondents mentioned there will believe this to be something very much more than a perfunctory expression of thanks, and that those many others who have given their assistance will accept my acknowledgements as well.

They will not be held responsible I am sure for the errors and shortcomings in this book. With all these blemishes upon it, however, this is perhaps the first attempt of its kind in the discipline known as Political Science. The editor, historian and political scientist turned student of bibliography and textual criticism, finds himself a little dazed by its results.

Not so much by the number and importance of the changes in the content of Locke's political doctrine which are shown up when his text is critically treated. These revisions have been few, and there are those who may well wonder whether they were worth the effort to recover and record. Critics such as these will perhaps agree however that the uncertainty which has surrounded the subject of exactly what Locke wrote has been so great that it was essential at any cost to establish it, even if it turned out to be not so very different from what he was always supposed to have written.

The surprises have been of a rather different kind. It turns out that the accepted interpretation of Locke's book as a historical document is quite indefensible in the face of the evidence, not all of it new evidence and some of it public for many years. In the Introduction the reader will find a discussion of the three dogmas which political science has maintained about this book ever since the study was begun. Each, so the editor believes, is demonstrably wrong. Locke did not write in 1689 to justify the Revolution of 1688. Locke did not write with Thomas Hobbes in hand or in mind, either to refute him as we all so recently supposed, or to adopt his doctrine without confessing it, as some authorities now claim. Locke did not write as a philosopher, applying to politics the implications of his view of reality as a whole.

To claim that these are the dogmas of Lockeian interpretation is of course to express an opinion. Moreover, the arguments invite refutation, refutation in detail, detail of the kind which is analysed here. No doubt the revised interpretations suggested in this edition will themselves have to be revised, some of them rejected. The editor is conscious that he is unsuited by temperament for an undertaking which tries in any degree to be definitive, accurate in every tiny point.

Nevertheless the point of substance remains. How is it possible that a work of such importance can have been treated with such looseness of thinking, such insouciant carelessness about evidence, such extraordinary credulity? These questions suggest others. Why have the canons of criticism traditionally applied to the classics, of the Ancient World and of modern literature, never before been applied to documents of modern political theory? Can we go on accepting a position which divorces this study of ours from scholarship as it is practised elsewhere?

The problems of political theory will never be solved by worrying about the positions of commas, and the responsibility of political scientists does not end with the composition of careful footnotes. Because this is true it is surely the more important that we should be quite confident that what we know is knowledge, that if it is history it really happened, if it is interpretation it is based on ascertained facts and tested hypotheses.

Anxiety over points like these, and from time to time the excitement of the chase itself, has kept the editor for nearly a decade at an intricate, wearisome, unrewarding task. Perhaps it would never have been completed if it had not turned out to be a fascinating story about an extraordinary man writing and concealing a book of enormous historical importance. It is presented as an example of the results of applying to one particular document used by political scientists the critical techniques which the editor believes should be applied to all comparable works. The job was done by an amateur, learning as he went. Professionals should find it easier and quicker.

It should be recorded here that this is not the first critical edition of Locke *on Government,* though it is the first in the English language. In 1948 Luigi Pareyson published an edition with footnotes throughout both treatises which have been freely drawn on here and have been very useful indeed. It is perhaps a further illustration of the points which have been laid down that the English speaking world should

have been content to wait until after such an edition had
appeared in the Italian language.

ACKNOWLEDGEMENTS

May I first mention those men and institutions who have
helped me with the bibliography and textual criticism. First
of all Julian Boyd ('Mr Jefferson', the prince of editors)
and many other librarians and scholars in the United States:
Mr Adams at the Pierpont Morgan Library in New York,
those at Harvard, Yale, the Library of Congress, the Union
Seminary, Princeton University, and elsewhere. The Bodleian Library has been extremely generous of its facilities,
and my own Cambridge colleges of Trinity, Peterhouse
and St John's have all freely helped.

To Trinity I owe a general debt, since it has been so
ready with its confidence in these Locke studies and with
special support for them. So indeed has the Rockefeller
Foundation, the Folger Shakespeare Library at Washing-
ton, that murmuring hive of seventeenth-century scholarship, the Institute for Advanced Study at Princeton and the
Fulbright Commission with its travelling fellowships. The
far-sighted, patient, sensitive patronage of these great American institutions continues to amaze the fortunate English-
man who is the object of it. Unobtrusive but important
assistance has come, also, from the Goldsmiths' Company
of London, and of course from the Cambridge University
Press—what tolerance it has shown. I must record too my
personal debts to Mr Arthur Houghton, Jr., of 5th Avenue,
New York, to Professor Lamprecht, late of Amherst College, to Herr Dr Klemmt of West Berlin, to Johan Gerritsen, of the Royal Library at The Hague, and to Mr R. G.
Lloyd, of Bembridge School.

Piero Sraffa of Trinity College has had more of a hand
in this book than I would guess he would care to admit,
and I hope that Herbert Butterfield, Ernest Barker, Jacob
Viner, Rosalie Colie, Louis Wright, Brough Macpherson,
Maurice Cranston, Michael Oakeshott, John Yolton, Wolfgang Von Leyden, Karl Friedrich, Caroline Robbins,
Tommy Cook, will recognize their handiwork and forgive
me where I have gone wrong. The three research workers
who have been with me whilst this book has been in preparation, Jock Salmon, Jasper Rose, Philip Abrams, will see
clearly how much more I have learnt from them. John
Pocock, Tony Jolowicz, Ralph Leigh, John Elliott, Clive
Parry, Esmond de Beer, Samuel Mintz and Professor

Thomas have given me specific help as well as general encouragement. Richard Schlatter has been a particular as well as a general friend to this book, and has read the proofs for me. Scholars in the languages faculty at Princeton have given last minute help. My wife worked at many, many things, the index especially. But my greatest debt of all in those myriad points of accuracy and of book consultation is to Mr John Harrison, of the University Library at Cambridge: for his friendship, too.

P.L.

THE INSTITUTE FOR ADVANCED STUDY
PRINCETON
May 1959

Foreword to the Second Impression

My debts have grown even further since this book appeared, and foremost comes what is now owed by all students of Locke to Mr Paul Mellon. In 1960 he bought from the Earl of Lovelace and presented to the Bodleian Library at Oxford the whole remaining literary inheritance of the family from John Locke. The manuscripts found at Ben Damph Forest are already in Oxford amongst the rest of the Lovelace MSS; Locke's books are housed in Mr Mellon's own library at Oak Spring, Upperville, Virginia, U.S.A., though they will finally go to Oxford too. This was an act of generosity unparalleled in the history of the Bodleian.

To those who have taken such pains in reviewing the original work and correcting its errors, my thanks are also due. I have pondered what they have said, and amended where I thought I could. But sometimes I felt they were so much in the right that to act on their advice would mean changing my Introduction more than would be allowable. This is especially so in Section V, where my friends Wolfgang von Leyden, Brough Macpherson, Raymond Polin and Philip Abrams have often made me feel that I was wrong and they are right.

I am grateful too for the help of Mr John Dunn, of King's College, Cambridge, for the addition of some details of fact. Nevertheless the Introduction and Notes stand almost entirely as they did, modified only slightly here and there so as to take into account work on Locke published since 1957. One additional manuscript source (now alas apparently lost) is used here in Locke's *Manifesto* of 1689 to Edward Clarke (see page 59). A detail must be further added to this Foreword, for the reader in Christ's College Library who recognized Locke's master-copy can now be identified as Professor Eric Stokes.

P.L.

TRINITY COLLEGE
CAMBRIDGE
March 1963

INTRODUCTION*

I

THE BOOK

'Property I have nowhere found more clearly explained, than in a book entitled, Two Treatises of Government.' This remark was made by John Locke in 1703, not much more than a year before he died. It must be a rare thing for an author to recommend one of his own works as a guide to a young gentleman anxious to acquire 'an insight into the constitution of the government, and real interest of his country'. It must be even rarer for a man who was prepared to do this, to range his own book alongside Aristotle's *Politics* and Hooker's *Ecclesiastical Polity,* to write as if the work were written by somebody else, somebody whom he did not know. Perhaps it is unique in a private letter to a relative.[1] What could possibly be the point of concealing this thing, from a man who probably knew it already?

Odd as it is, this statement of Locke's anticipates the judgment of posterity. It was not long before it was universally recognized that Locke on *Government* did belong in the same class as Aristotle's *Politics,* and we still think of it as a book about property, in recent years especially. It has been printed perhaps a hundred times since the 1st edition appeared with the date 1690 on the title-page. It has been translated into French, German, Italian, Russian, Spanish, Swedish, Nor-

---

* The system used for referring to sources and authorities is described on p. 168.
[1] The Rev. Richard King. Locke's letter to him of 25 August 1703 is printed in *Works*, 1801, X, 305. They had a mutual cousin in Sir Peter, later Lord King.

wegian and Hindi: probably into other languages too.[2] It is
an established classic of political and social theory, perhaps
not in the first flight of them all, but familiar to eight generations of students of politics all over the world, and the subject
of a great body of critical literature.

The prime reason for the importance attached to this book
of Locke's is its enormous historical influence. We shall not
be concerned here with the part which it played in the growth
to maturity of English liberalism, or in the development of
those movements which had their issue in the American Revolution, the French Revolution and their parallels in southern
America, in Ireland, in India—everywhere where government
by consent of the governed has made its impact felt. We shall
certainly have to decide whether or not the book was worthy
of the effect it has had, or perhaps to work out a criterion to
make such a decision possible. But our first object must be a
modest historian's exercise—to establish Locke's text as he
wanted it read, to fix it in its historical context, Locke's own
context, and to demonstrate the connection of what he thought
and wrote with the Locke of historical influence.

We may begin with Locke's own attitude to his own work
on government. Our direct evidence is meagre, for we have
only two further references to the book by name from Locke
himself. One is an exactly similar recommendation made in
the same year in *Some Thoughts Concerning Reading and
Study for a Gentleman*.[3] This makes no mention of property,
but the tendency is clear enough, and it marks his recognition
of the uses which the work would have, the same for *Two
Treatises of Government* as for everything else he published.
They were to be part of the assimilated atmosphere of the
English gentleman, the Member of Parliament, the administrator and politician, at home and overseas, but above all the
landowner, the local notable.

In the third and most important reference of all he finally
did acknowledge his authorship. He was addressing himself
to posterity rather than to his contemporaries, to us who can
only read him and not to those who could have known him:
it was made in a codicil to his will, signed only a week or two
before he died. He was listing his anonymous works for the
benefit of the Bodleian Library, and he wrote:

'I do hereby give to the public library of the University of

[2] See Appendix A (136–45) for a handlist of printings, English and
foreign.
[3] *Works*, 1801, III, 272.

Oxford. . . . *Two Treatises of Government* whereof Mr Churchill has published several editions but all very incorrect.'[4]

Without this final, almost accidental afterthought we should have no direct proof that he wrote the book at all.[5] His anxiety to keep the secret is the more remarkable in that his responsibility was widely suspected from the time of publication. It was talked of in Oxford in 1689, and in 1690 Molyneux was told in London that he wrote the work. In 1693 Bayle referred to Locke's authorship as if it were generally known, even on the continent. Although it would seem that his most hostile critic, John Edwards, was not in the secret in 1697, it was being referred to openly in print in the following year. Walter Moyle, in his *Essay on the Lacedaemonian Government*, declared: 'I would advise you to read first the answer that has been made to *Filmer* by Mr *Locke*, and his *Essay of the Original, Extent and End of Civil Government;* that piece contains the first Rudiments upon this subject. I know a Gentleman, who calls it the A.B.C. of *Politicks*.'

Molyneux in 1698 was not so frank, but even more complimentary: he called it 'An Incomparable *Treatise*, . . . said to be written by my Excellent Friend, JOHN LOCKE, *Esq*; Whether it be so or not, I know not; This I am sure, whoever is the Author, the greatest Genius in *Christendom* need not disown it.' In 1701 the most powerful and important of all Locke's friends, John, Lord Somers, cited the book with marked deference to its author: his clear implication was that he knew who wrote it and so did his readers.[6]

By then, no doubt, Locke had told the great man by word of mouth that the book indeed was his, as he had told Tyrrell and Molyneux, imploring all of them, everyone who challenged

[4] Will, dated 7 April 1704; codicil, 15 September 1704. Locke died 28 October 1704.

[5] Though the circumstantial evidence is quite conclusive. In the Whitehouse Collection there are papers of corrections in his hand for the 1694 printing.

[6] Tyrrell to Locke, 20 December 1689, 30 August 1690 (see below, 65 and 93); Molyneux to Locke, 27 August 1692 (*Works*, 1714, III, 502), and his *Case of Ireland*, 1698, 1720 ed., 23 and 130 where he refers to *Locke's Treat. Government* (in his reply Clement, 1698, complains of the abuse of 'Mr *Lock*, or whoever was the Author of that Excellent Treatise of Government'); Bayle to Minutoli, 14 September 1693, 1725, IV, 731. Moyle's *Essay* was printed in his *Works* in 1727 (see p. 58), and the date of original publication was given as 1698 by the editor, to whom it was dedicated, though I can find no other record of its appearance. For Somers's reference, see note to II, § 139. Other instances could be found, e.g., Cary, 1698; Leslie (?), 1698.

him with the secret, to keep his knowledge to himself and out of print.[7] And he persisted in all his other exasperating attempts to conceal it, in a way which can only be called abnormal, obsessive. He destroyed all his workings for the book and erased from his papers every recognizable reference to its existence, its composition, its publication, printing and reprinting. All the negotiations with both printer and publisher went on through a third party, who was instructed to refer to the author as 'my friend'. This in spite of the fact that the publisher was a personal acquaintance both of Locke and his agent, and handled nearly all of his other books. In Locke's own library, this book in all its editions was catalogued and placed on the shelves as anonymous, so that even a casual browser should find nothing to compromise the secret.

He showed a similar cautiousness over some of his other works. He was willing to risk a breach with his Dutch friend Limborch for letting it be known that he had written on toleration,[8] since this fact, as well as his responsibility for the *Reasonableness of Christianity*, was also reserved for final revelation in the codicil to his will. But nothing exceeded his cold fury towards Tyrrell, a lifelong associate, when he had reason to believe that he had betrayed him over *Two Treatises* in 1690. There is no parallel in the papers of this devious man for the labyrinthine methods he used when the book was reprinted in 1694, perhaps no parallel in literature.[9]

All this argues a peculiarity in Locke's personality as a man and in his personality as an author, particularly as a controversialist and especially as a commentator on political issues. This we will consider in its due place. The present importance of his anxiety to keep the secret about *Two Treatises* as long as he lived lies in the effect which it has had on the transmission of the text. His statement in his will betrays his vexation that this book had been mangled by the printer, and implies that he was anxious to leave behind him an authoritative text.

[7] Locke obviously told Tyrrell between August 1691 and August 1692 (see below, 92), and Molyneux when he visited him in England in 1698 (see Molyneux to Locke, 15 March 1698, and Locke to Molyneux, 6 April 1698, *Works*, 1801, IX, 450–4 and compare Bastide, 1907, 286).

[8] Locke, Limborch letters, April 1690, in King's *Locke*, 1830, II, 305–11. He never put his name on English printings of the *Education*, though it appeared on the French translation.

[9] Rand, 1927, 387–94, and the originals, with some unpublished items, in the Whitehouse Collection. Rand assumes that the only book referred to in these letters between Locke and Clarke is the *Essay*, but it can be shown that *Two Treatises* is intended in Locke's of 7 March, 12 March, 19 March (as well as the *Essay*) and 30 March 1694.

There is evidence to prove that he went to great pains to ensure that we should read him on politics in the exact words
which he used, and we must turn to the history of its printing
to see why it is that we do not do so. Our modern reprints of
Locke on *Government* represent a debasement of a form of
his book which he himself excoriated, and tried his best to
obliterate.[10]

This author lived most of his life amongst books. He was
well informed about printing and publishing, and the firm of
Awnsham and John Churchill, one of the great houses of his
day, came to be a part of his life. Yet he could write in June
1704:

> Books seem to me to be pestilent things, and infect all that
> trade in them . . . with something very perverse and brutal.
> Printers, binders, sellers, and others that make a trade and
> gain out of them have universally so odd a turn and corrup-
> tion of mind, that they have a way of dealing peculiar to them-
> selves, and not conformed to the good of society, and that
> general fairness that cements mankind.[11]

This profound suspicion of book tradesmen, rather than any
argued belief in liberty of expression, made John Locke the
champion of the freedom of the press. His bitter experience
with the publication of his own works was an important reason. It was certainly *Two Treatises of Government* which
irritated him most.

We have said that Locke carefully expunged from all his
records every overt mention of this book. It is not surprising,
then, that no manuscript version of it or any part of it has
ever been recovered. This is another indication that his anxiety
to conceal it went far beyond what he felt about his writings
on toleration, for example, since he preserved draft after draft
of his views on that subject. But although it has never been
seen we know that the manuscript on *Government* which
Locke sent to the press, or perhaps had copied for the printer,
in the late summer of 1689, had some interesting peculiarities.
It was a remnant: more than half of it had been lost. It was
probably written all over with corrections, amendments and
extensions: some recent, others going back six years and more.
We shall discuss these features of the original manuscript when
we come to the date of composition. The printed text of the
first, 1690, edition has the status which comes from being

[10] See Laslett, 1952 **(iv)**, 342, note 2, and 1954 (ii), note 1.
[11] *Works*, 1801, X, 291, Locke to Anthony Collins.

taken from a manuscript original, even though the cunning author may have made sure by using a copyist that his publisher did not recognize the hand.

This is only the beginning of the story which ends with the versions read today. The work of editing is complicated when only printed sources are available, especially when there were several editions in the author's lifetime, and printing difficulties as well. The 1st edition was botched, and no wonder, with such copy and such tortuous communications. We may never know in detail what happened, and the bibliographical problem is for specialists only. Locke certainly interrupted the press, and one of his objects was to change the title of the book and of each treatise, so as to alter the apparent relationship between them. The difficulty is to account for the fact that two sorts, or 'states',[12] of the finished book were produced. In the earlier state it had no paragraph 21 in the *Second Treatise*, and a few pages before the point where it should have appeared the ordinary print gave way to three pages in the larger type of the Preface. The second state was made to look normal: nothing is obviously missing, there is no large type. Modern editors in a hurry, just well enough informed to seek out the 1st edition to reproduce, have sometimes lighted on one state, sometimes on the other; hence a great deal of confusion and some mixed up references.[13]

This 1st printing, our first authority, was completely unsatisfactory to Locke. We have been able to use his personal copy for this edition. Apart from corrections of misprints, it has a few amendments in his hand.

The plot of the story begins to unfold, a story of repeated frustration of Locke's attempts to get out a clear text. The book sold, and in 1694 a new printing was wanted. By this time, we may expect, both his manuscript original and all handwritten copies had been destroyed. So Locke sent a cor-

---

[12] Called for reference 1X and 1R, see Laslett, 1952 (iv); Bowers, Gerritsen and Laslett, 1954; Johnston, 1956. Dr Gerritsen has now put forward an explanation which seems to me to make the earlier, more complicated conjectures unnecessary. Though its effects on the text are not important, it implies the following. The passage which is present in 1R and not in 1X was lost at the press and had to be rewritten by Locke. He may have been able to use an earlier copy of his text, or he may have been composing anew. It is therefore very interesting that this passage (see II, 20–21, and especially paragraph 20, 11–23 and note) should contain statements which refer so definitely to the revolutionary events of 1688. It is hoped that Dr Gerritsen's explanation will shortly appear in print.

[13] See notes on II, § 16, 1; § 17, 18; § 20, 3; § 21.

rected copy of the 1st printing on its roundabout way through Edward Clarke, his third party, and Churchill the publisher to the printer. It had over 150 alterations of sense or extensions, but the final text was worse than ever, so bad that Locke felt like abandoning the whole book. On 12 March 1694, he wrote to Clarke:

There is no contesting with everlasting unalterable neglect. If I receive that other paper I sent for I shall go on with it. If not I shall trouble myself no more about it. Its fate is it seems to be the worst printed that ever book was, and it is in vain for anyone to labour against it.[14]

The chastened Churchill offered to scrap the whole edition. But not before Clarke had been told to 'rub up his carelessness a little' for this second was 'ten times worse than the first edition'. They finally agreed to sell it very cheap, so that it should be 'scattered amongst common readers'. Meantime Locke would correct it more exactly, especially as to punctuation, and then Churchill would print it again with better type and on good paper. This is what seems to have happened, though we have no further correspondence which we can attach to the affair.[15] The 2nd edition of 1694, and it is in fact a cheap and nasty little book, price sixpence, held the field for four years, when it was sold out in its turn. Then the better quality reprint was issued as Locke had demanded, the 3rd edition, 1698. The modifications in the 2nd edition, and the very minor alterations in the 3rd, have been taken account of in our text.[16]

But even this did not satisfy Locke, who seems to have had a standard of perfection above the resources of the printers of his time. This 3rd printing of 1698 had its faults, but it is difficult not to feel that the exasperation which he showed in his will over all the printings of this work had an independent source in an inner anxiety about what he had

[14] Rand, 1927, 389. The 'other paper' was a missing page of corrections. The effect of Locke's vain attempts to clear up the worst of the muddle is to be found in the numbers of cancel leaves in this printing, see Johnston, 1956.

[15] The references to a book printed in 1698 quoted by Bowers, Gerritsen and Laslett, 1954, where the printer left out whole paragraphs 'in the former sheets of this very book' now seem to concern a different work.

[16] It had two cancel leaves. See Editorial Note (162) for the effect of these successive corrections. Where Locke retained them in his 'text for posterity' (see below) they appear in the present text as a matter of course, and occasionally where he omitted to reinsert them there. All variants are registered in the Collation (479).

written. As it became obvious to him that no version correct
enough to satisfy such meticulousness would ever appear in
his lifetime,[17] he made plans to ensure that it should do so
after his death. He corrected a copy of the printed version
in minute detail, scrutinizing the word-order, the italics, the
punctuation, even the spelling, as well as the general sense.
It seems that he intended to carry out this process in duplicate,
which is what we might expect in him. It seems also that
one of the copies he corrected may have been of the 2nd
printing of 1694, rather than the 3rd of 1698, which, though
slightly revised, was a page for page reprint of its predecessor.
The other copy, the text of the 3rd printing corrected between
the lines, in the margins and on the fly leaves, is the one
reproduced here. Locke himself did not get further than
the first few pages in the laborious correcting process, and
the rest is in the hand of his amanuensis, Pierre Coste,
though Locke's hand does appear occasionally throughout
the book. The indications are that Coste was copying from
the other master-copy.

Locke must have left directions behind him for the
publication of this text for posterity, just as he did in the
case of the *Essay on the Understanding*.[18] Presumably these
directions were left with Churchill, the publisher, though it
is a little difficult to understand why nine years were allowed
to elapse before the book appeared, for the posthumous
Essay took only two. It may be that Locke's heir and literary
executor was given the responsibility, or even Pierre Coste.[19]
But whoever it was who made the decision, in 1713 this
definitive text appeared over Churchill's imprint as the 4th
edition, and in the following year it was included in the 1st
edition of Locke's *Collected Works*, published by the same
firm. And whatever exactly took place between Locke's death
in 1704 and 1713, it is clear that the effect he desired was

---

[17] Though a new edition was entered in the *Term Catalogues* in 1699.
[18] The 5th edition, 1706, was obviously a posthumous fulfillment of
Locke's own directions, presumably to Churchill: see Yolton's *Everyman* edition, 1961. Introduction.
[19] But see a letter from La Motte to Desmaizeaux of November 1709
(British Museum, Sloan MSS. 4286, f. 91), inquiring for a copy of that
edition of *Two Treatises* 'qui a été faite après la mort de l'auteur, où l'on
a inséré les corrections dans l'exemplaire laissé à Mr. Coste'. The assumption here is that the text for posterity had already appeared, and it
seems to imply rather that someone other than Coste had been charged
with it. The context shows that a number of people, including Barberac,
knew of the existence of the master-text, and that Coste had a copy
of it.

brought about. A fairly reliable text of the book became established, and the earlier, imperfect printings were left behind.

As the eighteenth century wore on the work was sent to press again and again, about once every five years. Each new printing was usually set up from its immediate predecessor, and so the text inevitably declined in accuracy: it lost its original flavour. But in the 6th edition, 1764, this process was arrested. That fine republican eccentric, Thomas Hollis, had acquired in 'his private walks' the Coste master-copy and he published it. He then presented the volume itself to Christ's College, Cambridge, 'where Milton, the matchless John Milton' was bred.[20] The present text is a reproduction of this document, made possible by the generosity of the present Master and Fellows of Christ's. But it is not 'the copy from which Mr L hopes that his book will be printed after his death' [21] to which Coste himself refers. That other volume, the hypothetical second master-copy, has so far escaped a search for recovery begun in 1949. Even now, therefore, editorial work on this book could be overset by the discovery of a yet more authentic version.[22] So end attempts at perfection.

As his gentleman-scholarly habit was, Hollis did some editorial work on the book before he sent it to Christ's.[23] Subsequent reprints followed this fresh and better version. It was left to modern scholarship, and in particular to the editors of successive reprints after 1884, to go behind all this to the unsatisfactory printings of Locke's lifetime, and to create the prevalent confusion over the text. Hence the imperative need for doing Hollis's work over again, in accordance with our own standards of textual accuracy, presenting the book as the author intended us to read it, but registering his successive corrections. These have their own significance, for they show us how Locke's views in 1694, 1698 and in the period from about 1700 to 1704 differed in microscopic detail from those he originally published in

[20] On Hollis, see Robbins, 1950. Professor Robbins has been kind enough to communicate relevant extracts from the full, unpublished diary of Hollis.

[21] 'L'exemplaire sur lequel il [i.e. Mr L.] souhaite que son livre soit imprimé après sa mort', note in Coste's hand on the final fly of the Christ's copy: see note on II, § 172.

[22] See Editorial Note (162) for a discussion of the second master-copy.

[23] Blackburne's *Memoirs* of Hollis, 1780, 224, how he collated this copy with the first three printings 'with no little labour'.

1689.[24] Moreover the knowledge that he worked so hard and so often at his text is also important in itself. We must surely suppose that he meant to stand by what he finally approved for us to read. He certainly gave himself every opportunity to see and to revise those points of inconsistency and obscurity which have been seen in his text by so many of his commentators.

So John Locke has not escaped the consequences of the extraordinary attitude which he took up to his book on *Government*. There is an appropriate irony in the fact that the scholars of our own day have been confused by it, not the men of the eighteenth century. Though a study of this work must begin with this complicated story of determined anonymity and failure at the press, there is still more to be said. It was a different, a much modified version which entered into the main stream of European political thinking and affected French, even American revolutionism. Ever since it was translated into French, less than eighteen months after publication, the first of his English works to be put into the polite and universal language of that time, *Two Treatises* has led two quite independent lives. They have touched only at one point: in Boston, Massachusetts, in 1773.

In 1691 David Mazel, one of the Huguenot pastors living in Holland, translated the book.[25] He made a fair and literal version, adequate though not outstanding, but the book was transformed as well as translated. Locke's *Preface*, the entire *First Treatise*, the opening chapter of the *Second* connecting it with the *First*, were all left out. An *Avertissement* was prefixed, a fair enough statement of the drift and purpose of the text. The paragraphs were renumbered under chapters and not consecutively through the book; they were divided slightly differently.[26] A briefer work in an alien language and an altered shape, this essay 'Du Gouvernement Civil' was subtly changed in the direction of the Enlightenment and eighteenth-century Revolutionism. In this form it was reprinted a dozen times in the next century, more often as

[24] Though it bore the date 1690, it was actually printed in 1689 (see below, section III) and was on sale by November of that year. This was normal publishing practice then as it still is for our motor-car makers.

[25] There seems to be nothing to confirm, but nothing to upset, this traditional attribution.

[26] These paragraph numerations and divisions are recorded in the Collation.

an independent book in France than in England. In this form it was read by Montesquieu, Voltaire and Rousseau. From this version and not, until our day, from the English original, the translations into other languages were made. Did Locke know that his book was being altered in this way? Was he himself in any way responsible?

He may have been. He was presumably acquainted with the publisher, Abram Wolfgang, for he also published the periodical *La Bibliothèque Universelle*. During his recent exile in Holland, Locke had contributed to this journal.[27] Jean Leclerc, the editor, was one of Locke's closest friends in Holland, and he was no doubt acquainted with most of the protestant refugees, perhaps with Mazel himself though we have no evidence of such a connection. *Du Gouvernement Civil* was anonymous both as to author and to translator, but its preface gets very close to Locke's doctrine and object in writing.

Leclerc published a summary of the whole of *Two Treatises* in his periodical in 1691, from the English original. Nevertheless, the form of the French version may suggest Locke's responsibility, for the *Second Treatise* or *Essay of Civil Government* alone, independent of the *First,* is the form in which it has been read, even by those who have had the *First Treatise* in the volume in hand. We have already seen Locke emphasizing the disconnection between the two treatises when he changed the titles at such a late stage, and we shall present the case for supposing that the *Second Treatise* was the earlier work. I am prepared to believe from these indications that the French, the European and generally appreciated form of this book, was authenticated by Locke. Any overt recognition of the French form would of course have offended his passionate desire for anonymity.

This view has its difficulties, for it makes it necessary to ask why he did not adopt this form for subsequent English editions and in his text for posterity. It leaves open a decision on the extent to which he oversaw the French edition. Nevertheless we may believe that Locke would have been pleased to think that the French form, the independent

---

[27] See Laslett, 1957 (ii). Since this was written I have been able to see again Locke's copies of this journal, and find it was an error to attribute to him the articles marked in manuscript there. The hand seems to be Leclerc's, not Locke's, and Locke's part in the editorial work was less important than I had supposed.

Second Treatise, was to be received into the canon of classics on political theory.[28]

Whatever the status of the French version for Locke, it did not affect his corrections to the English versions, and he showed no sign that he realized the growing influence of the work on a readership far wider than his English public. That public, as the eighteenth century wore on, was no longer confined to readers of English in the British Isles, for it included those men in the North American colonies who were importing Locke's books, especially the collected editions, in such large numbers. When at last in 1773 the crucial relevance of Locke's political doctrine to the controversy over the rights of the Americans called forth a reprint from Boston, the text reproduced followed the standard English edition (Hollis's 6th edition, 1764). But the form of the book was the French form, not the English: no *First Treatise*, and the first chapter of the *Second* omitted.[29] What more intriguing example could be found of the well-known pathway of radical thinking from its origin in England, by way of French Protestants in Holland and French political criticism at home, to the new Englishmen of the New World?

So much for Locke's book as a book and the plot of its development to a giant of historical importance. The whole story could be told at much greater length. There is a striking illustration of Locke's attitude to the work, his unwillingness to own it and to take responsibility for its effects, in his failure to take any notice of Molyneux's *Case of Ireland*. Here a close friend was using the book as it was always going to be used, to justify a people in their demand for a voice in their own government. Locke's name appeared in the ensuing controversy. There are signs that Locke felt concern, perhaps even contemplated changing his text, yet he said nothing: his final corrections ignored the whole thing.[30]

---

[28] Locke's own copy of *Du Gouvernement Civil* has written in his hand on the title: *Pax ac Libertas*. He almost never wrote on the titles of his books, and this is the only known example of his adding to the title of one of his own. On the final page he has also added the personal sign which he used to authenticate his signature on financial documents. This sign is found on a dozen or so of Locke's books, and may have had a meaning to him which has not been recovered.

[29] See Appendix A: this printing has no chapter or paragraph numbers.

[30] Information from Mr John Dunn, of King's College, Cambridge. See references in note 6, p. 17 above, and compare Laslett, 1957 (i). Molyneux's reproduction of passages from Locke is recorded in the notes to II, §§ 4, 134, 177, 178, etc.

Or we could watch the interplay between editions of Locke and the crises of government and opinion. There was no American edition after 1773 until the twentieth century; a proposal for publication by subscription in 1806 apparently got no response. But during 'L'an III de la République Française' (1795) it appeared in revolutionary Paris in four different sizes, a neat tapering pile. Traditionalists in contemporary Britain were disturbed by the uses being made of the great philosopher of common sense and moderation by revolutionaries at home. In 1798 Bishop Thomas Elrington produced his edition of the book, introduced and annotated with remarks directed against citizen Thomas Paine so as to establish the distinction 'between the system of Locke and the theories of modern democrats'.[31] The first Spanish edition appeared in 1821, at the outset of the critical decade for the independence of the Spanish-American communities: in 1827 a further reprint was smothered in the press at Madrid.

Meanwhile the political theory of *Two Treatises of Government* had established its place in the minds of Montesquieu and Rousseau, Burke and Jefferson. We must now turn our attention to the personal qualities and the personal experience of the man who brought this system into being, and whose attitude to his own creation was such a singular one.

[31] Elrington was the only editor to notice the peculiarities of the 1st edition: his notes have been incorporated here.

II

LOCKE THE MAN AND LOCKE
THE WRITER

1. LOCKE AND OXFORD

John Locke lived from 1632 to 1704, from the seventh year
of the reign of Charles I to the third year of the reign of
Queen Anne: 1632 was the year of the birth of Sir Christopher
Wren in England, of Pufendorf and Spinoza on the continent.
In the course of his seventy-two years Locke saw the worlds
in which he spent his life, the intellectual and scientific world,
the political and economic world, change farther and faster
than any of his forefathers had done, and in England more
markedly than anywhere else. He was as much of a mere
Englishman as a universal genius could be, though he spent
two critical periods of his life abroad, in France from 1675 to
1679 and in Holland from 1683 to 1689. He was as private
and ordinary a man as could be expected of an individual
who was to help to change the philosophical and political
assumptions of humanity, but for two other periods he was
a directive political influence in his own right and something
of a public personality. This was between about 1667 and
1675 and again in 1679–82 when he was associated with
that overpowering political figure, the first earl of Shaftesbury,
and between 1694 and 1700 as the confidant of Lord Somers,
the chief figure of the government. He died a famous man

and he has remained one of the great English names ever since.

That fame was intellectual and literary; it still is. But he was a reluctant author, a professed 'enemy to the scribling of this age'. He was fifty-seven years old before a word of the works which have given him renown was published in print. When he went to France in 1675 he expected to die of what we should call tuberculosis of the lung, and the men of his time did die early. He could not have supposed he would live to see his disordered sketches on philosophy become the *Essay on Humane Understanding*, or his notes on religious and political society become the *Letters on Toleration* and *Two Treatises of Government*. He could not have anticipated then, nor at any time before his sixtieth birthday, that what he had noted in private would become famous in public as his *Thoughts on Education* and *Considerations* on money and economics. John Locke wrote and published as an old man, though he was quite confident that he would never live to be old. But like every other man, he thought his important thoughts when he was young. The fascination and difficulty of his career is to recognize the seeds and saplings burgeoning in his early and middle life and to watch them grow and spread into the mature forest trees which he left to posterity.

It could be said of the select group of great Englishmen in the century of our intellectual greatness that only one, John Locke, was a don by choice. Bacon was a lawyer and a politician, Hobbes was a teacher of noblemen, Newton was an academic by necessity until, with Locke's help, he got into the great world as an administrator. Locke went up to Oxford in 1652 at the age of twenty and he remained a full member of his college, if only nominally resident in later years, paying his fees and receiving his dues until he was ejected, illegally and against his will, in 1684 when he was fifty-two. He did his best to get back his place, and if we are to believe what he tells us himself he would have liked to have lived his whole life at the university. It was his career: for most of his earlier life it was the only thing which he thought he could excel in.

He reached Oxford by the most conventional of paths. He was a scholar, and no very distinguished scholar, of Westminster School under the fearsome Doctor Busby. He was there on that awful morning of 30 January 1649 when Charles I was executed, kept in school by his Royalist headmaster but within earshot of the awe-stricken crowd. There was a closed avenue for King's scholars of Westminster either to Trinity College, Cambridge, or to Christ Church, Oxford. John Dryden, of Northamptonshire, went to Trinity but his schoolmate, John Locke of Somerset, a westerner, a member of the Puritan network of families which were intertwined with the Royalist and predominating strands in that loyalist area, went to Christ Church. At the head of his college he found John Owen, the Independent and champion of toleration, all that was best in the Cromwellian attitude to learning and the Church. In his second year of residence Locke made his first appearance in print as an author: it was a salute to the Lord Protector on his victory over the Dutch in 1653, in a volume of academic poems edited by the admiring Owen.[1]

There was a great deal to attach this modestly rising academic to the Cromwellian regime and the good old cause of Puritan and Roundhead against King and Cavalier. Down in Somerset his father, John Locke senior, was a late Captain in the parliamentary armies, the second in line of a family recently risen to gentle rank by the exertions and good fortune of its members. Nicholas Locke, the grandfather, had made the money which set the family up as proprietors of some small consequence in the little villages of Chew Magna, and Pensford and Belluton, Belluton which became Locke's family home. Nicholas had succeeded in the familiar way as a clothier, a capitalist middleman, setting on work the cottagers of the countryside round the great port of Bristol and selling the cloth in that flourishing market. But his son, John Locke senior, we are told, was a loser rather than a gainer in the race for wealth and social consequence so typical of his class and time. A Calvinist attorney, Locke's father was, and Clerk to the Justices of Somerset, dependent for patronage on a much more powerful parliamentarian family, the Pophams.

It was the influence of the Pophams which had made it possible for Locke's father to mark out the scholarly calling for him at Westminster and at Christ Church. It was a recognized way up in the world; for the clever boy the most reliable. There were two children only, John and his younger brother who died a youth, and they were authoritatively handled. Although he paid his tribute to parental sternness, much later he was to say that he 'wish'd his Father had design'd

[1] Cranston, 1957, 36. Many other men contributed, including clandestine Royalists.

rather him for anything else than what he was destined to'.[2]
In 1661 the squire of Belluton died, and left his son a gentle-man of Somerset in his own right, the owner of farms and farmhouses and even a small Mendip mine. Academic, un-married, independent he was to remain, but it is very impor-tant that John Locke was always the titular representative of an English landed family.

At Oxford Locke was urbane, idle, unhappy and unremark-able, all these things at the same time and only just successful enough. He passed with fair credit up the steps: scholar; then Student or Fellow as it would be in other colleges; then the holder of the usual teaching offices. Next in order was ordination in the Church, if he were to stay at the University; but here he hesitated, wavered and refused. He found a way out in medicine, one of the Studentships reserved for doctors. He had played some little part in that remarkable upsurge of interest in 'natural philosophy' at Oxford which was so soon to give rise to the Royal Society, and was associated with Boyle in his laboratory in the High Street. He took up botany, the herbal side of medicine, in a systematic way, and duly proceeded to the bachelor's degree in medicine. Al-though he finally wriggled his way, as an unsympathetic contemporary put it, into a faculty place or medical Student-ship at Christ Church, he never became a full Doctor of Medicine. His academic career was checked by the mid-1660's, and, as it proved, it was checked for ever.

Locke did not begin as a philosopher and at Oxford he was never a philosopher at all. We can now piece together from the mass of papers he has left us what his earliest interests were. They were political. His correspondence, his reading, his notes and his sketches show that he was first concerned with the authority of the state in religion, then with the Natural Law which sanctioned that authority, and with the basis of Natural Law in experience. It was only after this, after he had ceased to spend his whole time at Oxford, that he proceeded to philosophy as such, to the problem of knowledge. Apart from his congratulatory poems, his first work written for publication was a polemical tract on the *Civil Magistrate;* it was never printed, but we have his manuscript. His addresses as a college official, and especially as Censor of Moral Philoso-phy in 1664, have similarly survived, and they are concerned

---

[2] Lady Masham, 1705, in Colie, 1955, 17.

with Natural Law.[3] The surprising thing is that his attitude to politics then was traditionalist and authoritarian.

Here we would seem to be faced with a clean break with his heritage and a vivid contrast with his final reputation. He firmly proclaims his submission to authority, and his whole position is that in indifferent things, the power of the magistrate is necessarily absolute because the nature of civil society requires it. He insists that each and every individual grants his whole liberty to the supreme legislative power, which is a necessary mark of all civil society, and is the representative of all. Its decisions bind the conscience of everyone, though they may not reach what he defines as his judgment and in case of conflict there is no remedy but passive obedience. Liberty is what is left untouched by regulation. As for the people, this is typical of what he says:

Nor will the largeness of the governor's power appear dangerous or more than necessary if we consider that as occasion requires it is employed upon the multitude that are as impatient of restraint as the sea, and whose tempests and overflows cannot be too well provided against. . . . To whom are we most likely to be a prey, to those whom the Scripture calls Gods, or those whom knowing men have always found and therefore call beasts?

Kings are called Gods in Scripture, and the people are beasts for the knowledgeable men, of Locke's day and before: no sharper conflict could be found with the doctrine of *Two Treatises of Government*. The uneasy, anarchical months between the death of Oliver Cromwell and the Stuart Restoration had made this slightly sceptical, unselfconfident Oxford don into the determined defender of authority, a man prepared to go to great lengths to secure quiet. But it was legal, not arbitrary authority which he championed, 'a body of laws so well composed' that their preservation 'was the only security of this nation's settlement'. Even in this, to us his earliest, his most authoritarian mood, Locke is revealed as a constitutionalist, and a man convinced of the fundamental

[3] Dr Von Leyden has published these writings as Locke's *Essays on the Law of Nature* (1954), with an admirable introduction. The two pieces on the *Magistrate* (MS. e. 7, in English, MS. c. 28, f. 3 ff. in Latin with a draft in e. 6) are now contained in the Dissertation of Mr P. Abrams, to be seen in the Cambridge University Library, and to be printed. The English tract was directed against Edward Bagshaw, also of Christ Church.

distinction between secular and spiritual power, political and religious authority. He was not tempted into that safest and most effective of illiberal positions, the Divine Right of Kings based on patriarchalism, though he does mention it.[4] Throughout these papers, in fact, he professed indifference as to the origin of political power, 'whether the magistrate's crown drops down on his head immediately from heaven or be placed there by the hands of his subjects', which was to be a main concern of his mature political writings. But searching examination of his manuscript shows that he did assume the popular origin of political power: his references to the possibility of Divine Right were evidently concessions to the outbursts of such sentiment which greeted the Restoration.[5]

These recent recoveries, then, reveal something quite unexpected in the intellectual development which led up to the writing of *Two Treatises*. We do not know why the polemical tract was not printed, but we may assume that its theories were made public to a certain extent, by being developed into a Latin address to members of Christ Church delivered between 1661 and 1664.[6] It is interesting in itself that Oxford students should have listened to an oration on such a subject, more interesting still to wonder whether they recognized certain elements in it which have a flavour of Hobbes, the archauthoritarian. No one who set out, as Locke did, to argue from consent to absolute authority, could have avoided arguing to some extent in parallel with the already infamous *Leviathan*. Hobbist notions were in the air: Locke must have absorbed them, more perhaps from the attacks on them than from direct acquaintance. The two men were closer then than at any other time, but beyond this point we should not go: the evidence will not bear it. It is to submit uncritically to the strong tradition which dictates that Locke should always be considered alongside of Hobbes and to go on to claim

[4] See Abrams, 1961, 236–56, and his statement on 255 about 'constitutional' in relation to 'arbitrary' positions. Locke took note of patriarchal theories. There is evidence that he already knew, even respected, Filmer's writings—see below, 46.

[5] See e.g. his corrections and overwriting on the first page of his English treatise, on page 4, and the passage deleted on p. 33.

[6] Von Leyden, 1954. He does not recognize the Latin treatise, undoubtedly the most important writing by Locke on political theory before *Two Treatises*, as one of the *Essays* which he publishes. Abrams (1961, 50–1) also suggests that it was one of the Latin *Essays* or *Lectures*, and stresses (cf. note on English treatise, p. 21) the Oxford context of the politics discussed in both tracts.

that he was a conscious Hobbesist at this time, too cautious to reveal himself.[7]

But Hobbes is not the only contemporary of Locke's earlier years whose writings are of importance to his development as a political thinker. The resemblance between Locke's final political doctrines and those of the English radicals writing and acting between 1640 and 1660 is most marked. It is so close in some respects that direct influence would seem obvious, through his personal experience amongst those of the 'honest party' and through his reading. He knew Henry Stubbe, for example, and wrote to him in praise of his *Essay on the Good Old Cause;* through him he could have been in contact with Harrington and the Rota men, and there are many other such possibilities. But we have no indication that he read radical literature at Oxford, or indeed much political literature at all apart from such highly respectable, academic authors as Grotius and Pufendorf, his coeval, whose first work appeared in 1660. Classical and polite learning occupied him, even the French romances. The fact is that as far as we know Locke never read Lilburne or the other Levellers, then or afterwards. He was brought back into the tradition which they began by an unexpected turn in his personal life. Thereafter politics came to mean something very different from scholastic exercises on things indifferent, and on the scope and authority of Natural Law.

He was never to get much further as a Natural Law theorist, and we shall point to this fact as critical to his whole development. Nevertheless these early writings can fairly be called the typical product of a mind capable of enormous expansion, as yet unable to expand at all. Something of the platform for his political theory had been set up, and he could have proceeded either in the authoritarian or in the liberal direction, but to no very important effect. It was not to be a simple question of unfolding the implications of

[7] This has been the tendency of those who have commented on these writings so far, see Gough, 1950, and Cranston, 1956, and 1957, 61–3: Von Leyden rightly sees certain of Hobbes's arguments absorbed into the discussions of natural law, but it is he who suggests that the influence came from contemporary discussion of them as much as from direct acquaintance. Abrams thinks that the resemblance of the sentence quoted by Cranston (1957, 62, see English treatise, p. 21) with Hobbes's famous description of life in a state of nature is no greater than with many such descriptions of life without government, and quotes one from a book known to have been in Locke's mind (Sanderson, *De Obligatione Conscientiae,* 1660, 1686 ed., 43). On Locke and Hobbes generally, see section IV below.

a particular starting point: it never really is for any thinker. As yet he had little sense of political reality, of policy itself. Indeed, a great deal was lacking in this meticulous Oxford bachelor, with his fine conversation, his keen mind and conventional views, lacking that is to *le Sage Locke,* Voltaire's idol, the universal philosopher with an attitude on all things. Something was to happen when his life was nearly half over, something which was to give him that firmness of intellectual tread which accounts for his giant reputation and to transform these early sentiments on authority, political and religious, into the Lockeian liberalism which presses on us still.

Oxford frustrated him, but he was not yet master of himself enough to make his way in the world there or outside. Locke had a name for disputation in the Schools, the established method of instruction and examination: 'Hogshearing' he called it, the laborious clipping of tiny hairs from the skins of vociferating animals, not swine apparently, but yearling lambs. Locke hated it, and he did it badly; his whole life work in one sense was a protest against it. This, he said later, was another reason why he 'pitched upon the study of physic', where he was at one remove from the Schools, and 'as far as might be from any public concerns'.[8] This second object, to keep away from public affairs, prevented him from pursuing the diplomatic career which opened up up in 1665 and 1666.

This was a whiff of Machiavelli's world, and might have convinced him that he had talents and a personality for other things than teaching, the pressing of flowers from the University Botanic Garden and the systematic filling out of a great series of notebooks. He went to Cleves, the capital of Brandenburg, as secretary to a special mission in 1665, and was so successful that he was offered a similar post in Madrid when he returned, and another post after that.[9] But he preferred to return to his students and his everlasting medical mixtures. His association with Shaftesbury was to change him profoundly, but never quite to convince him that his academic ambition was misplaced.

When that change had taken place, Oxford rejected him. As a traditionalist institution she mistrusted his politics, and the developed originality of his thought menaced her curriculum. All this was to happen twenty years later and more,

[8] Locke to the eighth earl of Pembroke, 3 December 1684, Christ Church MSS., printed Osler, 1914.
[9] See Cranston, 1957, ch. 7.

and his removal from his place was brought about neither by his college nor the university, but by the Crown as a piece of political vindictiveness. But though the inbred little society of clergymen at Christ Church in the 1680's were not actually responsible for expelling the ablest man amongst them, they were not guiltless in the matter. The good and scholarly Dr Fell, head of the house since 1660 and trusted by Locke, wrote thus to the Secretary of State:

> Mr Locke being 'a student of this house' . . . and 'suspected to be ill-affected to the Government, I have for divers years had an eye upon him. . . . Very frequently, both in public and in private, discourses have been purposely introduced, to the disparagement of his master, the Earl of Shaftesbury, his party, and designs, he could never be provoked to take any notice, or discover in word or look the least concern; so that I believe there is not in the world so great a master of taciturnity and passion'.[10]

The Royal order to remove Locke from his Studentship in 1684 was the first move against the universities in the final Stuart bid for personal government, which was to stumble over the obstinacy of the Fellows of Magdalen in 1688. It is ugly to see those who sat with him at table acting as *agents provocateurs*, but typical of the man that not a flicker of an eyelid could be used against him. Half a generation later the teachers of Oxford did greater harm to their university by refusing to acknowledge his books in their teaching.[11] So little can Oxford and the House justly claim him as their own that he was a power over the whole learned world before they would recognize him. The last days he spent amongst them illustrate his manner of going in a dramatic fashion.

On 21 July 1683 the University of Oxford in Convocation ordered to take place in the Court of the Schools, now the Bodleian Quadrangle, the last burning of books in the history of England. The decree was displayed in the halls and libraries of the colleges, and it anathematized doctrine after doctrine

[10] Fell to Sunderland, 8 November 1684, see King, 1830, I, 279. Prideaux, one of the Students, was passing information to government circles on Locke at this time, see *Letters*, 1875. It is fair to add that the full exchange with Sunderland shows that Fell was doing something to protect Locke, and that he was disturbed by what was forced upon him. See Lady Masham (Colie, 1956, 83).

[11] See Cranston, 1957, 466–9 and references, for the meeting of heads of houses in 1703 to consider the suppression of the new, Lockeian philosophy.

already written into *Two Treatises*. Amongst the authors they condemned to the fire were some of those on the books which then stood on the shelves of Locke's chamber at Christ Church. It seems that he was there himself, to watch the acrid smoke drifting up between the spires, tight lipped as ever and busy packing off his library into the country. Within a few weeks he had certainly left Oxford for the countryside where he was born, and by the autumn he was an exile in Holland. Locke never went to Oxford again in his life.[12]

2. LOCKE AND THE FIRST EARL
OF SHAFTESBURY

Anthony Ashley Cooper, of Wimbourne St Giles in Dorset, later first Lord Ashley and still later first earl of Shaftesbury, was one of the ablest and most extraordinary men alive in the England of Locke's lifetime. He was rich, rich in land and from political office, rich from investment at home and overseas. He was powerful, politically powerful both in the regional politics of the south-west and at Whitehall. It had been done by a series of swerves of allegiance: first for King, and then for Parliament; first a minister of Cromwell, then his great opponent, then an architect of the Restoration. He was one of the small, assertive men; a phenomenon of shrewdness and penetration, highly intelligent and critical, yet affected with delusions of grandeur and unscrupulous in his inconsistencies; superb as a leader and administrator, yet chronically ill, physically not psychologically, for he had the extraversion of Prime Minister Walpole.

His disease was a hydatid, an affection of the liver, fatal if

[12] The *Decree* can best be consulted in *Somers Tracts*, 1812, viii. Locke's movements can be traced in his diary and from the addresses of his letters, though he becomes very elusive in the weeks before he left for Holland, and it is impossible to be certain that he did not pass through Oxford in later life.

it should give rise to an abscess and the abscess not be removed. In July 1666, Lord Ashley, Chancellor of the Exchequer, convalescent after one of his attacks, rumbled down in his great coach to Oxford to try the waters of Astrop. They were to be brought to him in bottles, and the man who came into his presence with the twelve flasks was not the physician he expected, but the physician's friend, John Locke. This was how the two men first met, and at that moment a famous friendship began.

It was Locke's conversation which attracted the keen-sighted politician as well as his skill as a doctor. Courteous and modest, for Locke always knew his place with the great, he was penetrating and ironical, immensely well informed. Within a year he had taken up residence in the Ashley family, with his own apartment at Exeter House in the Strand, invited there to talk to the great man, to advise him and to doctor him and those about him. On the body of his noble patron he brought about one of the medical miracles of that age. He advised and directed an operation, an operation at a time when surgery was butchery, to remove the abscess on the liver and to insert a little pipe through the stomach wall as a drain to prevent another abscess from forming. Ashley wore the pipe for the rest of his life: to the satirists of the 1680's it became a great wooden tap to be mocked at, like the tap on a barrel of beer. In fact this pathetic little object was made at first of silver then of gold.[13]

This operation made Locke famous and it changed the whole course of his life. Ashley was convinced, and he had good reason to be, that he owed his life to Locke. An association which began casually and was continued on a pattern conventional at the time, since it was not unusual for the great to introduce men of Locke's stamp into their families, became a working association for all purposes for both of them. All that political influence could do was directed towards Locke's promotion in his profession of academic medicine, and he was provided for financially, though his obstinate independence evidently made it difficult for Ashley to go as far as he wanted. He was given offices, the secretaryship of the associated proprietors of the colony of Carolina, the secretaryship of Ashley's Board of Trade, the secretaryship for ec-

---

[13] On the operation, see Osler, 1914: a more recent medical opinion is that the drainage pipe was useless, but that it did save Shaftesbury's life and its success was almost miraculous.

clesiastical patronage when Ashley, now earl of Shaftesbury, became Lord Chancellor in November 1672. These were not great offices, and none of them led to the high political career which might well have developed out of this association.

We do not know why this was, though we may believe that it was Locke who held back rather than that Shaftesbury judged him unfitted for the highest promotion. For we do know that he was paid the highest compliment in the gift of a great politician.

My Lord imparted to him from time to time all the secretest affairs then in agitation and by my Lord's frequent discourse of state affairs, religion, toleration and trade, Mr Locke came to have a wonderful knowledge of these things. . . . He writ his book concerning Human Understanding whilst he lived with my Lord.

And again, from a source of the very highest authority, Shaftesbury's grandson and Locke's pupil, the third earl:

Mr Locke grew so much in esteem with my grandfather that, as great a man as he had experienced him in physic, he looked upon this but as his least part. He encouraged him to turn his thoughts another way. . . . He put him upon the study of the religious and civil affairs of the nation with whatsoever related to the business of a minister of state, in which he was so successful that my grandfather began soon to use him as a friend and consult with him on all occasions of that kind. . . . When my grandfather quitted the Court and began to be in danger from it, Mr Locke now shared with him in dangers as before in honours and advantages. He entrusted him with his secretest negotiations, and made use of his assistant pen in matters that nearly concerned the state, and were fit to be made public, to raise that spirit in the nation which was necessary against the prevailing Popish party.[14]

We owe *Two Treatises* to the wonderful knowledge of state affairs which Locke acquired from frequent discourse with the first earl of Shaftesbury; indeed the evidence suggests, as we shall see, that he actually wrote the book for Shaftes-

---

[14] The first extract comes from a document in the Shaftesbury Papers (P.R.O. 30/24, XLVII, 28, 3) endorsed 'F.C.' and copied in what looks like the third earl's hand into a fuller account. The second comes from the third earl's letter writtten for Jean Leclerc and based on documents like these—dated February 1705, printed 1851. Both have been modernized.

bury's purposes. The original meeting may not have been entirely a consulting-room accident. Shaftesbury's grandson tells us that he was recommended by the earl's steward, an important figure in the machinery of local influence.[15] Local politics, then, the association of families over wide areas and long periods of time, made this meeeting no unlikely thing, although no other connection has yet been found between the Lockes of Somerset and the great political family of the neighbouring county of Dorset. But its results were not simply political, nor were they confined to political and social theory. They are to be seen over the whole area of Locke's intellectual activity: without Shaftesbury, Locke would not have been Locke at all.

We have seen that Locke was never a pure philosopher at Oxford, and we have quoted the claim of a witness that his major work on philosophy was written in Shaftesbury's household. It is now known that this was indeed the case, though the actual work of composition took so long, nearly twenty years, that the finished work was never seen by Shaftesbury. Locke began his career as a philosopher in his chamber at Exeter House in the early months of 1671, and by July he had produced a draft of the embryonic *Essay* in one of his own notebooks. Before the end of the year he had rewritten and extended it, but meanwhile he had got someone to copy parts of the original and some of his workings for the information of the earl himself. We know this, and we know that this incomplete manuscript was looked on by Shaftesbury as a personal possession, because it was seized amongst his most private papers from his study when he was arrested in 1681: it has even been suggested that another such paper represented Shaftesbury's own sketched attempt at a theory of knowledge.[16] Here we have them, the statesman and his

[15] 'Mr Bennet of the town of Shaftesbury': he and his son were M.P.'s for the borough. Even the physician, David Thomas, who commissioned Locke with the water bottles, had a political identity. He was a strong Whig, and when the *Essay on Human Understanding* appeared, would have preferred a life of Shaftesbury. For even stronger emphasis on Locke's association with the Earl, see Viano, 1960, e.g. p. 543n.

[16] See Laslett, 1952 (i): the suggestion is Dr Von Leyden's and cannot be pursued because we have the first few words of the paper only. The subject of the first workings for the *Essay* is complex, see Cranston, 1957, 141–2, Aaron, *Locke*, 2nd ed. 1955, 50–5. Johnston, 1954, rightly corrects my suggestion that the Shaftesbury draft is the earliest still extant, but a detailed comparison between the two originals shows that they cannot be related as she supposes. The two other 1671 versions have been edited by Aaron and Gibb, 1936, and Rand, 1931.

medical, scholarly intimate, stimulating each other on the most abstract subject of all. It was not Locke the Oxford don who became a philosopher, but Locke the confidant of an eminent politician, living the political, social and intellectual life of Restoration London.

So it was with Locke the economist, the educationist, the theorist of toleration, even Locke the scientist and medical reformer. He became a Fellow of the Royal Society in November 1668, from Exeter House and not from Christ Church, sponsored by Sir Paul Neile, a founder of the Royal Society, but also a friend and political associate of Shaftesbury's. In London he met the great Sydenham, and helped in his medical practice and in his study of smallpox. He helped him also with his writings, leaving most of the relevant papers to join Shaftesbury's. Locke published nothing on medicine as such, but his views on education and economics both appeared in the 1690's in printed treatises, and it is quite clear that they had their origin in the work he did for, and in co-operation with, Shaftesbury. He was entrusted with the delicate and important task of finding a wife for the lumpish heir to the house of Ashley, and making sure that he produced an heir in his turn. What had begun as a medical undertaking, turned itself into an educational experiment, and the third earl tells us that he and his five brothers and sisters were all educated by Locke 'according to his own principles (since published by him)'.

He had shown no sign of an interest in the upbringing of children at Oxford, nor any trace of the economist's attitude. And yet within two years of his going to London he produced a paper on the rate of interest written 'at the direction of Lord Ashley' formulating the position which he consistently maintained for the rest of his life, with results of considerable consequence to the future of the British economy.[17] In economics he might be called a traditionalist, almost an Aristotelian, but on the subject of toleration his association with the acknowledged champion of religious freedom swiftly transformed the traditionalist and authoritarian views written into the Oxford treatises. In 1667, during the first months of his residence at Exeter House, he composed an *Essay on*

---

[17] See Laslett, 1957 (i), especially footnote 21. The draft, the first of a series, is MS. e. 8, dated 1688, compare Viano, 1960, 183 on, and refs.

Toleration [18] which turned his earlier arguments into a vigorous defence of the right of dissent, proceeding from analysis of the intellectual problem to positive recommendations about national policy. Advice of this sort was now expected of him, and he seems to have written similar policy documents on many or all of the objects of Shaftesbury's public career. Not the least of these new-born interests was colonial administration.[19]

Locke the man and Locke the writer make up a complicated personality, very difficult to separate from that of Shaftesbury himself in these truly formative years. Apart from the *Toleration* drafts, there are two published political works which have claims to be the result of literary co-operation between them. *The Fundamental Constitutions of Carolina*, privately and anonymously issued in 1669, and the *Letter from a Person of Quality*, anonymous, 1675, alike appear in an authoritative collection of Locke's works.[20] The manuscript of the *Constitutions* is in Locke's hand in the Shaftesbury papers, and a note of his written during or before composition has been found in one of his books: in 1679–80 he wrote to his French friends as if he were responsible for the work. No such evidence has come out about the other work, and in 1684 he seemed anxious to repudiate authorship. We shall perhaps never know exactly how far the *Constitutions* represented Locke's or Shaftesbury's views of how a society newly set up in the American wilderness should be ideally constituted, or how far it was a compromise between them and the other proprietors. The contrast of its doctrines with those of *Two Treatises* is intriguing. If Locke approved them in 1669, for English as well as colonial society, his

[18] Manuscript version in the Shaftesbury papers printed by Fox Bourne, 1876, I, 174–94. There are three other versions, and the relationship between them does not seem to be finally established (see the discussions in Cranston, 1957, III; Gough, 1950, corrected by Von Leyden, 1954; Johnston, 1956; Brown, 1933). But the evidence implies a close relationship in composition between Locke and Shaftesbury: one of the copies is in the same hand as is found in Shaftesbury's personal copy of the first workings on the philosophical *Essay* (see note 16, p. 40).

[19] See Laslett, 1957 (i).

[20] *A Collection of Several Pieces of Mr John Locke*, 1720. Desmaizeaux and Collins, who were responsible, were well placed to know what Locke had a hand in, but we shall not know definitely unless we can read the papers of his literary executor, Peter first Lord King. Both pieces are reprinted in collected Lockes from the 4th, 1740.

views on the people, who they were and how they were related to government, changed profoundly by 1679.

But it may be unprofitable simply to seek for consistency or inconsistency here, just as it is in comparing Locke at Oxford with Locke in Shaftesbury's entourage. These publications indicate one of the ways in which he acted as 'assistant pen' to his master in the first period of their association, before he left for France in 1675. He would also draft official papers, record conversations and negotiations, even prompt his master from behind his chair, as he is supposed to have done when Lord Chancellor Shaftesbury delivered the famous speech *Delenda est Carthago* against the Dutch enemy in 1673. But his important literary function was to write out for Shaftesbury's use an account of this or that political or social problem, telling him what had been thought or written about it, what arguments were likely to convince intelligent people of the correctness of a certain attitude to it. The successive drafts on toleration, economics, even perhaps on education and philosophy fit into this context, as well as being records of Locke's own intellectual development. They are supplemented by what he wrote in his diaries, his letters and his commonplace books. From these sources a remarkably complete record can be recovered of the story behind nearly all of his final books: the conspicuous exception is the work on *Government*.

In a sense, of course, all this material is relevant to Locke's development as a political theorist, especially the toleration file. We shall see that he began reading and making notes on political authority and the origin of political power as soon as he came under Shaftesbury's influence. It may be true that no draft on this subject was ever drawn up during this earlier period, to be subsequently destroyed.

For the issue of political obligation as such did not arise in an urgent form until 1679, when Shaftesbury found himself in need of a general, theoretical argument to justify a change in the constitution. There can be little doubt that Locke was summoned back from France early in 1679 to help his master. Shaftesbury was temporarily in office once again, trying to use the national scare over the Popish Plot to force on King Charles II the exclusion from the succession of his brother and heir apparent, the Catholic James, duke of York.[21] It is cer-

---

[21] 'In the year 79 the Earl of Shaftesbury being made Lord President of the Council Mr Locke (as it is said) was sent for home', Lady

tain that Locke knew all about what was going on, and that he took no opportunity to disapprove the forced confessions, the judicial murders, mob oratory and agitation. We do not know whether he 'believed in' the Popish Plot any more than we know if Shaftesbury did, but he never criticized Shaftesbury's actions at any time. He was always his loyal and whole-hearted admirer.

He went much further towards revolution and treason than his earlier biographers knew, anxious as they were to present him as a man of unspotted personal and political virtue.[22] When Parliament was summoned to meet at Oxford early in 1681, at a time when armed resistance seems to have been decided on if the Exclusion Bill failed again, Locke took an active part. He went from house to house finding accommodation for Shaftesbury's entourage, even for Rumsey, the chief of his desperadoes. He was in correspondence with Shaftesbury about influencing elections; he may even have written the famous 'Instructions to the Knights of the County of . . . for their Conduct in Parliament', which has claims to be the first modern party document in history.[23] When the parliamentary attempt had finally failed and Shaftesbury, after a period of imprisonment, had no other resort than to persuade his associates into consultations verging on treason, Locke went along with him and the others.

With his diary open to us we now know that Locke spent the whole of the summer of 1682 with Shaftesbury while these consultations proceeded. On 15 September he even went with him to Cassiobury, the seat of the earl of Essex, where a meet-

---

Masham, 1705. Another argument can be based on the fact that, though Locke had been away for four years, he was so busy with Shaftesbury's business directly he arrived in London, that it was seven months before he could get away to Oxford, and a year before he could go down to Somerset to visit his neglected property. There is a list of trials and confessions in MS. b. 2 and Locke sent a collection of literature of this sort to Thomas in Salisbury at his request.

[22] Mr Cranston has effectively demolished the belief of Locke's Victorian biographers in his 'political innocence', see especially chs. 14 and 16. Bastide, 1907, still maintained that 'he kept aloof from the struggle' (p. 68), but suspected that he may have helped Monmouth. I am prepared to believe that he was more deeply implicated in Monmouth's rebellion than even Cranston allows, and he misses the significance of the references to Cassiobury in Locke's diary.

[23] P.R.O. 30/24 VIB, Item, 399, endorsed 'The original of this wrote in Mr Locke's own hand'. On all this, see Christie, *Shaftesbury*, 1871.

ing of the Whig leaders was scheduled at the height of what is sometimes called the Insurrection Plot. Most significant of all, since it was the action of a man with an independent political personality for the first time, is the fact that he went there again on 24 April 1683, at the very time when preparations are supposed to have been under way for the Assassination, or Rye House, Plot.[24]

We can assume that he went on this second occasion entirely of his own choosing because Shaftesbury was dead, dead in exile in Holland, his last hours spent, so the tradition goes, in discussing the unorthodox religious doctrines implied in the later part of Locke's *Essay on Human Understanding*. Another frequent visitor to the earl of Essex in those dangerous days was Algernon Sidney, regicide and republican, a man who was to lose his head for his part in the Rye House Plot. Sidney had written at length in support of his views and in refutation of Sir Robert Filmer, the author whose works had become the official exposition of the Royal and Tory view of the basis of governmental power. Sidney's manuscript, later published as his *Discourses Concerning Government,* was an essential part of the case of the Crown at Sidney's trial later in the year.[25] As we have seen from what happened at Oxford, Locke was already a suspected man, and from the time of the discovery of the Rye House Plot he became a fugitive, quite soon in exile. Nothing specific was ever proved against him, but it was persistently believed that his treasonable activity had been writing against the government, just as Sidney had done.

We shall attempt to show that Locke had by this time written a work against the government, and that *Two Treatises of Government* was the book in question. The case will have to be presented in full because of the established dogma that it was written in or just after 1688.[26] We must now turn to such evidence as he has left us of his development as a political theorist whilst he was with Shaftesbury. We may believe if we wish that the train of thought which gave rise to *Two Treatises* departed from the following quotation from one of

[24] There is no reliable evidence of what was discussed on either occasion, but tyrannicide seems unlikely, since Essex was apparently quite unwilling to contemplate it, though he died in the Tower when a prisoner for his part in these preparations. Locke preserved a manuscript maintaining the Whig view that Essex did not commit suicide but was murdered, and he may well have been quite close to Essex.

[25] See Laslett, 1949, 36–7.

[26] See section III.

the works of Sir Robert Filmer, written by Locke into a note-book very early in his days at Exeter House.

Hobs

With noe small content I read Mr Hobs booke De Cive & his Leviathan about the rights of Soveraignty wch noe man yt I know hath soe amply & Judiciously handled. Filmore. Obser. preface: [27]

The list of books on politics, quotations from them and judgments of their value, from which this quotation comes, seems to have been drawn up in Shaftesbury's presence, for a very similar list has been found in Shaftesbury's own papers, in Locke's hand; [28] there are many items common to both. From this evidence we may conclude that the intellectual re-lationship between Locke and Shaftesbury in the matter of political theory was, as might be expected, much the same as for economics, toleration and so on. The association directed Locke's attention to the works of Milton, Campanella, Guic-cardini, Adam Contzen, as well as to such English champions of non-resistance as Heylyn, Dudley Digges and Filmer. Some of these authors were known to him already, and we may be-lieve that he had read, and praised, a work of Filmer's as early as the year 1659, though this was the first time he had been told that Filmer was its author.[29] It is clear that Shaftesbury's company was bringing him up against the questions he had

[27] Ms. f. 14, folio 16. For this manuscript, and for some of the titles on this list, see Appendix B. The quotation was obviously directly copied from Filmer's *Observations concerning the original of Government, Upon Mr Hobs* Leviathan . . ., London, 1652, first words of Preface.

[28] P.R.O. 30/24/47, no. 30, classified book list, section *Politici:* see Appendix B also. It is a curious fact that in both lists, Sir Robert Filmer, whose tracts had been printed anonymously, is called Sir Thomas Fil-more. This is the only occasion known to me when the name 'Filmer' was associated with these tracts before their collected publication in 1679, outside Sir Robert's family and his circle of friends. Locke and Shaftesbury named every one of Filmer's political tracts except his pieces on the *Power of Kings* and his *Freeholder*. Maclean, 1946, recognized that Locke read Filmer as early as 1667, but did not notice the parallel in the Shaftesbury pages.

[29] There are two references to another set of Filmer's *Observations*, his essay on Philip Hunton which had the title *The Anarchy of a Limited or Mixed Monarchy* (1648) in Locke's notebook entitled *Lemmata Ethica*. For this manuscript see Appendix B. Neither reference is dated, and most of the other entries in the book are later, and marked as such. But their position and context suggest that they were made very early in Locke's use of the book. One quotes the definition of absolute monarchy from p. 15 of Filmer's tract and adds appreciatively: 'hujusmodi monarchia optime defenditur.' No author is given.

deliberately left on one side at Oxford. What were the origins
of political power, how is it to be analysed, what are its limits
and what are the rights of the people?

That these questions were exercising Locke during his first
period with Shaftesbury, especially the possibility of a patriarchal origin for political power, is shown by another note made
in 1669.[30] There he made a point which he was to argue at
length in *Two Treatises*. In 1672 he schemed something out
on *Wisdom*, dividing his observations under the three headings
'Prudence', 'Theology' and 'Politics' (Politia). Politics in its
turn is divided into 'Fundamentals', 'The form of the State'
and 'Administration', and the two fundamentals are *Jus Paternum* and *Consensus Populi*.[31] This acceptance of patriarchalism alongside of popular consent is also to be found in the final
work, here no longer equally fundamental.

But though we know that this was the period of his development as a political theorist, the book itself comes as a revelation. The best illustration of this is the important issue of
property, for nothing in his literary remains from the years
leading up to his writing on *Government* suggests that property would be a major theme. It is mentioned, in a phrase
which fits in with his statement about it in his *Essay on the
Understanding*, in his Oxford *Essays on Natural Law;* but
what he says in his 1667 *Essay on Toleration* seems to imply
a general position which is very different from that presented
in *Two Treatises*.[32] These are only isolated references. The
fact would seem to be, and it can be confirmed for many of
the other subjects, that Locke simply had not thought in a
systematic way about property before 1679. He had not
worked out his justification of ownership in terms of labour.

The pre-history of *Two Treatises*, then, is a complex study
which cannot be taken further here. Enough has been said to
suggest the atmosphere in which its doctrines were formulated,
an atmosphere of political decisions and policy itself, with
Shaftesbury as the policy-maker and Locke as the confidential
co-adjutor, one amongst others but the most important. This
is not the atmosphere we associate with philosophy, and too
often with political thinking, nevertheless this was also the
time of Locke's philosophical maturation. *Two Treatises* and

[30] MS. c. 29, ff. 7–9, notes on Samuel Parker, *A Discourse of Ecclesiastical Politie*, 1670, printed in full by Cranston, 1957, 131–2.
[31] MS. c. 28, f. 41: 'Sapientia 72.' Compare Abrams, 1961, 311,
scheme of ? 1661.
[32] See below, 116.

the *Essay* were in gestation at the same time, and the political work reached its almost final form earlier, in spite of the fact that systematic work on it began seventeen years later.

We shall assign the important part of the work of composition to the years 1679–80. It was then, as we believe, that the book took shape, and took shape suddenly for an author with such slow, deliberate habits. Up till then the train of ideas which had been present in his mind from the beginning had developed in a desultory way, as a subordinate theme to that of toleration. It had been deliberately pushed aside when he wrote on Natural Law at Oxford, and can be seen only in such details as his registration of Filmer's agreement with Hobbes. Since he has left us no sketch, no early form of any part of the book we cannot tell what his earlier opinions had been on many of the subjects it covers, nor how they developed. He was certainly reflecting on them occasionally in his journeys through France between 1676 and 1679.

In February 1676, when he was at Montpellier, he made a note in his journal on the *Obligation of Penal Laws* which dealt rather obscurely with the problem of resistance. He is quite confident that civil laws do not necessarily oblige the individual conscience, but he maintains that there is a law of God 'which forbids disturbance or dissolution of governments'. Conscience is satisfied if a man 'obeys the magistrate to the degree, as not to endanger or disturb the government, under what form of government soever he live'.[33] Two and a half years later we find an abbreviated sketch of a complete theory, relating man to God, father to son, the individual to society, in familial, patriarchal terms: not Filmer's patriarchalism, but nevertheless closer to the notes of 1669 and 1672 than to *Two Treatises*. The heading he chose was Natural Law, *Lex Naturae*. Man, he noted, has 'a knowledge of himself, which the beasts have not' and this knowledge was 'given him for some use and end'. It shows men that a son should obey his father (although begot 'only in pursuance of his pleasure, without thinking of his son') and therefore they must obey God as the final 'author of their being'. It is similarly 'reasonable to punish' a child 'that injures another', and from this we may conclude that children, and all men, are expected by God 'to assist and help one another' as a duty. 'If he find that God

---

[33] Printed in King, 1830, I, 114–17: compare Lamprecht, 1916, 142–3, who seems slightly to exaggerate Locke's insistence here on passive obedience.

has made him and all other men in a state wherein they cannot subsist without society, and has given them judgment to discern what is capable of preserving and maintaining that society, can he but conclude that he is obliged, and that God requires him to follow those rules which conduce to the preserving of society?' [34]

He wrote this when travelling up the Loire in July 1678, a long way from London, Shaftesbury and the dreadful Popish Plot, and he wrote it for himself. We shall claim that his work on *Government* was an exercise on this same theme begun only about a year later, but written for his leader, written also for the public which both men wanted to persuade. Such is the measure of the difference between the Locke who wrote in solitude and the Locke who wrote for Shaftesbury.

But he also wrote for his patron in a way which is much more familiar and typical of his time, to honour and divert him. He presented his little volume on *The Growth of Vines and Olives* to his Lordship on 2 February 1680, and that eminent epicure and cultivator was overjoyed with the exquisite little manuscript volume. To the Countess on the same occasion, it was to celebrate his return from France, he dedicated his translation of the *Essais* of Nicole. In our anxiety to understand the harsh political reality in which these two friends lived their life together, we must not lose sight of its gracefulness, gentility and wit. Locke sat at the Chaplain's table in Lord Chancellor Shaftesbury's meticulously regulated dining hall: he had to trudge through the mud to support that megalomaniac imp when he went out in his coach on state occasions. But he also had a voice in the decoration of his houses, the layout of his gardens: he educated the grandchildren of his master in English gentility, that just and mellow blending of the practical man, with stoic virtue, understatement and a deep respect for learning. The ideal of the English gentleman is with us today, and in part it is Locke's invention. It grew out of his affection for Shaftesbury.

The last thing Locke wrote as literature was a life, a vindication, or an *Éloge* as the French were saying, of his great master. This was as it should be, for it was the final debt which all literary men owed to those who made the life of literature and thought possible for them. His own end came before he

---

[34] Journal for 1678, 201–2, modernized: compare, I, § 52 and note. In the note to II, § 58, is quoted a further note of importance to politics, written in his journal in Paris in March 1679.

could get further than the first few pages, but the Latin epitaph was finished:

Comitate, acumine, suadela, consilio, animo, constantia, fide,
    Vix parem invenias, superiorem certe nullibi.
Libertatis civilis, ecclesiasticae,
    Propugnator strenuus, indefessus.

Liberty, then, is the last word we are left with—a tireless, fierce fighter for liberty in religion, liberty in politics, the liberty of Locke's own work on *Government*.

3. LOCKE AND SOMERS

1689 was the year of the great climacteric in the life of Locke. As a result of the Revolution the obscure exile became a man of political influence, with powerful friends in high places. The minor figure in the republic of letters, something of a journalist in the Dutch intellectual community where he had been living, the multiplier of notes and writer of drafts, at last appeared as an author, first of the *Letter on Toleration*, then of *Two Treatises of Government*, both in print by the autumn of that year, but both anonymous. Then in December the John Locke who signed the Preface to *An Essay Concerning Human Understanding* became, by that very act, the John Locke of intellectual history. It turned him into a national institution and an international influence. In the fifteen years left to him he twisted his fingers round the haft of English intellectual life and got so firm a grasp that it pointed at last in the direction which he had chosen.

It was a philosophical reputation which he enjoyed, and it was because of the key position of philosophy that his intellectual domination was possible. Everything else which he wrote was important because he, Locke of the *Human Understanding*, had written it. It was so with his *Thoughts Concerning Education*, 1694, his works on *Money*, 1692 and 1695, and his polemic with Stillingfleet in defence of his *Essay* in 1697 and 1699. The anonymous works, the three letters on *Toleration* of 1689, 1690 and 1692, the *Reasonableness of Christianity* and its *Vindications* of 1695 and 1697, could not be associated with his philosophy by his contemporaries, or only by very few. It is surely significant that the work on *Government*, the most secret of all, went almost unscathed till its authorship was finally revealed.[35] But from the time of his death the relation of *Two Treatises* with the *Essay* has been its leading characteristic. Here is an important philosopher, the proposition goes, addressing himself to politics, so what he writes must be important political philosophy.

This way of looking at *Two Treatises of Government* has given rise to a convention of analysis which we shall have to criticize. There is a danger too in the very pattern of Locke's literary career: an apprenticeship of remarkable length leading up to a short final period in which six major works and nine lesser ones, were published, most of them in several editions, all by an ageing man, busily engaged with other things in his study, and in the world of politics and administration. It makes it look as if he deliberately planned his life in this way, and in the case of political theory this impression is hard to avoid. Here, it would seem, was a mind which trained itself first academically, then at the very seat of political power, and after two important periods of residence abroad, in France and in Holland, finally responded to the Revolution of 1688–9 with a work on *Government*.

The impression of a deliberate plan is of course an illusion, and I believe that he cannot have composed his book after 1683, but there is some value in this commentary on Locke the writer. He felt the need to ripen, particularly as a philosopher, before he appeared in print, and he was also both anxious to publish books and afraid of being criticized. In the final period of his life Locke overcame this fear, and when he found that what he published was a success, he published more. Criticism always disturbed him deeply, which must be one of the reasons for his refusing to acknowledge books which he knew would be controversial. The effect of all this was to make him publish late and enter into history only as an old man,

[35] Mr Dunn finds the earliest reply in Leslie, 1703, and what seems to be the second is *An Essay upon Government, wherein the Republican Schemes reviv'd by Mr Locke are Refuted*, London, 1705, author unknown. But it was noticed abroad: *Du Gouvernement Civil* was coolly reviewed by Basnage in his *Histoire des Ouvrages des Sçavans*, Tome VIII, June 1691, 457. 'C'est dommage', he says on p. 465, 'que l'Auteur n'a pas toûjours bien dégagé ses pensées, ni bien dévelopé ses sentimens.'

but it was not simply a matter of cumulative experience and above all it was not deliberate.

Calculated strategy is to be seen, however, in the way he went about the task of making sure that his ideas and opinions should affect the policy of governments in these years of his intellectual ascendancy. He had never wanted political office of the ordinary kind and once again he found himself refusing diplomatic posts. Hypochondriac as he was, his first need, as he said, was for a place of 'the highest convenience for a retired, single life'. He found obstacles in the way of getting back his Studentship at Christ Church, but a far more comfortable and delicate home for an ageing bachelor presented itself. By the middle of 1691 he was established in the household of Sir Francis Masham at his little moated manor house at Otes, in Essex, under the loving care of his lady, Damaris Masham, Locke's closest friend of all. Here twenty miles from London he spent his final, glorious years, his great and growing library around him, his special chair and desk, his cumbrous scientific apparatus, with his own servant and fodder for his own horse, all for one guinea a week.[36] His time went in writing, not simply the works he published in such numbers, but letters, letters to the learned world, to publishers, to stock-jobbers, and letters to politicians and to ministers and professional servants of the crown. The political influence he exercised in this way was truly extraordinary, and for the hundred warmest days in the year he exercised it in person from his London address in Lincoln's Inn Fields.

He did hold office of a sort, for from 1689 he was a Commissioner of Appeals and when the Board of Trade was founded in 1696 he was made a paid member. It has been shown, in fact, that Locke himself played a large part in the creation of this second body, the architect of the old Colonial System, and was directly responsible for the Great Recoinage of 1695–6, the expiry of the licensing of the press and many other measures too.[37] There was a knot of Lockeian members of parliament, a group cutting across political 'connection' as it is now beginning to be understood, 'the only known example of an association of politicians for the purpose of a set of rationally conceived policies, a programme based not only on

[36] For Locke at Otes, see Laslett, 1954 (i). From 1697 Locke had the literary assistance of Pierre Coste, who came to live at Otes as tutor to Lady Masham's son; hence the Christ's master-copy of *Two Treatises*.
[37] See Laslett, 1957 (i), summarized above: the full story has yet to be worked out.

common sentiment, but on superior information and abstract thinking'. It was all done by a typically Lockeian foundation called the 'College' whose main function was correspondence, but which met as a club when Locke was in London: its patron was John Somers, later Lord Somers, counsel for the Seven Bishops in 1688, Solicitor-General in 1689, Lord Keeper 1693, Lord Chancellor 1697 and the chief figure in William III's government until 1700.

Somers met Locke in the early 1680's and by 1689 looked to him so much as his mentor that he actually asked his advice on whether he should go on circuit or attend at parliament: in 1690 they exchanged views on the state of the currency. In fact, but with differences, Somers took on Shaftesbury's role for Locke. We need not dwell here on the importance and results of this association for government policy in the 1690's nor list the other noblemen, ministers and members who looked to him for advice and turned that advice into policy. The point of interest for Locke as a writer of political theory lies in the relation between the principles he had published, but not acknowledged, and the practical decisions which he advised so effectively and often helped to carry out. It would almost seem that during these years after the Revolution there was a sense in which liberal or Whig philosophy did in fact inform government and affect politicians in the person of Locke the Whig philosopher.

Such an interpretation cannot be taken too literally. Locke, as we have seen, seemed indifferent to the implications of *Two Treatises*, certainly for communities under English domination. There was a general change towards 'rationalism' over these years, and it is significant that Locke's part in it was not confined to thinking and writing: success and reputation came to him suddenly after 1688 because at that point a secular drift in the atmosphere became a rapid transformation. But historians are now careful not to call the events of 1688-9 the triumph of the Whigs, or even a revolution as that word is often used. Nevertheless it was the new general situation, as well as his own skill and good fortune, which enabled Locke to observe something of what we shall call his 'principle for policy' in action. The interesting thing is that he did not feel called upon to revise the text of his political theory in the light of this observation, although he did correct and recorrect its details and he can hardly have been unaware of its difficulties as a guide for ministers and administrators.

Outstanding in Locke's attitude and behaviour was his insistence on the citizen's duties in government: he looked upon himself and his friend Isaac Newton, Warden of the Mint, as contributing what an intellectual owed to government activity. If we are to understand Locke the political writer we must dwell for a little while on his peculiar relationship with the politicians.

In December 1684, he wrote from Holland a defensive letter to his patron at the time, the earl of Pembroke: it is a vindication of himself from the charges which had been used to justify his expulsion from Christ Church, and is an instructive commentary on several of the themes we have discussed. Talking of what he did in Shaftesbury's household, and hinting that as a practising physician he might have done better for himself materially, he continues:

> I never did anything undutifully against His Majesty or the government. . . . I have never been of any suspected clubs or cabals. I have made little acquaintance, and kept little company, in an house where so much came. . . . My unmeddling temper . . . always sought quiet, and inspired me with no other desires, no other aims, than to pass silently through this world with the company of a few good friends and books. . . . I have often wondered in the way that I lived, and the make that I knew myself of, how it could come to pass, that I was made the author of so many pamphlets, unless it was because I of all my Lord's family happened to have been bred most among books. . . . I here solemnly protest in the presence of God, that I am not the author, not only of any libel, but not of any pamphlet or treatise whatsoever in print, good, bad or indifferent. The apprehension and backwardness I have ever had to be in print even in matters very remote from anything of libellous or seditious, is so well known to my friends.[38]

We may raise our eyebrows at Locke's definition of being undutiful to government and feel he was prevaricating over his authorship of political works, but we must welcome this insight into his character as a writer and his attitude to his political patrons. It suggests a delicate and precise portrait of the intellectual in the company of men of action. Obviously fascinated with the consummate effectiveness of all that Shaftesbury thought and wrote, said and did; anxious, perhaps

---

[38] Locke to Pembroke, 3 December 1684, published Osler, 1914; probably not seen by Pembroke, but retained by Edward Clarke, through whom it was to be sent, and who was asked by Locke to destroy it. See his letter to Clarke of 1 January 1685 (Rand, 1927, 117–21), where he also repeats these assertions of his innocence, literary and political.

over-anxious, to identify himself with the power he wielded; Locke could not bring himself to share his whole personality with the politicians. There is a hint here of his uneasiness about their lack of scruple and the dusty triviality of political activity day by day. But this was not the inner reason why he held himself back; why he kept up his Oxford career while it lasted, paying token visits there in the summer when the great men were in the country, or insisted on his separate personality as a doctor and a thinker. He never overcame his inhibitions, although his situation in the 1690's made it possible for him to do what he wanted in spite of them. Wonderfully quick and effective as an expository talker and writer, a genius in the calm clarity with which he could see the shape of complicated things, he was not a man who could lose himself in the act of political doing, or even of intellectual creation. His was an effectiveness at one remove, a power to fascinate the men of action, and in his last years he enjoyed to the full the directive influence it gave him.

Locke died on 29 October 1704, in his study at Otes, a room walled in dark oily brown and dull white, the colours of the books which had been so much of his life. He is buried a long way from Oxford and from his ancestors in Somerset, and buried in somewhat strange company, for the Mashams who lie all round him at High Laver were Tories and courtiers of the next generation.[39] He died a gentleman: 'John Locke, Gent.' is the author's line on the title-pages of the endless reprints of his books which stood on the shelves of eighteenth-century libraries. This raises the final question which must be asked about him as the intimate of great politicians and the creator of political principle for the modern world. Can he be called, as so often he is, the spokesman of a rising class, the middle class, the capitalists, the bourgeoisie?

We cannot here pass judgment on the sociological system which regards this question as a critical one. Locke certainly satisfies some of the criteria which it has set up. He was born, as we have said, into the classical atmosphere of early capitalism, into what might well be called a Puritan rising family in the loose way in which the term is used, for he was brought up amongst the lawyers, officials and merchants who had found their way into the Somerset gentry and lived his life

[39] See Laslett, 1945 (i). Abigail Masham is there, the snivelling High Church chambermaid who insinuated Sarah Churchill out of the affections of Queen Anne.

as an absentee member. When he joined Shaftesbury, it could
be said that he passed from the *petite bourgeoisie* to the *haute
bourgeoisie*. He followed his wealthy patron into his invest-
ments—the Africa Company, the Lustring Company and finally the Bank of England. He invested in mortgages, lent
money all his life to his friends for their convenience and at
interest; although he protested that he 'never lov'd stock job-
bing' there is in his letters of 1700–1 a clear example of stock-
market profiteering in the shares of the Old and New East
India Companies. In his published works he showed himself
the determined enemy of beggars and the idle poor, who existed, he thought, because of 'the relaxation of discipline and
the corruption of manners'. He even implied that a working
family had no right to expect its children to be at leisure after
the age of three.[40]

But at the same time Locke profoundly mistrusted commerce and commercial men. He obviously welcomed the refusal of Somers to permit the control of national economic
policy by such men when they attempted to set up a parliamentary Board of Trade in 1695, and though he approved the
Bank of England, there is in his hand a curious dialogue expressing deep suspicions of the capitalists who floated it.[41]
Although he was a doctor, it is difficult to make him a representative of the emerging professions which are now taken
as symptomatic of the new order, for he despised medical men
just to the extent that they were a profession and he shared
Shaftesbury's contempt for lawyers. His expulsion from Oxford may have been symbolic of the clash of the new view of
the world with the old, but the crisis which actually brought
it about was a complex conflict of interests and beliefs leading
to violent political actions, and his own philosophical and general views were unpublished at the time.

It can be said nevertheless that Locke the individualist was
an individual, and this is to claim for him a more exceptional
social position than appears at first sight. The remarkable
thing about him was his freedom from engagement: family,
church, community, locality. To be free in all these directions
at that time posed a dilemma to him. This dilemma can be

---

[40] See his report to the Board of Trade on the poor, 1697, for these
details: printed by Fox Bourne, 1676, II, 377–90, compare Cranston,
1957, 424–5. His recommendations make it look as if the conditions
discovered in the early nineteenth century were not accidents, but the
result of deliberate policy.
[41] See Laslett, 1957 (i).

seen in his relations with Oxford and even with the household at Otes. That such a position was possible, for him and a growing number of others, was a development pregnant of the future. Locke was as free as a man could then be from solidarity with the ruling group, and yet he was not one of the ruled; this is the only intelligible definition of 'middle-class' as applied to him and it leaves out many of the things which that expression seems to imply. Ultimately the possibility of living like this did arise as a function of economic change, but Locke can only be made into the spokesman of that change by the use of a whole apparatus of unconscious motivation and rationalization. An order of free individuals is not a concerted group, not a cohesive assemblage actually bringing about change: no simple conception of 'ideology' will relate Locke's thought with social dynamics.

He is perhaps best described as an independent, free-moving intellectual, aware as others were not of the direction of social change. This is evident in the central issue of *Two Treatises*, which is primarily concerned with the structure of the family and its relevance to social and political authority. If ever men dealt with fundamentals, Filmer and Locke did in this polemic. That Locke should have been an innovator in his justification of property may seem even more significant, but in fact it makes a determinist view of his thinking more difficult. For the attempts to make his doctrine into a straight justification of capitalism have to be complex, too complex to be convincing.

So much for Locke's political writing as determined by social structure and his personal situation. We must now turn to our detailed examination of its chronological determination, the actual events which impelled him to write *Two Treatises of Government*.

III

'TWO TREATISES OF GOVERNMENT' AND THE REVOLUTION OF 1688[1]

Whilst he was waiting at Rotterdam for a ship to take him home after the Revolution, Locke received the following letter from The Hague:

I have been very ill this fortnight. The beginning was what is called disease of one's country, impatience to be there, but it ended yesterday with violence, as all great things do but kings. Ours went out like a farthing candle, and has given us by this Convention an occasion not only of mending the Government but of melting it down and making all new, which makes me wish you were there to give them a right scheme of government, having been infected by that great man Lord Shaftesbury.[2]

The writer was Lady Mordaunt, wife of his friend who was to become Earl of Monmouth and Earl of Peterborough and who was already in England with William III. The Convention she mentions was the Convention Parliament, then working out the constitutional future of England after James II had sputtered out. By 11 February Locke was in London:

[1] This section has been published in a slightly different form in the *Cambridge Historical Journal*, vol. XII, no. 1, March 1956, 40–55 (Laslett, 1956).

[2] Paraphrased: the original seems to read, e.g.: 'ours whent out: Lyke a farding candle: & has given us by this convension an occasion of mending the government but of melting itt down and make. . . .' Dated 31 January 1689.

on the 12th the Declaration of Right was completed:[3] on the 13th William and Mary were offered the crown.

This letter, except perhaps for its last phrase, aptly expresses the traditional view of the reasons why Locke sat down to write *Two Treatises of Government*. The book has 1690 on its title: 1689 had been a year of wavering in the face of a dangerous reaction. What was wanted was an argument, along with a scheme of government, an argument deep in its analysis and theoretical, even philosophical, in its premises, but cogent and convincing in its expression. In its second part, at any rate, *Two Treatises* presents precisely these things. The author's objects and the occasion of his writing are set out just as might be expected in the Preface. He hoped that the book would be:

> sufficient to establish the Throne of our Great Restorer, Our present King **William;** to make good his Title, in the Consent of the People, . . . and to justifie to the World, the People of England, whose love of their Just and Natural Rights, with their Resolution to preserve them, saved the Nation when it was on the very brink of Slavery and Ruine.

The case for supposing that the composition of this work belongs wholly and indissolubly with 1688, the year of the Glorious Revolution, is superficially convincing, therefore. It contains a statement which dates itself in that year.[4] It did in actual fact justify the Revolution to posterity, as well as to contemporaries. 'It is allowed on all hands,' wrote Josiah Tucker in 1781, 'and it has been a continual belief of the friends and admirers of Mr Locke, that he wrote his Essay on Government with a view to justify the Revolution.'[5] In

---

[3] This date makes it practically impossible that Locke had anything to do with its composition, or with any of the arguments offered to the Convention, though some of them look very like what he wrote in *Two Treatises* (compare, e.g., the *Proposals Offered to the Present Convention*, printed in *State Tracts*, 1692, with II, §§ 217, 219). Locke's papers contain nothing to suggest that he communicated his views from Holland to such writers or to members of the Convention.

[4] I, § 129, '*Judge Jefferies*, pronounced Sentence of Death in the late Times', the last phrase being in common use in 1689 to refer to James II's reign.

[5] Tucker, Josiah, *A treatise concerning civil government*, p. 72. In a paper written for Edward Clarke, his closest friend among the parliamentary gentry of England, Locke in fact himself issued *A call to the Nation for Unity*. It urged allegiance to William, oblivion for James II's supporters, and repudiation of Divine Right, in language apparently very close to the Preface to *Two Treatises*. It was sold with other Clarke papers at Sotheby's in 1922 and seen in the 1940's, but it has now been lost sight of.

the history books and the works on political theory, Locke on the English Revolution is still the supreme example of the way in which political events interplay with political thinking. This belief is far too deeply engrained, far, far too useful, to be easily abandoned. Nevertheless it is quite untrue.

Untrue, that is to say, in its most useful form. What Locke wrote did justify the Glorious Whig Revolution of 1688, if that phrase can be permitted at all. Some of the text undoubtedly was written in 1689 to apply to the situation then. But it cannot be maintained that the original conception of the book was the justification of a revolution which had been consummated. A detailed examination of the text and the evidence bearing on it goes to show that it cannot have been 1688 which fastened Locke's attention on the nature of society and politics, political personality and property, the rights of the individual and the ethical imperatives on government. The conjunction of events which set his mind at work on these things must be sought at an earlier period. *Two Treatises* in fact turns out to be a demand for a revolution to be brought about, not the rationalization of a revolution in need of defence.

It was suspected as long ago as 1876 that the *First Treatise* was composed several years before 1688, and that the *Second* cannot have been wholly subsequent to the Revolution.[6] But the evidence available at that time was even more fragmentary and difficult to interpret than it is today, and within a decade or two the dogma that Locke wrote to rationalize the events of 1688–9 became firmly established in the nascent study of political science.[7] Another reason why this came

[6] Fox Bourne, I, 466, and II, 166: he believed that the *First* was prepared in 1681 or 1682, and that the *Second,* from its tone and method, seemed to have been 'composed before, instead of after, King William's accession. . . . It may fairly be assumed that the whole work was substantially completed during the last year or so of Locke's residence in Holland'.

[7] Sir Leslie and Sir James Fitzjames Stephen, T. H. Green and Sir Frederick Pollock form the very distinguished group who seem to have been responsible, ignoring Fox Bourne and blandly accepting traditional dogma. Writing in 1876 itself, Sir Leslie Stephen merely said (II, 135) that 'Locke expounded the principles of the Revolution of 1688', but in 1879 Green was claiming in his famous *Lectures* that 'Locke wrote with a present political object in view . . . to justify the Revolution' (published 1895, 1931 ed., 76). Fowler was still following Fox Bourne in 1880, but Pollock was much more specific in reading the Revolution into the *Treatises* in his *Introduction to the History of the Science of Politics,* published originally in 1890. Sir James Stephen based his whole critique of the book on the fact that it had this as its occasion: he published this view in his *Horae Sabbaticae,* 2nd series,

about was that the reprints of the book which have circulated since that time have been so unsatisfactory.[8] Few of the students who have handled Locke on *Government* in recent generations were to know that he explained himself as he did in his *Preface,* or even that the work consists in two treatises, not one, the first breaking off in the middle of a sentence only a quarter of the way through its text. For the *Preface* has not been reprinted in England since 1854, and the *First Treatise* only once since 1884.[9] When we treat what we are pleased to call our great political classics like this, there can be little wonder that a minor mythology should grow around one of them.

Although Locke makes this statement in his *Preface* of 1689 expressing the hope that what he had written would serve to justify the Revolution, he does not elaborate it. Nothing he says there refers directly to the time at which the work was composed, but he does explain why it would not have been worth his while to rewrite the missing majority of his manuscript. We may take this to imply that the *First Treatise,* described on the title-page as a refutation of Filmer, had been composed some time before, and was not so much a thing of the moment when the *Preface* was being written. It is interesting to recognize that Locke originally wrote such an extensive analysis of the work of a man whom he wanted to regard as an obscure nonentity,[10] and that the book planned was similar in size and in purpose to Sidney's unmanageable *Discourses*. But it is quite understandable that he should have been unwilling to repeat the performance. Filmer's great vogue had been between 1679 and 1681, and only the lingering attachment to his principles of the passive obedience party

---

1892. In 1904 Pollock developed the case in definitive form in his address to the British Academy, and more recent commentators seem to have followed him uncritically here and in his claim that Locke was really and consciously attacking Hobbes. Bastide, 1907, went farthest in reading the events of 1688–9 into the *Second Treatise,* although he relied heavily on Fox Bourne, and accepted his date for the *First Treatise*—see especially pp. 255–72.

[8] See section I and especially references in note 10, p. 19.

[9] See Appendix A, Check List of Printings. The last English edition with both treatises and the Preface dates from 1824, but they presumably appeared in the last *Collected Locke* in 1854, which I have not seen and whose existence has been doubted. They are included in an American reprint of 1947 (Hafner).

[10] On Filmer, see Laslett, 1948 (i) and (ii), and 1949. The slightly apologetic tone of Locke's remarks about him in the *Preface* may be due to the fact that he knew his family in Kent.

in 1689 justified the appearance between the same covers of the *First* and *Second Treatise*.

More recent specialist students of Locke have used this evidence in favour of the view of the date or dates of composition originally proposed in 1876. They have freely granted that the *First Treatise* was written before 1683, before Locke left for Holland, and they explain the fact that it contains the only statement which undoubtedly belongs after 1688 (the reference to 'Judge Jefferies') as an insertion of 1689. But the second book, they seem to agree, must be much later, and can only be dated in the months surrounding the revolutionary events themselves, though they find it difficult to decide which passages came before and which came after William's triumph over James. It has been noticed that the books to which Locke directly refers in his text, though very few in number, were all in print before 1683. But in the absence of any detailed knowledge of the editions and copies he actually used to write any part of his text, this fact has not been taken to point to an earlier date of composition for the whole work. They concede that the drift of Locke's statements makes it look as if the Revolution was yet to come. Nevertheless they see nothing impossible in supposing that the *Second Treatise* was written in its entirety after the event: that is presumably between Locke's return in February 1689 and August of that year, when it must have been complete to receive the Licenser's stamp.[11]

In view of all the work on this point over the last eighty years it seems extraordinary that the traditional fallacy, that not one but both *Treatises* were written to justify the Revolution of 1688–9, should still survive. But before it is abandoned, it should be pointed out that there is evidence in its favour which has never been brought forward. In some ways it is a better explanation than the one which has just been summarized. If the wording of Locke's *Preface* is considered

[11] On 3 August 1689, the limiting date for the completion of the text. Among the Locke scholars referred to here are Gough, 1950, following Maclean, 1947 (i) and (ii), and Barker, 1948. Vaughan, 1925, conjectures from an argument about the inconsistency between the *Essay* and *Two Treatises*, an argument which is quite untenable in view of the history of the *Essay* as it has since become known, that '*Civil Government* . . . was written . . . in or shortly after 1680' (163, cf. 130). Driver, 1928, reaches a similar hypothesis on somewhat similar, though no more reliable grounds. Aaron, 1937 and 1955, is unwilling to pronounce, but he remarks that the aim of the book was 'to justify the Revolution' (1955, 270): Cranston, 1957, cites the present author's argument on the subject.

carefully, it will be seen that he talks of the book as a whole. He cannot be made to imply that it was written in two parts, on two occasions, separated by some years,[12] though the admission that so much of the manuscript had been lost would seem to invite some such statement. It is a 'Discourse concerning Government', with a beginning, a middle (now missing) and an end, not the two disparate essays which recent commentators seem to have in mind.

His cross-references tend to confirm that this was his view of it. They all occur in the first book, which is an interesting point, as we shall see. In § 66 he talks of something he will examine 'in its due place', which turns out to be the second book §§ 52–76: in § 87 he refers to a man's acquiring property, 'which how he . . . could do, shall be shewn in another place', that is in the second book, chapter 5: § 100 contains the words 'for which I refer my Reader to the Second Book'. This second book opens with the phrase 'It having been shewn in the foregoing Discourse', which means the text to be found in the preceding pages, not an earlier and separate discourse, for when unqualified that word refers to the complete work. When Locke wrote these phrases, he must surely have been quite clear about the content of his whole book, and their contexts make it very unlikely that they were later insertions.

We can add to these details Dr Gerritsen's very interesting discovery. Using the exact and subtle methods of analytical bibliography, he has shown that the title-page of the second book was a later insertion, made in the course of printing. The title to the whole, printed even later of course, was presumably brought into line with it.[13] It follows from this that Locke did not think of his volume originally as in two parts at all, any more than any work presented in two 'books'. The word 'Treatise', the expression 'Two Treatises', the title 'An Essay on Civil Government' applied to the second book were all afterthoughts, appearing finally on the title-pages, but never used in the text at all, not even in the cross-references. What Locke thought he was writing was a whole Discourse, set out in two books for his own literary purposes.

The book, then, was written as a whole. If it is permissible to infer from this that it was written within a relatively short

---

[12] Compare the *Epistle* introducing the *Essay on the Understanding*, explaining that it was 'written by incoherent parcels; and after long intervals . . . resumed again', etc.

[13] See Bowers, Gerritsen and Laslett, 1954.

time, then an exact chronological argument is possible about
the work he put into it, the work of original creation that is
to say, as distinct from addition and revision. Given evidence
to show that any considerable portion can only belong to the
situation of a few particular months, say in 1688–9, then the
whole belongs to those months.

But however willing men may have been to read the events
of 1688–9 into Locke's text, there are convincing signs that
the months of composition cannot have fallen then. The *First
Treatise,* as we have seen, was intended as a complete refutation of Filmer, *Patriarcha* and all, and in its original form
may well have covered all his propositions, except perhaps
his specifically historical argument about English institutions.
Moreover, the exhaustive contradiction of patriarchalism runs
right through the *Second Treatise* too: this is perhaps the
most important result of editing it critically. If we believe
that the whole book was written at one time, then we are
obliged to believe that it was written between 1679 and 1681,
or 1683 at the latest, since it is so obviously connected with
the controversy of those years over the republication of Filmer. We have already seen that it was this controversy which
set Sidney on work at his *Discourses,* which must have been
complete by mid-1683 and very probably earlier. It is well
known that in republishing Filmer, the Tories, champions of
the Monarchy against Shaftesbury and the Whig Exclusionists, scored a notable propaganda victory, and Sidney was
only one of a large number who took the risk of writing
against it.[14] If the *First Treatise* belongs to these earlier years
and the *Second Treatise* is part and parcel of it, then the
whole work was written before 1683, and there is an end of it.

Though a simple proof of this sort carries conviction to its
editor, the assumption that the book was composed over a
relatively short span of time is open to attack. It could be
maintained that it was the result of two separate impulses
from historical circumstances, although it was composed as
a whole. Granted that it was finished in some form when
Filmer's name was on everyone's lips, it could still be supposed that it was rewritten later, and altered so extensively
as to be a work of dual or multiple composition. This, as we
have seen, was how Locke wrote on the *Understanding* on
Toleration and on *Education.* Doubt could even be thrown on
the claim that the connection with Filmer must place the

14 See Laslett, 1948 (ii) and 1949: on the Whig Exclusionists, Furley,
1957; Pocock, 1957.

work in the early 1680's, for his name was still alive in 1688 and even later. The book, then, was composed as a whole, it might perhaps still be argued, but in the months up to August 1689; an author in a hurry might have started it as late as February of that year.

These possible objections make it necessary to go further into the evidence. Some of it can certainly be used against the position taken up here. There is force in the claim that it was still necessary for a Whig writer to go to some trouble to refute Filmer as late as 1689. His works were reissued in 1696, and any acquaintance with English political literature up to 1714 will show that Locke was not wasting his publisher's money by including the *First Treatise*. Locke's own correspondence makes this clear. James Tyrrell, who knew him best as a political writer, published *Patriarcha non Monarcha* against Filmer in 1680, but he found it necessary to return to the attack in 1691.[15] When he first saw *Two Treatises* in December 1689 he thought of it as an attack on patriarchalism, 'a very solid treatise cal'd of Government in which Sr R Filmers Principles are very well confuted'. In the previous June, Furly, the English Quaker who had been Locke's host in Rotterdam and was then in England, wrote thus to him: 'I met with a scrupulous Cambridge scholar that thought nothing could discharge him of the Oath of Allegiance that he had taken to James II and his successors. I had pleasant sport with him upon Sir R Filmers maggot.' [16]

But all this goes to show why it was that Locke published what he had written against Filmer in 1689, rather than to demonstrate that he actually composed his refutation then. It is just possible that a man could find time to do all that Locke is known to have done between February and August and also to begin and complete a work at such length against the patriarchal extremists. The tracts he acquired make it plain that he interested himself in all that was coming out for and against the new order of things at that critical time.[17]

[15] *Bibliotheca Politica*, 1st dialogue and passim.

[16] Tyrrell to Locke, 20 December 1689: Benjamin Furly to Locke, 10 June 1689, compare his letter of 26 October 1690, which confirms that he knew of the authorship of *Two Treatises*. The book was in circulation a little before Tyrrell saw it. It was advertised in the *London Gazette* for 14–18 November: I owe this reference to Mr L. W. Hanson.

[17] Locke bought political pamphlets only sporadically. Quite a number in his library catalogue date from 1679–82, though it is clear that at that time he was using some of Shaftesbury's copies of such works. A superficial survey shows that he bought for himself as much in 1689 as in all other years together, which bears on the nature and extent of the revision he made of *Two Treatises* for publication.

But it is very difficult indeed to believe that he allowed himself to be rushed into print in this way. If he did, he must have lost over half his manuscript immediately after he had finished writing, and this is almost inconceivable.

For we must never lose sight of his personality. 'Reader, Thou hast here the Beginning and End of a Discourse concerning Government; what Fate has otherwise disposed of the Papers that should have filled up the middle, and were more than all the rest, 'tis not worth while to tell thee' are the exact words he uses to explain the fragmentary nature of his text. Whatever this mysterious fate was, it cannot have been that Locke the precisionist had simply mislaid a whole sheaf of his own papers within the previous week or two, and he was not the man to allow an agent, a printer or a publisher to do such a thing.[18] Nor was he a man to do things in a hurry: we have seen how long and complicated was the process through which all his other books had to go before they appeared in print. To think of him as a man who would write for publication a rationalization of events which had just taken place is to misunderstand his character completely. This makes against the traditional interpretation in all its possible forms.

Did he compose the work, or at least the second book, in the leisurely, Lockeian manner during his Dutch exile, bringing it with him home for final revision and publication? This is the tendency of recent Locke scholarship, at least as to the *Second Treatise* and there is evidence for it. It accounts for the fact that his political comment reads for the most part as if it were made before and not after William's accession.[19] It allows for a much earlier date of germination. His connection with such architects of the Revolution as Mordaunt naturally gave rise to the expectation that he might write about it. He was pressed as early as 1687 to publish on

---

[18] This obvious point can be illustrated by his behaviour when a paper of his corrections was said to be mislaid in 1694, see above, 20–1 and note 14.

[19] It will be seen from the passage in the Preface quoted on p. 59 that Locke writes of William alone, and not his co-sovereign Mary. This may mark him as a supporter of William's sole sovereignty, an attitude typical of the Whigs who had been in exile, but one which ceased to be held by the latest date at which the Preface can have been written—October 1689.

Toleration,[20] and if he could go into print on this subject, why should he not be writing on politics? Any sign that he was actually engaged on *Two Treatises* in Holland in or just before 1688 would make this view formidable.

There is an entry in his journal in February 1687 which seems at first sight to provide just the detail to sanction such an interpretation. It is an extract from Garcilaso de la Vega which is also to be found in the *Second Treatise*, § 14.[21] But even this turns out to be quite inconclusive. For it so happens that the passage is present in the second state of the first edition only, and therefore could easily have been added when he made the modifications which turned the first into the second state in October 1689.[22] Nevertheless the possible implication of this one item and the necessity of finding positive confirmatory evidence of the view put forward here makes it very important that there should be a whole class of sources which has yet to be used. In Locke's notes on his reading, in his lists of books, in the books themselves and their whereabouts at the dates under discussion, we have indications of a much more specific and reliable kind than those so far cited.

But before we turn to this material we may refer to some obvious features of the text of the book. Quite apart from its unmistakable connection with the Filmer controversy of 1679–81, there are political references which make sense for those years and those years alone. In 1689 the phrase 'King James' with no number following could mean King James II and nobody else. Yet in the text printed in that year Locke

[20] Tyrrell to Locke, 6 May 1687: 'your Discourse about Liberty of Conscience would not do amiss now to dispose people's minds to pass it when the Parliament sits.' This 'Discourse' was not the final *Epistola*, which was composed in Holland in 1684–5 and was unknown to Tyrrell, and to everyone except Limborch, see Fox Bourne, 1876, II, 34. In Laslett, 1956, evidence is cited about a work which Locke was trying to get printed in 1687. Mr Cranston has now convinced me that it cannot have been *Two Treatises*.

[21] See II, § 14, 14–20 and note and Locke's diary for 2 February 1687.

[22] See Laslett, 1952 (iv) and 1954 (ii), for the two states. The item was either a MS. addition to author's copy, misunderstood by the compositor of the first state, or an alteration between the two states. Even if it were the former, it could have been done in 1689, when he modified his MS. in so many other respects. In fact this detail may confirm the view that Locke did not have his MS. with him in 1687 when he made the diary entry, but copied that entry into it two years later.

twice refers to 'King James' when he meant James I, surely a very significant anachronism and one which he corrected in later printings.[23] It seems strange that this should not have been noticed before, but even stranger that the parliamentary issues of the Exclusion Controversy have not been noticed in the constitutional discussion of the *Second Treatise*.

Except perhaps in the last chapter, Locke's chief concern there was the summoning and dissolution of Parliament. This was for him the crucial relationship between Legislative and Executive. It was this which could lead to '*a state of War*' (that is with the people) when the 'Executive Power shall make use of . . . force to hinder the *meeting* and *acting of the Legislative*' (II, § 155). Now this was not the major issue of 1688, nor of James II's reign. But it was typical of the years between 1678 (or even 1675) and 1681, when Shaftesbury with Locke so often at his side had made attempt after attempt to force Charles II either to dissolve a parliament long out of date, or to summon it after an intolerable series of prorogations. The 'long train of Abuses, Prevarications, and Artifices' of § 225 became a phrase in the American Declaration of Independence. It included underhand favouring of Catholicism '(though publickly proclaimed against)' (§ 210). These abuses were those of Charles II, not James II. He did not find it necessary either to be underhand in favouring Catholicism, or to proclaim against it.

We can go no further into the results of reducing Locke's theories to their revised historical context.[24] Let us begin our consideration of the evidence now open to us in Locke's books and reading by taking a straightforward example. His diary tells us that he was in London in August 1681, in Shaftesbury's house, though Shaftesbury was away, in the Tower. On the 29th he bought 'Knox, R^t Historical Relation of Ceylon, fol. London 81' for eight shillings (that is, Robert Knox on Ceylon, 1681). In § 92 of the *Second Treatise* he refers to 'the late Relation of *Ceylon*', and the word late here means, presumably, just published. Now we know that Locke kept this book in London, and that he lost sight of it in 1683 when he went to Holland. There is no

---

[23] *Second Treatise*, §§ 133 and 200, corrected in 1694 and 1698 respectively—see Collation. This perhaps should not be pressed too far. James I was also a literary figure and the omission of the number would not confuse the reader in obviously literary contexts.

[24] See footnotes to relevant paragraphs, and in general on Locke's thought in relation to Shaftesbury's policies, Viano, 1960, § 111.

sign that it was ever amongst the separate collection which he kept at Oxford, and which was transported to Tyrrell's house in 1684 when he was expelled from Christ Church. Knox does not appear in any document from the period of his exile; journal, book bill, book list or notebook. We have no evidence that he ever saw this copy, or any other copy, until the title appears in the catalogue he made of his London books in the summer of 1689 (see Appendix B). His Oxford books were not delivered to him by Tyrrell until 1691. It is, therefore, very unlikely that he wrote this phrase in the *Second Treatise* between 1683 and 1689, and very likely that he wrote it between 1681 and 1683.

'Very likely' could become 'certainly' only if we could exclude the possibility of access to another copy later, and we had cumulative evidence. It is in the nature of things that later access cannot be entirely excluded,[25] though in this and many other cases it is highly improbable. But cumulative evidence is just what we do possess. Although he refers to so few books directly in his text, we can work out a sizeable list of those he may have consulted and compare it with three other lists. One is the census of the books in his rooms at Christ Church which he wrote out in his diary under July 1681, another is the London list of 1689, and the third is Tyrrell's catalogue of the books returned in 1691. It appears that Locke's library of the early 1680's, divided between Shaftesbury's house and Christ Church, contained nearly all the works which he used for the writing of *Two Treatises*.

This can be supplemented from his records of his reading and purchases over the relevant years.[26] They show that between 1679 and 1682 Locke was more interested in publications on political theory and natural law than ever before or after. One or two of the critical titles, as we shall see, are to be found amongst those which Shaftesbury drew to his attention in 1679, and which were lent to him, or made available in London. It was only in the period before 1683 that Locke had convenient access to the particular books which he needed for writing on *Government*. Any other

[25] Maclean, 1947 (ii), ingeniously argues that a book which he believes is vital to *Two Treatises* (Lawson, 1657, see below) could have been used by Locke in Furly's house in Rotterdam. But though it has this Lawson and some other relevant items, the catalogue of Furly's library (*Bibliotheca Furleiana*, 1714) does not contain enough of the right titles to make it possible for Locke to have done his reading for the book there.
[26] See Appendix B for a summary of this evidence and the book lists.

suggested date of composition implies that he went painfully from friend to friend and library to library consulting them one by one.

We may take a further particular example in confirmation, a book of much greater importance to his political thinking than Knox—Hooker's *Ecclesiastical Polity*. He had read Hooker before, we know, though perhaps not far into that tall folio.[27] But it was not until 13 June 1681 that he bought in London 'Hooker Ecclesiasticall Politie fol Lond. 66'. He read in the book during the rest of the month, making lengthy extracts from it into his journal, some of them important for his philosophizing. Now, there are sixteen passages from Hooker quoted in the *Second Treatise*,[28] and in § 239 Locke explains why he had used the work. When the quotations in his diary are set alongside those in the *Second Treatise*, they are seen to alternate, never overlapping. The conclusion must be that in June 1681 Locke was working on the *Second Treatise*, incorporating extracts from Hooker into it, and at the same time copying into his diary other passages of philosophical interest.[29] These details are interesting not only for the implication that the Hooker quotations were added to the text after it had been begun, but also because they reveal Locke at work on *Two Treatises* and the *Essay on the Understanding* at the same time.

We have chosen these examples from books quoted in the *Second Treatise* only, and enough has been said to establish a presumption against assuming that only the *First Treatise* could have been in existence in 1681. For an exact demonstration that the whole book can be fixed down to particular months and limiting dates of composition we must turn to the copies Locke used of the works of Filmer, which enter into both treatises.

These tracts had originally been published separately in

---

[27] In his early essay on the *Civil Magistrate* he states that he had only read the Preface, see Abrams, 1961, p. 32, though within a few months he had read at least the first book, and Hooker appears occasionally in his notebooks up to 1681.

[28] Four in the text (§§ 15, 60, 61), eleven in Locke's notes, see §§ 74, 90, 91, 94 (two), 111, 134 (two passages quoted together), 135, 136 (same passage as in 134).

[29] A 1666 edition of Hooker appears in the London list and in an unfinished entry in his final master catalogue. This last, however, has a complete entry for the 1676 edition, which is still among his books. These volumes therefore may not be distinct. He had yet another Hooker dated 1632 in Oxford, though it is interesting that he did not use it to finish this work when he visited his rooms during July. He continued when he got back to London.

1648, 1652 and 1653, but Filmer's original writing, the famous *Patriarcha,* from which they finally derive, had never been printed.[30] About the middle of 1679 the printed tracts were hurriedly republished as a collection under the title *The Freeholders Grand Inquest,* each tract being individually paginated. In January 1680 this collection was printed again, with continuous pagination. At about the same time *Patriarcha* was first published. Locke bought this 1680 collection with *Patriarcha* bound up with it for 4s. 6d. on 22 January 1680,[31] and in his Preface to *Two Treatises* he tells us that these were the editions he used. He explains his references to Filmer thus: 'O for his Observations on Hobbs, Milton etc. . . . a bare Quotation of Pages always means Pages of his Patriarcha. Edit. 1680.' [32] This was presumably the volume short-titled 'Filmer' which was standing in his rooms in July 1681, for it was certainly the one which Tyrrell took charge of whilst Locke was in exile, and returned in 1691.

As we should expect with the meticulous Locke, these conventions are consistently respected. In the 200 or so references to Filmer in the *First Treatise,* a passage marked 'O 245' is always found on p. 245 of the 1680 Collection, and one marked '13' is always found on p. 13 of *Patriarcha.* But the single occasion on which he cites this author by page number in the *Second Treatise,* he breaks his convention.

He is discussing liberty as being 'for every one to do what he lists' in § 22, and he refers to 'what Sir *R.F.* tells us *O.A.* 55'. Now this will not work for the 1680 Collection. Nothing resembling what he quotes is to be seen on p. 55 of that volume. But it does work for a p. 55 of the 1679 Collection, p. 55 of the *Observations on Aristotle* which becomes p. 143 in the 1680 reprint, where Filmer does make this particular statement about liberty. It looks as if Locke must have been using the 1679 volume when he wrote § 22 of the *Second Treatise,* and so observing a different convention of reference. And it looks as if he had reached that paragraph before even reading *Patriarcha:* indeed the text of the *Second Treatise,* although written against patriarchism, could have

---

[30] See Laslett, 1949, especially 47–8, *Concise Bibliography of Filmer's Works.*

[31] This volume (Appendix B, no. 33) is in front of the present writer. Some of the leaves are folded up to indicate passages, but there are no marginal notes.

[32] 'Observations on Hobbs', etc. refers collectively to the tracts in the volume, with the exception of the *Freeholder,* printed first; Locke never refers to the *Freeholder* in *Two Treatises* as we now know it.

been originally composed without his having seen *Patriarcha* at all.

We have independent evidence that Locke was in fact reading the 1679 Collection in the year of its appearance, and that he was making extracts from the book in almost precisely the form found in the *Second Treatise*. A 'Tablet', or scribbling pad, of his has survived from this period, used for notes and references, some taken from Shaftesbury. On p. 119 he wrote under '79' (for 1679): 'Filmer to resolve the conscience O p. 59.' On p. 59 of Filmer's *Observations on Aristotle* in the 1679 Collection, resolving the conscience is discussed, discussed in fact in connection with the consent of the people to government, a major theme of the *Second Treatise*. This passage is only four pages away from the one we have just identified. We could not expect to discover more convincing circumstantial evidence than this, an exact indication that Locke was engaged on the early part of that essay in 1679.[33]

We can, therefore, make a general assertion on the basis of this precise, if complicated and tedious discussion. As early as 1679 Locke had begun a work on government, and a work with the immediate object of refuting Filmer. He had begun it, it would seem, with Shaftesbury's connivance, perhaps at his request and with his assistance in the matter of sources. But the work he had begun was not the *First Treatise*, but the *Second*. He had certainly reached paragraph number 22 of that *Treatise*, possibly number 57 and even number 236, almost the very end, when he changed his mind sometime in 1680, and decided to write the *First Treatise* too.[34] We need not look far for the reason why he did this. It was the appearance of *Patriarcha* in January 1680, together with the enor-

---

[33] The 'Tablet' is MS. f. 28. On p. 40 he notes, also under 1679, 'Shaftesbury: Lawson's book of the English Government', an entry later crossed through, showing, it is clear, that Shaftesbury made Locke a loan of this book, who crossed out the entry when he returned it (or it may have been Locke who lent, and Shaftesbury who returned). This makes it obvious that the two men were reading Lawson then, and that Maclean's supposition that Locke read him in 1687 in Holland is otiose. If Shaftesbury was the lender, it may be that he lent Locke the 1679 collection of Filmer too. Locke had Lawson, 1660, in Holland, and finally bought the 1689 reprint, see Appendix B, no. 50.

[34] See notes on these paragraphs. In § 57 he repeats, without reference, the phrase from Filmer used in § 22, and in § 236 inserts another quotation noted in his 'Tablet', this time under 1680. In the *First Treatise*, § 14, there is a phrase which might possibly imply that he read *Patriarcha* first, and the other tracts later, but statements in I §§ 6, 11 confirm the view taken here.

mous growth of Filmer's influence which went on during the rest of that year. The reply he had originally planned was insufficient because it left out of account the most important work of the man he was criticizing and did not contain the phrase-by-phrase refutation which he recognized was now needed. Exactly the same decision was taken at exactly the same time, with very similar results on his final text in refutation of Filmer, by his friend James Tyrrell.

The extraordinary literary relationship between John Locke and James Tyrrell enters at many points into the story of Locke as a political writer. They were friends from Locke's Oxford days, and mutually interested in primitive peoples, Natural Law and toleration as well as politics; they exchanged books, corresponded [35] and from time to time discussed. It was no even, undisturbed friendship, for Tyrrell, as will be seen, was not the most tactful of men. 'He never polished himself out of his sincerity', as his epitaph admits.

In the crisis years of 1680–3 Locke spent much of his time at Tyrrell's house at Shotover, some miles away from his suspicious college, and they engaged in collaborative writing: a critical commentary on Stillingfleet's *Unreasonableness of Separation* (1681).[36] We know that the first form of Tyrrell's *Patriarcha non Monarcha* was written by January 1680 and sent to an eminent Whig historian, William Petyt, reporting that it would have to be modified if it were to be published because 'There is lately come to this town a new treatise of Sir Robert Filmer's called *Patriarcha*'.[37] When Locke bought the printed book on 2 June 1680 he could have seen for himself the effects on the text of Tyrrell's change of plan: a new part had been added at the beginning to take *Patriarcha* into account. In fact Tyrrell had written a *First Treatise*.[38]

Locke and Tyrrell, then, were in close communication when, as we believe, both were engaged in refuting Filmer, and their

[35] Compare Von Leyden, 1954 (Tyrrell and Locke's natural law MSS.).

[36] MS. c. 34; Locke's, Tyrrell's and another hand (an amanuensis?) interspersed. Tyrrell actually made notes, on subjects of importance to political theory, in Locke's journal for 1680, see note on II, § 108, 7.

[37] Inner Temple MS. 583 (17), f. 302, Tyrrell to Petyt 'Jan. 12th', obviously 1680. See Pocock, 1957, 187–8: Mr Pocock helped with this reference.

[38] This book was divided at sheet L between two compositors, and the same point (Chap. IV) seems to mark the end of the rewritten passage. The second compositor began with page number 97, instead of 137 as he should, and this may imply that Tyrrell's revisions were made after the book had been cast off, and added some 40 pages in the earlier part.

writing plans followed a remarkably similar pattern. So close
were they, indeed, that some sort of collaboration would seem
possible, or even likely. But the remarkable thing is that the
evidence we have goes to show that Locke most certainly did
not let Tyrrell see his manuscript, or even know of its existence, and that Tyrrell seems to have been almost as guarded
about his too.[39] This is of some interest, since so many of
Tyrrell's positions against Filmer were also those of Locke,
more particularly the account of the right of property.[40] But
whatever the exact relationship of the two men over their two
books, it is clear that when Locke decided to add the *First*
to the *Second Treatise,* he did only what Tyrrell did and what
circumstances demanded.

For only in *Patriarcha,* and after January 1680, was the
authoritarian, patriarchal, Tory case at work on the minds of
the politically important as one influential whole. In his tracts
Filmer had commented on the constitution and on the origin
of government in separate contexts, so much so that it has
been widely believed that the *Freeholders Grand Inquest,* his
specifically constitutional work, was by a different author.[41]
Locke may have modified, rearranged, perhaps extensively rewritten the *Second Treatise* when he knew that the *First* would
be added: we have seen him working at it in this way in 1681
when he added the Hooker passages. He certainly made further additions and presumably modifications in 1689, and
the decision to print the treatises in their final order could
have been taken then. But much of it was left as originally
written, including the reference in § 22 which survived all his
repeated correction. From the point of view of our discussion,
the book as a response to political and literary circumstances,
it must belong to the autumn and winter of 1679–80, exactly
a decade earlier than it is traditionally supposed to have been

[39] Locke bought a copy of *Patriarcha non Monarcha* 'for Mr Tyrrell'.
No man buys a book to give it to its anonymous author, if he knows
who wrote it.
[40] See footnotes to text throughout, especially note on II, § 27.
Patriarcha non Monarcha is referred to appreciatively, by title if not by
author, in I, § 124. It can be argued from the facts presented here that
Tyrrell, not Locke, must be regarded as the initiator of the 'labour
theory of value', unless these two claims are accepted. One is that
Locke had written, or worked out, the substance of his text by 1679,
and the other is that he had communicated his conceptions to his
friend. It is, I believe, possible to be fairly certain of the first of these
claims, but the second is not so clearly established, and any assessment
of the 'originality' of any part of *Two Treatises* must take these facts
into account.
[41] See Laslett, 1949, and compare Allen, 1928.

written. *Two Treatises* is an Exclusion Tract, not a Revolution Pamphlet.

As it stands, Locke's book is cumbersome and uninviting: two hundred unreadable pages introducing an essay which is lively and convincing if a little laboured and repetitive. We can see why he arranged it thus, though we may feel aggrieved at his insensitivity. But there is no good reason for supposing that he thought his thoughts in such an unlikely order, or wrote them down like this. Every one of his positions is assumed in the *First Treatise,* but when he refers to them there he has to send us forward to the *Second.* Who would deliberately choose to begin the exposition of a complicated theme by the refutation of another man's system without laying down his own premises? I believe that a satisfactory account of the writing of the book must assume that the *Second Treatise,* the positive statement, was substantially complete when the *First,* the negative commentary, was begun.

This is as much as may be safely inferred from what is certainly known about the date and manner of composing *Two Treatises.* It leaves a great deal open to conjecture, and this interlude will be given up to conjecture. Only one guess will be made, but if it is a lucky guess it explains a great deal.

There is a document referred to in the papers of both Locke and Shaftesbury which had a history corresponding quite exactly with the history of the manuscript or manuscripts of *Two Treatises* as it has been worked out here. It had a cover name, *De Morbo Gallico,* a cant expression for syphilis, the French disease. This may seem vulgar, but Locke's medical identity must not be forgotten, and cover names are common in these papers, especially for secret, dangerous or embarrassing documents. Moreover Locke and Shaftesbury did think of despotism as a French disease, and when he wrote in 1679 Locke had just returned from France, from studying the French disease as a political system.

When Shaftesbury was arrested in July 1681 Locke was presumably in the house. But by the time lists had been drawn up of the papers which had been seized, Locke was in Oxford, making the catalogue of his books there. Amongst his folios, standing close to Hooker and to the big bound notebook containing his first draft on the *Understanding,* he entered *Tractatus de Morbo Gallico.*[42] Meanwhile in London the government

---

[42] This must be distinct from his old medical book with the title *Morbus Gallicus. Omnia quae extant de eo,* Venice, 1566, which was a folio too.

men were searching amongst Shaftesbury's papers, and they
had come across several Locke items. There was the Shaftesbury copy of the draft on the *Understanding,* the letter on the
Oxford Parliament, 'Mr Locke's book of fruit trees'. 'Notes
out of Mors Gallicus in my lord's hand' was another document
registered by them.[43] Shaftesbury must have had some reason
to go to the trouble of making these notes: he may conceivably have been a syphilitic, but this has never been suspected
before. Anyway Locke took his document with this title over
to Tyrrell's house on 17 July, and when he left for London on
the 18th wrote in shorthand in his diary 'Left with him De
Morbo Gallico'.

A year later Dr Thomas of Salisbury, his medical and political friend, wrote and told him that 'You may send your
Observations de Morbo Gallico' and named a messenger.[44]
If this was the same thing, it must have been something Locke
had himself written. It next appears in November 1683, in
a letter written to Clarke from Holland soon after he had
arrived, full of cryptic allusions to possessions left behind.

Honest Adrian writes me word that the chest that is now
in Mrs . . . custody was not opened, though he had the key
and directions to do it. Neither do I ask whether anything else
was in her custody was opened, only give me leave to tell you
that I either think or dreamt you enquired of me concerning
the title of a treatise, part whereof is in Mr Smith's hands, and
it is *Tractatus de Morbo Gallico.* If there were another copy
of it I should be glad to have that at any reasonable rate, for
I have heard it commended and shall apply myself close to
the study of physic by the fireside this winter. But of this I
shall write to you more hereafter, when I hear there are more
copies than one, for else it will not be reasonable to desire it.
I desire also to know whether Dr Sydenham hath published
anything this year.[45]

Locke seems to say that he wants another copy of a treatise
which exists in part in the keeping of someone he names, perhaps Mrs Smithsby his London landlady. But he is evidently
afraid that the cautious Clarke may have destroyed the full

[43] P.R.O. Shaftesbury Papers, 30/24 Bundle VIA, item 349, paper 3.
[44] Thomas to Locke, 25 July 1682: on 5 August he acknowledged
arrival of the man who was to bring 'your opinion *de Morbo Gallico*'.
[45] Locke to Clarke, 21 November (1683), Rand, 1927, 100. The 'Mrs'
whose name has perished may be Mrs Smithsby, and the same with the
later 'Mr Smith': 'Adrian' is Dr Thomas: the medical references look
like a blind. Unfortunately this and the next letter are missing from
the collection (now the Whitehouse Papers) as Rand knew it, and
his unreliable transcription cannot be checked.

copy. Well he might have, if this was the manuscript we are after, for in that very month Sidney was up at the Old Bailey for writing against Filmer: in his previous letter Locke had asked for 'what news the Old Bailey affords'.

The last context is mutilated but clearer. In a much later letter to Clarke of 18 February 1687, Locke writes: 'I beg also that the half . . . de Morbo Gallico, which I left with R. Smith sealed up in a little [box] about the length of a hand and about [half a] hand in breadth, may be sent into. . . .' And a little further on in the letter: 'Your may easily [perceive] why I would have that tract de Morbo Gallico. . . .' [46] It would seem that the full copy of the work had not been available, for it had evidently not been sent to him in Holland. It is tempting to suppose that the reason why he wanted the other half-copy was political, for only recently politics had begun to take up a great deal of his time.[47] Nothing with this title, or on a subject which would fit these references, has survived in Locke's voluminous papers, although other writings he found at Mrs Smithsby's when he returned to London in 1689 are still to be seen amongst them.

If this exercise in conjecture could be substantiated it would imply all these things. The first form of Two Treatises, under the name De Morbo Gallico, was originally written into a folio notebook, in the same way as Locke's first sketch of his Essay. Shaftesbury had seen and noted it before his arrest in July 1681, when it had already been placed on Locke's shelves at Christ Church amongst the books he used to write it. Tyrrell had charge of it for a while a little after this, though he did not know its identity: Thomas, who read it in 1682, and Clarke were let into the secret. It existed in two copies by 1683, but before Locke went to Holland, one of the copies had been halved and then left with Mrs Smithsby: Clarke had orders to destroy the other copy completely if it should seem advisable, with an eye to what was happening at the trial of Sidney.[48]

[46] Rand, 1927, 196–7. The dots represent passages which had perished when Rand saw the letter, and the square brackets his suggested readings.

[47] Locke to Limborch, 14 February 1687.

[48] Locke was in a high state of anxiety at this time and destroyed a great deal: it was probably then that he effaced the references to the writing of the book from his papers. Campbell (The Chancellors, 1845, III, 374) states that Locke ordered Shaftesbury's autobiography to be destroyed because of what happened to Sidney. No. 168 of the Whitehouse Collection, undated but obviously of this period, is a number cypher to be used to conceal names in Locke's correspondence with Clarke.

Clarke did dispose of the full copy, and Locke did not regain any part of this writing, as far as we know, before 1689, certainly not before 1687. We may identify the half of his manuscript which he left with Mrs Smithsby with the whole work as we now have it. His motive for destroying the remainder can easily be inferred. Presumably this area was the dangerous one. It came, it will be remembered, at the end, not in the middle, of the manuscript, since it was a continuation of the *First Treatise*. It contained those passages which he and his friends were afraid might be of use to a counsel for the Crown in persuading a court of justice that in writing this book John Locke had been as much of a traitor as Algernon Sidney. Such, then, in the words of the Preface was the 'Fate' which 'otherwise disposed of the Papers that should have filled up the middle'.

Quite apart from conjecture, the evidence presented here and further analysed in the footnotes to Locke's text [49] makes possible the following tentative reconstruction of the stages of composition. In the winter of 1679–80 the *Second Treatise* was written, perhaps only partially, perhaps as a completed work. Early in 1680 the *First Treatise* was added to it, and if Shaftesbury did read the book, he probably read it at this stage. Perhaps he or someone else suggested revisions to Locke, for he went at it again in the summer of 1681, adding the Hooker references and excerpts, and probably chapters XVI, XVII, XVIII and part of chapter VIII in the *Second Treatise*, in all some fifty paragraphs. The process of revision and extensions went on into 1682, it may be, and there are parts of chapter XVIII which seem to belong to 1683, with perhaps some or most of the final chapter. From February to August 1689 further revision and extension went on, as we have seen, throughout the volume, and continued until the very last possible printer's moment. In all, however, only the Preface, the titles and some twenty-five new paragraphs seem to have been written then, including the whole of chapters I, IX and XV in the *Second Treatise*. In these passages only, together with the considerable number of much briefer additions and modifications, can the book be said to belong to the year of the Glorious Revolution.

[49] An attempt has been made to assign each chapter of the *Second Treatise* to one of the conjectured periods of composition: see the notes on the first paragraph of each chapter. Where any particular paragraph or passage seems to be of different date from the surrounding text, this has been commented upon.

The writing of *Two Treatises of Government* as it has been reconstructed here can only belong to the association of Locke with Shaftesbury, and that association ended in trauma. The necessity of going into exile, the loss of his position at Christ Church, the threat of trial and perhaps even execution were all connected in the mind of this careful, introverted, timid man with his having written on politics. When he returned in 1689 and made up his mind to publish what he had written, it was not to a country whose political future seemed stable. The return of James II was a possibility throughout the 1690's: if he had returned, it would have meant exile for Locke, and perhaps, he must have argued, a harder fate for the known writer of this book. His own experience and the treatment of his friends and associates made it clear to him that a Catholic Stuart monarch would not hesitate to use anything found in his private papers against him. This begins to explain his extraordinary furtiveness about the writing of *Two Treatises*, and his persistent refusal to admit that he had written it.

But there may be another reason, much more interesting for political thinking and for its relation with philosophy. It is possible that Locke was unwilling to let it be known that the same man who wrote the *Essay concerning Humane Understanding* also wrote *Two Treatises of Government* because he was quite well aware that it was no simple matter to reconcile their doctrines. We have described a man who disliked criticism and shrank from controversy. There can be no doubt that he would have had to face both of these things if his contemporaries had been invited to compare the assumptions of his theory of knowledge with the assumptions of his political principles. The critical issue was his view of the Natural Law. The reputation of Thomas Hobbes had been blasted beyond recovery, and one of the reasons was that he had laid himself open in this way. It is time to examine the relationship of Hobbes and Locke as a subject in itself.

IV

LOCKE AND HOBBES

1. FILMER, LOCKE AND HOBBES.
'TWO TREATISES' AND CONTEMPORARY
POLITICAL WRITING

If Locke wrote his book as a refutation of Sir Robert Filmer, then he cannot have written it as a refutation of Thomas Hobbes. The mistake of supposing that he was arguing deliberately against *Leviathan* is almost as common as the chronological error we have just examined. We have tried to show that the book was a response to urgent political circumstances, although the circumstances were not those of 1688–9. There would have been no point whatsoever for the intellectual champion of the Whig exclusionists to produce one more criticism of Hobbes, the most rejected, and politically the least important, of all the absolutist writers. Filmer, on the other hand, was the man of the moment, a formidable and growing force with those whose political opinions mattered, and representing in himself the *ipsissima verba* of the established order. It was because this was so that Locke found himself impelled to write on this subject, and for that reason Filmer's thinking lies directly behind his political doctrines. Moreover, his controversy with patriarchalism has a significance in the history of political and social thinking, in the development of the structure of modern society, which we are only just beginning to appreciate.[1]

Locke rejected Hobbesian absolutism along with Filmer's, of course: the word 'Leviathan' occurs in his *Second Treatise,* and there are phrases and whole arguments which recall the Hobbesian position, and must have been intended in some sense as comments upon them.[2] Moreover, the thinking of Hobbes was of systematic importance to Locke and enters into his doctrines in a way which goes much deeper than a difference in political opinion. But this cannot alter the fact that Filmer's tracts occupy for the *Second Treatise* the position which has traditionally been reserved for the works of Hobbes. This has had some effects which have previously gone unnoticed.

Filmer influenced Locke, in the way all men influence those who choose to refute them. It was he, and not Locke himself, and decidedly not Hobbes, who set the terms of the argument. No doubt Locke would have found some opportunity to declare his belief in the freedom and equality of all men, but as it happened he was forced to do so at the very outset of his work on government, because Filmer had directly denied it, against Hobbes amongst others. It may well be that some of Locke's arguments would never have been developed at all if it had not been for Filmer. We have seen that he showed no sign of an interest in the theory of property before he sat down to his polemic, and found himself faced with an argument in favour of primitive communism which was very difficult to refute unless a new justification of ownership was devised.[3] Patriarchalism influenced him in a more straightforward way, and in his concessions to it we may see in his thinking some signs that he recognized the limitations of his own intellectualistic rationalism.[4]

If in fact *Two Treatises* had been directed against Hobbes

[1] See Laslett, 1949, 33–43. Bastide, 1907, especially 208–9, takes the view that Hobbes was an important political influence because of his purchase over Charles II and his courtiers, but his evidence is somewhat meagre. Pollock again seems to have done most to establish the view that Locke was really writing against Hobbes: see 1904, 238, and also Vaughan, 1925; Gough, 1950.

[2] See footnotes to II, §§ 19, 21, 98, 133, 211, 212.

[3] See above, p. 47 and note to II, § 25, 18–21. Tyrrell similarly developed many of his arguments only because of Filmer. Viano, 1960, esp. pp. 209 on, also insists on the importance of Filmer and patriarchalism to the understanding of both *Treatises.*

[4] See note to II, § 74, 16–41 and references.

and not Filmer it would have been a far less interesting, far
less influential work. To say this is not to claim that Locke
did succeed in annihilating Filmer as completely as he himself
believed, and as subsequent history seems to confirm. As a
piece of formal dialectic what he wrote is less complete and in
some ways less convincing, to his own contemporaries anyway, than the identical work of his friend Tyrrell.[5] It is true
that Locke completely outclassed his chosen opponent in
intellect and in scholarship. After he had added the detailed
argumentation of the *First Treatise* to the *Second,* we may
feel that nobody could any longer believe that the texts of
the Old Testament which Filmer had used to justify patriarchal
kingship could possibly apply to contemporary monarchs.
But what was the conscientious reader to believe about the
content of Revelation and its relationship with the political
world in which he lived, and about the origin of government?
For Locke was assuming that in some way Old Testament
history joined on, so to speak, with his account of what
happened, but unlike Filmer he was never prepared to say
quite how it did so.[6] 'We must not deny the truth of the
history of the creation', urged Filmer against Hobbes. Locke
would not admit he was doing this, when in reality he was
making use of rationalist arguments which simply could not
be contained in Filmer's world of Biblical politics.

Not only did Locke refuse to meet Filmer on his own
ground, and fail to recognize the full strength, antiquity and
importance of the patriarchal tradition,[7] he persistently ignored the searching counter-criticisms which are the strength
of Filmer's case. How could Locke's bland assertion of the
historicity of a state of nature, of an agreement or compact
behind all established government, of the justifiability of
assuming universal consent to political institutions, be defended against Filmer's sceptical commentary? It was Tyrrell,
not Locke, who recognized Filmer's needling effectiveness,
and admitted that there was really no stopping place between
the ground he and Locke occupied and logical individualism,
final democracy, the sharing of political power with women,

---

[5] *Patriarcha non Monarcha* is fairer to the opposing case and considers it within its whole literary context, which *Two Treatises* does not.
It is much more difficult to read, of course, and contains nothing
comparable as a positive political theory, but I should like to retract the
statement in Laslett, 1949, 38–9.
[6] See notes on I, § 130 and I, § 136.
[7] See e.g. note on I, § 64, 12–19.

children and servants.[8] All this is quite apart from Locke's failure to share Filmer's vision of the emotional togetherness implied by all political relationships, the physically, physiologically natural element which, as has been argued elsewhere, political thinking since Locke has misunderstood to the danger of us all.[9]

Locke certainly absorbed something from patriarchalism. It has been shown above that there had been a time when he went a very long way with this traditional argument. But he did not learn enough, not enough to understand such institutions as the family, the nation, the community of a neighbourhood, as we think they should be understood. And Hobbes could do nothing with the patriarchal attitude. To him patriarchal societies were those 'the concord whereof dependeth on natural lust', and that was all. He was unwilling to distinguish the authority of a father from the naked exercise of force. In all these respects, then, Hobbes, Locke, Tyrrell, Sidney and the others were on the one side, with Filmer and the tradition he stood for on the other. A controversy between Locke and Hobbes would have been within one party only, and could never have given rise to the characteristic political attitude of the modern world. A clash between two such men as Locke and Filmer was a symbolic, a necessary occurrence: it changed men's minds.

Nevertheless Hobbes and Filmer shared nearly every one of the attributes of absolutism as it was rejected by English parliamentarians—will as the source of all law and the form of all authority, the necessity of perpetual and absolute submission to the arbitrary dictates of an indivisible sovereign, the impossibility of mixed government. In so far as Locke's writing was directed against these things, it would not seem to have mattered whether it was Hobbes or Filmer he had in mind. But when his statements are examined closely it appears that the form of the absolutist propositions he was rejecting was almost always Filmer's.[10] If it had been the precise content and force of Hobbes's statements which he

---

[8] Tyrrell, 1681, 83–4; his only comment is that such a form of government had never existed. Locke's silence on this point laid him open to the extremist interpretations of the English supporters of the French Revolution; see the footnotes made by Elrington to the *Second Treatise*. It was this obtuseness, or inadvertence, or prudence, which makes it legitimate to describe him in colourful terms as a 'father of democracy', our sort of democracy.

[9] Laslett, 1949, 42–3.

[10] See e.g. notes on II, § 92, 8; II, § 95, 10.

wished to comment upon, then he would have quoted them verbatim.

We can say this with some confidence, for Locke was a meticulous and practised controversialist. We have seen that he had known of Filmer's agreement with Hobbes for over a decade when he wrote *Two Treatises*.[11] When in the earliest work he wrote he commented on Bagshaw, and when he defended himself against Stillingfleet and Proast much later on, Locke carefully cited paragraph and sentence of the book he was discussing. He did so, with exasperating tediousness, in the *First Treatise*, out of Filmer. There is no reason why we should expect him to behave differently in the *Second Treatise* if Hobbes had been his critical target there.

Locke's habits in controversy, and the facts we have cited about the importance of patriarchalism at this time, make it impossible to argue that Filmer was simply Locke's whipping boy, his opportunity for attacking Hobbes by proxy. No doubt there was something faintly ridiculous about Filmer even by the year 1679. But we have seen that both Locke and Shaftesbury seemed to take him quite seriously not very long before. It is even more ridiculous to suppose that the point of this public flagellation was to humiliate the Hobbesists among the spectators, a lash or two being aimed at them directly. Locke never called Filmer a Hobbesist, nor said anything to link the two names together, though Sidney did not hesitate to do so, and Tyrrell also commented on Hobbesian positions whilst engaged with Filmer's.[12]

Indeed it cannot be shown that when he wrote Locke had had any recent contact with *Leviathan* or with any other work of Hobbes at first hand.[13] If it were not for the passages in the *Second Treatise* which are Hobbesian in flavour or seem to have been directed particularly at him, we should not know that Locke was concerned in any way with Hobbes as a thinker at that time, for his notes, his diaries, his letters, his book lists and purchases show no sign of such an interest.

[11] See above, p. 46. The sentence from Filmer quoted there continues: 'I consent with him [Hobbes] about the rights of exercising government, but I cannot agree to his means of acquiring it.'

[12] See, e.g. Sidney, 1772, 5 and Tyrrell, 1681, 138–41, 2nd pagination. On p. 209 he accuses Filmer of directly borrowing from Hobbes, which is historically almost impossible.

[13] See Appendix B, numbers 42–4. He lent his *Leviathan* in 1674, and did not get it back till 1691. He possessed no other political or philosophical work of Hobbes.

His one overt mention of the word *Leviathan,* in paragraph 98 of the *Second Treatise,* is very far from specific: indeed if it were taken literally it would seem to imply a serious misunderstanding, or misremembrance, of Hobbes's doctrine.[14]

There is an interesting parallel to this in Locke's *Essay on the Understanding.* Again, he mentions Hobbes only once in the course of that lengthy work, which covers a great deal of the same ground as Hobbes had done, and which many commentators have also supposed was written with Hobbes in mind. And again he mistakes the Hobbesian case in a passage which was clearly also meant to be sarcastic and general.[15] Nevertheless his *Essay* shows clear signs of proximity to Hobbes, even on the critical subject of property and justice. ' "Where there is no property there is no justice" is a proposition as certain as any demonstration in Euclid', says Locke in his *Essay.*[16] 'Where there is no *Own,* that is no Propriety, there is no Injustice', says *Leviathan,*[17] and Hobbes goes on to a conclusion that Locke decisively rejected, not in the *Essay,* but in *Two Treatises,* that property cannot exist before and apart from government. Did Locke when he wrote this striking re-echo of a phrase of Hobbes consciously recollect

---

[14] 'Such a Constitution as this would make the mighty *Leviathan* of a shorter duration, than the feeblest Creatures.' The 'constitution' at issue would require universal consent to all the acts of a political body, though Hobbes accepted decision by a majority in assemblies. The passage is clearly ironic and general, not a comment on a passage in Hobbes, see note there.

[15] I, iii, 9 (1894, I, 69), where he claims that a Hobbesist kept his promise because the public required it and because of the fear of punishment by Leviathan. In fact, of course, the keeping of covenants was the third of the laws of nature, as Hobbes understood them. Some commentators on Hobbes might say that Locke was ultimately right in this reflection, but he surely would not have formulated this fundamental criticism in such an offhand way if it had been seriously intended.

[16] IV, iii, 18 (1894, II, 208). Locke had made a very similar statement many years before: 'Quid enim justitia ubi nulla proprietas aut dominium', eighth *Essay on the Law of Nature,* Von Leyden, 1954, p. 212, and he developed it in his *Education,* § 110: 'Children cannot well comprehend what injustice is, till they understand property' (*Works,* 1801, IX, 101, passage added in later editions). In the *Essay* Locke even hints at his justification of ownership in terms of industry: 'Just the same is it in moral knowledge: let a man have the idea of taking from others, without their consent, what their honest industry has possessed them of, and call this *justice* if he please' (1894, II, 234).

[17] Chapter 15, 1904, 97-8. It is probable that both Locke and Hobbes were here using 'property' in the wider sense, of which material possessions is only one part. See below, pp. 115-16.

its source? All these examples suggest that he did not. He seems to have been in the curious position of having absorbed Hobbesian sentiments, Hobbesian phraseology in such a way that he did not know where they came from: his early reading, never repeated, perhaps; or other men's books and the general discussion of Hobbes; or both.

The exact literary relationship between the two men, then, is an interesting and intricate study. Locke never escaped the shadow of *Leviathan,* and in the controversy over his views on Christianity which grew so violent in the late 1690's he found himself directly accused of reproducing Hobbesian positions. In 1697, Richard Willis, later Bishop of Winchester, claimed that the thesis of Locke's *Reasonableness of Christianity* (1695) was 'consonant to the words of the Leviathan, whence this doctrine is borrowed, Part IV Ch. 43',[18] and the more forthright John Edwards henceforth described his theological writings as written all over with Hobbesism. When the two passages are compared, the resemblance is surprisingly close: there is little verbal similarity, and the common use of some texts of scripture is to be expected, but the doctrine is almost identical. Locke replied to his critic at the very end of *A Second Vindication of the Reasonableness of Christianity,* 1697: 'I tell him, I . . . did not know those words, he quoted out of the Leviathan, were there, or any thing like them. Nor do I know yet, any farther than as I believe them to be there, from his quotation.' [19]

This may insinuate that he had never read *Leviathan,* as it certainly declares his unwillingness to do so much as open the book and check a reference when the challenge arose. Indeed the resemblance in this case could have been coincidence, a result of that rationalist attitude which the two men had in common, applied here to the Christian Revelation. Or it may likewise be a case of a man having read something many years before, having read it and forgotten it, which he then reproduced as a notion of his own. This view, the more sympathetic one, seems to me to be the more likely. When Locke wrote philosophy he 'utterly refused to read any books upon that subject' so as to keep other men's notions out of his

---

[18] *Occasional Paper No. 1,* 1697.
[19] *Works,* 1801, VII, 420. Locke may be prevaricating here, for in the same tract he denied all knowledge of Socinian literature which he certainly possessed and had almost certainly read.

head.[20] He said of politics 'This subject . . . requires more meditation than reading',[21] and when he wrote on political theory he may also have made a conscious effort to spin everything out of his own mind, to take nothing from the thoughts of other men. The result was that he reproduced some ideas from books which he had read, even books he had read to reject.

'I am not so well read in Hobbes or Spinosa', he said in 1698, and made an ironical comment about 'those justly decried names'.[22] He did read Hobbes nevertheless, although it is so difficult to say when, or how much. The cumulative body of Locke's notebooks is very considerable, and it consists to a very large extent of citations of the books of other men, referenced and arranged with monumental carefulness. It is a most remarkable fact that it has not been possible to find a single referenced extract from the works of Hobbes in the whole Lockeian corpus. Only one citation has so far come to light, and that is not found in a notebook, but on the flyleaf of a volume in his library, published in 1668: even then the famous passage from *Leviathan* written there is given without its source, and might appear to the unwary reader to have been a sentiment written by Locke himself.[23] We have seen that when he was young, when his tendency was authoritarian and his analysis at its closest to Hobbes, his acquaintance with him was as much, perhaps, through literature about him as through direct reading.[24]

The young Locke may well have gone through an experience which must have been common after 1651, when *Leviathan* appeared, and was much in demand, as Pepys tells us, in spite of its ugly reputation. Hobbes fascinated him, then and for the rest of his life. He found it an effort to

[20] This is independent testimony. Tyrrell to Locke, 18 March 1690.
[21] *Works*, 1801, X, 308.
[22] *Works*, 1801, IV, 477; compare Strauss, 1953, p. 211, and for Spinoza, see Appendix B, nos. 78, 79.
[23] It is in Locke's copy of Velschius, *Sylloge Observationum Medicinalium*, Ulm, 1668: 'In wrong or noe definitions, lyes the first abuse of speech, from wch. proceeds all false and uselesse Tenets; wch. make those men who take their instruction from the authority of books, not from their owne meditation to be as much below the condition of ignorant men, as men indued with true science are above it. For between true science and erroneous doctrines Ignorance is in the middle.' [*Leviathan*, chapter IV (I ed. 1651, 15).]
[24] See above, p. 33. Cox, 1960, lists several derivative references. There are other surprises in Locke's reading: e.g. his failure to get much further with Hooker than the first book (above, p. 70), his statement that he never read Sidney (*Works*, 1801, III, 272).

reject his doctrine, though he did reject it very early. When he wrote *Two Treatises,* then, *Leviathan* was an influence, a gravitational constant exercised by a large body though at a great distance. But an influence nevertheless, positive in its effects, and quite unlike the influence of Filmer, which, though negative in its direction, was a close up, documentary affair.

Under these circumstances it is idle to look for a direct source, or the source, of Locke's political thinking in Hobbes or anyone else. But of the writers he consulted when engaged on his book, Samuel Pufendorf was perhaps of the greatest use to him, in spite of the fact that their views on constitutional matters were in such contrast. He took advantage of Pufendorf's arguments, he reproduced his positions, and he describes his major work 'as the best book of that kind', better than the great Grotius on *War and Peace.*[25] Now this book of Pufendorf's, the *De Jure Naturae* (1672), had much to say about Hobbes. Here, and in his *Elementa* of 1660, Pufendorf criticized Hobbesian doctrine, but he accepted and appreciated something of the Hobbesian analysis. Locke possessed other critiques of Hobbes.[26] It is perhaps in this direction that we should look for the documentary connection between Hobbes and Locke in the *Two Treatises.*

This account can only be tentative, and it may seem unsatisfactory to those who expect such a literary relationship to fit a framework neatly fashioned from 'influence' and 'rejection', expect it to be a wholly conscious and independent affair. It never is. Hobbes and Locke were caught up within the living tissue, the innumerable threads and fibres growing together, which connects one intellectual generation with its successor in the same country, in the same small society. We have seen that it was from this source, from conversation and casual contact, not from documentary acquaintance, that Locke inherited the fruit of the radical writings of the

[25] *Works*, 1801, III, 272, *Thoughts Concerning Reading and Study.* He also recommended Pufendorf in his other list (X, 308). On Pufendorf as used by Locke, see Appendix B, numbers 66–8, and notes on II, 58, 65, 74 (Pufendorf and Tyrrell), 105 etc. In 1702 Barberac began a correspondence with Locke, asking his advice, and telling him of his intention to translate Pufendorf.

[26] Clarendon, 1676 (bought December 1681); Tenison. 1670; Lawson, 1657. Locke also had a positively Hobbesist work in Matthew Wren's *Monarchy Asserted* (no. 90 in Appendix B), which had been known to him from the time of its publication in 1659, and was on his shelves in 1681. Von Leyden (1954, p. 39) states that Locke had read Pufendorf's *Elementa* as early as 1660.

Civil War.[27] With his interests and with his experience, he could never have escaped the Hobbesian impact.

We must describe *Two Treatises,* then, as a deliberate and polemically effective refutation of the writings of Sir Robert Filmer, intellectually and historically important because of that fact and not in spite of it, related only in the indirect way we have discussed with the work of Hobbes, though antithetical in its political and constitutional doctrine. It was other things as well, of course, and it is as an independent treatise on politics that it has had its influence, although its connection with Hobbes has so often been distorted and exaggerated. It was intended to affect, and it most decidedly did affect, the political and constitutional beliefs of the Englishmen who created the constitution and the political habits under which we still live. But there was one thing it did not contain which every similar treatise included as a matter of course: there was one set of interests passionately pursued by the men who read it and accepted its doctrines, which it made no play upon; there was one 'Whig', or 'liberal', or anti-absolutist intellectual tradition about which it had nothing whatsoever to say. This tradition, these interests, this argument, made up the historical case for English liberty, for the Common Law, for the House of Commons, for the 'ancient constitution', a case which had exercised all Locke's like-minded predecessors since the days of Sir Edward Coke and which had suffered a severe reverse at the hands of Sir Robert Filmer himself.

In *Two Treatises* as we now have it Filmer's constitutional position is never mentioned at all. No reference is made by Locke to the later part of *Patriarcha* and to the *Freeholder's Grand Inquest* where the argument is presented, in spite of the fact that the *Freeholder* stood first in order of the works of Filmer as Locke considered them. When he set out his method of referring to Filmer's tracts,[28] he blandly ignored the existence of the *Freeholder*. In so far as Locke touched at all on the historical case which he, Shaftesbury and the Exclusionists

[27] See above, p. 34. Mr Abrams draws attention to the close personal link between Hobbes, Henry Stubbe and perhaps other students of Christ Church in the late 1650's, and cites Stubbe's letters to Hobbes; British Museum Add. MSS. 32553.
[28] See above, p. 71: Locke once cites the part of *Patriarcha* which deals with the constitution (Laslett's edition, 106–26: the citation is in I, § 8, 37–9 and quotes a passage from p. 113), but he does not comment on it. It is interesting that 60 per cent of all Locke's references to Filmer in the book as we now have it intend pp. 53–64 of *Patriarcha,* and 80 per cent this and four other passages only.

were all fighting for, it seems to have been in a chapter inserted later in order to overset the antithetical case based on conquest. But Filmer had not used that argument, and here Hobbes was one of the few possible targets, for Hobbes unlike Locke did attempt to demonstrate his case in terms of English historical fact.[29] As far as Locke was concerned, Filmer might never have made the statements which maintained that the House of Commons was not originally a part of Parliament, that it was first summoned in the forty-ninth year of Henry III and owed its existence, as did all English law, even the Common Law, to the Royal will.[30] To the constitutionalists of Locke's day and ours arguments of this sort mattered a very great deal: to Locke, apparently, they mattered not at all.

We must say 'apparently' because it should never be forgotten that more than half of Locke's text is lost. It may be that in the missing portion he did develop a case against Filmer's constitutional position and a direct commentary on the legal issues raised by the Exclusion controversy. If it is justifiable to suppose that he destroyed this very part of the text because it contained statements which might have cost him his head, then it would seem likely that it did concern matters much closer to the law of treason than did the rest of the *First Treatise*.[31] But in the brief sentence which Locke gave to constitutional and legal history in the *Second Treatise* he merely 'sent his readers' to a group of writers, whose works he did not own and evidently had never read. He repeated these titles in his lists of recommended books in 1703 and named one of two 'ancient lawyers', all Whig-tainted source books. He added the writings of some of the authors who had engaged in the controversy on the Whig side. He even used this phrase of them: 'wherein he will find the antient constitution of the government of England'.[32]

---

[29] See note on II, § 175 (chapter XVI) and on § 175 itself. There is no evidence whatsoever that Locke had read the lesser works of Hobbes listed there, or had them in mind at the time.

[30] See *Patriarcha*, pp. 106–26, especially p. 117, and the *Freeholder*, *passim*. It is Mr Pocock in his important book *The Ancient Constitution and the Feudal Law*, 1957, who has demonstrated how far-reaching were the effects of these statements and how difficult Filmer's opponents found it to answer them.

[31] See above, pp. 77–8.

[32] See II, § 239, 48–9 and note: *Works*, 1801, III, 272–3, and X, 308. Of the titles in these lists, Locke possessed, besides the works of Tyrrell, seven of those of Atwood; the worst of the Whig constitutional writers; Sadler's *Rights of the Kingdom*, 1682; the 1689 *State Tracts*; Chamber-

All that we learn from these details is that Locke was willing to let men believe in the historical myths so stubbornly defended by common lawyers and Whig writers. It would not be easy to make out a case for supposing that they all belong to a lengthy constitutional argument which originally formed most of *Two Treatises*. Locke's book has only to be compared with Tyrrell's to see how unlikely this is, and when we add to this our knowledge of the interests and reading of the two men it looks impossible.

As a political theorist, then, Locke made no appeal to history or tradition. Nothing in his book could be disproved by the discovery of new evidence about what had happened in England in 1066, or 1215 or 1642, or by a new and more convincing view of how ancient Greek, ancient Roman or medieval English society had actually worked. This was not only extraordinary in view of the way in which these things had been written about before in his own country and in view of the attitude and expectations of the men who first read it. It makes the book unique. It was at once a response to a particular political situation and a statement of universal principle, made as such and still read as such. This work, the authoritative statement of Anglo-Saxon political assumptions, the supreme literary expression of English history and English constitutional development, refers to England as 'a neighbour kingdom', and the Common Law as 'the municipal law of some countries'.[33] Neither Machiavelli, nor Hobbes, nor Rousseau succeeded in making the discussion of politics so completely independent of historical example, so entirely autonomous an area of discourse, yet Locke has affected the everyday activity of practising politicians more perhaps than any of them.

This is a tribute both to the effectiveness of the political theorist's technique in general and to Locke's particular exercise of it. Only a man of such endowment as an abstract thinker could have transformed the issues of a predominantly historical, highly parochial political controversy of this sort into a general political theory. That it should have been done in a sense in anticipation of events, so that from hindsight it has always looked as if it were a rationalization of something which had not yet occurred when it was written, emphasizes

layn's *Anglia Notitia*, 1700. He had no work of Coke or Bracton, nor the *Nirror, Fleta*, the *Modus Tenendi*, or anything of Petit or Brady. He did have one work of Spelman, the *Glossarium*, 1687.
[33] See I, § 90, 32–4; II, § 205, 11.

this quality still further, marks it perhaps with the distinctive sign of this particular discipline of the mind and the imagination. Locke's instinct in leaving the whole legal, historical and constitutional controversy on one side, in deciding, when something of this sort had to be undertaken, to place it apart from his analytic argument, was eminently correct and in this character. This is why his book is with us, and Filmer, Petit, Brady, even Tyrrell and Sidney, have sunk beneath the surface of our intellectual and literary tradition. We should expect that a man capable of this would be a philosopher, even if he turned out to be a philosopher unwilling to admit that he had written out a political theory.

But in what sense should we expect his philosophy to be related to his political theory? If we ask ourselves this question we can discover an exquisite contrast between the Civil Philosophy of Hobbes and Locke's Political Principle.

2. LOCKE THE PHILOSOPHER AND
LOCKE THE POLITICAL THEORIST

In August 1692 Tyrrell sent to Locke a copy of his newly published book on natural law, with this comment:

> I hope that this treatise may give the world sufficient satisfaction, or at least may excite your self, or some other thinking person, to give the world a better account of the Law of Nature and its obligation, than what hath been already performed, as also to confute with better reasons the Epicurean principles of Mr Hobbes. For the doing of which I know no man more capable than yourself if you please to undertake it, and shall no more resent it than the publishing of the *Two Treatises of Government* after *Patriarcha Non Monarcha*. Since, if truth can be better represented and improved by a greater hand, I shall not value my small performances [the less if they] serve for a foil to set it off.[34]

[34] Tyrrell to Locke, 9 August 1692, spelling and punctuation modernized, and words within square brackets supplied. The work was *A Brief Disquisition of the Law of Nature*, 1692, a paraphrase of Richard Cumberland's *De Legibus Naturae Disquisitio Philosophica*, 1672, with special emphasis on his polemic against Hobbes.

This letter hints at much of the relationship between a great literary figure and his less distinguished, less successful friend, as it shows that Tyrrell by this time was one of the few who certainly knew that Locke had written *Two Treatises*. But it also makes it clear that Tyrrell was not satisfied with what had been said on natural law in that work or in the *Essay on Humane Understanding*, and felt that Hobbes had still to be confounded, by Locke himself. And it comes at the end of an exchange between the two men which almost severed the friendship of a lifetime.

Between December 1689 and April 1690 Tyrrell wrote six times from Oxford to Locke in London, telling him how his *Essay* was being received, and reporting criticisms of it. In three of his letters he also asked the name of the author of *Two Treatises*, and though Locke seems to have replied four times, defending himself against the criticisms, he refused to answer that question. When Tyrrell told him that 'the people in Oxford had now found out a better author than I for it, viz. yourself, your answer was to this effect, that since they would not have you to be the author of a book that you owned' (this was the *Essay*, which his critics were saying was lifted from Descartes) 'you did not think it worth while to give them any satisfaction in those that you did not own at all'. In April Tyrrell came to London and faced him with his suspicions about the work on government, but Locke 'declined the discourse' and was told he must 'thank your own reservedness' if the results were unfortunate.[35] On his return in June, Tyrrell read the *Essay* again and discussed it 'with some thinking men at Oxford'; he found them 'dissatisfied with what you have said concerning the law of nature (or reason) whereby we distinguish moral good, from evil and virtue from vice'.[36]

The coincidence of these two things, the suspicion that he had written *Two Treatises* and that he was unsound on natural law, seems to have infuriated Locke, but the explosion was delayed a little while. He saw Tyrrell again in July, and gave him a paper of explanation which seems to have maintained that natural law 'since it did not proceed from God as a lawgiver . . . could not properly be called a law, and the not taking God into this hypothesis has been the

---

[35] Leibnitz was apparently informed by a London correspondent that Locke wrote *Patriarcha non Monarcha*.
[36] Tyrrell to Locke 30 June, 27 July, 30 August, 1960.

great reason of Mr Hobbeses mistake that the laws of nature
are not properly laws nor do oblige mankind to their observation when out of a civil state or commonwealth'. In August
Locke seems to have found reason to suppose that Tyrrell had
been spreading the report about his authorship of *Two
Treatises* and he lost his temper: he sent him an icy letter
repudiating the attack on the *Essay* and enclosed another
one, now destroyed, demanding an explanation about *Two
Treatises*.

The letter in defence of the *Essay* has always been regarded
as the most important source for Locke's attitude to his
critics,[36a] but its context has been previously unknown. If the
statements on natural law in *Two Treatises* are set alongside
those references in the *Essay* which are discussed in this correspondence, it will be seen why he had reason to be annoyed
with Tyrrell at this time. Throughout the political work the
expression natural law is used with suave assurance, as if
there could be no doubt of its existence, of its meaning, of
its content in the minds of author and reader. It is 'plain and
intelligible to all rational Creatures' (II, § 124), it is so much
a positive code that it governs the state of nature (II, § 6),
but its obligations 'cease not in Society'; all men everywhere
must be 'conformable to the Law of Nature, *i.e.* to the Will of
God' (II, § 135). In the *Essay* it is allowed, in parenthesis,
that natural law does not depend on the existence of innate
ideas: men should not deny 'that there is a law knowable by
the light of nature' (I, ii, 13). But when it comes (II, xxviii,
7–) to the description of the laws or rules which men actually
refer their actions to, no natural law is mentioned. In this
exchange of letters Locke fails to convince Tyrrell that
natural law can be equated with or made part of divine law,
civil law (the law of the law-courts) or the 'philosophic law'
(in later editions the 'law of opinion or reputation') which
he maintains are as a matter of fact the standards which men
use to judge of right and wrong. The *Essay* has no room for
natural law.

So sharp here is the contrast between two almost con-
temporaneous works by the same man that in one passage in
Two Treatises, perhaps in the second passage also, Locke uses

[36a] It was printed by King (1830, 366–73), from a copy preserved by
Locke, his only extant letter to Tyrrell, and now in Bodley, dated 4
August 1690. It may, indeed, have never been received by Tyrrell in this
form: perhaps a milder version was actually sent.

language on the subject of natural law which seems inconsistent with his own statements about innate ideas in the *Essay*.[37] Questioning on this point cannot be pressed too far, for we are told that 'it would be besides my present purpose, to enter here into the particulars of the Law of nature, or its *measure of punishment;* yet, it is certain there is such a Law, and that too, as intelligible and plain to a rational Creature, and a Studier of that Law, as the positive Laws of Commonwealths nay possibly plainer' (II, § 12). It seems that it was always 'beside his present purpose' for Locke to demonstrate the existence and content of natural law. He did not do so in his *Essay,* even in the 2nd edition where the passage in the second book which Tyrrell had complained of was rewritten. He would not do so by bringing out his early *Essays on the Law of Nature,* which Tyrrell asked him to do in the course of their exchange.[38] As Dr Von Leyden has shown, these earlier essays would not have provided a doctrine of natural law capable of reconciling the theory of knowledge in Locke's *Essay* with the ethical doctrine of that work and of *Two Treatises*. This, it is suggested, may have been one of the reasons why Locke was unwilling to be known as the author of both books.

Locke is, perhaps, the least consistent of all the great philosophers, and pointing out the contradictions either within any of his works or between them is no difficult task. Sometimes it seems quite clear that he was unconscious of his inconsistency, at other times, and this appears to be one of them, he himself realized his dilemma, but was unable to find a solution. The objective existence of a body of natural law is an essential presupposition of his political theory and when we find him using the phrase we should perhaps think of him as taking up what might be called a stance to a series of possible explanations. Natural law, in his system in *Two Treatises,* was at one and the same time a command of God, a rule of reason, and a law in the very nature of things as they are, by which they work and we work too. This conception of adopting a more or less conscious stand-pat attitude could perhaps be used as a general sympathetic approach towards the problem created by Locke's ethical statements, which point in many directions at the same time and which have

[37] See note on II, § 11, 31–2 ('so plain was it writ in the Hearts of all Mankind'), I, § 86, 21–4 and references.
[38] Tyrrell to Locke, 27 July 1690, compare Von Leyden, 1954, 9–10.

been much discussed.[39] It invites us to look upon *Two Treatises* as something very different from an extension into the political field of the general philosophy of the *Essay*, and reminds us that Locke differed in the character of his thinking from Hobbes. He did not reply to *Leviathan* because it was irrelevant to his purposes as a writer of political principle.

It is natural that posterity should have chosen to look upon the philosophical and the political work as complementary. But Locke himself, as we have shown, was perfectly willing, indeed very anxious, that they should be seen apart. It is easily demonstrated that the literary continuity between them was about as slight as it possibly could be under such circumstances. The close analysis of his text has revealed only one example of this author using identical material in both works,[40] and then in a passage probably inserted later. The style, the type of argument, the atmosphere are all recognizable as from the same writer, but in every other respect they differ remarkably. *Two Treatises* is not written on the 'plain, historic method' of the *Essay*. If it were, we might expect in the first place that it would insist on the limitations of our social and political understanding, for that is Locke's chief enterprise in the *Essay*, to portray the character of our knowledge by showing up its limits. Then the situations, the rights, the duties discussed, would have been presented recognizably as the 'complex ideas' or 'mixed modes' of Locke's system of knowledge, the product of ratiocination and therefore fixed and definite, capable of entering into a mathematically demonstrable morality. Just such a discussion is implied by, or even begun in, the statement about property we have quoted, and there are many other examples.[41]

[39] See, e.g. Leslie Stephen, 1876; James Stephen, 1892; Lamprecht, 1918; Vaughan, 1925; Kendall, 1941; Von Leyden, 1954 and 1956; Strauss, 1953; Simon, 1951; Yolton, 1955; Brogan, 1958; Polin, 1960; Singh, 1961; Abrams, 1961. The trouble was that Locke began by basing right and wrong on God's commands and punishments, but also adopted a hedonistic ethic as well, an ethic of the Hobbesian sort. Meanwhile he passionately believed in the possibility of demonstrating ethics mathematically, though he was perpetually complicating everything with his anthropological relativism, noting the variety of ethical values among the world's peoples and hinting that virtue and vice were simply customary.

[40] See note on I, § 57.

[41] See p. 85 and II, § 22, 9–10: the passage immediately following the sentence cited on p. 85 (the ideas of absolute liberty and government) is an even better illustration. For a different view of *Two Treatises* and the *Essay*, see Polin, 1961.

Some such construction as this might be made by a modern scholar attempting to create a theory of politics out of Locke's *Essay,* if, as so nearly happened, it had never become certainly known that *Two Treatises* was his. Such an exercise might have illuminating results, though it cannot be our subject here, for the implications of Locke's theory of knowledge for politics and political thinking were very considerable and acted quite independently of the influence of *Two Treatises.* The famous doctrine of the *tabula rasa,* for example, the blank sheet of the mind on which experience and experience alone can write, made men begin to feel that the whole world is new for everyone and we are all absolutely free of what has gone before.

The political results of such an attitude have been enormous. It was, perhaps, the most effective solvent of the natural-law attitude. In a sense these results were intended. For though Locke wrote the *Essay* about how men know things, his final object, the object he had in mind when he started, was to help men to know what to do. 'Our business here is not to know all things', his classic statement goes, 'but those which concern our conduct.' He keeps on slipping into this mood throughout the book, but the only work he actually produced on how men should behave was *Two Treatises.* And it cannot be said to represent his account of the implications for conduct, for politics, of the doctrines of the *Essay.* It was written for an entirely different purpose and in an entirely different state of mind.

None of the connecting links is present. It is extraordinary, for example, how little definition there is in the political work, though the *Essay* is, as it should be, much concerned with definition and though he reproaches Filmer for failing to define. *Two Treatises* relies heavily upon natural law, but the term, as we have seen, is never analysed there. It is all about freedom and consent, but they are nowhere discussed as subjects in themselves. It is the same with law, with reason, with will, with government itself. Political power is defined, and so is property (though it is used in two meanings, and Locke seems to pass from one to the other without warning), but not in philosophic terms, on nothing like the principles laid down in his *Essay* and insisted upon from his earliest writings.[42] Justice is scarcely mentioned, and the issue about

[42] On Filmer and definition, I, § 7 etc.; on meanings of property, pp. 114–15 below.

justice and property is never raised, though there is a reference to it in the *Education*. Even more singular, perhaps, is
the way in which Locke brushes aside the question of
conscience and political obligation, which had worried him
as a young man as it had worried all his predecessors and
contemporaries.[43]

If we try to pass from one work to another and use the
definitions offered in the *Essay* for the political discussion,
we find that they do not fit very well: at least one important
term, consent, is not defined even there. The political argument is not presented as a part of a general philosophy, and
does not seem to be intended to be read as such. There is a
note in Locke's journal which was written at the time when,
as we suppose, he was working over *Two Treatises*, and adding the Hooker quotations. It reads almost as a conscious
commentary on the relationship between philosophy, ethics
and politics. He had just expressed his belief in the possibility
of demonstrating ethics, and his scepticism about the poten-
tialities of natural science. He goes on:

The well management of public or private affairs depending
upon the various and unknown humours, interests and capacities of men we have to do with in the world, and not upon
any settled ideas of things physical, polity and prudence are
not capable of demonstration. But a man is principally
helped in them by the history of matter of fact, and a sagacity
of finding out an analogy in their operations and effects.
[The truths of mathematics are certain.] But whether this
course in public or private affairs will succeed well, whether
rhubarb will purge or quinquina cure an ague, is only known
by experience, and there is but probability grounded upon
experience, or analogical reasoning, but no certain knowledge
or demonstration.[44]

Empirical medicine, rather than philosophy, seems to be
the model for the man who sets out to comment on political
matters. Locke the doctor rather than Locke the epistemologist
is the man we should have in mind when we read his work

---

[43] See above, p. 85 note 16 on property in the *Education*, and note on
I, § 105, for Locke's slight and unimportant references to conscience.
[44] Journal, 1681, under 26 June, modernized: printed in full by Aaron
and Gibb, 1936, 116–18. Dugald Stewart seems first to have stressed the
importance of Locke's medical experience and attitude for his ethical
and political thought.

on *Government*. To call it 'political philosophy', to think of him as a 'political philosopher', is inappropriate.[45] He was, rather, the writer of a work of intuition, insight and imagination, if not of profound originality, who was also a theorist of knowledge.

He was also a writer on economics, toleration and education, active in many areas where political generalization had to be made. When the text of *Two Treatises* is put alongside these other works, the literary relationship is found to be somewhat closer than in the case of the *Essay*.[46] Religious freedom was a fundamental to Locke and the assumptions on which he based it are common to the writings in defence of it and to the writing on politics, yet it is not mentioned in *Two Treatises*.[47] His economic theory has some points in common with his political principle, and his educational theory has even more: there are details from the political text which can be seen developing in his later writings, especially the successive editions of the *Education*. But the inconsistencies are even more conspicuous. It would indeed be difficult to show that they entail one another, or that they all arise with a logical necessity from his theory of knowledge. Even between the *Essay* and the work on education, where the barrier of anonymity is absent on both sides and the connection is intimate, Locke makes no cross-references. It is pointless to look upon his work as an integrated body of speculation and generalization, with a general philosophy at its centre and as its architectural framework.

[45] Compare Strauss, 1953, 220–1. I am unable to follow him, however, when he claims that the *Treatises* are the 'civil' presentation of a political doctrine which could have been presented 'philosophically'. The passage which he cites from the *Essay* (III, IX, 3) seems to state quite clearly that the civil use of words in ordinary affairs can only be discussed by the philosophic use of words, and so *Two Treatises*, if it is not 'political philosophy', can only be philosophical in this sense. The passage which Strauss cites from II, § 52, 1–3 appears to me to repeat this assertion, though he evidently believes that it marks off the book as in 'civil' language. Like the other statements which Locke makes (see note on I, § 23, 26–9 and references) it insists that the language of the discussion of politics must be consistent and of clear definition, 'philosophic' in fact. Locke may have contradicted his own rules in practice, but there can be no doubt what those rules were and how they defined this book.
[46] On toleration see II, §§ 3, 87, 108, 134, 135. On economics see II, §§ 45–7.
[47] Freedom of expression is not mentioned either. Locke seems to have helped to bring about the freedom of the press without ever considering it as a political right.

This marks Locke off very sharply from the other political theorists of his generation, indeed from the traditional attitude which dominated political thinking before and after him. It separates him even more definitely from Thomas Hobbes. The heavy books of Grotius, Pufendorf, Hooker and the others, standing on Locke's shelves and dominating intellectual activity in this field, were all presentations of a single, synthetic system, a view of the world which proceeded from an account of reality to an account of knowledge, and so to an ethic and to politics. They varied in completeness and in the extent to which they relied on Christian revelation to fill out the great chain of being, or in the use which they made of historical examples and concrete political situations. But natural law was their common assumption, and in its terms they endeavoured to discover a closed system, a system which ideally would be complete and entirely consistent. We should be disposed to give the title 'philosopher' to very few of them, but the task they set themselves was a philosophical one. And in the mind of the ablest of them all philosophy was civil philosophy: Hobbes created a general determinist system, where political obligation, even the form and function of the state, was made to follow from a new definition of natural law. Locke was a philosopher too, but to him the system was an open one.

We cannot explore the various directions which this position lays open to view. It gives to Locke's thinking a somewhat unexpected precedent, for in Machiavelli and the writers of political advice, the reminiscent statesmen themselves, there did exist a counter-tradition to natural law, a convention of discussing politics and its theory outside the area of philosophy. Here the relationship between Shaftesbury the statesman and Locke the thinker comes very close to the surface, and it is recalled by a sentence in Locke's *Essay*. He is discussing the medieval scholarly doctors and he says: 'Notwithstanding these learned disputants, these all knowing doctors, it was to the unscholastic statesmen that the governments of the world owed their peace, defence, and liberties.' [48]

This opens out an inquiry of a different sort, the extent to which the actual doctrine of Locke's *Essay* allowed for the peculiar relationship of political theory with general philosophical inquiry by its very incompleteness, suggesting that

[48] II, X, 9: 1894, II, 128.

beyond its chosen limits the system was indeed an open matter. In this sense, its anti-synthetic quality, Locke's philosophy could be said to inform the whole of his thinking, but in quite the antithetical way from Hobbes and the natural-law theorists. He, and not Hobbes, could perhaps be looked upon as Machiavelli's philosopher, but most certainly not because the content of his philosophy entailed the content of Machiavellian political doctrine.

A great deal more could be said, then, of Locke the philosopher and Locke the political theorist to illuminate his position in the history of thought as well as the logic of the problem of philosophy and politics. The conventional description of Locke's thought as a peculiar and fertile admixture of empiricism and rationalism suggests the terms of the discussion. In his attitude these two elements were, so to speak, held in solution, only to be precipitated by the men who followed him, Berkeley and Hume in particular. If, then, there was not a Lockeian philosophy in the Hobbesian sense, there was a Lockeian attitude and this can be traced in all that he wrote. Natural law was, in this analysis, a part of his rationalism, his conviction that the universe is to be understood rationally, even the workings of the deity, even the relations of human beings, but at all points it must be compared with, made to fit into, the observed, the empirical facts about the created world and human behaviour.

This position is no easy one to occupy, even if it is taken up as a stance towards the problem in the way which has been suggested.[49] It led Locke later into his attempt to supplement his rationalism and empiricism with revelation. Although the laws of the rational heathens had enough of natural virtue to 'hold societies together', the holy scriptures, rationally interpreted, were to be used almost as sources of empirically verified facts for moral and political purposes. This was necessary because of the patent insufficiency of reason: 'It is plain, in fact, that human reason, unassisted failed men in its great and proper business of morality. It never from unquestionable principles, by clear deductions, made out an entire body of the "law of nature".'[50] This

[49] Von Leyden suggests that the difficulty arises from the ambiguity of natural law, but, like Polin, takes an opposite view to mine of Locke's attitude to it.

[50] *Reasonableness of Christianity*, 1697, *Works*, 1801, VII, 139–40: compare Strauss, 1953, 205, where Locke's proviso about heathen societies is ignored, as is his implied (though perhaps confused) distinction between natural law and moral law.

scepticism about natural law and about reason itself contrasts strangely once again with the easy confidence of *Two Treatises*. In this mood Locke doubted the efficacy of reason not simply because it had failed to demonstrate morality, but also because men obeyed it so little. In this particular, then, the Lockeian attitude led to the doubt and self-searching of which we now have so much evidence. But elsewhere it led to the comfortable certainties of eighteenth-century thought.

If a distinction between the philosophy and the attitude of Locke is legitimate, we could fill out the picture of him as a thinker; we could account, for example, for his unwillingness to push any argument to its extreme. But to do this is not to transfer parts of the content of his philosophy into his political theory: to claim, for instance, that there is more than accidental symmetry, an aesthetic coherence, between his atomic view of matter and his atomic view of society, or to imply that there is a relationship of cause and effect between his conceptualism (or nominalism, some would say) and his belief in toleration.[51] This is to assume that his political thinking was related to his philosophy as the part to the whole. It implies that a formal consistency, a purely logical interrelationship between parts, is always to be looked for in a thinker, who must be judged accordingly: where it is found wanting some more remote and unrealistic principle of reconciliation must be found to defend a great reputation. It is to lose sight of the possibility that the more successful a man is as a political thinker, the more difficult he will find it to come to terms with his view of the world as a whole. In fact it may be taken to lay it down that all political thought is meta-political thought, formal analysis of the way men discuss politics and never also intuitive explorations of what they do. If this is done the distinction between Locke and Hobbes is made somewhat obscure and Locke may even turn out to be a Hobbesian, a muddle-headed one. To complete our examination of the relationship between these two men, we must examine these terms more closely.

But before we do this we may look at what has already been said in the light, Locke's own unfailing light, of common sense. A great deal, perhaps too much, has been made of

---

[51] See Simon, 1951: even more extraordinary seems to be the question raised there as to why Locke's optimism survived his conversion to the Copernican hypothesis, as if it were literally true that the conception men have of the stars cannot help but be a directive influence on their beliefs.

Locke's inconsistencies.[52] But it must be remembered that all thinkers are inconsistent, and the latest and most ingenious exponent of Hobbes himself has no more than this to say of him on the question of consistency: 'He is not obviously more contradictory than Locke.'[53] We have chosen to expound the case in these terms because it arises more easily out of the documentary evidence, and because inconsistency, doubt, hesitation seem to be crucial to the position as it can be more positively examined in the *Essay* and *Two Treatises* themselves, in their sources and in the circumstances of their composition and publication. Then we have emphasized, perhaps over-emphasized, the distinction between Locke the philosopher and Locke the political theorist. But it is not true to say that to understand his political writing as philosophy is necessarily to misapprehend him. His influence as a political writer, as we have said,[54] probably arose because of his philosophical fame. Nevertheless it is of importance to see in Locke, the recognized point of departure for liberalism, the liberal dilemma already present, the dilemma of maintaining a political faith without subscribing to a total, holistic view of the world.

Hobbes's view of the world might have had its logical difficulties, but there can be no doubt that it was wholly Hobbesian. He was the greatest of all the meta-political writers, those who refine and analyse political language and elaborate axioms into axiologies. For this reason his influence on thought about politics has been enormous, but his purchase over what men do politically has been negligible. After he had written, this discipline became entirely different, but the political habits of his countrymen were changed not one little bit, except in so far as clarity of thinking in some men can modify the attitude of a whole society, and

[52] Polin, 1960, claims in opposition that Locke's doctrine is a coherent whole, and that only an extreme empiricist, an historian, could argue as above.

[53] Warrender, 1957, *Preface*. The subject of this book, the great difficulty of finding ethical continuity between Hobbes's state of nature and his state of society, shows Hobbes in an incoherency much more serious than any of Locke's.

[54] Above, p. 50. In his later years, Locke obviously looked on politics as related to philosophy in the traditional way. This comes out in his various letters of advice about reading for young men. 'True politics I look on as a part of moral philosophy, which is nothing but the art of conducting men right in society and supporting a community amongst its neighbours', he wrote in 1697 to Lady Mordaunt, now the Countess of Peterborough. 'A young man should begin with Aristotle and then read the moderns if he please.'

on Hobbes's own submission this is very little. The reason for his historical ineffectiveness is not very far to seek. A man who can say, as he did, that 'The skill of making, and maintaining Commonwealths, consisteth in certain rules, as doth Arithmetique and Geometry; not (as Tennis-play) on Practise only' [55] lacks what might be called a sense of policy. The skill, the consistency, the imagination and the insight with which he sets about discovering what those rules are and how they are related to each other and to knowledge in general must attract his readers, but they will read him as literature only, not literature which is also advice. His work is condemned to be rationalization, and the paradox of the relationship between Locke and Hobbes is that *Leviathan* is much more dated than *Two Treatises;* it is rationalization even of a historical situation. The complete failure of Hobbes as a political, as distinct from a literary and philosophical, realist, is shown up by the fact that he seems to have thought that *Leviathan* would be adopted as a political programme.

The secret of his success in transforming the way men study and write about politics lies in the fact that all political theory must be rationalization, must aspire to the status of philosophy, to some extent. A work of policy exclusively, a work which would deny *in toto* the aphorism which we have quoted from *Leviathan*, could never be written. When, therefore, John Locke set out in 1679 to convince his readers about 'the true original extent and end of civil government' he produced a book which was in some respects like *Leviathan*, although it was not a refutation of it. It was quite unlike it in doctrine, and for two reasons. He had rejected Hobbes's psychological assumptions and also his entirely rationalistic, unempirical view of natural law, which was widely felt to be a sophistry in any case: [56] with his instinct against synthetic thinking, therefore, he was under no logical necessity of considering its authoritarian conclusions and we have shown that there was no possible political motive for doing so. It differed very considerably in the form of its argument, because of these things, because of Filmer, and because of the Lockeian attitude we have discussed, so completely in contrast with the Hobbesian attitude. It contained just that ingredient which *Leviathan* lacked—policy; statement of guidance of what men will accept, respond to and pursue, of the limits of their loyalty

---

[55] *Leviathan*, chapter 20, last sentence.
[56] See Tyrrell's letter quoted on p. 93 above.

and the possible extent of generalization about their behaviour. But it was also the presentation of a cogitated case, a piece of intellectual persuasion, from a mind with a great deal in common with that of Hobbes, fully aware of the change which Hobbes had wrought.

It may not, we have seen, have been a matter of direct derivation, since it is quite possible that Locke made his own way along the same road trodden by Hobbes before him, aided only by derivative acquaintance with what Hobbes had said. Locke was a post-Hobbesian, in spite of the fact that so great a part of Hobbesian belief was so much an irrelevance to his purpose in writing on politics that he did not have to refute it. It is right to think of *Two Treatises* as a work of greater importance than *Leviathan* because of the pregnant difference in its relationship with philosophy; it was for this reason that its text could become a part of political habit, and incidentally create the paradox that in so far as Hobbes has done that at all, it is through Locke that he has done it.

In the political doctrines we shall now examine, Locke presented a set of principles of an entirely superior order of effectiveness than any before written in the English language.

V

THE SOCIAL AND POLITICAL THEORY OF 'TWO TREATISES OF GOVERNMENT'

When men think of themselves as organized with each other they must remember who they are. They do not make themselves, they do not own themselves, they do not dispose of themselves, they are the workmanship of God. They are his servants, sent into the world on his business, they are even his property (II, § 6). To John Locke this was a proposition of common sense, the initial proposition of a work which appeals to common sense throughout. It is an existentialist proposition, which men have not thought it worth while to question seriously until our own day, and it relies not so much on the proved existence of a Deity as upon the possibility of taking what might be called a synoptic view of the world, more vulgarly, a God's-eye view of what happens among men here on earth. If you admit that it is possible to look down on men from above, then you may be said to grant to Locke this initial position.

From this common-sense starting-point he proceeds to two inferences, that we are all free and we are all equal; free of each other, that is to say, and equal to each other, for we are not free of God's superiority and not equal to him. If God could be shown to have given any man, or any order of men, superiority over other men, then these inferences could not be drawn. It was because Sir Robert Filmer had claimed that there was to be found in Revelation a proof that God had set some men above other men, fathers above sons and men above women, the older above the younger and kings above all others that his doctrine was so dangerous and had to be refuted. It became necessary to show in minute detail, analysing text after text of the Scriptures, that this interpretation was quite wrong.

This is the logical function of the *First Treatise* in Locke's work on government, but he says nothing there which is not laid down in the *Second Treatise*. The polemic against Filmer had to be in the form of a Scriptural argument, but it is necessarily an argument from observation and reason as well, for the Scripture does not interpret itself.[1] Observation shows, says Locke the empiricist, that the superiority of fathers is temporary only, and observation combined with reason shows us why: such superiority is necessary for the preservation of mankind and its duration is determined by the zoological facts (II, §§ 80, 81). Filmer, following Grotius, had interpreted those facts to show that procreation, one individual creating another individual by begetting him, gave a right of superiority, subjection of will to will, even ownership. This is not only bad observation, but it is utterly unreasonable and moreover it offends against the first principle that man is the workmanship and property of God, not himself. Quite simply and quite literally, then, men were born free in Locke's view, as quite simply and quite literally they had been born unfree in Filmer's system, and in the patriarchal tradition.

No, Locke says; 'the Lord and Master of them all' has not 'by any manifest Declaration of his Will set one above another' (II, § 4), and we all have the same faculties, the same natural advantages; power and jurisdiction is and must be reciprocal amongst us. Again, you do not have to accept a theology to agree that this is all a matter of common sense. All that happens if you wish to disagree is that you find the task of proving something different uncomfortably thrust upon you.

But if it is true that God leaves us free, that nothing in the natural order can be shown to subject one man to another even apart from the revealed will of God, it may still be relevant to ask what positively makes us free, in what does this

[1] This is an important general position of Locke's, best known perhaps from his rejection of 'enthusiasm'. The *First Treatise* repeatedly argues from scripture on the one hand, and reason on the other—see e.g. §§ 4, 60 (Reason and Revelation), 112.

freedom consist. For absolute freedom has no meaning, it
must be defined—'*Where there is no Law, there is no freedom*'
(II, § 57). It is the law of nature which sets the bounds to
natural freedom (II, § 4) and since the law of nature is an
expression of God's will, God's omnipotence can be reconciled
with human freedom.[2] Moreover, God's positive direction is
known to all of us through our reason, since reason, as the
Platonists were saying in Locke's day, is '*the Voice of God*'
in man (I, § 86, see note there). But in the stance, as we have
called it, which Locke took up towards natural law, 'the Law
of Nature . . . is the Law of Reason' (I, § 101). It is our
reason, therefore, which promulgates to us the law of nature
and it is our reason which makes us free. 'We are *born Free*
as we are born Rational' (II, § 61), and the liberty of acting
according to our own will, never from compulsion by the will
of others, is grounded on the possession of reason (II, § 63).

But reason means even more than this and has further
consequences for natural liberty and equality. Conceived of
as a law (the law of nature), or almost as a power, it is
sovereign over all human action. It can dictate to a man as
conscience does (II, § 8) and to more than one man in the
social situation, since it is given by God to be the rule betwixt
man and man (II, § 172). It is a quality too, in fact it is the
human quality which places man above the brutes, and when
it is present to the full almost brings him up to the level of
the angels (I, § 58). This language is traditional and the distinction between man and beasts based on the presence or
absence of the quality reason goes back beyond Christianity
to the Stoics and Aristotle, but it was of peculiar significance
to Locke's generation, as witness the curious debate as to
whether brutes, which can work in the world although not
being human they do not have the quality, must therefore be
machines. And Locke makes full and peculiar use of it in his
account of state and society.

It justifies in the first place the subordinate position of children, who though they are born to the full state of equality
are not born in it (II, § 55). They only attain freedom when
they reach what we still call the age of reason. All this is obvious enough, and only has to be stated at the length Locke
gives to it because of Filmer, but it should be noticed that
even children under age are not subject to the will of their

---

[2] Quite how, is never shown. Locke is famous for his confession that
this problem was beyond him, and it is typical that he should never have
raised it in his work on political theory.

parents so much as without will, their parents will for them: reason is still sovereign over parent and child. This is one of the very few ways in which age, process or development is relevant to human relationships, though Locke admits that age, virtue, intelligence and blood (none of which seems easily described as a difference in rationality) in some way unimportant to his purpose can infringe natural equality (II, § 54). But the next consequence is more startling. When we look upon ourselves as God's workmanship, we recognize that we all possess reason because he gave it to us, and therefore any man who behaves unreasonably is to that extent an animal, and may be treated as such. Specifically, any man who seeks to get anyone else into his power, under his will, denying that this other person is as free as he is because he too possesses reason, refusing to recognize that reason is the rule between men, that man 'becomes liable to be destroied by the injured person and the rest of mankind, as any other wild beast, or noxious brute that is destructive to their being' (II, § 172).

This is a drastic argument, and we may think it somewhat crude. It serves to spell out in thick, black letters Locke's quite literal belief that reason is the mode of co-operation between men; reason, he had just said, is 'the common bond whereby humane kind is united into one fellowship and societie'. It is not an isolated statement, but a recurrent repetitive theme, perhaps developed in detail as a later insertion (see note on II, § 172), but essential to Locke's account of the maintenance of justice inside and outside organized society. It may be looked upon as his final judgment on the consequences to the actual relationships between men of the synthetic civil philosophy of Hobbes, for *Leviathan,* like the royal patriarch, did subordinate all human wills to one will, it made law and government a matter of will, therefore it did treat men as beasts and anyone pretending to its rights and powers could be treated as a beast. But the actual object which he had in mind seems to have been much more personal and political. When the passages presenting this argument are examined closely, Charles and James Stuart fit easily enough into the role of those 'wild Savage Beasts, with whom Men can have no Society nor Security',[3] for they had tried to rule

[3] II, § 11, 28–30. This is a reference to an aggressor in the state of nature, but the last phrase also appeared in the final text of II, § 172, 18. The subject of II, §§ 171 and 172 is clearly the established government of a country, Locke's country, and these are the words applied to it when it claims the right to 'Absolute, Arbitrary Power' ('Having quitted Reason' to do so).

England as despots, if not of the Hobbesian, then certainly of the patriarchal type.

In perfect freedom, equal to each other, capable of national behaviour and so able to understand and co-operate with each other, that is how we are born. It must be emphasized that we are all born this way, bond or free, savage or civilized, inside or outside society or the state, for it is a truly universal doctrine in Locke and he does not, for example, go on to argue from this dogmatic rationalist position that the basis of political life is the rule of the rational man over his irrational fellows.[4] There can be no arbitrary source of power of one man over another, not even a source in Revelation, for Divine right has already been disposed of as not proven. How then does it come about that there is such a thing as rulership in the world? How is government possible at all?

Locke answers this fundamental question, and it is significant of his radical individualism that it should ever arise in such an urgent form, by introducing what he calls a 'Strange Doctrine'. By this he may intend to warn us that he is innovating,[5] but what he says comes as no great surprise: '*every one*', he declares, '*has the Executive Power* of the Law of Nature' (II, §§ 6, 7, 8, 13). If anyone offends against the law of nature, everyone else has the right to punish him for it and exact retribution, not simply for his own damage but to vindicate the rule 'of *reason* and common Equity, which is that measure God has set to the actions of Men, for their mutual security' (II, § 8). We may do so individually, but we may and must co-operate with other individuals against this 'trespass against the whole Species'. On this natural right, which arises out of humanity itself, is based not simply the right of governing, but its power as well, for it is a collective

---

[4] Though he concedes wide inequality in capacity, reasoning capacity, see note on II, § 4, 13 and references. Locke took a sober, almost a gloomy view of the powers of most of the human race to follow an argument, to take part in 'rational society' at all in its sophisticated definition, and texts to illustrate this can be found throughout his works, the *Essay* especially: the title of 'optimistic rationalist' sits oddly upon him. Nevertheless it does not seem to me justifiable to read into his statements, certainly the statements of *Two Treatises*, any doctrine of differential rationality as has sometimes been done. Strictly the non-rational man was not a man at all and Locke never denies that any individual can be rational according to his capacity, he only insists that he is blameworthy if he is not. He may not be a consistent optimist, but he is no cynic: see Polin, 1961, 40n.

[5] Strauss, 1953, lays some stress on Locke's use of this phrase, but it seems to me to be not much more than a literary device to him. As Strauss points out, Locke's doctrine on the point differs only by a twist of emphasis from that of Pufendorf and Cumberland.

power which is used against an offender even if only one man wields it. The right of governing, and power to govern, is a fundamental, individual, natural right and power, set alongside that of preserving oneself and the rest of mankind (II, §§ 128–30). It is judicial in its nature, for it is the pronouncing and enforcing of a law, the law of nature which is the law of reason.

The whole of Locke's political theory is already in view, even the concept of trust and the separation of powers. We shall make general the implications of this position on the executive power of the law of nature under the title of a doctrine, the Lockeian doctrine of natural political virtue. Dogmatically presented as a 'strange doctrine', no demonstration of its truth is offered, but it is implied in a particular provision of the law of nature as distinct from the law of nature generally. This is the right and duty of every man to preserve himself and everybody else as much as possible, which is the only law of nature used in such a way.[6] Government, when first viewed from this position is simply a 'Magistrate, who by being Magistrate, hath the common right of punishing put into his hands' (II, § 11). But we have not yet reached the stage of established government. All the characteristics of men, and the relationship between them, which we have discussed so far belong to the state of nature.

The state of nature is simply the condition in which the executive power of the law of nature remains exclusively in the hands of individuals and has not been made communal. It can be inferred that it was the original condition of all humanity, because wherever established and permanent collective authority is found, it is always discovered to be the result of men taking thought, making deliberate arrangements to secure and establish the rule of rationality and the provisions of natural law. It is not an adequate reply to this to say that men are all observed in fact to live under government, because 'Government is everywhere antecedent to Records' (II, § 101, compare I, §§ 144, 145) and because primitive tribes are known to be living now without government, or very nearly so. But although these historical and anthropological facts are important, demonstrating as they do that individual

[6] Because of the particular attitude to the law of nature which we have described, Locke never lists the laws themselves and he never relates one law of nature with another, though this law of preservation is called 'fundamental'; see note on II, § 16, 9–10 and references, including a passage in his *Education*. In all these respects he is a very unconventional natural-law writer, much more so than Hobbes.

men have lived and do live with each other in the state of nature, it is much more significant that states themselves, and heads of states, can be related to each other in no other way, now or at any time. The King of France and the King of England can collaborate to maintain the peace of the world, so as to preserve mankind. For the most part they do, but each is individually executing the law of nature: there is no institution or authority for the purpose. This fact, and the persistence of areas of the earth in the state of nature, may also put private individuals into this state with each other even now. Such are the Swiss and the Indian bargaining for truck in the woods of America (II, § 14).[7]

The state of nature, therefore, has obvious disadvantages; it is to be expected that men will do their best to replace it, and we have seen that they are constituted in such a way that they are perfectly well able to do so. It leaves every man judge in his own case (II, § 13). He has the law of nature to guide him, but this law is unwritten, 'no where to be found but in the minds of Men', so that 'they who through Passion or Interest shall mis-cite, or mis-apply it, cannot so easily be convinced of their mistake where there is no establish'd Judge' (II, § 136). But this does not mean that the state of nature is a state of war, 'however some Men', meaning Hobbes, 'have confounded' them (II, § 19). War, in fact, is not a state but an incident, although a 'sedate setled Design' on life makes it permissible to use 'state' in describing it (II, § 16). War is indeed an incident apparently inseparable from human life, because it is the appeal to God in cases where men cannot settle things reasonably, and we have to recognize that such a final appeal is always a possibility even within highly developed political society, a possibility which has important consequences. It is to be expected that war should be much closer to the surface in a state of nature, as witness the frequency and importance of war in the international state of nature,

[7] The scattered references to primitive societies in *Two Treatises*, with the more extensive discussion in the *Essay*, cover an enormous amount of reading, a perpetual preoccupation and an intellectual dilemma. Locke may be said to have done more than anyone else to found the study of comparative anthropology, and he was well aware that the evidence did not demonstrate a 'state of nature' of the sort he described in his political theory. Once more, then, he had to take up a stance towards the problem. We may believe that this was his position: natural man cannot be proved to have lived universally in comparative peace, in imminent sociability, but the evidence does not make such an assumption impossible, and it certainly does not make it necessary to assume that he lived in a state of war.

but this cannot mean that war describes the state of nature, or that it is otherwise relevant to the distinction between the state of nature and the state of society.

'In the beginning all the World was *America*' (II, § 49) and a complete account of human development would show us that in the primitive, patriarchal, Old Testament stage in Europe we once lived as the American Indians now do (see notes on I, § 130). In fact this condition of living together according to reason without a common superior on earth, in mutual assistance, peace, goodwill and preservation (II, § 19), is the universal background against which government should be understood. It tells us what government is and what it does by showing us what it is not and what it does not do.[8] It even makes it possible to distinguish proper forms of government from improper ones. '*Absolute Monarchy*', for example, is '*inconsistent with Civil Society*, and so can be no Form of Civil Government at all' (II, § 90). It must be so, because an absolute monarch is judging in his own case, as all men must in the state of nature. Therefore in respect of him the whole society he rules is itself still in a state of nature; moreover he is substituting the rule of force and will, his force and will, for the rule of reason clothed in natural law. But this does not mean that there is no peace, no justice, no means of social and political co-operation within the society he rules, any more than the international state of nature precludes international peace and co-operation. For men are not like that. The state of nature is already social and political. The state of society never completely transcends the state of nature: the contrast is never complete.

These considerations undoubtedly complicate Locke's view of the state of nature, but the complication demonstrates his superior realism and allows room in his system for elements often supposed to be absent from him and from the individualist attitude generally.[9] At the point we have now reached,

[8] This is the analytic function of this concept in the political theory of early modern times, and can be criticized as the error of supposing that what is logically prior is historically previous and institutionally basic. That Locke was uneasy about its implications is shown by his unwillingness to do more than hint at the assimilation between Old Testament history and the condition of America in his day, and in any case the incompleteness of the contrast which he draws between the two states makes him somewhat less vulnerable than his predecessors.

[9] Locke's state of nature, with its immanent sociability and its acceptance of man as in principle a political animal, does in a sense incorporate the Aristotelian attitude. See Polin, 1961, 174, for the *theoretical* as distinct from the *actual* state of nature.

however, where the question arises why it should be that men ever do proceed from a state of nature to a state of society, he suddenly departs from all his predecessors, classical and medieval. Although his state of nature is inconvenient, and although his individual is perfectly capable of transcending it and we can already see why he and his fellows should wish to do so, Locke introduces here a motive for the establishment of political society which few had considered in the context of political origins, and none had given much prominence. He abruptly injects into the discussion the concept of property.

Property generally is justified ethically in Locke's system by arguments not unlike those of the other thinkers of the time. Mankind's right to the goods of nature derives from God's grant in the Scriptures, from man's rationality, from the fundamental natural law of self-preservation (II, § 25 on, I, §§ 86, 87). But on these grounds it is man as a species which has a right to own things, not an individual man. This means that the goods of nature were originally common, both because the Bible says so, and because universal freedom and equality must mean original communism. Locke and his fellows were in some difficulty in accounting for the fact that this original communism had given way to private property. They could and did argue from occupancy, 'findings is keepings', but in the end this must imply consent. In fact, as Filmer had argued with ingenuity and force, the only way out of original communism was to assume that in some way or other every individual in the world had consented to every act of property acquisition.

Locke's solution to the problem was to lay it down that 'every Man has a *Property* in his own *Person*' so that 'the *Labour* of his Body, and the *Work* of his Hands' are his. Therefore whatsoever 'he removes out of the State that Nature hath provided, and left it in, he hath mixed his *Labour* with . . . and thereby makes it his *Property*' (II, § 27). This famous passage, which almost contradicts his first principle that men belong to God, not themselves, together with the general claim that ' 'tis *Labour* indeed that *puts the difference of value* on every thing' (II, § 40) are perhaps the most influential statements he ever made.[10] Property so acquired was

[10] See note on II, § 27 for Tyrrell's very similar passage, probably however suggested to him by Locke, and note on II, § 28 for a further discussion of Locke as an innovator in this matter. It cannot be proved to have been entirely original to Locke, and is close to the traditional dogma that a labourer had an inalienable right to his tools. Polin, 1960, 255, prints a further reference to property and justice.

not unlimited, for it was confined originally to what a man and his family could consume or use, and must not be wasted (II, § 36). It extended to the land as well as to the fruits of it (II, §§ 32–40), but even in this form it must never be used as an instrument of oppression, as a means of getting others to submit to your will (I, §§ 42–3). The whole argument is intended to show that individual property did not arise from the common consent of all mankind, though in the end the actual distribution of it is held to be due to money, which is a matter of consent, perhaps even worldwide consent.[11] In the state of nature, then, the exertions of men and above all their invention of money had brought them all into relationships with each other which were not those of rational and conscious co-operation but sprang from their differing contact, almost physical contact, with the world of material things—from their property as thus defined.

In fact men were led to leave the state of nature and to set up society and political organization because they had to find a source of power 'for the Regulating and Preserving of Property' (II, § 3). As the *Second Treatise* goes on, more and more emphasis is laid on the 'great and *chief end* . . . of Mens uniting into Commonwealths, and putting of themselves under Government, *is the Preservation of their Property*. To which in the state of Nature there are many things wanting.'[12] Meanwhile it has become obvious that Locke's account of the origin of property cannot be intended to cover all meanings of the word. For it is not defined as material possessions, nor in units of the conveniences or necessities of life but much more generally as 'Lives, Liberties and Estates, which I call by the general name, *Property*' (II, § 123).[13] Except in the chapter on property, and in other cases where it is clear that material possessions are meant, the word 'property' in the *Second Treatise* is usually to be read in this sense. It is the sense in which Locke's contemporaries could talk of the protestant religion established by law as their 'property', and Richard Baxter maintain that 'men's *lives* and *Liberties* are the chief parts of their propriety' though he, like Locke,

[11] II, § 45, see especially 11. 22–4 and note, II, § 50, etc.

[12] II, § 124: compare II, § 94, 24–5 and note there on Tyrrell's similar statement: also II, §§ 127, 134, 138, etc.

[13] The occurrences of this wider definition are listed in the note to II, § 87, 5–6: it may be noteworthy that three of the contexts (those in §§ 87, 123 and 173) were possibly additions of 1689.

sought the origin of 'propriety in a man's industry'.[14]

Property, moreover, seems to give the political quality to personality. A slave lacks all political rights because he is incapable of property: despotical power, not properly political at all, can only be exercised over the propertyless (II, § 174). We well may complain that Locke does not make it sufficiently clear which definition of property he is using in which context. But the fact that he was prepared to allow material property, labour-mixed-with-natural-objects property, to stand for many or all the abstract rights of the individual does help us to understand why the concept as a whole enters into his account of the foundation of civil society.

For property to Locke seems to symbolize rights in their concrete form, or perhaps rather to provide the tangible subject of an individual's powers and attitudes. It is because they can be symbolized as property, something a man can conceive of as distinguishable from himself though a part of himself, that a man's attributes, such as his freedom, his equality, his power to execute the law of nature, can become the subject of his consent, the subject of any negotiation with his fellows. We cannot alienate any part of our personalities, but we can alienate that with which we have chosen to mix our personalities.[15] Whether Locke's mind was working quite in this way or not, it is clear from what he says elsewhere about civil as opposed to spiritual society that it can only concern itself with 'civil concernments', which on examination seem to be identical with 'property' in its extended meaning in the *Second Treatise*.[16] In some way, then, and it would

---

[14] See Baxter, 1680, passage noted under II, § 27. 'Propriety' and 'property' seem to have the same meaning, or combination of meanings, in Locke and in Baxter, though Locke occasionally substituted the second for the first in correcting his book (e.g. in title to 1*st Treatise*, chapter vii). The extended meaning of property has been noticed occasionally (Gough, 1950; Brogan, 1958) but I owe to Professor Viner of Princeton the demonstration that the extended meaning is to be taken as a normal usage both for Locke and his contemporaries. Professor Viner has been kind enough to communicate an unpublished paper on the subject. Locke's extraordinary vagueness about the use of this term is well illustrated in II, § 131, 7: see note there.

[15] The conventional judgment of Locke's view of property, that it described a natural, inalienable right, seems on this view to be exactly wrong. Property is precisely that part of our attributes (or, perhaps to be pedantic, that attribute of our attributes) which we can alienate, but only of course by our own consent.

[16] See passages cited in note on II, § 3 from Locke on *Toleration*. His whole argument on that subject is intended to prove that the subjective world of religious conviction is completely inaccessible to the objective world of 'civil concernments', of property in fact.

seem that it can only be in some symbolic way, it is through the theory of property that men can proceed from the abstract world of liberty and equality based on their relationship with God and natural law, to the concrete world of political liberty guaranteed by political arrangements.

To see a symbolic system in a writer so down-to-earth as Locke, however, may be to read more than should be read into an expedient forced upon him by the necessity of replying to Sir Robert Filmer. Property, both in the narrow and in the extended sense, is insufficiently protected and inadequately regulated in the state of nature and this is the critical inconvenience which induces men to 'enter into Society to make one People, one Body Politick under one Supreme Government . . . by setting up a Judge on Earth with Authority to determine all Controversies' (II, § 89). It is critical only in the cumulative sense, for it is to be added to the love and want of society (II, § 101) and to the danger of aggression from abroad (II, § 3) as well as to all the other inconveniences which arise from men being judges in their own cases, and which are so considerable that it can be said that 'God hath certainly appointed Government to restrain the partiality and violence of Men' (II, § 13). Once this stage is reached, Locke's political principle can be written out in full. But before this is done, we should perhaps review Locke's theory of property a little further since it has been the subject of so much criticism and misunderstanding.[17]

'God gave the World . . . to the use of the Industrious and Rational', says he (II, § 34), gave it to them in the state of nature that is, and appointed government also as a remedy for the inconveniences of that state. For by their very industriousness and rationality these people created inconveniences for themselves and the rest of mankind, setting up relationships between men through their ever-more-complicated contact with material things which defeated the control of individuals acting as lone executors of the law of nature. Conscious, co-operative control was set up, therefore, under governments where 'the Laws regulate the right of property, and the possession of land is determined by positive constitutions' (II, § 50).

---

[17] Locke's doctrine of property has been extensively discussed: see, e.g. Larkin, 1930; Czajkowski, 1941; Kendall, 1941 (the first to criticize the 'individualist' interpretation); Gough, 1950; Strauss, 1953; Cherno, 1957; Monson, 1958; Polin, 1960; Viano, 1961 (Locke's theory and Shaftesbury's policy); Macpherson 1951 and 1962.

This regulation of property and determination of land-ownership by political authority is not easy to interpret from Locke's text. His object seems to be to guarantee secure and quiet possession, however large the estate and whatever it contained. In spite of the statements presenting the 'labour theory of value', it would be extremely difficult to argue that he had any sort of doctrine in mind which we should call socialist. Nevertheless he never contradicts the assertion he made in 1667, that the magistrate can appoint ways of transferring properties from one man to another, and make what property laws he likes, provided they are equitable.[18] Even the minutest control of property by political authority can be reconciled with the doctrine of *Two Treatises*. The property he defends is never confined to substantial possessions, or looked on as what we (not Locke) call capital. He hints that even the poorest has enough to need society's protection for it (II, § 94 and note). If not complete communism, certainly redistributive taxation, perhaps nationalization could be justified on the principles we have discussed: all that would be necessary is the consent of the majority of the society, regularly and constitutionally expressed, and such a law would hold even if all the property-owners were in the minority.

On the other hand the whole tenor of his argument is in favour of those with a great deal to lose. It may be felt that his anxiety to make property rights independent of the universal consent of all mankind, even though property distribution through money is subject to it,[19] represents an interest more cogent than the necessity of answering Filmer. The same preoccupation with the absolute security of material property may be seen in the confusion left by his dual definition of the concept. If he was prepared to allow all his references to be taken in the sense of material possessions, then his whole position looks very like an uncompromising defence of wealth and its power. If it is permissible to look on his use of the concept 'property' as symbolic, as has been suggested, then the symbolic system seems to express all human rights as market commodities. He is perfectly willing to contemplate the continuous or permanent appropriation of the product of one man's labour by another, a servant's by a master.[20] Slave la-

---

[18] The 1667 *Essay on Toleration:* see note on II, § 120.

[19] See note 11 on p. 115 above.

[20] Macpherson, 1951, 560. It seems, however, to be an over-interpretation to say that a man can sell his labour in the sense of the propensity to work, and I cannot follow the statement (p. 564) that 'Locke has separated life and labor'. When Locke writes on the wage relationship in

bour in no way perturbs him. He fails to make any specific provision against the obvious consequences of allowing unlimited accumulation of precious stones, metals and money in all its forms, once consent had given them value.

Nevertheless it is gratuitous to turn Locke's doctrine of property into the classic doctrine of the 'spirit of capitalism', whatever that may be. It can only be done by explaining away all the statements which he makes about the origin and limitations of property as obstacles to his true meaning. All that he says about 'regulating' property, even though this is the first word he uses about it when it is introduced into the *Second Treatise* (II, § 3), has to be ignored. Half-conscious traditionalism or plain hypocrisy must be held to account for Locke's description of unlimited acquisitiveness as '*amor sceleratus habendi,* evil Concupiscence' (II, § 111). Above all it has to be done by denying point blank that Locke's consistent claim, 'The Obligations of the Law of Nature, cease not in Society, but only in many Cases are drawn closer' (II, § 135), can apply to property.[21] If we are prepared to treat historical texts in such a way we can prove just what we like from them.

In fact, of course, Locke was neither a 'socialist' nor a 'capitalist', though it is fascinating to find elements of both attitudes of ours in his property doctrine—more, perhaps, in what he left out or just failed to say than in the statements themselves. He was not even an advocate of land and landownership as the basis of political power, to be 'represented' in a nation's counsels. For all his enormous intellectual and political influence in the eighteenth century he was in these respects a barren field for anyone who wished to justify what

---

II, § 85, he uses the word 'service' not 'labour', and though he seems specific enough in II, § 28, 18–30 in making the master own his servant's labour, it is not clearly a matter of a wage relationship: see Laslett, 1964.

[21] Strauss, 1953, 240: see p. 246 for his reference to the spirit of capitalism. The case for Locke as a crypto-capitalist is presented with far greater exactness and subtlety by Macpherson, 1951, (see also 1962) from a point of view which scorns 'petty bourgeois socialism'. Interesting as it is, Strauss's view seems to be based on a reading of Lockeian texts which is so arbitrary and so much concerned to discover a 'real' meaning (generally a Hobbesist or a capitalist one) that it is quite unacceptable to an editor of *Two Treatises;* for a critique of some of his positions, see Yolton, 1958. The close and revealing analysis which Macpherson has given to what Locke said has clarified the issues remarkably, but it would seem that he could only have come to his thoroughly unrealistic and occasionally unhistorical conclusions because he set out to demonstrate that Locke's object could only have been to 'provide the ideological support for capitalist appropriation'.

once was called the Whig oligarchy. But he did use his property doctrine to give continuity to a political society, to join generation to generation.

Locke's doctrine of property was incomplete, not a little confused and inadequate to the problem as it has been analysed since his day, lacking the humanity and the sense of social co-operation to be found in the canonists who had preceded him. But it remains an original doctrine, particularly important in its bearing on the way men analysed social and political origins, and his own judgment on it must stand—no man has ever done quite this before or since.

We are now in a position to follow Locke's political principle through to its conclusion. Men may enter into society quite suddenly, and it is perhaps best to assume that any given company actually decided at some point in time to change their condition to this new state. But there can be degrees of 'community', a variety of ways in which political authority can be founded, and even apparently permanent conditions which cannot be called one or the other state. The most usual development is in fact patriarchal, where a large family grows into a political society and its hereditary head gives rise to a royal lineage. But this must not lead us into the mistake of supposing that patriarchal is political power, or to confuse the relation of man and wife, parent and child, master and servant, with the political relation. However political power comes into being, it can only be looked on as the formation of a community by a band of rational creatures, all with the power to punish transgression of the law of nature and offences against their property. Any number of them can exercise the power collectively, and they can replace their patriarchs or make their generals into elective kings as and when they please. The unmistakable sign of civil society having come into being is when every individual has resigned up to the society or the public his individual power to exercise the law of nature and protect his property. This is the social compact and it is fair to everybody, since everybody makes the same sacrifice for the same benefits. It sets up a judge on earth, with authority to determine all the controversies and redress the injuries that may happen to any member of the commonwealth, as it is now called.

All this will be done by consent, the consent of every individual concerned. The judge thus established will be a legislative power, able to pronounce on offences because it can promulgate settled, standing rules in accordance with the law of nature; rules, or laws, which are indifferent, and so fair to everybody, guaranteeing, defining and giving substance to everybody's freedom. To sanction those laws and judgments, this 'legislative', as we may call it, will have at its disposal the mingled force of all the members of society—an 'executive' power in fact. It will have a third power in virtue of the condition in which the community finds itself, a power of protection from foreign enemies and of communication with other such communities and with individuals in a state of nature. This is the 'federative' power. It will not need a separate judicial power, because, we have seen, the pronouncing of judgment is its general function. These three powers are distinct in themselves, and the executive and legislative are best kept in separate hands, except that the head of the executive may be a part of the legislative, with power of summons and prorogation. But there can be no doubt of the ultimate superiority of the legislative in the constitution.

Its establishment, and the form of government generally, are 'the fundamental Appointment of the Society', the Constitution as we should say (II, § 214). The original compact which set it up will imply majority rule, for the state is not simply a rightful power, it is a collective body, and a body which can only move on the side of the greater mass. Its gravitational logic requires that those who are a part of it shall not resist its final direction. Political power, now that it has arrived, will not be special in the sense that it is different from the power all men continue to exercise in preserving the law of nature where their governors cannot, or by agreement must not, intervene. It will be special only in the sense that it is collective, and so cannot be an attribute, least of all the property, of a single man or family. Every effort must be made to ensure that those who wield it shall never develop an interest separate from that of the community, the people. Any individual born outside the community is free to join it, or born inside can decide to leave for another community, or even to live in some part of the world still in a state of nature. When he is within the community he must accept the rulership of its governors and obey its laws.

But the governors are only entrusted with the power they have. Government comes into being at the same time and perhaps by the same act as that which established civil society, but its power is given for attaining an end and limited to it. If that end should be neglected, the government is dissolved and the power devolves to the people, or to the community which is all one. Now this does not restore a state of nature, or it does not necessarily do so. The people under these circumstances may themselves act as a 'legislative', and so maintain government, but it is likely that after a very short while they will set up new trustees for government, or change the form and conditions of governing. It is for the people only to decide whether or when their governmental trustees have acted contrary to their trust, or their legislative has been changed, and for the people as a whole to act as umpire in any dispute between the governors and a part of their body. If the governors resist such judgment, or behave in any way which threatens that the people will cease to be a community and become a confused multitude, then the state of nature is at hand, with all its disadvantages. This will seldom, perhaps never, happen for the people can be relied upon to be patient and long-suffering. If such an extreme situation does come about, and the question arises of who is to be the final judge, the answer brings us back to where Locke began. There is no final judge of these things on earth, the ultimate appeal can only be to God.

This is the major theme of Locke on *Government*,[22] and it is extended into a discussion of conquest, tyranny and other related subjects. It will be seen that the theme as a whole does develop out of the assertion that each individual possesses the executive power of the law of nature. We may look on his intention as being to lay down a doctrine in this way, a doctrine which we shall call that of natural political virtue. This would seem to be the most probable and sympathetic reading of the book, though not all that is said is quite consistent with it.

This doctrine lays it down that all individuals, whether grouped together formally or informally, or even when alone, will have some tendency [23] to allow for the existence, the desires, actions and needs of other men: this is what is to be expected if each is to be trusted with the means of maintaining the humanity of all. It accounts for the quasi-social character of the state of nature, and makes it possible to talk of 'all the Priviledges' of that 'ill condition' (II, § 127). It permits any number of men to set up a political society: 'when

[22] It has had to be interpreted somewhat for purposes of straight exposition; see below for trust, dissolution of government, etc.
[23] Almost the Aristotelian *nisus*, though Locke did not mean to make society natural in quite the Aristotelian way.

any number of Men have, by the consent of every individual, made a *Community*' (II, § 96); 'this any number of Men may do, because it injures not the Freedom of the rest' (II, § 95). This is important because it denies that there has to be a special shape for a body of men before they can take on ethical unity, as Filmer had claimed when he insisted that they must be a family under patriarchal will.

The doctrine of natural political virtue goes some way to justify in ethical terms Locke's rather perfunctory defence of majority rule in mechanical terms. For a majority, which is simply a random sample of those who voted, will under this doctrine tend to act with some responsibility towards those in the minority.[24] It can be seen most clearly in Locke's insistence that 'in well order'd Commonwealths' the men who wield the legislative power should be ordinary citizens, drawn from the main body of those for whom they legislate and reverting to that status when out of office (II, § 143, with note and references). Applied in this way the doctrine becomes an essential presupposition of representative government as it developed after Locke had written, essential to such things as virtual representation, which he implies at all points, and the rule of parties, which he never contemplated. It sanctions the right of a group of leaders to take revolutionary action, and it is always behind an individual acting alone in a political situation, a judge, a king, or a Speaker.[25]

It may be noted that in expounding this doctrine Locke is once more occupying a position which looks two ways at once, rather than selecting a unitary definition and pursuing its implications. We all possess natural political virtue, both because we are disposed favourably towards each other in our very make-up, our nature, and because, when we co-operate, when we discuss things together, the tendency of what we do and what we say will inevitably be towards the politically efficacious, that which will work out for all of us. We might distinguish the two facts of the phrase as 'naturalistic' and 'intellectualistic' respectively, and we must insist that Locke recognized both of them. In this he found himself very close to Hooker, and he was thus able to make very effective use

[24] Kendall, 1941, seems unable to concede such a doctrine to Locke, and interprets his statements in such a way as to make him a 'majority-rule authoritarian', though see his final chapter, 'The Latent Premise'.
[25] Safeguarded in all these cases, of course, by the concept of trust —see below.

of that respected name, so authoritative with his opponents.[26] But he does not base social life on love and sociability to any extent, for his rejection of patriarchalism made it difficult, though he does make concessions even over this. We have natural political virtue, he seems to say, primarily because of a symmetry in reason between all of us.

Locke's theories of political obligation and political freedom, in so far as he worked them out in any detail, can be looked on as developments of natural political virtue. The virtue which we all possess is outward-facing: we might use a later, utilitarian expression and call it 'other regarding'. We must stress the point that in Locke's system it is the power which men have over others, not the power which they have over themselves, which gives rise to political authority. Organized government is not to be regarded as a form of self-government. We do not dispose of ourselves, and so we have no right to give ourselves up to anybody or anything else. All that rational co-operation enables us to do is to give up our other-regarding powers to found political authority. We do this by an act of consent and it can even be said that 'the Judgments of the Commonwealth' are our own judgments, they being made by ourselves or our 'Representative' (II, § 88).

We cannot, then, be obliged by any government to which we have not given some sign of consent—walking on a road is enough (II, § 119), but owning property under its jurisdiction is much more tangible. And only this can give a man permanent membership of a society (II, § 122), where there has been no express declaration of allegiance. Nevertheless it is a little misleading to say that we are actually governed exclusively by our own consent. We come under the jurisdiction of the other-regarding powers of our fellow citizens when we cease to act rationally and socially, and in society this means that we must submit to the common executive power, the power of the state sanctioning natural law and those settled standing rules which it has established. We have consented to the establishment of that executive power, and through its character as a legislative we may be said to have had a voice in the codifying of those rules, more especially where the legislating body is a representative one. But we should be under the executive power of the law of nature in any case,

---

[26] See footnotes to *Second Treatise*, especially to § 5, see Polin, 1961, 105 etc.

as exercised by others over us. If this were not so, how could any government punish the crimes of aliens within its jurisdiction (II, § 9)? [27]

Property, on the other hand, is of such a nature that *'without a Man's own consent it cannot be taken away from him'* (II, § 193). In all matters of property, then, the warrant of a government's action must always be consent. Since Locke lays so much emphasis on the preservation of property as the reason for establishing the state, as the end of government, and since he assigns so many social and political functions to property ownership, it may seem that consent is the sole basis of obligation in his system. He has been read almost exclusively in this sense, but obligation does have an independent source in his doctrine of natural political virtue.

We may look on this position in another way and say that the passage from the state of nature to the state of society and government makes possible rule by consent, which is not possible in a state of nature. This is important because it lays stress on the fact that in Locke's theory freedom is not merely absence of restraint, it is positive. It is something which is enlarged by the creation of society and government, which is given substance by the existence of laws, the laws of the law courts. It can be negatively defined, therefore, as being under no other legislative power but that established by consent in the commonwealth (II, § 22), and positively as the progressive elimination of the arbitrary from political and social regulation. He is very insistent on this positive point, resting it originally on the right to preservation, and on the individual's inability to dispose of himself (II, §§ 22–3). He develops it into the denial that government can be a personal matter, a matter of will: it must always be an institutional matter, a matter of law. Law makes men free in the political arena, just as reason makes men free in the universe as a whole. It is progressively codified by a legislative brought into being by consent, it is expressive of and in harmony with the law of nature, which continues of course in society (II, § 135). For 'Law . . . is . . . *the direction of a free and intelligent Agent* to his proper Interest', and its end is *'to*

<hr>

[27] See Lewis, 1940 and, for criticism of Locke, see Plamenatz, 1936 and the discussion in Gough, 1950, chapter III. He does not even insist, as might be expected, on the necessity of a representative legislature for a government to be legitimate, though he seems to assume it and in III, § 176 talks of the 'native Right' of a people to have a legislative approved by a majority.

preserve and enlarge Freedom' (II, § 57). Locke is much closer here than was once recognized to Rousseau's position that men can be compelled to be free, compelled by the law of the legislative which they have consented to set up.[28]

Men cannot, however, be compelled by will, the individual will of a ruler or the general will of a society. Locke's insistence that government is defined and limited by the end for which political society is established, that it can never be arbitrary or a matter of will, can never be owned, is expressed in a particular and exact application of his doctrine of natural political virtue—the concept of trust. He tends to use the language of trust whenever he talks of the power of one man over another, even for fathers and children (II, § 59). 'Some Trust one in another' is an assumption of all who join to make up society (II, § 107). This must be so if the tendency of men is to be responsible, if governors and governed are interchangeable; we can and must trust each other if natural political virtue is a reality. But there is an easily discovered limit to the trust which can be accorded or assumed, and this limit is implied in the concept of trust itself. Trust is both the corollary and the safeguard of natural political virtue.

The concept of trust is very specific to Locke, though it is not original with him.[29] His actual words must be looked at if we are to see its function clearly, and yet not make him more precise than he intended to be. We may notice that the word 'contract' does not occur more than about ten times in his book, and it is hardly ever applied to political matters at all.[30] It is 'compact' or often mere 'agreement' which creates a society, a community (II, §§ 14, 97, 99, etc.), or political power (I, §§ 94, 113; II, §§ 102, 171, 173, etc.), even law (II, § 35). Now compact and agreement are more general than contract: they are further removed from the language of the law. Vague as Locke is, we seem to have here a deliberate attempt to avoid being specific and to leave legal models on one side. It may imply that the transmutation into

[28] See Gough, 1950, 32, commenting on Kendall, 1941; Abrams, 1961 (government *is* a matter of will), and Seliger, 1963 (ii) (consent and natural law).

[29] See the valuable discussion of the concept in Gough, 1950, chapter VII.

[30] But to legal and quasi-legal agreements, such a marriage (I, §§ 47, 98; II, §§ 81–2) or property arrangement (II, § 194), though compare, I, § 96.

the social and political condition must not be looked on in a legal way; it is a variable thing and a pretty loose one too.

The word 'trust' is much more frequent than either contract or compact, and it is a legal word.[31] But although Locke used it with legal overtones, and was as always quite willing to take advantage of all the suggestions it contained for his readers, we need not assume, as is often done, that he was trying to describe a formal trust deed for government. In applying the word trust to the various political powers in the state, the constitution, Locke draws an important distinction for us, perhaps two of them. He divides off the process of compact, which creates a community, from the further process by which the community entrusts political power to a government; although they may take place at the same time, these two are distinct. This puts his system amongst those which distinguish the 'contract of society' from the 'contract of government', though in Locke this second process is not a contract at all. And this may be his second point; to underline the fact that the relation between government and governed is not contractual, for a trust is not a contract.

If a contract is to be set up, or understood, it is necessary that the parties to it should each get something out of it, and applied to politics this would mean that the government got something out of governing which the subjects are bound to give. Now this is what Locke was most anxious to avoid. Although contractually related to each other, the people are not contractually obliged to government, and governors benefit from governing only as fellow members of the 'Politick Body' (I, § 93). They are merely deputies for the people, trustees who can be discarded if they fail in their trust (II, § 240). The property trusts which his landowning readers were so accustomed to were a little like this, but they contained no provisions about trustees being deputies, liable to be discarded by those for whose benefit the trust is established. This should convince us that Locke did not intend to go further in his references to trust than to make suggestive use of legal language.[32] He does not describe *a* trust at all; the

---

[31] The technical term for a lawyer's instrument much in use, we may note, in Chancery when Locke was himself a Chancery secretary—see above, p. 38.

[32] Gough, 1950, and Sir Ernest Barker, 1948, among others (compare Vaughan, 1925), see a formal trust in Locke's theory, with the people as both trustor and beneficiary, acting as defrauded beneficiaries when the government breaches its trust. Locke does talk of breach of trust

phrase itself is absent. It is always 'this', 'that' or 'their trust'
—'the trust of prerogative', 'this express or tacit trust', even
'double trust'. The stress is solely on the fiduciary nature of
all political power ('a Fiduciary Power' [II, § 149], 'a Fiduciary
Trust' [II, § 156]). He could even talk elsewhere of bishops
as trustees, trustees of religion on behalf of all the Christians
of the nation. The concept is obviously intended to make it
clear that all actions of governors are limited to the end of
government, which is the good of the governed, and to
demonstrate by contrast that there is no contract in it—a
fiduciary relationship, that is all.

When trust is substituted in this way for contract, constitutional change is sanctioned, even revolution; it secures
the sovereignty of the people, though that phrase must be
used with care, a perpetual residual power to cashier their
governors and remodel their government. '*Governments are
dissolved* . . . when the Legislative, or the Prince, either of
them act contrary to their Trust' (II, § 221), power reverts
to the people, who may then establish a new legislative and
executive (II, § 222). It is the people (the community, the
public) who decide when a breach of trust has occurred,
for only the man who deputes power can tell when it is
abused (II, § 240), and in case of dispute the final appeal
is to God—revolution. The people are able to do all these
things because their ability to act as a community survives
the dissolution of government, which does not itself bring
back the state of nature.

The trend of Locke's statements about the ultimate right
of the people to revolt is quite unmistakable. But close examination shows that it was not formulated with much pre-
cision, and its connection with the concept of trust has to be
filled in for him. In the chapter *of the Dissolution of Government* (II, ch. XIX) he is not at all explicit about what
actually happens when people find themselves at liberty to
entrust new hands with the government. Although we are
expressly told (II, § 211) to distinguish between the dissolution of government and the dissolution of society, and informed that overwhelming force from abroad is almost the

---

(II, § 222), but more often and more vaguely of acting contrary to their
trust (II, § 149, 155, 221, 226, 240). When governors do this it is the
government, not the trust, which is dissolved, and, though he does once
refer to forfeit of the trust itself (II, § 149), it is very difficult to make
sense of what he says if you try to interpret the actions of a people on
breach of trust as those of defrauded beneficiaries under a formal trust.

only thing which can dissolve political society itself, he often seems to talk as if the dissolution of government brings about a state of nature. James II, for it can only be he, is condemned for 'actually putting himself into a State of War with his People', dissolving the government and leaving them 'to that defence, which belongs to every one in the State of Nature' (II, § 205). This state of nature, moreover, sometimes looks less like the Lockeian than the Hobbesian condition, that miserable condition of war of all against all, where no such thing as an organized community could possibly exist, since 'the People become a confused Multitude, without Order or Connexion' (II, § 219).[33]

This is not so inconsistent as it may appear, for we have seen that Locke drew no very rigid distinction between the natural and the political condition, and his doctrine of natural political virtue could be manipulated so as to cover these cases. His intention in the rather confused argument of this chapter may have been to insist on the efficacy of a threat to return to the state of nature—a present sanction, we are to believe, both when government exists and when it does not, and particularly at that point of crisis when no one is quite sure, which is as far as what we call anarchy ever really goes. But this interpretation is suggested by the whole tenor of his doctrine, rather than demonstrated by his statements.

And it does not help us to understand quite how, or quite when, the trust relationship between the people and their government is brought into being. An original agreement undoubtedly made it a matter of trust that a specified form of government should be preserved, but we are not told whether this agreement is always part of the social compact.[34] He seems content, in fact, to suggest a continuing understanding between governed and governors. It is to be referred in its origin to the compact of society, because that was what gave

[33] It may be significant that both these passages, and others pointing in this direction, were very probably additions of 1689. Compare the discussion in Vaughan, 1925, and Strauss, 1953, 234 note 100. On the people, see Polin, 1961, 157–61, and, on their function as judges, 272 on (also Seliger, 1963 [i]).

[34] See e.g. II, §§ 239, 11–12 and 227, 1; compare I, § 96 (where power *is* based on contract). Elsewhere (II, §§ 134, 136, 142, 167, 171, 242) he seems to suppose an entrusting action, which took place in past time, taken by the 'first Framers of Government' (II, § 156). In his *Second Letter concerning Toleration* (1690) he talks of God as the final arbiter of the Magistrates' trust (1765, 114). For the most part, however, he talks of trust as a continuing relationship between governor and governed in the way described above.

the governed an identity, but it is continuously maintained
because the governed go on existing and go on entrusting. It
is a matter of suggestion rather than demonstration, relying
for its plausibility on the language of trust, on trust as a
concept.

This is not untypical of Locke as a political writer, and
though it makes exact analysis difficult, it helps to give him
his strength. Locke's impreciseness over the dissolution of
government has not led to any misunderstanding of his principles, and no more has his metaphor of trust. No man, no
nation, no exasperated colony about to throw off the insensi-
tive rule of men who had no acceptable policy for them,
could ever have sat down to ask whether the state of nature
had returned, and if so what it was like. But they have responded to the statements which Locke made with that
hypothetical, but vaguely conceived, situation in mind. And
they have been influenced by the trust image. This certificate
of responsibility still hangs above the desks of administrators,
especially of colonial administrators and trusteeship coun-
cillors; held there by the influence of British legal and constitutional precedent, and by Locke's own reputation. Once
more it is a question of the ethics of common sense in
politics. If you trust people, they will trust you, and you
and they will get things done together, but especially if all
your actions proceed on the recognition that your power is
not yours but a trust from them to you.

We have tried to show that the main theme of Locke's
book was the development of the implications of this doctrine
of natural political virtue, defined, checked and safeguarded
by the concept of trust. From time to time, and especially in
discussing majorities, we have found ourselves referring to a
different strand of argument, an argument in terms of power,
even of will. It might be incorrect to claim that these strains
are distinct in his thinking, or that Locke himself saw them
apart: what he says about power is in the way of an adjunct
to his other statements, not a different and parallel explanation. Nevertheless it is useful to look on this part of what
he said as independent, for its most important consequence,
the association of Locke with the historic doctrine of the
separation of powers, could not possibly have arisen out of
the theories which we have discussed so far.

Locke's initial definition is in terms of power (II, § 3) and
throughout his book he seems to be consciously discussing a
power system. It might be suggested that the reason for this

was his recognition that there were in his attitude recognizable anarchist elements, a disposition found in all individualists to regard state, society and government as unnecessary, or accidental, or just unfortunate. It is to be seen in his aside declaring that it was only corruption, viciousness, degeneracy in some men which made it necessary for humanity to set up communities 'separate from this great and natural Community' of all mankind (II, § 128). The doctrine of natural political virtue is anarchistic in its implications generally, and we have seen that Locke had to answer in a somewhat urgent form the question of why men set up states at all. His contemporaries, certainly Sir Robert Filmer, would have looked on the most important of all his claims as obviously anarchical, the claim that there is no final appeal in ultimate political questions, only God—which means combat, revolution.

But, Locke is anxious to convince us, this does not mean that the state which we set up and obey, which guarantees our property in all its forms and under all its definitions, lacks unity, direction, power. When we meet together to set up artificially that final judge which is lacking to us in the state of nature we create a rightful legislative authority, the nature of which is ethical and which we are bound to obey however weak its sanctions. But we create something else as well, we create a principle of unity, a 'living Body', out of our separate selves. In this paragraph (II, § 212) Locke goes on, in language we may think strange in him, to talk of the legislative as the '*Soul that gives Form, Life, and Unity* to the Commonwealth', and of 'the *Essence and Union of the Society* consisting in having one Will, the Legislative', which, when once it is broken, leaves every one 'at the disposure of his own Will' because 'the publick Will' is at a stand.[35] Here it may be thought he comes near to denying his own principle that government is not a matter of will, or even to concepts belonging to a quite different political system, a general will analysis. In fact, however, he seems to be doing no more than insist that when men come together politically they create power, which is available to them in institutional form for the purposes of their association, and which will find its first and highest expression in the making of law.

When, therefore, Locke talks of the various powers of the commonwealth, the supremacy of one and the derivative

[35] Compare the 'will' language used in II, § 151.

nature of the others, he should be taken in the simple sense of force, at least initially. The supreme power, the legislative, is supreme because it literally represents the united force of the commonwealth, and the commonwealth to remain one body can have only one supreme power. The executive power is thus inevitably inferior. It is distinguished from the legislative in that it cannot make law, and has for the most part only a delegated power. The legislative, being preferably a representative body, need not, should not be in continuous existence (II, §§ 152, 153). Now this does not exclude the possibility that both powers can be exercised by the same body or person. It supposes, in fact, that the executive will have a part to play in the legislative, as is the case in the constitution of England, which Locke so obviously had in mind.[36]

That he was looking on these powers in this straightforward sense is illustrated by the very nature of the third power, the federative. This was simply the power of the community directed outwards, towards other such communities in amicable relationship, or in protection against aggression. It is a distinct power, no doubt, but this outward direction is its only characteristic. It is almost essential, therefore, that it be in the same hands as that of the executive and be given the freest possible play for quick, arbitrary decision. It must have the greatest possible freedom from everyday control by the legislative or its laws—to which it is of course finally responsible.[37]

It is surely already obvious from this that Locke cannot be said to have had a doctrine in mind. There is here no theory of the importance and desirability of the perpetual residence of these powers in separate hands in order to preserve liberty, guarantee rights, or keep the constitution in harmony, unison and health. This is confirmed by two further considerations. One is that the judiciary, that separate power whose independence is recognized as an essential to constitutional government both by Locke's predecessors and by all his successors, whether they have expounded the separa-

---

[36] All this is insisted on at length (especially the points about the summoning of the legislature by the executive, the conditions which the constitution may lay down about the intervals at which it shall meet, and so on) because, as is suggested above, Locke was writing with Charles II and his parliaments in mind.

[37] On the federative power, see Laslett, 1957 (i), 396, and the discussion in Cox, 1960, where he makes exaggerated claims for the primacy of foreign policy in Locke.

tion of the powers or not, is never mentioned by Locke along with the other three. As we have said, the judiciary was no separate power, it was the general attribute of the state. It would not make sense to put it alongside the executive and legislative. Locke recognized that the judiciary should be indifferent and upright (II, § 131), known and authorized (II, § 136), or else nothing he wanted would come about: that is all. Finally, the proper functioning and just exercise of these powers is provided for by Locke, but not by any doctrine of necessary separation. It is done by the concept of trust, which applies to the legislative in its fullest force, but also to the prerogatives exercised by executive and federative.

Locke shared the traditional opinion about balancing the power of government by placing several parts of it in different hands (II, § 107). He seems to have attached some importance to the distinct natures of legislative, executive and federative, for they are introduced, by function if not all by name, immediately after he gives his first formal account of how the state comes into being (II, § 88). He even asserts that one of the reasons why an absolute monarchy can be no properly constituted political authority is because he has 'all, both Legislative and Executive Power in himself alone', so that 'there is no Judge' (II, § 91). This is as far as he goes.

It may be historically interesting that Montesquieu and later the American founders took him up in a sense which he cannot be said to have contemplated, just as it is interesting to find that Locke conspicuously ignored the clearest issue over the separation of powers which arose in our constitutional history, even though it involved him personally.[38] It is one example of the extraordinary fashion in which the thinking of Locke and the constitutional practice of Englishmen so soon began to coalesce in the minds of a posterity determined to benefit from both. The result was a mingled misunderstanding of the greatest possible historical consequence.

We cannot dwell on this subject, nor on Locke as an exponent of the English constitution of his day. In his analysis of politics in terms of force as well as in terms of rightful authority Locke is closer to the thought of our own day on

---

[38] Laslett, 1957 (i); this was the issue of whether the crown or the Commons should appoint the Board of Trade of 1696, of which Locke was a member.

the subject of sovereignty than he was to the assumptions of his own time. Behind the superior power of the legislative in his system there is always to be seen the finally supreme, all-important power of the people themselves, again conceived of as a force, though justified in its interferences once more by the concept of trust. It was a power which would only rarely display itself, and, as we have tried to show, there is considerable obscurity about the actual circumstances in which it could come into action and more about what it might achieve. Nevertheless this residual power must be called Locke's idea of what we now think of as popular sovereignty.

Locke reads as if his reflections on the true original, extent and end of civil government were directed towards political universals, instead of directed towards the highly specific situation of his own party, at a particular time and within the highly individual context of English politics. We have described this as an achievement, the achievement of a philosophic mind writing, in a sense, against its philosophic bent. It has inevitably led to his being criticized for raising expectations which he did not fulfil, for propounding theories, whose final implications he never contemplated. Some of these criticisms have been considered here, but one still remains. It is often said that Locke is the supreme representative of those individualist thinkers who stress rights instead of duties. As early as 1798 Bishop Elrington reproached him for not declaring that men had a duty to set up the state and to leave the condition of mere nature. But if his system as we have analysed it is sympathetically considered, this appears, perhaps, as the greatest of all the misapprehensions about him. Natural political virtue can only work if we obey the tendency within all of us, for it is a tendency, it is not the full description of ourselves. Trust is a matter of conscience, which may have its final and unlikely sanctions but which operates because of the sense of duty which Locke dogmatically, unthinkingly assumes in every man he contemplates.

Locke's psychological insight may be imperfect, his logic often odd, his general standpoint ungrateful to our generation and not easily understood even within his own personal historical context. His rationalist sociology may seem fantastic, even in comparison with the uncritical traditionalism of a man like Filmer. But after he had written and what he had written had had its enormous impact on the European mind, it was no longer possible to believe that politics went forward in a moral sphere in which the good man was the good citizen. Citizenship was now a specific duty, a personal challenge in a world where every individual either recognized his responsibility for every other, or disobeyed his conscience. Political duties have not changed since then.

APPENDIX A

CHECK-LIST OF PRINTINGS, 1689–1960

Note. This list records all printings, notices of printings and books of extracts known to the editor in 1963. It is intended as a guide only and is not bibliographically exact or exhaustive: it is least reliable in the nineteenth century and later printings. Every item has been inspected in at least one copy, except those marked 'not seen'. Many of them are rare, but locations are only given where not more than one or two copies have been traced. The abbreviations 1X and 1R are explained in Laslett, 1952 (ii), and the printing history of the book is discussed there and in Laslett, 1954 (i)—see above p. 20. 1T = First, 2T = Second Treatise (1T2T = both): 2Tf = 2T French form, see French Printings, no. 2. English names are used where possible for foreign places of publication.

1. BRITISH PRINTINGS

1. 1689/90 Two Treatises of Government, London, Awnsham Churchill, 1690.

Two States, 1X and 1R (identical except in Sheet Q), 8vo, 467 pp. 1T2T. Anonymous, 1st edition, licensed 23 August 1689.

2.   1694   Two Treatises of Government, The Second Edition Corrected, London, Awnsham and John Churchill, 1694.

8vo, 358 pp., 1T2T, anonymous.

3.   1698   Two Treatises of Government, London, Awnsham and John Churchill, 1698.

8vo, 358 pp., 1T2T, anonymous—page-for-page reprint of the 2nd edition.

4.   1713   Two Treatises of Government, By John Locke Esq., The Fourth Edition, London, John Churchill, 1713.

12mo, 379 pp. 1T2T—printing of one of Locke's master-copies; see Editorial Note.

5.   1714   Two Treatises, etc., in The Works of John Locke, London, John Churchill, MDCCXIV.

Fo, pp. 99–228 of 2nd of 3 vols., 1T2T—printing of one of Locke's master-copies; see Editorial Note. 1st Collected edition.

6.   1722   Two Treatises, etc., in The Works of John Locke, The Second Edition, London, A. Churchill and A. Manship, MDCCXXII.

Fo, 1T2T, 2nd Collected edition, reprint of 1st.

7.   1727   Two Treatises, etc., in The Works of John Locke, The Third Edition, London, A. Bettesworth, etc., MDCCXXVII.

Fo, 1T2T, 3rd Collected edition, reprint of 2nd.

8.   1728   Two Treatises of Government, By John Locke Esq., The Fifth Edition, London, A. Bettesworth, etc., MDCCXXVIII.

8vo, 308 pp., 1T2T—probably a reprint of 4th edition, same publishers as for 3rd Collected edition.

9.   1740   Two Treatises, etc., in The Works of John Locke, The Fourth Edition, London, Edmund Parker, etc., MDCCXL.

Fo, 1T2T, 4th Collected edition, reprint of 3rd.

10.   1751   Two Treatises, etc., in The Works of John Locke, The Fifth Edition, London, S. Birt, etc., MDCCLI.

Fo, 1T2T, 5th Collected edition, reprint of 4th.

11.   1753   Of Civil Polity, London, MDCCLIII.

Half-sheet 8vo, vi + 36 pp., extracts from 2T only. No author, printer, publisher. Copy in Bodley.

12.   1759   Two Treatises, etc., in The Works of John Locke, The Sixth Edition, London, D. Browne, etc., MDCCLIX.

Fo, 1T2T, 6th Collected edition, reprint of 5th.

13.   1764   Two Treatises of Government, By John Locke, London, Printed MDCLXXXVIIII, Reprinted the Sixth Time by A. Millar, etc., MDCCLXIIII.

8vo, 416 pp., 1T2T—printing of Christ's copy, edited by Thomas Hollis; see Editorial Note. 6th edition.

14.   1766   Two Treatises of Government, By John Locke, Dublin, Sarah Cotter and J. Sheppard, MDCCLXVI.

8vo, 331 pp., 1T2T, reprint of 6th edition, copy in possession of the editor.

15.   1768   Two Treatises, etc., in The Works of John Locke, The Seventh Edition, London, H. Woodfall, etc., MDCCLXVIII.

4to, 1T2T, pp. 135–312 of 2nd of 4 vols., 7th Collected edition, text of no. 13, 6th (Hollis's) edition.

16.   1772   Two Treatises of Government, By John Locke, London MDCLXXXVIII, Reprinted the Seventh Time by J. Whiston, etc. MDCCLXXII.

8vo, 376 pp., 1T2T. Reprint of 6th edition.

17.   1777   Two Treatises, etc., in The Works of John Locke, The Eighth Edition, London, W. Strahan, etc., MDCCLXXVII.

4to, 1T2T, 8th Collected edition, reprint of 7th.

18.   1779   Two Treatises of Government, By John Locke, Dublin, J. Sheppard and G. Nugent, MDCCLXXIX.

8vo, 331 pp., 1T2T—reprint of no. 14.

19.   1791   Two Treatises, etc., in The Works of John Locke, The Ninth Edition, London, T. Longman, etc., 1791.

8vo, 1T2T, 9th Collected edition, reprint of 8th, edited by Bishop Edmund Law.

20.   1794   Two Treatises of Government, By John Locke, Dublin, William Mackenzie.

8vo., 304 pp., 1T2T, text of 6th edition. Copy in possession of the editor.

21.   1794?   The Spirit of John Locke on Civil Government, Reviv'd by the Constitutional Society of Sheffield, Sheffield, Printed for the Society by J. Gales, no date.

Large 12mo in 6's, viii + 78 pp.—extracts from 2T, has been dated at 1800, copy in Library of Congress.

22.   1796   Two Treatises of Government, By John Locke, The Sixth Edition, Glasgow, R. Smith & D. Boag, 1796.

Large 12mo in 6's, 1T2T—text of 6th edition.

23.   1798   An Essay Concerning the True Original Extent and End of Civil Government, By John Locke, Dublin, George Bonham, 1798.

Large 12mo, vi + 210 pp., 2T only. Text of 6th edition, annotated by Thomas Elrington, the first annotated edition. Copy in Leeds University Library.

24.   1801   Two Treatises, etc., in The Works of John

Locke, The Tenth Edition, London, J. Johnson, etc., 1801.

8vo, pp. 207–486 of the 5th of 10 vols., 1T2T, 10th Collected edition, reprint of 9th.

25.   1812   Two Treatises, etc., in The Works of John Locke, The Eleventh Edition, London, W. Otridge & Son, etc., 1812.

8vo, 1T2T, 11th Collected edition, reprint of 10th.

26.   1814   An Essay Concerning the True Original, Extent and End of Civil Government, by John Locke, A New Edition, London, Printed at the Revived Apollo Press by John Bell, Proprietor of the Weekly Messenger, 1814.

12mo in 6's, 157 pp., 2T only, text of 6th edition.

27.   1821   Two Treatises of Government, By John Locke, A New Edition Corrected, London, Whitmore and Fenn, etc., MDCCCXXI.

8vo, 401 pp., 1T2T, text of 6th edition. (Preface signed January 1821, printed by B. W. and S. Gardiner.)

28.   1821   Two Treatises on Government, By John Locke, London, R. Butler, W. Reid, etc., 1821.

8vo, 401 pp., 1T2T, page-for-page reprint of no. 27, copy in possession of the editor. (Frontispiece dated 1 May 1821, printed by W. Wilson.)

29.   1823   Two Treatises, etc., in The Works of John Locke, A New Edition Corrected, London, Thomas Tegg, etc., 1823.

8vo, 1T2T, 12th Collected edition.

30.   1824   Two Treatises of Government, By John Locke, A New Edition, London, Rivington, Longman, etc., 1824.

8vo, 1T2T, text of 6th edition, copy at Harvard.

31.   1824   Two Treatises, etc., in The Works of John Locke, The Twelfth Edition, London, C. & J. Rivington, etc., 1824.

8vo, 1T2T, 13th Collected edition, reprint of 11th.

32.   1826   (Reprint in Collected edition of this year, a new issue of 12th Collected edition, 1823—not seen), 14th Collected edition.

[33.   1854   (Reprint in Collected edition of this year—not seen), 15th Collected edition—perhaps a ghost.]

34.   1884, 1887, etc.   Two Treatises on Civil Government, By John Locke, Preceded by Sir Robert Filmer's 'Patriarcha', Introduction by Henry Morley, London, Routledge, 1884, Morley's Universal Library.

8vo, 320 pp., 1T2T without Locke's Preface. Listed as published January 1884, but several issues, one dated 1887 ('The Second Edition'), others undated, not all in the Universal Library. Reprint of 1st edition, 1X version.

35. 1889, 1901, 1905, etc. Of Civil Government and Toleration, By John Locke, edited by Henry Morley, London, Cassell, Cassell's National Library and ditto New Series.

14–15 cm., 192 pp., 2T only, text of 4th edition, 1713.

36. [1924] Of Civil Government, Two Treatises, By John Locke, with an Introduction by W. F. Carpenter, London, Dent, The Everyman Library.

17½ cm., xx + 242 pp., no date but several issues up to 1949. Indifferent reprint of 1st edition, 1X version, 1T2T but with wrong paragraph numeration 2T 22 to 36.

37. 1946, 1948. The Second Treatise of Civil Government and a Letter Concerning Toleration, By John Locke, Edited by J. W. Gough, Oxford, Blackwell.

19½ cm., xxxvi + 165 pp., 2T only, text of American printing no. 4, with some additions and modifications from the 6th edition.

38. 1948 Social Contract, Locke, Hume, Rousseau, Oxford University Press, World's Classics, Introduction by Sir Ernest Barker.

15 cm., lxiii + 440 pp., 2T only, text of 1st edition, 1R version.

39. 1956 [Revised edition of 37, xli + 167 pp.]

2. AMERICAN PRINTINGS

1. 1773 An Essay Concerning the True Original, Extent and End of Civil Government, By the late learned John Locke, Boston, Edes & Gill, 1773.

Small 4to, 130 pp., 2T only—a reprint of British Printing 13, 14 or 16, in the French form, i.e. 1st chapter omitted. No paragraph numbers, no chapter numbers.

2. 1806 Locke on Civil Government. Proposals for Publishing by Subscription by B. B. Macanulty, Salem, 1806.

Fo, 1 leaf—the book itself did not appear. Copy at Harvard.

3. [1921] Selections from John Locke's Second Treatise of Government, by S. E. Morison, Boston, Old South Leaflet, no date.

23 pp., selections from no. 1 above, with chapter heads and paragraph numbers.

4. 1937 Treatise of Civil Government and A Letter Concerning Toleration, by John Locke, edited by C. L. Sherman, New York, Appleton, 1937.

19½ cm., xv + 224 pp., 2T only, reprint of 1st edition 1690, conflation of 1X and 1R versions.

5. 1939 An Essay, etc., in The English Philosophers from Bacon to Mill, ed. E. A. Burtt, The Modern Library, New York, 1939.

2T only, text from no. 4 above.

6. 1947 The Second Treatise of Civil Government, in John Locke on Politics and Education, ed. H. R. Penniman, Classics Club College Edition, New York, Van Nostrand, 1947.

2T only, text from Everyman edition (British Printing no. 35).

7. 1947 Two Treatises of Government, By John Locke, with Patriarcha by Sir Robert Filmer, New York, Hafner, 1947.

311 pp., 1T2T; text of British Printing 13, the best modern reprint, introduction by T. I. Cook.

8. 1948 Reprint in Great Books Series, Chicago, 1948.

2T only, text from no. 4 above.

9. 1952 Reprint in Library of Liberal Arts, New York, 1952.

2T only, text from no. 7 above, introduction by Thomas P. Peardon.

10. 1955 Reprint in Gateway Edition, Chicago, 1955.

2T only, text from no. 4 above, introduction by Russell Kirk.

3. FRENCH PRINTINGS

1. 1690 Epitome of both Treatises by Jean LeClerc under English titles of each in *Bibliothèque Universelle et Historique* de l'Année MDCXC, Tome 19me, Amsterdam, Wolfgang, MDCXCI.

12mo, 1T pp. 559–, 2T pp. 573–.

2. 1691 Du Gouvernement Civil, Traduit de l'Anglois, Amsterdam, Wolfgang, MDCXCI.

12mo, vi + 321 pp., 2T only in French form (Translation of 1st London edition, 1R version, 1st chapter omitted, numbered by chapter instead of continuously and slightly differently divided, with an Avertissement—abbr. 2Tf). Author and translator anonymous, French attributed to David Mazel.

3. 1724 Du Gouvernement Civil, Nouvelle Edition, Geneva, Du Villard and Jacquier, MDCCXXIV.

12mo, vii + 365 pp., 2Tf, anonymous, reprint of 2.

4. 1749 Du Gouvernement Civil de Mr Locke, Nouvelle Edition Revue et Corrigée, Brussels, MDCCXLIX.

12mo, xii + 360 pp., 2Tf with a supplement to advertisement, not much amended.

5.   1754   Du Gouvernement Civil, Brussels, MDCCLIV.

2Tf, page-for-page reprint of no. 4.

6.   1755   Du Gouvernement Civil par Mr Locke, Cinquième Edition exactement revue et corrigée sur la 5 Edition de Londres & augmentée de quelques Notes, par L.C.R.D.M.A.D.P., Amsterdam, J. Schreuder and P. Mortier, MDCCLV.

12mo, xviii + 328 pp. 2Tf, very little modified, but with an extra advertisement and 25 notes: editor unidentified.

7.   1780   Du Gouvernement Civil, Amsterdam, B. Ulam, MDCCLXXX.

12mo, 2Tf, page-for-page reprint of no. 6.

8.   1783   Du Gouvernement Civil, A Londres et se trouve à Paris chez Servière, MDCCLXXXIII.

12mo, xxiv + 384 pp., 2Tf, reprint of no. 6, but omits supplementary advertisement and includes a sketch of Locke's life.

9.   1790   Du Gouvernement Civil, par Locke. In *Bibliothèque de l'homme public,* edited by Condorcet, Peysonel and Le Chapelier, Tome 2, Paris, Buisson, 1790.

Large 8vo, the extended summary and paraphrase of 2Tf occupying the second half (pp. 136–212) of the volume.

10.   1795   Traité du Gouvernement Civil, par M. Locke, Revue et Corrigée exactement sur la dernière Edition de Londres, Paris, Desveux & Royez, An III [1795].

Three formats:

   12mo, [22] + v–xvi + 17–481 pp.
   8vo, [4] + v–xxx + [31]–368 pp.
   4to, ditto.

2Tf, probably a reprint of no. 8, but introductory matter slightly different, containing a notice of a reprint of other works of Locke's.

11.   1795   Du Gouvernement Civil par M. Locke, Septième Edition, Paris, André, An III (1795).

12mo, 16 + 342 + [2] pp., 2Tf, reprint of no. 6.

12.   1802   Du Gouvernement Civil, par Locke, Quatrième Edition Française, Londres et Paris chez Servière, An 10 (1082) [i.e. 1802].

12mo, xxiv + 384 pp., 2Tf, reprint of no. 8. Copy in Bodley.

13.   1802, Traité du Gouvernement Civil, Paris, Volland, 1802.

12mo, 2Tf, perhaps a reprint of no. 10—not seen.

14.   1953   Essai sur le Pouvoir Civil de John Locke, texte

traduit, présenté et annoté par J. L. Fyot, Bibliothèque de la Science Politique, Paris, Presses Universitaires, 1953.

23 cm., xvi + 223 pp., 2T only, translation of British Printing 13.

4. ITALIAN PRINTINGS

1. 1773   Il Governo Civile tradotto nell'Italiano Idioma, Amsterdam, MDCCLXXIII.

8vo, vii + 288 pp., translated from French version (2Tf), anonymous. Copy in Bodley.

2. 1925   Saggio sul Governo Civile, ed. & tr. V. Beonio-Brocchieri, Turin, Bocca, 1925.

8vo, 280 + 2 pp. A translation of 2T from the version in the London Collected editions, before 1759—not seen.

3. 1947   Saggio sul Governo Civile. Selections from 2T translated and edited by G. Preti.

8vo, 134 pp., Milan, 1947—not seen.

4. 1948   Due Trattati Sul Governo di John Locke, col Patriarca di Robert Filmer a cura di Luigi Pareyson, Turin, Unione Tipografico-Editrice, 1948.

24 cm., 555 pp., 1T2T. The only previous critical edition.

5. 1956 (2T translated and edited by Alfredo Sasetti)—not seen.

5. SPANISH PRINTINGS

1. 1821   Tratado del Gobierno Civil por Mr Locke, traducido de la septima edición francesa, por D.S.C. y L., Madrid, la Minerva Española, 1821.

16mo, 2Tf: the 7th French edition is French Printing no. 11 above, 1795—not seen.

2. 1827   Del Gobierno Civil, traducido por Don M.V.M., licenciado, Paris, Rosa.

12mo, 1827. In spite of its title, this book does not in fact contain Locke on Government, but a translation of his *Conduct of the Understanding* on pp. 1–178 where it should have appeared: the *Letter on Toleration* is included—not seen.

3. 1941   Ensayo sobre el Gobierno Civil; Traducción y Prefacio de José Carner, México, Fondo de cultura Económica, 1941.

Presumably 2T only, claims to be first direct translation from English—not seen.

Note. In 1920 Pablo de Azcárate translated Filmer's *Patriarcha* (Madrid, Calpe), evidently intending to go on to Locke on Government, but his second book does not seem to have appeared.

6. GERMAN PRINTINGS

1. 1718   Le Gouvernement Civil oder die Kunst wohl zu Regieren . . . John Locke . . . aus der Englischen und Französichen Sprache . . . übersetzt von G—, Frankfurt and Leipzig, Hartung, 1718.

Presumably a translation of 2Tf—not seen.

2. 1906   Zwei Abhandlungen über Regierung nebst 'Patriarcha' von Sir Robert Filmer. Deutsch von Hilmar Wilmanns, Halle, 1806.

8vo, viii + 384 pp., 1T2T, translated from Morley's volume of same content (British Printing no. 33).

7. SWEDISH PRINTING

1726   Johan Lockes Oförgripelige Tankar Om Werldslig Regering . . . Öwersatte i från Engelskan af Hans Harmens, Stockholm, Kongl. Tryckeriet, 1726.

In spite of title, this seems to be a translation of 2Tf. Copy at Harvard.

8. NORWEGIAN PRINTING

1947   Translation of 2T by K. P. Heggdal, part of the 'Politisk bibliotek: Klassikerne', Oslo, Dreyers Forlag, 1947.

20 cm., xx + 226 + [2] pp. Foreword by K. Foss, translation of text based on one of the master-copies.

9. RUSSIAN PRINTING

1902   (Translation of 2T, published by P. P. Soikin, St Petersburg, 1902.)

Copy in Fundamental Library of Social Science, Moscow—not seen.

10. HINDI PRINTING

1960   (Translation of 2T by Raghuveer Singh.)

11. HEBREW PRINTING

1959   (Translation of 2T by Joseph Ur, text of 1R, revised edition.)

APPENDIX B

SOURCES OF 'TWO TREATISES' IN LOCKE'S READING

It has been decided not to attempt here a full, concerted survey of the possible sources of *Two Treatises* for the following reasons. In a sense the whole of the Introduction is a commentary on this subject, and much more specific references are made in the footnotes to the text. An adequate discussion of every likely source, however, would have to be very lengthy because of the wealth of information which Locke left behind him.

Moreover it has become obvious that such a discussion in the case of Locke would be more than usually unsatisfactory. It is always difficult and seldom convincing to try to demonstrate that an author wrote thus and thus because he had just read this and that, or had read such things at a crucial time, or was under their influence without recognizing it, and so on. Locke's deliberate policy of making as few references as he could, his tendency to clear his head as far as possible of other men's notions (see above, pp. 85–8) and his generally elusive character as a writer, makes him peculiarly unsuited to this type of treatment. In a book of some 400 pages, obviously polemical and obviously concerned with other men's opinions and publications, he mentions only six writers by their names, two others by the titles of their works. In none of the numerous passages where the editor has found it possible to trace parallels, even patent signs of indebtedness (as in many contexts with Pufendorf, for example, or Sagard in

II, § 106), has it been possible to demonstrate exact reproduction of phrases or of sentiments.[1]

Nevertheless it has been claimed above that Locke did use a specific collection of books when he wrote *Two Treatises,* and this claim is important to the assigning of its composition to a particular time (see section III). Printed below is a list of ninety books certainly known to have been available to Locke during the periods when it is supposed that he worked at political theory, and in most cases books which he can be proved to have used, or at least possessed.[2] The evidence for these facts is also presented in tabular form.

It must be stated with strong emphasis that this list is a guide only and that it would be possible to extend it very considerably, no doubt to make it more exhaustive and exact. Only the more obvious authorities have been used here, and the information was acquired as an incidental rather than as an end in itself. The books registered are given short titles only, just enough to identify them. The full titles of those referred to elsewhere will be found in the List of Authorities. Entries in capitals are of works mentioned by author and/or title in the text of *Two Treatises.* What follows is a brief description of the sources in question.

Locke's 1667 Notebook (Column A)

MS. f. 14, notebook with 67 (1667) inside front cover. In the editor's opinion this list of books was drawn up in association with Shaftesbury during the year of its dating, and many of the titles entered appear also in the next source.

1667   Book-list in Shaftesbury MSS. (Column B)

Public Record Office 30/24, XLVII, 30. A book-list in Locke's hand under various heads, 'Politici, Historici, De Rebus Ecclesiasticis, etc.', undated but closely connected with the preceding and probably of about 1667. The entries recorded come mainly from the section 'Politici'.

1681, 1682   Lemmata Ethica (Column C)

A notebook formerly in Locke's library at Ben Damph Forest and kindly loaned to the editor by the Earl of Lovelace.

[1] In this sense Locke's book, although so clearly dependent on the thoughts and works of his predecessors, even on the public discussion of political issues, is most decidedly not a derivative one. If it is compared with the books of Filmer, or Tyrrell, or Molyneux, for example, this point becomes quite obvious.

[2] Some authors (e.g. Hobbes and Harrington) are included for a quite different reason, to show how uncertain it is that Locke was in contact with their books when he wrote.

It is dated 1659 inside the front cover, and some of the entries may come from that year or soon after (see above, p. 46). But most of the subsequent entries are dated, and those recorded here come mainly from the years 1681 and 1682, when the book was extensively used by Locke for purposes of political and social theory, and are marked as such. (Now in the Bodleian Library.)

1681 Book-list (Column D)

Found on pp. 92–103 of Locke's journal for 1681 (MS. f. 5) between the entries for 14 July and 19 July. Headed 'A Catalogue of my Books at Oxford'—see above, p. 69. Titles nearly all reproduced in the list of books returned by Tyrrell in 1691, see below.

1689–91 Books restored to Locke on return from Holland (Column E)

London Books. Listed in *Adversaria Physica,* 1693 (now also in Bodley), described in Harrison and Laslett's *Catalogue* of Locke's library, to be published by the Oxford University Press. List probably made between June and November, 1689, but added to until 1691.

Oxford Books. Listed by Tyrrell in MS. f. 17 (see also MS. b. 2 and MS. f. 16). Stored at Tyrrell's house and returned in 1691.

1694 Catalogue of Locke's Final Library (Column F)

This catalogue is being prepared by Mr John Harrison and the editor for publication by the Oxford Bibliographical Society. The numbers in column F (H. and L. numbers) are those given to entries in that catalogue: they also appear in the notes in the final column. It is based almost entirely on another manuscript, Locke's own master list of his books made when his collection was complete in his last years, now in Mr Mellon's library at Oak Spring, Virginia.

Under Notes in the final column all other sources for this information are given, and the entries in the other columns are explained if it is necessary. Apart from Locke's journal and letters (his letters have been made least use of for these purposes) the important manuscripts are MS. f. 28 and 29 (Locke's *Tablets,* used 1679–81, see above, p. 72) and MS. c. 33 'Memorandum of Books read', which seems to belong to the same period. There are some references to the catalogues of the third earl of Shaftesbury ('in Shaftesbury Library'), now in the Record Office (P.R.O. 30/24, xxix).

Author (and/or) title	A 1667 Notebook (MS. f. 14)	B 1667? Book-list in Shaftesbury Papers (P.R.O. 30/24, xLVII, 30)	C 1681, 1682 [and c. 1660] (Lemmata Ethica)	D 1681 (July) List of Books at Oxford (Journal MS. f. 5)	E 1689–91 *Books from Oxford (MS. b. 2, MS. f. 17); † London Books (Adversaria Physica)	F 1694– Final Library Catalogue (H. and L. numbers)	Notes (other sources, etc.)
1 ACOSTA, History of East and West Indies, 4to, 1604	—	*	—	*	*	859	Quoted II, § 102. Lent March 1681 (Journal). B 'one of the best works on the West Indies'. The Latin original is H. and L. 858
2 Acuna, Relation des Amazones, 12mo, Paris, 1682	—	—	—	—	*	16	Listed in 1682 (Journal)
3 AINSWORTH, Annotations on Books of Moses, Fo, 1639	—	—	—	—	*	41	Referred to, I § 28. Bought December 1681
4 Allestree, Gentleman's Calling, 8vo, 1660	—	—	—	*	*	1240	—
5 Amiramus, Scipio [sic, ?Ammirato, Scipione, Discorsi sopra Cornelio Tacito, 8vo, Florence, 1594]	*	—	—	*	—	85ᵃ	—
6 Aristotle, De Rhetorica, ed. Goulston, 4to, 1619	—	—	—	*	*	118	—

Author (and/or title)	A 1667 Notebook (MS. f. 14)	B 1667? Book-list in Shaftesbury Papers (P.R.O. xlvii, 30)	C 1681, 1682 [and c. 1660] (Lemmata Ethica)	D 1681 (July) List of Books at Oxford (Journal MS. f. 5)	E 1689–91 *Books from Oxford (MS. b. 2, MS. f. 17); † London Books (Adversaria Physica)	F 1694—Final Library Catalogue (H. and L. numbers)	Notes (other sources, etc.)
7 Bouhours, Entretiens d'Ariste et d'Eugène, 8vo, Amsterdam, 1671	—	—	*	—	—	—	H. and L. 1056 is edition of 1682
8 Atwood, Argumentum Anti-Normannicum, 8vo, 1682	—	—	—	—	*	113	—
9 Bacon, Essays, 4to, 1632	—	—	—	*	*	178	—
10 Bacon, Henry VII, Fo, 1641	—	—	—	—	*	162	—
11 Barclay, De Potestate Papae, and De Regno et Regali Potestate, 8vo, Hanover, 1612	*	—	—	*	*	203, 204	See II, §§ 232–9, I, § 4. Bought for Shaftesbury, 1680. Noted in Tablet (see p. 72) under 1680
12 Bentivoglio, Memorie, 8vo, Amsterdam, 1648	—	—	*	—	—	—	—
13 Bergerac, Cyrano de, Selenarchia, Government of the World in the Moon, 8vo, 1658	*	*	*['1660]	—	*	268ª	H. and L. 279 is Bergerac Satyrical Characters, 1658
14 Bernier, Voyage de Kachemire, 1671	—	—	*	—	*†	289	Cited in C under 1682. Two copies: one in Oxford, one in London

	A	B	C	D	E	No.	Notes
15 Bodin, *De Republica*	*	—	*	*	—	—	—
16 Brutus [*Vindiciae contra Tyrannos*]	—	—	—	—	—	[1856]	Bought 'Junius Brutus' for Tyrrell, May 1681: entry in D 'Brutus' amongst 8vo's. The *Vindiciae* was printed at the end of many editions of Machiavelli, *Princeps* (compare no. 54 below), and this may account for entry in D
17 Campanella *Monarchia Hispanica*, 16mo, Amsterdam, 1653	—	—	*	—	—	576	Both cited in B, with rest of Campanella's writings, as bearing on the Popish threat to England; a remark repeated in 1667 Journal. Locke bought no. 17 whilst he was in Holland
18 Campanella, *Civitas Solis*	—	—	*	—	—	—	—
19 Cardan, *Opera*, Fo, 1663	*	*	*	*	*	587	See note on I, §1: bound in 1680 (Journal)
20 Chillingworth, *Religion of Protestants*, Fo, 1674	—	—	*	*	†	685	Quoted several times in C; certainly read in 1682. 1684 edition bought in Holland, H. and L. 686
21 Commines, *Mém⋯*	*	—	*	*	—	—	Commended for 'arcana imperii'
22 Contzen [?*Politicorum libri 10*, Fo, 1621, or ...*The Plot of Contzen*, 4to, 1641]	—	—	*	—	—	—	Also cited for 'arcana imperii', and noted in 1667 Journal

Author (and/or) title	A 1667 Notebook (MS. f. 14)	B 1667? Book-list in Shaftesbury Papers (P.R.O. 30/24, xlvii, 30)	C 1681, 1682 [and c. 1660] (Lemmata Ethica)	D 1681 (July) List of Books at Oxford (Journal MS. f. 5)	E 1689–91 *Books from Oxford (MS. b. 2, †London Books (Adversaria Physica)	F 1694– Final Library Catalogue (H. and L. numbers)	Notes (other sources, etc.)
23 Cudworth, *True intellectual System*, Fo, 1678	—	—	—	—	†	896	Bought December 1681 and cited in Journal February 1682
24 Dandini, *Voyage du Mont Liban*, 12mo, 1675	—	—	*	*	*	*912*	Listed and probably bought in 1678, very frequently quoted in C, obviously read 1681–2. Lent to Tyrrell August 1679
25 Digges, Dudley, *Unlawfulness of taking up Arms*, 4to, 1648, 1662, etc.	*	*	—	—	—	—	—
26 Digges, Dudley, *A Review of Observations on His Majesty's Answers*, 4to, 1643	*	—	—	—	—	—	—
27 Doleman [Parsons], *Conference about Succession*, 8vo, 1681	—	—	—	—	†	987	—
28 Falkland, *Infallibility*, 4to, 1651	?	*	*	—	—	—	Quoted in A, B, C: perhaps c. 1660 in C
29 Filmer, *Anarchy* (On Hunton), 4to, 1648	*	*	*	—	—	—	C has references to *Anarchy* which may be of c. 1660.

No.	Entry						No.	Notes
30	FILMER, *Original* (On Hobbes, Milton, Grotius) 4to, 1652	*	—	—	—	—	—	Author called 'Sr Thomas Filmore' in A, B. Reference in *Tablet*, under date 1679, to another collected ed. published in that year—see pp. 71 and 72 above. H. and L. *1120–2* (1 volume) bought January 1680
31	FILMER, *Forms* (On Aristotle), 4to, 1652	*	—	—	*	—	—	
32	FILMER, *Advertisement* (On Witches), 4to, 1653	*	*	—	—	—	—	
33	FILMER [Collected Tracts], 8vo, 1680	—	—	—	*	*	*1120–2*	
34	Gage, *Survey of West Indies*, 3rd ed, 8vo, 1677	—	*	*	—	†	*1205*	Read in August 1680 (Journal)
35	Galileo, *Opere*, 4to, 1656	—	—	*	*	*	*1208*	Bound November 1679 (Journal)
36	Gee, *Divine Right and Original of Civil Magistrates*, 8vo, 1658	*	—	—	—	—	—	In Shaftesbury Library
37	Grotius, *De Veritate Religionis Christianae*	*	*	*	—	—	—	Much quoted in A, B, C: H. and L. *1339* is later edition, Amsterdam, 1680, acquired in Holland
38	Grotius, *De Jure Belli ac Pacis*, 8vo, Amsterdam, 1650	*	—	—	—	†	*1329a*	This work commended in *Education* and in letters of 1703, but see no. 65. He bought another edition in Holland, H. and L. *1329*
39	Guicciardini, *Hypomneses politicae*	*	*	—	—	—	—	Locke possessed three copies of Guicciardini's *Historia*, H. and L. *1357–1358a*

Author (and/or title)	A 1667 Notebook (MS. f. 14)	B 1667? Book-list in Shaftesbury Papers (P.R.O. 30/24, XLVII, 30)	C 1681, 1682 [and c. 1660] (Lemmata Ethica)	D 1681 (July) List of Books at Oxford (Journal MS. f. 5)	E 1689–91 *Books from Oxford (MS. b. 2, f. 17); †London Books Physica	F 1694– Final Library Catalogue (H. and L. numbers) (Adversaria)	Notes (other sources, etc.)
40 Harrington, *Oceana*	—	—	—	—	—	1388	Discussed in a letter of 1689. Read by Shaftesbury, 1674 (Journal). H. and L. 1388 is the edition of 1700. Locke also had *The Art of Lawgiving*, 1659, and Harrington's *Queries concerning Elections*, 1690
41 Heylyn	*	*	—	—	—	—	A, B refer to all Heylyn's works. H. and L. 1446ª is Heylyn on *France*, 1656
42 Hobbes, *Leviathan*, Fo, 1651	—	—	—	—	—	1465	Locke lent his *Leviathan* to Tyrrell in March 1674 (Journal), and it does not seem to have been in his possession in 1679–83, or until 1691. He bought a copy of no. 44 for Toinard, June 1679. He owned only these three books of Hobbes, and only one direct citation from any work of his has been found in Locke's papers—see note on p. 87
43 Hobbes, *Problemata physica*, 8vo, 1662	—	—	—	*	*	1466	
44 Hobbes, *De Mirabilibus Pecci*, 4to, 1666	—	—	—	*	—	1464	

45 HOOKER, *Ecclesiastical Polity*, Fo, 1632 and 1676 [and/or 1666]	—	—	*	*	*1490–2*	See above, p. 70
46 Jurieu, *Policy of Clergy of France*, 8vo, 1681; French edition, 12mo, Hague, 1682	—	*	—	*†	*2397* and *799*	English edition lent to Tyrrell, May 1681, and returned 1691. Other references are to French edition
47 Justin, 8vo, Paris, 1543	—	—	*	†	*1601*	Quoted II, § 103. Locke had three other editions, H. and L. *1600, 1602, 1602a*
48 Kettlewell, *Christ. Obedience*, 4to, 1681	—	—	—	*	*1631*	Bought May 1682 (Journal); for Shaftesbury, June 1682
49 Knox, *Ceylon*, Fo, 1681	—	—	—	†	*1649*	Referred to II, § 92. Bought August 1681; see above, p. 68
50 Lawson, *Politica sacra et civilis*, 4to, 1660. Or *Examination of Political Part of Leviathan*, 8vo, 1657	—	—	—	—	*1695a, 1696* or *1695*	Lawson's 'Book of Government' exchanged between Locke and Shaftesbury in 1679, see above, p. 72. H. and L. *1695a* is first (1660) ed. of *Politica*, bought in Holland but not retained: H. and L. *1696* is 1689 edition, bought in 1690. Locke also had Lawson on *Hebrews* and *Theopolitica* (H. and L. *1697, 1697a*)
51 Lery, *Voyage du Bresil*, 8vo, La Rochelle, 1578	—	—	—	†	*1718*	Entered as a book read, MS. c. 33

Author (and/or) title	A 1667 Notebook (MS. f. 14)	B 16677 Book-list in Shaftesbury Papers (P.R.O. 30/24, xLVII, 30)	C ˜681, 1682 [and c. 1660] (Lemmata Ethica)	D 1681 (July) List of Books at Oxford (Journal MS. f. 5)	E 1689–91 *Books from Oxford (MS. b. 2, MS. f. 17); † London Books (Adversaria Physica)	F 1694–Final Library Catalogue (H. and L. numbers)	Notes (other sources, etc.)
52 Leyser, Discursus politicus de Polygamia	*	*	—	—	—	[58]	In A and B referred to as if an English book written by Hales. H. and L. 58 is 2nd ed. Freiburg, 1676, returned by Tyrrell 1691
53 Machiavelli, Discourses, 12mo, 1636	—	—	—	*	*	1852	—
54 Machiavelli, Prince [Latin ed.], 12mo, Leiden, 1643	—	—	—	—	—	[18:6]	H. and L. 1856 was bought in Holland and included the Vindiciae, see no. 16 above. In 1691 Tyrrell also returned H. and L. 1848, the Opere, 1550 ed., bought in 1678, which may have been the other Machiavelli listed in D
55 Mariana, History of Spain	*	—	—	—	—	—	—
56 Marvel, Rehearsal Transprosed, 8vo, 1672	—	—	—	—	* †	1931, 1932	Copies of first two impressions, one in Oxford, one in London. On London list calls author 'Marvin'. Second part and books about this work also held

						No.	Notes
57 Milton	*	*	—	*	†	[1994] [1994a]	A lists *Areopagitica*, *Reformation*, *Divorce* and *Against Salmasius*, and first two are also quoted, B lists first three and C quotes *Reformation*. H. and L. *1994a* is 1689, 4to printing of Milton on *Sovereign Right*, from London list. H. and L. *1994* is *Works*, 1698
58 Montaigne, *Essays*, Fo, 1603	—	—	*	*	—	2029	Seems from C to have been read in 1681
59 Naudé, *Considérations politiques sur les coups d'estat*, 12mo, Rome, 1667	—	—	*	—	†	2074a	Read in 1681, repeatedly quoted in C
60 Neville, *Plato Redivivus*, 8vo, 1681	—	—	—	—	—	—	Lent to Tyrrell May 1681 (Journal). In Shaftesbury Library
61 Osborne, *Political Reflections on the Government of the Turks*, 8vo, 1656	—	—	—	—	*	2145	—
62 Ovagle, *Historica Relatione del Regn... di Cile*, Fo, Rome, 1646	—	—	—	*	*	2152	—
63 Parker, Sam., *Law of Nature*, 4to, 1681	—	—	—	—	†	2198	Bought 1682. For Locke on another work of Parker, see above, p. 47

Author (and/or) title	A 1667 Notebook (MS. f. 14)	B 1667? Book-list in Shaftesbury Papers (P.R.O. 30/24, XLVII, 30)	C 1681, 1682 [and c. 1660] (Lemmata Ethica)	D 1681 (July) List of Books at Oxford (Journal MS. f. 5)	E 1689–91 *Books from Oxford (MS. b. 2, MS. f. 17); † London Books (Adversaria Physica)	F 1694– Final Library Catalogue (H. and L. numbers)	Notes (other sources, etc.)
64 Pascal, Pensées, 12mo, Paris, 1678	—	—	—	*	*	2222	Sent to Tyrrell September 1682: another edition in London
65 Pufendorf, De Jure Naturae, 4to, Lund, 1672	—	—	—	*	*	2401	Bought June 1680: for Shaftesbury, June 1681. Commended in 1686 (preferred to Grotius, compare similar remark in Education), in 1698 and in 1703 ('best book of that kind'). H. and L. 2407 is Amsterdam ed., 1698
66 Pufendorf, De Officio Hominis et Civis, 8vo, Lund, 1673	—	—	*	—	*	2403	Frequently cited in C under 1681 and 1682. Commended in 1703
67 Pufendorf, Dissertationes academicae, 8vo, Lund, 1675, and 8vo, Uppsala, 1677	—	—	—	—	—	2402 and 2406	Both eds. bought after 1683
68 Pufendorf, Elementorum Jurisprudentiae, 8vo, Hague, 1660, and Cambridge, 1672	—	—	—	—	—	2404 and 2405	1660 ed. bought in Holland, 1672, though read very early. 1672 ed. bought May 1681, returned by Tyrrell 1691

#	Title						No.	Notes
69	Pyrard, *Voyage aux Indes Orientales*, 4to, Paris, 1679	—	—	—	*	*	2411	Noted as read in MS. c. 33. Lent to Tyrrell August 1679, bought for Shaftesbury September 1681 (Journal)
70	*A Remonstrance of the State of the Kingdom*, 4to, 1641 [15 December]	*	—	—	—	—	2465a	Thomason E 181 (a) : possessed in the 1690's. Another Civil War tract, Robinson's *People's Plea*, 1646 (E328 [3]), listed in B
71	Roger, *La Porte ouverte de la Religion des Bramines*, 4to, Amsterdam, 1670	—	—	*	—	*	2495	Repeatedly cited in C
72	Sagard, *Canada*, 1636, and *Voyage des Hurons*, 1632	—	—	—	*	*	2526, 2527	Both noted as read MS. c. 33. *Canada* extensively used in 1679 (Journal) : see notes on II, §§ 58, 106
73	Sandys, *Europae Speculum*, 12mo, 1638	—	—	—	*	*	2552	—
74	Selden, *De Jure naturali juxta Disciplinam Ebraeorum*, 4to, 1665	—	—	*	—	—	2603	Bought in Holland. Locke admired Selden and had other titles
75	Simon, *Histoire critique du Vieux Testament*, 4to, Paris, 1678	—	—	*	—	—	—	Very frequent references in C: clearly read in 1681, but bought later, in other editions. Locke had several books by Simon

Author (and/or) title	A 1667 Notebook (MS. f. 14)	B 1667? Book-list in Shaftesbury Papers (P.R.O. 30/24, XLVII, 30)	C 1681, 1682 [and c. 1660] (Lemmata Ethica)	D 1681 (July) List of Books at Oxford (Journal MS. f. 5)	E 1689–91 *Books from Oxford (MS. b. 2, MS. f. 17); †London Books (Adversaria Physica)	F 1694– Final Library Catalogue (H. and L. numbers)	Notes (other sources, etc.)
76 Smith, J., Description of New England, 4to, 1616	—	—	*	*	—	—	Frequently quoted in C: read in 1682
77 Somers, The Security of Englishman's Lives, 8vo, 1682	—	—	—	—	*	1308	In Tablet under 1681, headed 'Grand Jurys'
78 Spinoza, Tractatus theologico-politicus, 8vo, 1674	—	—	—	—	*	2743	Lent May 1674 (Journal). See above, p. 87
79 Spinoza	—	—	—	—	*	2742	Presumably Spinoza on Descartes. Locke bought his Opera Posthuma in Holland
80 Stubbe, Henry, Light out of Darkness, 4to, 1659	—	—	—	*	*	2798	—
81 Stubbe, Henry, Essay in Defence of the Good Old Cause, 8vo, 1659	—	—	—	—	*	2800a	Read by Locke in 1659
82 Terry, Voyage to East India, 8vo, 1655	—	—	—	*	*	2857	—

						No.	
83 Thesaurus politicus, Pts 1–3, 8vo, Cologne, 1609–11. [Transl. by G. Ens of Tesoro politico, raccolto per C. Ventura]	*	—	—	—	—	—	Described in A as 'a collection of very good prudential pieces'
84 [TYRRELL] Patriarcha non Monarcha, 8vo, 1681	—	—	—	—	—	2999	Bought June 1681 'for Mr Tyrrell' (Journal). See above, p.74
85 Valla, Ferdinand and Isabella	—	—	—	—	—	—	—
86 Valle, Viaggi, 12mo, Venice, 1667	*	*	—	*	—	3046	Frequently quoted in C: read in 1681 (Journal)
87 Vane, Henry, either Retired Man's Meditation, 1655, or Healing Question, 1656	*	*	—	*	—	3047 or 3048	—
88 VEGA, Garcilasco de la, Commentaire royale, 4to, Paris, 1633	*	*	*	*	—	3058	See I, §57, etc.: Locke had two copies. The title appears in Tablet, 1679 (Journal), is named in Paris, and in Journal of 1687, in Holland. Other works by Vega, H. and L. 3059–61
89 Ursino, Vindiciae pro capite Regis Angliae, 4to, Hague, 1650	*	—	—	—	—	3024	Quoted in A on Libertas
90 Wren, Matthew, Monarchy asserted, 8vo, Oxford, 1659	*	*	—	*	—	3188	Locke had two copies

EDITORIAL NOTE

1. THE TEXT

General. The attempt here is to present Locke's 'text for posterity' (see above, p. 22) from the Christ's corrected copy. It has been set up in type from a photograph of that document. The compositors have in fact worked from printer's copy prepared for the press between 1698 and 1704 by Locke himself and by Coste. Locke's hand appears only occasionally after the first few pages, and Coste seems to have been copying rather than taking his dictation: it seems possible that he may have been copying from another, very similar exemplar, the hypothetical second master-copy which is discussed below.

The decision to reproduce the Christ's copy, modified only in such particulars as were absolutely necessary, was the simplest, most consistent solution to an intricate editorial problem. The reader has before him the version which would have satisfied Locke at the time of his death, or something as close to that version as the editor can make it. He has also a record, complete in all essentials, but not absolutely exhaustive, of all the variants from that final version which were seen by Locke, and then rejected by him at one correcting stage or other. These variants are recorded in the collation.[1]

---

[1] See Note on Collation, below, p. 167.

Documents used. In order to appreciate why the editor has ventured to alter the Christ's copy in any way whatsoever, it is necessary to record the documents from which he has worked. They are:

(i) Locke's own copy of the 1st printing of 1689–90. This is in the 2nd state (1R, see above, p. 20 and references), complete with errata slip. Locke has entered the errata, and made a few further modifications of his own.

(ii) The 2nd printing, 1694, with its errata list.

(iii) The Christ's copy of the 3rd printing, 1698, with its errata list and the very extensive corrections in Locke's hand and in Coste's.

(iv) The 4th printing, 1713, reproducing Locke's text for posterity, possibly from the hypothetical second master-copy: it could, of course, have been the result of comparison between the Christ's copy and that copy, or with other, unknown authoritative sources.

(v) The printing in the 1st Collected edition, 1714, a reprint of (iv), but conceivably also influenced by other, unknown authoritative sources.

(vi) The 5th edition, 1727, reprinting the 4th, showing minor editorial clarification and important for (vii).

(vii) The 6th edition, 1764, Hollis's attempt to reproduce the Christ's copy, collating it (so he claimed) with (i), (ii) and (iii), but not apparently with (iv) or (v). The basic text is that of (vi).

(viii) Locke's own copy of the first French edition, 1691, not, however, marked in any way by him in the text.

Obscurities in (iii), the copy text, have been elucidated by comparison with all of the seven other documents, though some of them [especially (i), (ii), (iv), (v)] are obviously much more important than the others. In some cases the editor has been led to prefer a reading of his own to all of these. These obscurities are such as must arise in a text of this date and history, and, though they are fairly numerous, it must be stressed that they affect Locke's meaning only in very minor matters. Their main sources are as follows:

1. Faults in Locke's original manuscript appearing in the printings of 1689–90, 1694, 1698 and not corrected in the Christ's copy.

2. Faults in these printings not corrected in the Christ's copy.

3. Faults, of incompleteness, illegibility, etc., in the manuscript corrections in the Christ's copy.

Emendation. In emending these details in the Christ's copy the editor has been guided by an obvious principle. He has assumed that they only appear there because Locke failed to notice them in his final correction and he has corrected them as he supposed Locke would have done. Comparison with the first three printings has disposed of most of the obscurities, and a proper deference has been shown to the first printing, as being the closest to the original manuscript—especially in the form of the particular copy owned and corrected by the author. But since Locke corrected the book so extensively again in 1694 and 1698, a later reading has always been preferred to an earlier one, except where it seemed clear that it was due to compositor's blunder. Such blunders were common in both later printings and often went uncorrected in the Christ's copy.

In tackling the remaining textual obscurities the editor has turned for guidance to the 4th, Collected and 6th editions, since they were all alike attempts to do what he has tried to do, to reproduce Locke's 'text for posterity'. The status of these versions depends to a large extent on the possibility that one, some, or all of them derive (wholly or partially) from a source different from the Christ's copy, and even closer to Locke's textual intentions. The particular question to be answered is this. Does the 4th edition, on which all these versions seem to be based, represent the hypothetical second master-copy whose existence seems clearly to be implied by Coste's note on the final fly of the Christ's copy? There are subsidiary questions about the possible existence of other authoritative sources (and conceivable links between them and editions later than the 4th), but we have no evidence on these points and only this crucial question can be discussed here.

Second master-copy. The evidence suggesting that the 4th edition was not necessarily (or exclusively) based on the Christ's copy is as follows. In the first place Coste makes it quite clear that this particular document was *not* the one Locke wanted to be used for posthumous publication.[2] An editor in 1713, therefore, anxious to carry out Locke's directions, would have done his best to get hold of the other copy which Coste seems to have in mind and print from that.

---

[2] The letter of La Motte quoted in footnote 19 to p. 22 above presumably implies that a second, more authentic copy did exist, otherwise Coste would surely never have had the Christ's copy bequeathed to him.

Secondly, comparison shows that there are small particulars in which the 4th edition, and those based on it, differ from the Christ's copy (and sometimes from each other).

All these variant details are recorded in the Collation, but some may be cited here. I, § 154 shows variations from the Christ's copy which seem to derive from a different document. A correction to II, § 50 seems impossible to recover from the Christ's copy. A correction to II, § 13, present in the Christ's copy and so in the 6th edition, is omitted from the 4th edition and derived texts. On the other hand a word occurs in II, § 230 in the 4th edition, etc., which is not in the Christ's copy, but seems to be a genuine Locke insertion nevertheless. There are further details which suggest that the alternative source, of all these variations, if it existed, was a corrected exemplar of the 2nd, not the 3rd printing: a misspelling, for example, in II, § 16, and a passage in II, § 36.

On this evidence there is a possible case for supposing that the 4th edition was indeed a printing of the other 'exemplaire' referred to by Coste, that this was a copy of the 1694 printing more authoritatively corrected, and that a critical edition should be based on this text, corrected by comparison with the other authoritative documents, and not on the Christ's copy. But the difficulties of such a case are so formidable that it has been found impossible to accept it. For if the 4th edition and its derived texts do in fact represent Coste's other master-copy, then they should contain the very passage which he writes out from that other copy as a variant from his own version in his note on II, § 172. Neither the 4th edition, the Collected edition nor any derived text does print the passage in this way. Then, though the detailed evidence may seem convincing when cited alone, there is simply not enough of it. The number of variants to be expected between printings of this date is so great that the resemblances, omissions, additions on which the case rests could be coincidental. Finally, even if the 4th and derived texts were based on another authoritative source, we cannot say what that source (or sources) was. We have nothing but unconfirmed inference to persuade us that it was the authentic second master-copy.

For these reasons, therefore, the question has had to be left open here.[3] The editor is satisfied that a text presented on the basis of the hypothesis just discussed would not differ

---

[3] I have not gone so far as to undertake the minute, statistical analysis which might yield further evidence.

in any very important respects from the one given here. The Christ's master-copy is of unimpeachable authenticity; it has not been printed since 1764 and never comparatively; it clearly represents for us now the most obvious, authentic source for Locke's 'text for posterity'. There are even signs that some of its amendments were later than those in its hypothetical source (see Collation for I, § 34). It has been taken as the copy text, therefore, and these other authoritative sources have been used for its elucidation.[4]

Other modifications of copy text. Inevitably there have been problems which have had to be solved without reference to these other authoritative documents, some of them presumably arising from obscurities in what Locke originally wrote down. Wherever the editor has ventured a reading of his own, or supplied a word, square brackets have been used, and the fact noted in the Collation. Moreover, Locke's citations from the classics, the Bible, the works of Filmer and so on have been checked and amended. Only two further liberties have been taken with Locke's 'text for posterity'. After his citations of Filmer's page numbers, and whenever he quotes or refers to Filmer in a way which might require a modern reader to look up the original, the corresponding page number in the modern reprint of Filmer[5] has been inserted in square brackets. Locke's quotations from Hooker have been removed from the side and lower margins, where they appear in all three early printings without exact reference signs in the body of the text. They have been printed at the bottom of the page, with reference signs inserted where the editor believes Locke intended them to be.

Apart from these things, and it must be repeated that they are mostly of the smallest importance to Locke's meaning, the type of the 3rd printing has been followed as exactly as possible, up to the point where it might become a burden to

[4] Professor Bowers has pointed out that the perfect text, or super text, might have been brought about by taking the 1st printing as the copy, and modifying it by the corrections of 1694, 1698, of the Christ's copy and of the 4th edition and derived texts. This would be nearer to the manuscript of 1689, but it could hardly be said to represent Locke's 'text for posterity'. The printing style, for example, would be for the most part of 1690, and it is clear that in the years up to 1698 spelling and printing style altered, in ways which seem to inform some of Locke's corrections.

[5] *Patriarcha, and other Political Writings of Sir Robert Filmer, edited from the Original Sources,* by Peter Laslett. Blackwell's Political Texts, Oxford, 1949.

the twentieth-century reader. Its free use of capitals, its very extensive use of italics, its characteristic spelling, have all been retained, but the long 's' has been eliminated. The manuscript amendments have been reproduced precisely as they were intended to be, as an integral part of a running text.

2. THE COLLATION

The Collation is intended to show precisely what Locke did to his text to make it definitive, and to provide something of its history between its original publication and Locke's final correction. It is explained in a note printed on p. 479 and again on p. 507, where it will be found that the registration of variants has been limited to some extent.

The cumulative results of the Collation are of considerable interest, but on the whole the elaborate work of comparison and collation was disappointing in its detailed alterations. It is difficult to see why Locke inserted so many commas for his final version, for example, and even his substantial corrections seldom change his essential meaning. His extensive italicization does seem to have been intended to make quotation easier. But unimportant as the detailed results may appear to be, it is hoped that this work will not have to be done again. For what it is worth it has made available something like a variorum edition.

3. THE FOOTNOTES

The editorial footnotes elucidate the text and draw attention to variations to be found in the Collation, sometimes reproducing them when they are significant of changes of meaning.

They explain Locke's allusions,[6] draw attention to his sources, provide cross-references, and contain much of the evidence for the views expressed in the Introduction, especially about the history and dates of composition of the book.[7] They are not intended as a commentary on Locke's social and political ideas. The editor has spared himself many observations of this sort, except perhaps in Locke's treatment of Filmer and his relationship with Hobbes. A determined effort has been made to keep down the number and length of the footnotes, so as to make reading and consultation as convenient as possible. If the intricacy of the editorial problems has made them burdensome nevertheless, the editor can only apologize.

4. REFERENCES TO SOURCES AND AUTHORITIES

Much of the complication of footnote references arises from such expressions as *op. cit., ibid., loc. cit.* and so on. They have been eliminated here as far as possible. Internal references are mostly by page number throughout the book, except for the text itself, where they are by the paragraph number (I for the *First Treatise,* II for the *Second Treatise*) and sometimes line number. References to other works are made on a system more usual in scientific books and papers; that is, by author and date only, followed by a Roman figure in brackets if the author published in that year more than one work used here. A full description of each book or article appears in the List of Authorities on pp. 543–56. Locke's journal, letters referred to by the date only and manuscript sources prefixed simply by 'MS.' are all in the Lovelace Collection, Bodleian Library, Oxford. This collection is described in detail and the pressmarks given for all documents, in Long, P., 1959.

[6] Even to translating simple Latin phrases, and describing the familiar figures of ancient mythology. The editor's apology must be that he has tried to bear in mind the undergraduate reader, all over the English-speaking world.

[7] Little reference is made to the use of Locke's book by his successors: his influence has been so extensive that an attempt to represent it would obviously be impossible. The one exception is in the citation of Elrington's notes of 1798, the only previous English edition annotated on any scale.

TWO
TREATISES
OF

Government:

In the Former,

The False Principles and Foundation

OF

Sir *Robert Filmer*,

And His FOLLOWERS,

ARE

Detected and Overthrown.

The Latter is an

ESSAY

CONCERNING

The True Original, Extent, and End

OF

Civil-Government.

LONDON: Printed for *Awnsham* and *John Churchill*, at the
Black Swan in *Pater-Noster-Row.* 1 6 9 8.

An Englishman, a Lover of Liberty, Citizen of the World, is desirous of having the honor to deposite this Book in the Library of Christ College Cambridge.

To Dr Thomas
Master of Christ College Cambridge
April 20, 1764.

Letter of Thomas Hollis. The original is now pasted into the binding of the volume in Christ's College Library. It is typical of Hollis to describe himself in this way, without giving his name; see above, p. 23 and note 20. He presented a copy of his edition printed from this text to William Pitt, the elder, on 26 May, and the British Museum on 8 June 1764. Hugh Thomas was Master of Christ's from 1764–80.

Quod si nihil cum potentiore juris humani relinquitur inopi, at ego ad Deos vindices humanae superbiae confugiam: et precabor ut iras suas vertant in eos, quibus non suae res, non alienae satis sint quorum saevitiam non mors noxiorum exatiet: placari nequeant, nisi hauriendum sanguinem laniandaque viscera nostra praebuerimus.   Liv. Lib. ix. c. i.

Note on title-page. This is reproduced from the Christ's copy, i.e. the 1698 printing. An additional phrase *Pax ac Libertas* appears on the title-page of Locke's copy of the first French printing, where it is written in his hand (see above, p. 26 and note). The above quotation from Livy is written on the fly-leaf facing the title in the Christ's volume, and appears (in a rather more accurate version) on the title of the 4th edition, 1713, and the 5th edition, 1728, but not elsewhere (see Loeb edition, IV, 164, showing considerable variation). Its general meaning is as follows: 'But if, in dealing with the mighty, the weak are left no human rights, yet will I seek protection in the gods, who visit retribution on human pride. And I will beseech them that they turn their anger against those who are not content with their own, or with that of others, who will not be sated with the death of the guilty. They are not to be placated unless we yield to them our blood to drink and our entrails to tear out.' The surprising ferociousness of these sentiments may well be another expression of Locke's savagery against despotism in general and against Charles II and James II in particular, compare note on II, § 172 and references.

The PREFACE.

Reader,

*Thou hast here the Beginning and End of a Discourse
concerning Government; what Fate has otherwise disposed
of the Papers that should have filled up the middle, and
were more than all the rest, 'tis not worth while to tell thee.
These, which remain, I hope are sufficient to establish the* 5
Throne of our Great Restorer, Our present King William;
*to make good his Title, in the Consent of the People, which
being the only one of all lawful Governments, he has more
fully and clearly than any Prince in* Christendom: *And to
justifie to the World, the People of* England, *whose love* 10
*of their Just and Natural Rights, with their Resolution to
preserve them, saved the Nation when it was on the very
brink of Slavery and Ruine. If these Papers have that
evidence, I flatter my self is to be found in them, there will
be no great miss of those which are lost, and my Reader* 15
*may be satisfied without them. For I imagine I shall have
neither the time, nor inclination to repeat my Pains, and
fill up the wanting part of my Answer, by tracing Sir*
Robert *again, through all the Windings and Obscurities
which are to be met with in the several Branches of his* 20
*wonderful System. The King, and Body of the Nation,
have since so thoroughly confuted his* Hypothesis, *that, I
suppose, no Body hereafter will have either the Confidence
to appear against our Common Safety, and be again an
Advocate for Slavery; or the Weakness to be deceived* 25
*with Contradictions dressed up in a Popular Stile, and well
turned Periods. For if any one will be at the Pains himself,
in those Parts which are here untouched, to strip Sir*
Robert's *Discourses of the Flourish of doubtful Expressions, and endeavour to reduce his Words to direct, positive,* 30
*intelligible Propositions, and then compare them one with
another, he will quickly be satisfied there was never so*

The Preface. (Compare Locke's *Manifesto* written for Clarke; above, 59, n. 5.) Presumably written in 1689, about the month of August, after the preparation of the text for the press, but before the revision of the titles—see notes on titles and Introduction, section III. From line 38, however, it resembles the Preface to Tyrrell's *Patriarcha non Monarcha,* 1681, so closely that the final passages may have been written earlier.

1 *Discourse*—perhaps the original word for the book—see Introduction, 63, and II, § 15, 18–19; II, § 52, 2.

6 *Great Restorer*—in a letter to Mordaunt dated 21 February 1689, refusing the King's offer of an ambassadorship, Locke called William 'our great deliverer'.

7 Compare I, § 95, 16 and note.

much glib Nonsense put together in well sounding English.
If he think it not worth while to examine his Works all
35 *through, let him make an Experiment in that part where*
he Treats of Usurpation; and let him try whether he can,
with all his Skill, make Sir Robert *intelligible, and con-*
sistent with himself, or common sense. I should not speak
so plainly of a Gentleman, long since past answering, had
40 *not the Pulpit, of late Years, publickly owned his Doctrine,*
and made it the Currant Divinity of the Times. 'Tis
necessary those Men, who taking on them to be Teachers,
have so dangerously misled others, should be openly
shewed of what Authority this their Patriarch is, whom they
45 *have so blindly followed, that so they may either retract*
what upon so ill Grounds they have vented, and cannot be
maintained, or else justifie those Principles which they
Preachd up for Gospel; though they had no better an
Author than an English *Courtier. For I should not have*
50 *Writ against Sir* Robert, *or taken the pains to shew his*
mistakes, Inconsistencies, and want of (what he so much
boasts of, and pretends wholly to build on) Scripture-
proofs, were there not Men amongst us, who, by crying up
his Books, and espousing his Doctrine, save me from the
55 *Reproach of Writing against a dead Adversary. They have*
been so zealous in this Point, that if I have done him any
wrong; I cannot hope they should spare me. I wish, where
they have done the Truth and the Publick wrong, they
would be as ready to Redress it and allow its just Weight
60 *to this Reflection, viz. That, there cannot be done a greater*
Mischief to Prince and People, than the Propagating wrong
Notions concerning Government, that so at last all times
might not have reason to complain of the Drum *Ecclesi-*
astick. If any one, concerned really for Truth, undertake

33 Compare I, §§ 20, 110, etc. and Tyrrell's reference to Filmer's
'gentile stile'. These compliments to Filmer as a stylist puzzle the modern
reader; for though he has his merits as a phrasemaker, as a writer of
continuous, controversial prose Filmer is no more attractive than any of
his contemporaries.
39-41 Compare II, § 112, 9;13.
44-50 Modified and extended in 1698, see Collation, and the reference to 'courtier' inserted. Filmer himself was never at court; see note
on I, § 5, 8-9.
55 Filmer had died in 1653; see note on Introduction 71 and reference, and compare Tyrrell's very similar apology.
63-4 *Drum Ecclesiastick*—the pulpit: Tyrrell talks of the 'wind blown
theologue'.

the Confutation of my Hypothesis, *I promise him either to* 65
recant my mistake, upon fair Conviction; or to answer his
Difficulties. But he must remember two Things;

First, *That Cavilling here and there, at some Expression,
or little incident of my Discourse, is not an answer to my
Book.* 70

Secondly, *That I shall not take railing for Arguments, nor
think either of these worth my notice: Though I shall
always look on my self as bound to give satisfaction to any
one who shall appear to be conscienciously scrupulous in the
point, and shall shew any just Grounds for his Scruples.* 75

I have nothing more, but to advertise the Reader, that A
stands for our Author. O *for his Observations on* Hobbs,
Milton, *&c. And that a bare Quotation of Pages always
means Pages of his* Patriarcha. Edit. 1680.

The CONTENTS of BOOK I.

Chap. I.   *The Introduction*   Page 169

Chap. II.   *Of Paternal and Regal Power*   172

Chap. III. *Of* Adam's *Title to Sovereignty,
by Creation*   179

Chap. IV.   *Of* Adam's *Title to Sovereignty, by
Donation,* Gen. 1. 28.   184

Chap. V.   *Of* Adam's *Title to Sovereignty, by the
Subjection of* Eve   201

Chap. VI.   *Of* Adam's *Title to Sovereignty, by
Fatherhood*   206

Chap. VII. *Of Fatherhood and Propriety,
consider'd together as Fountains of Sovereignty*   225

Chap. VIII. *Of the Conveyance of* Adam's *Sovereign Monarchical Power*   230

Chap. IX.   *Of Monarchy, by Inheritance from*
Adam   233

Chap. X.   *Of the Heir to the Monarchical Power
of* Adam   247

Chap. XI.   *Who Heir?*   250

76–9 See Introduction, 71, for Locke's method of referring to Filmer.
The words 'Edit. 1680' were added in 1698.

The Contents of Book II.

Chap. I.   The Introduction   299
Chap. II.   Of the State of Nature   301
Chap. III.   Of the State of War   311
Chap. IV.   Of Slavery   316
Chap. V.   Of Property   319
Chap. VI.   Of Paternal Power   337
Chap. VII.   Of Political, or Civil Society   353
Chap. VIII.   Of the Beginning of Political Societies   366
Chap. IX.   Of the Ends of Political Society and
Government   386
Chap. X.   Of the Forms of a Commonwealth   391
Chap. XI.   Of the Extent of the Legislative Power   392
Chap. XII.   Of the Legislative, Executive, and
Federative Power of the Commonwealth   401
Chap. XIII.   Of the Subordination of the Powers
of the Comonwealth   404
Chap. XIV.   Of Prerogative   412
Chap. XV.   Of Paternal, Political, and Despotical
Power, considered together   418
Chap. XVI.   Of conquest   422
Chap. XVII.   Of Usurpation   436
Chap. XVIII. Of Tyranny   437
Chap. XIX.   Of the Dissolution of Governments   445

The End of the Contents.

BOOK I.

CHAP. I.

The Introduction

§ 1. Slavery is so vile and miserable an Estate of Man, and so directly opposite to the generous Temper and Courage of our Nation; that 'tis hardly to be conceived, that an *Englishman,* much less a *Gentleman,* should plead for't. And truly, I should have taken Sr. Rt: Filmer's *Patriarcha* as any 5 other Treatise, which would perswade all Men, that they are Slaves, and ought to be so, for such another exercise of Wit, as was his who writ the Encomium of *Nero,* rather than for a serious Discourse meant in earnest, had not the Gravity of the Title and Epistle, the Picture in the 10 Front of the Book, and the Applause that followed it, required me to believe, that the Author and Publisher were both in earnest. I therefore took it into my hands with all the expectation, and read it through with all the attention due to a Treatise, that made such a noise at its 15 coming abroad, and cannot but confess my self mightily surprised, that in a Book, which was to provide Chains for all Mankind, I should find nothing but a Rope of Sand, useful perhaps to such, whose Skill and Business it is to raise a Dust, and would blind the People, the better to 20 mislead them, but in truth not of any force to draw those into Bondage, who have their Eyes open, and so much Sense about them as to consider, that Chains are but an ill wearing, how much Care soever hath been taken to file and polish them. 25

§ 1   8   'the Encomium of *Nero*', *Encomium Neronis* by Jerome Cardan, 1546. Locke owned Cardan's *Opera,* Leyden, 1663 (Appendix B, no. 19).
    10   The title of Filmer's book was *Patriarcha: or the Natural Power of Kings,* and was prefixed by an epistle from his friend Peter Heylyn, the Royalist Divine. Van Hove's engraved portrait of Charles II was the frontispiece, marking the connection of its publication with the Royal Court. Compare I, § 14, 5–6 and I, § 129, 1, and on Heylyn see Laslett, 1948, 1949: on the publication of *Patriarcha,* and Locke's personal copy, see Introduction, 33 and note.
    Locke is disingenuous in implying that this was his first encounter with Filmer's works, see Introduction, 71.

§ 2. If any one think I take too much liberty in speaking so freely of a Man, who is the great Champion of absolute Power, and the Idol of those who Worship it; I beseech him to make this small allowance for once, to one,
5 who, even after the reading of Sir *Robert*'s Book, cannot but think himself, as the Laws allow him, a Freeman: And I know no fault it is to do so, unless any one better skill'd in the Fate of it, than I, should have it revealed to him, that this Treatise, which has lain dormant so long, was,
10 when it appeared in the World, to carry by strength of its Arguments, all Liberty out of it; and that from thenceforth our Author's short Model was to be the Pattern in the Mount, and the perfect Standard of Politics for the future. His System lies in a little compass, 'tis no more but this,

15   *That all Government is absolute Monarchy.*

And the Ground he builds on, is this,

          That no Man is Born free.

3. In this last age a generation of men has sprung up among us, who would flatter princes with an Opinion, that they have a Divine Right to absolute Power, let the Laws by which they are constituted, and are to govern, and the
5 Conditions under which they enter upon their Authority, be what they will, and their Engagements to observe them never so well ratified by solemn Oaths and Promises. To make way for this doctrine they have denied Mankind a Right to natural Freedom, whereby they have
10 not only, as much as in them lies, exposed all Subjects to the utmost Misery of Tyranny and Oppression, but have also unsettled the Titles, and shaken the Thrones of Princes: (For they too, by these Mens systeme, except only one, are all born Slaves, and by Divine Right, are Subjects
15 to *Adam*'s right Heir); As if they had design'd to make War upon all Government, and subvert the very Foundations of Human Society, to serve their present turn.

---

§2 9 *Patriarcha* was written *c*. 1637–8, not published till 1680: see Introduction, 71, and Laslett, 1949.
   12–13 'Pattern in the Mount', Heb. viii. 5, itself a reference to God's Commandments on Sinai.
   14–17 Filmer's system, summarized by him on p. 229 of Laslett's edition.

4. However we must believe them upon their own bare Words, when they tell us, we are all born Slaves, and we must continue so; there is no remedy for it: Life and Thraldom we enter'd into together, and can never be quit of the one, till we part with the other. Scripture or Reason 5 I am sure doe not any where say so notwithstanding the noise of divine right, as if Divine Authority hath subjected us to the unlimited Will of another. An admirable State of Mankind, and that which they have not had Wit enough to find out till this latter Age. For however Sir *Robert* 10 *Filmer* seems to condemn the Novelty of the contrary Opinion, *Patr. p.* 3 [53]. yet I believe it will be hard for him to find any other Age or Country of the World, but this which has asserted Monarchy to be *Jure Divino*. And he confesses, *Patr. p.* 4 [54]. That *Heyward, Blackwood, Bar-* 15 *clay, and others, that have bravely vindicated the Right of Kings in most Points,* never thought of this, *but with one Consent admitted the Natural Liberty and Equality of Mankind.*

5. By whom this Doctrine came at first to be broach'd, and brought in fashion amongst us, and what sad Effects it gave rise to, I leave to *Historians* to relate, or to the Memory of those who were Contemporaries with *Sibthorp* and *Manwering* to recollect. My business at present is 5 only to consider what Sir *R. F.* who is allowed to have carried this Argument farthest, and is supposed to have brought it to perfection, has said in it; for from him every one, who would be as fashionable as *French* was at Court, has learned, and runs away with this short System of 10

§ 4 15–16 For these authors see *Patriarcha* (Laslett, 1949), p. 54, and compare I, § 67, 31–3, Barclay is quoted in II, §§ 232–3, 235–9: Locke listed in 1681 Barclay's *De Potestate Papae* and his *De Regno et Regali Potestate* (Appendix B, no. 11)—see note on II, § 232.
§ 5 1 Paragraph number omitted in 1st edition, both states.
4–5 Refers to the famous sermons exalting the Royal Prerogative preached and published in 1627 by Robert Sybthorpe (*Of Apostolique Obedience*) and Roger Manwaring (*Religion and Allegiance*), see Allen, 1938, 176–80. They are also named by Sidney in somewhat the same way: 1772, 5.
8–9 Compare Preface 48–9 (added in 1698): Sir Robert Filmer's brother Edward was at the Court of Charles I and a francophile, a friend of Henrietta Maria's, and his son Edward was Gentleman of the Privy Chamber to Charles I and Charles II (see Laslett, 1948 [ii]), but he himself was never a courtier. In this sentence 'was' seems to have been changed from 'is' in 1689.

Politics, *viz. Men are not born free,* and *therefore could
never have the liberty to choose either Governors, or Forms
of Government. Princes have their Power Absolute, and
by Divine Right, for Slaves could never have a Right to*
15 *Compact or Consent. Adam was an absolute Monarch,
and so are all Princes ever since.*

CHAP. II.

Of Paternal and Regal Power.

6. Sir R. F.'s great Position is, that *Men are not naturally
free.* This is the Foundation on which his absolute
Monarchy stands, and from which it erects it self to an
height, that its Power is above every Power, *Caput inter
5 nubila,* so high above all Earthly and Human Things, that
Thought can scarce reach it; that Promises and Oaths,
which tye the infinite Deity, cannot confine it. But if this
Foundation fails, all his Fabric falls with it, and Governments must be left again to the old way of being made by
10 contrivance, and the consent of Men ('Ανθρωπίνη κτίσις)
making use of their Reason to unite together into Society.
To prove this grand Position of his, he tells us, *p.* 12 [57].
Men are born in subjection to their Parents, and therefore
cannot be free. And this Authority of Parents, he calls
15 *Royal Authority, p.* 12, 14 [57, 58]. *Fatherly Authority,
Right of Fatherhood, p.* 12, 20 [57, 61]. One would have
thought he would in the beginning of such a Work
as this, on which was to depend the Authority of Princes,
and the Obedience of Subjects, have told us expressly
20 what that Fatherly Authority is, have defined it, though

---

§ 6   4–5   *Caput inter nubila*—head in the clouds.
  7   Compare II, § 195, 7–8.
  8–11   I Peter ii. 13, 'submit yourselves to every ordinance of men'
(ἀνθρωπίνῃ κτίσει). Compare the second *Letter on Toleration* (1765 ed.
106).
  12–27   Implying that Locke had dealt with the 'Other Treatises' when
he decided to analyze *Patriarcha,* see above, p. 72, note 34 and references.

not limited it, because in some other Treatises of his he
tells us, 'tis Unlimited, and Unlimitable; * he should
at least have given us such an account of it, that we might
have had an entire Notion of this *Fatherhood*, or *Fatherly
Authority*, whenever it came in our way in his Writings. 25
This I expected to have found in the first Chapter of his
Patriarcha. But instead thereof, having, 1. *En Passant*,
Made his Obeysance to the *Arcana Imperii*, p. 5 [54]. 2.
Made his Compliment to the *Rights and Liberties of this,
or any other Nation*, p. 6. [55] which he is going presently 30
to null and destroy; And, 3. Made his Leg to those Learned
Men, who did not see so far into the Matter as himself,
p. 7 [55]. He comes to fall on *Bellarmine*, p. 8. [56] and,
by a Victory over him, Establishes his *Fatherly Authority*
beyond any question. *Bellarmine* being routed by his 35
own Confession, *p*. 11. [57] the day is clear got, and there
is no more need of any Forces: For having done that, I
observe not that he states the Question, or rallies up any
Arguments to make good his Opinion, but rather tells us
the Story, as he thinks fit, of this strange kind of domineer- 40
ing Phantom, called the *Fatherhood*, which whoever could
catch, presently got Empire, and unlimited absolute Power.
He assures us how this *Fatherhood* began in *Adam*, continued its course, and kept the World in order all the time
of the *Patriarchs* till the Flood, got out of the Ark with 45
Noah and his Sons, made and supported all the Kings of
the Earth till the Captivity of the *Israelites* in *Egypt*, and
then the poor *Fatherhood* was under hatches, till *God by
giving the Israelites Kings, Re-established the ancient and
prime Right of the Lineal Succession in Paternal Govern-* 50
ment. This is his business from *p*. 12 to 19 [57–60]. And
then obviating an Objection, and clearing a Difficulty or
two with one half Reason, *p*. 23. [62] *to confirm the Natural Right of Regal Power*, he ends the first Chapter. I

* *In Grants and Gifts that have their Original from God or Nature, as
the Power of the Father hath, no inferior Power of Man can limit, nor
make any Law of Prescription against them*, O. 158 [233].
The *Scripture teaches, that supreme Power was Originally in the
Father without any Limitation*, O. 245 [234].

33 Bellarmine. Filmer directed much of his argument against Cardinal Bellarmine's subordinating secular power to the papacy in his *De
Potestate Summi Pontifici*, 1610—see Laslett, 1949; McIlwain, 1918.
48–51 Not a quotation, but a summary of *Patriarcha*, 57–8.
54 'first Chapter', i.e. paragraphs i–viii of *Patriarcha* in Laslett's edition, where there are no chapters since it reproduces Filmer's manuscript
which lacks them.

55 hope 'tis no Injury to call an half Quotation an half Reason, for God says, *Honour thy Father and Mother;* but
our Author contents himself with half, leaves out *thy
Mother* quite, as little serviceable to his purpose. But of that
more in another place.

7.   I do not think our Author so little skill'd in the way
of writing Discourses of this nature, nor so careless of the
Point in hand, that he by oversight commits the fault that
he himself, in his *Anarchy of a mix'd Monarchy,* p. 239.
5 [280] objects to Mr *Hunton* in these words: *Where first I
charge the A. that he hath not given us any Definition, or
Description of Monarchy in general; for by the Rules of
Method, he should have first defin'd.* And by the like Rule
of Method Sir *Robert* should have told us, what his *Father-
10 hood* or *Fatherly Authority* is, before he had told us, in
whom it was to be found, and talked so much of it. But
perhaps Sir *Robert* found, that this *Fatherly Authority,*
this Power of Fathers, and of Kings, for he makes them
both the same, *p. 24.* [63] would make a very odd and
15 frightful Figure, and very disagreeing, with what either
Children imagine of their Parents, or Subjects of their
Kings, if he should have given us the whole Draught together in that Gigantic Form, he had painted it in his own
Phancy: and therefore like a wary Physician, when he
20 would have his Patient swallow some harsh or *Corrosive
Liquor,* he mingles it with a large quantity of that, which
may dilute it; that the scatter'd Parts may go down with
less feeling, and cause less Aversion.

8.   Let us then endeavour to find what account he gives
us of this *Fatherly Authority,* as it lies scatter'd in the
several Parts of his Writings. And first, as it was vested in
Adam, he says, *Not only* Adam, *but the succeeding Patri-
5 archs, had by Right of Fatherhood Royal Authority over
their Children,* p. 12 [57]. *This Lordship which* Adam *by
Command had over the whole World, and by Right descending from him the Patriarchs did enjoy, was as large*

59   'in another place'; see I, § 11, 35 note and references.
§ 7   4   Filmer's *Observations upon Mr Hunton's Treatise of Monarchy,
or, the Anarchy of a Limited or Mixed Monarchy* (Laslett, 1949, 277–
313). On Hunton's *Treatise of Monarchie* (1643) and Locke, see note
on II, § 168, 1–2.
19–21   This has the professional touch of Locke the physician.

and ample as the Absolute Dominion of any Monarch which hath been since the Creation, p. 13 [58]. *Dominion* 10 *of Life and Death, making War, and concluding Peace*, p. 13 [58]. Adam *and the Patriarchs had absolute Power of Life and Death*, p. 35 [76]. *Kings, in the Right of Parents, succeed to the Exercise of Supreme Jurisdiction*, p. 19 [61]. *As Kingly Power is by the Law of God, so it hath* 15 *no Inferior Law to Limit it,* Adam *was Lord of all*, p. 40 [78]. *The Father of a Family governs by no other Law, than by his own Will*, p. 78 [96]. *The Superiority of Princes is above Laws*, p. 79 [96]. *The unlimited Jurisdiction of Kings is so amply described by* Samuel, p. 80 [96]. *Kings* 20 *are above the Laws*, p. 93 [103]. And to this purpose, see a great deal more which our A——— delivers in *Bodin's* words: *It is certain, that all Laws, Priviledges, and Grants of Princes, have no Force, but during their Life; if they be not ratified by the express Consent, or by Sufferance of* 25 *the Prince following, especially Priviledges,* O. p. 279 [304]. *The reason why Laws have been also made by Kings, was this; When Kings were either busied with Wars, or distracted with public Cares, so that every private Man could not have Access to their Persons, to learn their Wills* 30 *and Pleasure, then were Laws of Necessity invented, that so every particular Subject might find his prince's Pleasure decypher'd unto him in the Tables of his Laws*, p. 92 [102]. *In a Monarchy, the King must by necessity be above the Laws*, p. 100 [105]. *A perfect Kingdom is that, wherein* 35 *the King rules all things according to his own Will*, p. 106 [105]. *Neither Common nor Statute Laws are, or can be, any Diminution of that General Power, which Kings have over their People by right of Fatherhood*, p. 115 [113]. Adam *was the Father, King, and Lord over his Family; a* 40 *Son, a Subject, and a Servant or Slave, were one and the same thing at first. The Father had Power to dispose or sell his Children or Servants; whence we find, that at the first reckoning up of Goods in Scripture, the Man-servant, and the Maid-servant, are numbred among the Possessions* 45

---

§ 8   9   'Absolute', 'absolutest' in original; these quotations are mainly accurate, though two passages are conflated.

    22–6   Filmer's works are studded with quotations from Bodin's *République*. Locke does not seem to have possessed any of Bodin's works, though he shows acquaintance with him—see Appendix B, no. 15 and compare note on I, § 56, 3.

    37–9   Locke's only citation of a passage from Filmer having to do with the constitution, see Introduction 89.

and Substance of the Owner, as other Goods were, O. Præf. [188]. *God also hath given to the Father a Right or Liberty, to alien his Power over his Children to any other; whence we find the Sale and Gift of Children to have been* 50 *much in use in the Beginning of the World, when Men had their Servants for a Possession and an Inheritance, as well as other Goods, whereupon we find the Power of Castrating and making Eunuchs much in use in Old Times,* O. p. 155 [231]. *Law is nothing else but the Will of him that hath* 55 *the Power of the Supream Father,* O. p. 223 [72]. *It was God's Ordinance that the Supremacy should be unlimited in* Adam, *and as large as all the Acts of his Will; and as in him, so in all others that have Supream Power,* O. p. 245 [284].

9.   I have been fain to trouble my Reader with these several Quotations in our A——'s own Words, that in them might be seen his own Description of his *Fatherly Authority,* as it lies scatter'd up and down in his Writings, 5 which he supposes was first vested in *Adam,* and by Right belongs to all Princes ever since. This *Fatherly Authority* then, or *Right of Fatherhood,* in our A——'s sence is a Divine unalterable Right of Sovereignty, whereby a Father or a Prince hath an Absolute, Arbitrary, Unlimited, and 10 Unlimitable Power, over the Lives, Liberties, and Estates of his Children and Subjects; so that he may take or alienate their Estates, sell, castrate, or use their Persons as he pleases, they being all his Slaves, and he Lord or Proprietor of every Thing, and his unbounded Will their Law.

10.   Our A—— having placed such a mighty Power in *Adam,* and upon that supposition, founded all Government, and all Power of Princes, it is reasonable to expect, that he should have proved this with Arguments clear and evi- 5 dent, suitable to the weightiness of the Cause. That since Men had nothing else left them, they might in Slavery have such undeniable Proofs of its Necessity, that their Consciences might be convinced, and oblige them to submit peaceably to that Absolute Dominion, which their Gov- 10 ernors had a Right to exercise over them. Without this, What Good could our A—— do, or pretend to do, by erecting such an unlimited Power, but flatter the Natural

47   'Praef.'—Indicates the Preface to Filmer's 'Forms'.

Vanity and Ambition of Men, too apt of it self to grow and
encrease with the Possession of any Power? And by perswading those, who, by the consent of their Fellow-Men, 15
are advanced to great, but limited degrees of it, that by that
part which is given them, they have a Right to all, that was
not so; and therefore may do what they please, because
they have Authority to do more then others, and so tempt
them to do what is neither for their own, nor the good of 20
those under their Care, whereby great Mischiefs cannot
but follow.

11. The Sovereignty of *Adam,* being that on which, as
a sure Basis, our A—— builds his mighty Absolute Monarchy, I expected, that, in his *Patriarcha,* this his main
Supposition would have been proved and established with
all that Evidence of Arguments, that such a Fundamental 5
Tenet required; and that this, on which the great stress of
the Business depends, would have been made out with Reasons sufficient to justifie the Confidence with which it was
assumed. But in all that Treatise, I could find very little
tending that way; the Thing is there so taken for granted 10
without Proof, that I could scarce believe my self, when
upon attentive reading that Treatise, I found there so
mighty a Structure rais'd upon the bare supposition of this
Foundation. For it is scarce credible, that in a Discourse
where he pretends to confute the *Erroneous Principle* of 15
Man's *Natural Freedom,* he should doe it by a bare supposition of *Adam's Authority,* without offering any Proof
for that Authority. Indeed he confidently says, that *Adam
had Royal Authority.* p. 12 [56], and 13 [57]. *Absolute
Lordship and Dominion of Life and Death,* p. 13 [58]. *An* 20
Universal Monarchy, p. 33 [75]. *Absolute Power of Life
and Death,* p. 35 [76]. He is very frequent in such Assertions, but what is strange in all his whole *Patriarcha,* I find
not one Pretence of a Reason to establish this his great
Foundation of Government; not any thing that looks like 25
an Argument, but these words: *To confirm this Natural
Right of Regal Power, we find in the Decalogue, that the
Law which injoyns Obedience to Kings, is delivered in the
Terms, Honour thy Father, as if all Power were Originally*

§ 11 3 etc. References to *Patriarcha*—see Introduction, 72–4. Locke
had found that Filmer did not demonstrate the sovereignty of Adam in
his tracts, discussed in the *Second Treatise,* and he now finds that
Patriarcha evades the issue.

30 *in the Father* [62]. And why may I not add as well, That
in the *Decalogue*, the Law that enjoyns Obedience to
Queens, is delivered in the Terms of *Honour thy Mother*,
as if all Power were originally in the Mother? The Argument, as Sir *Robert* puts it, will hold as well for one as
35 t'other. But of this, more in its due place.

12. All that I take notice of here, is, that this is all
our A—— says in this first, or any of the following Chapters, to prove the *Absolute Power of Adam*, which is his
great Principle; and yet, as if he had there settled it upon
5 sure Demonstration, he begins his *2d* Chapter with these
words, *By conferring these Proofs and Reasons, drawn
from the Authority of the Scripture* [63]. Where those
Proofs and Reasons for *Adam*'s Sovereignty are, bating
that of *Honour thy Father* above mentioned, I confess, I
10 cannot find, unless what he says, p. 11 [57]. *In these words
we have an evident Confession, viz. of Bellarmine, that
Creation made Man Prince of his Posterity,* must be taken
for Proofs and Reasons drawn from Scripture, or for any
sort of Proof at all: though from thence by a new way of
15 inference in the Words, immediately following, he concludes *the Royal Authority of Adam,* sufficiently settled
in him.

13. If he has in that Chapter, or any where in the
whole Treatise, given any other Proofs of *Adam's Royal
Authority,* other than by often repeating it, which, among
some Men, goes for Argument, I desire any body for him
5 to shew me the Place and Page, that I may be convinced
of my mistake, and acknowledge my oversight. If no such
Arguments are to be found, I beseech those Men, who have
so much cryed up this Book, to consider whether they do
not give the World cause to suspect, that it's not the Force
10 of Reason and Argument, that makes them for Absolute
Monarchy, but some other by Interest, and therefore are
resolved to applaud any Author, that writes in favour of
this Doctrine, whether he support it with Reason or no.
But I hope they do not expect that rational and indifferent
15 Men should be brought over to their Opinion, because this
their great Dr. of it, in a Discourse made on purpose, to

35 'in its due place'—compare I, § 6, 59: see I, § 60 on, § 52, 10–17
and II, § 64 on.
§ 12 2–3, 5 'Chapters', '2d Chapter'—see note on I, § 6, 54.

set up the *Absolute Monarchical Power of Adam,* in opposition to the *Natural Freedom* of Mankind, has said so little to prove it, from whence it is rather naturally to be concluded, that there is little to be said. 20

14. But, that I might omit no care to inform my self in our A——'s full Sense, I consulted his *Observations on Aristotle, Hobs, &c.* to see whether in disputing with others he made use of any Arguments, for this his darling Tenet of *Adam's Sovereignty,* since in his Treatise of the *Natural* 5 *Power of Kings,* he hath been so sparing of them. In his Observations on Mr. *Hob's Leviathan,* I think he has put, in short, all those Arguments for it together, which in his Writings I find him any where to make use of; his Words are these. *If God Created only* Adam, *and of a piece of* 10 *him made the Woman, and if by Generation from them two, as parts of them all Mankind be propagated: If also God gave to* Adam *not only the Dominion over the Woman and the Children that should Issue from them, but also over the whole Earth to subdue it, and over all the Crea-* 15 *tures on it, so that as long as* Adam *lived, no Man could claim or enjoy any thing but by Donation, Assignation, or Permission from him, I wonder,* &c. O. 165 [241]. Here we have the Sum of all his Arguments, for *Adam's Sovereignty,* and against *Natural Freedom,* which I find up and 20 down in his other Treatises; and they are these following; *God's Creation* of *Adam,* the *Dominion* he gave him *over Eve:* And the *Dominion* he had as *Father over his Children,* all which I shall particularly consider.

§ 14 2–3 'Observations . . .'—a collective reference to Filmer's works other than *Patriarcha* and the *Freeholder;* that is, Laslett's edition, 185–326. This phrase might be used against the view of the purpose and order of writing of the *Two Treatises* adopted here; compare note on I, § 11, 3 and reference.
5–6 'Natural Power of Kings'—sub-title of *Patriarcha.*
22–4 Locke deals with these three points in chapters 3, 5 and 6 of this treatise.

Of Adam's *Title to Sovereignty by Creation.*

15 Sir *Robert* in his Preface to his Observations on *Aristotle's* Politicks, tells us, *A Natural Freedom of Mankind cannot be supposed without the denial of the Creation of* Adam [188]: But how *Adam's* being Created, which was
5 nothing but his receiving a Being immediately from Omnipotency, and the hand of God, gave *Adam* a *Sovereignty* over any thing, I cannot see, nor consequently understand, how a *Supposition of Natural Freedom is a denial of* Adam's *Creation,* and would be glad any body else (since
10 our A—— did not vouchsafe us the favour) would make it out for him. For I find no difficulty to suppose the *Freedom of Mankind,* though I have always believed the *Creation of Adam;* He was Created, or began to exist, by God's immediate Power, without the Intervention of Parents or
15 the pre-existence of any of the same Species to beget him, when it pleased God he should; and so did the Lion, the Kings of Beasts before him, by the same Creating Power of God: and if bare existence by that Power, and in that way, will give Dominion, without any more ado, our
20 A——, by this Argument, will make the Lion have as good a Title to it as he, and certainly the Ancienter. No! for *Adam* had his Title *by the Appointment of God,* says our A—— in another place [289]. Then bare *Creation* gave him not Dominion, and one might have *supposed Mankind*
25 *Free* without *denying the Creation of Adam* since 'twas God's *Appointment* made him Monarch.

16. But let us see, how he puts his *Creation* and this *Appointment* together. *By the Appointment of God,* says Sir *Robert, as soon as* Adam *was Created he was Monarch of the World, though he had no Subjects, for though there*
5 *could not be actual Government till there were Subjects, yet by the Right of Nature it was due to* Adam *to be Governor of his Posterity: though not in act, yet at least in habit,* Adam *was a King from his Creation* [289]. I wish he had told us here what he meant *by God's Appointment.*
10 For whatsoever Providence orders, or the Law of Nature

directs, or positive Revelation declares, may be said to be
by God's Appointment, but I suppose it cannot be meant
here in the first Sense, *i.e.* by Providence; because that
would be to say no more, but that *as soon as Adam was
Created* he was *de facto* Monarch, because *by Right of* 15
Nature it was due to Adam, *to be Governor of his Posterity.* But he could not *de facto* be by Providence Constituted
the Governor of the World at a time, when there was
actually no Government, no Subjects to be governed, which
our *A——* here confesses. *Monarch of the world* is also 20
differently used by our Author, for sometimes he means
by it a Proprietor of all the World exclusive of the rest of
Mankind, and thus he does in the same page of his Preface before cited, *Adam*, says he, *being Commanded to
Multiply and People the Earth and to subdue it, and hav-* 25
*ing Dominion given him over all Creatures, was thereby
the Monarch of the whole World, none of his Posterity had
any Right to possess any thing but by his Grant or Permission, or by Succession from him* [187–8].

2. Let us understand then by *Monarch* Proprietor *of* 30
the World, and by *Appointment* God's actual Donation,
and revealed positive Grant made to *Adam*, 1 Gen. 28. as
we see Sir *Robert* himself does in this parallel place, and
then his Argument will stand thus, *by the positive Grant
of God; As soon as* Adam was *Created, he was Proprietor* 35
*of the World, because by the Right of Nature it was due
to Adam to be Governor of his Posterity.* In which way
of arguing there are two manifest Falshoods. *First*, It is
false that God made that Grant to *Adam*, as soon as he
was Created, since though it stands in the Text immediately 40
after his Creation, yet it is plain it could not be spoken to
Adam till after *Eve* was made and brought to him, and
how then could he be *Monarch by Appointment as soon
as Created*, especially since he calls, if I mistake not, that
which God says to *Eve*, 3 *Gen.* 16: *The original Grant of* 45
Government, which not being till after the Fall, when
Adam was somewhat, at least in time, and very much, distant in condition from his *Creation*, I cannot see, how our

§ 16   30   '2.'—presumably indicates the second part of the argument
of this paragraph, although there is no '1.'
    40–2   Compare I, § 29, 13–15. Tyrrell makes exactly this point in
Patriarcha non Monarcha, 1681, 101 (second pagination).
    44   'if I mistake not'—Hunton, not Filmer, used this text for this pur-
pose, though the phrase quoted in lines 45–6 occurs on p. 283 of Filmer.

A—— can say in this Sense, that *by God's Appointment,*
50 *as soon as* Adam *was Created he was Monarch of the*
World. Secondly, Were it true that God's actual Donation
appointed Adam *Monarch of the World as soon as he was*
Created, yet the Reason here given for it would not prove
it, but it would always be a false Inference, that God, by
55 a positive Donation *appointed* Adam *Monarch of the*
World, because by Right of Nature it was due to Adam
to be Governor of his Posterity: for having given him the
Right of Government by Nature, there was no need of a
positive Donation, at least it will never be a proof of such
60 a Donation.

17. On the other side the Matter will not be much
mended, if we understand by *God's appointment* the Law
of Nature, (though it be a pretty harsh Expression for it
in this place) and by *Monarch of the World,* Sovereign
5 Ruler of Mankind; for then the Sentence under Consideration must run thus: *By the Law of Nature, as soon as*
Adam *was Created he was Governor of Mankind, for by*
Right of Nature it was due to Adam *to be Governor of*
his Posterity, which amounts to this, He was *Governor by*
10 *Right of Nature,* because he was *Governor by Right of*
Nature. But supposing we should grant, that a Man is *by*
Nature Governor of his Children, *Adam* could not hereby
be Monarch as soon as Created; for this Right of Nature
being founded in his being their Father, how *Adam* could
15 have a *Natural Right* to be *Governor* before he was a
Father, when by being a father only he had that *Right,* is,
methinks, hard to conceive, unless he will have him to be
a Father before he was a Father, and to have a Title before he had it.

18. To this foreseen Objection, our A—— answers
very Logically, *He was Governor in Habit, and not in Act:*
A very pretty way of being a Governour without Government, a Father without Children, and a King without Sub-
5 jects. And thus Sir *Robert* was an Author before he writ
his Book, not *in Act* 'tis true, but *in Habit,* for when he
had once Publish'd it, it was due to him *by the Right of*
Nature, to be an Author, as much as it was *to Adam to*
be Governor of his Children when he had begot them;
10 And if to be such a *Monarch of the World,* an absolute
Monarch *in Habit, but not in Act,* will serve the turn, I

should not much envy it to any of Sir *Robert*'s Friends
that he thought fit graciously to bestow it upon, tho' even
this of *Act* and *Habit*, if it signified any thing but our
A——'s skill in distinctions, be not to his purpose in this 15
place. For the Question is not here about *Adam*'s actual
Exercise of Government, but actually having a Title to be
Governor: Government, says our A——, was *due to*
Adam *by the Right of Nature*. What is this Right of Nature? A Right Fathers have over their Children by beget- 20
ting them; *Generatione jus acquiritur parentibus in liberos,*
says our A—— out of *Grotius,* O. 223 [71]. The Right
then follows the begetting as arising from it, so that according to this way of reasoning or distinguishing of our
A——, *Adam,* as soon as he was Created, had a Title 25
only in Habit, and not in Act, which in plain *English* is,
He had actually no Title at all.

19.   To speak less Learnedly, and more Intelligibly, one
may say of *Adam,* he was in a possibility of being *Governor,* since it was possible he might beget Children, and
thereby acquire that Right of Nature, be it what it will,
to Govern them, that accrues from thence, but what Con-   5
nection has this with *Adam's Creation,* to make him say,
That *as soon as he was Created, he was Monarch of the
World?* For it may be as well said of *Noah,* that as soon as
he was born, he was Monarch of the World, since he was
in possibility (which in our A——'s Sense is enough to 10
make a Monarch, *a Monarch in Habit,*) to outlive all
Mankind but his own Posterity. What such necessary Connection there is betwixt *Adam's Creation* and his *Right to
Government,* so that a *Natural Freedom of Mankind cannot be supposed without the denial of the Creation of* 15
Adam, I confess for my part I do not see; Nor how those
words, *by the Appointment, &c.* O. 254. [289] how ever
explain'd, can be put together to make any tolerable Sense,
at least to establish this Position, with which they end, *viz.
Adam was a King from his Creation;* A King, says our 20
A——, *not in Act, but in Habit, i.e.* actually no King at all.

§§ 18–20 These paragraphs are typical of the least attractive features of
Locke on Filmer: he has the grace to apologize. Some parts of this
passage, especially in paragraph 20, are reminiscent of the *Preface,* and
may have been written in 1689. In the 1st edition § 19 is almost incomprehensible because of errors in the printing, corrected by Locke in his
copy—see Collation.

20. I fear I have tired my Reader's Patience, by dwelling longer on this Passage than the weightiness of any Argument in it, seems to require: but I have unavoidably been engaged in it by our A——'s way of writing, who
5 hudling several Suppositions together, and that in doubtful and general terms makes such a medly and confusion, that it is impossible to shew his Mistakes, without examining the several Senses, wherein his Words may be taken, and without seeing how, in any of these various Meanings, they
10 will consist together, and have any Truth in them; for in this present Passage before us, how can any one argue against this Position of his, that *Adam was a King from his Creation,* unless one examine, whether the Words, *from his Creation,* be to be taken, as they may, for the time of the
15 Commencement of his Government, as the foregoing words import, *as soon as he was Created he was Monarch,* or, for the cause of it, as he says, p. 11 [57]. *Creation made Man Prince of his Posterity?* How farther can one judge of the truth of his being thus King, till one has examined
20 whether King be to be taken, as the words in the beginning of this Passage would perswade, on supposition of his *Private Dominion,* which was by God's positive Grant, *Monarch of the World by Appointment;* or *King* on supposition of his *Fatherly Power* over his Off-spring which
25 was by Nature, *due by the Right of Nature,* whether, I say, King be to be taken in both, or one only of these two Senses, or in neither of them, but only this, that Creation made him Prince, in a way different from both the other? For though this assertion, that *Adam was King from his*
30 *Creation,* be true in no Sense, yet it stands here as an evident Conclusion drawn from the preceding words, though in truth it be but a bare assertion joyn'd to other assertions of the same kind, which confidently put together in words of undetermined and dubious meaning, look like a sort of
35 arguing, when there is indeed neither Proof nor Connection: A way very familiar with our A——, of which having given the Reader a taste here, I shall, as much as the Argument will permit me, avoid touching on hereafter, and should not have done it here, were it not to let the
40 World see, how Incoherencies in Matter, and Suppositions without Proofs put handsomly together in good Words and a plausible Style, are apt to pass for strong Reason and good Sense, till they come to be look'd into with Attention.

Of Adam's *Title to Sovereignty by Donation*, Gen. 1. 28.

21.   Having at last got through the foregoing Passage, where we have been so long detain'd, not by the Force of Arguments and Opposition, but the Intricacy of the Words, and the Doubtfulness of the Meaning; Let us go on to his next Argument, for *Adam*'s Sovereignty. Our A——— tells   5 us in the Words of Mr. *Selden,* that *Adam by Donation from God,* Gen. 1. 28. *was made the General Lord of all Things, not without such a private Dominion to himself, as without his Grant did exclude his Children. This Deter-mination of Mr.* Selden, says our A———, *is consonant to*   10 *the History of the Bible, and natural Reason,* O. 210 [63, 64]. And in his Pref. to his Obs: on *Arist.* he says thus; *The first Government in the World was Monarchical in the Father of all Flesh,* Adam *being commanded to Multiply and People the Earth, and to subdue it, and having Do-*   15 *minion given him over all Creatures, was thereby the Mon-arch of the whole World, none of his Posterity had any Right to possess any thing, but by his Grant or Permission, or by Succession from him; The Earth, saith the Psalmist, hath he given to the Children of Men, which shews the*   20 *Title comes from Fatherhood* [187, 188].

22.   Before I examine this Argument, and the Text on which it is founded, it is necessary to desire the Reader to observe, that our A———, according to his usual Method, begins in one Sense, and concludes in another; he begins here with *Adam*'s propriety, or *Private Dominion, by Do-*   5 *nation;* and his conclusion is, *which shews the Title comes from Fatherhood.*

23.   But let us see the Argument. The words of the Text are these; *And God Blessed them, and God said unto them, be Fruitful and Multiply and Replenish the Earth and sub-due it, and have Dominion over the Fish of the Sea, and over the Fowl of the Air, and over every living thing that*   5 *moveth upon the Earth,* 1 Gen. 28. From whence our

§ 21   6 'Selden'—on Filmer and Selden see Laslett, 1949. Filmer's quotations come from *Mare Clausum,* translated by M. Nedham, 1635, not owned by Locke, though he had several of the others—see, for example, Appendix B, no. 74.

A—— concludes, *that Adam, having here Dominion given
him over all Creatures, was thereby the Monarch of the
whole World*. Whereby must be meant, that either this
10 Grant of God gave *Adam* Property, or as our A—— calls
it, *Private Dominion* over the Earth, and all inferior or
irrational Creatures, and so consequently that he was
thereby *Monarch;* or 2°, that it gave him Rule and Dominion over all Earthly Creatures whatsoever, and thereby
15 over his Children, and so he was *Monarch:* for, as Mr.
Selden has properly worded it, *Adam was made General
Lord of all Things,* one may very clearly understand him,
that he means nothing to be granted to *Adam* here but
Property, and therefore he says not one word of *Adam's*
20 *Monarchy*. But our A—— says, *Adam was hereby Monarch of the World,* which properly speaking, signifies Sovereign Ruler of all the Men in the World, and so *Adam,*
by this Grant, must be constituted such a Ruler. If our
A—— means otherwise, he might, with much more clear-
25 ness have said, that *Adam was hereby Proprietor of the
whole World*. But he begs your Pardon in that point, clear
distinct Speaking not serving every where to his purpose,
you must not expect it in him, as in Mr. *Selden,* or other
such Writers.

24. In opposition therefore to our A——'s Doctrine,
that *Adam was Monarch of the whole World,* founded on
this Place, I shall shew.

1°. That by this Grant, 1 *Gen.* 28. God gave no im-
5 mediate Power to *Adam* over Men, over his Children, over
those of his own Species, and so he was not made Ruler,
or *Monarch* by this Charter.

2°. That by this Grant God gave him not *Private Dominion* over the Inferior Creatures, but right in common
10 with all Mankind; so neither was he *Monarch,* upon the
account of the Property here given him.

§ **23** 15–16 For Selden's wording, see *Mare Clausum,* translated by
Nedham, 1635, 20: Locke does not seem to have gone back to the
original. Tyrrell uses very similar arguments against Filmer, 1681, 98–
116 (second pagination).
26–9 The clearest connection of this polemic against Filmer with
Locke's philosophical writing is this insistence on fixed definitions and
distinct terms. Compare the *Essay,* III, ix, 10 (1894, II, 110), referring
to writers of their own opinions: 'if they do not use their words with
a due clearness and perspicuity, we may lay them aside, and without any
injury done them, resolve thus with ourselves, *Si non vis intelligi, debes
negligi*.' Compare I, § 108, I, § 109, II, § 52.

25. 1. That this Donation, 1 *Gen.* 28. gave *Adam* no power over Men, will appear if we consider the words of it. For since all Positive Grants convey no more than the express words they are made in will carry, let us see which of them here will comprehend Mankind, or *Adam*'s Poster-   5
ity; and those, I imagin, if any, must be these, *every living thing that moveth*, the words in *Hebrew* are, חיה הרמשת
i.e. Bestiam Reptantem, of which words the Scripture it self is the best interpreter. God having Created the Fishes and Fowles the 5*th* day, the beginning of the 6*th*, he 10
creates the Irrational Inhabitants of the dry Land, which, *v.* 24. are described in these words, *let the Earth bring forth the living Creature after his kind; Cattle and creep-ing things, and beasts of the Earth, after his kind, and* v. 2 *and God made the Beasts of the Earth after his kind,* 15
and Cattle after their kind, and every thing that creepeth on the Earth after his kind; Here in the Creation of the brute Inhabitants of the Earth, he first speaks of them all under one General Name, of *Living Creatures*, and then afterwards divides them into three ranks, 1. *Cattle*, or such 20
Creatures as were or might be tame, and so be the Private possession of Particular Men; 2. חיה which *ver.* 24 and 25 in our Bible, is Translated Beasts, and by the *Septuagint* θηρία, *Wild beasts*, and is the same word, that here in our Text, *ver.* 28. where we have this great Charter to *Adam*, 25
is Translated *Living thing*, and is also the same Word used, *Gen.* 9. 2. where this Grant is renewed to *Noah*, and there likewise Translated *Beast*, 3. The third Rank were the Creeping Animals, which *ver.* 24 and 25 are comprised under the word, הרמשת, the same that is used here *ver.* 30
28. and is Translated *moving*, but in the former Verses *Creeping*, and by the *Septuagint* in all these places, ἑρπετὰ, or Reptils; from whence it appears that the words which we Translate here in God's Donation, *ver.* 28. *Living Crea-tures moving*, are the same which in the History of the 35
Creation, *ver.* 24, 25. signify two Ranks of terrestrial Crea-tures, *viz. Wild Beasts* and *Reptils,* and are so understood by the *Septuagint.*

---

§ 25 Mr D. W. Thomas, Regius Professor of Hebrew in the University of Cambridge, states that Locke's Hebrew as displayed here and in paragraphs 26 and 27 is adequate to his purpose. But it adds very little to the argument. It is printed correctly in the 1st edition only. For a detailed examination, see Pareyson's Italian critical edition, 1948.
  1 '1'—the '2' is on line 1 of paragraph 29.

26. When God had made the Irrational Animals of the World, divided into three kinds, from the places of their Habitation, *viz. Fishes of the Sea, Fowls of the Air,* and *Living Creatures of the Earth,* and these again into Cattle, Wild Beasts, and Reptils, he considers of making Man, and the Dominion he should have over the Terrestrial World, *ver.* 26. and then he reckons up the Inhabitants of these three Kingdoms, but in the Terrestrial, leaves out the second Rank חיה, or wild Beasts: But here, *ver.* 28. where he actually executes this design, and gives him this Dominion, the Text mentions *the Fishes of the Sea, and Fowls of the Air,* and the *Terrestrial Creatures* in the words, that signifie the *Wild Beasts* and *Reptils,* though Translated *Living thing that moveth,* leaving out Cattle. In both which places, though the Word that signifies *Wild Beasts* be omitted in one, and that which signifies *Cattle* in the other, yet, since God certainly executed in one place, what he declares he designed in the other, we cannot but understand the same in both places, and have here only an account, how the Terrestrial irrational Animals, which were already created and reckon'd up at their Creation, in three distinct Ranks *of Cattle, Wild Beasts,* and *Reptils* were here, *ver.* 28. actually put under the Dominion of Man, as they were designed *ver.* 26. nor do these words contain in them the least appearance of any thing, that can be wrested, to signifie God's giving to one Man Dominion over another, *Adam* over his Posterity.

27. And this further appears from *Gen.* 9. 2. where God renewing this Charter to *Noah* and his Sons, he gives them Dominion over *the Fowls of the Air,* and *the Fishes of the Sea,* and *the Terrestrial Creatures,* expressed by חיה and הרמש Wild Beasts and Reptils, the same words that in the Text before us 1 *Gen.* 28. are Translated *every moving thing, that moveth upon the Earth,* which by no means can comprehend Man, the Grant being made to *Noah* and his Sons, all the Men then living, and not to one part of Men over another: Which is yet more evident from the very next words *ver.* 3. where God gives every רמש, *every moving thing,* the very words used *Ch.* 1. 28. to them for Food. By all which it is plain, that God's Donation to *Adam, Ch.* 1. 28. and his designation, *v.* 26. and his Grant again to *Noah* and his Sons, refer to, and contain in them, neither more nor less, than the Works of the

Creation the 5th day, and the Begininng of the 6th, as they
are set down from the 20th, to the 26th ver. inclusively
of the 1st Chap. and so comprehend all the Species of irrational Animals of the *Terraqueous Globe,* though all the 20
words whereby they are expressed in the History of their
Creation, are no where used in any of the following Grants,
but some of them omitted in one, and some in another.
From whence I think it is past all doubt, that Man cannot
be comprehended in this Grant, nor any Dominion over 25
those of his own Species be convey'd to *Adam.* All the
Terrestrial irrational Creatures are enumerated at their
Creation, *ver.* 25. under the Names, *Beasts of the Earth,*
Cattle and creeping things, but Man being not then Created,
was not contained under any of those Names, and there- 30
fore, whether we understand the *Hebrew* words right or
no, they cannot be supposed to comprehend Man in the
very same History, and the very next Verses following,
especially since that *Hebrew* word רמש which if any in
this Donation to *Adam, Ch.* 1. 28. must comprehend Man, 35
is so plainly used in contradistinction to him, as *Gen.* 6.
20; 7. 14. 21. 23; *Gen.* 8. 17, 19. And if God made all
Mankind slaves to *Adam* and his Heirs, by giving *Adam*
Dominion over *every living thing that moveth on the Earth,*
Chap. 1. 28. as our A—— would have it, methinks Sir 40
Robert should have carried his Monarchical Power one
step higher, and satisfied the World, that Princes might eat
their Subjects too, since God gave as full Power to *Noah*
and his Heirs, *Chap.* 9. 2. to eat *every Living thing that*
moveth, as he did to *Adam* to have Dominion over them, 45
the *Hebrew* words in both places being the same.

28.   *David,* who might be supposed to understand the
Donation of God in this Text, and the Right of Kings too,
as well as our A——, in his Comment on this place, as the
Learned and Judicious *Ainsworth* calls it, in the 8th Psalm,
finds here no such Charter of Monarchical Power, his words 5
are, *Thou hast made him, i.e.* Man the Son of Man, *a*
little lower than the Angels, thou mad'st him to have Do-

<hr>

§ 28   4   'Ainsworth'—see Henry Ainsworth, *Annotations upon the Five*
Books of Moses, the booke of the Psalmes . . . 1622 (1639), Appendix
B, no. 3. Locke bought this book at Cooper's auction in December
1681: it was an edition of a collection of commentaries originally
published separately. On Gen. i. 28, Ainsworth says 'For this state of
Man . . . David laudeth the Lord in Psal. 8'.

minion over the works of thy hands, thou hast put all things
under his Feet, all Sheep and Oxen and the Beasts of the
10 *Field, and the Fowl of the Air, and Fish of the Sea, and*
whatsoever passeth through the paths of the Sea. In which
words, if any one can find out that there is meant any
Monarchical Power of one Man over another, but only
the Dominion of the whole Species of Mankind, over the
15 inferior Species of Creatures, he may, for ought I know,
deserve to be one of Sir *Robert's Monarchs in habit,* for
the rareness of the discovery. And by this time, I hope it
is evident, that he that gave *Dominion over every Living*
thing that moveth on the Earth, gave *Adam* no Mo-
20 narchical Power over those of his own Species, which will
yet appear more fully in the next thing I am to shew.

29. 2. Whatever God gave by the words of this
Grant, 1 *Gen.* 28. it was not to *Adam* in particular, exclusive of all other Men: whatever *Dominion* he had
thereby, it was not a *Private Dominion,* but a Dominion
5 in common with the rest of Mankind. That this Donation
was not made in particular to *Adam,* appears evidently
from the words of the Text, it being made to more than
one, for it was spoken in the Plural Number, God blessed
them, and said unto *them,* Have Dominion. God says unto
10 *Adam* and *Eve,* Have Dominion; *thereby,* says our *A.,*
Adam was Monarch of the World: But the Grant being
to them, *i.e.* spoke to *Eve* also, as many Interpreters think
with reason, that these words were not spoken till *Adam*
had his Wife, must not she thereby be Lady, as well as
15 he Lord of the World? If it be said that *Eve* was subjected
to *Adam,* it seems she was not so subjected to him, as to
hinder her *Dominion* over the Creatures, or *Property* in
them: for shall we say that God ever made a joint Grant
to two, and one only was to have the benefit of it?

30. But perhaps 'twill be said, *Eve* was not made till
afterward: Grant it so, What advantage will our *A.* get by
it? The Text will be only the more directly against him,
and shew that God in this Donation, gave the World to
5 Mankind in common, and not to *Adam* in particular. The
word *Them* in the Text must include the Species of Man,

§ 29   1   '2.'—refers back to '1' on line 1 of paragraph 25.
13–14   Compare I, § 16, 41.

for 'tis certain *Them* can by no means signifie *Adam* alone.
In the 26*th* Verse, where God declares his intention to
give this Dominion, it is plain it meant, that he would
make a Species of Creatures, that should have Dominion 10
over the other Species of this Terrestrial Globe: The words
are, *And God said, Let us make Man in our Image, after
our likeness, and let them have Dominion over the Fish,*
&c. *They* then were to have Dominion. Who? even those
who were to have the *Image* of God, the Individuals of 15
that Species of *Man* that he was going to make, for that
Them should signifie *Adam* singly, exclusive of the rest,
that should be in the World with him, is against both
Scripture and all Reason: And it cannot possibly be made
Sense, if *Man* in the former part of the *Verse* do not sig- 20
nifie the same with *Them* in the latter, only *Man* there, as
is usual, is taken for the Species, and *them* the individuals
of that Species: and we have a Reason in the very Text.
God makes him *in his own Image after his own Likeness*,
makes him an intellectual Creature, and so capable of *Do-* 25
minion. For wherein soever else the *Image of God* consisted, the intellectual Nature was certainly a part of it,
and belong'd to the whole Species, and enabled them to
have *Dominion* over the inferiour Creatures; and therefore
David says in the 8*th* Psalm above cited, *Thou hast made* 30
him little lower than the Angels, thou hast made him to
have Dominion. 'Tis not of *Adam* King *David* speaks here,
for *Verse* 4. 'tis plain, 'tis of *Man, and the Son of Man*,
of the Species of Mankind.

31.   And that this Grant spoken to *Adam* was made to
him, and the whole Species of Man, is clear from our *A*'s
own Proof out of the *Psalmist. The Earth*, saith the Psalmist, *hath he given to the Children of Men; which shews the*
Title comes from Fatherhood: These are Sir *Robert*'s 5
words in the Preface before cited, and a strange Inference
it is he makes, *God hath given the Earth to the Children*
of Men, ergo *the Title comes from Fatherhood*. 'Tis pity
the Propriety of the *Hebrew* Tongue had not used *Fathers*

§ 30   19–23   Pareyson comments that Locke is right and the patri-
archalists wrong here, because in Hebrew, which the Authorized Version follows very closely, and in English a singular can be a collective.
   30   'above cited'—I, § 28, 6–11.
§ 31   6   'Preface . . . '—the Preface to Filmer's 'Forms', last cited
I, § 21, 12.

10 *of Men* instead of *Children of Men*, to express Mankind:
then indeed our *A.* might have had the countenance of the
sound of the words, to have placed the *Title* in the *Fatherhood*. But to conclude, that the *Fatherhood* had the Right
to the Earth, because God gave it *to the Children of Men*,
15 is a way of arguing peculiar to our *A.* And a Man must
have a great mind to go contrary to the Sound as well as
Sense of the Words, before he could light on it. But the
Sense is yet harder, and more remote from our *A's* purpose: For as it stands in his Preface [187–188], it is to
20 prove *Adam's* being Monarch, and his reasoning is thus,
God gave the Earth to the Children of Men, ergo *Adam
was Monarch of the World.* I defie any Man to make a
more pleasant Conclusion than this, which cannot be ex-
cused from the most obvious Absurdity, till it can be shewn,
25 that by *Children of Men*, he who had no Father, *Adam*,
alone is signified; but whatever our *A.* does, the Scripture
speaks not Nonsense.

32.   To maintain this *Property and Private Dominion*
of Adam, our *A.* labours in the following Page [64] to
destroy the Community granted to *Noah* and his Sons, in
that parallel place, 9 *Gen.* 1, 2, 3. and he endeavours to
5 do it two ways.

1°.   Sir *Robert* would perswade us against the express
words of the Scripture, that what was here granted to *Noah*,
was not granted to his Sons in common with him. His
words are; *As for the general Community between* Noah
10 *and his Sons, which Mr.* Selden *will have to be granted
to them*, 9. Gen. 2. *the Text doth not warrant it* [64].
What *Warrant* our *A.* would have, when the plain express
words of Scripture, not capable of another meaning, will
not satisfie him, who pretends to build wholly on Scripture,
15 is not easie to imagine. The Text says, *God blessed* Noah
and his Sons, and said unto them, i.e. as our *A.* would
have it, *unto him: For*, saith he, *although the Sons are
there mentioned with* Noah *in the Blessing, yet it may best
be understood, with a Subordination or Benediction in Suc-
20 cession*, O. 211 [64]. That indeed is *best*, for our *A.* to be
understood, which best serves to his purpose, but that truly
may best be understood by any body else, which best agrees
with the plain construction of the words, and arises from
the obvious meaning of the place, and then *with Subordina-
25 tion* and *in Succession*, will not *be best understood*, in a

Grant of God, where he himself put them not, nor mentions any such Limitation. But yet, our *A.* has reasons, why
it *may best be understood so. The Blessing,* says he in the
following words, *might truly be fulfilled, if the Sons either
under or after their Father, enjoy'd a private Dominion,* O. 30
211. [64] which is to say, that a Grant, whose express words
give a joynt Title in present (for the Text says, into your
hands they are delivered) *may best be understood with a
Subordination* or in *Succession:* because 'tis possible,
that in *Subordination,* or *Succession* it may be enjoy'd. 35
Which is all one as to say, that a Grant of any thing
in present possession, *may best be understood* of reversion:
because 'tis possible one may live to enjoy it in reversion.
If the Grant be indeed to a Father, and to his Sons after
him, who is so kind as to let his Children enjoy it presently 40
in common with him, one may truly say, as to the event
one will be as good as the other: but it can never be true,
that what the express words grant in possession, and in
common, *may best be understood,* to be in reversion. The
sum of all his reasoning amounts to this: God did not 45
give to the Sons of *Noah* the World in common with their
Father, because 'twas possible they might enjoy it under,
or after him. A very good sort of Argument, against an express Text of Scripture: but God must not be believed,
though he speaks it himself, when he says he does any thing, 50
which will not consist with Sir *Robert's* Hypothesis.

33. For 'tis plain, however he would exclude them,
That part of this *Benediction,* as he would have it in *Succession,* must needs be meant to the Sons, and not to *Noah*
himself at all. *Be Fruitful, and Multiply, and Replenish the
Earth,* says God, in this Blessing. This part of the Benedic- 5
tion, as appears by the sequel, concerned not *Noah* himself at all: for we read not of any Children he had after
the Flood, and in the following Chapter, where his Posterity is reckon'd up, there is no mention of any, and so
this *Benediction in Succession,* was not to take place till 10
350 Years after, and to save our *A's* imaginary *Monarchy,*
the Peopling of the World must be deferr'd 350 Years; for
this part of the *Benediction* cannot be understood with
Subordination, unless our *A.* will say, that they must ask

§ 33   8   'following Chapter'—Gen. x.
     11 and 12   '350 Years'—the time Noah lived after the Flood.

15 leave of their Father *Noah* to lie with their Wives. But
in this one point our *A.* is constant to himself in all his
Discourses, he takes great care there should be Monarchs
in the World, but very little that there should be People:
and indeed his way of Government is not the way to People
20 the World. For how much Absolute Monarchy helps to
fulfil this great and primary Blessing of God Almighty,
Be fruitful, and multiply, and replenish the Earth, which
contains in it the improvement too of Arts and Sciences,
and the conveniences of Life, may be seen in those large
25 and rich Countries, which are happy under the *Turkish*
Government, where are not now to be found ⅓, nay in
many, if not most parts of them ¹⁄₃₀, perhaps I might say
not ¹⁄₁₀₀ of the People, that were formerly, as will easily
appear to any one, who will compare the Accounts we have
30 of it at this time, with Antient History. But this by the by.

34. The other Parts of this *Benediction* or Grant are so
expressed, that they must needs be understood to belong to
Noah and his Sons, to them as much as to him, and not
to his Sons *with a subordination or in Succession. The fear
5 of you, and the dread of you,* says God, *shall be upon
every Beast,* &c. Will any Body but our *A.* say, that the
Creatures feared and stood in awe of *Noah* only, and not
of his Sons without his leave, or till after his death? And
the following words, *into your hands they are delivered,*
10 are they to be understood as our *A.* says, if your Father
please, or they shall be deliver'd into your hands hereafter.
If this be to argue from Scripture, I know not what may
not be proved by it, and I can scarce see how much this
differs from that *Fiction and Phansie,* or how much a
15 surer Foundation it will prove than the opinions of *Philosophers and Poets,* which our *A.* so much condemns in his
Preface.

15–30 The point about absolute monarchy and depopulation is taken
up again in I, § 41, and in II, § 42, 24–32—an addition made in the late
1690's. This passage may itself be an addition of 1689. Increase of
population was an important aim of policy for Locke, insisted upon in
his economic writings.
§ 34 13–17 In his Preface to the *Forms,* Filmer says (188) 'there
never was any such thing as an independent multitude, who at first
had a natural right to a community: this is but a fiction, or fancy of
too many in these days, who please themselves in running after the
opinions of philosophers and poets'. See I, § 154.

35. But our *A——* goes on to prove, that *it may best be understood with a Subordination or a Benediction in Succession*, for, says he, *it is not probable, that the private Dominion which God gave to* Adam, *and by his Donation, Assignation or Cession to his Children, was Abrogated, and a Community of all things instituted between* Noah *and his Sons.* —— Noah *was left the sole Heir of the World, why should it be thought that God would disinherit him of his Birthright, and make him of all Men in the World the only Tenant in Common with his Children*, O. 211 [64]. 10

36. The Prejudices of our own ill grounded Opinions, however by us called *Probable*, cannot Authorize us to understand Scripture contrary to the direct and plain meaning of the Words. I grant, 'tis not probable that *Adams private Dominion was* here *Abrogated;* because it is more than improbable (for it will never be proved) that ever *Adam* had any such *Private Dominion:* And since parallel places of Scripture are most probable to make us know, how they *may be best understood*, there needs but the comparing this Blessing here to *Noah* and his Sons after the Flood, with that to *Adam* after the Creation, 1 *Gen.* 28. to assure any one that God gave *Adam* no such *Private Dominion.* 'Tis *Probable*, I confess, that *Noah* should have the same Title, the same Property and Dominion after the Flood, that *Adam* had before it. But since *Private Dominion* cannot consist with the Blessing and Grant God gave to him and his Sons in Common, 'tis a sufficient Reason to conclude that *Adam* had none, especially since in the Donation made to him, there is no words that express it, or do in the least favour it; And then let my Reader judge whether *it may best be understood*, when in the one place there is not one word for it, not to say, what has been above proved, that the Text it self proves the contrary, and in the other, the Words and Sense are directly against it.

37. But our *A.* says, *Noah was the sole Heir of the World, why should it be thought that God would disinherit him of his Birth-right?* Heir, indeed, in *England*, signifies the Eldest Son, who is by the Law of *England* to have all his Fathers Land, but where God ever appointed any such *Heir of the World*, our *A.* would have done well to have shewed us, and how *God disinherited him of his Birth-right*, or what harm was done him if God gave his Sons

a Right to make use of a part of the Earth for the support
10 of themselves and Families, when the whole was not only
more then *Noah* himself, but infinitely more than they all
could make use of, and the Possessions of one could not
at all Prejudice, or as to any use streighten that of the other.

38.   Our *A*. probably foreseeing he might not be very
successful in persuading People out of their Senses, and
say what he could, Men would be apt to believe the plain
words of Scripture, and think, as they saw, that the Grant
5 was spoken to *Noah* and his Sons jointly. He endeavours
to insinuate, as if this Grant to *Noah*, conveyed no Property, no Dominion; because, *Subduing the Earth and
Dominion over the Creatures are therein omitted, nor the
Earth once named*. And therefore, says he, *there is a
10 considerable difference between these two Texts, the first
Blessing gave* Adam *a Dominion over the Earth and all
Creatures, the latter allows* Noah *Liberty to use the Living
Creatures for Food, here is no alteration or diminishing
of his Title, to a Property of all Things, but an Enlarge-
15 ment only of his Commons*, O. 211 [64]. So that in our
A's Sense, all that was said here to *Noah* and his Sons,
gave them no Dominion, no Property, but only *Enlarged*
the *Commons;* Their *Commons*, I should say since, God
says, *to you are they given*, though our *A*. says *his*, for
20 as for *Noah*'s Sons, they it seems by Sir *Robert*'s appointment during their Fathers Life time, were to keep Fasting
days.

39.   Any one but our *A*. would be mightily suspected,
to be blinded with Prejudice, that in all this Blessing to
Noah and his Sons, could see nothing but *only* an Enlargement of Commons. For as to *Dominion* which our
5 *A*. thinks omitted, *the fear of you, and the dread of you*,
says God, *shall be upon every Beast*, which I suppose,
expresses the *Dominion*, or Superiority was designed Man
over the living Creatures, as fully as may be, for in that
fear and dread, seems chiefly to consist what was given
10 to *Adam,* over the inferiour Animals; who as absolute a
Monarch as he was, could not make bold with a Lark
or a Rabbet to satisfie his hunger, and had the Herbs but
in common with the Beasts, as is plain from 1 Gen. 29.
and 30. In the next place, 'tis manifest that in this Blessing
15 to *Noah* and his Sons, Property is not only given in clear

words, but in a larger extent than it was to *Adam*. *Into
your hands they are given*, says God, to *Noah* and his
Sons, which Words, if they give not Property, nay, Property in Possession, 'twill be hard to find Words that can,
since there is not a way to express a Man's being possessed 20
of any thing more Natural, nor more certain, than to say,
it is delivered into his Hands. And, *Verse* 3d, to shew,
that they had then given them the utmost Property Man
is capable of, which is to have a right to destroy any thing
by using it; *Every moving thing that Liveth*, saith God, 25
shall be Meat for you, which was not allowed to *Adam*
in his Charter. This our *A*. calls, *a Liberty of using them
for Food, and only an Enlargement of Commons*, but *no
alteration of Property*, O. 211 [64]. What other Property
Man can have in the Creatures, but the *Liberty of using* 30
them, is hard to be understood: So that, if the first
Blessing, as our *A*. says, gave *Adam Dominion over the
Creatures*, and the Blessing to *Noah* and his Sons, gave
them *such a Liberty to use them*, as *Adam* had not; it
must needs give them something that *Adam* with all his 35
Soveraignty wanted, something that one would be apt to
take for a greater Property; for certainly he has no absolute Dominion over even the Brutal Part of the Creatures, and the Property he has in them is very narrow and
scanty, who cannot make that use of them, which is per- 40
mitted to another. Should any one, who is Absolute Lord
of a Country, have bidden our *A. Subdue the Earth*, and
given him Dominion over the Creatures in it, but not have
permitted him to have taken a Kid or a Lamb out of the
Flock, to satisfie his hunger, I guess he would scarce have 45
thought himself Lord or Proprietor of that Land, or the
Cattel on it: But would have found the difference between
having Dominion, which a Shepherd may have, and having full Property as an Owner. So that, had it been his
own *Case*, Sir *Robert* I believe, would have thought here 50
was an *Alteration*, nay, an enlarging of *Property*, and
that *Noah* and his Children had by this Grant, not only
Property given them, but such a property given them in
the Creatures, as *Adam* had not; for however, in respect
of one another, Men may be allowed to have propriety in 55
their distinct Portions of the Creatures; yet in respect of
God the Maker of Heaven and Earth, who is sole Lord
and Proprietor of the whole World, Mans Propriety in the
Creatures is nothing but that *Liberty to use them*, which

60 God has permitted, and so Man's property may be altered
and enlarged, as we see it was here, after the Flood, when
other uses of them are allowed, which before were not.
From all which I suppose, it is clear, that neither *Adam*
nor *Noah,* had any *Private Dominion,* any Property in
65 the Creatures, exclusive of his Posterity, as they should
successively grow up into need of them, and come to be
able to make use of them.

40. Thus we have Examined our *A*'s Argument for
Adam's *Monarchy,* founded on the Blessing pronounced,
1 *Gen.* 28. Wherein I think 'tis impossible for any sober
Reader, to find any other but the setting of Mankind above
5 the other kinds of Creatures, in this habitable Earth of
ours. 'Tis nothing but the giving to Man, the whole Species
of Man, as the chief Inhabitant, who is the Image of his
Maker, the Dominion over the other Creatures. This lies
so obvious in the plain words, that any one but our *A.*
10 would have thought it necessary to have shewn, how these
words that seem'd to say the quite contrary, gave *Adam*
Monarchical Absolute Power over other Men, or the
Sole Property in all the Creatures, and methinks in a
business of this moment, and that whereon he Builds all
15 that follows, he should have done something more than
barely cite words which apparently make against him;
for I confess, I cannot see any thing in them, tending to
Adam's *Monarchy,* or *Private Dominion,* but quite the
contrary. And I the less deplore the dulness of my ap-
20 prehension herein, since I find the Apostle seems to have
as little notion of any such *Private Dominion of Adam*
as I, when he says, God *gives us all things richly to enjoy,*
which he could not do, if it were all given away already,
to Monarch *Adam,* and the Monarchs his Heirs and Suc-
25 cessors. To conclude, this Text is so far from proving
Adam Sole Proprietor, that on the contrary, it is a Confirmation of the Original Community of all things amongst
the Sons of Men, which appearing from this Donation of
God, as well as other places of Scripture; the Soveraignty
30 of *Adam,* built upon his *Private Dominion,* must fall, not
having any Foundation to support it.

§ 40   16   'apparently'—means 'obviously' here.
    22   'God, who giveth richly all things to enjoy', I Tim. vi. 17, also
quoted in II, § 31, 7. Locke nowhere cites biblical texts *proving* original
communism.

41. But yet, if after all, any one will needs have it so, that by this Donation of God, *Adam* was made sole Proprietor of the whole Earth, what will this be to his Soveraignty? And how will it appear, that *Property* in Land gives a Man Power over the Life of another? Or how will the Possession even of the whole Earth, give any one a Soveraign Arbitrary Authority over the Persons of Men? The most specious thing to be said, is, that he that is Proprietor of the whole World, may deny all the rest of Mankind Food, and so at his pleasure starve them, if they will not acknowledge his Soveraignty, and Obey his Will. If this were true, it would be a good Argument to prove, that there was never any such *Property*, that God never gave any such *Private Dominion;* since it is more reasonable to think, that God who bid Mankind increase and multiply, should rather himself give them all a Right, to make use of the Food and Rayment, and other Conveniencies of Life, the Materials whereof he had so plentifully provided for them; than to make them depend upon the Will of a Man for their Subsistence, who should have Power to destroy them all when he pleased, and who being no better than other Men, was in Succession likelier by want and the dependance of a scanty Fortune, to tye them to hard Service, than by liberal Allowance of the Conveniencies of Life, to promote the great Design of God, *Increase* and *Multiply:* He that doubts this, let him look into the Absolute Monarchies of the World, and see what becomes of the Conveniencies of Life, and the Multitudes of People.

42. But we know God hath not left one Man so to the Mercy of another, that he may starve him if he please: God the Lord and Father of all, has given no one of his Children such a Property, in his peculiar Portion of the things of this World, but that he has given his needy Brother a Right to the Surplusage of his Goods; so that it cannot justly be denied him, when his pressing Wants call for it. And therefore no Man could ever have a just

§ **41**   26–9   Compare I, § 33, 15–30, note and references: this may be an addition of 1689. Paragraphs 41–3 mark an important limitation on men's rights in property, see Introduction, 115, and compare Polin, 1960, 195 on.
§ **42**   6   Locke may here have in mind the injunction in Luke xi. 41.

Power over the Life of another, by Right of property in
10 Land or Possessions; since 'twould always be a Sin in any
Man of Estate, to let his Brother perish for want of af-
fording him Relief out of his Plenty. As *Justice* gives
every Man a Title to the product of his honest Industry,
and the fair Acquisitions of his Ancestors descended to
15 him; so *Charity* gives every Man a Title to so much out
of another's Plenty, as will keep him from extream want,
where he has no means to subsist otherwise; and a Man
can no more justly make use of another's necessity, to
force him to become his Vassal, by with-holding that Re-
20 lief, God requires him to afford to the wants of his Brother,
than he that has more strength can seize upon a weaker,
master him to his Obedience, and with a Dagger at his
Throat offer him Death or Slavery.

43.   Should any one make so perverse an use of God's
Blessings poured on him with a liberal Hand; should any
one be Cruel and Uncharitable to that extremity, yet all
this would not prove that Propriety in Land, even in this
5 Case, gave any Authority over the Persons of Men, but
only that Compact might; since the Authority of the Rich
Proprietor, and the Subjection of the Needy Beggar began
not from the Possession of the Lord, but the Consent of
the poor Man, who preferr'd being his Subject to starving.
10 And the Man he thus submits to, can pretend to no more
Power over him, than he has consented to, upon Compact.
Upon this Ground a Man's having his Stores filled in a
time of Scarcity, having Money in his Pocket, being in a
Vessel at Sea, being able to Swim, &c. may as well be
15 the Foundation of Rule and Dominion, as being Possessor
of all the Land in the World, any of these being sufficient
to enable me to save a Mans Life who would perish if
such Assistance were denied him; and any thing by this
Rule that may be an occasion of working upon anothers
20 necessity, to save his Life, or any thing dear to him, at
the rate of his Freedom, may be made a Foundation of
Sovereignty, as well as Property. From all which it is
clear, that tho' God should have given *Adam Private*

---

§ **42** 12–17 On Justice and Charity, see II, § 5. This passage hints at
the labour theory of property, stated at length in *Second Treatise*, ch. v,
paragraph 27 on: 'honest industry' is mentioned in II, § 42, 29.

Dominion, yet that *Private Dominion* could give him no
Sovereignty; But we have already sufficiently proved, that
God gave him no *Private Dominion.*   25

CHAP. V.

Of Adam's *Title to Sovereignty by the Subjection of* Eve.

44.   The next place of Scripture we find our *A.* Builds
his Monarchy of *Adam* on, is 3. *Gen.* 16. *And thy desire
shall be to thy Husband, and he shall rule over thee. Here
we have* (says he) *the Original Grant of Government,*
from whence he concludes, in the following part of the   5
Page *O.* 244 [283]. *That the Supream Power is settled in
the Fatherhood, and limited to one kind of Government,
that is to Monarchy:* For let his premises be what they
will, this is always the conclusion, let *Rule* in any Text,
be but once named, and presently *Absolute Monarchy* is   10
by Divine Right Establish'd. If any one will but carefully
Read our *A*'s own reasoning from these Words, *O.* 244.
[283] and consider among other things, *the Line and
Posterity of* Adam, as he there brings them in, he will find
some difficulty, to make Sense of what he says; but we   15
will allow this at present, to his peculiar way of Writing,
and consider the Force of the Text in hand. The Words
are the Curse of God upon the Woman, for having been
the first and forwardest in the Disobedience, and if we
will consider the occasion of what God says here to our   20
first Parents, that he was Denouncing Judgment, and
declaring his Wrath against them both, for their Disobedience, we cannot suppose that this was the time,
wherein God was granting *Adam* Prerogatives and Priviledges, investing him with Dignity and Authority, Elevat-   25

---

§ 44 6–8 Quotation not quite literal: Locke has turned up this page
of his Filmer.

ing him to Dominion and Monarchy: For though as a
helper in the Temptation, as well as a Partner in the
Transgression, *Eve* was laid below him, and so he had
accidentally a Superiority over her, for her greater Pun-
30 ishment, yet he too had his share in the fall, as well as the
sin, and was laid lower, as may be seen in the following
Verses, and 'twould be hard to imagine, that God, in the
same Breath, should make him Universal *Monarch* over
all Mankind, and a day labourer for his Life; turn him
35 out of *Paradice, to till the Ground, ver.* 23. and at the
same time, advance him to a Throne, and all the Priviledges and Ease of Absolute Power.

45. This was not a time, when *Adam* could expect any
Favours, any grant of Priviledges, from his offended
Maker. If this be *the Original Grant of Government*, as
our *A*—— tells us, and *Adam* was now made Monarch,
5 whatever Sir *Robert* would have him, 'tis plain, God made
him but a very poor Monarch, such an one, as our *A*——
himself would have counted it no great Priviledge to be.
God sets him to work for his living, and seems rather to
give him a Spade into his hand, to subdue the Earth, than
10 a Scepter to Rule over its Inhabitants. *In the Sweat of thy
Face thou shalt eat thy Bread*, says God to him, *ver.* 19.
This was unavoidable, may it perhaps be answered, because he was yet without Subjects, and had no body to
work for him, but afterwards living as he did above 900
15 Years, he might have People enough, whom he might
command, to work for him; no, says God, not only
whilst thou art without other help, save thy Wife, but
as long as thou livest, shalt thou live by thy Labour. *In
the Sweat of thy Face, shalt thou eat thy Bread, till thou
20 return unto the Ground, for out of it wast thou taken, for
dust thou art, and unto dust shalt thou return, v.* 19. It
will perhaps be answered again, in Favour of our *A*——,
that these words are not spoken Personally to *Adam*, but
in him, as their Representative, to all Mankind, this being
25 a Curse upon Mankind, because of the fall.

46. God, I believe, speaks differently from Men, because he speaks with more Truth, more Certainty: but
when he vouchsafes to speak to Men, I do not think, he

§ 45 8 Compare II, § 32, 12–14.

speaks differently from them, in crossing the Rules of
language in use amongst them. This would not be to 5
condescend to their Capacities, when he humbles himself
to speak to them, but to lose his design in speaking, what
thus spoken, they could not understand. And yet thus
must we think of God, if the Interpretations of Scripture,
necessary to maintain our A———s Doctrine, must be re- 10
ceived for good. For by the ordinary Rules of Language,
it will be very hard to understand, what God says; If
what he speaks here, in the Singular Number to *Adam*,
must be understood to be spoken to all Mankind, and
what he says in the Plural Number, 1 *Gen.* 26. and 28. 15
must be understood of *Adam* alone, exclusive of all others,
and what he says to *Noah* and his Sons Joyntly, must be
understood to be meant to *Noah* alone, *Gen.* 9.

47. Farther it is to be noted, that these words here
of 3 *Gen.* 16. which our *A.* calls *the Original Grant of
Government* were not spoken to *Adam*, neither indeed
was there any Grant in them made to *Adam*, but a Punishment laid upon *Eve:* and if we will take them as they 5
were directed in particular to her, or in her, as their representative to all other Women, they will at most concern
the Female Sex only, and import no more but that Subjection they should ordinarily be in to their Husbands: But
there is here no more Law to oblige a Woman to such a 10
Subjection, if the Circumstances either of her Condition
or Contract with her Husband should exempt her from
it, then there is, that she should bring forth her Children
in Sorrow and Pain, if there could be found a Remedy
for it, which is also a part of the same Curse upon her: 15
for the whole Verse runs thus, *Unto the Woman he said,
I will greatly multiply thy sorrow and thy conception; In
sorrow thou shalt bring forth Children, and thy desire
shall be to thy Husband, and he shall rule over thee.*
'Twould, I think, have been a hard matter for any Body, 20
but our *A.* to have found out a Grant of *Monarchical
Government to Adam* in these Words, which were neither
spoke to, nor of him: neither will any one, I suppose, by
these Words, think the weaker Sex, as by a Law so subjected to the Curse contained in them, that 'tis their duty 25
not to endeavour to avoid it. And will any one say, that
Eve, or any other Woman, sinn'd, if she were brought to
Bed without those multiplied Pains God threatens her

here with? Or that either of our Queens *Mary* or *Eliza-*
30 *beth*, had they Married any of their Subjects, had been
by this Text put into a Political Subjection to him? or
that he thereby should have had *Monarchical Rule* over
her? God, in this Text, gives not, that I see, any Authority
to *Adam* over *Eve*, or to Men over their Wives, but only
35 foretels what should be the Womans Lot, how by his
Providence he would order it so, that she should be subject to her husband, as we see that generally the Laws
of Mankind and customs of Nations have ordered it so;
and there is, I grant, a Foundation in Nature for it.

48. Thus when God says of *Jacob* and *Esau*, That
the Elder should serve the Younger, 25 *Gen.* 23. no body
supposes that God hereby made *Jacob Esau*'s Sovereign,
but foretold what should *de facto* come to pass.
5 But if these words here spoke to *Eve* must needs be
understood as a Law to bind her and all other Women
to Subjection, it can be no other Subjection than what
every Wife owes her Husband, and then if this be the
Original Grant of Government and the *Foundation of*
10 *Monarchical Power*, there will be as many Monarchs as
there are Husbands. If therefore these words give any
Power to *Adam*, it can be only a Conjugal Power, not
Political, the Power that every Husband hath to order the
things of private Concernment in his Family, as Proprietor
15 of the Goods and Land there, and to have his Will take
place before that of his wife in all things of their common Concernment; but not a Political Power of Life and
Death over her, much less over any body else.

49. This I am sure: If our *A.* will have this Text to
be a *Grant, the Original Grant of Government*, Political
Government, he ought to have proved it by some better
Arguments than by barely saying, That *thy desire shall be*
5 *unto thy Husband*, was a Law whereby *Eve* and *all that
should come of her*, were subjected to the absolute Monarchical Power of *Adam* and his Heirs. *Thy desire shall*

---

§ 47   29–30   Mary and Elizabeth Tudor are clearly meant, and it seems
unlikely that Locke would have written like this after April 1689, when
Mary Stuart was crowned joint sovereign with William III: compare
references to James II, II, § 133, 12; II, § 200, 3–4, and Introduction, 68.
Locke's attitude towards the curse on women in childbearing is typical
of his progressive, humanitarian rationalism.

be to thy Husband, is too doubtful an expression, of whose
signification Interpreters are not agreed, to build so confidently on, and in a Matter of such moment, and so great 10
and general Concernment: But our *A.* according to his
way of Writing, having once named the Text, concludes
presently without any more ado, that the meaning is, as
he would have it. Let the words *Rule* and *Subject* be
but found in the Text or Margent, and it immediately 15
signifies the Duty of a Subject to his Prince, the Relation
is changed, and though God says *Husband,* Sir *Robert* will
have it *King; Adam* has presently *Absolute Monarchical
Power* over *Eve,* and not only over *Eve,* but *all that
should come of her,* though the Scripture says not a word 20
of it, nor our *A.* a word to prove it. But *Adam* must for
all that be an Absolute Monarch, and so down to the end
of the Chapter. And here I leave my Reader to consider,
whether my bare saying, without offering any Reasons to
evince it, that this Text gave not *Adam* that *Absolute* 25
Monarchical Power, our *A.* supposes, be not as sufficient
to destroy that Power, as his bare Assertion is to Establish
it, since the Text mentions neither *Prince* nor *People,*
speaks nothing of *Absolute* or *Monarchical Power,* but
the Subjection of *Eve* to *Adam,* a Wife to her Husband. 30
And he that would trace our *A.* so all through, would
make a short and sufficient answer to the greatest part of
the Grounds he proceeds on, and abundantly confute them
by barely denying; It being a sufficient answer to Assertions
without Proof, to deny them without giving a Reason. 35
And therefore should I have said nothing but barely deny'd
that by this Text *the Supreme Power was setled and
founded by God himself, in the Fatherhood, Limited to
Monarchy, and that to* Adam's *Person and Heirs,* all which
our *A.* notably concludes from these words, as may be 40
seen in the same Page, *O.* 244. [283] it had been a sufficient answer; should I have desired any sober Man only
to have read the Text, and considered to whom, and on
what occasion it was spoken, he would no doubt have
wondered how our *A.* found out *Monarchical absolute* 45

---

§ **49** 15 'Margent'—presumably refers to the margins of the Authorized Version, with its references and sub-headings; compare I, § 66, 23
and note.

22-3 'down to the end of the Chapter', that is the first chapter of
Patriarcha; see note on I, § 6, 54. It ends in the middle of section VII
(p. 63).

Power in it, had he not had an exceeding good Faculty
to find it himself, where he could not shew it others. And
thus we have examined the two places of Scripture, all
that I remember our *A.* brings to prove *Adam*'s *Sov-*
50 *ereignty,* that *Supremacy,* which he says, *it was Gods*
Ordinance should be unlimited in Adam, *and as large as*
all the Acts of his Will, O. 245. [284] viz. 1 *Gen.* 28. and
3. *Gen.* 16. one whereof signifies only the Subjection of
the Inferior Ranks of Creatures to Mankind, and the other
55 the Subjection that is due from a Wife to her Husband,
both far enough from that which Subjects owe the Governours of Political Societies.

CHAP. VI.

Of Adam*'s Title to Sovereignty by Fatherhood.*

50. There is one thing more, and then I think I have
given you all that our *A.* brings for proof of *Adam*'s
Sovereignty, and that is a Supposition of a natural Right
of Dominion over his Children, by being their Father, and
5 this Title of *Fatherhood* he is so pleased with, that you
will find it brought in almost in every Page, particularly,
he says, *Not only* Adam, *but the succeeding Patriarchs*
had by Right of Fatherhood Royal Authority over their
Children, p. 12 [57]. And in the same page, *This Subjec-*
10 *tion of Children being the Fountain of all Regal Authority,*
&c. This being, as one would think by his so frequent
mentioning it, the main Basis of all his Frame, we may well
expect clear and evident Reason for it, since he lays it
down as a Position necessary to his purpose, That *every*
15 *Man that is born is so far from being free, that by his very*
Birth he becomes a Subject of him that begets him, O. 156
[232]. So that *Adam* being the only Man Created, and all
ever since Being Begotten, no body has been born free.

---

§ 50   9–10 '*Subjection*'—Subordination in Filmer.
  15 '*free*'—free-born in Filmer.

If we ask how *Adam* comes by this Power over his Children, he tell us here 'tis by begetting them: And so again, 20 *O.* 223 [71]. *This Natural Dominion of* Adam, *says he, may be proved out of* Grotius *himself, who teacheth, That* generatione jus acquiritur parentibus in liberos. And indeed the Act of begetting being that which makes a Man a Father, his Right of Father over his Children can nat- 25 urally arise from nothing else.

51. *Grotius* tells us not here how far this *jus in liberos,* this Power of Parents over their Children extends; but our *A.* always very clear in the point, assures us, 'tis *Supreme Power,* and like that of Absolute Monarchs over their Slaves, Absolute Power of Life and Death. He that 5 should demand of him, How, or for what Reason it is, that begetting a Child gives the Father such an Absolute Power over him, will find him answer nothing: we are to take his word for this as well as several other things, and by that the Laws of Nature and the Constitutions of 10 Government must stand or fall. Had he been an Absolute Monarch, this way of talking might have suited well enough; *pro ratione voluntas,* might have been of force in his mouth, but in the way of proof or argument is very unbecoming and will little advantage his plea for Absolute 15 Monarchy. Sir Robert has to much lessen'd a Subjects authority to leave himself the hopes of establishing any thing by his bare saying it. One Slave's Opinion without proof is not of weight enough to dispose of the Liberty and fortunes of all Mankind: If all Men are not, as I think 20 they are, naturally equal, I'm sure all Slaves are; and then I may without presumption oppose my single Opinion to his, and be confident that my Saying, *That Begetting of Children makes them not Slaves to their Fathers,* as cer-

---

22 'Grotius'—'by generation a right over children is acquired by the parents' is quoted by Filmer from Grotius in that part of his *Original* which he devotes to Grotius, and in that passage of his tract which was taken from the original *Patriarcha* manuscript as printed by Laslett, see pp. 71–2.

21–6 Compare II, § 52, 12, note and references.

§ 51 1 Grotius analyses the rights of parents over their children in *De Jure Belli ac Pacis,* II, V (1712 ed. 234–): the phrase under discussion occurs in section I. But his concern here is with the three periods into which the relationship of parent and child should be divided, and it is quite clear that Locke was justified in accusing Filmer of making what he wanted stand in the place of argument (*pro ratione voluntas,* line 13) in the use he made of Grotius.

25 tainly sets all Mankind Free; as his affirming the contrary makes them all Slaves. But that this Position, which is the Foundation of all their Doctrine, who would have Monarchy to be *Jure Divino,* may have all fair play, let us hear what Reasons others give for it, since our *A.* offers 30 none.

52. The Argument, I have heard others make use of, to prove that Fathers, by begetting them, come by an Absolute Power over their Children, is this; That *Fathers have a Power over the Lives of their Children, because* 5 *they give them Life and Being,* which is the only proof it is capable of, since there can be no reason, why naturally one Man should have any claim or pretence of Right over that in another, which was never his, which he bestowed not, but was received from the bounty of another. 10 1°. I answer, That everyone who gives another any thing, has not always thereby a Right to take it away again. But, 2°. They who say the *Father* gives Life to his Children, are so dazled with the thoughts of Monarchy, that they do not, as they ought, remember God, who is *the Author* 15 *and Giver of Life: 'Tis in him alone we live, move, and have our Being.* How can he be thought to give Life to another, that knows not wherein his own Life consists? Philosophers are at a loss about it after their most diligent enquiries; And Anatomists, after their whole Lives and 20 Studies spent in Dissections, and diligent examining the Bodies of Men, confess their Ignorance in the Structure and Use of many parts of Mans Body, and in that Operation wherein Life consists in the whole. And doth the Rude Plough-Man, or the more ignorant Voluptuary, frame or 25 fashion such an admirable Engine as this is, and then put

§ 52 In this paragraph and down to number 55 there are evident traces of Locke's medical studies and of his scientific scepticism, attaching here to embryology as it does to the constitution of matter in his *Essay.* His answer to Filmer has an impressiveness here that it lacks elsewhere, though it is not strictly relevant as refutation, and is in contrast with Tyrrell's comments on the same point, for he merely denies that procreation gives absolute power to fathers because the mother would get a greater right from it. Man as the workmanship of God is a major theme of the *Second Treatise,* see II, §§ 6, 56, etc., and Introduction, 106. Pufendorf (1672, VI, ii, 4) contradicts Grotius here, and insists as Locke does (see also note in 1678 journal, Introduction, 49 and I, § 54, 4–5) that in procreation parents usually seek merely their own pleasure, and therefore it is the occasion not the foundation of parental power.

Life and Sense into it? Can any Man say, He formed the
parts that are necessary to the Life of his Child? Or can
he suppose himself to give the Life, and yet not know what
Subject is fit to receive it, nor what Actions or Organs are
necessary for its Reception or Preservation?   30

53.   To give Life to that which has yet no being, is
to frame and make a living Creature, fashion the parts,
and mould and suit them to their uses, and having proportion'd and fitted them together, to put into them a
living Soul. He that could do this, might indeed have   5
some pretence to destroy his own Workmanship. But is
there any one so bold, that dares thus far Arrogate to
himself the Incomprehensible Works of the Almighty?
Who alone did at first, and continues still to make a living
Soul, He alone can breathe in the Breath of Life. If any   10
one thinks himself an Artist at this, let him number up
the parts of his Childs Body which he hath made, tell
me their Uses and Operations, and when the living and
rational Soul began to inhabit this curious Structure, when
Sense began, and how this Engine which he has framed   15
Thinks and Reasons: If he made it, let him, when it is
out of order, mend it, at least tell wherein the defects lie.
Shall he that made the Eye not see? says the Psalmist,
Psalm 94. 9. See these Mens Vanities: The Structure of
that one part is sufficient to convince us of an All-wise   20
Contriver, and he has so visible a claim to us as his Work-
manship, that one of the ordinary Appellations of God in
Scripture is, *God our Maker,* and *the Lord our Maker.*
And therefore though our *A.* for the magnifying his
Fatherhood, be pleased to say, *O* 159. [233] *That even*   25
the Power which God himself exerciseth over Mankind
is by Right of Fatherhood, yet this Fatherhood is such an
one as utterly excludes all pretence of Title in Earthly
Parents; for he is *King* because he is indeed Maker of us
all, which no Parents can pretend to be of their Children.   30

54.   But had Men Skill and Power to make their Chil-
ren, 'tis not so slight a piece of Workmanship, that it can
be imagined they could make them without designing it.
What Father of a Thousand, when he begets a Child,
thinks farther then the satisfying his present Appetite?   5

§ 54   Compare I, § 52 note and references.

God in his infinite Wisdom has put strong desires of Copulation into the Constitution of Men, thereby to continue
the race of Mankind, which he doth most commonly without the intention, and often against the Consent and Will
10 of the Begetter. And indeed those who desire and design
Children, are but the occasions of their being, and when
they design and wish to beget them, do little more towards
their making, than *Ducalion* and his Wife in the Fable did
towards the making of Mankind, by throwing Pebbles
15 over their Heads.

55. But grant that the Parents made their Children,
gave them Life and Being, and that hence there
followed an Absolute Power. This would give the *Father*
but a joynt Dominion with the Mother over them. For
5 no body can deny but that the Woman hath an equal
share, if not the greater, as nourishing the Child a long
time in her own Body out of her own Substance. There
it is fashion'd, and from her it receives the Materials and
Principles of its Constitution; And it is so hard to imagine
10 the rational Soul should presently Inhabit the yet un-
formed Embrio, as soon as the Father has done his part
in the Act of Generation, that if it must be supposed to derive any thing from the Parents, it must certainly owe
most to the Mother: But be that as it will, the Mother
15 cannot be denied an equal share in begetting of the Child,
and so the Absolute Authority of the Father will not arise
from hence. Our *A——* indeed is of another mind; for
he says, *We know that God at the Creation gave the
Sovereignty to the Man over the Woman, as being the
20 Nobler and Principal Agent in Generation,* O. 172 [245].
I remember not this in my Bible, and when the place is
brought where God at the *Creation* gave the Sovereignty
to Man over the Woman, and that for this Reason, because *he is the Nobler and Principal Agent in Generation,*
25 it will be time enough to consider and answer it: But it
is no new thing for our *A——* to tell us his own Fancies
for certain and Divine Truths, though there be often a
great deal of difference between his and Divine Revela-

§ 54 6–8 Compare II, § 66, 9–11.
13 Deucalion's story corresponds in Greek mythology to Noah's. He
and his wife made an ark to survive the deluge, and afterwards were
told by the oracle to throw stones behind them. Those thrown by
Deucalion became men, those thrown by his wife became women, and
so the world was repopulated.

tions: for God in the Scripture says, *his Father and his*
Mother that begot him.   30

56. They who alledge the Practice of Mankind, for
exposing or selling their Children, as a Proof of their
Power over them, are with Sir *Rob.* happy Arguers, and
cannot but recommend their Opinion by founding it on the
most shameful Action, and most unnatural Murder, hu- 5
mane Nature is capable of. The Dens of Lions and
Nurseries of Wolves know no such Cruelty as this: These
Savage Inhabitants of the Desert obey God and Nature
in being tender and careful of their Off-spring: They will
Hunt, Watch, Fight, and almost Starve for the Preserva- 10
tion of their Young, never part with them, never forsake
them till they are able to shift for themselves; And is it
the Priviledge of Man alone to act more contrary to
Nature than the Wild and most Untamed part of the
Creation? Doth God forbid us under the severest Penalty, 15
that of Death, to take away the Life of any Man, a
Stranger, and upon Provocation? and does he permit us
to destroy those he has given us the Charge and Care of,
and by the dictates of Nature and Reason, as well as his
Reveal'd Command, requires us to preserve? He has in 20
all the parts of the Creation taken a peculiar care to
propagate and continue the several Species of Creatures,
and makes the Individuals act so strongly to this end, that
they sometimes neglect their own private good for it, and

§ 55   29–30 '*his Father and his Mother that begot him*', from Zech, xiii.
3, where parents punish their children with death for prophesying.
§ 56   3 'happy Arguers'—in *Patriarcha* (77–8) Filmer shows, with an
example from Roman history, that fathers could punish their children
with death, and in the *Directions* (231) he says: 'God also hath given
to the Father a right . . . to alien his power over his children . . .
whence we find the sale and gift of children . . . much in use in the
beginning of the world . . . the power of castrating . . . much in use.'
These statements come unaltered from Bodin's *République*, where it is
said that it is 'needful to restore unto parents . . . their power of life
and death over their children' (Knolles's translation, p. 22). Bodin must
have been among the 'happy Arguers', but there were others perhaps
even as late as Montesquieu (see *Esprit des Lois*, v, 7). Tyrrell is more
straightforward than Locke over this, and tackles Bodin direct, as does
Sidney. It is notable that only Locke in answering Filmer failed to go
behind him to his source, for Bodin is of the very greatest importance
to all that Filmer wrote—see Laslett, 1949.
20–31 There is an echo of the medieval bestiary in this paragraph:
on natural love for children compare II, § 60, 19–23; II, § 63; II, § 67,
17–23 and II, § 170. On preservation of self or offspring compare I,
§ 88, 15–20, and Strauss, 1953, 227, where Locke's slight vacillation here
is made into a Hobbesian insistence on the primacy of self.

25 seem to forget that general Rule which Nature teaches
all things of self Preservation, and the Preservation of
their Young, as the strongest Principle in them over rules
the Constitution of their particular Natures. Thus we see
when their Young stand in need of it, the timorous become
30 Valiant, the Fierce and Savage Kind, and the Ravenous
Tender and Liberal.

57. But if the Example of what hath been done, be
the Rule of what ought to be, History would have furnish'd
our A—— with instances of this *Absolute Fatherly Power*
in its heighth and perfection, and he might have shew'd
5 us in *Peru*, People that begot Children on purpose to
Fatten and Eat them. The Story is so remarkable, that I
cannot but set it down in the A——'s Words. 'In some
'Provinces, *says he*, they were so liquorish after Mans
'Flesh, that they wou'd not have the patience to stay till
10 'the Breath was out of the Body, but would suck the
'Blood as it ran from the Wounds of the dying Man; they
'had publick Shambles of Man's Flesh, and their Mad-
'ness herein was to that degree, that they spared not their
'own Children which they had Begot on Strangers taken
15 'in War: For they made their Captives their Mistresses
'and choisly nourished the Children they had by them,
'till about thirteen Years Old they Butcher'd and Eat
'them, and they served the Mothers after the same fashion,
'when they grew past Child bearing, and ceased to bring
20 'them any more Roasters, *Garcilasso de la vega hist. des
'yncas de* Peru, I, 1. c. 12.'

58. Thus far can the busie mind of Man carry him
to a Brutality below the level of Beasts, when he quits
his reason, which places him almost equal to Angels.
Nor can it be otherwise in a Creature, whose thoughts
5 are more than the Sands, and wider than the Ocean, where

§ 57 20–1 The French translation of the *Comentarios Reales* of
Garcilaso de la Vega, published in 1633, seems to have been a favourite
book, and it was in Locke's Oxford study in 1681, see Appendix B,
no. 88. It is frequently quoted in his diaries and published works: indeed
the very passage used here is also to be found, somewhat differently
translated, in his *Essay on the Understanding*, I, iii, 9 (1894, 1, 73).
It was probably added to both works in 1689: here it has no particular
relevance and seems to have been dragged in to make a sensation. But
see Introduction, 67, and compare I, § 153, 21–3 and note.
§ 58 This paragraph forms an important declaration of the essential
rightness of 'Natural Man' and reads almost like Rousseau, the Rousseau

fancy and passion must needs run him into strange courses,
if reason, which is his only Star and compass, be not that
he steers by. The imagination is always restless and suggests variety of thoughts, and the will, reason being laid
aside, is ready for every extravagant project; and in this 10
State, he that goes farthest out of the way, is thought
fittest to lead, and is sure of most followers: And when
Fashion hath once Established, what Folly or craft began,
Custom makes it Sacred, and 'twill be thought impudence
or madness, to contradict or question it. He that will 15
impartially survey the Nations of the World, will find so
much of their Governments, Religions, and Manners
brought in and continued amongst them by these means,
that he will have but little Reverence for the Practices
which are in use and credit amongst Men, and will have 20
Reason to think, that the Woods and Forests, where the
irrational untaught Inhabitants keep right by following
Nature, are fitter to give us Rules, than Cities and Palaces,
where those that call themselves Civil and Rational, go
out of their way, by the Authority of Example. If prece- 25
dents are sufficient to establish a rule in the case, our
A—— might have found in holy writ Children sacrificed
by their parents and this amongst the people of God
themselves. The Psalmist tells us *Psalm. cvi. 38. They
shed innocent bloud even the bloud of their sons and of* 30
*their daughters when they sacrificed unto the Idols of
Canaan.* But God judgd not of this by our A——s rule,
nor allowd of the authoritie of practise against his righteous Law, but as it follows there, *The Land was polluted
with bloud, therefore was the wrath of the Lord kindled* 35
*against his people in so much that he abhorred his own
inheritance.* The killing of their Children, though it were
fashionable, was charged on them as *innocent bloud,* and
so had, in the account of God, the guilt of murder, as the
offering them to Idols had the guilt of Idolatry.   40

59. Be it then as Sir *Robert* says, that *Anciently,* it
was *usual* for Men *to sell and Castrate their Children,* O.

---

of the *Discours sur l'Inégalité;* compare II, § 6. In talking here of the
strength of fashion, Locke touches on a determinist strain which runs
through his thought about society: compare the *Essay,* II, xxviii, especially section 12, 'the greatest part of mankind govern themselves
chiefly, if not solely, by this *law of fashion*', which in section 10 was
'the *law of opinion or reputation*', in the earlier editions of the *Essay*
even the '*philosophical law*' (1894, 1, 476–80, compare Introduction, 95).

155 [231]. Let it be, that they exposed them; Add to it,
if you please, for this is still greater Power, that they
5 begat them for their Tables to fat and eat them: If this
proves a right to do so, we may, by the same Argument,
justifie Adultery, Incest and Sodomy, for there are examples of these too, both Ancient and Modern; Sins,
which I suppose, have their Principal Aggravation from
10 this, that they cross the main intention of Nature, which
willeth the increase of Mankind, and the continuation of
the Species in the highest perfection, and the distinction of
Families, with the Security of the Marriage Bed, as necessary thereunto.

60. In confirmation of this Natural Authority of the
Father, our *A.* brings a lame Proof, from the positive
Command of God in Scripture; His words are, *to confirm*
the Natural Right of Regal Power, we find in the Deca-
5 *logue, that the Law which injoyns Obedience to Kings,*
is delivered in the Terms, Honour thy Father, p. 23 [62].
Whereas many confess, that Government only in the Ab-
stract, is the Ordinance of God, they are not able to prove
any such Ordinance in the Scripture, but only in the
10 *Fatherly Power, and therefore we find the Commandment,*
that injoyns Obedience to Superiors, given in the Terms,
Honour thy Father; so that not only the Power and Right
of Government, but the Form of the Power Governing,
and the Person having the Power, are all the Ordinances
15 *of God. The first Father had not only simply Power, but*
Power Monarchical, as he was Father immediately from
God, O. 254 [289]. To the same purpose, the same Law is
cited by our *A.* in several other places, and just after the
same Fashion, that is, *and Mother,* as Apocriphal Words,
20 are always left out; a great Argument of our *A's* ingenuity, and the goodness of his Cause, which required in
its Defender Zeal to a degree of warmth, able to warp the
Sacred Rule of the Word of God, to make it comply with
his present occasion; a way of proceeding, not unusual to

§ **60**   3–17   These quotations differ in detail from Filmer's text: 'several
other places' in line 18 presumably refers to 188, 283.
     19   *'and Mother'*—this discussion of Filmer's omission of 'Mother' in
his use of the Fifth Commandment occupies Locke until paragraph 66
and fulfils the promise of I, §§ 6 and 11. The argument is stated in
II, §§ 52, 53. Sidney and Tyrrell do not make such use of this obvious
equivocation, indeed Sidney implies that Filmer omitted 'Mother' by
accident (1772, 57).

those, who imbrace not Truths, because Reason and Revela- 25
tion offer them; but espouse Tenets and Parties, for ends
different from Truth, and then resolve at any rate to defend
them; and so do with the Words and Sense of Authors,
they would fit to their purpose, just as *Procrustes* did with
his guests, lop or stretch them, as may best fit them to the 30
size of their Notions: And they always prove like those,
so served, Deformed, Lame, and useless.

61. For had our *A.* set down this Command without
Garbling, as God gave it, and joyned *Mother* to Father,
every Reader would have seen that it had made directly
against him, and that it was so far from Establishing the
Monarchical Power of the Father, that it set up the *Mother* 5
equal with him, and injoyn'd nothing but what was due in
common, to both Father and Mother: for that is the
constant Tenor of the Scripture, *Honour thy Father and
thy Mother,* Exod. 20. *He that smiteth his Father or
Mother, shall surely be put to Death,* 21. 15. *He that* 10
curseth his Father or Mother, shall surely be put to Death,
Ver. 17. Repeated *Lev.* 20. 9. and by our Saviour, *Matth.*
15. 4. *Ye shall fear every Man his Mother and his Father,*
Lev. 19. 3. *If a Man have a Rebellious Son, which will not
Obey the Voice of his Father, or the Voice of his Mother;* 15
*then shall his Father and his Mother, lay hold on him, and
say, this our Son is Stubborn and Rebellious, he will not
Obey our Voice,* Deut. 21. 18, 19, 20, 21. *Cursed be he
that setteth Light by his Father or his Mother,* 27. 16. *My
Son, hear the Instructions of thy Father, and forsake not* 20
the Law of thy Mother, are the Words of *Solomon* a King,
who was not ignorant of what belonged to him, as a
Father or a King, and yet he joyns *Father* and *Mother*
together, in all the Instructions he gives Children quite
through his Book of *Proverbs, Wo unto him, that sayeth* 25
*unto his Father, what begettest thou, or to the Woman, what
hast thou brought forth,* Isa. 45. ver. 10. *In thee have they
set Light by Father or Mother,* Ezek. 22. 7. *And it shall
come to pass, that when any shall yet Prophesie, then his
Father and his Mother that begat him, shall say unto him,* 30
thou shalt not live, and his Father and his Mother that

29 'Procrustes'—the legendary brigand of Eleusis who trimmed or
stretched his victims to the length of a bed.
§ 61 Four of the texts cited here are quoted less exactly in II, § 52,
17–21, see note there.

begat him, shall thrust him through when he Prophesieth,
Zech. 13. 3. Here not the Father only, but Father and
Mother joyntly, had Power in this Case of Life and
35 Death. Thus ran the Law of the Old Testament, and in
the New they are likewise joyn'd, in the Obedience of their
Children, *Eph.* 6. 1. The Rule is, *Children Obey your
Parents,* and I do not remember, that I any where read,
Children Obey your Father and no more. The Scripture
40 joyns *Mother* too in that Homage, which is due from
Children, and had there been any Text, where the Honour
or Obedience of Children had been directed to the *Father*
alone, 'tis not likely that our *A.,* who pretends to Build
all upon Scripture, would have omitted it. Nay, the
45 Scripture makes the Authority of *Father and Mother,*
in respect of those they have begot, so equal, that in some
places it neglects, even the Priority of Order, which is
thought due to the Father, and the *Mother* is put first,
as *Lev.* 19. 3. From which so constantly joyning Father
50 and Mother together, as is found quite through the
Scripture, we may conclude that the Honour they have
a Title to from their Children, is one common Right
belonging so equally to them both, that neither can claim
it wholly, neither can be excluded.

62. One would wonder then how our *A.* infers from
the 5th Commandment, that all *Power was originally in the
Father.* How he finds *Monarchical Power of Government,
settled and fixed by the Commandment, Honour thy
5 Father* and thy Mother. If all the Honour due by the
Commandment, be it what it will, be the only right of
the *Father,* because he, as our *A——* says, *has the
Soveraignty over the Woman, as being the Nobler and
Principal Agent in Generation* [245], why did God after-
10 wards all along joyn the *Mother* with him, to share in this
Honour? Can the Father, by this Sovereignty of his, discharge the Child from paying this *Honour* to his *Mother?*
The Scripture gave no such License to the Jews, and yet
there were often Breaches wide enough betwixt Husband
15 and Wife, even to Divorce and Separation, and, I think,
no Body will say a Child may withhold Honour from his
Mother, or, as the Scripture terms it, *set light by her,*

49 '*Lev.* 19. 3'.—'Ye shall fear every man his mother and father',
cited II, § 52, 19.
§ **62** 15–22 This point is made in II, § 69, 10–13.

though his Father should command him to do so, no more
than the Mother could dispense with him, for neglecting
to *Honour* his Father, whereby 'tis plain, that this Com- 20
mand of God, gives the Father no Sovereignty, no Supremacy.

63. I agree with our *A——*, that the Title to this
Honour is vested in the Parents by Nature, and is a right
which accrews to them, by their having begotten their
Children, and God by many positive Declarations has
confirm'd it to them: I also allow our *A——*s Rule, *that* 5
in Grants and Gifts, that have their Original from God
and Nature, as the Power of the Father (let me add *and*
Mother, for whom God hath joyned together, let no Man
put asunder) *no inferior Power of Men can limit, nor*
make any Law of Prescription against them, O. 158. [233] 10
so that the Mother having by this Law of God, a right to
Honour from her Children, which is not Subject to the Will
of her Husband, we see this *Absolute Monarchical Power*
of the Father, can neither be founded on it, nor consist with
it; And he has a Power very far from *Monarchical,* very 15
far from that Absoluteness our *A——* contends for,
when another has over his Subjects the same Power he
hath, and by the same Title: And therefore he cannot
forbear saying himself that *he cannot see how any Mans*
Children can be free from Subjection to their Parents, p. 20
12. [57] which, in common Speech, I think, signifies *Mother*
as well as *Father,* or if *Parents* here signifies only *Father,*
'tis the first time I ever yet knew it to do so, and by such an
use of Words, one may say any thing.

64. By our *A——*s Doctrine, the Father having Absolute Jurisdiction over his Children, has also the same over
their Issue, and the consequence is good, were it true, that
the Father had such a Power: And yet I ask our *A——*
whether the Grandfather, by his Sovereignty, could dis- 5
charge the Grand-child from paying to his Father the
Honour due to him by the *5th* Commandment. If the
Grandfather hath by *right of Fatherhood,* sole Sovereign
Power in him, and that Obedience which is due to the
Supreme Magistrate, be Commanded in these Words, 10

§ 64   4–7 This argument was used against Filmer by both Sidney
(chapter 1, section 15) and by Tyrrell (1681, 3), though not so
pointedly.

Honour thy Father, 'tis certain the Grandfather might
dispense with the Grand-sons Honouring his Father, which,
since 'tis evident in common Sense, he cannot, it follows
from hence that, *Honour thy Father and Mother,* cannot
15 mean an absolute Subjection to a Sovereign Power, but
something else. The right therefore which Parents have
by Nature, and which is confirmed to them by the *5th*
Commandment, cannot be that political Dominion, which
our *A——* would derive from it: For that being in every
20 Civil Society Supreme somewhere, can discharge any
Subject from any Political Obedience to any one of his
fellow Subjects. But what Law of the Magistrate, can
give a Child liberty, not to *Honour his Father and
Mother?* 'Tis an Eternal Law annex'd purely to the relation
25 of Parents and Children, and so contains nothing of the
Magistrates Power in it, nor is subjected to it.

65. Our *A——* says, *God hath given to a Father, a
Right or Liberty to alien his Power over his Children to
any other,* O. 155 [231]. I doubt whether he can *Alien*
wholly the right of *Honour* that is due from them; But
5 be that as it will, this I am sure, he cannot *Alien,* and
retain the same Power, if therefore the Magistrates Sovereignty be as our *A——* would have it, *nothing but the
Authority of a Supreme Father, p.* 23. [62] 'tis unavoidable,
that if the Magistrate hath all this Paternal Right as he
10 must have if *Fatherhood* be the Fountain of all Authority,
then the Subjects though Fathers, can have no Power over
their Children, no right to Honour from them: for it
cannot be all in anothers hands, and a part remain with
the Parents. So that according to our *A——s* own Doctrine,
15 *Honour thy Father and Mother* cannot possibly be understood of Political Subjection and Obedience; since the
Laws both in the Old and New Testament, that Commanded Children to *Honour and obey their Parents,* were

12–19 In denying, as he seems to do here, that the Fifth Commandment has anything to do with political obedience, Locke was
repudiating far more than the principles of Filmer. He was attacking a
tradition of Christianity, and particularly of Protestant Christianity.
Luther, for example, develops his whole doctrine of political and social
authority as a commentary on the Fifth Commandment (*Von den Guten
Werken,* 1520 [1888]), and Tynsdale argues in a precisely similar manner
in his *Obedience of a Christian Man,* 1528 (1848). See the discussion
in Laslett, 1949, 20–33.
§ 65 3–14 Compare II, § 71, 1–8.

given to such, whose Fathers were under civil Government, and fellow Subjects with them in Political Societies; 20
and to have bid them *Honour and obey their Parents* in our
A——s Sense, had been to bid them be Subjects to those
who had no Title to it, the right to Obedience from Subjects, being all vested in another: and instead of teaching
Obedience, this had been to foment Sedition, by setting up 25
Powers that were not. If therefore this Command, *Honour
thy Father and Mother,* concern Political Dominion, it
directly overthrows our *A——s* Monarchy; it being since
to be paid by every Child to his Father, even in Society,
every Father must necessarily have Political Dominion, 30
and there will be as many Sovereigns as there are Fathers:
besides that the Mother too hath her Title, which destroys
the Sovereignty of one Supream Monarch. But if *Honour
thy Father and Mother* mean something distinct from
Political Power, as necessarily it must, it is besides our 35
A——s business, and serves nothing to his purpose.

66.   *The Law that enjoyns Obedience to Kings is delivered,* says our *A——,* *in the Terms, Honour thy Father,
as if all Power were Originally in the Father,* p. 23 [62].
And that Law is also delivered, say I, in the Terms,
Honour thy Mother, as if all Power were Originally in the 5
Mother. I appeal whether the Argument be not as good on
one side as the other, *Father and Mother* being joyned all
along in the Old and New Testament where ever Honour
or Obedience is injoyn'd Children. Again our *A——*
tells us, O. 254. [289] *that this Command, Honour thy* 10
*Father gives the right to govern, and makes the Form of
Government, Monarchical.* To which I answer, that, if
by *Honour thy Father* be meant Obedience to the Political
Power of the Magistrate, it concerns not any duty we owe
to our natural Fathers who are Subjects: because they, by 15
our *A——s* Doctrine, are divested of all that Power, it
being placed wholly in the Prince, and so being equally
Subjects and Slaves with their Children, can have no right
by that Title, to any such *Honour or Obedience,* as contains in it Political Subjection: If *Honour thy Father and* 20

30–1 Compare Sidney, 1772, 21: 'This paternal power must necessarily accrue to every father: he is a king by the same right as the sons
of Noah.' See also Tyrrell, 1681, for example, 38.
§ 66   3   'p. 23'—Locke wrote 'O. 254', assimilating it with the next
reference, line 10. His quotations and references are careless in this
part of the text.

Mother signifies the duty we owe our Natural Parents, as by our Saviour's Interpretation, *Matth.* 15. 4. and all the other mentioned places, 'tis plain it does, then it cannot concern Political Obedience, but a duty that is
25 owing to Persons, who have no Title to Sovereignty, nor any Political Authority as Magistrates over Subjects. For the Person of a private Father, and a Title to Obedience, due to the Supreme Magistrate, are things inconsistent; and therefore this Command, which must necessarily
30 comprehend the Persons of our Natural Fathers, must mean a duty we owe them distinct from our Obedience to the Magistrate, and from which the most Absolute Power of Princes cannot absolve us: What this Duty is, we shall in its due place examine.

67.   And thus we have at last got through all that in our *A.* looks like an Argument for that *Absolute Unlimited Sovereignty* described, Sect. 8. which he supposes in *Adam,* so that Mankind ever since have been all born *Slaves,*
5 without any Title to Freedom. But if *Creation* which gave nothing but a Being, made not *Adam Prince of his Posterity:* If *Adam, Gen.* 1. 28. was not constituted Lord of Mankind, nor had a *Private Dominion* given him exclusive of his Children, but only a Right and Power over the Earth,
10 and inferiour Creatures in common with the Children of Men: If also *Gen.* 3. 16. God gave not any Political Power to *Adam* over his Wife and Children, but only subjected *Eve* to *Adam,* as a punishment, or foretold the Subjection of the weaker Sex, in the ordering the com-
15 mon concernments of their Families, but gave not thereby to *Adam,* as to the Husband, Power of Life and Death, which necessarily belongs to the Magistrate: If Fathers by begetting their Children acquire no such Power over them: And if the Command, *Honour thy Father and*
20 *Mother,* give it not, but only enjoyns a Duty owing to Parents equally, whether Subjects or not, and to the *Mother* as well as the *Father;* If all this be so, as I think,

22–3 See Matt. xv. 4: 'For God commanded, saying, Honour thy father and mother: and He that curseth father or mother, let him die the death', compare I, § 49, 15. The Authorized Version has eleven 'mentioned places' in the margin, all in the Old Testament.

34 The 'due place' is evidently the *Second Treatise,* chapter VI (§§ 52–76), see Introduction, 63.

§ 67 3 'Sect. 8.'—that is, section V (60–1) of *Patriarcha* in Laslett's edition.

by what has been said, is very evident, then Man has a
Natural Freedom, notwithstanding all our *A.* confidently
says to the contrary, since all that share in the same com- 25
mon Nature, Faculties and Powers, are in Nature equal,
and ought to partake in the same common Rights and
Priviledges, till the manifest appointment of God, who is
Lord over all, Blessed for ever, can be produced to shew
any particular Persons Supremacy, or a Mans own consent 30
subjects him to a Superior. This is so plain, that our *A.*
confesses, that Sir *John Hayward, Blackwood* and *Barclay,
the great Vindicators of the Right of Kings,* could not deny
it, but *admit with one consent the Natural Liberty and
Equality of Mankind,* for a Truth unquestionable. And our 35
A. hath been so far from producing any thing, that may
make good his great Position, That *Adam was Absolute
Monarch,* and so *Men are not Naturally Free,* that even
his own Proofs make against him; so that to use his own
way of Arguing, *This first erroneous Principle failing, the* 40
whole Fabrick of this vast Engine of Absolute Power
and Tyranny, *drops down of it self,* and there needs no
more to be said in answer to all that he builds upon so
false and frail a Foundation.

68. But to save others the Pains, were there any need,
he is not sparing himself to shew, by his own Contradictions, the weakness of his own Doctrine. *Adam*'s Absolute
and Sole Dominion is that which he is every where full of,
and all along builds on, and yet he tells us, *pag.* 12. [57] 5
*That as Adam was Lord of his Children, so his Children
under him had a Command and Power over their own
Children.* The unlimited and undivided Sovereignty of
Adam's Fatherhood, by our *A*'s Computation, stood but
a little while, only during the first Generation, but as soon as 10
he had Grand-Children, Sir *Rob.* could give but a very ill
account of it. *Adam, as Father of his Children,* saith he,

25–30 A striking re-echo of the language of II, § 4, setting forth the
basis of human equality, see Introduction, 19.
    29 Rom. xi. 5: 'Christ . . . who is over all, God blessed for ever.'
    31–3 *Patriarcha,* 54: on these authors see the previous citation in I,
§ 4, note and references.
    40–2 Locke is refuting Filmer in his own words, substituting
'Absolute Power and Tyranny' for 'Popular Sedition'. The phrase as
Locke modifies it occurs on p. 4 of the 1680 printing, but in the
manuscript Filmer had written 'the main foundation of popular sedition
would be taken away', Laslett's edition, p. 54.

*hath an Absolute, Unlimited Royal Power over them, and
by virtue thereof over those that they begot, and so to all*
15 *Generations* [57]; and yet *his Children*, viz. *Cain* and
Seth, have a Paternal Power over their Children at the
same time: so that they are at the same time *Absolute
Lords*, and yet *Vassals and Slaves: Adam* has all the
Authority, as *Grand-Father of the People*, and they have
20 a part of it as Fathers of a part of them: He is Absolute
over them and their Posterity, by having begotten them,
and yet they are Absolute over their Children by the same
Title. *No*, says our *A.*, *Adam's Children under him, had
Power over their own Children, but still with Subordination*
25 *to the first Parent* [57]. A good distinction that sounds
well, and 'tis pity it signifies nothing, nor can be reconciled with our *A.*'s Words. I readily grant, that supposing
Adam's Absolute Power over his Posterity, any of his
Children might have from him a delegated, and so a
30 *Subordinate* Power over a part, or all the rest: But that
cannot be the Power our *A.* speaks of here, it is not a
Power by Grant and Commission, but the Natural Paternal
Power he supposes a Father to have over his Children. For
1°, he says, *As* Adam *was Lord of his Children, so his*
35 *Children under him had a Power over their own Children:*
They were then Lords over their own Children after the
same manner, and by the same Title, that *Adam* was, *i.e.*
by right of Generation, by right of *Fatherhood*. 2°. 'Tis
plain he means the Natural Power of Fathers, because he
40 limits it to be only *over their own Children;* a delegated
Power has no such limitation, as only over their own
Children, it might be over others, as well as their own
Children. 3°. If it were a delegated Power, it must appear
in Scripture: but there is no ground in Scripture to affirm,
45 that *Adam's* Children had any other Power over theirs,
than what they Naturally had as Fathers.

69. But that he means here Paternal Power, and no
other, is past doubt from the Inference he makes in these
words immediately following, *I see not then how the Children of* Adam, *or of any Man else can be free from*
5 *Subjection to their Parents* [57]: whereby it appears, that
the *Power* on one side, and the *Subjection* on the other,
our *A.* here speaks of, is that *Natural Power* and *Subjection* between Parents and Children. For that which every
Mans Children owed, could be no other: and that our *A.*

always affirms to be Absolute and Unlimited. This Natural 10
Power of Parents over their Children, *Adam* had over his
Posterity, says our *A.*, and this *Power* of Parents over their
Children, his Children had over theirs in his Life-time,
says our *A.* also: so that *Adam*, by a Natural Right of
Father, had an Absolute, Unlimited Power over all his 15
Posterity, and at the same time his Children had by the
same Right Absolute Unlimited Power over theirs. Here
then are two Absolute Unlimited Powers existing together,
which I would have any body reconcile one to another,
or to common Sense. For the *Salvo* he has put in of 20
Subordination, makes it more absurd: To have one *Absolute, Unlimited*, nay *Unlimitable Power* in Subordination
to another, is so manifest a Contradiction, that nothing
can be more. Adam *is Absolute Prince with the Unlimited
Authority of Fatherhood over all his Posterity;* All his 25
Posterity are then absolutely his Subjects, and, as our *A.*
says, his *Slaves*, Children and Grand-Children, are equally
in this State of Subjection and Slavery, and yet, says our
A. the Children of Adam *have Paternal,* i.e. Absolute,
Unlimited *Power over their own Children:* which in plain 30
English is, they are Slaves and Absolute Princes at the same
time, and in the same Government, and one part of the
Subjects have an Absolute Unlimited Power over the other
by the Natural Right of Parentage.

70. If any one will suppose in favour of our *A.* that
he here meant, that Parents, who are in Subjection themselves to the Absolute Authority of their Father, have yet
some Power over their Children: I confess he is something
nearer the Truth: But he will not at all hereby help our *A.* 5
For he no where speaking of the Paternal Power, but as an
Absolute Unlimited Authority, cannot be suppos'd to understand any thing else here, unless he himself had limited it, and
shewed how far it reach'd. And that he means here Paternal
Authority in that large Extent, is plain from the immediate 10
following words; *This Subjection of Children being,* says
he, *the Fountain of all Regal Authority,* p. 12 [57]. *The
Subjection,* then that in the former Line he says, *every
Man is in to his Parents,* and consequently what *Adam*'s
Grand-Children were in to their Parents, was that which 15
was the Fountain of all *Regal Authority, i.e.* According to
our *A., Absolute, Unlimitable* Authority. And thus *Adam*'s
Children had *Regal Authority* over their Children, whilst

they themselves were Subjects to their Father, and Fellow-
20 Subjects with their Children. But let him mean as he
pleases, 'tis plain he allows *Adam's Children to have
Paternal Power,* p. 12. [57] as also all other Fathers to
have *Paternal Power over their Children,* O. 156 [232].
From whence one of these two things will necessarily fol-
25 low, that either *Adam's* Children, even in his lifetime, had,
and so all other Fathers have, as he phrases it, *p. 12* [57].
*By Right of Fatherhood Royal Authority over their
Children,* or else, that *Adam, by Right of Fatherhood,
had not Royal Authority:* For it cannot be but that *Paternal
30 Power* does, or does not, give *Royal Authority* to them
that have it: If it does not, then *Adam* could not be
Sovereign by this Title, nor any body else, and then there
is an end of all our *A's* Politics at once; If it does give
Royal Authority, then every one that has *Paternal Power*
35 has *Royal Authority,* and then by our *A's* Patriarchical
Government, there will be as many Kings as there are
Fathers.

71.   And thus what a Monarchy he hath set up, let him
and his Disciples consider. Princes certainly will have great
Reason to thank him for these new Politics, which set up
as many Absolute Kings in every Country as there are
5 Fathers of Children. And yet who can blame our *A.*
for it, it lying unavoidably in the way of one discoursing
upon our *A's* Principles? For having placed an *Absolute
Power* in *Fathers by Right of Begetting,* he could not easily
resolve how much of this Power belong'd to a Son over
10 the Children he had begotten; And so it fell out to be a very
hard matter to give all the Power, as he does, to *Adam,*
and yet allow a part in his Lifetime to his Children, when
they were Parents, and which he knew not well how to
deny them. This makes him so doubtful in his Expressions,
15 and so uncertain where to place this Absolute Natural
Power, which he calls *Fatherhood;* sometimes *Adam* alone
has it all, as *p. 13.* [58] *O.* 244, 245 [282/3]. & *Pref.* [188].
  Sometimes *Parents* have it, which word scarce signifies
the Father alone, *p. 12.* [57] 19 [61].
20 Sometimes *Children* during their Fathers Lifetime, as
p. 12 [57].
  Sometimes *Fathers* of *Families,* as *p. 78* [96], and 79 [96].
  Sometimes *Fathers* indefinitely, *O.* 155 [231].
  Sometimes the *Heir to Adam, O.* 253 [289].

Sometimes *the Posterity of Adam,* 244 [283], 246 [284]. 25
Sometimes *prime Fathers, all Sons or Grand-Children of Noah, O.* 244 [283].
Sometimes *the eldest Parents, p.* 12 [57].
Sometimes all Kings, *p.* 19 [60].
Sometimes all that have Supreme Power, *O.* 245 [281].   30
Sometimes *Heirs to those first Progenitors, who were at first the Natural Parents of the whole People, p.* 19 [61].
Sometimes an Elective King, *p.* 23 [62].
Sometimes those whether a few or a multitude that Govern the *Commonwealth, p.* 23 [62].   35
Sometimes he that can catch it, an Usurper, *p.* 23. [62] *O.* 155 [232].

72.   Thus this *New Nothing,* that is to carry with it all Power, Authority, and Government; This *Fatherhood* which is to design the Person, and Establish the Throne of Monarchs, whom the People are to obey, may, according to Sir *Robert,* come into any Hands, any how, and so by his 5 Politicks give to Democracy Royal Authority, and make an Usurper a Lawful Prince. And if it will do all these fine Feats, much good do our Author and all his Followers with their Omnipotent *Fatherhood,* which can serve for nothing but to unsettle and destroy all the Lawful Govern- 10 ments in the World, and to Establish in their room Disorder, Tyranny, and Usurpation.

§ 72   1   *'New Nothing'*—a conventional phrase for an empty novelty: in Victorian Oxford they used the expression 'A silver new nothing and a tantadling tart'.

Of Fatherhood and Property Considered together as Fountains of Sovereignty.

73.   In the foregoing Chapters we have seen what *Adam's* Monarchy was, in our *A's* Opinion, and upon what Titles he founded it. The Foundations which he lays the chief stress on, as those from which he thinks he may best derive Monarchical Power to future Princes, are two, *viz.* *Fatherhood and Property*, and therefore the way he proposes to *remove the Absurdities and Inconveniences of the Doctrine of Natural Freedom*, is, *to maintain the Natural and Private Dominion of Adam*, O. 222 [71]. Conformable hereunto, he tells us, the *Grounds and Principles of Government necessarily depend upon the Original of Property*, O. 108 [204]. *The Subjection of Children to their Parents is the Fountain of all Regal Authority*, p. 12 [57]. And *all Power on Earth is either derived or usurped from the Fatherly Power, there being no other Original to be found of any Power whatsoever*, O. 158 [233]. I will not stand here to examine how it can be said without a Contradiction, that the *first Grounds and Principles of Government necessarily depend upon the Original of Property*, and yet, *that there is no other Original of any Power whatsoever, but that of the Father:* It being hard to understand how there can be *no other Original* but *Fatherhood*, and yet that the *Grounds and Principles of Government depend upon the Original of Property; Property and Fatherhood* being as far different as Lord of a Mannor and Father of Children. Nor do I see how they will either of them agree with what our *A.* says, *O.* 244 [283] of God's Sentence against *Eve, Gen.* 3. 16. *That it is the Original Grant of Government:* so

§ 73 Title to chapter VII—'*Property*' substituted for '*Propriety*' by Locke after 1698, a correction frequently made elsewhere, though it is difficult to see why, unless the language had changed between 1680 and 1700.

that if that were the *Original*, Government had not its 30
Original by our *A*'s own Confession, either from *Property*
or *Fatherhood;* and this Text which he brings as a proof of
Adam's Power over *Eve*, necessarily contradicts what he
says of the *Fatherhood*, that it is the *Sole Fountain of all
Power*. For if *Adam* had any such Regal Power over *Eve*, 35
as our *A*. contends for, it must be by some other Title
than that of begetting.

74.   But I leave him to reconcile these Contradictions
as well as many others, which may plentifully be found in
him by any one, who will but read him with a little Attention, and shall come now to consider how these two
Originals of Government, *Adam*'s *Natural* and *Private* 5
Dominion, will consist, and serve to make out and Establish
the Titles of succeeding Monarchs, who, as our *A*. obliges
them, must all derive their Power from these *Fountains*.
Let us then suppose *Adam* made *by God's Donation* Lord
and Sole Proprietor of the whole Earth, in as large and 10
ample a manner as Sir *Robert* could wish; let us suppose
him also *by Right of Fatherhood* Absolute Ruler over his
Children with an unlimited Supremacy, I ask then upon
Adam's Death what becomes of both his *Natural* and
Private Dominion, and I doubt not 'twill be answered, that 15
they descended to his next Heir, as our *A*. tells us in
several places; But this way 'tis plain, cannot possibly
convey both his *Natural* and *Private Dominion* to the same
Person. For should we allow that all the Property, all the
Estate of the Father ought to descend to the Eldest Son, 20
(which will need some proof to Establish it) and so he
has by that Title all the *Private Dominion* of the Father,
yet the Father's *Natural Dominion*, the Paternal Power
cannot descend to him by Inheritance. For it being a Right
that accrews to a Man only by *begetting*, no Man can have 25
this Natural Dominion over any one he does not *beget:*
unless it can be suppos'd, that a man can have a Right to
any thing, without doing that upon which that Right
is solely founded. For if a Father by *begetting*, and no other
Title, has *Natural Dominion* over his Children, he that does 30
not beget them, cannot have this *Natural Dominion* over
them: and therefore be it true or false that our *A*. says,
O. 156. [232] That *every Man that is born, by his very
Birth becomes a Subject to him that begets him*, this necessarily follows, *viz*. That a Man by his Birth cannot become 35

a Subject to his Brother, who did not beget him: unless it
can be suppos'd that a Man by the very same Title can
come to be under the *Natural and Absolute Dominion*
of two different Men at once, or it be Sense to say, that
40 a Man by Birth is under the *Natural Dominion* of his
Father, only because he begat him, and a Man by Birth
also is under the *Natural Dominion* of his Eldest Brother,
though he did not beget him.

75. If then the *Private Dominion* of *Adam*, i.e. his
Property in the Creatures, descended at his Death all
entirely to his Eldest Son, his Heir; (for if it did not,
there is presently an end of all Sir *Robert's* Monarchy)
5 and his *Natural Dominion*, the Dominion a Father has
over his Children by begetting them, belong'd immediately
upon *Adam's* decease equally to all his Sons who had
Children, by the same Title their Father had it, the
Sovereignty founded upon *Property*, and the Sovereignty
10 founded upon *Fatherhood*, come to be divided: since
Cain as Heir had that of *Property* alone, *Seth* and the
other Sons that of *Fatherhood* equally with him. This is
the best can be made of our *A's* Doctrine, and of the
two Titles of Sovereignty he sets up in *Adam*, one of them
15 will either signifie nothing, or if they both must stand,
they can serve only to confound the Rights of Princes,
and disorder Government in his Posterity. For by building
upon two Titles to Dominion, which cannot descend together, and which he allows may be separated (for he
20 yields that *Adam's Children had their distinct Territories
by Right of Private Dominion*, O. 210. [54] *p.* 40 [78]) he
makes it perpetually a doubt upon his Principles where the
Sovereignty is, or to whom we owe our Obedience, since
Fatherhood and *Property* are distinct Titles, and began
25 presently upon *Adam's* Death to be in distinct Persons.
And which then was to give way to the other?

76. Let us take the account of it, as he himself gives it
us. He tells us out of *Grotius*, That *Adam's Children by
Donation, Assignation, or some kind of Cession before
he was dead, had their distinct Territories by Right of*

§ 76 2 '*Grotius*'—a mistake. In the passage quoted, Filmer was
using Selden's *Mare Clausum* to contradict Grotius. Tyrrell gets it
right, 1681, 101 (second pagination).

private Dominion; Abel *had his Flocks and Pastures for* 5
them; Cain *had his Fields for Corn, and the Land of*
Nod *where he built him a City,* O. 210 [63/64]. Here 'tis
obvious to demand which of these two after *Adam*'s
Death, was Sovereign? *Cain,* says our *A. p.* 19 [61]. By
what Title? As *Heir; for Heirs to Progenitors, who were* 10
Natural Parents of their People, are not only Lords of their
own Children, but also of their Brethren, says our *A. p.*
19 [61]. What was *Cain* Heir to? Not the entire Possessions,
not all that which *Adam* had *Private Dominion* in, for our
A. allows that *Abel* by a Title derived from his Father, 15
had his distinct Territory for Pasture by Right of Private
Dominion. What then *Abel* had by *Private Dominion* [64],
was exempt from *Cain*'s Dominion. For he could not have
Private Dominion over that, which was under the Private
Dominion of another, and therefore his Sovereignty over 20
his Brother is gone with this *Private Dominion,* and so
there are presently two Sovereigns, and his imaginary Title
of *Fatherhood* is out of doors, and *Cain* is no Prince
over his Brother: Or else if *Cain* retain his Sovereignty over
Abel, notwithstanding his *Private Dominion,* it will follow 25
that the *first Grounds and Principles of Government* have
nothing to do with *Property,* whatever our *A.* says to the
contrary. 'Tis true, *Abel* did not out-live his Father *Adam,*
but that makes nothing to the Argument, which will hold
good against Sir *Robert* in *Abel*'s Issue, or in *Seth,* or any 30
of the Posterity of *Adam,* not descended from *Cain.*

77. The same inconvenience he runs into about *the*
three Sons of Noah, who, as he says, *p.* 13. [58] *had the*
whole World divided amongst them by their Father. I ask
then in which of the three shall we find *the Establishment*
of Regal Power after *Noah*'s Death? If in all three, as our 5
A. there seems to say; then it will follow, that Regal Power
is founded in Property of Land, and follows *Private*
Dominion, and not in *Paternal Power* or *Natural Dominion,*
and so there is an end of Paternal Power as the Fountain
of Regal Authority, and the so much magnified *Fatherhood* 10
quite vanishes. If the *Regal Power* descended to *Shem* as

§ 76 5–7 See Gen. iv. 16–17. This argument is used in II, § 38, and this
part of the text has some importance for Locke's own account of the
relation of property to government. Filmer's inconsistency on the
subject is grosser than Locke's, but Locke's offhand superiority is hardly
justifiable.

Eldest, and Heir to his Father, then *Noah's Division of
the World by Lot to his Sons, or his Ten Years Sailing
about the Mediterranean to appoint each Son his part,*
15 which our *A.* tells of, *p. 15.* [59] was labour lost, his
Division of the World to them, was to ill, or to no purpose.
For his Grant to *Cham* and *Japhet* was little worth if *Shem,*
notwithstanding this Grant, as soon as *Noah* was dead, was
to be Lord over them. Or, if this Grant of *Private Dominion*
20 to them over their assigned Territories, were good, here
were set up two distinct sorts of Power, not Subordinate
one to the other, with all those Inconveniences which he
musters up against the *Power of the People,* O. 158 [233]
which I shall set down in his own words, only changing
25 *Property* for *People. All Power on Earth is either derived
or usurped from the Fatherly Power, there being no other
Original to be found of any Power whatsoever: For if there
should be granted two sorts of Power, without any Subordination of one to the other, they would be in perpetual
30 strife which should be Supreme, for two Supremes cannot
agree: If the Fatherly Power be Supreme, then the Power
grounded on Private Dominion must be subordinate, and
depend on it; and if the Power grounded on Property be
Supreme, then the Fatherly Power must submit to it, and
35 cannot be exercised without the License of the Proprietors,
which must quite destroy the Frame and Course of Nature.*
This is his own arguing against two distinct Independent
Powers, which I have set down in his own words, only
putting Power rising from Property, for *Power of the
40 People;* and when he has answered what he himself has
urged here against two distinct Powers, we shall be better
able to see how, with any tolerable Sense, he can derive
all Regal Authority *from the Natural and Private Dominion
of* Adam, from *Fatherhood* and *Property* together, which
45 are distinct Titles that do not always meet in the same
Person; and 'tis plain, by his own Confession, presently
separated as soon both as *Adam's* and *Noah's* Death made
way for Succession: Though our *A.* frequently in his
Writings jumbles them together, and omits not to make
50 use of either, where he thinks it will sound best to his
purpose. But the Absurdities of this will more fully appear
in the next Chapter, where we shall examine the ways of
conveyance of the Sovereignty of *Adam,* to Princes that
were to Reign after him.

Of the Conveyance of Adam's *Sovereign Monarchical Power.*

78.   Sir *Robert,* having not been very happy in any Proof
he brings for the Sovereignty of *Adam,* is not much more
fortunate in conveying it to future Princes, who, if his
Politicks be true, must all derive their Titles from that
first Monarch. The ways he has assigned, as they lie   5
scatter'd up and down in his Writings, I will set down
in his own Words: In his Preface he tells us [188], That
*Adam being Monarch of the whole World, none of his
Posterity had any right to possess any thing, but by his
Grant or Permission, or by Succession from him:* Here he 10
makes two ways of conveyance of any thing *Adam* stood
possessed of, and those are *Grant* or *Succession.* Again he
says *All Kings either are, or are to be reputed, the next
Heirs to those first Progenitors, who were at first the
Natural Parents of the whole People,* p. 19 [60, 61]. *There* 15
*cannot be any Multitude of Men whatsoever, but that in
it, consider'd by it self, there is one Man amongst them,
that in Nature hath a Right to be the King of all the rest,
as being the next Heir to* Adam, O. 253 [288, 289]. Here
in these places *Inheritance* is the only way he allows of 20
conveying Monarchical Power to Princes. In other places
he tells us *O.* 155. [232] *All Power on Earth is either
derived or usurped from the Fatherly Power,* O. 158. [233]
*All Kings that now are, or ever were, are or were either
Fathers of their People, or the Heirs of such Fathers or* 25
Usurpers of the Right of such Fathers, O. 253 [288]. And
here he makes *Inheritance* or *Usurpation* the only ways
whereby Kings come by this Original Power: But yet he
tells us, *This Fatherly Empire, as it was of it self Hereditary, so it was alienable by Patent, and seizable by an* 30
Usurper, O. 190 [256]. So then here Inheritance, Grant or
Usurpation will convey it. And last of all, which is most

§ **78**   22   '*O.* 155'—redundant reference. The preceding words are an
insertion of Locke's in the Christ's copy, but he did not strike out this
reference. It is clear from such things as this that he did not make
his final revision, after 1698, with Filmer's book in his hand.
   30   '*by Patent*'—Filmer wrote '*by the Parent*' in his manuscript (1949
ed., p. 256).

admirable, he tells us, *p.* 100. [106] *It skills not which way Kings come by their Power, whether by Election, Donation,*
35 *Succession, or by any other means, for it is still the Manner of the Government by Supreme Power, that makes them properly Kings, and not the Means of obtaining their Crowns.* Which I think is a full answer to all his whole *Hypothesis,* and Discourse about *Adam*'s Royal
40 Authority, as the Fountain from which all Princes were to derive theirs: And he might have spared the trouble of speaking so much, as he does, up and down of Heirs and Inheritance, if to make any one *properly a King,* needs no more but *Governing by Supreme Power, and it matters*
45 *not by what Means he came by it.*

79. By this notable way, our *A.* may make *Oliver* as *properly King,* as any one else he could think of: And had he had the Happiness to live under *Massanello's* Government, he could not by this his own Rule have forborn to
5 have done Homage to him, with *O King live for ever,* since the Manner of his Government by Supreme Power, made him *properly* King, who was but the Day before *properly* a Fisherman. And if *Don Quixot* had taught his Squire to Govern with Supreme Authority, our *A.* no doubt could
10 have made a most Loyal Subject in *Sancho Pancha's Island:* and he must needs have deserved some Preferment in such Governments, since I think he is the first Politician, who, pretending to settle Government upon its true Basis, and to establish the Thrones of lawful Princes, ever told the
15 World, That he was *properly a King, whose Manner of Government was by Supreme Power, by what Means soever he obtained it;* which in plain *English* is to say, that

41–5 This gives Filmer's whole case away: cf. Salmon, 1959, 111 n.
§ **79** 1 '*Oliver*'—Oliver Cromwell. It may be worth noting that Filmer actually wrote his justification for obedience to usurpers under Cromwell, in particular his *Directions* (231–5). It is a little unsympathetic of Locke to reproach him perpetually with statements made under such necessity, especially since the only work he himself had actually published at this time was his poetic eulogy of Cromwell—see Introduction, 30, compare I, § 121, 14.
3 See *Cambridge Modern History* (1906), IV, 656–7. The revolt of Tommaso Aniello (Masaniello) in 1647 in Naples against the Spanish government became a symbol for mob rule all over Europe for the next few generations. In the Hilary Term 1682/3, for example, a poem was published in London entitled 'Massanello, or a Satyr against the Association'.
10 See Cervantes, *Don Quixote,* Part I, chapters 37, 38, 42, 45, etc. Locke possessed four editions, two in French and two in English.

Regal and Supreme Power is properly and truly his, who
can by any Means seize upon it: and if this be, to be
properly a King, I wonder how he came to think of, or 20
where he will find, an *Usurper.*

80. This is so strange a Doctrine, that the surprize of
it hath made me pass by, without their due Reflection, the
Contradictions he runs into, by making sometimes *Inheritance* alone, sometimes only *Grant* or *Inheritance,* sometimes only *Inheritance* or *Usurpation,* sometimes all these 5
three, and at last *Election,* or *any other means,* added to
them, the ways whereby *Adam's* Royal *Authority,* that is,
his right to Supreme Rule, could be convey'd down to future Kings and Governors, so as to give them a Title to
the Obedience and Subjection of the People. But these 10
Contradictions lie so open, that the very reading of our
A's own Words, will discover them to any ordinary Understanding: and though what I have quoted out of him
(with abundance more of the same Strain and Coherence
which might be found in him) might well excuse me from 15
any farther trouble in this Argument, yet having proposed
to my self, to examine the main parts of his Doctrine, I
shall a little more particularly consider how *Inheritance,*
Grant, Usurpation or *Election,* can any way make out
Government in the World upon his Principles; or derive 20
to any one a right of Empire, from this Regal Authority of
Adam, had it been never so well proved, that he had been
Absolute Monarch, and Lord of the whole World.

CHAP. IX.

Of Monarchy, by Inheritance from Adam.

81. Though it be never so plain that there ought to be
Government in the World, nay should all Men be of our
A——s mind, that Divine appointment had ordained it to
be *Monarchical,* yet since Men cannot obey any thing,

5 that cannot command, and Ideas of Government in
the Fancy, though never so perfect, though never so right,
cannot give Laws, nor prescribe Rules to the Actions of
Men; it would be of no behoof for the setling of Order, and
Establishment of Government in its Exercise and Use
10 amongst Men, unless there were a way also taught how to
know the Person, to whom it belonged to have this Power,
and Exercise this Dominion over others. 'Tis in vain then
to talk of Subjection and Obedience, without telling us
whom we are to obey. For were I never so fully perswaded,
15 that there ought to be Magistracy and Rule in the World,
yet I am nevertheless at Liberty still, till it appears who
is the Person that hath Right to my Obedience: since if
there be no Marks to know him by, and distinguish him,
that hath Right to Rule from other Men, it may be my
20 self, as well as any other. And therefore though Submission to Government be every ones duty, yet since that signifies nothing but submitting to the Direction and Laws of
such Men, as have Authority to Command, 'tis not enough
to make a Man a Subject, to convince him that there is
25 *Regal Power* in the World, but there must be ways of designing, and knowing the Person to whom this *Regal Power*
of Right belongs, and a Man can never be oblig'd in Conscience to submit to any Power, unless he can be satisfied
who is the Person, who has a Right to Exercise that Power
30 over him. If this were not so, there would be no distinction
between Pirates and Lawful Princes, he that has Force is
without any more ado to be obey'd, and Crowns and Scepters would become the Inheritance only of Violence and
Rapine. Men too might as often and as innocently change
35 their Governours, as they do their Physicians, if the Person cannot be known, who has a right to direct me, and
whose Prescriptions I am bound to follow. To settle therefore Mens Consciences under an Obligation to Obedience,
'tis necessary that they know not only that there is a Power
40 somewhere in the World, but the Person who by Right is
vested with this Power over them.

82. How successful our *A——* has been in his attempts,
to set up a *Monarchical Absolute Power* in *Adam*, the
Reader may judge by what has been already said: but were
that *Absolute Monarchy* as clear as our *A——* would de-
5 sire it, as I presume it is the contrary, yet it could be of no

use to the Government of Mankind now in the World,
unless he also make out these two things.

First, That this *Power of Adam* was not to end with him,
but was upon his Decease conveyed intire to some other
Person, and so on to Posterity.   10

Secondly, That the Princes and Rulers now on Earth,
are possessed of this *Power of Adam,* by a right way of conveyance derived to them.

83. If the first of these fail, the *Power of Adam,* were
it never so great, never so certain, will signifie nothing to
the present Governments and Societies in the World, but
we must seek out some other Original of Power for the
Government of Politys then this of *Adam,* or else there   5
will be none at all in the World. If the latter fail, it will
destroy the Authority of the present Governours, and absolve the People from Subjection to them, since they having no better a Claim then others to that Power, which is
alone the Fountain of all Authority, can have no Title to   10
Rule over them.

84. Our *A——* having Fansied an Absolute Sovereignty in *Adam,* mentions several ways of its conveyance
to Princes, that were to be his Successors, but that which
he chiefly insists on, is, that of *Inheritance,* which occurs
so often in his several Discourses, and I having in the fore- 5
going Chapter quoted several of these passages, I shall not
need here again to repeat them. This Sovereignty he erects,
as has been said upon a double Foundation, *viz.* that of
Property, and that of *Fatherhood.* One was the right he
was supposed to have in all Creatures, a right to possess   10
the Earth with the Beasts, and other inferior Ranks of
things in it for his Private use, exclusive of all other Men.
The other was the Right he was supposed to have, to Rule
and Govern Men, all the rest of Mankind.

85. In both these Rights, there being supposed an exclusion of all other Men, it must be upon some Reason
peculiar to *Adam,* that they must both be founded.

That of his *property* our *A.* supposes to arise from God's
immediate *Donation, Gen.* 1. 28. and that of *Fatherhood*   5
from the Act of *Begetting:* Now in all Inheritance, if the
Heir succeed not to the reason, upon which his Father's

Right was founded, he cannot succeed to the Right which
followeth from it: For Example, *Adam* had a Right of
10 Property in the Creatures, upon the *Donation* and *Grant*
of God Almighty, who was Lord and Proprietor of them
all, let this be so as our *A——* tells us, yet upon his Death
his Heir can have no Title to them, no such right of Property in them, unless the same reason, *viz.* God's *Donation*,
15 vested a right in the *Heir* too. For if *Adam* could have
had no Property in, nor use of, the Creatures without this
positive *Donation* from God, and this *Donation*, were only
personally to *Adam*, his *Heir* could have no right by it,
but upon his death, it must revert to God the Lord and
20 Owner again: for positive Grants give no Title farther than
the express words convey it, and by which only it is held.
And thus, if as our *A——* himself contends, that *Donation, Gen.* 1. 28. were made only to *Adam* personally his
Heir could not succeed to his property in the Creatures:
25 and if it were a Donation to any but *Adam*, let it be shewn,
that it was to his Heir in our *A*'s Sense, *i.e.* to one of his
Children exclusive of all the rest.

86.   But not to follow our *A——* too far out of the way,
the plain of the Case is this. God having made Man, and
planted in him, as in all other Animals, a strong desire of
Self-preservation, and furnished the World with things fit
5 for Food and Rayment and other Necessaries of Life, Subservient to his design, that Man should live and abide for
some time upon the Face of the Earth, and not that so
curious and wonderful a piece of Workmanship by its own
Negligence, or want of Necessaries, should perish again,
10 presently after a few moments continuance: God, I say,
having made Man and the World thus, spoke to him, (that
is) directed him by his Senses and Reason, as he did the
inferior Animals by their Sense, and Instinct, which he
had placed in them to that purpose, to the use of those
15 things, which were serviceable for his Subsistence, and
given him as means of his *Preservation*. And therefore I
doubt not, but before these words were pronounced, 1 *Gen.*
28, 29. (if they must be understood Literally to have been
spoken) and without any such Verbal *Donation*, Man had
20 a right to a use of the Creatures, by the Will and Grant of

§ 86   8   'Workmanship'—see note on I, § 52, and references.

God. For the desire, strong desire of Preserving his Life
and Being having been Planted in him, as a Principle of
Action by God himself, Reason, *which was the Voice of
God in him,* could not but teach him and assure him, that
pursuing that natural Inclination he had to preserve his 25
Being, he followed the Will of his Maker, and therefore
had a right to make use of those Creatures, which by his
Reason or Senses he could discover would be serviceable
thereunto. And thus Man's *Property* in the Creatures, was
founded upon the right he had, to make use of those things, 30
that were necessary or useful to his Being.

87. This being the Reason and Foundation of *Adams
Property* gave the same Title, on the same Ground, to all
his Children, not only after his death, but in his life time:
So that here was no Priviledge of his *Heir* above his other
Children, which could exclude them from an equal Right 5
to the use of the inferior Creatures, for the comfortable
preservation of their Beings, which is all the *Property* Man
hath in them: and so *Adams* Sovereignty built on *property,*
or as our *A.* calls it, *Private Dominion* comes to nothing.
Every Man had a right to the Creatures, by the same Title 10
Adam had, *viz.* by the right every one had to take care of,
and provide for their Subsistence: and thus Men had a
right in common, *Adams* Children in common with him.
But if any one had began, and made himself a Property
in any particular thing, (which how he, or any one else, 15

21–4 These lines raise a number of important problems in Locke's
political theory in relation to his philosophy (see Introduction, section
IV, 2). Preservation, of oneself and all mankind, is a natural law for
Locke, perhaps the natural law, here presented as 'a Principle of
Action' planted by God in man. This would seem to contradict chapter
III of Book I of his *Essay,* headed 'No Innate Practical Principles',
but the language here is very close to the exception he makes (1894,
1, 67) for the 'desire for happiness' an 'innate practical principle', see
Yolton, 1956, 'Reason' as *'the Voice of God'* is a famous neoplatonism,
see II, § 56, 5–6 and Locke's *Reasonableness* (1695) where reason is
called 'a spark of the divine nature', 'the candle of the Lord' (*Works,*
1801, VII, 133), and on reason generally, see Polin, 1960, 25 etc.

21–31 This, and the following paragraph, state Locke's ultimate
justification of property, here typified by property in animals; see Introduction, 114. Compare II, § 30, 1–4, where the labour theory is called
the 'Law of reason', and compare and contrast his eighth *Essay on the
Law of Nature* where possession of private property (*res sua, res
privata*) is said to be protected by the law of nature (Von Leyden,
1954, 206–7).

§ **87** 15–16 A clear cross-reference to the fifth chapter of the *Second
Treatise,* see Introduction, 63.

could do, shall be shewn in another place) that thing, that
possession, if he dispos'd not otherwise of it by his positive
Grant, descended Naturally to his Children, and they had
a right to succeed to it, and possess it.

88.   It might reasonably be asked here, how come Children by this right of possessing, before any other, the
properties of their Parents upon their Decease. For it being
Personally the Parents, when they dye, without actually
Transferring their Right to another, why does it not return
again to the common stock of Mankind? 'Twill perhaps be
answered, that common consent hath disposed of it, to the
Children. Common Practice, we see indeed does so dispose
of it but we cannot say, that it is the common consent of
Mankind; for that hath never been asked, nor actually
given: and if common tacit Consent hath establish'd it, it
would make but a positive and not Natural Right of Children to Inherit the Goods of their Parents: But where the
Practice is Universal, 'tis reasonable to think the Cause
is Natural. The ground then, I think, to be this. The first
and strongest desire God Planted in Men, and wrought
into the very Principles of their Nature being that of Self-
preservation, that is the Foundation of a right to the Creatures, for the particular support and use of each individual
Person himself. But next to this, God Planted in Men a
strong desire also of propagating their Kind, and continuing themselves in their Posterity, and this gives Children
a Title, to share in the *Property* of their Parents, and a
Right to Inherit their Possessions. Men are not Proprietors
of what they have meerly for themselves, their Children have a Title to part of it, and have their Kind of
Right joyn'd with their Parents, in the Possession which
comes to be wholly theirs, when death having put an end
to their Parents use of it, hath taken them from their Possessions, and this we call Inheritance. Men being by a like
Obligation bound to preserve what they have begotten, as
to preserve themselves, their issue come to have a Right in
the Goods they are possessed of. That Children have such
a Right is plain from the Laws of God, and that Men are
convinced, that Children have such a Right, is evident from
the Law of the Land, both which Laws require Parents to
provide for their Children.

89.   For Children being by the course of Nature, born

weak, and unable to provide for themselves, they have by
the appointment of God himself, who hath thus ordered
the course of nature, a Right to be nourish'd and maintained by their Parents, nay a right not only to a bare Sub- 5
sistence but to the conveniences and comforts of Life, as
far as the conditions of their Parents can afford it. Hence
it comes, that when their Parents leave the World, and so
the care due to their Children ceases, the effects of it are
to extend as far as possibly they can, and the Provisions 10
they have made in their Life time, are understood to be
intended as nature requires they should, for their Children,
whom after themselves, they are bound to provide for,
though the dying Parents, by express Words, declare nothing about them, nature appoints the descent of their Prop- 15
erty to their Children, who thus come to have a Title, and
natural Right of Inheritance to their Fathers Goods, which
the rest of Mankind cannot pretend to.

90.   Were it not for this Right of being Nourished, and
Maintained by their Parents, which God and Nature has
given to Children, and obliged Parents to, as a Duty, it
would be reasonable, that the Father should Inherit the
Estate of his Son, and be preferr'd in the Inheritance be- 5
fore his Grand Child. For to the Grand Father, there is
due a long Score of Care and Expences laid out upon the
Breeding and Education of his Son, which one would think
in Justice ought to be paid. But that having been done in
Obedience to the same Law, whereby he received Nourish- 10
ment and Education from his own Parents, this Score of
Education received from a Man's Father, is paid by taking
care, and providing for his own Children; is paid, I say, as
much as is requir'd of Payment by Alteration of Property,
unless present necessity of the Parents require a return of 15
Goods for their necessary Support and Subsistence. For
we are not now speaking of that Reverence, Acknowledg-
ment, Respect and Honour that is always due from Children to their Parents, but of Possessions and Commodities

§ 90 15–20 Professor Viner (see Introduction, 116) regards this
passage as providing a clear example of Locke's distinction between
property as a general category, which could include 'Reverence, . . . Respect and Honour' and property specifically defined as 'Possessions and
commodities of Life valuable by Money'. Contrast II, § 87, 5–6, note and
references.

20 of Life valuable by Money. But tho' it be incumbent on
parents to bring up and provide for their children, yet this
Debt to the Children does not quite cancel the Score due
to the Parents, but only is made by Nature preferable to
it. For the Debt a Man owes his Father, takes place, and
25 gives the Father a Right to Inherit the Sons Goods, where
for want of Issue, the Right of Children doth not exclude
that Title. And therefore a Man having a Right to be maintain'd by his Children where he needs it, and to enjoy also
the comforts of Life from them, when the necessary Pro-
30 vision due to them, and their Children will afford it, if
his Son dye without Issue, the Father has a Right in Nature to possess his Goods, and Inherit his Estate (whatever
the Municipal Laws of some Countries, may absurdly direct otherwise,) and so again his Children and their Issue
35 from him, or for want of such, his Father and his Issue.
But where no such are to be found, *i.e.* no Kindred, there
we see the Possessions of a Private Man revert to the Community, and so in Politic Societies come into the Hands
of the Public Magistrate: but in the State of Nature be-
40 come again perfectly common, no body having a right to
Inherit them: nor can any one have a Property in them,
otherwise then in other things common by Nature, of which
I shall speak in its due place.

91. I have been the larger in shewing upon what ground
Children have a Right to succeed to the Possession of their
Fathers Properties, not only because by it, it will appear,
that if *Adam* had a Property (a Titular insignificant use-
5 less Property; for it could be no better, for he was bound
to Nourish and Maintain his Children and Posterity out
of it) in the whole Earth and its Product, yet all his Children coming to have by the Law of Nature and Right of
Inheritance a joynt Title, and Right of Property in it after
10 his Death, it could convey no Right of Sovereignty to any
one of his Posterity over the rest: Since every one having

§ 90 32–4 Locke seems to have in mind the 'Municipal Laws' of his
own country (compare II, § 205, 1), which direct that land ('Estate')
cannot be inherited by a man's father, or anyone in the ascending
line, though this is not true of goods. See Holdsworth, *History of
English Law*, 1923, II, 171–85, especially p. 175, and compare I, § 123,
12–14, and II, § 12, 19. In this discussion, and in I, § 89 also, Locke
may have in mind Grotius, 1625, III, iii.
    42–3 A cross-reference to chapter V of the *Second Treatise*, see I,
§ 87, 15–16 and reference.

a Right of Inheritance to his Portion, they might enjoy
their Inheritance, or any part of it in common, or share
it, or some parts of it by Division, as it best liked them.
But no one could pretend to the whole Inheritance, or any 15
Sovereignty supposed to accompany it, since a Right of Inheritance gave every one of the rest, as well as any one,
a Title to share in the Goods of his Father. Not only upon
this Account, I say, have I been so particular in examining
the Reason of Childrens inheriting the Property of their 20
Fathers, but also because it will give us farther Light in the
Inheritance of *Rule* and *Power,* which in Countries where
their particular Municipal Laws give the whole Possession
of Land entirely to the First Born, and Descent of Power
has gone so to Men by this Custom, some have been apt 25
to be deceived into an Opinion, that there was a Natural
or Divine Right of Primogeniture, to both *Estate* and
Power; and that the Inheritance of both *Rule* over Men
and *Property* in things, sprang from the same Original, and
were to descend by the same Rules. 30

92.   Property, whose Original is from the Right a Man
has to use any of the Inferior Creatures, for the Subsistence
and Comfort of his Life, is for the benefit and sole Advantage of the Proprietor, so that he may even destroy the
thing, that he has Property in by his use of it, where need 5
requires: but Government being for the Preservation of
every Mans Right and Property, by preserving him from
the Violence or Injury of others, is for the good of the
Governed. For the Magistrates Sword being for a *Terror
to Evil Doers,* and by that Terror to inforce Men to ob- 10
serve the positive Laws of the Society, made conformable
to the Laws of Nature, for the public good, *i.e.* the good
of every particular Member of that Society, as far as by
common Rules, it can be provided for; the Sword is not
given the Magistrate for his own good alone. 15

---

§ **91**   23   Locke obviously has the English Common Law in mind here
also; compare I, § 90, 32–4 and note I, § 37, 3–4.
§ **92**   1–4   Here, Locke assimilates all property to rights over animals,
justified in I, § 86: see lines 21–2 of that paragraph, and II, § 6 note.
     6–7   A major theme of the *Second Treatise;* see, for example, II,
§ 124, 1–3.
     9–10, 14–15   Phrases from the famous thirteenth chapter of Romans,
verses 3–4: 'For rulers are not a terror to good works, but to evil . . .
for he beareth not the sword in vain.'

93. Children therefore, as has been shew'd, by the dependance they have on their Parents for Subsistence, have a Right of Inheritance to their Fathers Property, as that which belongs to them for their proper good and behoof, 5 and therefore are fitly termed Goods, wherein the First Born has not a sole or peculiar Right by any Law of God and Nature, the younger Children having an equal Title with him founded on that Right they all have to maintenance, support and comfort from their Parents, and noth- 10 ing else. But Government being for the benefit of the Governed, and not the sole advantage of the Governors (but only for theirs with the rest, as they make a part of that Politick Body, each of whose parts and Members are taken care of, and directed in its peculiar Functions for the good 15 of the whole, by the Laws of the Society) cannot be inherited by the same Title that Children have to the Goods of their Father. The Right a Son has to be maintained and provided with the necessaries and conveniences of Life out of his Fathers Stock, gives him a Right to succeed to his 20 Fathers *Property* for his own good, but this can give him no Right to succeed also to the *Rule,* which his Father had over other Men. All that a Child has Right to claim from his Father is Nourishment and Education, and the things nature furnishes for the support of Life: But he has 25 no Right to demand *Rule* or *Dominion* from him: He can subsist and receive from him the Portion of good things, and advantages of Education naturally due to him, without *Empire* and *Dominion.* That (if his Father hath any) was vested in him, for the good and behoof of others, and 30 therefore the Son cannot Claim or Inherit it by a Title, which is founded wholly on his own private good and advantage.

94. We must know how the first Ruler, from whom any one claims, came by his Authority, upon what ground any one has *Empire,* what his Title is to it, before we can know who has a right to succeed him in it, and inherit it from 5 him. If the Agreement and consent of Men first gave a Scepter into any ones hand, or put a Crown on his Head, that also must direct its descent and conveyance. For the same Authority, that made the first a Lawful *Ruler,* must make the Second too, and so give Right of Succession: in 10 this Case Inheritance or Primogeniture, can in its self have no Right, no pretence to it, any farther then that Consent,

which Established the Form of the Government, hath so
settled the Succession. And thus we see the Succession of
Crowns, in several Countries places it on different Heads,
and he comes by Right of Succession, to be a Prince in one 15
place, who would be a Subject in another.

95.   If God by his positive Grant and revealed Declaration, first gave *Rule* and *Dominion* to any man, he that will
Claim by that Title, must have the same positive Grant of
God for his Succession. For if that has not directed the
Course of its descent and conveyance down to others, no 5
body can succeed to this Title of the first Ruler; Children
have no Right of Inheritance to this; and Primogeniture
can lay no Claim to it, unless God the Author of this Constitution hath so ordained it. Thus we see the pretensions
of *Sauls* Family, who received his Crown from the imme- 10
diate Appointment of God, ended with his Reign; and *David*
by the same Title that *Saul* Reigned, *viz.* Gods Appointment, succeeded in his Throne, to the exclusion of *Jona-
than,* and all pretentions of Paternal Inheritance. And if
Salomon had a Right to Succeed his Father, it must be by 15
some other Title, then that of Primogeniture. A *Cadet,* or
Sisters Son, must have the Preference in Succession, if he
has the same Title the first Lawful Prince had: and in Dominion that has its Foundation only in the positive appointment of God himself, *Benjamin* the youngest, must 20
have the Inheritance of the Crown, if God so direct as well
as one of that Tribe had the first possession.

96.   *If Paternal Right,* the Act of *Begetting,* give a Man
Rule and *Dominion,* Inheritance or Primogeniture can give
no Title. For he that cannot succeed to his Fathers Title,
which was *Begetting,* cannot succeed to that Power over
his Brethren, which his Father had by Paternal Right over 5
them. But of this I shall have occasion to say more in an-

§ 95   16–21   This passage may mark §§ 93, 94, 95 (wholly or partially)
as an insertion of 1689. William was a 'Cadet, or Sister's Son' with
respect to the English Royal line, his mother being a sister of Charles
II and James II. If this is the intention, William's claim is upheld as
on a level with that of 'the first Lawful Prince'. Compare the Preface,
line 7 and Lamprecht, 1918, 140.
§ 96   6–7   'in another place'—this reads 'bye and bye' in the 1st edition.
It seems to refer, then, to a later part of the *First Treatise,* and not to
the *Second,* for chapter VI there, 'Of Paternal Power', contains no
specific discussion of the political rights of an eldest brother. The most
likely area of the text is I, §§ 110–19, though it is just conceivable that
Locke intended some part of the lost portion.

other place. This is plain in the mean time, that any
Government, whether supposed to be at first founded in *Paternal Right, Consent of the People,* or the *positive Ap
10 pointment of God himself,* which can supersede either of
the other, and so begin a new Government upon a new
Foundation, I say, any Government began upon either of
these, can by Right of Succession come to those only, who
have the Title of him, they succeed to. Power founded on
15 *Contract,* can descend only to him, who has Right by that
Contract: Power founded on *Begetting,* he only can have
that *Begets:* And Power founded on the positive *Grant* or
Donation of God, he only can have by Right of Succession,
to whom that Grant directs it.

97. From what I have said, I think this is clear, that
a Right to the use of the Creatures, being founded Originally in the Right a Man has to subsist and enjoy the conveniences of Life, and the natural Right Children have to
5 inherit the Goods of their Parents, being founded in the
Right they have to the same Subsistence and Commodities
of Life, out of the Stock of their Parents, who are therefore taught by Natural Love and Tenderness to provide
for them, as a part of themselves: and all this being only
10 for the good of the Proprietor, or Heir; it can be no Reason for Childrens Inheriting of *Rule* and *Dominion,* which
has another Original and a different end. Nor can Primogeniture have any Pretence to a Right of solely Inheriting
either *Property* or *Power,* as we shall, in its due place, see
15 more fully. 'Tis enough to have shew'd here, that *Adam*'s
Property, or *Private Dominion,* could not convey any Sovereignty or Rule to his Heir, who not having a Right to
inherit all his Fathers Possessions, could not thereby come
to have any Sovereignty over his Brethren: and therefore
20 if any Sovereignty on account of his *Property,* had been
vested in *Adam,* which in Truth there was not; yet it would
have Died with him.

98. As *Adam*'s Sovereignty, if by vertue of being Proprietor of the whole World, he had any Authority over

§ 97 1–4 See I, § 92, 1–4, note and references.
14–15 Compare note on I, § 96, 6–7, though here the reference seems
probably to be to I, § 111 on.

Men, could not have been inherited by any of his Children over the rest, because they had the same Title to divide the Inheritance, and every one had a Right to a Portion of his Fathers Possessions: So neither could *Adam's* Sovereignty by Right of *Fatherhood*, if any such he had, descend to any one of his Children. For it being in our *A*'s Account, a Right acquired by *Begetting* to Rule over those he had begotten, it was not a Power Possible to be Inherited, because the Right being consequent to, and built on, an Act perfectly Personal, made that Power so too, and impossible to be Inherited. For Paternal Power, being a Natural Right rising only from the relation of Father and Son, is as impossible to be Inherited as the Relation itself, and a Man may pretend as well to Inherit the Conjugal Power the Husband, whose Heir he is, had over his Wife, as he can to Inherit the Paternal Power of a Father over his Children. For the Power of the Husband being founded on Contract, and the Power of the Father on *Begetting*, he may as well Inherit the Power obtained by the conjugal contract, which was only Personal, as he may the Power obtained by Begetting, which could reach no farther then the Person of the Begetter, unless Begetting can be a Title to Power in him, that does not beget.

99. Which makes it a reasonable question to ask, Whether *Adam*, dying before *Eve*, his Heir (suppose *Cain* or *Seth*) should have had, by Right of Inheriting *Adam's Fatherhood*, Sovereign Power over *Eve* his Mother. For *Adam's Fatherhood* being nothing but a Right he had to Govern his Children, because he begot them, he that inherits *Adam's Fatherhood*, inherits nothing, even in our *A*'s Sense, but the Right *Adam* had to Govern his Children, because he begot them: So that the Monarchy of the Heir would not have taken in *Eve*, or if it did, it being nothing but the *Fatherhood of Adam* descended by inheritance, the Heir must have Right to Govern *Eve*, because *Adam* begot her; for *Fatherhood* is nothing else.

100. Perhaps it will be said with our *A——* [231], that a Man can alien his Power over his Child, and what may be transfer'd by compact, may be possessed by Inheritance. I answer, a Father cannot alien the Power he has over his Child, he may perhaps to some degrees forfeit it, but cannot transfer it: and if any other Man acquire it, 'tis not

by the Fathers Grant, but by some Act of his own. For
Example, a Father, unnaturally careless of his Child, sells
or gives him to another Man; and he again exposes him:
10 a third Man finding him, breeds up, cherishes and provides
for him as his own. I think in this Case, no body will doubt
but that the greatest part of filial Duty and Subjection was
here owing, and to be paid to this Foster-Father: and if
any thing could be demanded from the Child, by either
15 of the other, it could be only due to his Natural Father:
who perhaps might have forfeited his Right to much of
that Duty comprehended in the Command, *Honour your
Parents,* but could transfer none of it to another. He that
purchased, and neglected, the Child, got by his Purchase
20 and Grant of the Father, no Title to Duty or Honour from
the Child, but only he acquired it, who by his own Authority, performing the Office and Care of a Father, to the
forlorn and Perishing Infant, made himself by Paternal
Care, a Title to proportionable Degrees of Paternal Power.
25 This will be more easily admitted upon Consideration of
the Nature of Paternal Power, for which I refer my Reader
to the Second Book.

101.   To return to the Argument in hand: This is evident, That Paternal Power arising only from *Begetting,*
for in that our *A.* places it alone, can neither be *transfer'd,*
nor *inherited:* And he that does not beget, can no more
5 have Paternal Power which arises from thence, than he can
have a Right to any thing who performs not the Condition,
to which only it is annexed. If one should ask, By what
Law has a Father Power over his Children? It will be answered, no doubt, by the Law of Nature, which gives such
10 a Power over them, to him that begets them. If one should
ask likewise, By what Law does our *A*'s Heir come by a
Right to Inherit? I think it would be answered, By the
Law of Nature too. For I find not that our *A.* brings one
word of Scripture to prove the Right of such an Heir he

§ **100**   7–11   Compare II, § 65, 6–7 and Tyrrell, 1681, 16. The whole
discussion of the rights of fathers, foster-fathers and so on springing
from their duty of *educating* children is very similar in Locke and
Tyrrell, and may have a common source in Grotius, who denies that the
jus paternum can be entirely alienated (1625, II, V, 26), though in section 5 he admits that under certain conditions a child can be pledged or
sold.
   26–7   This is the only reference in the *First Treatise* to the *Second
Treatise* by name. See the Introduction, 63.

speaks of: Why then the Law of Nature gives Fathers Pa- 15
ternal Power over their Children, because they did *beget*
them, and the same Law of Nature gives the same Paternal
Power to the Heir over his Brethren, who did not *beget*
them: whence it follows, that either the Father has not his
Paternal Power by begetting, or else that the Heir has it not 20
at all: For 'tis hard to understand how the Law of Nature,
which is the Law of Reason, can give the Paternal Power to
the Father over his Children, for the only Reason of
Begetting, and to the first-born over his Brethren without
this only Reason, *i.e.* for no Reason at all: and if the Eldest, 25
by the Law of Nature, can inherit this Paternal Power,
without the only Reason that gives a Title to it, so may the
Youngest as well as he, and a Stranger as well as either; for
where there is no Reason for any one, as there is not, but
for him that begets, all have an equal Title. I am sure our 30
A. offers no Reason, and when any body does, we shall see
whether it will hold or no.

102.   In the mean time 'tis as good Sense to say, that by
the Law of Nature a Man has Right to inherit the Property
of another, because he is of Kin to him, and is known to be
of his Blood, and therefore by the same Law of Nature, an
utter Stranger to his Blood, has Right to inherit his Estate: 5
As to say that by the Law of Nature he that begets them,
has Paternal Power over his Children, and therefore by
the Law of Nature the Heir that begets them not, has this
Paternal Power over them: or supposing the Law of the
Land gave Absolute Power over their Children, to such only 10
who nursed them, and fed their Children themselves, could
any body pretend that this Law gave any one, who did no
such thing, Absolute Power over those, who were not his
Children?

103.   When therefore it can be shew'd, that conjugal
Power can belong to him that is not an Husband, it will also
I believe be proved, that our A——'s Paternal Power acquired by begetting, may be inherited by a Son, and that a
Brother as Heir to his Fathers Power, may have Pa- 5
ternal Power over his Brethren, and by the same Rule
conjugal Power too, but till then, I think we may rest
satisfied, that the Paternal Power of *Adam,* this Sovereign
Authority of *Fatherhood,* were there any such, could not
descend to, nor be inherited by, his next Heir. *Fatherly* 10

Power I easily grant our A—— if it will do him any good,
can never be lost, because it will be as long in the World
as there are Fathers: but none of them will have *Adam*'s
Paternal Power, or derive theirs from him, but every one
15 will have his own, by the same Title *Adam* had his, *viz.*
by *Begetting,* but not by Inheritance or Succession, no more
then Husbands have their conjugal Power by Inheritance
from *Adam.* And thus we see as *Adam* had no such *Property,* no such *Paternal Power,* as gave him *Sovereign* Juris-
20 diction over Mankind; so likewise his Sovereignty built
upon either of these Titles, if he had any such, could not
have descended to his Heir, but must have ended with him.
Adam therefore, as has been proved, being neither Monarch, nor his imaginary Monarchy hereditable, the Power
25 which is now in the World, is not that which was *Adam*'s,
since all that *Adam* could have upon our *A*'s grounds,
either of *Property* or *Fatherhood,* necessarily Died with
him, and could not be convey'd to Posterity by Inheritance.
In the next place we will consider whether *Adam* had any
30 such Heir, to inherit his Power, as our *A.* talks of.

CHAP. X.

Of the Heir to Adam's *Monarchical Power.*

104. Our *A.* tells us, *O.* 253. [288, 289] *That it is a truth
undeniable, that there cannot be any Multitude of Men
whatsoever, either great or small, tho' gathered together
from the several corners and remotest Regions of the
5 World, but that in the same Multitude considered by its
self, there is one Man amongst them, that in Nature hath
a Right to be King of all the rest, as being the next Heir
to* Adam, *and all the other Subject to him, every Man
by Nature is a King or a Subject.* And again, p.
10 20. [61] *If Adam himself were still living, and now ready
to die, it is certain that there is one Man, and but one in*

the World who is next Heir. Let this *Multitude of Men* be, if our *A.* pleases, all the Princes upon the Earth, there will then be by our *A*'s Rule, *one amongst them, that in Nature hath a Right to be King of all the rest, as being the* 15 *Right Heir to* Adam; an excellent way to Establish the Thrones of Princes, and settle the Obedience of their Subjects, by setting up an Hundred, or perhaps a Thousand Titles (if there be so many Princes in the World) against any King now Reigning, each as good upon our *A*'s 20 Grounds, as his who wears the Crown. If this Right of *Heir* carry any weight with it, if it be the *Ordinance of God,* as our *A.* seems to tell us, *O.* 244. [283] must not all be subject to it, from the highest to the lowest? Can those who wear the Name of Princes, without having the 25 Right of being *Heirs to* Adam, demand Obedience from their Subjects by this Title, and not be bound to pay it by the same Law? Either Governments in the World are not to be claim'd and held by this Title of *Adam*'s Heir, and then the starting of it is to no purpose, the being or not 30 being *Adam*'s Heir signifies nothing as to the Title of Dominion; or if it really be, as our *A.* says, the true Title to Government and Sovereignty, the first thing to be done, is to find out this true Heir of *Adam,* seat him in his Throne, and then all the Kings and Princes of the World ought to 35 come and resign up their Crowns and Scepters to him, as things that belong no more to them, than to any of their Subjects.

105. For either this Right in Nature, of *Adam*'s Heir, to be King over all the race of Men, (for altogether they make one *Multitude*) is a Right not necessary to the mak-

§ 105 On the argument of this paragraph, compare Sidney, *Discourses,* 1, 12, 24–5. Compare *First Treatise,* § 81, 27–30; § 110, 12–13; § 119, 36–7; § 120, 2–3; § 122, 2; § 125, 11; § 126, 31–2. In all these contexts the issue of conscience and government is confined to the straightforward question of recognizing who it is that the citizen must obey, and all the more complex and difficult discussion, so important to Locke's predecessors and his own generation, is left on one side. This is in marked contrast with such writers as Pufendorf, even with the younger Locke himself, for in his Latin essay on the civil magistrate he had put forward quite complicated arguments about conscience and obligation. Even in the notes he made on Filmer in 1679 (see Introduction, 71) 'resolving the conscience' was a point he picked upon. There are three further references in the *Second Treatise* (§ 8, 6; § 21, 26; § 209, 5) but little is added by them: conscience is neither defined nor discussed in this book, compare Introduction, 98.

ing of a Lawful King, and so there may be Lawful Kings
5 without it, and then Kings Titles and Power depend not
on it, or else all the Kings in the World but one are not
Lawful Kings, and so have no Right to Obedience: Either
this Title of Heir to *Adam* is that whereby Kings hold their
Crowns, and have a Right to Subjection from their Sub-
10 jects, and then one only can have it, and the rest being
Subjects can require no Obedience from other Men, who
are but their fellow Subjects, or else it is not the Title
whereby Kings Rule, and have a Right to Obedience from
their Subjects, and then Kings are Kings without it, and
15 this Dream of the Natural Sovereignty of *Adam*'s Heir is
of no use to Obedience and Government. For if Kings have
a Right to Dominion, and the Obedience of their Subjects,
who are not, nor can possibly be, Heirs to *Adam*, what
use is there of such a Title, when we are obliged to Obey
20 without it? If Kings, who are not Heirs to *Adam*, have no
Right to Sovereignty, we are all free till our *A.* or any
body for him, will shew us *Adam*'s right Heir. If there be
but one Heir of *Adam*, there can be but one Lawful King
in the World, and no body in Conscience can be obliged
25 to Obedience till it be resolved who that is; for it may be
any one who is not known to be of a Younger House, and
all others have equal Titles. If there be more than one Heir
of *Adam*, every one is his Heir, and so every one has Regal
Power. For if two Sons can be Heirs together, then all the
30 Sons are equally Heirs, and so all are Heirs, being all Sons,
or Sons Sons of *Adam*. Betwixt these two the Right of Heir
cannot stand: for by it either but one only Man, or all
Men are Kings. Take which you please, it dissolves the
Bonds of Government and Obedience: since if all Men are
35 Heirs, they can owe Obedience to no body; if only one,
no body can be obliged to pay Obedience to him, till he
be known and his Title made out.

Who HEIR?

106. The great Question which in all Ages has disturbed Mankind, and brought on them the greatest part of those Mischiefs which have ruin'd Cities, depopulated Countries, and disordered the Peace of the World, has been, Not whether there be Power in the World, nor whence it came, 5 but who should have it. The settling of this point being of no smaller moment than the security of Princes, and the peace and welfare of their Estates and Kingdoms, a Reformer of Politicks, one would think, should lay this sure, and be very clear in it. For if this remain disputable, all 10 the rest will be to very little purpose; and the skill used in dressing up Power with all the Splendor and Temptation Absoluteness can add to it, without shewing who has a Right to have it, will serve only to give a greater edge to Man's Natural Ambition, which of it self is but too keen. 15 What can this do but set Men on the more eagerly to scramble, and so lay a sure and lasting Foundation of endless Contention and Disorder, instead of that Peace and Tranquility, which is the business of Government, and the end of Humane Society? 20

107. This Designation of the person our *A.* is more than ordinarily obliged to take care of, because he, affirming that *the Assignment of Civil Power is by Divine Institution,* hath made the Conveyance as well as the Power it self Sacred: so that no Consideration, no Act or Art of 5 Man can divert it from that Person, to whom by this Divine Right, it is assigned, no Necessity or Contrivance can substitute another Person in his room. For if the *Assignment of Civil Power be by Divine Institution;* and *Adam's Heir* be he, to whom it is thus Assigned, as in the foregoing 10

§ **107** 9 At this point ends a passage covering five pages in the 1st edition (133–7 of its pages, beginning at § 104) minutely corrected by Locke for the 2nd—see Collation.

10–11 This cannot refer to a foregoing chapter of *Patriarcha,* since Locke has only discussed the first chapter, and in his text as we have it he never goes further. It must then intend Locke's own previous chapter, chapter X. This reference is the result of a correction for the 2nd edition, 1694.

Chapter our *A.* tells us, it would be as much Sacriledge for
any one to be King, who was not *Adam*'s Heir, as it would
have beeen amongst the *Jews,* for any one to have been
Priest, who had not been of *Aarons* Posterity: For *not*
15 *only* the Priesthood *in general being by Divine Institution,
but the Assignment of it* to the Sole Line and Posterity of
Aaron, made it impossible to be enjoy'd or exercised by
any one, but those Persons, who are the Off-spring of
Aaron: whose Succession therefore was carefully observed,
20 and by that the Persons who had a Right to the Priesthood
certainly known.

108.   Let us see then what care our *A.* has taken, to
make us know who is this *Heir,* who *by Divine Institution,
has a right to be King over all Men.* The first account of
him we meet with is *p.* 12. [57] in these words: *This Sub-*
5 *jection of Children, being the Fountain of all Regal Au-*
thority, by the Ordination of God himself; it follows, that
Civil Power not only in general, is by Divine Institution,
but even the Assignment of it specifically to the Eldest
Parents. Matters of such Consequence as this is, should be
10 in plain words, as little liable as might be to Doubt or
Equivocation; and I think if Language be capable of expressing any thing distinctly and clearly, that of Kindred,
and the several Degrees of nearness of Blood, is one. It
were therefore to be wish'd, that our *A.* had used a little
15 more intelligible Expressions here, that we might have better known who it is, to whom the *Assignment of Civil*
Power is made by *Divine Institution,* or at least would have
told us what he meant by *Eldest Parents.* For I believe if
Land had been Assigned or Granted to him, and the *Eldest*
20 *Parents* of his Family, he would have thought it had needed
an Interpreter, and 'twould scarce have been known to
whom next it belong'd.

109.   In propriety of Speech, and certainly Propriety
of Speech is necessary in a Discourse of this Nature, *Eld-*
est Parents signifies either the Eldest Men and Women that
have had Children, or those who have longest had Issue:
5 and then our *A*'s Assertion will be, That those Fathers and
Mothers who have been longest in the World, or longest
Fruitful, have by *Divine Institution* a Right to *Civil Power.*
If there be any Absurdity in this, our *A.* must answer for

§ **109** 1–2 On this and I, § 108 compare I, § 23, 26–9 and note.

it: and if his Meaning be different from my Explication, he is to be blam'd, that he would not speak it plainly. This 10 I am sure, *Parents* cannot signifie Heirs Male, nor *Eldest Parents* an Infant Child: who yet may sometimes be the true Heir, if there can be but one. And we are hereby still as much at a loss, who *Civil Power* belongs to, notwithstanding this *Assignment by Divine Institution*, as if there 15 had been no such *Assignment* at all, or our *A*. had said nothing of it. This of *Eldest Parents* leaving us more in the dark, who by *Divine Institution* has a Right to *Civil Power*, than those who never heard any thing at all of *Heir*, or descent, of which our *A*. is so full. And though 20 the chief matter of his Writings be to teach Obedience to those who have a Right to it, which he tells us is conveyed by descent, yet who those are to whom this Right by descent belongs, he leaves like the Philosophers Stone in Politicks, out of the reach of any one to discover from his 25 Writings.

110. This obscurity cannot be imputed to want of Language in so great a Master of Style as Sir *Robert* is, when he is resolved with himself what he would say: and therefore, I fear, finding how hard it would be to settle Rules of descent by Divine Institution, and how little it would be 5 to his purpose, or conduce to the clearing and establishing the Titles of Princes, if such Rules of descent were settled, he chose rather to content himself with doubtful and general terms, which might make no ill sound in Mens Ears, who were willing to be pleas'd with them, rather than offer 10 any clear Rules of descent of this *Fatherhood* of *Adam*, by which Mens Consciences might be satisfied to whom it descended, and know the Persons who had a Right to Regal Power, and with it to their Obedience.

111. How else is it possible, that laying so much stress as he does upon *descent*, and *Adam*'s *Heir, next Heir, true Heir*, he should never tell us what *Heir* means, nor the way to know who the *next* or *true Heir* is. This I do not remember he does any where expressly handle, but where it 5

24 'the Philosophers Stone', the substance capable of changing baser material into gold or silver, the supreme object of alchemy. For all his rationalistic contempt of Filmer, Locke was interested in alchemy, and it is a remarkable fact that Robert Boyle left to Locke and Newton a recipe for increasing gold, which Locke seems to have worked at. See Cranston, 1957.

comes in his way very warily and doubtfully touches:
though it be so necessary that without it all Discourses of
Government and Obedience upon his Principles would be
to no purpose, and *Fatherly Power*, never so well made
out, will be of no use to any body. Hence he tells us, *O.*
244. [283] *That not only the Constitution of Power in general, but the limitation of it to one kind,* (i.e.) *Monarchy
and the Determination of it to the individual Person and
Line of* Adam, *are all three Ordinances of God, neither*
Eve *nor her Children could either limit* Adam's *Power,
or joyn others with him; and what was given unto* Adam
was given in his Person to his Posterity. Here again our
A. informs us, that the *Divine Ordinance* hath limited the
descent of *Adam*'s Monarchical Power. To whom? *To*
Adam's *Line and Posterity,* says our *A.* A notable *Limitation,* a *Limitation* to all Mankind. For if our *A.* can find
any one amongst Mankind that is not of the *Line* and
Posterity of Adam, he may perhaps tell him who this next
Heir of *Adam* is: But for us, I despair how this *Limitation*
of *Adam*'s Empire to his *Line* and *Posterity* will help us
to find out *one Heir.* This *Limitation* indeed of our *A.* will
save those the labour who would look for him amongst the
Race of Bruits, if any such there were; but will very little
contribute to the discovery of *one next Heir* amongst Men,
though it make a short and easie determination of the
Question about the descent of *Adam*'s Regal Power, by
telling us, that the *Line* and *Posterity* of *Adam* is to have
it, that is in plain *English,* any one may have it, since there
is no Person living that hath not the Title of being of the *Line*
and *Posterity* of *Adam,* and while it keeps there, it keeps
within our *A*'s Limitation by God's Ordinance. Indeed, *p.*
19. [61] he tells us, that *such Heirs are not only Lords of
their own Children, but of their Brethren,* whereby, and by
the words following, which we shall consider anon, he seems
to insinuate that the Eldest Son is *Heir:* but he no where,
that I know, says it in direct words, but by the instances of
Cain and *Jacob* that there follow, we may allow this to be
so far his Opinion concerning Heirs, that where there are
divers Children, the Eldest Son has the Right to be *Heir.*
That Primogeniture cannot give any Title to Paternal Power
we have already shew'd. That a Father may have a Natural
Right to some kind of Power over his Children, is easily
granted, but that an Elder Brother has so over his Brethren
remains to be proved. God or Nature has not any where,

that I know, placed such Jurisdiction in the First-born, nor 50
can Reason find any such Natural Superiority amongst
Brethren. The Law of *Moses* gave a double Portion of the
Goods and Possessions to the Eldest, but we find not any
where that naturally, or by *God's Institution,* Superiority
or Dominion belong'd to him, and the Instances there 55
brought by our *A.* are but slender Proofs of a Right to
Civil Power and Dominion in the First-born, and do rather
shew the contrary.

112.   His words are in the forecited place [61]: *And
therefore we find God told* Cain *of his Brother* Abel; *his
desire shall be Subject unto thee, and thou shalt Rule over
him.* To which I answer,

1.   These words of God to *Cain,* are by many Inter- 5
preters with great Reason, understood in a quite different
Sense than what our *A.* uses them in.

2.   Whatever was meant by them, it could not be, that
Cain as Elder, had a natural Dominion over *Abel;* for the
words are conditional: *If thou dost well* and so personal to 10
Cain, and whatever was signified by them, did depend on
his Carriage and not follow his Birth-right, and therefore
could by no means be an Establishment of Dominion in the
First-born in general. For before this *Abel* had his *distinct
Territories by Right of Private Dominion,* as our *A.* him- 15
self confesses, *O.* 210. [64] which he could not have had to
the prejudice of the Heirs Title, *If by Divine Institution,*
Cain as Heir were to inherit all his Father's Dominion.

3.   If this were intended by God as the Charter of
Primogeniture, and the Grant of Dominion to Elder 20
Brothers in general as such, by Right of Inheritance, we
might expect it should have included all his Brethren. For
we may well suppose, *Adam,* from whom the World was
to be peopled, had by this time, that these were grown up
to be Men, more Sons than these two: whereas *Abel* him- 25
self is not so much as named; and the words in the Original,
can scarce, with any good Construction, be applied to him.

4.   It is too much to build a Doctrine of so mighty consequence upon so doubtful and obscure a place of Scripture, which may be well, nay better, understood in a quite 30
different Sense, and so can be but an ill Proof, being as
doubtful as the thing to be proved by it, especially when
there is nothing else in Scripture or Reason to be found,
that favours or supports it.

113. It follows, *p.* 19. [61] *Accordingly when Jacob bought his Brothers Birth-right, Isaac blessed him thus; be Lord over thy Brethren, and let the Sons of thy Mother bow before thee.* Another instance I take it, brought by 5 our *A.* to evince Dominion due to Birth-right, and an admirable one it is. For it must be no ordinary way of reasoning in a Man, that is pleading for the natural Power of Kings, and against all compact to bring for Proof of it, an example where his own account of it founds all the 10 right upon compact, and settles Empire in the Younger Brother, unless buying and selling be no compact; for he tells us, *when Jacob bought his Brothers Birth-right.* But passing by that, let us consider the History it self, with what use our *A.* makes of it, and we shall find these fol- 15 lowing Mistakes about it.

1°. That our *A.* reports this, as if *Isaac* had given *Jacob* this Blessing, immediately upon his Purchasing the *Birth-right;* for he says, *when Jacob bought Isaac blessed him,* which is plainly otherwise in the Scripture. For it ap- 20 pears there was a distance of time between, and if we will take the Story in the order it lies, it must be no small distance; all *Isaac*'s Sojourning in *Gerar,* and Transactions with *Abimelech, Gen.* 26. coming between, *Rebeka* being then Beautiful and consequently young, but *Isaac* when 25 he Blessed *Jacob,* was old and decrepit; And *Esau* also complains of *Jacob, Gen.* 27. 36. that *two times* he had Supplanted him, *he took away my Birth-right,* says he, *and behold now he hath taken away my Blessing;* words, that I think signifie distance of time and difference of Action.

30 2.° Another mistake of our *A*'s, is, that he supposes *Isaac* gave *Jacob* the *Blessing,* and bid him be *Lord over his Brethren,* because he had the *Birth-right:* for our *A.* brings this Example to prove, that he, that has the *Birth-right,* has thereby a right to *be Lord over his Brethren.* 35 But it is also manifest by the Text, that *Isaac* had no consideration of *Jacobs* having bought the Birth-right, for when he blessed him, he considered him not as *Jacob,* but took him for *Esau.* Nor did *Esau* understand any such connection between *Birth-right* and the *Blessing,* for he 40 says, *he hath Supplanted me these two times, he took away my Birth-right, and behold now he hath taken away my Blessing:* whereas had the *Blessing,* which was to be *Lord over his Brethren,* belong'd to the *Birth-right, Esau* could not have complain'd of this second as a Cheat, *Jacob*

having got nothing but what *Esau* had sold him, when 45
he sold him his *Birth-right:* so that it is plain, Dominion, if
these words signifie it, was not understood to belong to the
Birth-right.

114. And that in those days of the Patriarchs, Dominion
was not understood to be Right of the Heir, but only a
greater Portion of Goods, is plain from *Gen.* 21. 10. for
Sarah taking *Isaac* to be Heir, says, *Cast out this Bond-*
woman and her Son, for the Son of this Bond-woman 5
shall not be Heir with my Son: whereby could be meant
nothing, but that he should not have a pretence to an
equal share of his Fathers Estate after his death, but should
have his Portion presently and be gone. Accordingly we
read, *Gen.* 25. 5, 6. That *Abraham gave all that he had* 10
unto Isaac, but unto the Sons of the Concubines which
Abraham had, Abraham gave Gifts and sent them away
from Isaac his Son, while he yet lived: That is, *Abraham*
having given Portions to all his other Sons, and sent them
away, that which he had reserved, being the greatest 15
part of his Substance, *Isaac* as Heir Possessed after his
Death, but by being Heir, he had no Right to be *Lord*
over his Brethren; for if he had, why should *Sarah* endeavour to Rob him of one of his *Subjects,* or lessen the
number of his *Slaves,* by desiring to have Ishmael sent 20
away.

115. Thus, as under the Law, the Priviledge of *Birth-*
right was nothing but a double Portion, so we see that
before *Moses* in the Patriarchs time, from whence our *A.*
pretends to take his Model, there was no knowledge, no
thought, that Birth-right gave Rule or Empire, Paternal 5
or Kingly Authority, to any one over his Brethren. If this
be not plain enough in the Story of *Isaac* and *Ishmael,*
he that will look into 1 *Chron.* 5. 1. 2. may there read these
words, *Ruben was the first Born, but forasmuch as he*
defiled his Fathers Bed, his Birth-right was given unto the 10
Sons of Joseph, the Son of Israel, and the Genealogy is
not to be reckon'd after the Birth-right; for Judah prevailed
above his Brethren, and of him came the chief Ruler, but
the Birth-right was Joseph's: what this Birth-right was, *Jacob*
Blessing *Joseph, Gen.* 48. 22. telleth us in these words, 15
Moreover I have given thee one Portion above thy Brethren,
which I took out of the Hand of the Amorite, with my

Sword and with my Bow. Whereby it is not only plain, that
the Birth-right was nothing but a double Portion, but the
20 Text in *Chron.* is express against our *A*'s Doctrine, and
shews that Dominion was no part of the Birth-right. For
it tells us that *Joseph* had the Birth-right, but *Judah* the
Dominion. One would think our *A.* were very fond of the
very name of *Birth-right* when he brings this Instance of
25 *Jacob* and *Esau*, to prove that Dominion belongs to the
Heir over his Brethren.

116. 1°. Because it will be but an ill example to
prove, that Dominion by God's Ordination belonged to
the Eldest Son, because *Jacob* the Youngest here had it,
let him come by it how he would. For if it prove any
5 thing, it can only prove against our *A.* that the *Assignment
of Dominion to the Eldest, is not by Divine Institution*,
which would then be unalterable. For if by the Law of
God, or Nature, Absolute Power and Empire belongs to
the Eldest Son and his Heirs, so that they are Supream
10 Monarchs, and all the rest of their Brethren Slaves, our *A.*
gives us reason to doubt whether the Eldest Son has a
Power to part with it, to the Prejudice of his Posterity,
since he tells us, *O.* 158. [233] That *in Grants and Gifts
that have their Original from God or Nature, no inferior
15 Power of Man can limit, or make any Law of Prescription
against them*.

117. 2°. Because this place, *Gen.* 27. 29. brought
by our *A.* concerns not at all the Dominion of one Brother
over the other, nor the Subjection of *Esau* to *Jacob*. For
'tis plain in the History, that *Esau* was never Subject to
5 *Jacob*, but lived a part in Mount *Seir*, where he founded a
distinct People and Government, and was himself Prince
over them, as much as *Jacob* was in his own family. This
Text if considered, can never be understood of *Esau*
himself, or the Personal Dominion of *Jacob* over him: For
10 the words *Brethren* and *Sons of thy Mother*, could not be
used literally by *Isaac*, who knew *Jacob* had only one

§ 117 5 'Mount *Seir*'—compare II, § 38, 34–6. The foundation of
a 'distinct People and Government' by one man and his family is described at length in chapter VIII of the *Second Treatise*, 'Of the Beginning of Political Societies'; see especially § 105 on.

Brother; and these words are so far from being true in
a literal Sense, or Establishing any Dominion in *Jacob*
over *Esau,* that in the Story we find the quite contrary,
for *Gen.* 32. *Jacob* several times calls *Esau* Lord and him- 15
self his Servant, and *Gen.* 33. *he bowed himself seven
times to the ground to* Esau. Whether *Esau* then were a
Subject and Vassal, nay (as our *A.* tells us, all Subjects are)
Slaves to *Jacob,* and *Jacob* his Sovereign Prince by Birth-
right, I leave the Reader to Judge; and to believe if he 20
can, that these words of *Isaac, be Lord over thy Brethren,
and let thy Mothers Sons bow down to thee,* confirm'd
Jacob in a Sovereignty over *Esau,* upon the account of
the *Birth-right* he had got from him.

118. He that reads the Story of *Jacob* and *Esau,* will
find there was never any Jurisdiction or Authority, that
either of them had over the other after their Father's
Death: they lived with the Friendship and Equality of
Brethren, neither *Lord,* neither *Slave* to his Brother, but 5
independent each of other, were both heads of their
distinct Families, where they received no Laws from one
another, but lived separately, and were the Roots out of
which sprang two distinct Peoples, under two distinct
Governments. This Blessing then of *Isaac,* whereon our *A.* 10
would Build the Dominion of the Elder Brother, signifies
nor more but what *Rebecca* had been told from God, *Gen.*
25. 23. *Two Nations are in thy Womb, and two manner of
People, shall be separated from thy Bowels, and the one
People shall be stronger than the other People, and the* 15
Elder shall serve the Younger; And so *Jacob* Blessed *Judah,
Gen.* 49. and gave him the Scepter and Dominion, from
whence our *A.* might have argued as well, that Jurisdiction
and Dominion belongs to the third Son over his Brethren,
as well as from this Blessing of *Isaac,* that it belonged to 20
Jacob: Both these places contain only Predictions of what
should long after happen to their Posterities, and not any
declaration of the Right of Inheritance to Dominion in
either. And thus we have our *A*'s two great and only
Arguments to prove, that *Heirs are Lords over their* 25
Brethren.

1°. Because God tells *Cain, Gen.* 4. That however sin
might set upon him, he ought or might be Master of it:
For the most Learned Interpreters understand the words
of sin, and not of *Abel,* and give so strong Reasons for it, 30

that nothing can convincingly be inferr'd from so doubtful
a Text, to our *A*'s purpose.

2°.   Because in this of *Gen.* 27. *Isaac* foretels that the
Israelites, the Posterity of *Jacob*, should have Dominion
35 over the *Edomites*, the Posterity of *Esau;* therefore says
our *A. Heirs are Lords of their Brethren:* I leave any one
to judge of the Conclusion.

119.   And now we see how our *A.* has provided for
the descending and conveyance down of *Adam*'s Monarchical Power, or Paternal Dominion to Posterity, by the
Inheritance of his *Heir,* succeeding to all his Father's
5 Authority, and becoming upon his Death as much Lord
as his Father was, *not only over his own Children, but
over his Brethren,* and all descended from his Father, and
so *in infinitum.* But yet who this Heir is, he does not once
tell us; and all the light we have from him in this so
10 Fundamental a Point, is only that in his instance of *Jacob,*
by using the word *Birth-right,* as that which passed from
Esau to *Jacob,* he leaves us to guess, that by Heir, he means
the Eldest Son, though I do not remember he any where
mentions expresly the Title of the First-born, but all along
15 keeps himself under the shelter of the indefinite Term
Heir. But taking it to be his meaning, that the Eldest
Son is Heir, (for if the Eldest be not, there will be no
pretence why the Sons should not be all Heirs alike) and
so by Right of Primogeniture has Dominion over his
20 Brethren; this is but one step towards the Settlement of
Succession, and the difficulties remain still as much as ever,
till he can shew us who is meant by Right Heir, in all
those cases which may happen where the present Possessor
hath no Son. This he silently passes over, and perhaps
25 wisely too: For what can be wiser after one has affirm'd,

§ 119 24 'This he silently passes over'—Pareyson comments here that
Filmer does in fact provide for such a case in his section on the *Escheat-
ing of Kingdoms* (61–2), where 'heads of families and Princes of
provinces . . . have power to consent in the uniting or conferring of their
fatherly right'. Sidney comments on this in *Discourses*, 1, 19, and
Tyrrell (1681), 54, but Locke does not in the text we now have, although it raises the whole issue between natural and conventional in
the origin of political power. It seems not unlikely that Locke did comment, and at length, on Filmer's concession to election and consent in
this case, but in the lost part of his work. Here he is merely registering
Filmer's unwillingness to be specific about the rules of inheritance, which
Tyrrell also notices: 'he nowhere positively answers this important Question' (1681, 45).

That *the Person having that Power, as well as the Power and Form of Government, is the Ordinance of God,* and *by Divine Institution,* vid. *O.* 254. [289] *p.* 12. [57] than to be careful, not to start any Question concerning the Person, the resolution whereof will certainly lead him into a Confession, that God and Nature hath determined nothing about him. And if our A. cannot shew who by Right of Nature, or a clear positive Law of God, has the next right to inherit the Dominion of this Natural Monarch, he has been at such pains about, when he died without a Son, he might have spared his pains in all the rest, it being more necessary for the setling Mens Consciences, and determining their Subjection and Allegiance, to shew them who by Original Right, Superior and Antecedent to the Will, or any Act of Men, hath a Title to this *Paternal Jurisdiction,* than it is to shew that by Nature there was such a *Jurisdiction:* it being to no purpose for me to know there is such a *Paternal Power,* which I ought, and am disposed to obey, unless where there are many Pretenders, I also know the Person that is rightly invested and endow'd with it.

120. For the main matter in question being concerning the Duty of my Obedience, and the Obligation of Conscience I am under to pay it to him that is of right my Lord and Ruler, I must know the Person that this Right of Paternal Power resides in, and so impowers him to claim Obedience from me. For let it be true what he says, *p.* 12. [57] That *Civil Power not only in general is by Divine Institution, but even the assignment of it specifically to the Eldest Parents;* and *O.* 254. [289] *That not only the Power or Right of Government, but the Form of the Power of Governing, and the person having that power, are all the Ordinance of God;* yet unless he shew us in all Cases who is this Person, *Ordain'd* by God, who is this *Eldest Parent,* all his Abstract Notions of Monarchical Power will signifie just nothing, when they are to be reduced to Practice, and Men are conscientiously to pay their Obedience. For *Paternal Jurisdiction* being not the thing to be obeyed, because it cannot command, but is only that which gives one Man a Right, which another hath not, and if it come by Inheritance, another Man cannot have, to command and be Obey'd; it is ridiculous to say, I pay Obedience to the *Paternal Power,* when I obey him, to whom Paternal

Power gives no Right to my Obedience; for he can have
no Divine Right to my Obedience, who cannot shew his
25 Divine Right to the Power of ruling over me, as well as
that by Divine Right, there is such a Power in the World.

121.   And hence not being able to make out any Princes
Title to Government, as Heir to *Adam,* which therefore is
of no use, and had been better let alone, he is fain to
resolve all into present Possession, and makes Civil
5 Obedience as due to an *Usurper* as to a lawful King; and
thereby the *Usurper's* Title as good. His words are, *O.* 253.
[289] And they deserve to be remembred: *If an Usurper
dispossess the true Heir, the Subjects Obedience to the
Fatherly Power must go along and wait upon God's Provi-*
10 *dence.* But I shall leave his Title of Usurpers to be
examin'd in its due place, and desire my sober Reader to
consider what thanks Princes owe such Politicks as this,
which can suppose *Paternal Power* (*i.e.*) a Right to Government in the Hands of a *Cade,* or a *Cromwel,* and so all
15 Obedience being due to Paternal Power, the Obedience of
Subjects will be due to them by the same Right, and upon
as good Grounds as it is to lawful Princes; and yet this,
as dangerous a Doctrine as it is, must necessarily follow
from making all Political Power to be nothing else but
20 *Adam's* Paternal Power by Right and *Divine Institution,*
descending from him, without being able to shew to whom
it descended, or who is Heir to it.

122.   To settle Government in the World, and to lay
Obligations to Obedience on any Mans Conscience, it is as
necessary (supposing with our *A.* that all Power be nothing
but the being possessed of *Adam's Fatherhood*) to satisfie
5 him, who has a Right to this Power, this *Fatherhood,* when
the Possessor dies without Sons to succeed immediately
to it, as it was to tell him that upon the death of the

§ 121   11 The 'due place' was almost certainly a part of the lost con-
tinuation of the *First Treatise;* see the reference to usurpation in Locke's
Preface, where he implies that this subject was discussed there, lines 35–7.
In his two-paragraph chapter XVII of the *Second Treatise,* 'Of
Usurpation', Locke does not discuss 'his', that is Filmer's, 'Title of
Usurpers'.
    14 'Cromwel' is discussed in the note to I, § 79, 1: Jack Cade was the
leader of the Kentish uprising of 1450, which had also become a symbol
for popular revolt, compare the note on Masaniello, I, § 79, 3. In 1680
John Crowne published a play about Cade, *The Misery of Civil War,*
acted in 1681.

Father, the Eldest Son had a Right to it: For it is still to
be remember'd, that the great Question is, (and that
which our *A.* would be thought to contend for, if he did 10
not sometimes forget it) what Persons have a Right to be
obeyed, and not whether there be a Power in the World,
which is to be called *Paternal,* without knowing in whom
it resides: for so it be a Power, *i.e.* Right to Govern, it
matters not, whether it be termed *Paternal,* or *Regal;* 15
Natural, or *acquired;* whether you call it *Supreme Fatherhood,* or *Supreme Brotherhood,* will be all one provided
we know who has it.

123. I go on then to ask whether in the inheriting of
this *Paternal Power,* this *Supreme Fatherhood,* The Grand-
Son by a Daughter, hath a Right before a Nephew by a
Brother? Whether the Grand-Son by the Eldest Son, being
an Infant, before the Younger Son a Man and able? 5
Whether the Daughter before the Uncle? or any other
Man, descended by a Male Line? Whether a Grand-Son
by a Younger Daughter, before a Grand-Daughter by an
Elder Daughter? Whether the Elder Son by a Concubine,
before a Younger Son by a Wife? From whence also will 10
arise many Questions of Legitimation, and what in Nature
is the difference betwixt a Wife and a Concubine? For as
to the Municipal or Positive Laws of Men, they can
signifie nothing here. It may farther be asked, Whether
the Eldest Son being a Fool, shall inherit this *Paternal* 15
Power, before the Younger a wise Man? And what Degree

§ 123 The objections in the paragraph look a little far-fetched, since
Filmer and his supporters had assumed the validity of the rules which
in fact governed the succession of the English Crown. The important
point is hinted at in lines 11–13, where Locke implies that on Filmer's
premises such rules cannot merely be the 'Municipal or Positive Laws'
of one country (compare note on I, § 90, 32–4), but must be a part
of natural law: Tyrrell (1681, 54 on) spends a great deal of time showing that 'there is nothing but custom in the case' and Sidney (*Discourses,*
1, 18) takes Filmer up on it. Such issues were a standard subject of the
natural-law theorists, and these questions of Locke's could almost have
been translated from the section headings XXX–XXXVII of chapter VII
of the Second Book of Grotius, *De Jure Belli.* It must be remembered
that the issues of 'the Elder Son by a Concubine' (9) and 'the difference
between a Wife and a Concubine' (12) were crucial to Locke when he
wrote this, because the claimant to the throne adopted by Shaftesbury
against the future James II was the Duke of Monmouth, Charles II's
eldest son by a concubine. To establish the precedency of Monmouth
over all other claimants, William Lawrence was enabled by Shaftesbury
in 1681 to publish the second part of his *Marriage by the Morall Law
of God* (see Furley, 1957, 21, note 11). Locke owned this book.

of Folly it must be, that shall exclude him? And who shall
be judge of it? Whether the Son of a Fool excluded for his
Folly, before the Son of his wise Brother who Reign'd?
20 Who has the *Paternal Power,* whilst the Widow-Queen is
with Child by the deceased King, and no body knows
whether it will be a Son or a Daughter? Which shall be
Heir of two Male-Twins, who by the Dissection of the
Mother, were laid open to the World? Whether a Sister by
25 the half Blood, before a Brothers Daughter by the whole
Blood?

124.   These, and many more such Doubts, might be
proposed about the Titles of Succession, and the Right
of Inheritance; and that not as idle Speculations, but such
as in History we shall find, have concerned the Inheritance
5 of Crowns and Kingdoms; and if ours want them, we need
not go farther for famous Examples of it, than the other
Kingdom in this very Island, which having been fully related
by the Ingenious and Learned Author of *Patriarcha non
Monarcha,* I need say no more of. Till our *A.* hath re-
10 solved all the Doubts that may arise about the next Heir,
and shewed that they are plainly determin'd by the Law
of Nature, or the revealed Law of God, all his Suppositions of a *Monarchical, Absolute, Supreme, Paternal
Power* in *Adam,* and the descent of that Power to his
15 Heirs, would not be of the least use to Establish the
Authority, or make out the Title of any one Prince now on
Earth, but would rather unsettle and bring all into question:

§ 124   6 and 8–9   James Tyrrell was of course the author of *Patriarcha
non Monarcha* (1681), published late in 1680 and acquired by Locke
on 2 June 1681; see Introduction, 71–4, for this book and for the relationship between Locke and Tyrrell when it was being written. This is
the only specific acknowledgement to the work, but the parallel passages between it and Locke's noted in this edition show how close the
two men were. In Tyrrell's letter of 20 December 1689 referring to *Two
Treatises* (see Introduction, 65) he says, evidently with this reference
in mind, that the writer concerned 'speaks of the author of *Patriarcha
non Monarcha* more respectfully than he deserves', and writing to
Locke on 30 August 1690 he adds that the author of *Two Treatises*
'agreed perfectly with my conceptions in *Patriarcha non Monarcha*
(which he had quoted)'.
   Locke presumably intended here pp. 54–60 of Tyrrell's book, dealing
with the succession of uncle or nephew, son or grandson, bastard or
legitimate in Navarre, Castile, Portugal, among the Moguls of India and
especially, and at length, in Scotland—'the other Kingdom of this very
Island', which was also Lawrence's favourite source of illustration—see
note on I, § 123.

For let our *A.* tell us as long as he please, and let all Men
believe it too, that *Adam* had a *Paternal,* and thereby *a
Monarchical Power;* That this (the only Power in the
World) *descended to his Heirs,* and that there is no other
Power in the World but this: let this be all as clear Demon-
stration, as it is manifest Error, yet if it be not past doubt,
to whom this *Paternal Power descends,* and whose now it
is, no body can be under any Obligation of Obedience,
unless any one will say, that I am bound to pay Obedience
to *Paternal Power* in a Man, who has no more *Paternal
Power* than I my self; which is all one as to say, I obey a
Man, because he has a Right to Govern, and if I be asked,
How I know he has a Right to Govern, I should answer,
It cannot be known, that he has any at all. For that cannot
be the reason of my Obedience, which I know not to be
so; much less can that be a reason of my Obedience, which
no body at all can know to be so.

125.   And therefore all this ado about *Adam's Fatherhood,* the greatness of its Power, and the necessity of its
supposal, helps nothing to Establish the Power of those
that Govern, or to determine the Obedience of Subjects,
who are to obey, if they cannot tell whom they are to
obey, or it cannot be known who are to Govern, and who
to Obey. In the State the world now is, irrecoverably ignorant who is *Adam's* heir, this *Fatherhood,* this *Monarchical Power of Adam* descending to his Heirs, would be of
no more Use to the Government of Mankind, than it would
be to the quieting of Mens Consciences, or securing their
Healths, if our *A.* had assured them, that *Adam* had a
Power to forgive Sins or cure Diseases, which by Divine
Institution descended to his *Heir,* whilst this Heir is impossible to be known. And should not he do as rationally, who
upon this assurance of our *A.* went and confessed his Sins,
and expected a good Absolution, or took Physick with
expectation of Health from any one who had taken on
himself the Name of Priest or Physician, or thrust himself
into those Employments, saying, I acquiesce in the Ab-
solving Power descending from *Adam,* or I shall be cured
by the Medicinal Power descending from *Adam;* as he
who says, I submit to, and obey the *Paternal Power*
descending from *Adam,* when 'tis confessed all these
Powers descend only to his single Heir, and that Heir is
unknown.

126. 'Tis true, the Civil Lawyers have pretended to
determine some of these Cases concerning the Succession
of Princes; but by our *A*'s Principles, they have medled
in a matter that belongs not to them: For if all Political
5 Power be derived only from *Adam,* and be to descend
only to his Successive Heirs, by the *Ordinance of God* and
Divine Institution, this is a Right Antecedent and Paramount to all Government; and therefore the positive Laws
of Men, cannot determine that which is it self the Founda-
10 tion of all Law and Government, and is to receive its
Rule only from the Law of God and Nature. And that
being silent in the Case, I am apt to think there is no such
Right to be conveyed this way: I am sure it would be to
no purpose if there were, and Men would be more at a
15 loss concerning Government and Obedience to Governours,
then if there were no such Right: since by positive Laws
and Compact, which *Divine Institution* (if there be any)
shuts out, all these endless inextricable Doubts, can be
safely provided against; but it can never be understood,
20 how a Divine Natural Right, and that of such moment as is
all Order and Peace in the World, should be convey'd
down to Posterity, without any Plain Natural or Divine
Rule concerning it. And there would be an end of all
Civil Government, if the *Assignment* of Civil Power were
25 by *Divine Institution* to the Heir, and yet *by that Divine
Institution,* the Person of the Heir could not be known.
This *Paternal Regal Power,* being by Divine Right only his,
it leaves no room for humane prudence, or consent to
place it any where else: for if only one Man hath a Divine
30 Right to the Obedience of Mankind, no body can claim
that Obedience, but he that can shew that Right; nor can
Mens Consciences by any other pretence be obliged to it.
And thus this Doctrine cuts up all Government by the
Roots.

127. Thus we see how our *A.* laying it for a sure
Foundation, that the very *Person* that is to Rule, is *the
Ordinance* of God, and by *Divine Institution,* tells us at

§ **126** 1 'Civil Lawyers', the professors of the Civil or Roman Law
of Locke's day, and right back to the age of Justinian: writers such as
Grotius and Pufendorf are probably intended to be included here. Filmer quotes the Civil Law frequently, but not on the point of succession,
but Locke was indifferent to Roman Law as such, though he possessed
his *Institutes* and *Corpus Juris Civilis.* On this paragraph compare
Tyrrell (1681), 54, and Sidney, I, § 18.

large, only that this Person is the *Heir*, but who this Heir is,
he leaves us to guess; and so this *Divine Institution* which   5
Assigns it to a Person, whom we have no Rule to know,
is just as good as an Assignment to no body at all. But
whatever our *A.* does, *Divine Institution* makes no such
ridiculous Assignments: nor can God be supposed to make
it a Sacred Law, that one certain Person should have a   10
Right to something, and yet not to give Rules to mark out,
and know that Person by, or give an *Heir* a Divine Right to
Power, and yet not point out who that *Heir* is. 'Tis rather
to be thought, that an *Heir*, had no such Right by *Divine
Institution*, than that God should give such a Right to the   15
Heir, but yet leave it doubtful, and undeterminable who
such Heir is.

128. If God had given the Land of *Canaan* to *Abraham*,
and in general Terms to some body after him, without
naming his Seed, whereby it might be known, who that
somebody was, it would have been as good and useful an
Assignment, to determine the Right to the Land of *Canaan*,   5
as it would to the determining the Right of Crowns, to give
Empire to *Adam* and his Successive Heirs after him, without telling who his Heir is: For the word *Heir*, without a
Rule to know who it is, signifies no more than somebody,
I know not whom. God making it a *Divine Institution*,   10
that Men should not marry those who were *near of Kin*,
thinks it not enough to say, *none of you shall approach
to any that is near of Kin to him, to uncover their Nakedness:* But Moreover, gives Rules to know who are those
near of Kin, forbidden by *Divine Institution*, or else that   15
Law would have been of no use: it being to no purpose to
lay restraint, or give Privileges, to Men, in such general
Terms, as the Particular Person concern'd cannot be known
by. But God not having any where said, the next Heir shall
Inherit all his Fathers Estate or Dominion, we are not to   20
wonder that he hath no where appointed who that Heir
should be, for never having intended any such thing, never
designed any Heir in that Sense, we cannot expect he
should any where nominate, or appoint any Person to it,
as we might, had it been otherwise. And therefore in   25
Scripture, though the word *Heir* occur, yet there is no such
thing as Heir in our *A*'s Sense, one that was by Right of

§ **128**   12–15   See Lev. xviii: the text quoted comes from verse 6, and
the specified incestuous relationships in the rest of the chapter.

Nature to Inherit all that his Father had, exclusive of
his Brethren. Hence *Sarah* supposes, that if *Ishmael* staid in
30 the House, to share in *Abrahams* Estate after his Death,
this Son of a bond woman might be Heir with *Isaac:* and
therefore, says she, *cast out this Bond-woman and her Son,*
for the Son of this Bond-woman shall not be Heir with my
Son; But this cannot excuse our *A*——, who telling us
35 there is in every Number of Men, one who is *Right* and
next *Heir* to *Adam* [288–9], ought to have told us what
the Laws of descent are. He having been so sparing to
instruct us by Rules, how to know who is *Heir,* let us see
in the next place, what his History out of Scripture, on
40 which he pretends wholly to build his Government, gives
us in this necessary and Fundamental point.

129. Our *A.* to make good the Title of his Book, *p.*
13. [58] begins the History of the descent of *Adams*
Regal Power, *p.* 13. in these words: *This Lordship which*
Adam *by command had over the whole World, and by*
5 *Right descending from him, the Patriarchs did enjoy was*
as large, &c. How does he prove that the Patriarchs by
descent did enjoy it? for *Dominion of Life and Death,*
says he, *we find* Judah *the Father pronounced Sentence*
of Death against Thamar *his Daughter-in-Law for playing*
10 *the Harlot, p.* 13 [58]. How does this prove that *Judah*
had Absolute and Sovereign Authority, *He pronounced*
Sentence of Death? The pronouncing of Sentence of Death
is not a certain mark of Sovereignty, but usually the Office

32–4   See Gen. xxi. 10, noted previously in I, § 114.
§ 129   1   This can only be intended to refer to the title *Patriarcha, or*
the Natural Power of Kings, and is one of the indications that the *First*
Treatise, as distinct from the *Second,* was directed at *Patriarcha* particularly—see Introduction 74 and compare, I, § 1, 10 and note.
4   '*by command*'—thus in the 1680 printing of *Patriarcha:* the manuscript reads '*by creation*' (58).
12–18   Filmer in claiming that the power to pronounce on life and
death was a certain mark of sovereignty was following Bodin's classic
definition: in his *Methodus,* probably behind the references to sovereignty in the Latin Tract of 1664: see p. 6 and note in Abrams' edition,
compare Von Leyden, 1954, p. 20. 'The power of life and death when
the law itself leaves no room for extenuating' was the fifth and final
mark of sovereignty. Comparison with such passages as I, § 131, II, § 3,
II, § 11, 7–9 (see note there) and II, § 65 shows that Locke did argue
about 'marks of sovereignty' in somewhat Bodin's way. It seems quite
unjustifiable to maintain as Green did that Locke never used the term
sovereignty in the way his contemporaries did (1931, 75) or that he
avoided it because of the use Hobbes had made of the word (see
Gough, 1950, 41).

of Inferior Magistrates. The Power of making Laws of Life
and Death, is indeed a Mark of Sovereignty, but pronounc- 15
ing the Sentence according to those Laws may be done by
others, and therefore this will but ill prove that he had
Sovereign Authority: As if one should say, *Judge Jefferies,*
pronounced Sentence of Death in the late Times, therefore *Judge Jefferies,* had Sovereign Authority: But it will 20
be said, *Judah* did it not by Commission from another, and
therefore did it in his own Right. Who knows whether he
had any Right at all? heat of Passion might carry him to
do that which he had no Authority to do. *Judah had
Dominion of Life and Death,* how does that appear? he 25
exercised it, he *pronounced Sentence of Death against*
Thamar, our *A——* thinks it is very good Proof, that
because he did it, therefore he had a Right to do it; He lay
with her also: By the same way of Proof, he had a Right
to do that too: If the consequence be good from doing 30
to a Right of doing. *Absalon* too may be reckon'd amongst
our *A-s* Sovereigns, for he pronounced such a Sentence
of Death against his Brother *Amnon,* and much upon a
like occasion, and had it executed too; if that be sufficient
to prove a Dominion of Life and Death. 35

But allowing this all to be clear Demonstration of
Sovereign Power, who was it that had this *Lordship by
Right descending to him from* Adam, *as large and ample
as the Absolutest Dominion of any Monarch* [58]? Judah,
says our *A——, Judah* a younger Son of *Jacob,* his Father 40
and Elder Brethren living: so that if our *A——s* own
Proof be to be taken, a younger Brother may in the Life
of his Father and Elder Brothers, *by Right of descent,* enjoy
Adams Monarchical Power; and if one so qualified may
be Monarch by descent, why may not every man? if *Judah,* 45
his Father and Elder Brother living were one of *Adams*
Heirs, I know not who can be excluded from this Inheritance; all Men by Inheritance may be Monarchs as
well as *Judah.*

130.   *Touching War, we see that* Abraham *Commanded
an Army of* 318 *Souldiers of his own Family, and* Esau *met
his Brother* Jacob *with* 400 *Men at Arms; For matter of*

18–20 The reference to Judge Jeffreys 'in the late Times' must have
been inserted after the end of James II's reign and is the only sentence
in *Two Treatises* which dates itself, in 1689. See Introduction 59.
31–3 For Absolom and Amnon see II Sam. xiii.

Peace; Abraham *made a League with* Abimilech, &c. *p.* 13
5 [58]. Is it not possible for a Man to have 318 Men in his
Family, without being Heir to *Adam?* A Planter in the *West
Indies* has more, and might, if he pleased (who doubts)
Muster them up and lead them out against the *Indians,*
to seek Reparation upon any Injury received from them,
10 and all this without the *Absolute Dominion of a Monarch,
descending to him from Adam.* Would it not be an admirable Argument to prove, that all Power by Gods Institution descended from *Adam* by Inheritance, and that
the very Person and Power of this Planter were the *Ordi-
15 nance of God,* because he had Power in his Family over
Servants, born in his House, and bought with his Money?
For this was just *Abrahams* Case: Those who were rich
in the *Patriarchs* Days, as in the *West-Indies* now, bought
Men and Maid Servants, and by their increase as well as
20 purchasing of new, came to have large and numerous
Families, which though they made use of in War or Peace,
can it be thought the Power they had over them was an
Inheritance descended from *Adam,* when 'twas the Purchase of their Money? A Mans Riding in an expedition
25 against an Enemy, his Horse bought in a Fair, would be
as good a Proof that the owner *enjoyed the Lordship which*
Adam *by command had over the whole World, by Right
descending to him,* as *Abrahams* leading out the Servants
of his Family is, that the Patriarchs enjoy'd this Lordship
30 by descent from *Adam:* since the Title to the Power, the
Master had in both Cases, whether over Slaves or Horses,
was only from his purchase; and the getting a Dominion
over any thing by Bargain and Money, is a new way of
proving one had it by Descent and Inheritance.

§ 130   6–7 'A Planter in the *West Indies*'—compare I, § 131, 2–11.
Locke speaks here from his personal knowledge as secretary to the
proprietors of Carolina, which was regarded as an extension of the West
Indies (compare I, § 144, 27 and note), and as Secretary to Shaftesbury's Board of Trade and Plantations, see Introduction, 38–9. It is interesting that both Locke and Filmer, whose brother was a planter in
Virginia, accepted the political character of the family under such circumstances, as did Tyrrell who talks much as Locke does, but his
planter is in the Barbadoes (1681, 105). All of them to varying degrees
imply in this way that the position of the colonial planter can be assimilated to that of the Biblical patriarch. It may be permissible to guess
that the planters themselves, although they acquired their subjects (slaves
and indentured servants) by purchase, as Locke says, would have regarded their power as patriarchal as Filmer claimed, rather than as
resting finally on consent, and that Filmer's Biblical arguments would
have appealed to them more than Locke allowed.

131. *But making War and Peace are marks of Sovereignty* [58]. Let it be so in Politick Societies. May not therefore a Man in the *West-Indies,* who hath with him Sons of his own, Friends, or Companions, Soldiers under Pay, or Slaves bought with Money, or perhaps a Band made 5 up of all these, make War and Peace, if there should be occasion, and *ratifie the Articles too with an Oath* [58], without being a Sovereign, an Absolute King over those who went with him? he that says he cannot, must then allow many Masters of Ships, many private Planters to be 10 Absolute Monarchs, for as much as this they have done. War and Peace cannot be made for Politick Societies, but by the Supream Power of such Societies; because War and Peace, giving a different Motion to the force of such a Politick Body, none can make War or Peace, but 15 that which has the direction of the force of the whole Body, and that in Politick Societies is only the Supream Power. In voluntary Societies for the time, he that has such a Power by consent, may make War and Peace, and so may a single Man for himself, the State of War 20 not consisting in the number of *Partysans,* but the enmity of the Parties, where they have no Superiour to appeal to.

132. The actual making of War or Peace is no proof of any other Power, but only of disposing those to exercise or cease Acts of enmity for whom he makes it, and this Power in many Cases any one may have without any Politick Supremacy. And therefore the making of War 5 or Peace will not prove that every one that does so is a Politick Ruler, much less King; for then Common-wealths must be Kings too, for they do as certainly make War and Peace as Monarchical Government.

133. But granting this *a mark of Sovereignty* in *Abraham,* Is it a proof of the Descent to him, of *Adam's Sovereignty* over the whole World? If it be, it will surely

§ 131   1–2   Declaring war and peace was Bodin's third mark of sovereignty, *Methodus,* 1945, 172, compare I, § 129, 12–18 and note.
    22   The lack of a common superior, as characterizing the state of nature is discussed at length in the *Second Treatise,* chapter II, 'Of the State of Nature', and references in this paragraph to war supplement the following chapter there, 'Of the State of War', see especially §§ 20–1. In the relationships within and between planters' families in America, we have a model for the origin and nature of the Lockeian state, and its contrast with the state of nature—see Introduction.

be as good a proof of the *descent of Adam's Lordship*
5 to others too. And then Common-wealths, as well as
Abraham, will be *Heirs of Adam*, for they make *War and
Peace*, as well as he. If you say, that the *Lordship of Adam*
doth not by Right descend to Common-wealths, though
they make War and Peace, the same say I of *Abraham*, and
10 then there is an end of your Argument; if your stand to
your Argument, and say those that do make War and
Peace, as Common-wealths do without doubt, do *inherit
Adam's Lordship*, there is an end of your Monarchy,
unless you will say, that Common-wealths *by descent*
15 *enjoying Adam's Lordship* are Monarchies, and that indeed
would be a new way of making all the Governments in the
World Monarchical.

134. To give our *A.* the honour of this new invention,
for I confess it is not I have first found it out by tracing
his Principles, and so charged it on him, 'tis fit my Readers
know that (as absurd as it may seem) he teaches it himself,
5 *p.* 23. [62] where he ingeniously says, *In all Kingdoms
and Common-wealths in the World, whether the Prince
be the Supream Father of the People, or but the true Heir
to such a Father, or come to the Crown by Usurpation or
Election, or whether some few or a Multitude Govern the
10 Common-wealth: yet still the Authority that is in any one,
or in many, or in all these is the only Right, and natural
Authority of a Supream Father*, which Right of *Fatherhood*
he often tells us, is *Regal and Royal Authority;* as particularly, *p.* 12. [57] the page immediately preceding this
15 Instance of *Abraham*. This Regal Authority, he says, those
that Govern Common-wealths have: and if it be true, that
Regal and Royal Authority be in those that govern Common-wealths, it is as true, that Common-wealths are
govern'd by Kings: for if Regal Authority be in him that
20 Governs, he that Governs must needs be a King, and so all
Common-wealths are nothing but down-right Monarchies,
and then what need any more ado about the matter? the
Governments of the World are as they should be, there
is nothing but Monarchy in it. This without doubt, was
25 the surest way our *A.* could have found, to turn all other
Governments, but Monarchical, out of the World.

135. But all this scarce proves *Abraham*, to have been
a King as Heir to *Adam*. If by Inheritance he had been

King, *Lot*, who was of the same Family, must needs have
been his Subject, by that Title before the Servants in his
Family: but we see they liv'd as Friends and Equals, and
when their Herdsmen could not agree, there was no pretence of Jurisdiction or Superiority between them, but they
parted by consent, *Gen.* 13. hence he is called both by
Abraham, and by the Text *Abraham's Brother*, the Name
of Friendship and Equality, and not of Jurisdiction and
Authority, though he were really but his Nephew. And if
our *A.* knows that *Abraham* was *Adam*'s Heir, and a King,
'twas more it seems then *Abraham* himself knew, or his
Servant whom he sent a wooing for his Son; for when he
sets out the advantages of the Match, 24 *Gen.* 35. thereby
to prevail with the Young-woman and her Friends, he says,
I am Abrahams Servant, and the Lord hath Blessed my
Master greatly, and he is become great, and he hath given
him Flocks and Herds and Silver and Gold, and Men-Ser-
vants and Maid-servants, and Camels and Asses, and Sarah
my Masters Wife, bare a Son to my Master when she was old,
and unto him he hath given all he hath. Can one think that a
discreet Servant, that was thus particular to set out his Master's Greatness, would have omitted the Crown *Isaac* was to
have, if he had known of any such? Can it be imagin'd he
should have neglected to have told them on such an occasion as this that *Abraham* was a King, a Name well
known at that time, for he had nine of them his Neighbours, if he or his Master had thought any such thing, the
likeliest matter of all the rest, to make his Errand Successful?

136.   But this discovery it seems was reserved for our
A. to make 2 or 3000 Years after, and let him injoy the
Credit of it, only he should have taken care that some of
Adam's Land should have descended to this his *Heir*, as
well as all *Adam*'s Lordship, for though his Lordship which
Abraham, (if we may believe our *A.*) as well as the other
Patriarchs, *by Right descending to him did enjoy, was as*
large and ample as the Absolutest Dominion of any Mon-

---

§ **135** 7–8 'they parted by consent'—II, § 38, 33–4 'they, by consent, as
Abraham and Lot did, . . . separated': see note there.

16 The young woman was Rebeccah.

28 These nine kings are listed in Gen. xiv. 1–2, and cited by Filmer,
59.

arch which hath been since the Creation [58]. Yet his Es-
10 tate, his Territories, his Dominions were very narrow and
scanty, for he had not the Possession of a Foot of Land,
till he bought a Field and a Cave of the Sons of *Heth* to
bury *Sarah* in.

137.   The Instance of *Esau* joyn'd with this of *Abraham*,
to prove that the *Lordship which* Adam *had over the whole
World, by Right descending from him, the Patriarchs did
enjoy*, is yet more pleasant then the former: *Esau met his*
5 *Brother Jacob with* 400 *Men at Arms* [58]; He therefore
was a King by Right of Heir to *Adam*. 400 Arm'd Men
then however got together are enough to prove him that
leads them to be a King and *Adam*'s Heir. There have been
Tories in *Ireland*, (whatever there are in other Countries)
10 who would have thankt our *A*. for so honourable an Opinion of them, especially if there had been no body near with
a better Title of 500 Armed Men, to question their Royal
Authority of 400. 'Tis a shame for Men to trifle so, to say
no worse of it, in so serious an Argument. Here *Esau* is
15 brought as a Proof that *Adam's Lordship, Adam's absolute
Dominion, as large as that of any Monarch descended by
Right to the Patriarchs*, and in this very *Chap. p.* 19. [61]
Jacob is brought as an instance of one, that by *Birth-right
was Lord over his Brethren*. So we have here two Brothers

§ **136** 12 Gen. xxiii for the burial of Sarah. Compare II, § 35, 9–23
and note: Sidney makes the same point about the restricted territory
of Abraham and the other patriarchs in *Discourses*, 1, 8. According to
Usher's chronology, in the margins of the Authorized Version, it took
place in 1872 B.C., about 2500 years before Locke and Filmer, and the
reference in line 2 shows that Locke was accepting this chronology:
compare, I, § 147, 59, I, § 150, 11 and notes. This he did in general,
though both he and Newton found it so difficult to reconcile with their
cosmology, and in Locke's case, with his comparative anthropology.
MS. c. 27 shows that he was working at the chronology of the Old
Testament in the year 1680.
§ **137** 8–9 This would seem to be the only direct reference to Locke's
political opponents, the Royalists, traditionalists or tories, in his book,
and it is tempting to look on it as a jibe at the opponents of the Revolution of 1688–9. But though it is just possible that the phrase in
parentheses, where 'other Countries' means England of course, was added
in 1689, the sentence itself can only have been written in 1679–81, when
'tory' was still an opprobrious nickname for Irish bog-trotters, and had
not become irrevocably attached to a body of English political opinion.
17 'this very *Chap.*'—Chapter I of *Patriarcha* (53–63), see note on
I, § 6, 54. The form of this reference implies that Locke, in the lost continuation of the *First Treatise*, may have commented on the second and
third chapters of Filmer's *Patriarcha*, as printed in 1680, see Introduction, Section III.

Absolute Monarchs by the same Title, and at the same time 20
Heirs to *Adam:* The Eldest Heir to *Adam,* because he met
his Brother with 400 Men, and the youngest Heir to *Adam*
by *Birth-right:* Esau *injoy'd the Lordship which* Adam *had
over the whole World by Right descending to him, in as
large and ample manner, as the absolutest Dominion of* 25
any Monarch, and at the same time, *Jacob Lord over him,
by the Right Heirs have to be Lords over their Brethren.*
Risum teneatis? I never, I confess, met with any Man of
Parts so Dexterous as Sir *Robert* at this way of Arguing:
But 'twas his Misfortune to light upon an hypothesis that 30
could not be accommodated to the Nature of things, and
Human Affairs, his principles could not be made to agree
with that Constitution and Order which God had settled
in the World, and therefore must needs often clash with
common Sense and Experience.   35

138. In the next Section, he tells us [58], *This Patriarchal Power continued not only till the Flood, but after it,
as the name Patriarchs doth in part prove.* The word Patriarch doth more then *in part prove,* that *Patriarchal Power*
continued in the World as long as there were Patriarchs, 5
for 'tis necessary that Patriarchal Power should be whilst
there are Patriarchs, as it is necessary there should be Paternal or Conjugal Power whilst there are Fathers or Husbands: but this is but playing with Names. That which he
would fallaciously insinuate is the thing in question to be 10
proved, viz. that the *Lordship which* Adam *had over the
World,* the supposed Absolute Universal Dominion of
Adam by *Right descending from him the Patriarchs did
enjoy.* If he affirms such an Absolute Monarchy continued
to the Flood, in the World, I would be glad to know what 15
Records he has it from; for I confess I cannot find a word
of it in my Bible: If by *Patriarchal Power,* he means any
thing else, it is nothing to the matter in hand: And how the
name *Patriarch in some part proves,* that, those, who are
called by that name, had Absolute Monarchical Power, I 20
confess, I do not see, and therefore I think needs no answer, till the Argument from it be made out a little clearer.

---

28 '*Risum teneatis?*'—'can you help laughing', Horace, *Ars Poetica,*
5, though probably a conventional phrase in academic disputation.
§ **138** 1 'next Section'—section 5 of the 1680 printing, section III and
part of section IV (58–60) in Laslett's edition.

139. *The three Sons of Noah had the World,* says our
A., *divided amongst them by their Father, for of them was
the whole World overspread,* p. 14 [58]. The World might
be overspread by the Off-spring of *Noah*'s Sons, though he
5 never divided the World amongst them; For the *Earth*
might be *Replenished* without being divided, so that all our
A——'s Argument here, proves no such Division. However I allow it to him, and then ask, the World being divided amongst them, which of the three was *Adam*'s Heir?
10 If *Adam*'s *Lordship, Adam*'s *Monarchy,* by Right descended
only to the Eldest, then the other two could be but his
Subjects, his Slaves; If by Right it descended to all three
Brothers, by the same Right, it will descend to all Mankind,
and then it will be impossible what he says, *p.* 19. [61] that
15 *Heirs are Lords of their Brethren,* should be true, but all
Brothers, and consequently all Men will be equal and independent, all Heirs to *Adam*'s Monarchy, and consequently all Monarchs too, one as much as another. But
'twill be said *Noah* their Father divided the World amongst
20 them, so that our *A.* will allow more to *Noah,* than he will
to God Almighty, for *O.* 211. [64] he thought it hard, that
God himself should give the World to *Noah* and his Sons,
to the prejudice of *Noah*'s Birth-right, his words are, *Noah
was left Sole Heir to the World, why should it be thought
25 that God would disinherit him of his Birth-right, and make
him of all Men in the World, the only Tenant in common
with his Children?* and yet here he thinks it fit, that *Noah*
should disinherit *Shem* of his Birth-right, and divide the
World betwixt him and his Brethren, so that this *Birth-right,*
30 when our *A.* pleases, must, and when he pleases, must not,
be sacred and inviolable.

140. If *Noah* did divide the World between his Sons,
and his Assignment of Dominions to them were good, there
is an end of Divine Institution; all our *A*'s Discourse of
Adam's Heir, with whatsoever he builds on it, is quite out
5 of doors; and the Natural Power of Kings falls to the
ground; and then *the form of the Power Governing, and
the Person having that Power,* will not be (as he says they
are *O.* 254 [289]) *the ordinance of God,* but they will be
Ordinances of man. For if the right of the Heir be the Or-
10 dinance of God, a Divine Right, no Man, Divine, or not
Father, can alter it: If it be not a Divine right, it is only
Human depending on the Will of Man: and so where

Human Institution gives it not, the First-born has no right at all above his Brethren; and Men may put Government into what hands, and under what form, they please. 15

141. He goes on, *Most of the civillest Nations of the Earth, labour to fetch their Original from some of the Sons or Nephews of Noah*, p. 14 [58]. How many do most of the civillest Nations amount to? and who are they? I fear the *Chineses*, a very great and civil People, as well as sev- 5 eral other People of the *East*, *West*, *North* and *South*, trouble not themselves much about this matter. All that believe the Bible, which I believe are our *A's most of the civillest Nations*, must necessarily derive themselves from *Noah*, but for the rest of the World, they think little of 10 his Sons or Nephews. But if the Heralds and Antiquaries of all Nations, for 'tis these Men generally that labour to find out the Originals of Nations, or all the Nations themselves should *labour to fetch their Original from some of the Sons or Nephews of* Noah, what would this be to prove, 15 that the *Lordship which* Adam *had over the whole World, by right descended to the Patriarchs?* Whoever, Nations, or Races of Men, *labour to fetch their Original from,* may be concluded to be thought by them, Men of Renown, famous to Posterity for the Greatness of their Virtues and 20 Actions; but beyond these they look not, nor consider who they were Heirs to, but look on them as such as raised themselves by their own Virtue to a Degree that would give a Lustre to those, who in future Ages could pretend to derive themselves from them. But if it were *Ogygis,* 25 *Hercules, Brama, Tamberlain, Pharamond;* nay, if *Jupiter* and *Saturn* were the Names, from whence divers Races of Man, both Ancient and Modern, have labour'd to derive their Original; will that prove that those Men *enjoyed the Lordship of Adam, by right descending to them?* If not, 30 this is but a flourish of our *A*'s to mislead his Reader, that in it self signifies nothing.

§ **141** 25–7 Ogygis, first king of Thebes, reigning at the time of the flood, and so connected with a new race of Greeks: Hercules, Heracles, from whom the Dorians of Ancient Greece thought themselves descended: Brama, Brahma, from whom the Brahmans—the dominant caste of India—claimed divine descent: Tamberlain, Timur, the Mongol leader, from whom Locke perhaps supposes that the Mongols or even the Russians claimed descent: Pharamond, the Merovingian legendary king, may be included as a fabulous father of the French, and Jupiter and Saturn as originators of the Romans.

142. To as much purpose, is, what he tells us, *p. 15.*
[59] concerning this Division of the World, *That some say
it was by lot, and others that* Noah *sail'd round the* Mediterranean *in Ten Years, and divided the World into* Asia,
5 Afric *and* Europe, Portions for his three Sons. *America*
then, it seems, was left to be his that could catch it. Why
our *A.* takes such pains to prove the Division of the World
by *Noah* to his Sons, and will not leave out an Imagination, though no better than a Dream, that he can find any
10 where to favour it, is hard to guess, since such a *Division,*
if it prove any thing, must necessarily take away the Title
of *Adam*'s Heir: unless three Brothers can altogether be
Heirs of *Adam;* And therefore the following Words, *How-
soever the manner of this Division be uncertain, yet it is*
15 *most certain the Division it self was by Families from*
Noah *and his Children, over which the Parents were Heads
and Princes, p. 15.* [59] if allow'd him to be true, and of
any force to prove, that all the Power in the World is
nothing but the Lordship *of* Adam's *descending by Right,*
20 they will only prove that the Fathers of the Children are
all Heirs to this Lordship of *Adam.* For if in those days
Cham and *Japhet,* and other Parents besides the Eldest
Son were Heads and Princes over their Families, and had
a right to divide the Earth by Families, what hinders
25 Younger Brothers, being Fathers of Families, from having
the same Right? If *Cham* and *Japhet* were Princes by Right
descending to them, notwithstanding any Title of Heir in
their Eldest Brother, Younger Brothers by the same Right
descending to them are Princes now, and so all our *A*'s
30 Natural Power of Kings will reach no farther than their
own Children, and no Kingdom by this Natural Right, can
be bigger than a Family. For either this *Lordship of Adam
over the whole World,* by Right descends only to the Eldest Son, and then there can be but one Heir, as our *A.* says,
35 *p. 19* [60/61]. Or else, it by Right descends to all the Sons
equally, and then every Father of a Family will have it,
as well as the three Sons of *Noah:* Take which you will,
it destroys the present Governments and Kingdoms, that
are now in the World, since whoever has this *Natural
40 Power of a King,* by Right descending to him, must have
it either, as our A. tells us, *Cain* had it, and be Lord over
his Brethren, and so be alone King of the whole World,
or else as he tells us here, *Shem, Cham* and *Japhet* had it,
three Brothers, and so be only Prince of his own Family,

and all Families independent one of another; All the World 45
must be only one Empire by the right of the next Heir,
or else every Family be a distinct Government of it self,
by the *Lordship of Adam's descending to Parents of Families.* And to this only tends all the Proofs he here gives us
of the descent of *Adam's* Lordship: For continuing his 50
Story of this descent he says;

143.   *In the dispersion of* Babel, *we must certainly find
the Establishment of Royal Power, throughout the Kingdoms of the World,* p. 14 [58]. If you must find it, pray
do, and you will help us to a new piece of History: But
you must shew it us before we shall be bound to believe, 5
that Regal Power was Established in the World upon your
Principles. For, that Regal Power was Established *in the
Kingdoms of the World,* I think no body will dispute, but
that there should be Kingdoms in the World, whose several Kings enjoy'd their Crowns, *by right descending to* 10
them from Adam, that we think not only *Apocrypha,* but
also utterly impossible. If our A. has no better Foundation
for his Monarchy than a supposition of what was done at
the dispersion of *Babel,* the Monarchy he erects thereon,
whose top is to reach to Heaven to unite Mankind, will 15
serve only to divide and scatter them as that Tower did;
and instead of establishing civil government and order in
the World will produce nothing but confusion.

144.   For he tells us, the *Nations* they were divided
into, *were distinct Families, which had Fathers for Rulers
over them; whereby it appears, that even in the confusion,
God was careful to preserve the Fatherly Authority, by
distributing the Diversity of Languages, according to the* 5
Diversity of Families, p. 14 [58]. It would have been a
hard matter for any one but our *A.* to have found out
so plainly in the Text, he here brings, that all the Nations
in that dispersion were governed by *Fathers,* and that *God
was careful to preserve the Fatherly Authority.* The words 10
of the Text are; *These are the Sons of* Shem *after their
Families, after their Tongues in their Lands, after their
Nations;* and the same thing is said of *Cham* and *Japhet,*
after an Enumeration of their Posterities: in all which
there is not one word said of their Governors, or Forms 15
of Government; of *Fathers,* or *Fatherly Authority.* But
§ 144   9   The text is Gen. x. 31.

our *A.* who is very quick sighted, to spy out *Fatherhood,*
where no body else could see any the least glimpses of
it, tells us positively their *Rulers were Fathers, and God*
20 *was careful to preserve the Fatherly Authority;* and why?
Because those of the same Family spoke the same Language, and so of necessity in the Division kept together.
Just as if one should argue thus; *Hanibal* in his Army, consisting of divers Nations, kept those of the same Language
25 together, therefore Fathers were Captains of each Band,
and *Hanibal* was careful of the *Fatherly Authority.* Or
in Peopling of *Carolina,* the *English, French, Scotch,* and
Welch that are there, Plant themselves together, and by
them the Country is divided *in their Lands after their*
30 *Tongues, after their Families, after their Nations;* therefore
care was taken of the *Fatherly Authority.* Or because in
many parts of *America,* every little Tribe was a distinct
People, with a different Language, one should infer, that
therefore *God was careful to preserve the Fatherly Au-*
35 *thority,* or that therefore their Rulers *enjoy'd Adam's*
Lordship by right descending to them, though we know
not who were their Governors, nor what their Form of
Government, but only that they were divided into little
Independent Societies, speaking different Languages.

145.   The Scripture says not a word of their Rulers or
Forms of Government, but only gives an account, how
Mankind came to be divided into distinct Languages and
Nations; and therefore 'tis not to argue from the Authority
5 of Scripture, to tell us positively, *Fathers* were their *Rulers,*
when the Scripture says no such thing, but to set up Fancies of ones own Brain, when we confidently aver Matter
of Fact, where Records are utterly silent. Upon a like
ground, *i.e.* none at all he says, *That they were not con-*
10 *fused Multitudes without Heads and Governors, and at*
liberty to choose what Governors or Governments they
pleased [58].

27 'Peopling of Carolina'—compare I § 130, 6–7 and note. The *Fun-*
damental Constitutions of Carolina makes no provision for, nor refere-
ence to, the peopling of individual 'counties' or 'manors' in this way, but,
as was natural, English, French, Welsh and Scots did tend to settle the
area of the colony so.
33–9 This amplifies Locke's view of a state of nature as described
in his *Second Treatise* in an interesting way. If he was right, primitive
America should be just like this. Compare I, § 153, 21.
§ **145** 8 Compare I, § 144, 36–8; II, § 101, 12–13.

146. For I demand, when Mankind were all yet of one Language, all Congregated in the Plain of *Shinar*, were they then all under one Monarch, *who enjoy'd the Lordship of Adam by Right descending to him?* If they were not, there was then no thoughts, 'tis plain, of *Adam*'s Heir,   5 no Right to Government known then upon that Title, no Care taken by God or Man, of *Adam*'s *Fatherly Authority*. If when Mankind were but one People, dwelt altogether, and were of one Language, and were upon Building a City together; and when 'twas plain, they could not but know 10 the Right Heir, for *Shem* lived till *Isaac*'s time, a long while after the Division at *Babel;* If then, I say, they were not under the Monarchical Government of *Adam*'s Fatherhood, by Right descending to the Heir, 'tis plain there was no regard had to the *Fatherhood*, no Monarchy acknowl- 15 edg'd due to *Adam*'s *Heir*, no Empire of *Shem*'s in *Asia*, and consequently no such Division of the World by *Noah*, as our A. has talked of. As far as we can conclude any thing from Scripture in this matter, it seems from this place, that if they had any Government, it was rather a 20 Commonwealth than an Absolute Monarchy: For the Scripture tells us, *Gen.* 11. *They said.* 'Twas not a Prince commanded the Building of this City and Tower, 'twas not by the Command of one *Monarch,* but by the Consultation of many, a Free People, *Let us build us a City;* They 25 built it for themselves as Free-man, not as Slaves for their Lord and Master: *That we be not scattered abroad;* having a City once built, and fixed Habitations to settle our Abodes and Families. This was the Consultation and Design of a People, that were at liberty to part asunder, but 30 desired to keep in one Body, and could not have been either necessary or likely in Men tyed together under the Government of one Monarch, who if they had been, as our *A.* tells us, all *Slaves* under the Absolute Dominion of a Monarch, needed not have taken such care to hinder themselves 35

§ **146**   19–21   In the 1st Edition, I, § 147, 39–42 is more explicit than this: 'God himself says they were a Commonwealth'—see Collation and cf. II § 133, 3–4. In his early *Essay on the Civil Magistrate* Locke denied that God laid down in Scripture any rules of government or bounds to political power, except only the government of the Jews which he had himself constituted (English treatise, f. 33). There had been controversy over the constitution of the Israelites since the mid-sixteenth century —compare for example the *Vindiciae,* see Appendix B, no. 16. Locke may have discussed the point further in the missing section, together with Filmer's use of Old Testament monarchical history. Compare I, § 165, 3 and note.

from wandering out of the reach of his Dominion. I demand whether this be not plainer in Scripture than any thing of *Adam's Heir* or *Fatherly Authority?*

147. But if being, as God says, *Gen.* 11. 6. one People, they had one Ruler, one King by Natural Right, Absolute and Supreme over them, *what care had God to preserve the Paternal Authority of the Supreme Fatherhood* [58],
5 if on a suddain he suffers 72 (for so many our A. talks of [58]) *distinct Nations,* to be erected out of it, under distinct Governors, and at once to withdraw themselves from the Obedience of their Sovereign. This is to entitle God's care how, and to what we please. Can it be Sense to say,
10 that God was careful to preserve the *Fatherly Authority* in those who had it not? For if these were Subjects under a Supreme Prince, what Authority had they? Was it an instance of God's care to preserve the *Fatherly Authority,* when he took away the true *Supreme Fatherhood* of the
15 Natural Monarch? Can it be reason to say, That God, for the Preservation of *Fatherly Authority,* lets several new Governments with their Governors start up, who could not all have *Fatherly Authority?* and is it not as much reason to say, That God is careful to destroy *Fatherly Authority,*
20 when he suffers one who is in Possession of it, to have his Government torn in pieces, and shared by several of his Subjects? Would it not be an Argument just like this, for Monarchical Government, to say, when any Monarchy was shatter'd to pieces, and divided amongst revolted Subjects,
25 that God was careful to preserve Monarchical Power, by rending a settled Empire into a Multitude of little Governments? If any one will say, that what happens in Providence to be preserved, God is careful to preserve as a thing therefore to be esteemed by Men as necessary or useful,
30 'tis a peculiar Propriety of Speech, which every one will not think fit to imitate: but this I am sure is impossible to be either proper, or true speaking, that *Shem,* for example (for he was then alive) should have *Fatherly Authority,* or Sovereignty by Right of *Fatherhood* over that one People at *Babel,* and that the next moment *Shem* yet living,
35 72 others should have *Fatherly Authority,* or Sovereignty by Right of Fatherhood over the same People, divided into so many distinct Governments; either these 72 Fathers actually were Rulers, just before the Confusion, and then

§ **147**   39–42   See note on I, § 146, 19–38.

they were not one People, but that God himself says they 40
were; or else they were a Common-wealth, and then where
was Monarchy? or else these 72 Fathers had *Fatherly Authority*, but knew it not. Strange! that *Fatherly Authority*
should be the only Original of Government amongst Men,
and yet all Mankind not know it; and stranger yet, that the 45
confusion of Tongues should reveal it to them all of a sudden, that in an instant these 72 should know that they had
Fatherly Power, and all others know that they were to
obey it in them, and every one know that particular
Fatherly Authority to which he was a Subject. He that can 50
think this Arguing from Scripture, may from thence make
out what Model of an *Eutopia* will best suit with his Fancy
or Interest, and this *Fatherhood* thus disposed of, will justifie both a Prince who claims an Universal Monarchy, and
his Subjects, who being Fathers of Families, shall quit all 55
Subjection to him, and *Canton* his Empire into less Governments for themselves: For it will always remain a doubt
in which of these the Fatherly Authority resided, till our
A. resolves us, whether *Shem*, who was then alive, or these
72 new Princes, beginning so many new Empires in his 60
Dominions, and over his Subjects, had right to govern,
since our *A.* tells us, that both one and t'other had *Fatherly*,
which is Supreme, Authority, and are brought in by him
as Instances of those, who did *enjoy the Lordship of Adam
by right descending to them, which was as large and ample* 65
as the Absolutest Dominion of any Monarch [58]. This at
least is unavoidable, that if *God was careful to preserve
the Fatherly Authority, in the 72 New erected Nations*
[58], it necessarily follows, that he was as careful to destroy
all pretences of *Adams* Heir; since he took care, and 70
therefore did preserve the Fatherly Authority in so many,
at least 71, that could not possibly be *Adams* Heirs, when
the right Heir (if God had ever ordained any such Inheritance) could not but be known, *Shem* then living,
and they being all one People.   75

52   '*Eutopia*'—a reference to the *Utopia* of Sir Thomas More (1516),
already current as a collective name for all fanciful political models.
Utopia was the only work of More's which Locke possessed; the Oxford,
Latin edition of 1663.
56   '*Canton*'—to split up into independent political units, or cantons.
59   Shem, Noah's eldest son and so, as Filmer would say, the natural
heir to his power and possessions, lived for 600 years, and so would
have seen all these events—see Gen. xi. 11–12. This is another example
of Locke's accepting Biblical chronology, see I, § 136, 12 and note.

148. *Nimrod* is his next instance of enjoying this Patriarchal Power, *p.* 16. [59] but I know not for what Reason
our *A.* seems a little unkind to him, and says, that he
against Right enlarged his Empire, by seizing violently on
5 *the Rights of other Lords of Families:* These *Lords of*
Families here were called *Fathers of Families,* in his account of the dispersion at *Babel:* but it matters not how
they were called, so we know who they are; for this Fatherly
Authority must be in them, either as Heirs to *Adam,* and
10 so there could not be 72, nor above one at once, or else
as natural Parents over their Children, and so every Father
will have *Paternal Authority* over his Children by the same
Right, and in as large extent as those 72 had, and so be
Independent Princes over their own Off-spring. Taking his
15 *Lords of Families,* in this latter sense (as 'tis hard to give
those words any other sense in this place) he gives us a
very pretty account of the Original of Monarchy in these
following words, *p.* 16. [59] *And in this Sense he may be*
said to be the Author and Founder of Monarchy, viz. As
20 against Right seizing violently on the Rights of Fathers
over their Children, which Paternal Authority, if it be in
them by right of Nature; (for else how could those 72
come by it) no body can take from them without their
own consents, and then I desire our *A.* and his Friends to
25 consider how far this will concern other Princes, and
whether it will not according to his conclusion of that Paragraph, resolve all Regal Power of those, whose Dominions
extend beyond their Families, either into Tyranny and
Usurpation, or Election and Consent of Fathers of Fam-
30 ilies, which will differ very little from Consent of the People.

§ **148** 1 '*Nimrod*'—the story of Nimrod (Gen. x. 1–10), Noah's
grandson but not in the elder line, was commonly used by those who
founded political power, particularly monarchy, on force or conquest.
Filmer deals with this interpretation in the paragraph Locke is criticizing
here, admitting in 'his conclusion of that paragraph' (see lines 26–7 of this
one) that he was a usurper. Sidney follows the sixteenth- and early
seventeenth-century interpreters whom Filmer had in mind, using their
case to insinuate, of course, that all kings were usurpers by violence of
the rights of the people: see *Discourses*, 1, 8, headed 'Nimrod was the
first King'.

18 '*p.* 16'.—omitted in the 1st edition. This may imply that Locke
had his Filmer beside him when he corrected the 1st edition for the
2nd in 1694, although he did not when he made the final corrections
which appear in the Christ's copy. Compare notes on I, § 157, 2 and
I, § 78, 22.

149.   All his Instances, in the next *Section, p.* 17. [59]
of the 12. Dukes of *Edom,* the 9. Kings in a little corner
of *Asia* in *Abrahams* days, the 31 Kings in *Canaan* destroyed by *Joshua,* and the care he takes to prove that these
were all Sovereign Princes, and that every Town in those   5
days had a King, are so many direct Proofs against him,
that it was not the *Lordship of* Adam *by Right descending*
to them that made Kings: For if they had held their Royal-
ties by that Title, either there must have been but one
Sovereign over them all, or else every Father of a Family   10
had been as good a Prince, and had as good a claim to
Royalty as these: For if all the Sons of *Esau,* had each of
them, the Younger as well as the Eldest, the right of
Fatherhood, and so were Sovereign Princes after their
Fathers Death, the same Right had their Sons after them,   15
and so on to all Posterity, which will limit all the natural
Power of Fatherhood, only to be over the Issue of their
own Bodies, and their descendants, which Power of Fatherhood dies with the head of each Family, and makes way
for the like power of Fatherhood to take place, in each of   20
his Sons, over their respective Posterities, whereby the
Power of Fatherhood will be preserv'd indeed, and is intelligible, but will not be at all to our *A*——s purpose:
None of the instances he brings, are proofs of any Power
they had, as Heirs of *Adam*'s Paternal Authority, by the   25
title of his fatherhood descending to them, no—nor of any
power they had by Vertue of their own: For *Adams Fatherhood* being over all Mankind, it could descend but to one
at once, and from him to his right Heir only, and so there
could by that Title be but one King in the World at a time;   30
And by Right of Fatherhood, not descending from *Adam,*
it must be only as they themselves were Fathers, and so
could be over none but their own Posterity: So that if
those 12 Dukes of *Edom;* If *Abraham* and the 9 Kings
his Neighbours; If *Jacob* and *Esau* and the 31 Kings in   35
Canaan, the 72 Kings mutilated by *Adonibeseck,* the 32
Kings that came to *Benhadad,* the 70 Kings of *Greece*
making War at *Troy,* were as our *A.* contends [60], all of
them Sovereign Princes; 'tis evident that Kings deriv'd their
Power from some other Original *then Fatherhood,* since   40

§ 149   1   'in the next *Section*'—see note on I, § 138, 1: Section 7 of
the 1680 printing begins on p. 17. Locke seems to have felt that he had
got through two sections, 5 and 6, of *Patriarcha* in paragraphs 138–48.

some of these had Power over more than their own Posterity, and 'tis Demonstration, they could not be all Heirs
to *Adam:* For I challenge any Man to make any pretence
to Power by right of *Fatherhood,* either intelligible or pos-
45 sible in any one, otherwise, than either as *Adams* Heir, or
as Progenitor over his own Descendants, naturally sprung
from him. And if our *A.* could shew that any one of these
Princes, of which he gives us here so large a Catalogue,
had his Authority by either of these Titles, I think I might
50 yield him the cause: though 'tis manifest they are all impertinent and directly contrary to what he brings them to
prove, *viz.* That the *Lordship which* Adam *had over the
World by Right descended to the Patriarchs.*

150.   Having told us, *p.* 16. [59, 60] That *the Patriarchal Government continued in* Abraham, Isaac, *and* Jacob,
until the Egyptian Bondage, p. 17. [60] he tells us, *By
manifest Footsteps we may trace this Paternal Government
5 unto the* Israelites *coming into* Egypt, *where the exercise
of Supream Patriarchal Government was intermitted, because they were in Subjection to a stronger Prince.* What
these Footsteps are of paternal Government, in our *A*'s
Sense, *i.e.* of Absolute Monarchical Power descending from
10 *Adam,* and exercised by Right of *Fatherhood* we have
seen, that is for 2290 Years no Footsteps at all: since in
all that time he cannot produce any one Example of any
Person who claim'd or Exercised Regal Authority by right
of *Fatherhood;* or shew any one who being a King was
15 *Adams* Heir. All that his Proofs amount to, is only this,
that there were Fathers, Patriarchs and Kings in that Age
of the World; but that the Fathers and Patriarchs had any
Absolute Arbitrary Power, or by what Title those Kings
had theirs, and of what extent it was, the Scripture is wholly
20 silent; 'tis manifest by Right of *Fatherhood* they neither
did, nor could claim any Title to Dominion and Empire.

151.   To say, *that the Exercise of Supream Patriarchal
Government was intermitted, because they were in Subjection to a stronger Prince,* proves nothing but what I

§ 150   11   '2290 Years'—from the Creation (4004 B.C.) to the Exile in
Egypt (706 B.C.) according to Usher's chronology in the Authorized
Version. Compare note on I, § 136, 12, though here Locke follows the
chronology with startling exactness.

before suspected, *viz.* That *Patriarchal Jurisdiction or Government* is a fallacious expression, and does not in our *A.* 5
signifie (what he would yet insinuate by it) *Paternal* and
Regal Power; such an Absolute Sovereignty, as he supposes
was in *Adam.*

152.   For how can he say that *Patriarchal Jurisdiction
was intermitted in Egypt,* where there was a King, under
whose Regal Government the *Israelites* were, if *Patriarchal*
were *Absolute Monarchical Jurisdiction?* And if it were
not, but something else, why does he make such ado about 5
a Power not in question, and nothing to the purpose? The
Exercise of *Patriarchal* Jurisdiction, if *Patriarchal* be *Regal,*
was not intermitted whilst the *Israelites* were in *Egypt.*
'Tis true, the Exercise of *Regal* Power was not then in the
hands of any of the promised Seed of *Abraham,* nor before 10
neither that I know, but what is that to the intermission
of *Regal Authority, as descending from Adam,* unless our
A. will have it, that this chosen Line of *Abraham,* had the
Right of Inheritance to *Adams* Lordship? And then to what
purpose are his instances of the 72 Rulers, in whom the 15
Fatherly Authority was preserv'd in the Confusion at
Babel? Why does he bring the 12 Princes Sons of *Ismael;*
and the Dukes of *Edom,* and joyn them with *Abraham,
Isaac,* and *Jacob,* as examples of the exercise of true *Patriarchal Government,* if the exercise of *Patriarchal Jurisdic-* 20
tion were intermitted in the World, whenever the Heirs of
Jacob had not Supream Power? I fear *Supream Patriarchal
Jurisdiction* was not only *intermitted,* but from the time of
the Egyptian Bondage quite lost in the World, since 'twill
be hard to find from that time downwards, any one who 25
exercised it as an Inheritance descending to him from the
Patriarchs *Abraham, Isaac,* and *Jacob.* I imagined Monarchical Government would have served his turn in the
hands of *Pharaoh* or any Body. But one cannot easily
discover in all places what his discourse tends to, as par- 30
ticularly in this place, it is not obvious to guess what he
drives at, when he says, *the exercise of Supream Patriarchal
Jurisdiction* in *Egypt,* or how this serves to make out the
descent of *Adams* Lordship to the Patriarchs or any Body
else.   35

§ 152   This paragraph was extensively modified in 1694 by Locke: the
page is a cancel in the 2nd edition of that year, but it is further corrected in the Errata, and again in the Christ's copy. See the Collation.

153. For I thought he had been giving us out of Scripture, Proofs and Examples of Monarchical Government, founded on Paternal Authority, descending from *Adam;* and not an History of the *Jews:* amongst whom yet we 5 find no Kings, till many Years after they were a People: and when Kings were their Rulers, there is not the least mention or room for a pretence that they were Heirs to *Adam* or Kings by Paternal Authority. I expected, talking so much as he does of Scripture, that he would have pro- 10 duced thence a Series of Monarchs, whose Titles were clear to *Adams Fatherhood,* and who, as Heirs to him, own'd and exercised Paternal Jurisdiction over their Subjects, and that this was the true Patriarchical Government: whereas he neither proves, that the Patriarchs were Kings, nor that 15 either Kings or Patriarchs were Heirs to *Adam,* or so much as pretended to it: and one may as well prove, that the Patriarchs were all Absolute Monarchs; that the Power both of Patriarchs and Kings was only Paternal; and that this Power descended to them from *Adam;* I say all these 20 Propositions may be as well proved by a confused account of a multitude of little Kings in the *West-Indies,* out of *Ferdinando Soto,* or any of our late Histories of the *Northern America,* or by our *A*-s 70 Kings of *Greece,* out of *Homer,* as by any thing he brings out of Scripture, in that 25 Multitude of Kings he has reckon'd up.

154. And Methinks he should have let *Homer* and his Wars of *Troy* alone, since his great Zeal to Truth or Monarchy carried him to such a pitch of transport against *Philosophers and Poets,* that he tells us in his Preface [188], 5 that there *are too many in these days, who please themselves in running after the Opinions of Philosophers and*

§ 153   21   'multitude of little Kings'—compare I, § 144, 33–9 and note.

     22–3   'Ferdinando Soto', 'Histories of Northern America'. The reference to Soto could apply to any of the three accounts of that famous explorer published in French, Spanish or Portuguese in various editions. The most likely book is another work of Garcilaso (see note on I, § 57, 20–1), Richelet's French translation of his *La Florida del Inca*, 1605, *Histoire de la Floride, ou Rélation . . . de Ferdinand de Soto*, 1670, which Locke owned (see Appendix B, no. 88). The American histories might be Sagard's *Canada*, 1636, or his *Voyages des Hurons*, 1632—even John Smith's *Description of New England*, 1616, all of which Locke is known to have read when working at this book (Appendix B, nos. 72 and 76). His final library included many other likely titles.

§ 154   4, 31   'his Preface'—the Preface to Filmer's *Forms;* see note on I, § 8, 47.

*Poets, to find out such an Original of Government, as might
promise them some Title to Liberty, to the great Scandal
of Christianity, and bringing in of Atheism.* And yet these
Heathens, Philosopher *Aristotle,* and Poet *Homer,* are not 10
rejected by our zealous Christian Politician, whenever they
offer any thing that seems to serve his turn, whether to
the great Scandal of Christianity, and bringing in of Atheisme; let him looke. This I cannot but observe in Authors
who ('tis visible) write not for truth, how ready zeale for 15
interest and party is to entitle *Christianity* to their design,
and to charge *Atheisme* on those who will not without examining, submit to their Doctrines, and blindly swallow
their nonsense.

But to return to his Scripture History, our *A.* farther 20
tells us, *p.* 18. [60] that *after the return of the* Israelites
out of Bondage, *God out of a special care of them, chose*
Moses *and* Joshua *Successively to Govern as Princes in
the place and stead of the Supream Fathers.* If it be true,
that they *returned out of Bondage,* it must be into a State 25
of Freedom, and must imply, that both before and after
this *Bondage* they were free, unless our *A.* will say, that
changing of Masters, is returning *out of Bondage,* or that
a Slave *returns out of Bondage,* when he is removed from
one Gally to another. If then they *returned out of Bondage,* 30
'tis plain that in those days, whatever our *A.* in his Preface
[188] says to the contrary, there was difference between
a *Son,* a *Subject,* and a *Slave;* and that neither the *Patriarchs* before, nor their Rulers after this *Egyptian Bondage,
numbered their Sons or Subjects amongst their Possessions,* 35
and disposed of them with as Absolute a Dominion, as they
did *their other Goods.*

155. This is evident in *Jacob,* to whom *Reuben* offered
his two Sons as Pledges, and *Judah* was at last surety for
Benjamin's safe return out of *Egypt:* Which all had been
vain, superfluous, and but a sort of mockery, if *Jacob* had
had the same Power over every one of his Family as he 5

12–19 Passage added in Christ's copy, see Collation and note there.
The rather biting tone may betray his resentment of the attacks being
made on him in his last years as an enemy of Christianity—Filmer is
here classed with men like John Edwards (see Introduction, 86) though
his sentiment recalls that of his earliest political writing.

25–7 Locke seems to be playing on the ambiguity of the word 'freedom', freedom as national independence and as government by consent.
§ 155 See Gen. xlii–xliii.

had over his Ox or his Ass, as an *Owner* over his *Substance;* and the offers that *Reuben* or *Judah* made had been such a Security for returning of *Benjamin,* as if a Man should take two Lambs out of his Lords flock, and
10 offer one as security, that he will safely restore the other.

156. When they were out of this *Bondage,* what then? *God out of a special care of them, the Israelites* [60]. 'Tis well that once in his Book, he will allow God to have any care of the People, for in other places he speaks of Man-
5 kind, as if God had no care of any part of them, but only of their Monarchs, and that the rest of the People, the Societies of Men, were made as so many Herds of Cattle, only for the Service, Use, and Pleasure of their Princes.

157. *Chose* Moses *and* Joshua *Successively to Govern as Princes* [60]; A shreud Argument our *A.* has found out to prove Gods care of the Fatherly Authority, and *Adams* Heirs, that here as an expression of his care of his own
5 People, he chooses those for Princes over them, that had not the least pretence to either. The Persons chosen were, *Moses* of the Tribe of *Levy,* and *Joshua* of the Tribe of *Ephraim,* neither of which had any Title of *Fatherhood:* But says our *A.* they were in the place and stead of the Su-
10 pream Fathers: If God had any where, as plainly declared his choise of such *Fathers* to be Rulers, as he did of *Moses* and *Joshua,* we might believe *Moses* and *Joshuah* were in *their place and stead,* but that being the question in de-bate, till that be better proved, *Moses* being chosen by God
15 to be Ruler of his People, will no more prove that Govern-ment belong'd to *Adam's Heir* or to the *Fatherhood,* than God's choosing *Aaron* of the Tribe of *Levy* to be Priest, will prove that the Priesthood belong'd to *Adam's* Heir or the *Prime-fathers,* since God could choose *Aaron* to be
20 Priest, and *Moses* Ruler in *Israel,* though neither of those Offices, were settled on *Adam's Heir* or the *Fatherhood.*

§ 156 Locke compares the subjects of absolute monarchies to herds of animals in II, § 93, 8–16; compare also II, § 163, 21–7 and note on II, § 172, 11–22.
§ 157 2 In the Christ's copy 'p. 18' is deleted, a reference to Filmer which came after 'out' and which was inserted at the 2nd printing, see Collation. The passage indicated (Laslett's edition, 60) begins in the first line of I, § 156, and is completed here. This perhaps implies that the whole of I, § 156 after '*Israelites*' in line 2 is an insertion of 1689: compare I, §§ 159, 160 and note.

158.   Our *A.* goes on. *And after them likewise for a time he raised up Judges, to defend his People in time of peril*, p. 18 [60]. This proves Fatherly Authority to be the original of Government, and that it descended from *Adam* to his Heirs, just as well as what went before: only here   5
our *A.* seems to confess, that these Judges, who were all the Governours, they then had, were only Men of valour, whom they made their Generals to defend them in time of peril; and cannot God raise up such Men, unless Father-hood have a Title to Government?   10

159.   But says our *A. When God gave the* Israelites *Kings, he re-established the ancient and prime Right of Lineal Succession to Paternal Government*, p. 18 [60].

160.   How did God *re-establish* it? By a Law, a positive command? We find no such thing. Our *A.* means then, that when God gave them a King, in giving them a King, he *re-established the Right, &c.* To re-establish *de facto* the Right of Lineal Succession to Paternal Government, is to   5
put a Man in Possession of that Government which his Fathers did enjoy, and he by Lineal Succession had a Right to. For, first, if it were another Government, than what his Ancestors had, it was not succeeding to an *Ancient Right,* but beginning a new one. For if a Prince should   10
give a Man, besides his Ancient Patrimony, which for some Ages his Family had been disseiz'd of, an additional Estate, never before in the Possession of his Ancestors, he could

---

§ **158**   5–8   The view that the first monarchs, like the Judges of the Israelites, were military leaders is put forward at length in the *Second Treatise*, §§ 105–10, especially 109.

§§ **159, 160**   The paragraph number '159' was omitted from the 2nd and 3rd printings and not restored in Locke's final correction—159 was printed as if it continued 158. In fact, of course, 159 is simply the quotation from Filmer on which 160 is a commentary, just as 156 was orig-inally a quotation criticized in 157—see note on 157. It seems possible that these two quotations were made to stand alone as paragraphs in order to keep numeration continuous in an area of extensive correction, deletion and perhaps even losses. The paragraphs from 160 to 169, espe-cially 161, 162, were recorrected for punctuation in 1694, 1698 and after 1698—see Collation. All this betrays confusion in Locke's manu-script, and may be connected with the imminent breaking off of the *First Treatise*, or even with the peculiarities of the first printing of the early part of the *Second*. Moreover, the text hereabouts seems to consist simply in comments on Filmer's sentences, prolonging the chapter to twice the size of its predecessors, and wandering far from its title 'Who Heir?' It may represent a stringing together of surviving fragments of the lost portion of Locke's original manuscript.

not be said to *re-establish the Right of Lineal Succession*
15 to any more, than what had been formerly enjoy'd by his
Ancestors. If therefore the Power the kings of *Israel* had,
were any thing more than *Isaac* or *Jacob* had, it was not
the *re-establishing* in them the Right of Succession to a
Power, but giving them a new Power, however you please
20 to call it *Paternal* or not: and whether *Isaac* and *Jacob*
had the same Power, that the Kings of *Israel* had, I desire
any one, by what has been abovesaid, to consider, and I
do not think they will find that either *Abraham, Isaac,* or
Jacob had any Regal Power at all.

161. Next, there can be no *Re-establishment of the
Prime and Ancient Right of Lineal Succession* to any thing,
unless he, that is put in Possession of it has the right to
succeed, and be the true and next Heir to him he suc-
5 ceeds to. Can that be a Re-establishment, which begins in
a new Family? or that the *Re-establishment of an Ancient
Right of Lineal Succession,* when a Crown is given to one,
who has no Right of Succession to it, and who, if the Lineal
Succession had gone on, had been out of all possibility of
10 pretence to it? *Saul* the first King that God gave the
Israelites, was of the Tribe of *Benjamin.* Was the *Ancient
and Prime Right of Lineal Succession Re-established* in
him? The next was *David* the Youngest Son of *Jesse,* of
the Posterity of *Judah, Jacob's* third Son. Was the *Ancient
15 and Prime Right of Lineal Succession to Paternal Government Re-established* in him? Or in *Solomon* his younger
Son and Successor in the Throne? Or in *Jeroboam* over
the ten *Tribes?* Or in *Athaliah* a Woman, who Reigned six
Years an utter Stranger to the Royal Blood? *If the Ancient
20 and Prime Right of Lineal Succession to Paternal Government,* were *Re-established* in any of these or their Posterity, *the Ancient and Prime Right of Lineal Succession to
Paternal Government* belongs to Younger Brothers as well
as Elder, and may be Re-established in any Man living:
25 For whatever Younger Brothers, by *Ancient and Prime
Right of Lineal Succession,* may have as well as the Elder,
that every Man living may have a Right to, by Lineal Succession, and Sir *Robert* as well as any other. And so what
a brave Right of Lineal Succession, to his *Paternal* or
30 *Regal* Government, our *A.* has *Re-establish'd* for the securing the Rights and Inheritance of Crowns, where every
one may have it, let the World consider.

162. But says our *A*. however, *p*. 19. [60] *Whensoever God made choice of any special Person to be King, he intended that the Issue also should have benefit thereof, as being comprehended sufficiently in the Person of the Father, although the Father was only named in the Grant*. This yet will not help out Succession; for if, as our *A*. says, the benefit of the Grant be intended to the *Issue* of the Grantee, this will not direct the Succession; Since if God give any thing to a Man and his *Issue* in general, the Claim cannot be to any one of that *Issue* in particular, every one that is of his Race will have an equal Right. If it be said, our *A*. meant *Heir*, I believe our *A*. was as willing as any Body to have used that word, if it would have served his turn; but *Solomon* who succeeded *David* in the Throne, being no more his Heir than *Jeroboam*, who succeeded him in the Government of the Ten Tribes, was his Issue; our *A*. had reason to avoid saying, that God intended it to the *Heirs*, when that would not hold in a Succession, which our *A*. could not except against, and so he has left his Succession as undetermined, as if he had said nothing about it. For if the Regal Power be given by God to a Man and his *Issue*, as the Land of *Canaan* was to *Abraham* and his Seed, must they not all have a Title to it, all share in it? And one may as well say, that by God's Grant to *Abraham* and his Seed, the Land of *Canaan* was to belong only to one of his Seed exclusive of all others, as by God's Grant of Dominion to a man and his *Issue*, this Dominion was to belong in peculiar to one of his *Issue* exclusive of all others.

163. But how will our *A*. prove, that whensoever God made choice of any special Person to be a King, he intended that *the* (I suppose he means *his*) *Issue* also should have benefit thereof*. Has he so soon forgot *Moses* and *Joshua* whom in this very *Section* [60], he says, *God out of a special care chose to govern as Princes*, and the Judges that God raised up? Had not these Princes, having the Authority of the *Supream Fatherhood*, the same Power that the Kings had, and being specially chosen by God himself, should not their Issue have the benefit of that choice, as well as *David's* or *Solomon's*? If these had the

§ **163** 5 'Section'—section v of the 1680 printing; see note on I, § 138, 1.

Paternal Authority put into their hands immediately by
God, why had not their *Issue* the benefit of this Grant in
a Succession to this Power? Or if they had it as *Adam*'s
15 Heirs, why did not their Heirs enjoy it after them by Right
descending to them? For they could not be Heirs to one
another. Was the Power the same, and from the same Original in *Moses*, *Joshua* and the *Judges*, as it was in *David*
and the *Kings*, and was it inheritable in one and not in
20 the other? If it was not *Paternal Authority*, then God's own
People were govern'd by those that had not *Paternal Authority*, and those Governours did well enough without it:
If it were *Paternal Authority* and God chose the Persons
that were to exercise it, our *A*'s Rule fails, that *whensoever*
25 *God makes choice of any Person to be Supream* Ruler
(for I suppose the name King has no Spell in it, 'tis not
the Title, but the Power makes the difference) *he intends
that the Issue also should have the benefit of it*, since from
their coming out of *Egypt* to *David*'s time, 400 Years, the
30 *Issue* was never *so sufficiently comprehended in the Person
of the Father* [60], as that any Son after the Death of his
Father, succeeded to the Government amongst all those
Judges that judged *Israel*. If to avoid this, it be said, God
always chose the Person of the Successor, and so trans-
35 ferring the *Fatherly Authority* to him, excluded his Issue
from succeeding to it, that is manifestly not so in the Story
of *Jephtha*, where he Articled with the People, and they
made him Judge over them, as is plain, *Judg.* 11.

164. 'Tis in vain then to say [60], that *whensoever God
chooses any special Person* to have the exercise of *Paternal
Authority* (for if that be not to be King, I desire to know
the difference between a King and one having the exercise
5 of *Paternal Authority*,) *he intends the Issue also should
have the benefit of it*, since we find the Authority, the Judges
had, ended with them, and descended not to their *Issue*,
and if the Judges had not *Paternal Authority*, I fear it will
trouble our *A*. or any of the Friends to his Principles, to
10 tell who had then the *Paternal Authority*, that is, the
Government and Supream Power amongst the *Israelites*;

29 '400 Years'—that is, 1491 B.C. to *c.* 1050 B.C. in Usher's chronology; see note on I, § 136, 11.
36–7 On the story of Jephthah, critical to Locke's use of Scripture to
sanction his political theory, see II, § 21, 11 and 20, note and references.

and I suspect they must confess that the chosen People of
God continued a People several hundreds of Years, without
any Knowledge or Thought of this *Paternal Authority*, or
any appearance of Monarchical Government at all.   15

165. To be satisfied of this, he need but read the Story
of the *Levite*, and the War thereupon with the *Benjamites*,
in the 3 last *Chapt.* of *Jud.*: and when he finds, that the
Levite appeals to the People for Justice; that it was the
Tribes and the Congregation, that debated, resolved, and   5
directed all that was done on that occasion, he must conclude, either that *God* was not *careful to preserve the
Fatherly Authority* amongst his own chosen People; or
else that the *Fatherly Authority* may be preserved, where
there is no Monarchical Government; If the latter, then it   10
will follow that though *Fatherly Authority* be never so well
proved, yet it will not infer a necessity of Monarchical
Government; If the former, it will seem very strange and
improbable that God should ordain *Fatherly Authority*
to be so Sacred amongst the Sons of Men, that there could   15
be no Power or Government without it, and yet that
amongst his own People, even whilst he is providing a
Government for them, and therein prescribes Rules to the
several States and Relations of Men, this Great and Fundamental one, this most material and necessary of all the   20
rest should be concealed, and lye neglected for 400 Years
after.

166. Before I leave this, I must ask how our *A.* knows
that *whensoever God makes choice of any special Person
to be King, he intends that the Issue should have the benefit thereof?* [60] does God by the Law of Nature or Revelation say so? By the same Law also he must say, which of   5
his *Issue* must enjoy the Crown in Succession, and so point

§ 165   3   These chapters, Judg. xix, xx, xxi, were much relied upon
by that body of seventeenth-century opinion which held that the Israelites had a representative form of government; see the *Vindiciae Contra
Tyrannos*, Selden's *Mare Clausum* and Sidney's, *Discourses*, chapter II,
section 9, headed 'The Government instituted by God over the Israelites
was Aristocratical', especially 1772, 105. Locke hints at this argument
in I, § 146. The appeal of the Levite to the people for justice occurs in
Judg. xx. 7.
21–2   The 400 years were from the events under the Judges to the
anointing of Saul, 1406–1095 B.C. in Usher's chronology; see note on
I, § 136, 12.

out the Heir, or else leave his *Issue* to divide or scramble
for the Government: both alike absurd, and such as will
destroy the benefit of such Grant to the *Issue*. When any
10 such Declaration of God's Intention is produced, it will
be our Duty to believe God intends it so, but till that be
done, our *A*. must shew us some better Warrant, before we
shall be obliged to receive him as the Authentick Revealer
of God's Intentions.

167.   *The Issue*, says our *A*. *is comprehended sufficiently in the Person of the Father, although the Father
only was named in the Grant* [60]: And yet God, when
he gave the Land of *Canaan* to *Abraham*, *Gen*. 13. 15.
5 thought fit to put *his Seed* into the Grant too. So the
Priesthood was given to *Aaron and his Seed;* And the
Crown God gave not only to *David*, but *his Seed* also:
And however our *A*. assures us that *God intends, that the
Issue should have the benefit of it, when he chooses any
10 Person to be King,* yet we see that the Kingdom which
he gave to *Saul*, without mentioning his Seed after him,
never came to any of his *Issue;* and why when God chose
a Person to be King, he should intend that his *Issue*
should have the benefit of it, more than when he chose
15 one to be Judge in *Israel*, I would fain know a reason;
or why does a Grant of *Fatherly Authority* to a King
more comprehend the *Issue*, than when a like Grant is
made to a Judge? Is *Paternal Authority* by Right to descend to the *Issue*, of one and not of the other? There will
20 need some Reason to be shewn of this difference, more
than the name, when the thing given is the same *Fatherly
Authority*, and the manner of giving it, God's choice of
the Person the same too; for I suppose our *A.*, when he
says, *God raised up Judges*, will by no means allow, they
25 were chosen by the People.

168.   But since our *A*. has so confidently assured us of
the care of God to preserve the *Fatherhood*, and pretends
to build all, he says, upon the Authority of the Scripture,
we may well expect that the People whose Law, Con-

§ **167** 12 'chose'—at this word sheet P begins in the first printing,
1689. This sheet contained the text up to II, § 8, lines 6–7; see note there:
Locke's interference in the course of printing in 1689 could conceivably
have affected the text at any point from here to the end of Sheet S; see
note on II, § 51.

stitution and History is chiefly contained in the Scripture, 5
should furnish him with the clearest Instances of God's
care of preserving of the Fatherly Authority, in that
People who 'tis agreed he had a most peculiar care of. Let
us see then what State this *Paternal Authority* or Government was in amongst the *Jews,* from their beginning to 10
be a People. It was omitted by our *A's* confession, from
their coming into *Egypt,* till their return out of that Bondage, above 200 Years. From thence till God gave the
Israelites a King about 400 Years more, our *A.* gives but
a very slender account of it, nor indeed all that time are 15
there the least Footsteps of Paternal or Regal Government amongst them. But then says our *A.* [60] *God Re-
established the Ancient and Prime Right of Lineal Succession to Paternal Government.*

169. What a *Lineal Succession to Paternal Government* was then Established, we have already seen. I only
now consider how long this lasted, and that was to their
Captivity about 500 Years: From thence to their Destruction by the *Romans,* above 650 Years after, the 5
*Ancient and Prime Right of lineal Succession to Paternal
Government* was again lost, and they continued a People
in the promised Land without it. So that of 1150 Years
that they were God's peculiar People, they had Hereditary
Kingly Government amongst them, not one third of the 10
time, and of that time there is not the least Footstep of
one moment of *Paternal Government, nor the Re-establishment of the Ancient and Prime Right of Lineal Succession
to it,* whether we suppose it to be derived, as from its
Fountain, from *David, Saul, Abraham,* or which upon 15
our *A's* Principles is the only true; From *Adam.* ****

§§ **168, 169** Here the chronological argument becomes the main theme,
see I, § 136, 12: it presumably occupied the early part of the missing
portion.
　It will be seen that the *First Treatise* breaks off abruptly in the middle
of a phrase, obviously where Locke's manuscript reached the foot of a
page. In the later eighteenth-century editions and on, the stars were
omitted and, although it made nonsense, the final phrase seemed to end
a sentence.

THE SECOND TREATISE
OF GOVERNMENT

AN
E S S A Y

Concerning the

True Original, Extent, and End

OF

Civil Government

Title. The title-page was an insertion in the course of printing, as subtly demonstrated by Gerritsen, 1954. The original title, not allotted a page to itself in the printing as first planned, was presumably simply the 'Book II' at the head of the first page of its text, the *First Treatise* having 'Book I'. The title to the whole volume seems to have been altered to take account of this new title to the second book. See Introduction, 63.

The correct title to this second book, then, is either 'The Second Treatise of Government', to conform with that of the whole volume, or the full title given here, abbreviated 'Of Civil Government' (or alternatively 'An Essay Concerning Civil Government'). It was entitled thus in the French translation, the first appearance of the *Second Treatise* independently, perhaps with Locke's aproval (see Introduction, 24–5) —'Du Gouvernement Civil'. The title in common use is a solecism: 'The Second Treatise on (or of) Civil Government.' It may have arisen because the collected editions from the first (1714) on, and the individual editions from the 6th (1764) on, had the running title 'Of Government' for the *First Treatise* and 'Of Civil Government' for the *Second*—a distinction without meaning or usefulness.

BOOK II.

CHAP. I.

1. It having been shewn in the foregoing Discourse,

1°. That *Adam* had not either by natural Right of Fatherhood, or by positive Donation from God, any such Authority over his Children, or Dominion over the World as is pretended.   5

2°. That if he had, his Heirs, yet, had no Right to it.

3°. That if his Heirs had, there being no Law of Nature nor positive Law of God that determines, which is the Right Heir in all Cases that may arise, the Right of Succession, and consequently of bearing Rule, could not 10 have been certainly determined.

4°. That if even that had been determined, yet the knowledge of which is the Eldest Line of *Adam*'s Posterity, being so long since utterly lost, that in the Races of Mankind and Families of the World, there remains not to one 15 above another, the least pretence to be the Eldest House, and to have the Right of Inheritance.

All these premises having, as I think, been clearly made out, it is impossible that the Rulers now on Earth, should make any benefit, or derive any the least shadow of Au- 20 thority from that, which is held to be the Fountain of all Power, *Adam's Private Dominion and Paternal Jurisdic-*

§ 1 *Chapter* I.—obviously written by Locke to bridge the gap between the fragmentary *First Treatise* and the *Second*, presumably in 1689. As originally composed, this book must have started at § 4 (chapter II), or perhaps at an introductory paragraph to this one, now cancelled— see note on II, § 54, 1. Locke may, of course, have modified this area of the text considerably in 1689.

This chapter is omitted from the French version of 1691, and so from all editions in French and other languages until recent years—see Appendix A, 'Check List of Printings'. It was also left out of the early American edition, Boston, 1773—see Introduction, 27.

tion, so that, he that will not give just occasion, to think
that all Government in the World is the product only of
25 Force and Violence, and that Men live together by no
other Rules but that of Beasts, where the strongest carries
it, and so lay a Foundation for perpetual Disorder and
Mischief, Tumult, Sedition and Rebellion, (things that the
followers of that Hypothesis so loudly cry out against)
30 must of necessity find out another rise of Government,
another Original of Political Power, and another way of
designing and knowing the Persons that have it, then what
Sir *Robert F.* hath taught us.

2. To this purpose, I think it may not be amiss, to
set down what I take to be Political Power. That the
Power of a *Magistrate* over a Subject, may be distinguished
from that of a *Father* over his Children, a *Master* over his
5 Servant, a *Husband* over his Wife, and a *Lord* over his
Slave. All which distinct Powers happening sometimes
together in the same Man, if he be considered under these
different Relations, it may help us to distinguish these
Powers one from another, and shew the difference betwixt
10 a Ruler of a Common-wealth, a Father of a Family, and a
Captain of a Galley.

3. *Political Power* then I take to be *a Right* of making
Laws with Penalties of Death, and consequently all less
Penalties, for the Regulating and Preserving of Property,
and of employing the force of the Community, in the
5 Execution of such Laws, and in the defence of the Common-wealth from Foreign Injury, and all this only for the
Publick Good.

23–7 This has been taken as a covert reference to Hobbes, and in
fact may be a reminiscence of Filmer's attack on the Hobbesian state
of nature: 'It is not to be thought that God would create man in a
condition worse than any beast, as if he had made men to no other
end by nature but to destroy one another' (Laslett's edition, 241). Filmer was Hobbes's first critic, and Locke had read and noted this work
of his at least as early as 1667—see Introduction, 46. Compare II, § 93,
33–6.

27–8 Compare I, §§ 3; 83; 106, 17–18; § 143.
§ 3 Compare the definition of *respublica* in Locke's *Epistola de Tolerantia* (1689, that is, closer to this chapter than to the text as a
whole): 'The commonwealth seems to me to be a society of men constituted only for procuring, preserving their own *civil interests* (bona
civilia) . . . therefore is the magistrate armed with the force and
strength of all his subjects (toto scilicet subditorum robore) in order
to the punishment of those that violate any other man's rights' (1765,
p. 5, and pp. 35–6 for Popple's English translation). Here external se-

Of the State of Nature.

4. To understand Political Power right, and derive it from its Original, we must consider what State all Men are naturally in, and that is, a *State of perfect Freedom* to order their Actions, and dispose of their Possessions, and Persons as they think fit, within the bounds of the Law 5 of Nature, without asking leave, or depending upon the Will of any other Man.

A *State* also *of Equality,* wherein all the Power and Jurisdiction is reciprocal, no one having more than another: there being nothing more evident, than that Crea- 10 tures of the same species and rank promiscuously born to all the same advantages of Nature, and the use of the same faculties, should also be equal one amongst another without Subordination or Subjection, unless the Lord and Master of them all, should by any manifest Declaration of 15 his Will set one above another, and confer on him by an evident and clear appointment an undoubted Right to Dominion and Sovereignty.

---

curity is omitted and property is replaced by *bona civilia,* defined as 'life, liberty, health and indolency of body; and the possession of outward things, such as money, lands, houses, furniture and the like (vitam, libertatem, corporis integritatem, et indolentiam, et rerum externarum possessiones, ut sunt latifundia, pecunia, supellex etc.)'. See Introduction, 116; and on capital laws, see I, § 129, 12–18 and note, II, §§ 87–9, 171. Elrington (1798) remarks on the distinction between power and right in this paragraph, implying that Locke confuses them.

§ 4 *Chapter* II The French and other versions begin with this chapter, and in Locke's original text there may have been only one paragraph before this point, introducing the whole work; see note on II, § 54, 1. Although it was extended when Locke added his Hooker material (see §§ 5 and 15) and certainly corrected to some extent, perhaps a great deal, in 1689—see, for example, § 14, 14–20—there is no reason to suppose that it was not substantially completed in 1679.

3 'are'—Seliger points out that this means the state of nature was *not* past history.

10–12 A reference to the Creation, compare I, §§ 25–7, etc.

10–13 Quoted verbatim by Molyneux, *Case of Ireland,* 1698 (1720 ed., 127).

13 'should'—to be read as imperative in feeling, for Locke recognized inequality in capacity. See II, § 54, and *The Conduct of the Understanding:* 'there is, it is visible, a great variety in men's understandings, and their natural constitutions . . . the woods of America, as well as the schools of Athens, produce men of several abilities in the same kind'. In the same work, however, he is prepared to use the example

5. This *equality* of Men by Nature, the Judicious *Hooker* looks upon as so evident in it self, and beyond all question, that he makes it the Foundation of that Obligation to mutual Love amongst Men, on which he Builds
5 the Duties they owe one another, and from whence he derives the great Maxims *of Justice* and *Charity*. His words are;

The like natural inducement, hath brought Men to know that it is no less their Duty, to Love others than them-
10 *selves, for seeing those things which are equal, must needs all have one measure; If I cannot but wish to receive good, even as much at every Man's hands, as any Man can wish unto his own Soul, how should I look to have any part of my desire herein satisfied, unless my self be careful to*
15 *satisfie the like desire, which is undoubtedly in other Men, being of one and the same nature? to have any thing offered them repugnant to this desire, must needs in all respects grieve them as much as me, so that if I do harm, I must look to suffer, there being no reason that others*
20 *should shew greater measure of love to me, than they have by me, shewed unto them; my desire therefore to be*

---

of the natural equality of men for the purpose of illustrating the necessity of bottoming, that is discovering a 'truth well settled in the understanding' (*Works*, 1801, III, 189 and 259). Compare Hobbes, *Elements of Law* (1928, 54): 'men considered in mere nature ought to admit amongst themselves equality', and the similar statements in *Leviathan* (chapter 13) and *De Cive*, though the context and grounds of this statement of Locke's are very different.

§ 5 1–2 It was probably Locke, slavishly followed by his friend Molyneux, who did most to give currency to the title 'judicious' to Richard Hooker. He was genuinely indebted to him both in his philosophy and his political theory, and in his lists of recommended reading for young men he talks of the *Ecclesiastical Polity* as one of 'the most talked of books on politics, and requires thorough study of 'the judicious Hooker's first book' (*Works*, 1801, III, 272; X, 308). But the reference to him here and throughout the *Second Treatise* was also intended to lend respectability to his position and to turn the flank of his opponents, especially the good churchmen amongst them.

9–28 *Ecclesiastical Polity*, Book I, ch. VIII, § 7 (Keble ed. 1836, I, 288–9), not quite exactly quoted. Compare I, § 42 on Justice and Charity.

Like the other quotations from Hooker, this, and the rest of the paragraph with it, was added after the body of the text had been written (see Introduction, 70 and II, § 239, 51 and note), probably on 28 June 1681, on which date Locke copied into his diary extracts from just before and just after this one. All came from pp. 80–2 of the *Ecclesiastical Polity* which he had bought on 13 June—Appendix B, no. 45. This was probably the 1676 edition, and it is referred to as such in these footnotes, but it could have been that of 1666, see Introduction, 70 and note.

*lov'd of my equals in nature, as much as possible may be,
imposeth upon me a natural Duty of bearing to themward,
fully the like affection; From which relation of equality
between our selves and them, that are as our selves, what* 25
*several Rules and Canons, natural reason hath drawn for
direction of Life, no Man is ignorant.* Eccl. Pol. Lib. 1.

6. But though this be a *State of Liberty*, yet it is *not
a State of Licence*, though Man in that State have an un-
controleable Liberty, to dispose of his Person or Possessions, yet he has not Liberty to destroy himself, or so
much as any Creature in his Possession, but where some 5
nobler use, than its bare Preservation calls for it. The
State of Nature has a Law of Nature to govern it, which
obliges every one: And Reason, which is that Law, teaches
all Mankind, who will but consult it, that being all equal
and independent, no one ought to harm another in his 10
Life, Health, Liberty, or Possessions. For Men being all
the Workmanship of one Omnipotent, and infinitely wise
Maker; All the Servants of one Sovereign Master, sent into
the World by his order and about his business, they are
his Property, whose Workmanship they are, made to last 15
during his, not one anothers Pleasure. And being furnished
with like Faculties, sharing all in one Community of
Nature, there cannot be supposed any such *Subordination*
among us, that may Authorize us to destroy one another,
as if we were made for one anothers uses, as the inferior 20
ranks of Creatures are for ours. Every one as he is *bound
to preserve himself*, and not to quit his Station wilfully;
so by the like reason when his own Preservation comes not
in competition, ought he, as much as he can, *to preserve
the rest of Mankind*, and may not unless it be to do Justice 25
on an Offender, take away, or impair the life, or what
tends to the Preservation of the Life, Liberty, Health,
Limb or Goods of another.

§ 6   4   But compare II, § 23 and note.
    11–16   On man as God's workmanship see I, §§ 30; 52–4; 86, and as
God's property I, § 85, 11–12; compare II, § 56, 13–16, and English
Tract of 1660, 11.
    16–21   Compare I, §§ 86; 87; 92, 1–4 note; II, § 135, 15–20. These
statements are generally taken as directed against Hobbes, especially the
thirteenth chapter of *Leviathan*, but there is no verbal resemblance.
    20   'made for another's use'—Brogan, 1958, suggests a Kantian
parallel.

7. And that all Men may be restrained from invading others Rights, and from doing hurt to one another, and the Law of Nature be observed, which willeth the Peace and *Preservation of all Mankind*, the *Execution* of the
5 Law of Nature is in that State, put into every Mans hands, whereby every one has a right to punish the transgressors of that Law to such a Degree, as may hinder its Violation. For the *Law of Nature* would, as all other Laws that concern Men in this World, be in vain, if there were no body
10 that in the State of Nature, had a *Power to Execute* that Law, and thereby preserve the innocent and restrain offenders, and if any one in the State of Nature may punish another, for any evil he has done, every one may do so. For in that *State of perfect Equality*, where naturally
15 there is no superiority or jurisdiction of one, over another, what any may do in Prosecution of that Law, every one must needs have a Right to do.

8. And thus in the State of Nature, *one Man comes by a Power over another;* but yet no Absolute or Arbitrary Power, to use a Criminal when he has got him in his hands, according to the passionate heats, or boundless extrava-
5 gancy of his own Will, but only to retribute to him, so far as calm reason and conscience dictates, what is proportionate to his Transgression, which is so much as may serve for *Reparation* and *Restraint*. For these two are the only reasons, why one Man may lawfully do harm to an-
10 other, which is that we call *punishment*. In transgressing the Law of Nature, the Offender declares himself to live by another Rule, than that of *reason* and common Equity, which is that measure God has set to the actions of Men, for their mutual security: and so he becomes dangerous to
15 Mankind, the tye, which is to secure them from injury and violence, being slighted and broken by him. Which being a trespass against the whole Species, and the Peace and Safety of it, provided for by the Law of Nature, every man upon this score, by the Right he hath to preserve
20 Mankind in general, may restrain, or where it is necessary,

§ 8 6–7 'proportionate'—at this word sheet P ends and sheet Q begins in the first printing. This sheet exists in variant states (see Laslett, 1952 [iv], and Bowers, Gerritsen and Laslett, 1954 [ii]). Even more than in the case of the latter part of sheet P (see I, § 167, 12 and note), any part of it may be the result of Locke's last-minute modifications. It ends with the last word of § 21.

destroy things noxious to them, and so may bring such evil on any one, who hath transgressed that Law, as may make him repent the doing of it, and thereby deter him, and by his Example others, from doing the like mischief. And in this case, and upon this ground, every *Man hath* 25 *a Right to punish the Offender, and be Executioner of the Law of Nature.*

9. I doubt not but this will seem a very strange Doctrine to some Men: but before they condemn it, I desire them to resolve me, by what Right any Prince or State can put to death, or *punish an Alien,* for any Crime he commits in their Country. 'Tis certain their Laws by 5 vertue of any Sanction they receive from the promulgated Will of the Legislative, reach not a Stranger. They speak not to him, nor if they did, is he bound to hearken to them. The Legislative Authority, by which they are in Force over the Subjects of that Common-wealth, hath no 10 Power over him. Those who have the Supream Power of making Laws in *England, France* or *Holland,* are to an *Indian,* but like the rest of the World, Men without Authority: And therefore if by the Law of Nature, every Man hath not a Power to punish Offences against it, as 15 he soberly judges the Case to require, I see not how the Magistrates of any Community, can *punish an Alien* of another Country, since in reference to him, they can have no more Power, than what every Man naturally may have over another. 20

10. Besides the Crime which consists in violating the Law, and varying from the right Rule of Reason, whereby a Man so far becomes degenerate, and declares himself

§ 9 1–2 'strange Doctrine'—this seems to be Locke's way of announcing that his doctrine of punishment was, or was intended by him to be, a novelty; compare II, § 13, 1; II § 180, 6 and Introduction, 110. It is certainly in subtle contrast with Hobbes's doctrine in chapter 28 of *Leviathan,* with which it is often compared. The whole of Locke's *Second Letter on Toleration* (1690) is concerned with punishment as a means of '*Reparation* and *Restraint*'.
11–14 That is to say the Indian is in a state of nature with respect to all established political power, which implies that there is no international law (see Cox, 1960, 138).
§ 10 On this paragraph, Elrington comments (1798) that throughout the whole of this treatise Locke's 'zeal for liberty has very frequently led him to speak of men's *duties* as *rights* which they may exercise or renounce at pleasure'.

to quit the Principles of Human Nature, and to be a
5 noxious Creature, there is commonly *injury* done to some
Person or other, and some other Man receives damage by
his Transgression, in which Case he who hath received
any damage, has besides the right of punishment common
to him with other Men, a particular Right to seek *Repara-*
10 *tion* from him that has done it. And any other Person who
finds it just, may also joyn with him that is injur'd, and
assist him in recovering from the Offender, so much as
may make satisfaction for the harm he has suffer'd.

11.   From these *two distinct Rights,* the one of *Punish-*
ing the Crime *for restraint,* and preventing the like Offence,
which right of punishing is in every body; the other of
taking *reparation,* which belongs only to the injured party,
5 comes it to pass that the Magistrate, who by being Magistrate, hath the common right of punishing put into his
hands, can often, where the publick good demands not
the execution of the Law, *remit* the punishment of Criminal Offences by his own Authority, but yet cannot *remit*
10 the satisfaction due to any private Man, for the damage he
has received. That, he who has suffered the damage has a
Right to demand in his own name, and he alone can
remit: The damnified Person has this Power of appropriating to himself, the Goods or Service of the Offender, by
15 *Right of Self-preservation,* as every Man has a Power to
punish the Crime, to prevent its being committed again,
by the Right he has of Preserving all Mankind, and doing
all reasonable things he can in order to that end: And
thus it is, that every Man in the State of Nature, has a
20 Power to kill a Murderer, both to deter others from doing
the like Injury, which no Reparation can compensate, by
the Example of the punishment that attends it from every
body, and also *to secure* Men from the attempts of a
Criminal, who having renounced Reason, the common
25 Rule and Measure, God hath given to Mankind, hath by
the unjust Violence and Slaughter he hath committed
upon one, declared War against all Mankind, and there-

5 'noxious Creature'—compare II, § 172, 11–22, note and references.
§ 11 7–9 Compare II, § 159, 28–9. The power of pardon was the
fourth mark of sovereignty (Bodin, *Methodus,* 1945, 173, see I, § 129,
12–18, note and references, II, § 88, 4–7) and Locke may be following
the traditional argument here.

fore may be destroyed as a *Lyon* or a *Tyger,* one of those
wild Savage Beasts, with whom Men can have no Society
nor Security: And upon this is grounded the great Law 30
of Nature, *Who so sheddeth Mans Blood, by Man shall
his Blood be shed.* And *Cain* was so fully convinced, that
every one had a Right to destroy such a Criminal, that
after the Murther of his Brother, he cries out, *Every one
that findeth me, shall slay me;* so plain was it writ in the 35
Hearts of all Mankind.

12. By the same reason, may a Man in the State of
Nature *punish the lesser breaches* of that Law. It will
perhaps be demanded, with death? I answer, Each Transgression may be *punished* to that *degree,* and with so
much *Severity* as will suffice to make it an ill bargain to 5
the Offender, give him cause to repent, and terrifie others
from doing the like. Every Offence that can be committed
in the State of Nature, may in the State of Nature be also
punished, equally, and as far forth as it may, in a
Common-wealth; for though it would be besides my pres- 10
ent purpose, to enter here into the particulars of the Law
of Nature, or its *measures of punishment;* yet, it is certain
there is such a Law, and that too, as intelligible and plain
to a rational Creature, and a Studier of that Law, as the
positive Laws of Common-wealths, nay possibly plainer; 15
As much as Reason is easier to be understood, than the
Phansies and intricate Contrivances of Men, following

28–30   Compare II, § 172, 20–2 (verbal parallel), note and references.
    31–2   Genesis ix. 6: a divine command is equated here with a law
of nature.
    34–5   Genesis iv. 14. The final phrase is the most conspicuous in-
stance in the whole book of Locke's willingness here to take advantage
of the belief in innate ideas and innate practical principles, excoriated
in Book I of his *Essay concerning Humane Understanding.* The words
'writ in the Hearts' are typical of what Yolton (1956, section II) calls
the naïve form of the belief, and the principle at issue cannot well be
explained as an exception, as in the case of a similar passage in I, § 86,
21–4—see note and references there. He would seem to imply here
that his whole 'strange doctrine' about punishment was part of innate
knowledge, a possibility he had rejected as early as 1659–64, see Von
Leyden, 1954.
§ 12   10–12   For Locke's attitude to the law of nature and the claim
that it was always beside his present purpose to give its particulars, see
Introduction, 94.
    12–14   Compare II, § 124, 9–11, verbal parallel.
    16–22   This passage is indicative of Locke's hostility to those who
would multiply laws, indeed to the law, law-courts and lawyers, especially the Common Lawyers, in general (compare I, § 90, 32–4, note

contrary and hidden interests put into Words; For so
truly are a great part of the *Municipal Laws* of Countries,
20 which are only so far right, as they are founded on the
Law of Nature, by which they are to be regulated and
interpreted.

13.   To this strange Doctrine, *viz.* That *in the State of
Nature, every one has the Executive Power* of the Law
of Nature, I doubt not but it will be objected, That it is
unreasonable for Men to be Judges in their own Cases,
5 that Self-love will make Men partial to themselves and
their Friends. And on the other side, that Ill Nature,
Passion and Revenge will carry them too far in punishing
others. And hence nothing but Confusion and Disorder
will follow, and that therefore God hath certainly ap-
10 pointed Government to restrain the partiality and violence
of Men. I easily grant, that *Civil Government* is the proper
Remedy for the Inconveniences of the State of Nature,
which must certainly be Great, where Men may be Judges
in their own Case, since 'tis easily to be imagined, that
15 he who was so unjust as to do his Brother an Injury, will
scarce be so just as to condemn himself for it: But I
shall desire those who make this Objection, to remember
that *Absolute Monarchs* are but Men, and if Government
is to be the Remedy of those Evils, which necessarily
20 follow from Mens being Judges in their own Cases, and
the State of Nature is therefore not to be endured, I
desire to know what kind of Government that is, and
how much better it is than the State of Nature, where
one Man commanding a multitude, has the Liberty to be

and references). This he shared with the 1st Earl of Shaftesbury: see
the 79th and 80th *Fundamental Constitutions of Carolina,* which provide that all statute laws should be null after a century, and that no
comments upon the *Constitutions* should be permitted. Elrington (1798)
comments that this criterion of a nation's law in terms of natural law,
and not the will of a majority, 'points out the true principles of civil
government'.
18–22   Compare II, § 135, 27–30, and the striking parallels pointed
out by Von Leyden in the *Essays on the Laws of Nature,* 118–19, 188–
9, of his 1954 edition.
§ 13 1–3   See II, § 9, 1–2, note and references. Pollock, 1904, 241–2,
comments on a 'strange verbal parallel in that strangest of medieval
vagaries the *Mirror of Justices* . . . "Ordinary jurisdiction has every
one who is not deprived of it by sin, for every one may judge his neighbour according to the holy rules of right", Book IV, chap. II.' On the
Mirror see II, § 239, 49 and note.

Judge in his own *Case*, and may do to all his Subjects 25
whatever he pleases, without the least liberty to any one
to question or controle those who Execute his Pleasure?
And in whatsoever he doth, whether led by Reason, Mistake or Passion, must be submitted to? Much better it is
in the State of Nature wherein Men are not bound to 30
submit to the unjust will of another: And if he that judges,
judges amiss in his own, or any other *Case*, he is an-
swerable for it to the rest of Mankind.

14. 'Tis often asked as a mighty Objection, *Where are,*
or ever were, there any *Men in such a State of Nature?*
To which it may suffice as an answer at present; That
since all *Princes* and Rulers of *Independent* Governments
all through the World, are in a State of Nature, 'tis plain 5
the World never was, nor ever will be, without Numbers
of Men in that State. I have named all Governors of
Independent Communities, whether they are, or are not,
in League with others: For 'tis not every Compact that
puts an end to the State of Nature between Men, but only 10
this one of agreeing together mutually to enter into one
Community, and make one Body Politick; other Promises
and Compacts, Men may make one with another, and
yet still be in the State of Nature. The Promises and
Bargains for Truck, *&c.* between the two Men in the 15
Desert Island, mentioned by *Garcilasso De la vega,* in his

26–31   Modified by Locke in his final corrections, see Collation.
§ 14   1–3   Compare II, § 101, where the full answer is given, perhaps
as a later extension—see note there.
1–9   Governments in a state of nature with each other: compare II,
§ 183, 8–9, II, § 184, 35–6 (an aside in both cases). It is often assumed
that Locke was following Hobbes here, perhaps consciously: compare
Leviathan, chapter 13 (1904, 85), where the sequence of thought is
much the same. But Gierke insists that this conception was a commonplace with the natural-law theorists of the time (1934, i, 97): he cites
ten authorities on the point (ii, 288), including Pufendorf's *Elementa* and
De Jure Naturae. If Locke had any writer specifically in mind, it seems
most likely that it was Pufendorf. See Introduction, 88, and Appendix
B, nos. 65 and 68.
14–20   In the first state of the 1st edition this passage reads differently, and is the most important variation between the two states. The
bargains for truck there are 'Between the two Men in *Soldania,* in or
between, a *Swiss* and an *Indian*' and Garcilaso's desert island is not
mentioned (see Collation). It is clear that Locke did not simply add,
in the second state, a phrase omitted in the first, because Soldania (Sal-
danha Bay in South Africa) is not mentioned by Garcilaso, who is
concerned with America. He seems to have decided to omit this imper-

History of *Peru*, or between a *Swiss* and an *Indian*, in the Woods of *America*, are binding to them, though they are perfectly in a State of Nature, in reference to one
20 another. For Truth and keeping of Faith belongs to Men, as Men, and not as Members of Society.

15. To those that say, There were never any Men in the State of Nature; I will not only oppose the Authority of the Judicious *Hooker, Eccl. Pol. Lib.* I. *Sect.* 10. where he says, *The Laws which have been hitherto mentioned,*
5 i.e. the Laws of Nature, *do bind Men, although they have never any settled fellowship, never any Solemn Agreement amongst themselves what to do or not to do, but for as much as we are not by our selves sufficient to furnish our selves with competent store of things, needful for such a*
10 *Life, as our Nature doth desire, a Life, fit for the Dignity of Man; therefore to supply those Defects and Imperfections which are in us, as living singly and solely by our selves, we are naturally induced to seek Communion and Fellowship with others, this was the Cause of Mens uniting*
15 *themselves, at first in Politick Societies.* But I moreover affirm, That all Men are naturally in that State, and remain so, till by their own Consents they make themselves Members of some Politick Society; And I doubt not in the Sequel of this Discourse, to make it very clear.

---

fect reference to Soldania altogether, and to substitute for it this incident from Book I, chapter 8 of Garcilaso's *Commentarios Reales* (34–43 of his French translation of 1633, Appendix B, no. 88); (see note on I, § 57, 20–1 and compare I, § 153, 22–3 and note). He made the following note in his diary on 8 February 1687: 'Pedro Serrano that lived three years in a desolate island alone and after that time another shipwrecked man came to him and being but two they could not agree. Garcilasso de la Vega, Histoire des Incas I. I. c. 8.' This correction, therefore, raises the possibility that Locke wrote this passage in 1687, which is considered in the Introduction, 67. The original reference to the Hottentots of Soldania was genuine enough, for Locke frequently cited the example of this people as having no belief in God: these references (in the *Essay* and elsewhere) are listed in Von Leyden, 1954, 65, 81, for Locke cited this region along with Brazil as early as his fifth *Essay on the Law of Nature* (early 1660's, *op. cit.* 174). His information probably came from Terry's *Voyage to East India*, 1655, which was on his shelves in 1681—Appendix B, no. 82.

20–1 Compared by Von Leyden with the first and seventh *Essays on the Law of Nature* (1954, 81).

§ 15 4–15 Hooker, ed. Keble, 1836, 298–9, fairly accurately quoted, with alterations of punctuation. It comes from p. 85 of Locke's 1676 edition, a little after a passage copied into his diary on 28 June 1681; see note on II, § 5, 9–28.

Of the State of War.

16.   The *State of War* is a State of Enmity and Destruction; And therefore declaring by Word or Action, not a
passionate and hasty, but a sedate settled Design, upon
another Mans Life, *puts him in a State of War* with him
against whom he has declared such an Intention, and so   5
has exposed his Life to the others Power to be taken away
by him, or any one that joyns with him in his Defence,
and espouses his Quarrel: it being reasonable and just I
should have a Right to destroy that which threatens me
with Destruction. For *by the Fundamental Law of Nature,* 10
Man being to be preserved, as much as possible, when
all cannot be preserv'd, the safety of the Innocent is to
be preferred: And one may destroy a Man who makes
War upon him, or has discovered an Enmity to his being,
for the same Reason, that he may kill a *Wolf* or a *Lyon;* 15
because such Men are not under the ties of the Common
Law of Reason, have no other Rule, but that of Force
and Violence, and so may be treated as Beasts of Prey,

§ 16   *Chapter* III   In the same way as chapter II (see note on § 4)
this was presumably substantially written in 1679, but certainly amended
and extended in 1689 (see, for example, § 17, 20–4 and note) and its
text was the subject of the printing confusion in that year.
1   The large type, which is the most conspicuous feature distinguishing the first from the second state of the 1st edition, begins at this point
and continues until line 17 of § 17. It may well be the result of the cutting out of part of the text by Locke during the course of printing,
but this cannot be confirmed bibliographically, and even if it happened
the passage excised need not have come from this area of large type
—see Introduction, 20, Laslett, 1952 (iv), and Bowers, Gerritsen and
Laslett, 1954. In the second state of the 1st edition the type of this area
is of normal size, but it has two variant readings in this paragraph—see
Collation.
10–11   Compare II, § 6, 24–5; § 7, 4; § 128, 3–4; § 129, 1–2; § 135,
36–7; § 149, 27–8; § 159, 20–1; § 171, 13, etc., and Tyrrell, 1681, 15. On
Locke's tendency to regard this law of universal preservation as the
fundamental natural law, see Introduction, 111. In his *Education* (1695)
he says, 'And truly, if the preservation of all mankind, as much as in
him lies, were every one's persuasion, as indeed it is every one's duty,
and the true principle to regulate our religion, politics and morality
by, the world would be much quieter and better-natured, than it is'
(*Works*, 1801, IX, 113).
18–19   'Beasts of Prey . . . noxious Creatures'—compare II, § 172,
20–2, note and references: 'and so' to the end of the paragraph may
be an addition of 1689.

those dangerous and noxious Creatures, that will be sure
20 to destroy him, whenever he falls into their Power.

17. And hence it is, that he who attempts to get
another Man into his Absolute Power, does thereby *put
himself into a State of War* with him; It being to be
understood as a Declaration of a Design upon his Life.
5 For I have reason to conclude, that he who would get
me into his Power without my consent, would use me as
he pleased, when he had got me there, and destroy me
too when he had a fancy to it: for no body can desire to
have me in his Absolute Power, unless it be to compel me
10 by force to that, which is against the Right of my Freedom, *i.e.* make me a Slave. To be free from such force
is the only security of my Preservation: and reason bids
me look on him, as an Enemy to my Preservation, who
would take away that *Freedom,* which is the Fence to it:
15 so that he who makes an *attempt to enslave* me, thereby
puts himself into a State of War with me. He that in the
State of Nature, *would take away the Freedom,* that belongs to any one in that State, must necessarily be supposed to have a design to take away every thing else, that
20 *Freedom* being the Foundation of all the rest: As he that
in the State of Society, would take away the *Freedom*
belonging to those of that Society or Common-wealth,
must be supposed to design to take away from them every
thing else, and so be looked on as *in a State of War*.

18. This makes it Lawful for a Man to *kill a Thief,*
who has not in the least hurt him, nor declared any design upon his Life, any farther than by the use of Force,
so to get him in his Power, as to take away his Money,
5 or what he pleases from him: because using force, where
he has no Right, to get me into his Power, let his pretence
be what it will, I have no reason to suppose, that he, who
would *take away my Liberty,* would not when he had me
in his Power, take away every thing else. And therefore
10 it is Lawful for me to treat him, as one who has put

§ **17**   18 'State'—end of large type in first state of 1st edition, see II,
§ 16, 1.
    20–4 This last sentence may be an interpolation of 1689, an im-
plication that James II was 'in a State of War' with Englishmen. Indeed
§ 18 follows more naturally on to § 16, and the whole paragraph may
have been inserted.
§ **18**   1 Compare II, § 207, 15.

himself into a State of War with me, *i.e.* kill him if I can;
for to that hazard does he justly expose himself, whoever
introduces a State of War, and is *aggressor* in it.

19.   And here we have the plain *difference between the
State of Nature, and the State of War*, which however
some Men have confounded, are as far distant, as a State
of Peace, Good Will, Mutual Assistance, and Preservation,
and a State of Enmity, Malice, Violence, and Mutual De-   5
struction are one from another. Men living together according to reason, without a common Superior on Earth,
with Authority to judge between them, is *properly the
State of Nature*. But force, or a declared design of force
upon the Person of another, where there is no common 10
Superior on Earth to appeal to for relief, *is the State of
War:* And 'tis the want of such an appeal gives a Man the
Right of War even against an *aggressor*, though he be in
Society and a fellow Subject. Thus a *Thief*, whom I cannot harm but by appeal to the Law, for having stolen all 15
that I am worth, I may kill, when he sets on me to rob
me, but of my Horse or Coat: because the Law, which
was made for my Preservation, where it cannot interpose
to secure my Life from present force, which if lost, is
capable of no reparation, permits me my own Defence, 20
and the Right of War, a liberty to kill the aggressor, because the aggressor allows not time to appeal to our
common Judge, nor the decision of the Law, for remedy
in a Case, where the mischief may be irreparable. *Want
of a common Judge with Authority, puts all Men in a* 25
*State of Nature: Force without Right, upon a Man's
Person, makes a State of War,* both where there is, and
is not, a common Judge.

§ **19** 1–6 A comma should be understood after 'which'. Locke altered
the last phrase of this sentence, but then restored the previous reading,
see Collation. The 'some men' can only be the Hobbesists. Compare II,
§§ 6 and 7 for the general position and Locke's *Essays on the Law of
Nature, c.* 1661. In his fifth *Essay* he leaves it as a possibility that 'there
is in the state of nature a general war and a perpetual and deadly hatred
among men' as is maintained by some (quod aliqui volunt)—Von Leyden's edition, 1954, 162–3. But in his eighth *Essay* he pronounces
against those 'some'. For if by the law of nature men are in a state of
war, 'all society is abolished, and all faith, which is the bond of society'
(tollitur omnis societas et societatis vinculum fides); see II, § 212, 10–14,
and the Introduction. The peaceful condition of the state of nature
should be compared with the dangers etc. talked of in II, §§ 13, 92,
101, 123–4, etc.
    14–24 Compare II, § 182, 25.

20. But when the actual force is over, the *State of War* ceases between those that are in Society, and are equally on both sides Subjected to the fair determination of the Law; because then there lies open the remedy of 5 appeal for the past injury, and to prevent future harm: but where no such appeal is, as in the State of Nature, for want of positive Laws, and Judges with Authority to appeal to, *the State of War once begun, continues*, with a right to the innocent Party, to destroy the other when-10 ever he can, until the aggressor offers Peace, and desires reconciliation on such Terms, as may repair any wrongs he has already done, and secure the innocent for the future: nay where an appeal to the Law, and constituted Judges lies open, but the remedy is deny'd by a manifest 15 perverting of Justice, and a barefaced wresting of the Laws, to protect or indemnifie the violence or injuries of some Men, or Party of Men, *there* it *is* hard to imagine any thing but *a State of War*. For wherever violence is used, and injury done, though by hands appointed to 20 administer Justice, it is still violence and injury, however colour'd with the Name, Pretences, or Forms of Law, the end whereof being to protect and redress the innocent, by an unbiassed application of it, to all who are under it; wherever that is not *bona fide* done, *War is made* upon 25 the Sufferers, who having no appeal on Earth to right them, they are left to the only remedy in such Cases, an appeal to Heaven.

§ 20 3 'sides'—at this point begins the passage which is present in the second state of the 1st edition, but absent in the first state, see Introduction, 20, Laslett, 1952 (iv) and Bowers, Gerritsen and Laslett, 1954. In the first state the text goes straight on to 'And therefore in such Controversies, . . .' at the beginning of line 17 in § 21, thus: '20. But when the actual force is over, the State of War ceases between those that are in Society, and are equally on both sides Subject to the Judge: And therefore in such controversies . . .' (and so on, identically with the text in the second state to the end of the paragraph, starting the next as § 22. No sign for a § 21 is present). This anomaly has been variously dealt with by editors of the text; see footnote 2 to p. 342 of Laslett, 1952 (iv) and footnote 1 to p. 83 of Laslett, 1954 (iv). W. S. Carpenter, the editor of the *Everyman* text (*c*. 1924, with many subsequent printings) misnumbered all the paragraphs from this point to II, §§ 36, 37; see note on line 16 of II, § 36. Elrington (1798) first noticed this peculiarity, and has a note here on it.

13–27 This passage may well be an addition of 1689, directly referring to the events of the Revolution: the final 'appeal to Heaven' being most significant. It contains (line 17) the phrase which inspired Elrington to the following protest against Locke's theory of resistance, or perhaps the interpretation put on it by Thomas Paine and others.

21. To avoid this State of War (wherein there is no appeal but to Heaven, and wherein every the least difference is apt to end, where there is no Authority to decide between the Contenders) is one great *reason of Mens putting themselves into Society,* and quitting the State of Nature. For where there is an Authority, a Power on Earth, from which relief can be had by *appeal,* there the continuance of the State of War is excluded, and the Controversie is decided by that Power. Had there been any such Court, any superior Jurisdiction on Earth, to determine the right between *Jephtha* and the *Ammonites,* they had never come to a State of War, but we see he was forced to appeal to *Heaven. The Lord the Judge* (says he) *be Judge this day between the Children of* Israel, *and the Children of* Ammon, *Judg.* 11. 27. and then Prosecuting, and relying on his *appeal,* he leads out his Army to Battle: And therefore in such Controversies, where the question is put, *who shall be Judge?* It cannot be meant, who shall decide the Controversie; every one knows what *Jephtha* here tells us, that *the Lord the Judge,* shall judge. Where there is no Judge on Earth, the *Appeal* lies to God in Heaven. That Question then cannot mean, who shall judge? whether another hath put himself in a State of War with me, and whether I may as *Jephtha* did, appeal to Heaven in it? Of that I my self can only be Judge in my own Conscience, as I will answer it at the great Day, to the Supream Judge of all Men.

'But what shall we say of a theory which thus invests an individual with a right of throwing a whole society in confusion for the purpose of redressing his own particular grievance?'

§ 21   1–6 Hobbes had also made the social state a remedy for the state of war, and this sentence might be called Locke's closest formal approach to him in his political theory. It is interesting that it occurs in a passage omitted from one state of the 1st edition (see Laslett, 1952 [iv]), but it cannot be shown that the two facts are connected.

17 'And'—end of missing passage; see II, § 20, 3, note.

20 'Jephtha'—Locke evidently regarded the story of Jephthah as crucial to the scriptural foundations of his case about civil society and justice. See I, § 163, 36–7; II, § 109, 1–13, II, § 176, 31 and compare note on II, § 168, and references. Grotius and St Augustine before him had used the Jephthah story for political analysis, and Locke may have in mind the Calvinist position expressed by Jurieu (1689, 365) that the Judges, Jephthah among them, represented a stage between the anarchy of primeval innocence and established sovereignty, a stage which inevitably passed because of the effects of the Fall.

Of SLAVERY.

22. The *Natural Liberty* of Man is to be free from any Superior Power on Earth, and not to be under the Will or Legislative Authority of Man, but to have only the Law of Nature for his Rule. The *Liberty of Man, in*
5 *Society,* is to be under no other Legislative Power, but that established, by consent, in the Common-wealth, nor under the Dominion of any Will, or Restraint of any Law, but what the Legislative shall enact, according to the Trust put in it. *Freedom* then is not what Sir *R. F.* tells
10 us, *O.A.* 55 [224]. *A Liberty for every one to do what he lists, to live as he pleases, and not to be tyed by any Laws:* But *Freedom of Men under Government,* is, to have a standing Rule to live by, common to every one of that Society, and made by the Legislative Power erected in it;
15 A Liberty to follow my own Will in all things, where the Rule prescribes not; and not to be subject to the inconstant, uncertain, unknown, Arbitrary Will of another Man. As *Freedom of Nature* is to be under no other restraint but the Law of Nature.

§ 22 *Chapter* IV There is positive evidence for this chapter, as distinct from presumption in the case of chapters II and III, of composition in 1679 (see note on lines 9–10 below) and of revision in 1689.

1 At this point sheet R begins in the 1st edition; compare notes on II, § 8, 6–7: there are no further obvious printing peculiarities after this point in the 1st edition.

9–10 'what Sir R. F. tells us, *O.A.* 55'. The only reference to Filmer's works in the *Second Treatise,* though his name is mentioned at II, § 1, 33 and II, § 61, 17. The statement is repeated in II, § 57, 25–6; see note there and on II, § 236. It is one of the many signs that this work, as well as the *First Treatise,* was written with the object of refuting Filmer, in particular against his tracts, whilst the *First* was written against *Patriarcha.* In the Introduction, 71–4 this anomalous form of reference to Filmer—for it will be seen to be quite different from that used in the *First Treatise*—is used as an important part of the demonstration that the *Second Treatise* was written in 1679–80 in some form, and as the clue to the priority in writing of the *Second* to the *First.* The entry in Locke's *Tablet* which makes it possible to date the time of writing of this paragraph is relevant to the argument here. It refers to a passage in Filmer's *Forms* (Laslett's edition, 226) which reads: 'amongst all them that plead the necessity of the consent of the people, none hath ever touched upon these so necessary doctrines [that is, of the manner of obtaining it]; it is a task it seems too difficult, otherwise surely it would not have been neglected, considering how necessary it is to re-

23. This *Freedom* from Absolute, Arbitrary Power, is so necessary to, and closely joyned with a Man's Preservation, that he cannot part with it, but by what forfeits his Preservation and Life together. For a Man, not having the Power of his own Life, *cannot,* by Compact, or his 5 own Consent, *enslave himself* to any one, nor put himself under the Absolute, Arbitrary Power of another, to take away his Life, when he pleases. No body can give more Power than he has himself; and he that cannot take away his own Life, cannot give another power over it. Indeed 10 having, by his fault, forfeited his own Life, by some Act that deserves Death; he, to whom he has forfeited it, may (when he has him in his Power) delay to take it, and make use of him to his own Service, and he does him no injury by it. For, whenever he finds the hardship of his 15 Slavery out-weigh the value of his Life, 'tis in his Power, by resisting the Will of his Master, to draw on himself the Death he desires.

24. This is the perfect condition of *Slavery,* which *is* nothing else, but *the State of War continued, between a*

---

solve the conscience, touching the manner of the peoples passing their consent'.

Such, then, was the statement which Locke had in mind when he wrote in his *Tablet* 'Filmer to resolve the conscience' and went on to compose this part of the *Second Treatise.* The same point about law and freedom appears also in his *Essay concerning Humane Understanding,* IV, iii, 18: ' "No government allows absolute liberty." The idea of government being the establishment of society upon certain rules or laws which require conformity to them; and the idea of absolute liberty being for any one to do whatever he pleases; I am as capable of being certain of the truth of this proposition as of any in mathematics' (1894, II, 208–9)—see Introduction 96. Elrington (1798) is disturbed by the implications of this paragraph and finds it contradictory. He concludes that the great *desideratum* is an agreed definition of liberty: 'Whether Locke has given such a definition the reader will judge.'

§ 23 This paragraph invites comparison and contrast with Hobbes *Leviathan,* chapter 20, especially pp. 142–3 (1904 edition). Hobbes did maintain that a man can enslave himself by compact and consent, because he can bargain away the power over his own life. Locke, however, seems to contradict himself in his last sentence by justifying indirect suicide; compare also II, § 6, 3–5; § 135, 11–15 (a parallel passage); and § 17, 5–7, note and reference. Elrington (1798) urges this against him, and also objects to 'the indefinite continuance of a right to take away the life of another'.

§ 24 1–9 This, with § 23 and § 85, 9–18, is Locke's justification of slavery. It may seem unnecessary, and inconsistent with his principles, but it must be remembered that he writes as the administrator of slave-owning colonies in America. As Leslie Stephen pointed out (1902, II, 139), the *Fundamental Constitutions of Carolina* provide that every

lawful Conquerour, and a Captive. For, if once *Compact*
enter between them, and make an agreement for a limited
5 Power on the one side, and Obedience on the other, the
State of War and *Slavery* ceases, as long as the Compact
endures. For, as has been said, no Man can, by agreement, pass over to another that which he hath not in himself, a Power over his own Life.

10   I confess, we find among the *Jews*, as well as other
Nations, that Men did sell themselves; but, 'tis plain, this
was only to *Drudgery, not to Slavery.* For, it is evident,
the Person sold was not under an Absolute, Arbitrary,
Despotical Power. For the Master could not have power
15 to kill him, at any time, whom, at a certain time, he was
obliged to let go free out of his Service: and the Master
of such a Servant was so far from having an Arbitrary
Power over his Life, that he could not, at pleasure, so
much as maim him, but the loss of an Eye, or Tooth,
20 set him free, *Exod.* XXI.

---

freeman 'shall have absolute power and authority over his negro slaves'
(cx); compare notes on I, § 130, 6–7, and I, § 144, 27. The Instructions
to Governor Nicholson of Virginia, which Locke did so much to draft
in 1698 (see Laslett, 1957 [i]), regard negro slaves as justifiably en-
slaved because they were captives taken in a just war, who had forfeited
their lives 'by some Act that deserves Death' (§ 23, 11–12; compare Tyrrell, 1681, 62). Locke seems satisfied that the forays of the Royal Africa
Company were just wars of this sort, and that the negroes captured had
committed such acts. The best discussion of Locke on slavery is in
Polin, 1960, 277–81.

10–20   In Exod. xxi the Mosaic law regulates the treatment of bought
servants; they are to be freed in the seventh, Jubilee year, not to be
killed, to be freed if maimed by their masters. Hobbes notices this and
Grotius calls it 'imperfecta servitus', II, v, 30 (1712, 264).

CHAP. V.

Of PROPERTY.

25. Whether we consider natural *Reason*, which tells us, that Men, being once born, have a right to their Preservation, and consequently to Meat and Drink, and such other things, as Nature affords for their Subsistence: Or *Revelation*, which gives us an account of those Grants God made 5 of the World to *Adam*, and to *Noah*, and his Sons, 'tis very clear, that God, as King *David* says, *Psal.* CXV. xvi. *has given the Earth to the Children of Men,* given it to Mankind in common. But this being supposed, it seems to some a very great difficulty, how any one should ever 10 come to have a *Property* in any thing: I will not content my self to answer, That if it be difficult to make out *Property*, upon a supposition, that God gave the World to *Adam* and his Posterity in common; it is impossible that any Man, but one universal Monarch, should have 15 any *Property*, upon a supposition, that God gave the World to *Adam*, and his Heirs in Succession, exclusive of all the rest of his Posterity. But I shall endeavour to shew, how Men might come to have a *property* in several parts of that which God gave to Mankind in common, and that 20 without any express Compact of all the Commoners.

§ 25 *Chapter* V This important chapter is obviously integral to Locke's argument, and it is also obviously part of his polemic against Filmer—see note on lines 18–21 below, and on II, § 38, 10–13, etc. There is nothing to indicate a date of composition in 1689, or at any time later than the first form of the book, though it was perhaps subsequently amended, and it will be remembered that it falls within that part of the 1st edition which could have been modified in the course of printing. Apart from this, there is no reason to doubt that the chapter is to be dated in 1679.

1–4 This discussion of property is referred to in I, § 87, 15–16, and I, § 86, 1–5 echoes the language used here. Kendall, 1941, 77, notes the illogical transition from 'men' here, meaning individuals, to 'mankind' in line 9.

6–9 The biblical evidence for original communism, or rather against the primacy of private property, is discussed at length in the *First Treatise;* see I, § 21 and on: the text from Psalm cxv is cited in I, § 31 as part of a reference to Filmer's case.

9–18 This argument against the supposition that God gave the world to Adam and his posterity is developed in the *First Treatise.*

18–21 This sentence confirms that this paragraph, and the whole chapter on property which follows, were written with Filmer's works in mind, and as a direct refutation of them. For it was Filmer who has

26. God, who hath given the World to Men in common, hath also given them reason to make use of it to the best advantage of Life, and convenience. The Earth, and all that is therein, is given to Men for the Support and
5 Comfort of their being. And though all the Fruits it naturally produces, and Beasts it feeds, belong to Mankind in common, as they are produced by the spontaneous hand of Nature; and no body has originally a private Dominion, exclusive of the rest of Mankind, in any of them, as they
10 are thus in their natural state: yet being given for the use of Men, there must of necessity be a means *to appropriate* them some way or other before they can be of any use, or at all beneficial to any particular Man. The Fruit, or Venison, which nourishes the wild *Indian,* who knows no
15 Inclosure, and is still a Tenant in common, must be his, and so his, *i.e.* a part of him, that another can no longer have any right to it, before it can do him any good for the support of his Life.

27. Though the Earth, and all inferior Creatures be common to all Men, yet every Man has a *Property* in his own *Person*. This no Body has any Right to but himself.

---

raised the difficulty that original communism could not give way to private property without the universal consent of mankind. The discussions in Hobbes (the *Epistola Dedicatoria* of *De Cive,* 1647, presents the issue most clearly), Grotius (1625, II, ii, 2) and Pufendorf (1672, IV, 3) do not discuss this crux as Filmer does. The passage which Locke seems to have in mind occurs on p. 273 of Laslett's edition.
§ **26** Compare and contrast the discussion of the goods of nature in this paragraph with Pufendorf, *De Jure Naturae,* 1672, IV, iv, 13, and Locke's own earlier sentiments in his eighth *Essay on the Law of Nature,* which are markedly different: Von Leyden, 1954, 210–11.
§ **27** Compare Locke's introduction of the proposition about labour and property in this paragraph, its predecessor and those following, with that of Tyrrell: 'Supposing the Earth and the fruits thereof to have been at first bestowed in Common on all its inhabitants; yet since God's first command to man was, encrease and multiply, if he hath a right to perform the end, he hath certainly a right to the means of his preservation, and the propagation of his species, so that though the fruits of the earth, or beasts, for food, were all in common, yet when once any man had by his own labour acquired such a proportion of either as would serve the necessities of himself and Family, they became so much his own as that no man could without manifest injustice rob him of those necessities' (1681, 99–100, second pagination). Tyrrell goes on to talk of 'this sort of community' being retained among the Americans, the wild beast the Indian kills (compare II, § 30, 1–2), the fish he takes up (*ibid.* 9), the fruit of his trees and his venison (II, § 26, 14). But he talks in this parallel way in a different context. Following Grotius, he refers to the Stoic axiom about seats in the theatre,

The *Labour* of his Body, and the *Work* of his Hands, we
may say, are properly his. Whatsoever then he removes 5
out of the State that Nature hath provided, and left it in,
he hath mixed his *Labour* with, and joyned to it something
that is his own, and thereby makes it his *Property*. It
being by him removed from the common state Nature
placed it in, hath by this *labour* something annexed to it, 10
that excludes the common right of other Men. For this
Labour being the unquestionable Property of the Labourer,
no Man but he can have a right to what that is once
joyned to, at least where there is enough, and as good left
in common for others. 15

28. He that is nourished by the Acorns he pickt up
under an Oak, or the Apples he gathered from the Trees

---

and cites many other arguments about property, ignored by Locke: for
him the labour proposition is not the one rational method of making
use of the earth's produce, but rather a ground for retaining property
acquired, and he does not talk of a man owning himself (compare note
on II, § 32, 1–8). These points and the known relationship between
them (see above, 89–95), may imply that Locke suggested this line of
thinking to Tyrrell, who followed it without quite realizing what it
meant to Locke. It is not impossible that they arrived at this position
independently, for in a work published in 1680 but described on the
title as 'Mostly written many years past' Richard Baxter writes in vaguer
but in similar terms: '*Propriety is naturally antecedent to Government,*
which doth not *Give it*, but *regulate it* to the *Common good:* Every
man is born with a propriety in his *own members,* and nature giveth
him a propriety in *his Children,* and his *food* and other just *acquisitions*
of his industry. Therefore no Ruler can justly deprive men of their
propriety, unless it be by some *Law of God* (as in execution of justice
on such as forfeit it) or by their *own consent,* by *themselves* or their
Delegates or *Progenitors;* And men's *lives* and *Liberties* are the chief
parts of their propriety. That is the peoples just *reserved Property,* and
Liberty, which neither *God taketh from them,* by the power which his
own Laws give the Ruler, nor is *given away* by their *own* foresaid consent' (Baxter, 1680, 54–5; see Schlatter, 1957, 39, and compare passage
from Baxter's *Holy Commonwealth,* cited by Gough, 1950, 80).

What Baxter says here about life, liberty and property shows that he
had the same combined definition of property as Locke, both an extended and a specific definition; see Introduction, 115–16 and note on II,
§ 87, 5–6. It is possible to find many much vaguer hints at what is too
loosely called the labour theory of value (in Petty, 1662, for example,
of which Locke had the 1667 printing, or even in Hobbes; see Gough,
1950, 81) but these are the only passages in books he may have read
known to me which seem to show a systematic resemblance. See also
the hint in I, § 42, 12–17.

2–3   Repeated in II, § 173, 5–6; cf. Walwyn, the Leveller quoted Macpherson, 1962, 140.

§ 28   1–4   Compare Pufendorf, *De Jure Naturae,* 1672, IV, iv, 13,
'Quercus erat nullius: quae deciderant glandes ejus fiebant, qui legisset'.

in the Wood, has certainly appropriated them to himself.
No Body can deny but the nourishment is his. I ask then,
5 When did they begin to be his? When he digested? Or
when he eat? Or when he boiled? Or when he brought
them home? Or when he pickt them up? And 'tis plain,
if the first gathering made them not his, nothing else
could. That *labour* put a distinction between them and
10 common. That added something to them more than Nature, the common Mother of all, had done; and so they
became his private right. And will any one say he had
no right to those Acorns or Apples he thus appropriated,
because he had not the consent of all Mankind to make
15 them his? Was it a Robbery thus to assume to himself
what belonged to all in Common? If such a consent as
that was necessary, Man had starved, notwithstanding the
Plenty God had given him. We see in *Commons,* which
remain so by Compact, that 'tis the taking any part of
20 what is common, and removing it out of the state Nature
leaves it in, which *begins the Property;* without which the
Common is of no use. And the taking of this or that part,
does not depend on the express consent of all the Commoners. Thus the Grass my Horse has bit; the Turfs my
25 Servant has cut; and the Ore I have digg'd in any place
where I have a right to them in common with others,
become my *Property,* without the assignation or consent of
any body. The *labour* that was mine, removing them out
of that common state they were in, hath *fixed* my *Property*
30 in them.

Gough, 1950, draws attention to this parallel, and to Blackstone's account of the clash between Locke on the one hand and both Pufendorf
and Grotius on the other in their views on the origin of property. For
in spite of the above coincidence about acorns, Pufendorf follows Grotius in assigning the origin of property to universal agreement, not labour. Barbeyrac, in his edition of Pufendorf's *De Jure Naturae,* registers
his agreement with Locke's views on this matter, and maintains that
Locke was the first to formulate it, earlier than the only other author
he quotes, C. G. Titius of Leipzig (1661–1714). He also notes that
Locke's discussion grew out of his refutation of Filmer: Barbeyrac,
1734, I, 576–7. Barbeyrac corresponded with Locke (see Introduction,
88), and no man in the early eighteenth century was in a generally
better position than he to know about the relationship of his writings
with the natural-law jurists and with the whole tradition of social and
political theory.
18–30 Locke is using here the language of agrarian enclosure, the
parcelling out of the common fields of the traditional manor as private
property, which was so marked a feature of English economic history

29. By making an explicit consent of every Commoner, necessary to any ones appropriating to himself
any part of what is given in common, Children or Servants
could not cut the Meat which their Father or Master had
provided for them in common, without assigning to every 5
one his peculiar part. Though the Water running in the
Fountain be every ones, yet who can doubt, but that in
the Pitcher is his only who drew it out? His *labour* hath
taken it out of the hands of Nature, where it was common,
and belong'd equally to all her Children, and *hath* thereby 10
appropriated it to himself.

30. Thus this Law of reason makes the Deer, that
Indian's who hath killed it; 'tis allowed to be his goods
who hath bestowed his labour upon it, though before, it
was the common right of every one. And amongst those
who are counted the Civiliz'd part of Mankind, who have 5
made and multiplied positive Laws to determine Property,
this original Law of Nature for the *beginning of Property*,
in what was before common, still takes place; and by vertue thereof, what Fish any one catches in the Ocean, that
great and still remaining Common of Mankind; or what 10
Ambergriese any one takes up here, is *by* the *Labour* that
removes it out of that common state Nature left it in,
made his *Property* who takes that pains about it. And
even amongst us the Hare that any one is Hunting, is
thought his who pursues her during the Chase. For being 15
a Beast that is still looked upon as common, and no Man's
private Possession; whoever has imploy'd so much *labour*
about any of that kind, as to find and pursue her, has
thereby removed her from the state of Nature, wherein
she was common, and hath *begun a Property*. 20

---

in the sixteenth century, in his own time to some extent, and even more
in the eighteenth century; see also II, § 32, 8–12; § 35; §42, 20–2;
§ 37, 12–32. It is not quite consistent with his statement about enclosure
and the Indians in II, § 26, 13–18, for the Indian lived in a state of
nature, before compact had taken place. Here 'Commons' must mean
the common land of the traditional manorial system, remaining so 'by
Compact'. As Locke makes clear in II, § 35, only the men of the manor,
and not just anyone, could usually graze, turf and mine on the common land, and then only if the custom of the manor allowed. It is a
bad example of communism. Lines 28–30 contain the only example of
Locke transferring labour from one man to another. See the discussion
in Macpherson, 1961, Laslett, 1964.
§ 30 1–4 Compare I, § 86, 21–31, note and references.

31. It will perhaps be objected to this, That if gathering the Acorns, or other Fruits of the Earth, &c. makes a right to them, then any one may *ingross* as much as he will. To which I Answer, Not so. The same Law of Nature, that does by this means give us Property, does also *bound* that *Property* too. *God has given us all things richly,* 1 Tim. vi. 17. is the Voice of Reason confirmed by Inspiration. But how far has he given it us? *To enjoy.* As much as any one can make use of to any advantage of life before it spoils; so much he may by his labour fix a Property in. Whatever is beyond this, is more than his share, and belongs to others. Nothing was made by God for Man to spoil or destroy. And thus considering the plenty of natural Provisions there was a long time in the World, and the few spenders, and to how small a part of that provision the industry of one Man could extend it self, and ingross it to the prejudice of others; especially keeping within the *bounds,* set by reason of what might serve for his *use;* there could be then little room for Quarrels or Contentions about Property so establish'd.

32. But the *chief matter of Property* being now not the Fruits of the Earth, and the Beasts that subsist on it, but the *Earth it self;* as that which takes in and carries with it all the rest: I think it is plain, that *Property* in that too is acquired as the former. *As much Land* as a Man Tills, Plants, Improves, Cultivates, and can use the Product of, so much is his *Property*. He by his Labour does, as it were, inclose it from the Common. Nor will it invalidate his right to say, Every body else has an equal Title to it; and therefore he cannot appropriate, he cannot inclose, without the Consent of all his Fellow-Commoners, all Mankind. God, when he gave the World in common to all Mankind, commanded Man also to labour, and the penury of his Condition required it of him. God and his Reason commanded him to subdue the Earth, *i.e.*

§ **31** 7 Compare I, § 40, 22.
§ **32** 1–8 Tyrrell extends the labour theory to the possession of land in the same way as Locke, but with the same difference. Labour confirms a man's property in what he rightfully possesses, 'since the owner hath possessed himself of this land, and bestowed his Labour and Industry upon it' no man can take it away (1681, 112, 2nd pagination). See note on II, § 27.
8–12 The language of agrarian enclosure, see II, § 28, 18–30, and references.
12–14 Compare I, § 45.

improve it for the benefit of Life, and therein lay out something upon it that was his own, his labour. He that in Obedience to this Command of God, subdued, tilled and sowed any part of it, thereby annexed to it something that was his *Property,* which another had no Title to, nor 20 could without injury take from him.

33. Nor was this *appropriation* of any parcel of *Land,* by improving it, any prejudice to any other Man, since there was still enough, and as good left; and more than the yet unprovided could use. So that in effect, there was never the less left for others because of his inclosure for 5 himself. For he that leaves as much as another can make use of, does as good as take nothing at all. No Body could think himself injur'd by the drinking of another Man, though he took a good Draught, who had a whole River of the same Water left him to quench his thirst. And 10 the Case of Land and Water, where there is enough of both, is perfectly the same.

34. God gave the World to Men in Common; but since he gave it them for their benefit, and the greatest Conveniencies of Life they were capable to draw from it, it cannot be supposed he meant it should always remain common and uncultivated. He gave it to the use of the 5 Industrious and Rational, (and *Labour* was to be *his Title* to it;) not to the Fancy or Covetousness of the Quarrelsom and Contentious. He that had as good left for his Improvement, as was already taken up, needed not complain, ought not to meddle with what was already 10 improved by another's Labour: If he did, 'tis plain he desired the benefit of another's Pains, which he had no right to, and not the Ground which God had given him in common with others to labour on, and whereof there was as good left, as that already possessed, and more than 15 he knew what to do with, or his Industry could reach to.

35. 'Tis true, in *Land* that is *common* in *England,* or any other Country, where there is Plenty of People under

§ 35   Here Locke seems to recognize the inappropriateness of agrarian enclosure to his argument (see note on II, § 28, 18-30), but he persists. His statements are accurate, but vague, and it is interesting that the words 'Countrey' and 'Parish' are used where 'Manor' might be expected (line 9).

Government, who have Money and Commerce, no one
can inclose or appropriate any part, without the consent
5 of all his Fellow-Commoners: Because this is left common by Compact, *i.e.* by the Law of the Land, which is
not to be violated. And though it be Common, in respect
of some Men, it is not so to all Mankind; but is the joint
property of this Countrey, or this Parish. Besides, the re-
10 mainder, after such inclosure, would not be as good to
the rest of the Commoners as the whole was, when they
could all make use of the whole: whereas in the beginning
and first peopling of the great Common of the World, it
was quite otherwise. The Law Man was under, was rather
15 for *appropriating*. God Commanded, and his Wants forced
him to *labour*. That was his *Property* which could not be
taken from him where-ever he had fixed it. And hence
subduing or cultivating the Earth, and having Dominion,
we see are joyned together. The one gave Title to the
20 other. So that God, by commanding to subdue, gave
Authority so far to *appropriate*. And the Condition of
Humane Life, which requires Labour and Materials to
work on, necessarily introduces *private Possessions*.

36. The measure of Property, Nature has well set, by
the Extent of Mens *Labour, and the Conveniency of Life*:
No Mans Labour could subdue, or appropriate all: nor
could his Enjoyment consume more than a small part; so
5 that it was impossible for any Man, this way, to intrench
upon the right of another, or acquire, to himself, a Property,
to the Prejudice of his Neighbour, who would still have
room, for as good, and as large a Possession (after the other
had taken out his) as before it was appropriated. This
10 *measure* did confine every Man's *Possession,* to a very
moderate Proportion, and such as he might appropriate to
himself, without Injury to any Body in the first Ages of
the World, when Men were more in danger to be lost, by
wandering from their Company, in the then vast Wilderness
15 of the Earth, than to be straitned for want of room to

9 'property'—altered by Locke from "propriety' in 1698; compare
title to chapter VII of the *First Treatise*.
§ 36 9–28 The smallness of men's possessions in early Biblical times
is commented on in I, § 136, 9–12. This passage is a direct statement of
Locke's assumption that the state of nature in contemporary America
can be assimilated to the conditions of patriarchal times, compare note
on I, § 130.

plant in. And the same *measure* may be allowed still, without prejudice to any Body, as full as the World seems. For supposing a Man, or Family, in the state they were, at first peopling of the World by the Children of *Adam,* or *Noah;* let him plant in some in-land, vacant places of 20 *America,* we shall find that the *Possessions* he could make himself upon the *measures* we have given, would not be very large, nor, even to this day, prejudice the rest of Mankind, or give them reason to complain, or think themselves injured by this Man's Incroachment, though the Race 25 of Men have now spread themselves to all the corners of the World, and do infinitely exceed the small number [which] was at the beginning. Nay, the extent of *Ground* is of so little value, *without labour,* that I have heard it affirmed, that in *Spain* it self, a Man may be permitted to 30 plough, sow, and reap, without being disturbed, upon Land he has no other Title to, but only his making use of it. But, on the contrary, the Inhabitants think themselves beholden to him, who, by his Industry on neglected, and consequently waste Land, has increased the stock of Corn, 35 which they wanted. But be this as it will, which I lay no stress on; This I dare boldly affirm, That the same *Rule of Propriety,* (*viz.*) that every Man should have as much as he could make use of, would hold still in the World, without straitning any body, since there is Land 40 enough in the World to suffice double the Inhabitants had not the *Invention of Money,* and the tacit Agreement of Men to put a value on it, introduced (by Consent) larger Possessions, and a Right to them; which, how it has done, I shall, by and by, shew more at large. 45

37. This is certain, That in the beginning, before the desire of having more than Men needed, had altered the intrinsick value of things, which depends only on their

16 The *Everyman* text, having misnumbered its paragraphs since II, § 20, starts a new paragraph (§ 36) after 'plant in.', omitting the 'And'—see note on II, § 20, 3.

29–39 Private appropriation of waste land in this way was possible all over Spain in Locke's day, and is apparently still the custom in Andalusia. In Aragon the land, in the mountain area, had to be cleared within sixty days to become the property of the cultivator: in Catalonia such ownership became absolute once the plot had been worked, but lapsed if it was left uncultivated for three years: in Castile the labourer could only take enough for himself and his family. See Costa, 1898, 250–63. I owe this reference and information to Dr J. H. Elliott. Compare II, § 184, 30–2.

44–5 See II, § 45 and note: II, § 46 on.

usefulness to the Life of Man; or [Men] had *agreed, that*
5 *a little piece of yellow Metal,* which would keep without
wasting or decay, should be worth a great piece of Flesh,
or a whole heap of Corn; though Men had a Right to
appropriate, by their Labour, each one to himself, as much
of the things of Nature, as he could use: Yet this could
10 not be much, nor to the Prejudice of others, where the
same plenty was still left, to those who would use the same
Industry. To which let me add, that he who appropriates
land to himself by his labour, does not lessen but increase
the common stock of mankind. For the provisions serving
15 to the support of humane life, produced by one acre of
inclosed and cultivated land, are (to speak much within
compasse) ten times more, than those, which are yeilded by
an acre of Land, of an equal richnesse, lyeing wast in
common. And therefor he, that incloses Land and has a
20 greater plenty of the conveniencys of life from ten acres,
than he could have from an hundred left to Nature, may
truly be said, to give ninety acres to Mankind. For his
labour now supplys him with provisions out of ten acres,
which were but the product of an hundred lying in com-
25 mon. I have here rated the improved land very low in
making its product but as ten to one, when it is much
nearer an hundred to one. For I aske whether in the wild
woods and uncultivated wast of America left to Nature,
without any improvement, tillage or husbandry, a thousand
30 acres will yeild the needy and wretched inhabitants as many
conveniencies of life as ten acres of equally fertile land
doe in Devonshire where they are well cultivated?

Before the Appropriation of Land, he who gathered as
much of the wild Fruit, killed, caught, or tamed, as many
35 of the Beasts as he could; he that so employed his Pains
about any of the spontaneous Products of Nature, as any
way to alter them, from the state which Nature put them
in, *by* placing any of his *Labour* on them, did thereby

§ **37**   4 'Men'—added by editor.
    12–32 Passage added in two parts in the Christ's copy (see Colla-
tion), also recalling English agrarian enclosure, or even justifying it;
see note on II, § 28, 18–30. It is taken by Macpherson (1951, 559 and
1962, 212 on) to have been inserted by Locke to remove the 'sufficiency
limitation' on the acquisition of property, which obtained before money
was introduced.
    35–45 Cited by Kendall, 1941, 72, as a conspicuous example of 'the
"public" right to interfere with the liberty and property of private
persons', making against the individualist interpretation of Locke's
theory of property; see Introduction, 114.

acquire a Property in them: But if they perished, in his
Possession, without their due use; if the Fruits rotted, or 40
the Venison putrified, before he could spend it, he offended
against the common Law of Nature, and was liable to be
punished; he invaded his Neighbour's share, for he had
no Right, farther than his Use called for any of them,
and they might serve to afford him Conveniencies of Life. 45

38. The same *measures* governed the *Possession of
Land* too: Whatsoever he tilled and reaped, laid up and
made use of, before it spoiled, that was his peculiar Right;
whatsoever he enclosed, and could feed, and make use of,
the Cattle and Product was also his. But if either the Grass 5
of his Inclosure rotted on the Ground, or the Fruit of
his planting perished without gathering, and laying up,
this part of the Earth, notwithstanding his Inclosure,
was still to be looked on as Waste, and might be the
Possession of any other. Thus, at the beginning, *Cain* 10
might take as much Ground as he could till, and make it
his own Land, and yet leave enough to *Abel*'s Sheep to
feed on; a few Acres would serve for both their Possessions. But as Families increased, and Industry inlarged
their Stocks, their *Possessions inlarged* with the need of 15
them; but yet it was commonly *without any fixed property
in the ground* they made use of, till they incorporated,
settled themselves together, and built Cities, and then,
by consent, they came in time, to set out the *bounds of
their distinct Territories,* and agree on limits between 20
them and their Neighbours, and by Laws within themselves,
settled the *Properties* of those of the same Society. For
we see, that in that part of the World which was first
inhabited, and therefore like to be best peopled, even as
low down as *Abraham*'s time, they wandred with their 25
Flocks, and their Herds, which was their substance, freely
up and down; and this *Abraham* did, in a Country where
he was a Stranger. Whence it is plain, that at least, a great
part of the *Land lay in common;* that the Inhabitants valued
it not, nor claimed Property in any more than they made 30
use of. But when there was not room enough in the same
place, for their Herds to feed together, they, by consent,
as *Abraham* and *Lot* did, *Gen.* xiii. 5. separated and in-

§ **38**   10–13 These four lines are a paraphrase of a quotation by
Filmer from Selden's *Mare Clausum;* see Laslett's edition, 63–4. The
passage is given in full in I, § 76 and commented upon; see note there.
   33–4 See I, § 135, 7–8, verbal parallel.

larged their pasture, where it best liked them. And for the
35 same Reason *Esau* went from his Father, and his Brother,
and planted in *Mount Seir,* Gen. xxxvi. 6.

39. And thus, without supposing any private Dominion,
and property in *Adam,* over all the World, exclusive of all
other Men, which can no way be proved, nor any ones
Property be made out from it; but supposing the *World*
5 given as it was to the Children of Men *in common,* we see
how *labour* could make Men distinct titles to several
parcels of it, for their private uses; wherein there could be
no doubt of Right, no room for quarrel.

40. Nor is it so strange, as perhaps before consideration
it may appear, that the *Property of labour* should be able
to over-ballance the Community of Land. For 'tis *Labour*
indeed that *puts the difference of value* on every thing; and
5 let any one consider, what the difference is between an
Acre of Land planted with Tobacco, or Sugar, sown with
Wheat or Barley; and an Acre of the same Land lying in
common, without any Husbandry upon it, and he will find,
that the improvement of *labour makes* the far greater part
10 of *the value.* I think it will be but a very modest Computation to say, that of the *Products* of the Earth useful to the
Life of Man $\frac{9}{10}$ are the *effects of labour:* nay, if we will
rightly estimate things as they come to our use, and cast up
the several Expenses about them, what in them is purely
15 owing to *Nature,* and what to *labour,* we shall find, that
in most of them $\frac{99}{100}$ are wholly to be put on the account
of *labour.*

41. There cannot be a clearer demonstration of any
thing, than several Nations of the *Americans* are of this,
who are rich in Land, and poor in all the Comforts of Life;
whom Nature having furnished as liberally as any other
5 people, with the materials of Plenty, *i.e.* a fruitful Soil, apt
to produce in abundance, what might serve for food,
rayment, and delight; yet for want of improving it by

35–6 See I, § 117, 5–6. It is obvious from these parallels that this
paragraph was written with Filmer's argument and Filmer's text in
mind. Locke is sketching his account of the passage from a state of
nature to a state of society in terms of biblical history.
§ 39 Also clearly directed against Filmer: its argument occupies a
great deal of the *First Treatise,* which surely would have been referred
to here if it had been written at the time.

labour, have not one hundredth part of the Conveniencies we enjoy: And a King of a large fruitful Territory there feeds, lodges, and is clad worse than a day Labourer in 10 *England*.

42. To make this a little clearer, let us but trace some of the ordinary provisions of Life, through their several progresses, before they come to our use, and see how much they receive of their *value from Humane Industry*. Bread, Wine and Cloth, are things of daily use, 5 and great plenty, yet notwithstanding, Acorns, Water, and Leaves, or Skins, must be our Bread, Drink and Clothing, did not *labour* furnish us with these more useful Commodities. For whatever *Bread* is more worth than Acorns, *Wine* than Water, and *Cloth* or *Silk* than Leaves, Skins, 10 or Moss, that is wholly *owing to labour* and industry. The one of these being the Food and Rayment which unassisted Nature furnishes us with; the other provisions which our industry and pains prepare for us, which how much they exceed the other in value, when any one hath 15 computed, he will then see, how much *labour makes the far greatest part of the value* of things, we enjoy in this World: And the ground which produces the materials, is scarce to be reckon'd in, as any, or at most, but a very small, part of it; So little, that even amongst us, Land that is left 20 wholly to Nature, that hath no improvement of Pasturage, Tillage, or Planting, is called, as indeed it is, *wast;* and we shall find the benefit of it amount to little more than nothing. This shews, how much numbers of men are to be preferd to largenesse of dominions, and that the increase of 25 lands and the right imploying of them is the great art of

§ 42 20–4 A further reference to open-field tillage in England; see II, § 28, 18–30, note and references. The *'wast'* (waste) of line 22 was the manorial land outside the fields, often a grazing area of some value, and Locke's implied criticism of the system is once more a little out of place in this context, though it is interesting that he should have made it.

    24–32 A marginal addition in the Christ's copy, dating from the later 1690's (probably after 1698) and belonging therefore to the period of Locke's activities at the Board of Trade—see Laslett, 1957 (i). It is very significant of his attitude to that institution and his policy for it, and for King William III's government in its struggle with France, particularly the insistence on increased population (compare I, § 33, 15–30 and note) as against territory as a source of power, and the criticism of the 'narrownesse of Party'. The reference to a 'wise and godlike' Prince (compare II, § 166, 1), reveals the sense in which Locke, the enemy of divine-kingship, accepted the metaphor of divinity for the ruler as he thought of him.

government. And that Prince who shall be so wise and
godlike as by established laws of liberty to secure protection
and incouragement to the honest industry of Mankind
30 against the oppression of power and narrownesse of Party
will quickly be too hard for his neighbours. But this bye
the bye. To return to the argument in hand.

43.   An Acre of Land that bears here Twenty Bushels
of Wheat, and another in *America*, which, with the same
Husbandry, would do the like, are without doubt, of the
same natural, intrinsick Value. But yet the Benefit Man-
5 kind receives from the one, in a Year, is worth 5 *l.* and
from the other possibly not worth a Penny, if all the
Profit an *Indian* received from it were to be valued, and
sold here; at least, I may truly say, not $\frac{1}{1000}$. 'Tis *Labour*
then which *puts the greatest part of Value upon Land*,
10 without which it would scarcely be worth any thing: 'tis
to that we owe the greatest part of all its useful Products:
for all that the Straw, Bran, Bread, of that Acre of Wheat,
is more worth than the Product of an Acre of as good
Land, which lies wast, is all the Effect of Labour. For
15 'tis not barely the Plough-man's Pains, the Reaper's and
Thresher's Toil, and the Bakers Sweat, is to be counted into
the *Bread* we eat; the Labour of those who broke the
Oxen, who digged and wrought the Iron and Stones, who
felled and framed the Timber imployed about the Plough,
20 Mill, Oven, or any other Utensils, which are a vast
Number, requisite to this Corn, from its being seed to be
sown to its being made Bread, must all be *charged on*
the account of *Labour*, and received as an effect of that:
Nature and the Earth furnished only the almost worthless
25 Materials, as in themselves. 'Twould be a strange *Catalogue
of things, that Industry provided and made use of, about
every Loaf of Bread*, before it came to our use, if we
could trace them; Iron, Wood, Leather, Bark, Timber,
Stone, Bricks, Coals, Lime, Cloth, Dying-Drugs, Pitch,
30 Tar, Masts, Ropes, and all the Materials made use of in
the Ship, that brought any of the Commodities made use
of by any of the Workmen, to any part of the Work,
all which, 'twould be almost impossible, at least too long,
to reckon up.

44.   From all which it is evident, that though the things
of Nature are given in common, yet Man (by being

Master of himself, and *Proprietor of his own Person,* and the actions or *Labour* of it) had still in himself *the great Foundation of Property;* and that which made up the great 5 part of what he applied to the Support or Comfort of his being, when Invention and Arts had improved the conveniencies of Life, was perfectly his own, and did not belong in common to others.

45. Thus *Labour,* in the Beginning, *gave a Right of Property,* where-ever any one was pleased to imploy it, upon what was common, which remained, a long while, the far greater part, and is yet more than Mankind makes use of. Men, at first, for the most part, contented themselves 5 with what un-assisted Nature Offered to their Necessities: and though afterwards, in some parts of the World, (where the Increase of People and Stock, with the *Use of Money*) had made Land scarce, and so of some Value, the several *Communities* settled the Bounds of their distinct Territories, 10 and by Laws within themselves, regulated the Properties of the private Men of their Society, and so, *by Compact* and Agreement, *settled the Property* which Labour and Industry began; and the Leagues that have been made between several States and Kingdoms, either expressly or 15 tacitly disowning all Claim and Right to the Land in the others Possession, have, by common Consent, given up their Pretences to their natural common Right, which originally they had to those Countries, and so have, by *positive agreement, settled a Property* amongst themselves, 20 in distinct Parts and parcels of the Earth: yet there are still *great Tracts of Ground* to be found, which (the Inhabitants thereof not having joyned with the rest of Mankind, in the consent of the Use of their common Money) *lie waste,* and are more than the People, who dwell on it, do, or can 25 make use of, and so still lie in common. Tho' this can scarce happen amongst that part of Mankind, that have consented to the use of Money.

§ **45** Beginning of the argument promised in II, § 36, 44–5, continued until § 51; compare II, § 184.

22–4 It is all mankind, not a particular collection or society, which consents to the use of money, that is precious metals. Locke had stated this in his first writing on money (see note on § 46, 6–8), but this fact is used somewhat obscurely in this paragraph to relate the origin of the property of individuals in objects and the land with the ownership of areas of the earth by nations or states. It was traditional to consider these two forms of ownership side by side, for example, in Grotius and Pufendorf.

46. The greatest part of *things really useful* to the Life
of Man, and such as the necessity of subsisting made the
first Commoners of the World look after, as it doth the
Americans now, *are* generally things *of short duration;*
5 such as, if they are not consumed by use, will decay and
perish of themselves: Gold, Silver, and Diamonds, are
things, that Fancy or Agreement hath put the Value on,
more then real Use, and the necessary Support of Life. Now
of those good things which Nature hath provided in com-
10 mon, every one had a Right (as hath been said) to as
much as he could use, and had a Property in all that he
could affect with his Labour: all that his Industry could
extend to, to alter from the State Nature had put it in,
was his. He that *gathered* a Hundred Bushels of Acorns
15 or Apples, had thereby a *Property* in them; they were his
Goods as soon as gathered. He was only to look that he
used them before they spoiled; else he took more then his
share, and robb'd others. And indeed it was a foolish
thing, as well as dishonest, to hoard up more than he
20 could make use of. If he gave away a part to any body
else, so that it perished not uselesly in his Possession, these
he also made use of. And if he also bartered away Plumbs
that would have rotted in a Week, for Nuts that would
last good for his eating a whole Year, he did no injury; he
25 wasted not the common Stock; destroyed no part of the
portion of Goods that belonged to others, so long as
nothing perished uselesly in his hands. Again, if he would
give us Nuts for a piece of Metal, pleased with its colour;
or exchanged his Sheep for Shells, or Wool for a sparkling
30 Pebble or a Diamond, and keep those by him all his Life,
he invaded not the Right of others, he might heap up as
much of these durable things as he pleased; the *exceeding
of the bounds of his* just *Property* not lying in the largeness of his Possession, but the perishing of any thing
35 uselesly in it.

§ 46 6–8 Compare Locke's *Considerations of Interest and Money,*
written about 1668, published in 1692 (see Introduction, 41 and note).
'For mankind, having consented to put an imaginary value upon gold
and silver, by reason of their durableness, scarcity, and not being
very liable to be counterfeited, have made them, by general consent,
the common pledges.' It is universal consent, world-wide, for foreigners
are insisted on (*Works*, 1801, v, 22). There is some resemblance between Locke's account of the origin and functions of money and that
of Matthew Wren, *Monarchy Asserted*, 1660 (Appendix B, no. 90)—
see p. 22 on.

47. And thus *came in the use of Money*, some lasting thing that Men might keep without spoiling, and that by mutual consent Men would take in exchange for the truly useful, but perishable Supports of Life.

48. And as different degrees of Industry were apt to give Men Possessions in different Proportions, so this *Invention of Money* gave them the opportunity to continue to enlarge them. For supposing an Island, separated from all possible Commerce with the rest of the World, wherein 5 there were but a hundred Families, but there were Sheep, Horses and Cows, with other useful Animals, wholsome Fruits, and Land enough for Corn for a hundred thousand times as many, but nothing in the Island, either because of its Commonness, or Perishableness, fit to supply the 10 place of *Money:* What reason could any one have there to enlarge his Possessions beyond the use of his Family, and a plentiful supply to its Consumption, either in what their own Industry produced, or they could barter for like perishable, useful Commodities, with others? Where 15 there is not something both lasting and scarce, and so valuable to be hoarded up, there Men will not be apt to enlarge their *Possessions of Land*, were it never so rich, never so free for them to take. For I ask, What would a Man value Ten Thousand, or an Hundred Thousand Acres of 20 excellent *Land*, ready cultivated, and well stocked too with Cattle, in the middle of the in-land Parts of *America*, where he had no hopes of Commerce with other Parts of the World, to draw *Money* to him by the Sale of the Product? It would not be worth the inclosing, and we 25 should see him give up again to the wild Common of Nature, whatever was more than would supply the Conveniencies of Life to be had there for him and his Family.

49. Thus in the beginning all the World was *America*, and more so than that is now; for no such thing as *Money* was any where known. Find out something that hath the *Use and Value of Money* amongst his Neighbours, you shall see the same Man will begin presently to *enlarge* his 5 *Possessions*.

50. But since Gold and Silver, being little useful to the

§ 47 Compare *Considerations:* 'Money has a value, as it is capable, by exchange, to procure us the necessaries of conveniences of life, and in this it has the nature of a commodity' (1801, 5, 34).
§ 49 1 Compare II, § 108, 1–2.

Life of Man in proportion to Food, Rayment, and Carriage, has its *value* only from the consent of Men, whereof Labour yet makes, in great part, *the measure*, it is plain, that
5 Men have agreed to disproportionate and unequal Possession of the Earth, they having by a tacit and voluntary consent found out a way, how a man may fairly possess more land than he himself can use the product of, by receiving in exchange for the overplus, Gold and Silver,
10 which may be hoarded up without injury to any one, these metalls not spoiling or decaying in the hands of the possessor. This partage of things, in an inequality of private possessions, men have made practicable out of the bounds of Societie, and without compact, only by putting
15 a value on gold and silver and tacitly agreeing in the use of Money. For in Governments the Laws regulate the right of property, and the possession of land is determined by positive constitutions.

51.   And thus, I think, it is very easie to conceive without any difficulty, *how Labour could at first begin a title of Property* in the common things of Nature, and how the spending it upon our uses bounded it. So that there
5 could then be no reason of quarrelling about Title, nor any doubt about the largeness of Possession it gave. Right and conveniency went together; for as a Man had a Right to all he could imploy his Labour upon, so he had no temptation to labour for more than he could make use of. This
10 left no room for Controversie about the Title, nor for Incroachment on the Right of others; what Portion a Man carved to himself, was easily seen; and it was useless as well as dishonest to carve himself too much, or take more than he needed.

§ 50 4–18 Passage extensively corrected in the Christ's copy, in such a way as to make parts of text in lines 5–10 unintelligible except by comparison with text in 1st Collected edition, 1714, and 4th edition, 1713; see Collation. The original printed version reads very oddly, containing such phrases as 'the consent of Men have agreed', which has been the subject of some learned commentary—for example, Kendall, 1941, 84.

§ 51 Von Leyden compares this paragraph and §§ 31 and 36 with the statements about property in Locke's eighth *Essay on the Law of Nature* (1954, 204–15).

1–3 This curiously repetitive phrase may also be a result of confusion in Locke's manuscript, here uncorrected.

14 With the end of this paragraph and chapter also ends the section of the 1st edition which could have been involved in the printing difficulties of 1689; compare note on I, § 167, 12, and Laslett 1952 (iv), 1954 (ii).

CHAP. VI.

Of Paternal Power.

52. It may perhaps be censured as an impertinent Criticism in a discourse of this nature, to find fault with words and names that have obtained in the World: And yet possibly it may not be amiss to offer new ones when the old are apt to lead Men into mistakes, as this of *Paternal* 5
Power probably has done, which seems so to place the Power of Parents over their Children wholly in the *Father*, as if the *Mother* had no share in it, whereas if we consult Reason or Revelation, we shall find she hath an equal Title. This may give one reason to ask, Whether this might 10 not be more properly called *Parental Power.* For whatever obligation Nature and the right of Generation lays on Children, it must certainly bind them equal to both the concurrent Causes of it. And accordingly we see the positive Law of God every where joyns them together, 15 without distinction, when it commands the Obedience of Children, *Honour thy Father and thy Mother,* Exod. 20. 12. *Whosoever curseth his Father or his Mother,* Lev. 20. 9. *Ye shall fear every Man his Mother and his Father,* Lev. 19. 3. *Children obey your Parents,* &c. Eph. 6. 1. is the stile 20 of the Old and New Testament.

§ 52 *Chapter* VI. This chapter is obviously directed against Filmer, who is mentioned by name in § 61, and so seems clearly to belong to the original writing of 1679. Its argument is presented at greater length in the *First Treatise:* there are repetitions of phrases and of biblical citations.

1–3 Compare I, § 23, 26–9, note and references: Strauss, 1953, 221, sees in this a hint by Locke at the status of the 'discourse'; see Introduction, 99, note 45.

9–21 The argument that the mother's authority is equal with that of the father is developed extensively in the *First Treatise,* and a cross-reference is given in I, § 6, 59, again in I, § 11, 35—see, in general, chapter VI of that treatise (§§ 50–73). The appeal to reason is made in I, § 55, and to revelation in I, § 61, where these four texts are cited.

11 'Parental'—see II, § 69, 1 and note.

12 'right of Generation'—particularly attacked in I, § 52: in I, § 18, 20–1 and I, § 50, 22, Grotius is attacked by implication, since Filmer uses him, but there is no reason to suppose that Locke had anyone but Filmer in mind. Hobbes's similar argument in *Leviathan,* chapter 20, looks coincidental: it was attacked by Filmer, 245.

53. Had but this one thing been well consider'd without looking any deeper into the matter, it might perhaps have kept Men from running into those gross mistakes, they have made, about this Power of Parents: which however it might,
5 without any great harshness, bear the name of Absolute Dominion, and Regal Authority, when under the Title of *Parental Power* it seem'd appropriated to the Father, would yet have sounded but odly, and in the very name shewn the Absurdity, if this supposed Absolute Power over Children
10 had been called *Parental*, and thereby have discover'd, that it belong'd to the *Mother* too; for it will but very ill serve the turn of those Men who contend so much for the Absolute Power and Authority of the *Fatherhood*, as they call it, that the *Mother* should have any share in it. And it would
15 have but ill supported the *Monarchy* they contend for, when by the very name it appeared that that Fundamental Authority from whence they would derive their Government of a single Person only, was not plac'd in one, but two Persons joyntly. But to let this of Names pass.

54. Though I have said above, Chap. II, *That all Men by Nature are equal*, I cannot be supposed to understand all sorts of *Equality: Age* or *Virtue* may give Men a just Precedency: *Excellency of Parts and Merit* may place
5 others above the Common Level: *Birth* may subject some, and *Alliance* or *Benefits* others, to pay an Observance to those to whom Nature, Gratitude or other Respects may have made it due; and yet all this consists with the *Equality*, which all Men are in, in respect of Jurisdiction or Dominion
10 one over another, which was the *Equality* I there spoke of, as proper to the Business in hand, being that *equal Right* that every Man hath, *to his Natural Freedom*, without being subjected to the Will or Authority of any other Man.

55. *Children,* I confess are not born in this full state of *Equality*, though they are born to it. Their Parents have a sort of Rule and Jurisdiction over them when they come into the World, and for some time after, but 'tis but a
5 temporary one. The Bonds of this Subjection are like

§ 54 1 'Chap. II'—a late correction from '(2)'—see Collation. Originally, perhaps, a paragraph rather than a chapter reference, to what is now II, § 4; see note there.

the Swadling Cloths they are wrapt up in, and supported by, in the weakness of their Infancy. Age and Reason as they grow up, loosen them till at length they drop quite off, and leave a Man at his own free Disposal.

56. *Adam* was created a perfect Man, his Body and Mind in full possession of their Strength and Reason, and so was capable from the first Instant of his being to provide for his own Support and Preservation, and govern his Actions according to the Dictates of the Law of Reason 5 which God had implanted in him. From him the World is peopled with his Descendants, who are all born Infants, weak and helpless, without Knowledge or Understanding. But his Off-spring having another way of entrance into Improvement of Growth and Age hath removed them, 10 *Adam* and *Eve*, and after them all *Parents* were, by the Law of Nature, *under an obligation to preserve, nourish, and educate the Children,* they had begotten, not as their own Workmanship, but the Workmanship of their own Maker, the Almighty, to whom they were to be accountable 15 for them.

57. The Law that was to govern *Adam*, was the same that was to govern all his Posterity, the *Law of Reason.* But this Off-spring having another way of entrance into the World, different from him, by a natural Birth, that produced them ignorant and without the use of *Reason,* 5 they were not presently *under that Law:* for no Body can be under a Law, which is not promulgated to him; and this Law being promulgated or made known by *Reason* only, he that is not come to the Use of his *Reason,* cannot be said to be *under this Law;* and *Adam*'s Children being not 10 presently as soon as born, *under this Law of Reason* were not presently *free.* For *Law,* in its true Notion, is not so much the Limitation as *the direction of a free and*

§ 56 4–6 Compare I, § 86, 21–4 and note.
  13–16 Compare II, § 6, 11–16, note and references.
§ 57 This famous paragraph was apparently directed against Filmer, rather than Hobbes, in spite of the verbal resemblance noted under lines 18–19. This is shown by the other details recorded here. Locke made niggling corrections to it, but none alters the sense—see Collation.
  1–12 The references to Adam and his posterity criticize Filmer, who had made all Adam's children subject to his will, and all children subject to the will of their fathers, reason or no reason. Compare II, § 60, and the seventh *Essay on the Law of Nature* (Von Leyden, 1954, 202–3).

intelligent Agent to his proper Interest, and prescribes no
15 farther than is for the general Good of those under that
Law. Could they be happier without it, the *Law,* as an
useless thing would of it self vanish; and that ill deserves
the Name of Confinement which hedges us in only from
Bogs and Precipices. So that, however it may be mistaken,
20 *the end of Law* is not to abolish or restrain, but *to preserve
and enlarge Freedom:* For in all the states of created beings
capable of Laws, *where there is no Law, there is no
Freedom.* For *Liberty* is to be free from restraint and
violence from others which cannot be, where there is no
25 Law: But Freedom is not, as we are told, *A Liberty for
every Man to do what he lists:* (For who could be free,
when every other Man's Humour might domineer over
him?) But a *Liberty* to dispose, and order, as he lists, his
Person, Actions, Possessions, and his whole Property,
30 within the Allowance of those Laws under which he is;
and therein not to be subject to the arbitrary Will of
another, but freely follow his own.

58. The *Power,* then, *that Parents have* over their
Children, arises from that Duty which is incumbent on
them, to take care of their Off-spring, during the imperfect
state of Childhood. To inform the Mind, and govern the
5 Actions of their yet ignorant Nonage, till Reason shall
take its place, and ease them of that Trouble, is what the
Children want, and the Parents are bound to. For God
having given Man an Understanding to direct his actions,
has allowed him a freedom of Will, and liberty of Acting,

18–19 Compare *Leviathan,* chapter 30: 'For the use of Lawes is . . . to
direct and keep [the People] in such a motion, as not to hurt themselves
. . . as Hedges are set, not to stop Travellers, but to keep them in the
way.' Presumably a verbal coincidence or an unconscious re-echo,
though see Gough, 1950, 32.
19–32 Elrington, 1798, uses the statement about law and freedom
to claim that men are free if governed by just laws, even if they were
not consulted in their framing, and quotes Plato against the 'unsettled
fancies of modern theorists'.
25 'as we are told'—that is, by Filmer, who makes the statement
quoted, which is also quoted in II, § 22, 9–11; see note there and
references.
§ 58 Tyrrell's account of the origin and nature of parental power is
very similar to Locke's; see 1681, 15 and on. Both writers stress the
parental duty of education, though Tyrrell is much more specific than
Locke. In his diary for 1679 Locke made a note on the point from
Sagard's *Canada* (1636, Appendix B, no. 72), under the title *'Pietas':*

as properly belonging thereunto, within the bounds of that 10
Law he is under. But whilst he is in an Estate, wherein he
has not *Understanding* of his own to direct his *Will*, he
is not to have any Will of his own to follow: He that
understands for him, must *will* for him too; he must
prescribe to his Will, and regulate his Actions; but when 15
he comes to the Estate that made his *Father a Freeman*,
the *Son is a Freeman* too.

59. This holds in all the Laws a Man is under, whether
Natural or Civil. Is a Man under the Law of Nature?
What made him free of that Law? What gave him a free
disposing of his Property according to his own Will, within
the compass of that Law? I answer; State of Maturity 5
wherein he might be suppos'd capable to know that Law,
that so he might keep his Actions within the Bounds of it.
When he has acquired that state, he is presumed to know
how far that Law is to be his Guide, and how far he may
make use of his *Freedom*, and so comes to have it; till 10
then, some Body else must guide him, who is presumed
to know how far the Law allows a Liberty. If such a state
of Reason, such an Age of Discretion *made him free*, the
same shall make his Son free too. Is a Man under the Law
of *England*? *What made him free* of that Law? That is, 15
to have the Liberty to dispose of his Actions and Possessions according to his own Will, within the Permission of
that Law? A capacity of knowing that Law. Which is
supposed by that Law, at the Age of one and twenty years,
and in some cases sooner. If this *made* the Father *free*, 20
it shall *make* the Son *free* too. Till then we see the Law
allows the Son to have no Will, but he is to be guided by
the Will of his Father or Guardian, who is to understand
for him. And if the Father die, and fail to substitute a Deputy
in this Trust, if he hath not provided a Tutor to govern 25
his Son during his Minority, during his want of Under-

---

education, not generation, gave the obligation, he wrote, and compared
the Hurons with the Janissaries, initialling the note as his (compare II,
§ 106, 18–20 and note). The classical discussion is in Grotius (*De Jure
Belli*, II, V), rejected by Filmer but characteristically close to the
surface in Tyrrell: Pufendorf's commentary on the position of Grotius
may well have been in Locke's mind—see especially *De Jure Naturae*
(1672), VI, ii, De Protestate Patria.

11–13 Elrington (1798) uses this phrase about the understanding
and will to justify the political inferiority of adults who lack intellectual
attainments.

standing, the Law takes care to do it; some other must
govern him, and be a Will to him, till he hath *attained to a
state of Freedom,* and his Understanding be fit to take
30 the Government of his Will. But after that, the Father
and Son are equally *free* as much as Tutor and Pupil after
Nonage; equally Subjects of the same Law together, without
any Dominion left in the Father over the Life, Liberty, or
Estate of his Son, whether they be only in the State and
35 under the Law of Nature, or under the positive Laws of
an Establish'd Government.

60. But if through defects that may happen out of the
ordinary course of Nature, any one comes not to such a
degree of Reason, wherein he might be supposed capable
of knowing the Law, and so living within the Rules of it,
5 he is *never capable of being a Free Man,* he is never let
loose to the disposure of his own Will (because he knows
no bounds to it, has not Understanding, its proper Guide)
but is continued under the Tuition and Government of
others, all the time his own Understanding is uncapable
10 of that Charge. And so *Lunaticks* and *Ideots* are never set
free from the Government of their Parents; *Children, who
are not as yet come unto those years whereat they may
have; and Innocents which are excluded by a natural defect
from ever having;* Thirdly, *Madmen, which for the present
15 cannot possibly have the use of right Reason to guide
themselves, have for their Guide, the Reason that guideth
other Men which are Tutors over them, to seek and
procure their good for them,* says Hooker, Eccl. Pol. Lib.
1. Sect. 7. All which seems no more than that Duty, which
20 God and Nature has laid on Man as well as other Creatures,
to preserve their Off-spring, till they can be able to shift
for themselves, and will scarce amount to an instance or
proof of *Parents* Regal Authority.

61. Thus we are *born Free,* as we are born Rational;
not that we have actually the Exercise of either: Age
that brings one, brings with it the other too. And thus
we see how *natural Freedom and Subjection to Parents*
5 may consist together, and are both founded on the same

§ **60** 11–18 Keble's *Hooker,* 1836, 1, 276–7: 1676, 78, some lines
after a passage copied into Locke's diary on 26 June 1681. Probably
added after composition of the paragraph; see note on II, § 5, 9–28.
19–23 Compare I, § 56, 20–31.

Principle. A *Child* is *Free* by his Father's Title, by his Father's Understanding, which is to govern him, till he hath it of his own. The *Freedom of a Man at years of discretion*, and the *Subjection* of a Child *to his Parents*, whilst yet short of that Age, are so consistent, and so distinguishable, that the most blinded Contenders for Monarchy, *by Right of Fatherhood*, cannot miss this *difference*, the most obstinate cannot but allow their consistency. For were their Doctrine all true, were the right Heir of *Adam* now known, and by that Title settled a Monarch in his Throne, invested with all the Absolute, Unlimited Power Sir *R.F.* talks of; if he should die as soon as his Heir was born, must not the *Child*, notwithstanding he were never so free, never so much Sovereign, be in subjection to his Mother and Nurse, to Tutors and Governors, till Age and Education brought him Reason and Ability to govern himself, and others? The Necessities of his Life, the Health of his Body, and the Information of his Mind would require him to be directed by the Will of others and not his own: and yet will any one think, that this Restraint and Subjection were inconsistent with, or spoiled him of that Liberty or Sovereignty he had a Right to, or gave away his Empire to those who had the Government of his Nonage? This Government over him only prepared him the better and sooner for it. If any body should ask me, When my Son is *of Age to be free?* I shall answer, Just when his Monarch is of Age to govern. *But at what time*, says the judicious *Hooker*, Eccl. Pol. Lib. 1. Sect. 6. *a Man may be said to have attain'd so far forth the use of Reason, as sufficeth to make him capable of those Laws whereby he is then bound to guide his Actions; this is a great deal more easie for sense to discern, than for any one by Skill and Learning to determine.*

62. Common-wealths themselves take notice of, and allow that there is *a time when Men* are to *begin to act like Free Men*, and therefore till that time require not

§ 61 17 'Sir *R.F.*'—Sir Robert Filmer, an overt indication that Locke is here writing specifically against him; see note on II, § 52 (chapter VI) and II, § 22, 9–10 and note. This passage reads very like much of the *First Treatise*.
32–8 Keble's *Hooker*, 1836, 1, 273, accurately cited: 1676, 77, a few lines after a passage quoted in the *Essay concerning Humane Understanding* (1894, 402–3). Evidently inserted after the composition of the paragraph; see note on II, § 5, 9–28 (and on II, § 5, 1 for 'judicious').

Oaths of Fealty, or Allegiance, or other publick owning
5 of, or Submission to the Government of their Countreys.

63. The *Freedom* then of Man and Liberty of acting
according to his own Will, is *grounded on* his having
Reason, which is able to instruct him in that Law he is
to govern himself by, and make him know how far he is
5 left to the freedom of his own will. To turn him loose to
an unrestrain'd Liberty, before he has Reason to guide him,
is not the allowing him the priviledge of his Nature, to be
free; but to thrust him out amongst Brutes, and abandon
him to a state as wretched, and as much beneath that of
10 a Man, as theirs. This is that which puts the *Authority*
into the *Parents* hands to govern the *Minority* of their
Children. God hath made it their business to imploy this
Care on their Off-spring, and hath placed in them suitable
Inclinations of Tenderness and Concern to temper this
15 power, to apply it as his Wisdom designed it, to the
Childrens good, as long as they should need to be under it.

64. But what reason can hence advance this Care of the
Parents due to their Off-spring into an *Absolute Arbitrary
Dominion* of the Father, whose power reaches no farther,
than by such a Discipline as he finds most effectual to give
5 such strength and health to their Bodies, such vigour and
rectictude to their Minds, as may best fit his Children
to be most useful to themselves and others; and, if it be
necessary to his Condition, to make them work when
they are able for their own Subsistence. But in this power
10 the *Mother* too has her share with the *Father*.

65. Nay, this *power* so little belongs to the *Father*
by any peculiar right of Nature, but only as he is Guardian
of his Children, that when he quits his Care of them, he
loses his power over them, which goes along with their
5 Nourishment and Education, to which it is inseparably
annexed, and it belongs as much to the *Foster-Father* of

§ 64 4–10 These sentiments recall Locke on *Education* (already
formulated though not written when this was composed, see Introduction, 35), and even his insistence in his paper for the Board of Trade
that the children of the poor must work (Introduction, 56): compare
Tyrrell, 1681, 19.
§ 65 6–7 Compare I, § 100, 7–11 and Tyrrell, 1681, 16: in lines 26–7
of I, § 100 Locke makes a cross-reference to the *Second Treatise,*
evidently with such passages in this chapter in mind.

an exposed Child, as to the Natural Father of another:
So little power does the bare *act of begetting* give a Man
over his Issue, if all his Care ends there, and this be all
the Title he hath to the Name and Authority of a Father. 10
And what will become of this *Paternal Power* in that part
of the World where one Woman hath more than one
Husband at a time? Or in those parts of *America* where
when the Husband and Wife part, which happens frequently, the Children are all left to the Mother, follow her, 15
and are wholly under her Care and Provision? If the Father
die whilst the Children are young, do they not naturally
every where owe the same Obedience to their *Mother,*
during their Minority, as to their Father were he alive?
And will any one say, that the *Mother* hath a Legislative 20
Power over her Children? that she can make standing Rules,
which shall be of perpetual Obligation, by which they
ought to regulate all the Concerns of their Property, and
bound their Liberty all the course of their Lives? Or can she
inforce the observation of them with Capital Punishments? 25
For this is the proper *power of the Magistrate,* of which
the Father hath not so much as the shadow. His Command
over his Children is but temporary, and reaches not their
Life or Property. It is but a help to the weakness and im-
perfection of their Nonage, a Discipline necessary to their 30
Education: And though a *Father* may dispose of his own
Possessions as he pleases, when his Children are out
of danger of perishing for want, yet *his power* extends
not to the Lives or Goods, which either their own industry,
or anothers bounty has made theirs; nor to their Liberty 35
neither, when they are once arrived to the infranchisement
of the years of discretion. The *Father's Empire* then ceases,
and he can from thence forwards no more dispose of the
liberty of his Son, than that of any other Man: And it must
be far from an absolute or perpetual Jurisdiction, from 40
which a Man may withdraw himself, having Licence from
Divine Authority to *leave Father and Mother and cleave
to his Wife.*

20–7 Locke's references here imply denials of the marks of political
sovereignty which Filmer found in fatherly power; see I, § 129, 12–18
and note, II, § 3 and note. On the right of children to their property,
compare Grotius, 1625, II, v, 2 and Pufendorf, 1672, VI, ii, 8: Locke's
whole argument here and in II, § 69 (q.v.) is close to Pufendorf's.
42–3 Gen. ii. 24, quoted in Matt. xix. 5, etc., and used by Tyrrell,
1681, 31.

66. But though there be a time when a *Child* comes
to be as *free* from subjection to the Will and Command
of his Father, as the father himself is free from subjection
to the Will of any body else, and they are each under no
5 other restraint but that which is common to them both,
whether it be the Law of Nature, or municipal Law of their
Country: yet this freedom exempts not a Son from that
honour which he ought, by the Law of God and Nature,
to pay his *Parents*. God having made the Parents Instru-
10 ments in his great design of continuing the Race of
Mankind, and the occasions of Life to their Children, as
he hath laid on them an obligation to nourish, preserve,
and bring up their Off-spring; So he has laid on the
Children a perpetual Obligation of *honouring their Parents*,
15 which containing in it an inward esteem and reverence to
be shewn by all outward Expressions, ties up the Child
from any thing that may ever injure or affront, disturb,
or endanger the Happiness or Life of those, from whom
he received his; and engages him in all actions of defence,
20 relief, assistance and comfort of those, by whose means he
entred into being, and has been made capable of any
enjoyments of life. From this Obligation no State, no Freedom, can absolve Children. But this is very far from giving
Parents a power of command over their Children, or an
25 Authority to make Laws and dispose as they please, of their
Lives or Liberties. 'Tis one thing to owe honour, respect,
gratitude and assistance; another to require an absolute
obedience and submission. The *honour due to Parents*,
a Monarch in his Throne owes his Mother, and yet this
30 lessens not his Authority, nor subjects him to her Government.

67. The subjection of a Minor places in the Father a
temporary Government, which terminates with the minority
of the Child: and the *honour due from a Child*, places in
the Parents a perpetual right to respect, reverence, support
5 and compliance too, more or less, as the Father's care,
cost and kindness in his Education, has been more or less.
This ends not with minority, but holds in all parts and conditions of a Man's Life. The want of distinguishing these
two powers; viz. that which the Father hath in the right

§ **66**   7–9   Compare I, § 63, 1–2; I, § 66, 22–3 and Tyrrell, 1681, 19,
etc., following Grotius and Pufendorf.
9–11   Compare I, § 54, 6–8, verbal parallel.

of *Tuition,* during Minority, and the right of *Honour* all 10
his Life, may perhaps have caused a great part of the
mistakes about this matter. For to speak properly of them,
the first of these is rather the Priviledge of Children, and
Duty of Parents, than any Prerogative of Paternal Power.
The Nourishment and Education of their Children, is a 15
Charge so incumbent on Parents for their Childrens good,
that nothing can absolve them from taking care of it. And
though the *power of commanding and chastising* them go
along with it, yet God hath woven into the Principles
of Humane Nature such a tenderness for their Off-spring, 20
that there is little fear that Parents should use their power
with too much rigour; the excess is seldom on the severe
side, the strong byass of Nature drawing the other way.
And therefore God Almighty when he would express
his gentle dealing with the *Israelites,* he tells them, that 25
tho' he chasten'd them, *he chasten'd them as a Man
chastens his Son,* Deut. 8. 5. *i.e.* with tenderness and
affection, and kept them under no severer Discipline than
what was absolutely best for them, and had been less kindness to have slacken'd. This is that power to which 30
Children are commanded *Obedience,* that the pains and
care of their Parents may not be increased, or ill rewarded.

68. On the other side, *honour* and support, all that
which Gratitude requires to return for the Benefits received by and from them is the indispensible Duty of the
Child, and the proper Priviledge of the Parents. This is
intended for the Parents advantage, as the other is for the   5
Childs; though Education, the Parents Duty, seems to have
most power, because the ignorance and infirmities of Childhood stand in need of restraint and correction; which is a
visible exercise of Rule, and a kind of Dominion. And that
Duty which is comprehended in the word *honour,* requires 10
less Obedience, though the Obligation be stronger on
grown than younger Children. For who can think the
Command, *Children obey your Parents,* requires in a Man
that has Children of his own the same submission to his
Father, as it does in his yet young Children to him; and 15
that by this Precept he were bound to obey all his Father's
Commands, if out of a conceit of Authority he should have
the indescretion to treat him still as a Boy?

§ 67   17–23   Compare I, § 56, 20–31.

69. The first part then of *Paternal* Power, or rather Duty, which is *Education,* belongs so to the Father that it terminates at a certain season; when the business of Education is over it ceases of it self, and is also alienable before. For
5 a Man may put the Tuition of his Son in other hands; and he that has made his Son an *Apprentice* to another, has discharged him, during that time, of a great part of his Obedience both to himself and to his Mother. But all the *Duty of Honour,* the other part, remains never the less
10 entire to them; nothing can cancel that. It is so inseparable from them both, that the Father's Authority cannot dispossess the Mother of this right, nor can any Man discharge his Son from *honouring* her that bore him. But both these are very far from a power to make Laws, and
15 inforcing them with Penalties that may reach Estate, Liberty, Limbs and Life. The power of Commanding ends with Nonage; and though after that, *honour* and respect, support and defence, and whatsoever Gratitude can oblige a Man to for the highest benefits he is naturally
20 capable of, be always due from a Son to his Parents; yet all this puts no Scepter into the Father's hand, no Sovereign Power of Commanding. He has no Dominion over his Sons Property or Actions, nor any right, that his Will should prescribe to his Sons in all things; however it may become
25 his Son in many things, not very inconvenient to him and his Family, to pay a Deference to it.

70. A Man may owe *honour* and respect to an ancient, or wise Man; defence to his Child or Friend; relief and support to the Distressed; and gratitude to a Benefactor, to such a degree, that all he has, all he can do, cannot
5 sufficiently pay it: But all these give no Authority, no right to any one of making Laws over him from whom they are owing. And 'tis plain, all this is due not to the bare Title of Father; not only because, as has been said, it is owing to the Mother too; but because these Obligations to
10 Parents, and the degrees of what is required of Children, may be varied, by the different care and kindness, trouble

---

§ **69**   1   '*Paternal* Power'—Locke seems already to have forgotten his determination in II, § 52, 11 to call it '*Parental*'; compare II, § 170, 1.

6   '*Apprentice*'—this association of the filial relationship with apprenticeship is very significant for the social structure of seventeenth-century England; compare II, § 85, 9–18.

10–13   Compare I, § 62, 15–22.

16–26   Compare II, § 65, 20–7, and references, especially Pufendorf.

and expence, which is often imployed upon one Child, more than another.

71. This shews the reason how it comes to pass, that *Parents in Societies*, where they themselves are Subjects, retain a *power over their Children,* and have as much right to their Subjection, as those who are in the state of Nature, which could not possibly be, if all Political Power were only 5 Paternal, and that in truth they were one and the same thing: For then, all Paternal Power being in the Prince, the Subject could naturally have none of it. But these two *Powers, Political* and *Paternal, are so perfectly distinct* and separate; are built upon so different Foundations, and 10 given to so different Ends, that every Subject that is a Father, has as much a *Paternal Power* over his Children, as the Prince has over his; And every Prince that has Parents owes them as much filial Duty and Obedience as the meanest of his Subjects do to theirs; and can therefore 15 contain not any part or degree of that kind of Dominion, which a Prince, or Magistrate has over his Subject.

72. Though the Obligation on the Parents to *bring up* their Children, and the Obligation on Children to *honour* their Parents, contain all the Power on the one hand, and Submission on the other, which are proper to this Relation; yet there is *another Power* ordinarily *in the Father,* whereby 5 he has a tie on the Obedience of his Children: which though it be common to him with other Men, yet the occasions of shewing it, almost constantly happening to Fathers in their private Families, and the Instances of it elsewhere being rare, and less taken notice of, it passes in 10 the World for a part of *Paternal Jurisdiction.* And this is the Power Men generally have to *bestow their Estates* on those, who please them best. The Possession of the Father being the Expectation and Inheritance of the Children ordinarily in certain proportions, according to the Law and 15 Custom of each Country; yet it is commonly in the Father's Power to bestow it with a more sparing or liberal hand, according as the Behaviour of this or that Child hath comported with his Will and Humour.

§ 71 1–8 Compare I, § 65, 3–14.

73. This is no small Tye on the Obedience of Children: And there being always annexed to the Enjoyment of Land, a Submission to the Government of the Country, of which that Land is a part; It has been commonly suppos'd, That 5 a *Father* could *oblige his Posterity to that Government,* of which he himself was a Subject, and that his Compact held them; whereas, it being only a necessary Condition annex'd to the Land, and the inheritance of an Estate which is under that Government, reaches only those who will take 10 it on that Condition, and so is no natural Tye or Engagement, but a voluntary Submission. For *Every Man's Children* being by Nature as *free* as himself, or any of his Ancestors ever were, may, whilst they are in that Freedom, choose what Society they will join themselves to, what Com- 15 mon-wealth they will put themselves under. But if they will enjoy the *Inheritance* of their Ancestors, they must take it on the same terms their Ancestors had it, and submit to all the Conditions annex'd to such a Possession. By this Power indeed Fathers oblige their Children to Obedi- 20 ence to themselves, even when they are past Minority, and most commonly too subject them to this or that Political Power. But neither of these by any peculiar right of *Fatherhood,* but by the Reward they have in their hands to inforce and recompence such a Compliance; and is no more 25 Power than what a *French-man* has over an *English-man,* who by the hopes of an Estate he will leave him, will certainly have a strong Tye on his Obedience: And if when it is left him, he will enjoy it, he must certainly take it upon the Conditions annex'd to the *Possession of Land* in 30 that Country where it lies, whether it be *France* or *England.*

74. To conclude then, though the *Father's Power* of commanding extends no farther than the Minority of his Children, and to a degree only fit for the Discipline and Government of that Age: And though that *Honour* and 5 Respect, and all that which the *Latins* called *Piety,* which they indispensibly owe to their Parents all their Life times,

§ 73 This paragraph represents perhaps the weakest point of Locke's argument against Filmer. Compare note on II, § 45, 22–4, II, § 118, 23–9 and see Introduction, 83. Elrington, 1798, seizes on Locke's denial of a 'natural Tye' (line 10) to maintain that "it cannot be concluded that no degree of obligation whatsoever is imposed on a man by the acts of his ancestors', and this is the burden of Burke's criticism of Lockeian politics, especially as they were interpreted in Revolutionary France.

and in all Estates, with all that Support and Defence [which]
is due to them, gives the Father no Power of Governing,
i.e. making Laws and enacting Penalties on his Children;
Though by all this he has no Dominion over the Property 10
or Actions of his Son: yet 'tis obvious to conceive how
easie it was in the first Ages of the World, and in places
still, where the thinness of People gives Families leave to
separate into unpossessed Quarters, and they have room
to remove and plant themselves in yet vacant Habitations, 15
for the *Father of the Family* to become the Prince of it; †
he had been a Ruler from the beginning of the Infancy of
his Children: and since without some Government it would

† *It is no improbable Opinion, therefore, which the* Arch-Philosopher
*was of, That the chief Person in every Household was always, as it were,
a King: So when Numbers of Households joyn'd themselves in Civil
Societies together, Kings were the first kind of Governours amongst
them, which is also, as it seemeth, the reason why the name of Fathers
continued still in them, who, of Fathers, were made Rulers; as also the
ancient Custom of Governours to do as* Melchizedec, *and being Kings,
to exercise the Office of Priests, which Fathers did, at the first, grew
perhaps by the same Occasion. Howbeit, this is not the only kind of
Regiment that has been received in the World. The Inconveniences of
one kind have caused sundry other to be devised; so that in a word, all
publick Regiment of what kind soever, seemeth evidently to have risen
from the deliberate Advice, Consultation and Composition between
Men, judging it convenient, and behoveful; there being no impossibility
in Nature, considered by it self, but that Man might have lived without
any publick Regiment.* Hooker's Eccl. P. I. 1. Sect. 10.

§ 74 7 'which'—inserted by editor to make sense.

16–41 This passage, and the two succeeding paragraphs (compare
II, §§ 105–12), make considerable concessions to patriarchalism, and
represent the direct influence on Locke of Filmer and traditional attitudes. But not only is Locke's argument very close to Tyrrell's (1681,
35–9), but also to that of Pufendorf, *De Jure Naturae* (1672), VII, iii,
De Generatione Summi Imperii Civilis, see especially § 7 (904–5).
Tyrrell cites 'Mr Pufendorf a late judicious writer of great judgment and
learning' at this point (p. 37, words added in the copy Tyrrell corrected
for Locke), and also Sir William Temple's *Essay of Government*
(published in *Miscellanea*, 1680), for Temple was the great exponent of
patriarchalism tempered with consent and apart from Divine Right.
Locke does not seem to have read or possessed Temple's book, and these
sentiments seem to be the result of his consideration of Filmer, and
perhaps his acquaintance with Pufendorf.

16 The reference sign is inserted by the editor at this point to
show where it seems most likely that Locke wished to draw the attention of his reader to the passage in Hooker, printed without reference
sign in the margins of the 1st and later editions. All subsequent citations
from Hooker appear in the margins in this way, which marks them even
more obviously as later additions, made perhaps about June 1681 after
the original text was complete (see note on II, § 5, 9–28 and references).
The passage is found on pp. 303–4 of Keble's *Hooker*, 1836, vol. I and
on p. 86 of Locke's 1676 Hooker. The 'Arch-Philosopher' is of course
Aristotle; see the passages in *Politics*, 1, especially 1252b, which Filmer
had made use of.

be hard for them to live together, it was likeliest it should,
20 by the express or tacit Consent of the Children, when they
were grown up, be in the Father, where it seemed without
any change barely to continue; when indeed nothing more
was required to it, than the permitting the *Father* to exercise alone in his Family that executive Power of the Law
25 of Nature, which every Free-man naturally hath, and by
that permission resigning up to him a Monarchical Power,
whilst they remained in it. But that this was not by any
Paternal Right, but only by the Consent of his Children,
is evident from hence, That no Body doubts but if a
30 Sranger, whom Chance or Business had brought to his Family, had there kill'd any of his Children, or committed any
other Fact, he might Condemn and put him to Death, or
otherwise have punished him as well as any of his Children: which it was impossible he should do by virtue of
35 any Paternal Authority over one, who was not his Child,
but by virtue of that Executive Power of the Law of Nature, which, as a Man he had a right to: And he alone
could punish him in his Family, where the respect of his
Children had laid by the Exercise of such a Power, to give
40 way to the Dignity and Authority, they were willing should
remain in him, above the rest of his Family.

75. Thus 'twas easie, and almost natural for Children
by a tacit, and scarce avoidable consent to make way for
the *Father's Authority and Government.* They had been
accustomed in their Childhood to follow his Direction, and
5 to refer their little differences to him, and when they were
Men, who fitter to rule them? Their little Properties, and
less Covetousness seldom afforded greater Controversies;
and when any should arise, where could they have a fitter
Umpire than he, by whose Care they had every one been
10 sustain'd, and brought up, and who had a tenderness for
them all? 'Tis no wonder, that they made no distinction
betwixt Minority, and full Age; nor looked after one and
Twenty, or any other Age, that might make them the free
Disposers of themselves and Fortunes, when they could
15 have no desire to be out of their Pupilage. The Government they had been under, during it, continued still to be
more their Protection than restraint: And they could no

24–5 'executive Power of the Law of Nature'—see II, § 9, 1–2, note
and references.

where find a greater security to their Peace, Liberties, and Fortunes, than in the *Rule of a Father*.

76. Thus the natural *Fathers of Families*, by an insensible change, became the *politick Monarchs* of them too: And as they chanced to live long, and leave able, and worthy Heirs, for several Successions, or otherwise; So they laid the Foundations of Hereditary, or Elective Kingdoms, 5 under several Constitutions, and Manners, according as Chance, Contrivance, or Occasions happen'd to mould them. But if Princes have their Titles in the Fathers Right, and it be a sufficient proof of the natural *Right of Fathers* to Political Authority, because they commonly were those, 10 in whose hands we find, *de facto*, the Exercise of Government: I say, if this Argument be good, it will as strongly prove that all Princes, nay Princes only, ought to be Priests, since 'tis as certain, that in the Beginning, *The Father of the Family was Priest, as that he was Ruler in his own* 15 *Houshold*.

CHAP. VII.

Of Political or Civil Society.

77. God having made Man such a Creature, that, in his own Judgment, it was not good for him to be alone, put

§ 77 *Chapter* VII All the evidence goes to show that this chapter formed a part of the original critique of Filmer; compare note on chapter VI, II, § 52. There are references to men who can only be Filmer and his followers (§ 90) and arguments directly pointed at Filmer's text (§§ 92, 93): it is closely parallel to Tyrrell's discussion which was overtly directed against Filmer. There is no positive indication of insertions or revision in 1689, though the cross-reference in § 84, 3, may imply some revision at an earlier date.

1–4 Compare the fourth *Essay on the Law of Nature*. Man 'feels himself . . . urged to enter into society by a certain propensity of nature, and to be prepared for the maintenance of society by the gift of speech and through the intercourse of language' (Von Leyden, 1954, 156–7).

2 Gen. ii. 18: 'God said, it is not good that the man should be alone.'

him under strong Obligations of Necessity, Convenience,
and Inclination to drive him into *Society*, as well as fitted
5 him with Understanding and Language to continue and
enjoy it. The *first Society* was between Man and Wife,
which gave beginning to that between Parents and Children; to which, in time, that between Master and Servant
came to be added: And though all these might, and com-
10 monly did meet together, and make up but one Family,
wherein the Master or Mistress of it had some sort of Rule
proper to a Family; each of these, or all together came
short of *Political Society*, as we shall see, if we consider
the different Ends, Tyes, and Bounds of each of these.

78.   *Conjugal Society* is made by a voluntary Compact
between Man and Woman: and tho' it consist chiefly in
such a Communion and Right in one anothers Bodies, as
is necessary to its chief End, Procreation; yet it draws with
5 it mutual Support, and Assistance, and a Communion of
Interest too, as necessary not only to unite their Care, and
Affection, but also necessary to their common Off-spring,
who have a Right to be nourished and maintained by them,
till they are able to provide for themselves.

79.   For the end of *conjunction between Male and Female*, being not barely Procreation, but the continuation
of the Species, this conjunction betwixt Male and Female
ought to last, even after Procreation, so long as is necessary
5 to the nourishment and support of the young Ones, who
are to be sustained by those that got them, till they are
able to shift and provide for themselves. This Rule, which
the infinite wise Maker hath set to the Works of his hands,
we find the inferiour Creatures steadily obey. In those vi-
10 viparous Animals which feed on Grass, the *conjunction between Male and Female* lasts no longer than the very Act

---

6–14   Compare II, § 2, and also Aristotle's *Politics,* 1, especially
1252a and b.
§ 78   Compare Tyrrell, 1681, 14: 'Marriage, which is a mutual Compact between a Man and a Woman for their Cohabitation, the generation of Children, and their joint care and provision for them.'
§ 79   Natural history of this sort was a persistent pre-occupation of
Locke's, and he possessed many of the standard works. The pre-
Linnaean, pre-Darwinian system of classification comes out clearly
here, as it does in the *First Treatise*.

of Copulation: because the Teat of the Dam being sufficient to nourish the Young, till it be able to feed on Grass,
the Male only begets, but concerns not himself for the Female or Young, to whose Sustenance he can contribute 15
nothing. But in Beasts of Prey the *conjunction* lasts longer:
because the Dam not being able well to subsist her self,
and nourish her numerous Off-spring by her own Prey
alone, a more laborious, as well as more dangerous way of
living, than by feeding on Grass, the Assistance of the 20
Male is necessary to the Maintenance of their common
Family, which cannot subsist till they are able to prey for
themselves, but by the joynt Care of Male and Female.
The same is to be observed in all Birds (except some domestick ones, where plenty of food excuses the Cock from 25
feeding, and taking care of the young Brood) whose Young
needing Food in the Nest, the Cock and Hen continue
Mates, till the Young are able to use their wing, and provide for themselves.

80.   And herein I think lies the chief, if not the only
reason, *why the Male and Female in Mankind are tyed to
a longer conjunction* than other Creatures, *viz.* because
the Female is capable of conceiving, and *de facto* is commonly with Child again, and Brings forth too a new Birth 5
long before the former is out of a dependancy for support
on his Parents help, and able to shift for himself, and has
all the assistance is due to him from his Parents: whereby
the Father, who is bound to take care for those he hath
begot, is under an Obligation to continue in Conjugal So- 10
ciety with the same Woman longer than other Creatures,
whose Young being able to subsist of themselves, before
the time of Procreation returns again, the Conjugal Bond
dissolves of it self, and they are at liberty, till *Hymen,* at
his usual Anniversary Season, summons them again to 15
chuse new Mates. Wherein one cannot but admire the
Wisdom of the great Creatour, who having given to Man
foresight and an Ability to lay up for the future, as well
as to supply the present necessity, hath made it necessary,
that *Society of Man and Wife should be more lasting,* than 20
of Male and Female amongst other Creatures; that so their
Industry might be encouraged, and their Interest better
united, to make Provision, and lay up Goods for their common Issue, which uncertain mixture, or easie and frequent
Solutions of Conjugal Society would mightily disturb. 25

81. But though these are Ties upon *Mankind*, which make the *Conjugal Bonds* more firm and lasting in Man, than the other Species of Animals; yet it would give one reason to enquire, why this *Compact*, where Procreation and
5 Education are secured, and Inheritance taken care for, may not be made determinable, either by consent, or at a certain time, or upon certain Conditions, as well as any other voluntary Compacts, there being no necessity in the nature of the thing, nor to the ends of it, that it should always
10 be for Life; I mean, to such as are under no Restraint of any positive Law, which ordains all such Contracts to be perpetual.

82. But the Husband and Wife, though they have but one common Concern, yet having different understandings, will unavoidably sometimes have different wills too; it therefore being necessary, that the last Determination, *i.e.* the
5 Rule, should be placed somewhere, it naturally falls to the Man's share, as the abler and the stronger. But this reaching but to the things of their common Interest and Property, leaves the Wife in the full and free possession of what by Contract is her peculiar Right, and gives the Hus-
10 band no more power over her Life, than she has over his. The *Power of the Husband being* so far from that of an absolute Monarch, that the *Wife* has, in many cases, a Liberty to *separate* from him; where natural Right, or their Contract allows it, whether that Contract be made by them-
15 selves in the state of Nature, or by the Customs or Laws of the Countrey they live in; and the Children upon such Separation fall to the Father or Mother's Lot, as such Contract does determine.

§ 81 5–8 This guarded hint at the justifiability of divorce was too much for the clerical Elrington, who says: 'To make the conjugal union determinable by consent, is to introduce a promiscuous concubinage.' Locke was prepared to go much further than this, as is seen in the notes in his diary for 1678, 1679, 1680 under the heading *Atlantis*. He suggests that 'He that is already married may marry another woman with his left hand. . . . The ties, duration and conditions of the left hand marriage shall be no other than what is expressed in the contract of marriage between the parties' (*Diary,* 1678, 199). On Locke's *Atlantis,* see de Marchi, 1955.
§ 82 5–6 Elrington says that this implies that the right of the husband arises solely from superior power, as indeed it does in Hobbes's *Leviathan,* chapter 20, which Locke's discussion resembles to some extent.

83. For all the ends of *Marriage* being to be obtained under Politick Government, as well as in the state of Nature, the Civil Magistrate doth not abridge the Right, or Power of either naturally necessary to those ends, *viz.* Procreation and mutual Support and Assistance whilst they are 5 together; but only decides any Controversie that may arise between Man and Wife about them. If it were otherwise, and that absolute *Sovereignty* and Power of Life and Death naturally belong'd to the Husband, and were *necessary to the Society between Man and Wife,* there could be no 10 Matrimony in any of those Countries where the Husband is allowed no such absolute Authority. But the ends of Matrimony requiring no such Power in the Husband, the Condition of *Conjugal Society* put it not in him, it being not at all necessary to that State. *Conjugal Society* could 15 subsist and obtain its ends without it; nay, Community of Goods, and the Power over them, mutual Assistance, and Maintenance, and other things belonging to *Conjugal Society,* might be varied and regulated by that Contract, which unites Man and Wife in that Society, as far as may 20 consist with Procreation and the bringing up of Children till they could shift for themselves; nothing being necessary to any Society, that is not necessary to the ends for which it is made.

84. The *Society betwixt Parents and Children,* and the distinct Rights and Powers belonging respectively to them, I have treated of so largely, in the foregoing Chapter, that I shall not here need to say any thing of it. And I think it is plain, that it is far different from a Politick Society. 5

85. *Master* and *Servant* are Names as old as History, but given to those of far different condition; for a Freeman makes himself a Servant to another, by selling him for a certain time, the Service he undertakes to do, in exchange for Wages he is to receive: And though this com- 5 monly puts him into the Family of his Master, and under the ordinary Discipline thereof; yet it gives the Master but a Temporary Power over him, and no greater, than what

§ 83   13–22   Passage rewritten for the 2nd edition, see Collation: little difference of sense, except that 'Community of Goods' (lines 16–17) is introduced.
§ 84   3   'foregoing Chapter'—chapter VI; see note on II, § 77 (chapter VII).

is contained in the *Contract* between 'em. But there is an-
10 other sort of Servants, which by a peculiar Name we call
Slaves, who being Captives taken in a just War, are by the
Right of Nature subjected to the Absolute Dominion and
Arbitrary Power of their Masters. These Men having, as
I say, forfeited their Lives, and with it their Liberties, and
15 lost their Estates; and being in the *State of Slavery*, not
capable of any Property, cannot in that state be considered
as any part of *Civil Society;* the chief end whereof is the
preservation of Property.

86. Let us therefore consider a *Master of a Family*
with all these subordinate Relations of *Wife, Children,
Servants* and *Slaves* united under the Domestick Rule of a
Family; which what resemblance soever it may have in its
5 Order, Offices, and Number too, with a little Commonwealth, yet is very far from it, both in its Constitution,
Power and End: Or if it must be thought a Monarchy,
and the *Paterfamilias* the absolute Monarch in it, absolute
Monarchy will have but a very shattered and short Power,
10 when 'tis plain, by what has been said before, That the
Master of the Family has a very distinct and differently
limited *Power,* both as to time and extent, over those several Persons that are in it; for excepting the Slave (and
the Family is as much a Family, and his Power as *Pater-*
15 *familias* as great, whether there be any Slaves in his Family
or no) he has no Legislative Power of Life and Death
over any of them, and none too but what a *Mistress of a
Family* may have as well as he. And he certainly can have
no absolute Power over the whole *Family,* who has but a
20 very limited one over every individual in it. But how a
Family, or any other Society of Men, differ from that,
which is properly *Political Society,* we shall best see, by
considering wherein *Political Society* it self consists.

87. Man being born, as has been proved, with a Title
to perfect Freedom, and an uncontrouled enjoyment of all

§ 85 9-18 On slavery compare II, § 24, 1-9 and references: here is
added the claim that slaves are outside civil society. 'Servants' in this
paragraph, we must not forget, covered many now classed as industrial
or agricultural workers, and that Locke and all his contemporaries looked
upon them as under domestic authority is significant of very different
social assumptions; compare II, § 69, 6, 'Apprentice'.
§ 87 On this paragraph compare the *Third Letter for Toleration,* 1765,
163.

the Rights and Privileges of the Law of Nature, equally
with any other Man, or Number of Men in the World, hath
by Nature a Power, not only to preserve his Property, that   5
is, his Life, Liberty and Estate, against the Injuries and
Attempts of other Men; but to judge of, and punish the
breaches of that Law in others, as he is perswaded the Offence deserves, even with Death it self, in Crimes where
the heinousness of the Fact, in his Opinion, requires it.   10
But because no *Political Society* can be, nor subsist without having in it self the Power to preserve the Property,
and in order thereunto punish the Offences of all those of
that Society; there, and there only is *Political Society*,
where every one of the Members hath quitted this natural   15
Power, resign'd it up into the hands of the Community in
all cases that exclude him not from appealing for Protection to the Law established by it. And thus all private
judgement of every particular Member being excluded, the
Community comes to be Umpire, by settled standing Rules,   20
indifferent, and the same to all Parties; and by Men having
Authority from the Community, for the execution of those
Rules, decides all the differences that may happen between
any Members of that Society, concerning any matter of
right; and punishes those Offences, which any Member   25
hath committed against the Society, with such Penalties as
the Law has established: Whereby it is easie to discern
who are, and who are not, in *Political Society* together.
Those who are united into one Body, and have a common
establish'd Law and Judicature to appeal to, with Authority   30
to decide Controversies between them, and punish Offenders, *are in Civil Society* one with another: but those
who have no such common Appeal, I mean on Earth, are
still in the state of Nature, each being, where there is no
other, Judge for himself, and Executioner; which is, as I   35
have before shew'd it, the perfect *state of Nature*.

88. And thus the Commonwealth comes by a Power
to set down, what punishment shall belong to the several

5–6 'that is, his Life, Liberty and Estate'—compare this extended
definition of property with I, § 9, 10; II, §§ 57, 29; 59, 33–4; 85, 14–15;
123, 18; 131, 6–7; 135, 17–18; 137, 19–20; 173, 4–6; 209, 6;
221, 8–9; 222, 22–3; and see Introduction, 115. Contrast also II, § 13,
1–7 and note, I, § 90, 15–20.
20–3 Passage rewritten for 2nd edition; see Collation.

transgressions which they think worthy of it, committed amongst the Members of that Society, (which is the *power* 5 *of making Laws*) as well as it has the power to punish any Injury done unto any of its Members, by any one that is not of it, (which is the *power of War and Peace*;) and all this for the preservation of the property of all the Members of that Society, as far as is possible. But though every 10 Man who has enter'd into civil Society, and is become a member of any Commonwealth, has thereby quitted his power to punish Offences against the Law of Nature, in prosecution of his own private Judgment; yet with the Judgment of Offences which he has given up to the Legis-15 lative in all Cases, where he can Appeal to the Magistrate, he has given a right to the Commonwealth to imploy his force, for the Execution of the Judgments of the Commonwealth, whenever he shall be called to it; which indeed are his own Judgments, they being made by himself, or his 20 Representative. And herein we have the original of the *Legislative* and *Executive Power* of Civil Society, which is to judge by standing Laws how far Offences are to be punished, when committed within the Commonwealth; and also to determin, by occasional Judgments founded on the 25 present Circumstances of the Fact, how far Injuries from without are to be vindicated, and in both these to imploy all the force of all the Members when there shall be need.

89. Where-ever therefore any number of Men are so united into one Society, as to quit every one his Executive Power of the Law of Nature, and to resign it to the publick, there and there only is a *Political, or Civil Society*. And 5 this is done where-ever any number of Men, in the state of Nature, enter into Society to make one People, one Body Politick under one Supreme Government, or else when any one joyns himself to, and incorporates with any Govern-

§ **88** 4–5 and 7 Marks of sovereignty again hinted at; see II, § 11, 7–9 and references.

14–15 Elrington (1798) castigates this as leaving it optional that men should resign up their power to political authority.

16–20 Used by Kendall to demonstrate Locke's 'collectivism', along with II, § 120; see note there, and on II, § 151, 22–5, for 'representative'.

§ **89** 1–2 'Men are so united'—in 1 ed. active mood, 'Men so unite'; see Collation.

6 'People': first occurrence of this word, cf. Polin, 1960, 156.

ment already made. For hereby he authorizes the Society, or which is all one, the Legislative thereof to make Laws 10 for him as the publick good of the Society shall require; to the Execution whereof, his own assistance (as to his own Decrees) is due. And this *puts Men* out of a State of Nature *into* that of a *Commonwealth*, by setting up a Judge on Earth, with Authority to determine all the Controversies, 15 and redress the Injuries, that may happen to any Member of the Commonwealth; which Judge is the Legislative, or Magistrates appointed by it. And where-ever there are any number of Men, however associated, that have no such decisive power to appeal to, there they are still *in the state* 20 *of Nature*.

90.   Hence it is evident, that *Absolute Monarchy*, which by some Men is counted the only Government in the World, is indeed *inconsistent with Civil Society*, and so can be no Form of Civil Government at all. For the *end of Civil Society*, being to avoid, and remedy those inconveniencies of the State of Nature, which necessarily follow from every Man's being Judge in his own Case, by setting up a known Authority, to which every one of that Society may Appeal upon any Injury received, or Controversie that may arise, and which every one of the Society ought 10 to obey; † where-ever any persons are, who have not such an Authority to Appeal to, for the decision of any difference between them, there those persons are still *in the state of Nature*. And so is every *Absolute Prince* in respect of those who are under his *Dominion*.   15

---

† *The publick Power of all Society is above every Soul contained in the same Society; and the principal use of that power is to give Laws unto all that are under it, which Laws in such Cases we must obey, unless there be reason shew'd which may necessarily inforce, that the Law of Reason, or of God, doth injoyn the contrary,* Hook. Eccl. Pol. 1. I. Sect. 16.

14–21 Here Locke talks of the Legislative where the Judiciary might be expected; compare II, § 88, 13–15, and Introduction, 132. The whole paragraph should be contrasted with Hobbes's *Leviathan*, chapter 18.

§ 90 2 'some Men', that is Filmer and his followers, certainly not Hobbes to whom monarchy was decidedly not the only form of government. See II, § 77 (chapter VII).

11 Reference sign for Hooker quotation inserted by editor; see note on II, § 74, 16. Passage on p. 353 of Keble's *Hooker*, 1836, I, and Locke's 1676 edition 101–2, slightly modified in transcription here.

91. For he being suppos'd to have all, both Legislative
and Executive Power in himself alone, there is no Judge
to be found, no Appeal lies open to any one, who may
fairly, and indifferently, and with Authority decide, and
5 from whose decision relief and redress may be expected of
any Injury or Inconveniency, that may be suffered from
the Prince or by his Order: So that such a Man, however
intitled, *Czar*, or *Grand Signior*, or how you please, is as
much *in the state of Nature*, with all under his Dominion,
10 as he is with the rest of Mankind. For where-ever any two
Men are, who have no standing Rule, and common Judge
to Appeal to on Earth for the determination of Controversies of Right betwixt them, there they are still *in the
state of Nature*, and under all the inconveniencies of it,‡
15 with only this woful difference to the Subject, or rather
Slave of an Absolute Prince: That whereas, in the ordinary
State of Nature, he has a liberty to judge of his Right, and
according to the best of his Power, to maintain it; now
whenever his Property is invaded by the Will and Order
20 of his Monarch, he has not only no Appeal, as those in
Society ought to have, but as if he were degraded from the
common state of Rational Creatures, is denied a liberty to
judge of, or to defend his Right, and so is exposed to all
the Misery and Inconveniencies that a Man can fear from
25 one, who being in the unrestrained state of Nature, is yet
corrupted with Flattery, and armed with Power.

‡ *To take away all such mutual Grievances, Injuries and Wrongs,*
i.e. *such as attend Men in the State of Nature. There was no way but
only by growing into Composition and Agreement amongst themselves,
by ordaining some kind of Government publick, and by yielding themselves subject thereunto, that unto whom they granted Authority to
Rule and Govern, by them the Peace, Tranquility, and happy Estate of
the rest might be procured. Men always knew that where Force and
Injury was offered, they might be Defenders of themselves; they knew
that however Men may seek their own Commodity; yet if this were done
with Injury unto others, it was not to be suffered, but by all Men, and
all good Means to be withstood. Finally, they knew that no Man might
in reason take upon him to determine his own Right, and according to
his own Determination proceed in maintenance thereof, in as much as
every Man is towards himself, and them whom he greatly affects,
partial; and therefore that Strifes and Troubles should be endless,
except they gave their common Consent, all to be ordered by some,
whom they should agree upon, without which Consent there would be
no reason that any Man should take upon him to be Lord or Judge
over another.* Hooker's Eccl. Pol. I. 1. Sect. 10.

§ 91   14   Reference sign for Hooker's quotation inserted by editor;
see note on II, § 74, 16. See Keble's *Hooker*, 1836, 1, 302, Locke's 1676
edition, 86, slightly modified. Compare English treatise 1660, and
Abrams' note: Polin, 1961, 105.

92. For he that thinks *absolute Power purifies Mens Bloods,* and corrects the baseness of Humane Nature, need read but the History of this, or any other Age to be convinced of the contrary. He that would have been insolent and injurious in the Woods of *America,* would not probably be much better in a Throne; where perhaps Learning and Religion shall be found out to justifie all, that he shall do to his Subjects, and the Sword presently silence all those that dare question it. For what the *Protection of Absolute Monarchy* is, what kind of Fathers of their Countries it makes Princes to be, and to what a degree of Happiness and Security it carries Civil Society where this sort of Government is grown to perfection, he that will look into the late Relation of *Ceylon,* may easily see.

93. *In Absolute Monarchies* indeed, as well as other Governments of the World, the Subjects have an Appeal to the Law, and Judges to decide any Controversies, and restrain any Violence that may happen betwixt the Subjects themselves, one amongst another. This every one thinks necessary, and believes he deserves to be thought a declared Enemy to Society and Mankind, who should go about to take it away. But whether this be from a true Love of Mankind and Society, and such a Charity as we owe all one to another, there is reason to doubt. For this is no more, than what every Man who loves his own Power, Profit, or Greatness, may, and naturally must do, keep those Animals from hurting or destroying one another who labour and drudge only for his Pleasure and Advantage, and so are taken care of, not out of any Love the Master has for them, but Love of himself, and the Profit they bring him. For if it be asked, what Security, *what Fence* is there in such a State, *against the Violence and Oppression of this Absolute Ruler?* The very Question can scarce be born. They are ready to tell you, that it deserves Death only to ask after Safety. Betwixt Subject and Subject, they will

§ **92**   8   'presently'—immediately. This condemnation of absolute power is often supposed to be directed against Hobbes (for example, *Leviathan,* chapter 18, 1904, 128), but it is as appropriate against Filmer and the phrase 'Fathers of their Countries' in line 10 confirms that it was Filmer's absolute, patriarchal monarch which was in Locke's mind.

13–14   'the late Relation of *Ceylon*'—*An Historical Relation of the Island of Ceylon* by Robert Knox, 1680, bought by Locke on 29 August 1681; Appendix B, no. 49.

§ **93**   8–16   Compare I, § 156 note and references.

grant, there must be Measures, Laws, and Judges, for their
mutual Peace and Security: But as for the *Ruler*, he ought
to be *Absolute*, and is above all such Circumstances: be-
25 cause he has Power to do more hurt and wrong, 'tis right
when he does it. To ask how you may be guarded from
harm, or injury on that side where the strongest hand is to
do it, is presently the Voice of Faction and Rebellion. As
if when Men quitting the State of Nature entered into So-
30 ciety, they agreed that all of them but one, should be under
the restraint of Laws, but that he should still retain all the
Liberty of the State of Nature, increased with Power, and
made licentious by Impunity. This is to think that Men are
so foolish that they take care to avoid what Mischiefs may
35 be done them by *Pole-Cats*, or *Foxes*, but are content, nay
think it Safety, to be devoured by *Lions*.

94.   But whatever Flatterers may talk to amuze Peoples
Understandings, it hinders not Men, from feeling: and
when they perceive, that any Man, in what Station soever,
is out of the Bounds of the Civil Society which they are of;
5 and that they have no Appeal on Earth against any harm
they may receive from him, they are apt to think themselves in the state of Nature, in respect of him, whom they
find to be so; and to take care as soon as they can, to have
that *Safety and Security in Civil Society*, for which it was
10 first instituted, and for which only they entered into it.
And therefore, though perhaps at first, (as shall be shewed
more at large hereafter in the following part of this Discourse) some one good and excellent Man, having got a
Preheminency amongst the rest, had this Deference paid
15 to his Goodness and Vertue, as to a kind of Natural Authority, that the chief Rule, with Arbitration of their differ-

36 This whole paragraph, and particularly this last statement, are
often quoted as Locke's judgment on Hobbes; see, for example, Gough,
1950, 36. This is perhaps because of Hobbes's insistence that the claim
that the sovereign was not under the law led to the dissolution of civil
society; see *Leviathan*, chapter 29. But it seems much more likely to
refer to Filmer, who repeatedly maintains that 'A King according to law
makes no kind of government', Laslett's edition, 304. Locke makes a
generally similar statement in his first *Essay on the Law of Nature*, Von
Leyden, 1954, 118–19.
§ **94** 1–10 This is the first mention of revolutionism; compare II, §§ 168,
210.
1 'amuze' = mislead.
11–12 Perhaps §§ 105–112 are meant, or even chapter XIV, 'Of
Prerogative'.

ences, by a tacit Consent devolved into his hands, without
any other caution, but the assurance they had of his Up-
rightness and Wisdom: yet when time, giving Authority,
and (as some Men would perswade us) Sacredness to Cus- 20
toms, which the negligent, and unforeseeing Innocence of
the first Ages began, had brought in Successors of another
Stamp, the People finding their Properties not secure under
the Government, as then it was, (whereas Government has
no other end but the preservation of Property) could never 25
be safe nor at rest, *nor think themselves in Civil Society,*
till the Legislature was placed in collective Bodies of Men,
call them Senate, Parliament, or what you please.† By
which means every single person became subject, equally
with other the meanest Men, to those Laws, which he him- 30
self, as part of the Legislative had established: nor could
any one, by his own Authority, avoid the force of the Law,
when once made, nor by any pretence of Superiority, plead
exemption, thereby to License his own, or the Miscarriages
of any of his Dependants. *No Man in Civil Society can be* 35

---

† *At the first, when some certain kind of Regiment was once appointed, it may be that nothing was then farther thought upon for the
manner of governing, but all permitted unto their Wisdom and Discretion, which were to Rule, till by experience they found this for all parts
very inconvenient, so as the thing which they had devised for a Remedy,
did indeed but increase the Sore, which it should have cured. They saw,
that to live by one Man's Will, became the cause of all Mens misery.*
This constrained them to come unto Laws wherein all Men might see
their Duty beforehand, and know the Penalties of transgressing them.
Hooker's Eccl. Pol. I. 1. Sect. 10.

24–5 This is Locke's strongest assertion of the preservation of
property as the end of government, though it could be a later insertion:
see the discussion in Introduction, especally p. 115 and references.
Tyrrell, characteristically, puts his similar point in the context of
previous discussion: 'I hope this great difficulty which hath puzled
some Divines, which is *prior in nature,* Propriety or civil Government
is now cleared, since it is apparent, Propriety, understood either as the
application of natural things to the uses of particular Men, or else as the
general agreement of many men in the division of a Territory, or
Kingdom, must be before Government, one main end of which is to
maintain the Dominion or Property before agreed on' (1681, 2nd
pagination, 116).
27 'Legislature'—changed by Locke from 'Legislative'; see Collation. It means the power of law-making, not the law-making body;
compare II, § 153, 17; § 154, 4.
28 Reference sign for Hooker quotation inserted by editor; see note
on II, § 74, 16: Keble's *Hooker,* 1836, i, 304–5; Locke's 1676 edition,
86–7, coming a little after the passage given in the footnote to II,
§ 74. It is a remarkable fact that the same passage appears again in the
footnote to II, § 111, 9.

exempted from the Laws of it.‡ For if any Man may do, what he thinks fit, and there be no Appeal on Earth, for Redress or Security against any harm he shall do; I ask, Whether he be not perfectly still in the State of Nature, 40 and so can be *no part or Member of that Civil Society:* unless any one will say, the State of Nature and Civil Society are one and the same thing, which I have never yet found any one so great a Patron of Anarchy as to affirm.

CHAP. VIII.

Of the Beginning of Political Societies.

95.   Men being, as has been said, by Nature, all free, equal and independent, no one can be put out of this Estate, and subjected to the Political Power of another, without his own *Consent.* The only way whereby any one devests him-

---

‡ *Civil Law being the Act of the whole Body Politick, doth therefore over-rule each several part of the same Body.* Hooker ibid.

36   Reference sign inserted as above: Keble, 314; 1676, 90, one slight variant. Elrington, 1798, contrasts this passage and Locke's appeal to it with II, § 12, 16–22, and complains that it leads too directly to government by the will of the people. It certainly implies that the 'meanest man' (l. 30) has property and so a political personality.

§ 95   *Chapter* VIII. This chapter clearly formed part of the original critique of Filmer, whose positions are cited and whose language is paraphrased; see notes on § 95, 10; § 98, 13–16; § 101, 25–8; § 103, 11–20; § 112, 9–13; § 114, 5–9; etc.; compare note on II, § 77, chapter VII. But it seems possible that §§ 100–22 were not written in the original composition, but added a little later, after the composition of the *First Treatise,* perhaps in the summer of 1681 when he seems to have added the quotations from Hooker (see note on § 111, 9), or even after that. The evidence for this is the fact that § 132 seems to follow on to § 99, and that chapter IX (§§ 123–31) is a still later addition, perhaps of 1689; see note there. There is no evidence to show that any part of this chapter VIII was written in 1689, though it is possible, of course, that these discontinuities came about through a much more radical rearrangement of the text in that year.

2   'this Estate'—the third printing, not altered by Locke in the Christ's master-copy, reads 'his Estate': corrected by editor with authority of later editions, see Collation.

self of his Natural Liberty, and *puts on the bonds of Civil* 5
Society is by agreeing with other Men to joyn and unite
into a Community, for their comfortable, safe, and peaceable living one amongst another, in a secure Enjoyment of
their Properties, and a greater Security against any that are
not of it. This any number of Men may do, because it in- 10
jures not the Freedom of the rest; they are left as they were
in the Liberty of the State of Nature. When any number
of Men have so *consented to make one Community* or
Government, they are thereby presently incorporated, and
make *one Body Politick,* wherein the *Majority* have a Right 15
to act and conclude the rest.

96.   For when any number of Men have, by the consent of every individual, made a *Community,* they have
thereby made that *Community* one Body, with a Power to
Act as one Body, which is only by the will and determination of the *majority.* For that which acts any Community, 5
being only the consent of the individuals of it, and it being
necessary to that which is one body to move one way; it
is necessary the Body should move that way whither the
greater force carries it, which is the *consent of the majority:* or else it is impossible it should act or continue one 10
Body, *one Community,* which the consent of every individual that united into it, agreed that it should; and so every
one is bound by that consent to be concluded by the *ma-*

§ 95   10 'any number of Men may do'—a contradiction of a very
characteristic claim of Sir Robert Filmer's (see Laslett, 1949, 16) and it
is against Filmer that Locke's arguments about majorities are formulated. Though it invites contrast with Hobbes's famous paragraph on
'The Generation of a Commonwealth' (*Leviathan,* chapter 17, 1904, 118–
19), Filmer, not Hobbes, was in Locke's mind. Elrington (1798) objects
to this that it is not a question of what men may do, but what they are
'under a direct obligation', moral obligation, to do, and to Locke's statement about majorities (lines 15–16) that the numerical reasoning is fanciful; he makes power the foundation of right.
12–16   For an exhaustive discussion of this passage, which he calls
the most concise of all statements of 'the faith of majority-rule democrats', see Kendall, 1941, chapter VII.
§ 96   The general relationship between Locke's views and those of
George Lawson is well brought out by the similar content, but quite
different demonstration, of their attitude to the majority principle. In
his *Examination of Hobbes,* 1657, Lawson says that in all assemblies
and societies, the major part concludes and determines the whole, to avoid
confusion and dissension and to preserve order (p. 25). A common
source for both their views, and that of Tyrrell, could well have been
the very well known discussion by Grotius, *De Jure Belli,* Prolegomena
(1712, p. x), and II, V, 17.

jority. And therefore we see that in Assemblies impowered
15 to act by positive Laws where no number is set by that
positive Law which impowers them, the *act of the Majority*
passes for the act of the whole, and of course determines,
as having by the Law of Nature and Reason, the power
of the whole.

97.   And thus every Man, by consenting with others to
make one Body Politick under one Government, puts himself under an Obligation to every one of that Society, to
submit to the determination of the *majority*, and to be con-
5 cluded by it; or else this *original Compact*, whereby he
with others incorporates into *one Society,* would signifie
nothing, and be no Compact, if he be left free, and under
no other ties, than he was in before in the State of Nature. For what appearance would there be of any Compact?
10 What new Engagement if he were no farther tied by any
Decrees of the Society, than he himself thought fit, and
did actually consent to? This would be still as great a liberty, as he himself had before his Compact, or any one else
in the State of Nature hath, who may submit himself and
15 consent to any acts of it if he thinks fit.

98.   For if *the consent of the majority* shall not in reason, be received, *as the act of the whole,* and conclude
every individual; nothing but the consent of every individual can make any thing to be the act of the whole: But
5 such a consent is next impossible ever to be had, if we
consider the Infirmities of Health, and Avocations of Business, which in a number, though much less than that of
a Common-wealth, will necessarily keep many away from
the publick Assembly. To which if we add the variety of
10 Opinions, and contrariety of Interests, which unavoidably
happen in all Collections of Men, the coming into Society
upon such terms, would be only like *Cato*'s coming into the

§ 97   The effect, if not the sense and phraseology, of this paragraph
is very close to that of Hobbes, *Leviathan*, chapter 18, headed *No man
can without injustice protest against the Institution of the Soveraigne
declared by the major part* (1904, 122). See note on II, § 98, 13–16.
§ 98   This paragraph was extensively modified by Locke in the Christ's
copy (see Collation) though not in such a way as to alter the sense.
   12   Martial, *Epigrammaton*, 1, Praef.:
            'Cur in theatrum, Cato severe, venisti,
              An ideo tantum veneras, ut exires?'
A common anecdote about Cato of Utica; information from Mr E. J.
Kenney.

Theatre, only to go out again. Such a Constitution as this would make the mighty *Leviathan* of a shorter duration, than the feeblest Creatures; and not let it outlast the day 15 it was born in: which cannot be suppos'd till we can think, that Rational Creatures should desire and constitute Societies only to be dissolved. For where the *majority* cannot conclude the rest, there they cannot act as one Body, and consequently will be immediately dissolved again.   20

99.   Whosoever therefore out of a state of Nature unite into a *Community*, must be understood to give up all the power, necessary to the ends for which they unite into Society, to the *majority* of the Community, unless they expressly agreed in any number greater than the majority. 5 And this is done by barely agreeing to *unite into one Political Society*, which is *all the Compact that* is, or needs be, between the Individuals, that enter into, or make up a *Commonwealth*. And thus that, which begins and actually *constitutes any Political Society*, is nothing but the consent 10 of any number of Freemen capable of a majority to unite and incorporate into such a Society. And this is that, and that only, which did, or could give *beginning* to any *lawful Government* in the World.

100.   To this I find two Objections made.

First, *That there are no Instances to be found in Story of a Company of Men independent and equal one amongst another, that met together, and in this way began and set up a Government.*   5

§ 98 13–16 A deliberate invocation of the critical language of Hobbes, clearly sarcastic and not intended as a critical comment on the theory of *Leviathan*, nor on any particular passage in it; see Introduction, 84. Locke and Hobbes were agreed on the necessity of the consent of the majority being taken for the act of the whole, and it was Filmer who denied it; see passages cited in note on II, § 95, 10. His defence of the majority principle against Filmer must be pronounced unsatisfactory, for he responded to the challenge to prove 'by some law of nature that the major part have the power to rule over the rest of the multitude' (Filmer, 82) by simply asserting that it is 'by the Law of Nature and Reason' (II, § 96, 18); compare Allen, 1928.

§ 100 It is possible that the paragraphs from this point to II, § 131, were added after the original composition, perhaps in 1681, for § 132 seems to follow on to § 99. See note on II, §§ 95 (ch. VIII); 101; 111, 9; 123 (ch. IX); 132 (ch. X).

Secondly, *'Tis impossible of right that Men should do so, because all Men being born under Government, they are to submit to that, and are not at liberty to begin a new one.*

101. To the first there is this to Answer. That it is not at all to be wonder'd, that *History* gives us but a very little account of Men, *that lived together in the State of Nature.* The inconveniencies of that condition, and the love, and
5 want of Society no sooner brought any number of them together, but they presently united and incorporated, if they designed to continue together. And if we may not suppose *Men* ever to have been *in the State of Nature,* because we hear not much of them in such a State, we may as well sup-
10 pose the Armies of *Salmanasser,* or *Xerxes* were never Children, because we hear little of them, till they were Men, and imbodied in Armies. Government is every where antecedent to Records, and Letters seldome come in amongst a People, till a long continuation of Civil Society has, by
15 other more necessary Arts provided for their Safety, Ease, and Plenty. And then they begin to look after the History of their *Founders,* and search into their *original,* when they have out-lived the memory of it. For 'tis with *Commonwealths* as with particular Persons, they are commonly
20 *ignorant of their own Births* and *Infancies:* And if they know any thing of their *Original,* they are beholding, for it, to the accidental Records, that others have kept of it. And those that we have, of the beginning of any Polities in the World, excepting that of the *Jews,* where God himself
25 immediately interpos'd, and which favours not at all Paternal Dominion, are all either plain instances of such a beginning, as I have mentioned, or at least have manifest footsteps of it.

§ 100   6–9   See II, § 112, 20–1. Both the obvious objections registered here occur in Filmer, for example, 81 and 232.
§ 101   This paragraph begins the fuller answer about the actual existence of a state of nature preceding the establishment of civil societies, hinted at in II, § 14, 4. It seems possible that in 1681 Locke decided to elaborate his argument on this point, and that this was why he extended the text here—see note II, § 100 and references.
10   '*Salmanasser*'—the Assyrian conqueror (ninth century B.C.); '*Xerxes*'—the Persian conqueror (defeated at Salamis 480 B.C.).
12–13   Compare I, § 145, 8 and I, § 144, 36–8.
25–8   These phrases show that Locke has Filmer in mind, and 'manifest footsteps' is Filmer's own expression (60) ridiculed in I, § 150.

102. He must shew a strange inclination to deny evident matter of fact, when it agrees not with his Hypothesis,
who will not allow that the *beginning* of *Rome* and *Venice*
were by the uniting together of several Men free and independent one of another, amongst whom there was no 5
natural Superiority or Subjection. And if *Josephus Acosta*'s
word may be taken, he tells us, that in many parts of
America there was no Government at all. *There are great
and apparent Conjectures,* says he, *that these Men,* speaking
of those of *Peru, for a long time had neither Kings nor* 10
*Common-wealths, but lived in Troops, as they do this day
in* Florida, *the* Cheriquanas, *those of* Bresil, *and many
other Nations, which have no certain Kings, but as occasion is offered in Peace or War, they choose their Captains
as they please,* l. I. c. 25. If it be said, that every Man 15
there was born subject to his Father, or the head of his
Family. That the subjection due from a Child to a Father,
took not away his freedom of uniting into what Political
Society he thought fit, has been already proved. But be
that as it will, these Men, 'tis evident, were actually *free;* 20
and whatever superiority some Politicians now would place
in any of them, they themselves claimed it not; but by consent were all *equal,* till by the same consent they set Rulers
over themselves. So that their *Politick Societies* all *began*
from a voluntary Union, and the mutual agreement of Men 25
freely acting in the choice of their Governours, and forms
of Government.

103. And I hope those who went away from *Sparta*
with *Palantus,* mentioned by *Justin l. 3, c.* 4 will be allowed
to have been *Freemen independent* one of another, and to
have set up a Government over themselves, by their own
consent. Thus I have given several Examples out of His- 5

§ 102 3 Locke is contradicting Filmer here, see 206 *et seq.*, 220 *et seq.*
6–15 A citation from Edward Grimestone's translation of Acosta,
The naturall and morall historie of the Indies, 1604, a popular book
with Locke, and by his side in 1681; see Appendix B, no. 1. The passage
is found on 1, 72 of the 1880 reprint. The Cheriquanas are spelt with
a 'g' in the original: 'a wild tribe in forests to the east of the Andes'.
16–7 A reminiscence of Filmer; see passage quoted in note to II,
§ 114, 5–9.
§ 103 2 Palantus was the leader of the Spartans who founded the
city of Tarentum in Italy in the eighth century B.C. The account given
by Trogus Pompeius is known only from the epitome of his universal
history made by Justin in the second or third century A.D. The reference
here is probably to the Paris edition of 1543 (Appendix B, no. 47).

tory, of *People free and in the State of Nature,* that being
met together incorporated and *began a Common-wealth.*
And if the want of such instances be an argument to prove
that *Government* were not, nor could not be so *begun,* I
10 suppose the Contenders for Paternal Empire were better
let it alone, than urge it against natural Liberty. For if
they can give so many instances out of History, of *Gov-*
ernments begun upon Paternal Right, I think (though at
best an Argument from what has been, to what should of
15 right be, has no great force) one might, without any great
danger, yield them the cause. But if I might advise them in
the Case, they would do well not to search too much into
the *Original of Governments,* as they have begun *de facto,*
lest they should find at the foundation of most of them,
20 something very little favourable to the design they promote,
and such a power as they contend for.

104. But to conclude, Reason being plain on our side,
that Men are naturally free, and the Examples of History
shewing, that the *Governments* of the World, that were
begun in Peace, had their beginning laid on that founda-
5 tion, and were *made by the Consent of the People;* There
can be little room for doubt, either where the Right is, or
what has been the Opinion, or Practice of Mankind, about
the *first erecting of Governments.*

105. I will not deny, that if we look back as far as
History will direct us, towards the *Original of Common-*
wealths, we shall generally find them under the Government and Administration of one Man. And I am also apt
5 to believe, that where a Family was numerous enough to
subsist by it self, and continued entire together, without
mixing with others, as it often happens, where there is
much Land and few People, the Government commonly

11–20 A further reference to Filmer and his followers with their
'Paternal Right'.
§ **104** 3–4 On the limitation to governments begun in peace, see II,
§ 112, 16–17 and note.
§ **105** With this paragraph begins a passage continuing to II, § 112
which repeats and extends Locke's concessions to patriarchalism; compare II, § 74, 16–41 and note. Again his argument is close to that of
Tyrrell (for example, 1681, 83 on) and perhaps even closer to Pufendorf—see *De Jure Naturae,* 1672, VII, i, entitled *De Causa Impulsitiva*
Instituendae Civitatis, especially § 5. He follows Edward Gee, Filmer's
first critic (1658, p. 150), in these comments on Filmer's patriarchalism,
see Appendix B.

began in the Father. For the Father having, by the Law
of Nature, the same Power with every Man else to punish, 10
as he thought fit, any Offences against that Law, might
thereby punish his transgressing Children even when they
were Men, and out of their Pupilage; and they were very
likely to submit to his punishment, and all joyn with him
against the Offender, in their turns, giving him thereby 15
power to Execute his Sentence against any transgression,
and so in effect make him the Law-maker, and Governour
over all, that remained in Conjunction with his Family.
He was fittest to be trusted; Paternal affection secured their
Property, and Interest under his Care, and the Custom of 20
obeying him, in their Childhood, made it easier to submit
to him, rather than to any other. If therefore they must
have one to rule them, as Government is hardly to be
avoided amongst Men that live together; who so likely to
be the Man, as he that was their common Father; unless 25
Negligence, Cruelty, or any other defect of Mind, or Body
made him unfit for it? But when either the Father died, and
left his next Heir for want of Age, Wisdom, Courage, or
any other Qualities, less fit for Rule: or where several
Families met, and consented to continue together: There, 30
'tis not to be doubted, but they used their natural freedom,
to set up him, whom they judged the ablest, and most
likely, to Rule well over them. Conformable hereunto we
find the People of *America,* who (living out of the reach
of the Conquering Swords, and spreading domination of 35
the two great Empires of *Peru* and *Mexico*) enjoy'd their
own natural freedom, though, *cæteris paribus,* they commonly prefer the Heir of their deceased King; yet if they
find him any way weak, or uncapable, they pass him by
and set up the stoutest and bravest Man for their Ruler. 40

106. Thus, though looking back as far as Records give
us any account of Peopling the World, and the History of
Nations, we commonly find the *Government* to be in one
hand, yet it destroys not that, which I affirm, (*viz.*) That
the *beginning of Politick Society* depends upon the consent 5
of the Individuals, to joyn into and make one Society;
who, when they are thus incorporated, might set up what

19 Elrington (1798) comments here that men had a *duty* to trust
the heads of families and no arbitrary right to reject them, and on II,
§ 106 that Locke does not maintain that men have an arbitrary right
over their most important moral actions.

form of Government they thought fit. But this having
given occasion to Men to mistake, and think, that by
10 Nature Government was Monarchical, and belong'd to
the Father, it may not be amiss here to consider, why
People in the beginning generally pitch'd upon this form,
which though perhaps the Father's Preheminency might
in the first institution of some Common-wealths, give a
15 rise to, and place, in the beginning, the Power in one hand;
Yet it is plain, that the reason, that continued the Form
of *Government in a single Person*, was not any Regard,
or Respect to Paternal Authority; since all petty Monarchies, that is, almost all *Monarchies*, near their Original,
20 have been commonly, at least upon occasion, *Elective*.

107.   First then, in the beginning of things, the Father's
Government of the Childhood of those sprung from him,
having accustomed them to the *Rule of one Man*, and
taught them that where it was exercised with Care and
5 Skill, with Affection and Love to those under it, it was
sufficient to procure and preserve to Men all the Political
Happiness they sought for, in Society. It was no wonder,
that they should pitch upon, and naturally run into that
Form of Government, which from their Infancy they had
10 been all accustomed to; and which, by experience they
had found both easie and safe. To which, if we add, that
Monarchy being simple, and most obvious to Men, whom
neither experience had instructed in Forms of Government,
nor the Ambition or Insolence of Empire had taught to
15 beware of the Encroachments of Prerogative, or the Inconveniencies of Absolute Power, which Monarchy, in
Succession, was apt to lay claim to, and bring upon them,
it was not at all strange, that they should not much trouble
themselves to think of Methods of restraining any Ex-
20 orbitances of those, to whom they had given the Authority over them, and of ballancing the Power of Government, by placing several parts of it in different hands.
They had neither felt the Oppression of Tyrannical Do-

§ **106** 18–20 Compare II, § 132, 11–14. In his journal under 25
March 1679 (compare Introduction, 47) and under the heading *Politia*,
Locke quotes from Sagard's *Canada* (1636, Appendix B, no. 72: compare II, § 58 note) on the elective kingship of that region, which nevertheless usually permits the son to succeed to the father's throne. 'Their
kings are rather obliged by consent and persuasion than compulsion, the
public good being the reason of their authority . . . and this seems to
be the state of regal authority in its original in all that part of the
world', he writes, and initials the note (B.M. Add. MSS. 15642).

minion, nor did the Fashion of the Age, nor their Pos- 25
sessions, or way of living (which afforded little matter for
Covetousness or Ambition) give them any reason to ap-
prehend or provide against it: and therefore 'tis no
wonder they put themselves into such a *Frame of Government,* as was not only as I said, most obvious and sim- 30
ple, but also best suited to their present State and Condition; which stood more in need of defence against foreign
Invasions and Injuries, than of multiplicity of Laws. The
equality of a simple poor way of liveing confineing their
desires within the narrow bounds of each mans smal 35
propertie made few controversies and so no need of many
laws to decide them: And there wanted not of Justice
where there were but few Trespasses, and few Offenders.
Since then those, who liked one another so well as to joyn
into Society, cannot but be supposed to have some Ac- 40
quaintance and Friendship together, and some Trust one
in another; they could not but have greater Apprehensions
of others, than of one another: And therefore their first
care and thought cannot but be supposed to be, how to
secure themselves against foreign Force. 'Twas natural 45
for them to put themselves under a *Frame of Government,* which might best serve to that end; and chuse the
wisest and bravest Man to conduct them in their Wars,
and lead them out against their Enemies, and in this
chiefly be their *Ruler.*

108. Thus we see, that the *Kings* of the *Indians* in
America, which is still a Pattern of the first Ages in *Asia*
and *Europe,* whilst the Inhabitants were too few for the
Country, and want of People and Money gave Men to
Temptation to enlarge their Possessions of Land, or con- 5
test for wider extent of Ground, are little more than
Generals of their Armies; and though they command

§ **107** 32–7 Rewritten by Locke in the Christ's copy, but differences immaterial; see Collation. The text is considerably modified
in minute detail in this area, almost entirely for punctuation.
§ **108** 1–3 Compare II, § 49, 1.
7 '*Generals of their Armies*'—Locke shared with Tyrrel the view
that a frequent origin of kingship was in the military leader, and that
the dominance of such a leader may be a transitional stage between
the state of nature and of society. See Tyrrell, 1681, 85 (the early
kings of the Goths, Vandals, and 'our Saxons') and 92–3, referring
to the 'Caciques', of the Caribbean Islands and Brazil. Indeed Tyrrell
actually made a note on the point in Locke's journal for 1680, about
the King amongst the inhabitants of the Hudson Bay area, who was

absolutely in War, yet at home and in time of Peace they
exercise very little Dominion, and have but a very mod-
10 erate Sovereignty, the Resolutions of Peace and War,
being ordinarily either in the People, or in a Council.
Though the War it self, which admits not of Plurality of
Governours, naturally devolves the Command into the
King's sole Authority.

109. And thus in *Israel* it self, the *chief Business of
their Judges, and first Kings* seems to have been *to be
Captains in War*, and Leaders of their Armies; which,
(besides what is signified by *going out and in before the
5 People*, which was, to march forth to War, and home again
in the Heads of their Forces) appears plainly in the Story
of *Jephtha*. The *Ammonites* making War upon *Israel*, the

'only captain of so many families'. Acosta and Lery (Appendix B, nos.
1 and 51) were probably their other sources, but the most straightforward statement is to be found in the *Histoire naturelle et Morale
des Iles Antilles* (probably by Rochefort, but also attributed to Du
Tertre and De Poincy), Rotterdam, 1658, which Locke possessed; see
463–4. The discussion in Grotius, 1625, I, iii, 8, may be compared
and contrasted.

The argument is repeated in the *Letters on Toleration*: 'There are
nations in the *West Indies*, which have no other end of their society
but their mutual defence against their common enemies. In these their
captain, or prince, is sovereign commander in time of war; but in time
of peace, neither he nor any body else has any authority over any of
the society' (*Second Letter*, 1690, 1765, 107). 'Let me ask you,
Whether it be not possible that men, to whom the rivers and woods
afforded the spontaneous provisions of life, and so with no private
possessions of land, had no inlarged desires after riches or power,
should live in one society, make one people of one language under one
Chieftain, who shall have no other power to command them in time
of common war against their common enemies, without any municipal
laws, judges, or any person with superiority established amongst them,
but ended all their private differences, if any arose, by the extempory
determination of their neighbours, or of arbitrators chosen by the
parties. I ask you, whether in such a commonwealth, the Chieftain,
who was the only man of authority amongst them, had any power to
use the force of the commonwealth to any other end but the defence
of it against an enemy, though other benefits were attainable by it?'
(*Third Letter*, 1692, 1765, 171). This second passage, written in
vindication of the first, is a most interesting exposition of Locke's
views on the state of nature, or of such a state mixed with a state of
society.
§ 109 This assimilation of biblical history with the history of primitive
peoples is characteristically Lockeian; compare I, § 158, 5–8, and see
II, § 36, 9–28 and references.
4–5 '*going out and in before the People*'—a common old Testament
phrase for leading the Israelites to war; see, for example, Numbers
xxvii. 17.
7–19 'the Story of *Jephtha*'—see II, § 21, 20, with note and references.

Gileadites, in fear send to *Jephtha,* a Bastard of their
Family, whom they had cast off, and article with him,
if he will assist them against the *Ammonites,* to make 10
him their Ruler; which they do in these words, *And the
People made him head and captain over them,* Judg. 11.
11. which was, as it seems, all one as to be *Judge. And
he judged Israel,* Judg. 12. 7. that is, was their *Captain-
General, six Years.* So when *Jotham* upbraids the *Schechem-* 15
ites with the Obligation they had to *Gideon,* who had
been their *Judge* and Ruler, he tells them, *He fought for
you, and adventured his life far, and delivered you out of
the hands of Midian,* Judg. 9. 17. Nothing mentioned of
him, but what he did as a *General,* and indeed that is all 20
is found in his History, or in any of the rest of the Judges.
And *Abimelech* particularly is called *King,* though at most
he was but their *General.* And when, being weary of the
ill Conduct of *Samuel's* Sons, the Children of *Israel*
desired a King, *like all the nations to judge them, and to* 25
go out before them, and to fight their battels, 1 Sam. 8.
20. God granting their Desire, says to *Samuel, I will send
thee a Man, and thou shalt anoint him to be Captain over
my People Israel, that he may save my People out of the
hands of the Philistines,* c. 9. v. 16. As if the only *busi-* 30
ness of a *King* had been to lead out their Armies, and
fight in their Defence; and accordingly at his Inauguration,
pouring a Vial of Oyl upon him, declares to *Saul,* that
*the Lord had anointed him to be Captain over his inheri-
tance,* c. 10. v. 1. And therefore those, who after *Saul's* 35
being solemnly chosen and saluted *King* by the *Tribes* at
Mispah, were unwilling to have him their King, make no
other Objection but this, *How shall this Man save us?*
v. 27. as if they should have said, This Man is unfit to
be our *King,* not having Skill and Conduct enough in War, 40
to be able to defend us. And when God resolved to transfer the Government to *David,* it is in these Words, *But
now thy kingdom shall not continue: The Lord hath sought
him a Man after his own heart, and the Lord hath commanded him to be Captain over his People,* c. 13. v. 14. 45
As if the whole *Kingly Authority* were nothing else but
to be their *General:* And therefore the *Tribes* who had
stuck to *Saul's* Family, and opposed *David's* Reign, when
they came to *Hebron* with terms of Submission to him,
they tell him, amongst other Arguments they had to sub- 50
mit to him as to their King, That he was in effect their

*King in Saul's time, and therefore they had no reason but
to receive him as their King now. Also* (say they) *in time
past, when Saul was King over us, thou wast he that*
55 *leddest out and broughtest in Israel, and the Lord said
unto thee, thou shalt feed my People Israel, and thou shalt
be a Captain over Israel.*

110.   Thus, whether *a Family* by degrees *grew up into
a Common-wealth,* and the Fatherly Authority being continued on to the elder Son, every one in his turn growing
up under it, tacitly submitted to it, and the easiness and
5 equality of it not offending any one, every one acquiesced,
till time seemed to have confirmed it, and settled a right
of Succession by Prescription: or whether several Families,
or the Descendants of several Families, whom Chance,
Neighbourhood, or Business brought together, uniting into
10 Society, the need of a General, whose Conduct might defend them against their Enemies in War, and the great
confidence the Innocence and Sincerity of that poor but
vertuous Age (such as are almost all those which begin
Governments, that ever come to last in the World) gave
15 Men one of another, made the first Beginners of Common-wealths generally put the Rule into one Man's hand,
without any other express Limitation or Restraint, but
what the Nature of the thing, and the End of Government
required: which ever of these it was, that at first put the
20 rule into the hands of a single person, certain it is that
no body was ever intrusted with it but for the publick
Good and Safety, and to those Ends in the Infancies of
Commonwealths those who had it, commonly used it:
And unless they had done so, young Societies could not
25 have subsisted: without such nursing Fathers tender and
carefull of the publick weale, all Governments would have

53–7 II Sam. v. 2.
§ 110 18–26 Modified and partially rewritten in the Christ's copy; see
Collation. On 'nursing Fathers, and his other quasi-patriarchal statements, compare II, § 105, note and references.
    21–2 For Locke's doctrine of trust, see Introduction, 126 on, and
compare in this passage in particular the early words of his *Essay
Concerning Toleration* of 1667: 'The whole trust, power and authority
of the magistrate is vested in him for no other purpose, but to be made
use of for the good, preservation, and peace of men in that society
over which he is set, and therefore this ought to be the standard and
measure, according to which he ought to square and proportion his laws,
model and frame his government' (Fox Bourne, 1876, 1, 174).

sunk under the Weakness and Infirmities of their Infancy;
and the Prince and the People had soon perished together.

111.   But though the *Golden Age* (before vain Ambition, and *amor sceleratus habendi,* evil Concupiscence,
had corrupted Mens minds into a Mistake of true Power
and Honour) had more Virtue, and consequently better
Governours, as well as less vicious Subjects; and there 5
was then *no stretching Prerogative* on the one side to
oppress the People; *nor* consequently on the other any
Dispute about Priviledge, to lessen or restrain the Power
of the Magistrate; † and so no contest betwixt Rulers and
People about Governours or Government: Yet, when Am- 10
bition and Luxury, in future Ages would retain and increase the Power, without doing the Business, for which
it was given, and aided by Flattery, taught Princes to have
distinct and separate Interests from their People, Men
found it necessary to examine more carefully *the Original* 15
and Rights of *Government;* and to find out ways to *re-*

† *At first, when some certain kind of Regiment was once approved,
it may be nothing was then further thought upon for the manner of
governing, but all permitted unto their Wisdom and Discretion which
were to Rule, till by experience they found this for all parts very inconvenient, so as the thing which they had devised for a Remedy, did
indeed but increase the Sore which it should have cured. They saw,
that to live by one Man's Will, became the cause of all Mens misery.*
This constrained them to come unto Laws wherein all Men might see
their Duty before-hand, and know the Penalties of transgressing them.
Hooker's Eccl. Pol. I. 1. Sect. 10.

§ 111 2 The Latin tag is from Ovid, *Metamorphoses,* 1, 131. This
hint of a golden age is a highly traditional element, and is usually
assumed to be a description of Locke's state of nature; see Leslie
Stephen 1876 (1902), II, 137, followed, for example, by Strauss, 1953,
216. If this is the intention it is in sharp contrast with the Hobbesian
view of the state of nature, though, as Strauss points out, rather difficult
to reconcile with Locke's own account of the Fall, for example, I,
§§ 44, 45. Lamprecht, 1918, 127, however, takes the view that it
refers not to the state of nature but to the early, virtuous years of
established government. As always, Locke's language is inexact, but a
close and sympathetic reading of this paragraph and II, §§ 107, 110
seems to confirm this as the correct view.
 9 Reference sign for Hooker quotation inserted by editor; seee note
on II, § 74, 16. This quotation is also used to illustrate II, § 94, 28;
see note there. Its reappearance here may be due to the fact that §§ 100–
31 were added after the original composition (see note on II, § 95
(chapter VIII) and references), though it may indicate some confusion
in Locke's manuscript, or some misunderstanding by the compositor of
the 1st edition not subsequently corrected. The quotation is fairly appropriate in both places; it shows some variants from Hooker's text,
including Locke's underlining of a critical phrase, and between the two
printings of it.

strain the Exorbitances, and *prevent the Abuses* of that
Power which they having intrusted in another's hands
only for their own good, they found was made use of to
20 hurt them.

112.   Thus we may see how probable it is, that People
that were naturally free, and by their own consent either
submitted to the Government of their Father, or united
together, out of different Families to make a Government,
5 should generally put the *Rule into one Man's hands,* and
chuse to be under the Conduct of a *single Person,* without
so much as by express Conditions limiting or regulating
his Power, which they thought safe enough in his Honesty
and Prudence. Though they never dream'd of Monarchy
10 being *Jure Divino,* which we never heard of among Mankind, till it was revealed to us by the Divinity of this last
Age; nor ever allowed Paternal Power to have a right to
Dominion, or to be the Foundation of all Government.
And thus much may suffice to shew, that as far as we have
15 any light from History, we have reason to conclude, that
all peaceful beginnings of *Government* have been *laid in
the Consent of the People.* I say *peaceful,* because I shall
have occasion in another place to speak of Conquest,
which some esteem a way of beginning of Governments.
20   *The other Objection I find urged against the beginning
of Polities, in the way I have mentioned, is this, viz.*

113.   *That all Men being born under Government,
some or other, it is impossible any of them should ever
be free, and at liberty to unite together, and begin a new
one, or ever be able to erect a lawful Government.*
5   If this Argument be good; I ask, how came so many
lawful Monarchies into the World? For if any body, upon
this supposition, can shew me any one Man in any Age of
the World *free* to begin a lawful Monarchy; I will be

§ 112 9–13 The 'Divinity of this last Age' was Filmer's patriarchal
doctrine, publicly owned by the pulpit and made 'the *Currant Divinity
of the Times';* see the Preface, 43–4. It is possible that lines 9–19 here
were an addition of 1689.
   20–1 See II, § 100, 6–9: these four lines were obviously intended to
stand out of the paragraph numeration, hence the odd beginning of
§ 113.
§ 113 1–7 Compare note on II, § 100. This objection is not found
stated in such a general form by Filmer, but it is a position consistently
implied by him; see especially his *Forms* (Laslett, 1949, 185–229).

bound to shew him Ten other *free Men* at Liberty, at the
same time to unite and begin a new Government under a 10
Regal, or any other Form. It being demonstration, that
if any one, *born under the Dominion* of another, may be
so *free* as to have a right to command others in a new and
distinct Empire; every one that is *born under the Dominion* of another may be so *free* too, and may become a 15
Ruler, or Subject, of a distinct separate Government.
And so by this their own Principle, either all Men, however *born*, are *free*, or else there is but one lawful Prince,
one lawful Government in the World. And then they
have nothing to do but barely to shew us, which that is. 20
Which when they have done, I doubt not but all Mankind
will easily agree to pay Obedience to him.

114.   Though it be a sufficient Answer to their Objection to shew, that it involves them in the same difficulties
that it doth those they use it against; yet I shall endeavour
to discover the weakness of this Argument a little farther. 5
All Men, say they, *are born under Government, and
therefore they cannot be at liberty to begin a new one.
Every one is born a Subject to his Father, or his Prince,
and is therefore under the perpetual tye of Subjection and
Allegiance.* 'Tis plain Mankind never owned nor con- 10
sidered any such natural *subjection, that they were born
in*, to one or to the other, that tied them, without their
own Consents, to a Subjection to them and their Heirs.

115.   For there are no Examples so frequent in History,
both Sacred and Prophane, as those of Men withdrawing
themselves, and their Obedience, from the Jurisdiction
they were born under, and the Family or Community
they were bred up in, and *setting up new Govern-* 5
ments in other places; from whence sprang all that number of petty Common-wealths in the beginning of Ages,
and which always multiplyed, as long as there was room
enough, till the stronger, or more fortunate swallowed
the weaker; and those great ones again breaking to pieces, 10

§ 114   5–9 A paraphrase of Filmer (Laslett's edition, 232): 'Every
man that is born, is so far from being free-born, that by his very birth
he becomes a subject to him that begets him: under which subjection,
he is always to live, unless by immediate appointment from God, or
by the grant or death of his Father, he become possessed of that power
to which he was subject', ridiculed in the *First Treatise;* compare II,
§ 102, 16–17.

dissolved into lesser Dominions. All which are so many
Testimonies against Paternal Sovereignty, and plainly
prove, That it was not the natural right of the Father
descending to his Heirs, that made Governments in the
15 beginning, since it was impossible, upon that ground,
there should have been so many little Kingdoms; all must
have been but only one Universal Monarchy, if Men had
not been *at liberty to separate* themselves from their Families, and the Government, be it what it will, that was set
20 up in it, and go and make distinct Common-wealths and
other Governments, as they thought fit.

116. This has been the practice of the World from
its first beginning to this day: Nor is it now any more
hindrance to the freedom of Mankind, that they are
born under constituted and ancient Polities, that have
5 established Laws and set Forms of Government, than if
they were born in the Woods, amongst the unconfined
Inhabitants that ran loose in them. For those who would
perswade us, that *by being born under any Government,
we are naturally Subjects to it,* and have no more any
10 title or pretence to the freedom of the State of Nature,
have no other reason (bating that of Paternal Power,
which we have already answer'd) to produce for it, but
only because our Fathers or Progenitors passed away their
natural Liberty, and thereby bound up themselves and
15 their Posterity to a perpetual subjection to the Government, which they themselves submitted to. 'Tis true, that
whatever Engagements or Promises any one has made for
himself, he is under the Obligation of them, but *cannot
by any Compact whatsoever, bind his Children* or Pos-
20 terity. For this Son, when a Man, being altogether as free
as the Father, any *act of the Father can no more give
away the liberty of the Son,* than it can of any body else:
He may indeed annex such Conditions to the Land, he
enjoyed as a Subject of any Commonwealth, as may oblige
25 his Son to be of that Community, if he will enjoy those
Possessions which were his Fathers; because that Estate
being his Fathers Property, he may dispose or settle it as
he pleases.

§ 116   11–12   This parenthesis demonstrates that Locke is still arguing
against Filmer (compare § 115, 11–13): 'already answer'd' seems to
refer to the text immediately preceding, rather than to the *First
Treatise.*

117. And this has generally given the occasion to mistake in this matter; because Commonwealths not permitting any part of their Dominions to be dismembred, nor to be enjoyed by any but those of their Community, the Son cannot ordinarily enjoy the Possessions of his 5 Father, but under the same terms his Father did; by becoming a Member of the Society: whereby he puts himself presently under the Government, he finds there established, as much as any other Subject of that Commonwealth. And thus *the Consent of Free-men, born under Government,* 10 which only *makes them Members of it,* being given separately in their turns, as each comes to be of Age, and not in a multitude together; People take no notice of it, and thinking it not done at all, or not necessary, conclude they are naturally Subjects as they are Men. 15

118. But, 'tis plain, *Governments* themselves understand it otherwise; they *claim no Power over the Son, because of that they had over the Father;* nor look on Children as being their Subjects, by their Fathers being so. If a Subject of *England* have a Child by an *English* 5 Woman in *France,* whose Subject is he? Not the King of *England*'s; for he must have leave to be admitted to the Priviledges of it. Nor the King of *France*'s; For how then has his Father a liberty to bring him away, and breed him as he pleases? And who ever was judged as a *Traytor* 10 or *Deserter,* if he left, or warr'd against a Country, for being barely born in it of Parents that were Aliens there? 'Tis plain then, by the Practice of Governments themselves, as well as by the Law of right Reason, that *a Child*

§ 118 Leslie Stephen comments that this paragraph 'leads straight to anarchy', 1902, II, 140. I am indebted to Mr Parry, of Downing College, Cambridge, in the following notes.

5–6 In Locke's day, as in our own, a child of British subjects born in France was a British citizen, under the statute *De natis ultra mare* of 25 Edward III, and it was decided by a case of 1627 that either father or mother would suffice.

7–8 This does not seem to have been a general rule, but there were cases of foreign-born children of British parents being formally naturalized in the seventeenth century; see Parry, 1954.

13–15 Pollock comments that this is an 'opinion which no modern lawyer will accept, least of all a continental one', 1904, 244. Since, however, there was no right to nationality in the law of Locke's day, he is not necessarily wrong in what he says. He was strongly in favour of the naturalization of aliens on social and economic grounds; see Laslett, 1957 (i), 393.

15 *is born a Subject of no Country or Government.* He is
under his Fathers Tuition and Authority, till he come to
Age of Discretion; and then he is a Free-man, at liberty
what Government he will put himself under; what Body
Politick he will unite himself to. For if an *English-Man's*
20 Son, born in *France,* be at liberty, and may do so, 'tis
evident there is no Tye upon him by his Father being a
Subject of this Kingdom; nor is he bound up, by any
Compact of his Ancestors. And why then hath not his
Son, by the same reason, the same liberty, though he be
25 born any where else? Since the Power that a Father hath
naturally over his Children, is the same, where-ever they
be born; and the Tyes of Natural Obligations, are not
bounded by the positive Limits of Kingdoms and Common-wealths.

119.   *Every Man* being, as has been shewed, *naturally
free,* and nothing being able to put him into subjection
to any Earthly Power, but only his own Consent; it is to
be considered, what shall be understood to be *a sufficient
5 Declaration of* a Mans *Consent, to make him subject* to
the Laws of any Government. There is a common distinction of an express and a tacit consent, which will concern
our present Case. No body doubts but an *express Consent,*
of any Man, entring into any Society, makes him a perfect
10 Member of that Society, a Subject of that Government.
The difficulty is, what ought to be look'd upon as a *tacit
Consent,* and how far it binds, *i.e.* how far any one shall
be looked on to have consented, and thereby submitted
to any Government, where he has made no Expressions
15 of it at all. And to this I say, that every Man, that hath
any Possession, or Enjoyment, of any part of the Dominions of any Government, doth thereby give his *tacit
Consent,* and is as far forth obliged to Obedience to the
Laws of that Government, during such Enjoyment, as
20 any one under it; whether this his Possession be of Land,
to him and his Heirs for ever, or a Lodging only for a
Week; or whether it be barely travelling freely on the
Highway; and in Effect, it reaches as far as the very being
of any one within the Territories of that Government.

§ 119   8–10   The *Fundamental Constitutions of Carolina,* Articles 117–
18, make provision for just such an express declaration.

120. To understand this the better, it is fit to consider, that every Man, when he, at first, incorporates himself into any Commonwealth, he, by his uniting himself thereunto, annexed also, and submits to the Community those Possessions, which he has, or shall acquire, that do not 5 already belong to any other Government. For it would be a direct Contradiction, for any one, to enter into Society with others for the securing and regulating of Property: And yet to suppose his Land, whose Property is to be regulated by the Laws of the Society, should be exempt 10 from the Jurisdiction of that Government, to which he himself the Proprietor of the Land, is a Subject. By the same Act therefore, whereby any one unites his Person, which was before free, to any Commonwealth; by the same he unites his Possessions, which were before free, to it also; and they be- 15 come, both of them, Person and Possession, subject to the Government and Dominion of that Commonwealth, as long as it hath a being. *Whoever* therefore, from thenceforth, by Inheritance, Purchase, Permission, or otherways *enjoys any part of the Land*, so annext to, and under the 20 Government *of that Commonwealth, must take it with the Condition* it is under; that is, *of submitting to the Government of the Commonwealth*, under whose Jurisdiction it is, as far forth, as any Subject of it.

121. But since the Government has a direct Jurisdiction only over the Land, and reaches the Possessor of it, (before he has actually incorporated himself in the Society) only as he dwells upon, and enjoys that: *The Obligation* any one is under, by Virtue of such Enjoyment, 5 *to submit to the Government, begins and ends with the Enjoyment;* so that whenever the Owner, who has given nothing but such a *tacit Consent* to the Government, will, by Donation, Sale, or otherwise, quit the said Possession, he is at liberty to go and incorporate himself into any 10 other Commonwealth, or to agree with others to begin

§ 120 Kendall infers from this passage that society vouchsafes property to the individual. Compare II, § 139, 5–6 and statements in the works on toleration. Locke's *1st Letter* of 1689 implies that the magistrate may 'change propriety among fellow-subjects', and the *Essay* of 1667 says 'The magistrate having a power to appoint ways of transferring proprieties from one man to another, may establish any, so they be universal, equal and without violence and suited to the welfare of that society' (quoted here from the Huntington MS. The words underlined are omitted in that printed by Fox Bourne (1876, 1, 183)).

a new one, *in vacuis locis,* in any part of the World, they
can find free and unpossessed: Whereas he, that has once,
by actual Agreement, and any *express* Declaration, given
15 his *Consent* to be of any Commonweal, is perpetually and
indispensably obliged to be and remain unalterably a
Subject to it, and can never be again in the liberty of the
state of Nature; unless by any Calamity, the Government,
he was under, comes to be dissolved; or else by some
20 publick Act cuts him off from being any longer a Member of it.

122. But submitting to the Laws of any Country, living quietly, and enjoying Priviledges and Protection under
them, *makes not a Man a Member of that Society:* This
is only a local Protection and Homage due to, and from
5 all those, who, not being in a state of War, come within
the Territories belonging to any Government, to all parts
whereof the force of its Law extends. But this no more
makes a Man a Member of that Society, a perpetual Subject of that Commonwealth, than it would make a Man a
10 Subject to another in whose Family he found it convenient
to abide for some time; though, whilst he continued in it,
he were obliged to comply with the Laws, and submit to
the Government he found there. And thus we see, that
Foreigners, by living all their Lives under another Gov-
15 ernment, and enjoying the Priviledges and Protection of
it, though they are bound, even in Conscience, to submit
to its Administration, as far forth as any Denison; yet do
not thereby come to be *Subjects or Members of that
Commonwealth.* Nothing can make any Man so, but his
20 actually entering into it by positive Engagement, and
express Promise and Compact. This is that, which I think,
concerning the beginning of Political Societies, and that
Consent which makes any one a Member of any Commonwealth.

§ **121**   19–21   Final phrase added in 2nd edition, 1694; see Collation.

Of the Ends of Political Society and Government.

123. If Man in the State of Nature be so free, as has been said; If he be absolute Lord of his own Person and Possessions, equal to the greatest, and subject to no Body, why will he part with his Freedom? Why will he give up this Empire, and subject himself to the Dominion and 5 Controul of any other Power? To which 'tis obvious to Answer, that though in the state of Nature he hath such a right, yet the Enjoyment of it is very uncertain, and constantly exposed to the Invasion of others. For all being Kings as much as he, every Man his Equal, and the 10 greater part no strict Observers of Equity and Justice, the enjoyment of the property he has in this state is very unsafe, very unsecure. This makes him willing to quit a Condition, which however free, is full of fears and continual dangers: And 'tis not without reason, that he seeks 15 out, and is willing to joyn in Society with others who are already united, or have a mind to unite for the mutual *Preservation* of their Lives, Liberties and Estates, which I call by the general Name, *Property*.

124. The great and *chief end* therefore, of Mens uniting into Commonwealths, and putting themselves under Government, *is the Preservation of their Property*. To

§ **123** *Chapter IX.* There is nothing in this short chapter to connect it with what goes before, or what comes after, which seems to be a continuation of the original text from § 99—see notes on II, § 95 (chapter VIII), II, § 100 and II, § 132 (chapter X). There are no references to connect it with the critique of Filmer, though some parallels (see § 124, 9–11; § 125, 1–5; § 129, 4) with other statements in the *Second Treatise.* In form it is a short restatement of his whole position, in brief paragraphs, all leading up to a judgment on James II—see § 131. It seems, therefore, like chapter XV (see note on II, § 169) to be an insertion of 1689.

2–3 Compare II, § 6, 3–4 and Strauss, 1953, 227.

18–19 On the extended definition of property set out here, see II, § 87, 5–6 note and references. The whole paragraph should be compared and contrasted with the first paragraph of *Leviathan,* chapter 17, and with II, § 19, 4–5 and references.

§ **124** 1–3 The *locus classicus* for Locke's view of property in relation to government. Viner (see Introduction, 116) insists that property must here be taken to mean not simply material possessions, but property in the extended sense, the 'Lives, Liberties and Estates' of II, § 123, 18. In the *Epistola de Tolerantia* Locke puts the same

which in the state of Nature there are many things want-
5 ing.

First, There wants an *establish'd*, settled, known *Law*,
received and allowed by common consent to be the Standard of Right and Wrong, and the common measure to
decide all Controversies between them. For though the
10 Law of Nature be plain and intelligible to all rational
Creatures; yet Men being biassed by their Interest, as well
as ignorant for want of study of it, are not apt to allow
of it as a Law binding to them in the application of it to
their particular Cases.

125. *Secondly*, In the State of Nature there wants a
known and indifferent Judge, with Authority to determine
all differences according to the established Law. For every
one in that state being both Judge and Executioner of the
5 Law of Nature, Men being partial to themselves, Passion
and Revenge is very apt to carry them too far, and with
too much heat, in their own Cases; as well as negligence,
and unconcernedness, to make them too remiss, in other
Mens.

126. *Thirdly*, In the state of Nature there often wants
Power to back and support the Sentence when right, and
to *give* it due *Execution*. They who by any Injustice offended, will seldom fail, where they are able, by force

---

point somewhat differently, with material possessions more to the fore-
front: 'But the pravity of mankind being such that they had rather
injuriously prey upon the fruits of another mans labours (lieno labore
partis frui) than take pains to provide for themselves, the necessity
of preserving men in the possession of what honest industry has
already acquired, and also of preserving their liberty and strength,
whereby they may acquire what they further want, obliges men to enter
into society one with another (ideo homini parta, ut opes et facultates; vel
ea quibus parantur, ut corporis libertatem et robur, tuendi gratia,
ineunda est cum aliis societas) that by mutual assistance and joint
force they may secure unto each other their properties, in the things
that contribute to the comfort and happiness of this life (ut mutuo
auxilio et junctis viribus harum rerum ad vitam utilium sua cuique
privata et secura sit possessio)' (1765, 21, 56–7). Compare Macpherson, 1951, 551.
    9–11 Compare II, § 12, 12–14.
§ 125 1–3 Compare II, § 136, 9–10.
    3–5 Compare II, § 7.
    5–6 The mention of 'Passion' recalls Hobbes, *Leviathan*, chapter
17 (1904, 115, etc.), and the insistence on partiality recalls Hooker
(1836, I, 305, compare II, § 91 and *English Tract* of 1660, 10). It is
not demonstrable that Locke had either writer in mind.

to make good their Injustice: such resistance many times 5
makes the punishment dangerous, and frequently destructive, to those who attempt it.

127. Thus Mankind, notwithstanding all the Priviledges of the state of Nature, being but in an ill condition, while they remain in it, are quickly driven into
Society. Hence it comes to pass, that we seldom find any
number of Men live any time together in this State. The 5
inconveniencies, that they are therein exposed to, by the
irregular and uncertain exercise of the Power every Man
has of punishing the transgressions of others, make them
take Sanctuary under the establish'd Laws of Government,
and therein seek *the preservation of their Property*. 'Tis 10
this makes them so willingly give up every one his single
power of punishing to be exercised by such alone as shall
be appointed to it amongst them; and by such Rules as
the Community, or those authorised by them to that purpose, shall agree on. And in this we have the original 15
right and rise of both *the Legislative and Executive Power*,
as well as of the Governments and Societies themselves.

128. For in the State of Nature, to omit the liberty he
has of innocent Delights, a Man has two Powers.
The first is to do whatsoever he thinks fit for the preservation of himself and others within the permission of the
Law of Nature: by which Law common to them all, he 5
and all the rest of *Mankind are one Community*, make up
one Society distinct from all other Creatures. And were
it not for the corruption, and vitiousness of degenerate
Men, there would be no need of any other; no necessity
that Men should separate from this great and natural 10
Community, and by positive agreements combine into
smaller and divided associations.
The other power a Man has in the State of Nature, is
the *power to punish the Crimes* committed against that
Law. Both these he gives up, when he joyns in a private, 15
if I may so call it, or particular Political Society, and incorporates into any Commonwealth, separate from the rest
of Mankind.

129. The first *Power, viz. of doing whatsoever he
thought fit for the Preservation of himself,* and the rest of

§ **127**   11   'Single'—i.e. 'individual', not 'only'; see Kendall, 1941, 103.

Mankind, *he gives up* to be regulated by Laws made by the Society, so far forth as the preservation of himself, and the rest of that Society shall require; which Laws of the Society in many things confine the liberty he had by the Law of Nature.

130. *Secondly,* the *Power of punishing* he wholly *gives up,* and engages his natural force, (which he might before imploy in the Execution of the Law of Nature, by his own single Authority, as he thought fit) to assist the Executive Power of the Society, as the Law thereof shall require. For being now in a new State, wherein he is to enjoy many Conveniencies, from the labour, assistance, and society of others in the same Community, as well as protection from its whole strength; he is to part also with as much of his natural liberty in providing for himself, as the good, prosperity, and safety of the Society shall require: which is not only necessary, but just; since the other Members of the Society do the like.

131. But though Men when they enter into Society, give up the Equality, Liberty, and Executive Power they had in the State of Nature, into the hands of the Society, to be so far disposed of by the Legislative, as the good of the Society shall require; yet it being only with an intention in every one the better to preserve himself his Liberty and Property; (For no rational Creature can be supposed to change his condition with an intention to be worse) the power of the Society, or *Legislative* constituted by them, *can never be suppos'd to extend farther than the common good;* but is obliged to secure every ones Property by providing against those three defects above-mentioned, that made the State of Nature so unsafe and uneasie. And

§ 129   4 This limitation is elaborated in II, § 149, especially lines 25–8.

3, 6 Elrington, 1798, comments here that a man is bound to give up this power: he is compelled by the law of nature itself to quit the state of nature, and he can lose no liberty by it, since this would imply that civil law was distinct from natural law.

§ 131 13–23 These statements, especially lines 13–16, seem likely to be a reference to the actions of James II and the view he took of his position, for they are less appropriate than his other political judgments to the actions of Charles II. This may mark this paragraph, and indeed the whole chapter, as an insertion of 1689; see note on II, § 123, chapter IX, and compare Abram's note on *English Tract* of 1660, p. 19.

so whoever has the Legislative or Supream Power of any
Common-wealth, is bound to govern by establish'd *stand-* 15
ing Laws, promulgated and known to the People, and not
by Extemporary Decrees; by *indifferent* and upright *Judges*,
who are to decide Controversies by those Laws; And to
imploy the force of the Community at home, *only in the
Execution of such Laws*, or abroad to prevent or redress 20
Foreign Injuries, and secure the Community from Inroads
and Invasion. And all this to be directed to no other *end*,
but the *Peace, Safety*, and *publick good* of the People.

CHAP. X.

Of the Forms of a Common-wealth.

132. The Majority having, as has been shew'd, upon
Mens first uniting into Society, the whole power of the
Community, naturally in them, may imploy all that power
in making Laws for the Community from time to time,
and Executing those Laws by Officers of their own ap- 5
pointing; and then the *Form* of the Government is a perfect *Democracy:* Or else may put the power of making
Laws into the hands of a few select Men, and their Heirs
or Successors; and then it is an *Oligarchy:* Or else into
the hands of one Man, and then it is a *Monarchy:* If to 10
him and his Heirs, it is an *Hereditary Monarchy:* If to
him only for Life, but upon his Death the Power only
of nominating a Successor to return to them; an *Elective*

§ **132** *Chapter* X This can be dated before 1685 (see note on § 133,
12), and since it follows on from § 99, which can be concluded from
the words of its first line, is presumably the continuation and completion of chapter VIII (see notes on §§ 77, 100), written as part of
the original critique of Filmer.

Monarchy. And so accordingly of these the Community
15 may make compounded and mixed Forms of Government,
as they think good. And if the Legislative Power be at
first given by the Majority to one or more Persons only
for their Lives, or any limited time, and then the Supream
Power to revert to them again; when it is so reverted, the
20 Community may dispose of it again anew into what hands
they please, and so constitute a new Form of Government.
For the *Form of Government depending upon the placing*
the Supreme Power, which is the *Legislative,* it being impossible to conceive that an inferiour Power should pre-
25 scribe to a Superiour, or any but the Supreme make Laws,
according as the Power of making Laws is placed, such
is *the Form of the Common-wealth.*

133. By *Common-wealth,* I must be understood all
along to mean, not a Democracy, or any Form of Government, but *any Independent Community* which the *Latines*
signified by the word *Civitas,* to which the word which
5 best answers in our Language, is *Commonwealth,* and most
properly expresses such a Society of Men, which Community or Citty in *English* does not, for there may be
Subordinate Communities in a Government; and City
amongst us has a quite different notion from Common-
10 wealth: And therefore to avoid ambiguity, I crave leave
to use the word *Commonwealth* in that sense, in which I
find it used by King *James the First,* and I take it to be
its genuine signification; which if any Body dislike, I consent with him to change it for a better.

14–27 These statements are point-blank denials of what Filmer had
said, and of what Hobbes had said also (*Leviathan,* chapter 19). They
blandly ignore Filmer's acute critique of mixed government in his
Anarchy of a Limited or Mixed Monarchy (Laslett's edition, 277–313),
though Locke shared with Filmer the traditional analysis of sovereignty;
compare note on I, § 129, 12–18 and references.
22–7 Compare II, § 150.
§ 133 3–4 Compare 'that great LEVIATHAN called a COMMON-WEALTH
OR STATE (in latine CIVITAS)' (1904, XVIII), perhaps a re-echo, perhaps
a coincidence; see II, § 212 and note.
12 'King *James the First*'—1st edition, 'by K. *James* himself',
changed in 1694. This is a striking indication that he wrote this passage
before the accession of James II in 1685, see Introduction, 67–8, compare a second instance in II, § 200, 3–4, and 'either of our Queens' in I,
§ 47, 29–30. Locke is probably referring to the speeches of 1603 and 1609
quoted in II, § 200, for 'Commonwealth' occurs in both (II, § 200, 6
and 37–8). He quotes a maxim of 'King James', i.e. James I, in a letter
of 17 March 1684 (Rand, 1927, 107).

Of the Extent of the Legislative Power.

134. The great end of Mens entring into Society, being
the enjoyment of their Properties in Peace and Safety, and
the great instrument and means of that being the Laws
establish'd in that Society; the *first and fundamental posi-*
tive Law of all Commonwealths, *is the establishing of the* 5
Legislative Power; as the *first and fundamental natural*
Law, which is to govern even the Legislative it self, is *the*
preservation of the Society, and (as far as will consist
with the publick good) of every person in it. This *Legis-*
lative is not only *the supream power* of the Common- 10
wealth, but sacred and unalterable in the hands where the
Community have once placed it; nor can any Edict of
any Body else, in what Form soever conceived, or by what
Power soever backed, have the force and obligation of a
Law, which has not its *Sanction from* that *Legislative,* 15
which the publick has chosen and appointed. For without
this the Law could not have that, which is absolutely
necessary to its being a *Law, the consent of the Society,*
over whom no Body can have a power to make Laws, but
by their own consent, † and by Authority received from 20

† *The lawful Power of making Laws to Command whole Politick So-*
cieties of Men belonging so properly unto the same intire Societies, that
for any Prince or Potentate of what kind soever upon Earth, to exercise
the same of himself, and not by express Commission immediately and
personally received from God, or else by Authority derived at the first
from their consent, upon whose persons they impose Laws, it is no better
than meer Tyranny. Laws they are not therefore which publick Appro-
bation hath not made so. Hooker's Eccl. Pol. I. 1. Sect. 10. *Of this point*
therefore we are to note, that sith Men naturally have no full and per-
fect Power to Command whole Politick Multitudes of Men, therefore
utterly without our Consent, we could in such sort be at no Mans Com-
mandment living. And to be commanded we do consent when that
Society, whereof we be a part, hath at any time before consented, with-
out revoking the same after by the like universal agreement.
Laws therefore humane, of what kind soever, are available by consent.
Ibid.

§ 134 *Chapter XI* There is no obvious internal evidence to date the
composition of this chapter. It is far less clearly connected with the
polemic against Filmer than other parts of the text, but its statements
are consistent with the attitude Locke takes up in that controversy and it
is probably best regarded as part of the first form of the text, before
1681. There is nothing whatever to indicate that any part of it was an
addition of 1689.

1–12 Compare the very similar passage in Locke's *Epistola de*

them; and therefore all the *Obedience,* which by the most
solemn Ties any one can be obliged to pay, ultimately
terminates in this *Supream Power,* and is directed by those
Laws which it enacts: nor can any Oaths to any Foreign
25 Power whatsoever, or any Domestick Subordinate Power,
discharge any Member of the Society from his *Obedience
to the Legislative,* acting pursuant to their trust, nor oblige
him to any Obedience contrary to the Laws so enacted,
or farther than they do allow; it being ridiculous to im-
30 agine one can be tied ultimately to *obey* any *Power* in
the Society, which is not *the Supream.*

135. Though the *Legislative,* whether placed in one or
more, whether it be always in being, or only by intervals,
tho' it be the *Supream* Power in every Common-wealth;
yet,
5 *First,* It is *not,* nor can possibly be absolutely *Arbitrary*
over the Lives and Fortunes of the People. For it being
but the joynt power of every Member of the Society given
up to that Person, or Assembly, which is Legislator, it
can be no more than those persons had in a State of
10 Nature before they enter'd into Society, and gave up to
the Community. For no Body can transfer to another
more power than he has in himself; and no Body has an
absolute Arbitrary Power over himself, or over any other,
to destroy his own Life, or take away the Life or Property
15 of another. A Man, as has been proved, cannot subject
himself to the Arbitrary Power of another; and having
in the State of Nature no Arbitrary Power over the Life,

Tolerantia, 1689, translated thus by Popple in the *Letter concerning
Toleration* (1765, 21, 57). 'This is the original, this is the use, and these
are the bounds of the legislative, which is the supreme power in every
commonwealth. I mean, that provision may be made for the security of
each man's private possessions; for the peace, riches, and public commodities of the whole people; and, as much as possible, for the increase
of their inward strength, against foreign enemies.' On the priority of the
legislative, compare II, § 212, especially lines 17–19: in the Latin
treatise on the civil magistrate (1661) Locke insists that the supreme
power is always in the legislative, see page 12.
20 Reference sign for Hooker quotations inserted by editor; see
note on II, § 74, 16. Passages in Keble, 1836, II, 307–8, Locke's 1676
edition, 87–8, fairly exactly quoted. Molyneux (1698) cites the first part
of this passage to exactly the same effect as Locke.
§ 135 13–15 Compare II, § 6, 26–8; the two paragraphs are quite
close in sentiment and expression.

Liberty, or Possession of another, but only so much as
the Law of Nature gave him for the preservation of himself, and the rest of Mankind; this is all he doth, or can 20
give up to the Common-wealth, and by it to the *Legislative
Power,* so that the Legislative can have no more than
this. Their Power in the utmost Bounds of it, is *limited
to the publick good* of the Society. It is a Power, that
hath no other end but preservation, and therefore can 25
never have a right to destroy, enslave, or designedly to
impoverish the Subjects. † The Obligations of the Law of
Nature, cease not in Society but only in many Cases are
drawn closer, and have by Humane Laws known Penalties
annexed to them, to inforce their observation. Thus the 30
Law of Nature stands as an Eternal Rule to all Men,
Legislators as well as others. The *Rules* that they make
for other Mens Actions, must, as well as their own and
other Mens Actions, be conformable to the Law of Nature, *i.e.* to the Will of God, of which that is a Declara- 35
tion, and the *fundamental Law of Nature* being *the preservation of Mankind,* no Humane Sanction can be good,
or valid against it.

† *Two Foundations there are which bear up publick Societies, the one
a natural inclination, whereby all Men desire sociable Life and Fellowship; the other an Order, expressly or secretly agreed upon, touching
the manner of their union in living together; the latter is that which
we call the Law of a Common-weal, the very Soul of a Politick Body,
the parts whereof are by Law animated, held together, and set on work
in such actions as the common good requireth. Laws politick, ordain'd
for external order and regiment amongst Men, are never framed as they
should be, unless presuming the will of Man to be inwardly obstinate,
rebellious, and averse from all Obedience to the sacred Laws of his
Nature; in a word, unless presuming Man to be in regard of his de-
praved Mind, little better than a wild Beast, they do accordingly provide
notwithstanding, so to frame his outward Actions, that they be no hindrance unto the common good, for which Societies are instituted. Unless they do this they are not perfect.* Hooker's Eccl. Pol. I. 1. Sect. 10.

20–7   Compare *Third Letter on Toleration* (1692), 1765, 164: 'The
power that is in the civil sovereign is the force of all the subjects of the
commonwealth, which supposing it sufficient for other ends, than the
preserving the members of the commonwealth in peace from injury and
violence: yet if those who gave him that power, limited the application
of it to that sole end, no opinion of any other benefits attainable by it
can authorize him to use it otherwise.'

27   Reference sign for Hooker quotation inserted by editor; see
note on II, § 74, 16. See Keble's *Hooker,* 1836, 1, 299, Locke's 1676
edition, 85, coming just after the passage quoted in II, § 15, 4–15, and
fairly exactly transcribed.

27–30   Compare II, § 12, 18–22 and references.

136. *Secondly*, The *Legislative*, or Supream Authority, cannot assume to its self a power to Rule by extemporary Arbitrary Decrees, † but *is bound to dispense
Justice*, and decide the Rights of the Subject *by promul-
5 gated standing Laws, and known Authoris'd Judges*. For
the Law of Nature being unwritten, and so no where to
be found but in the minds of Men, they who through
Passion or Interest shall mis-cite, or misapply it, cannot
so easily be convinced of their mistake where there is no
10 establish'd Judge: And so it serves not, as it ought, to
determine the Rights, and fence the Properties of those
that live under it, especially where every one is Judge,
Interpreter, and Executioner of it too, and that in his own
Case: And he that has right on his side, having ordinarily
15 but his own single strength, hath not force enough to
defend himself from Injuries, or to punish Delinquents.
To avoid these Inconveniencies which disorder Mens
Properties in the state of Nature, Men unite into Societies,
that they may have the united strength of the whole
20 Society to secure and defend their Properties, and may
have *standing Rules* to bound it, by which every one may
know what is his. To this end it is that Men give up all
their Natural Power to the Society which they enter into,
and the Community put the Legislative Power into such

---

† *Humane Laws are measures in respect of Men, whose actions they
must direct, howbeit such measures they are as have also their higher
Rules to be measured by, which Rules are two, the Law of God, and
the Law of Nature; so that Laws Humane must be made according to
the general Laws of Nature, and without contradiction to any positive
Law of Scripture, otherwise they are ill made.* Ibid. 1. 3. Sect. 9.

To constrain Men to any thing inconvenient doth seem unreasonable.
Ibid. l. I. Sect. 10.

§ **136**   3   Reference sign for Hooker quotations inserted by editor; see
note on II, § 74, 16. The first passage is found in vol. I, p. 483 of Keble's
Hooker and p. 142 of Locke's 1676 edition. It is the only reference to
any book of the *Ecclesiastical Polity* other than the 1st and the Preface:
it is one of the few indications in any Locke context which shows that
he ever got further than the 1st Book—see Introduction, 70. It is the
more remarkable, then, that the passage is acknowledged by Hooker to
be a quotation from Aquinas, *Summa Theologiae*, I, ii, 95, Conclusio
(1624, 624B) Quaest. 95 Art. 3, where these words are found: 'Lex
autem humana . . . est quaedam regula vel mensura regulata vel men-
surata quaedam superiori mensura; quae quidem est duplex, scilicet
divina lex, et lex naturae.' The second passage comes from Keble, I,
306, and 1676, 87: both are quoted with insignificant variations.

5–8   Compare II, § 124, 9–14.
9–10   Compare II, § 125, 1–3: Locke is here recapitulating what he
had written there.

hands as they think fit, with this trust, that they shall be 25
govern'd by *declared Laws,* or else their Peace, Quiet,
and Property will still be at the same uncertainty, as it
was in the state of Nature.

137. Absolute Arbitrary Power, or Governing without
settled standing Laws, can neither of them consist with
the ends of Society and Government, which Men would
not quit the freedom of the state of Nature for, and tie
themselves up under, were it not to preserve their Lives, 5
Liberties and Fortunes; and by *stated Rules* of Right and
Property to secure their Peace and Quiet. It cannot be
supposed that they should intend, had they a power so
to do, to give to any one, or more, an *absolute Arbitrary
Power* over their Persons and Estates, and put a force 10
into the Magistrates hand to execute his unlimited Will
arbitrarily upon them: This were to put themselves into a
worse condition than the state of Nature, wherein they
had a Liberty to defend their Right against the Injuries
of others, and were upon equal terms of force to maintain 15
it, whether invaded by a single Man, or many in Combination. Whereas by supposing they have given up themselves
to the *absolute Arbitrary Power* and will of a Legislator,
they have disarmed themselves, and armed him, to make
a prey of them when he pleases. He being in a much worse 20
condition who is exposed to the Arbitrary Power of one
Man, who has the Command of 100000. than he that is
expos'd to the Arbitrary Power of 100000. single Men: no
Body being secure, that his Will, who has such a Command, is better, than that of other Men, though his Force 25
be 100000. times stronger. And therefore whatever Form
the Common-wealth is under, the Ruling Power ought to
govern by *declared* and *received Laws,* and not by extemporary Dictates and undetermined Resolutions. For then
Mankind will be in a far worse condition, than in the 30
State of Nature, if they shall have armed one or a few
Men with the joynt power of a Multitude, to force them
to obey at pleasure the exorbitant and unlimited Decrees

§ 137 This argument is irrelevant to Filmer, since he had denied the
possibility of a state of nature, though Locke consistently overlooks this
position, one of the strong points of patriarchalism. It is, however, relevant to Hobbes, and even recalls Filmer's own criticisms of Hobbes,
239–50, though not exactly tied to any Hobbesian proposition. This is
typical of the Hobbes/Locke relationship—see Introduction, 80–92.

of their sudden thoughts, or unrestrain'd, and till that
35 moment unknown Wills without having any measures set
down which may guide and justifie their actions. For all
the power the Government has, being only for the good
of the Society, as it ought not to be *Arbitrary* and at
Pleasure, so it ought to be exercised by *established and*
40 *promulgated Laws:* that both the People may know their
Duty, and be safe and secure within the limits of the
Law, and the Rulers too kept within their due bounds, and
not to be tempted, by the Power they have in their hands,
to imploy it to such purposes, and by such measures, as
45 they would not have known, and own not willingly.

138. *Thirdly,* The *Supream Power cannot take* from
any Man any part of his *Property* without his own consent.
For the preservation of Property being the end of Government, and that for which Men enter into Society, it neces-
5 sarily supposes and requires, that the People should *have*
Property, without which they must be suppos'd to lose that
by entring into Society, which was the end for which they
entered into it, too gross an absurdity for any Man to own.
Men therefore *in Society having Property,* they have such
10 a right to the goods, which by the Law of the Community
are theirs, that no Body hath a right to take their substance,
or any part of it from them, without their own consent;
without this, they have no *Property* at all. For I have
truly no *Property* in that, which another can by right take
15 from me, when he pleases, against my consent. Hence it
is a mistake to think, that the Supream or *Legislative*
Power of any Commonwealth, can do what it will, and
dispose of the Estates of the Subject *arbitrarily,* or take

§ **138** 1–2 Elrington, 1798, notes here the duty of each individual to
pay taxes.
5–8 Compare *Jura Populi Anglicani*, 1701, 30: 'The supreme Power
cannot take from any man any part of his Property without his own
consent' . . . (as a Very Learned and Ingenious Author tells us)', with
a footnote to 'The Author of two Treatises of Government, pag. 277'.
This is presumably a slip for p. 274 of the 1694 or 1698 printing, where
this paragraph appears. The author of the tract is generally recognized
as Lord Somers, Locke's close friend and patron, and it is very Lockeian
in tone, and even more forthright about property and consent, since
Locke leaves it possible to suppose that consent is collective, not individual.
14–19 Contrast Hobbes: '*Mine,* and *Thine* and *His;* that is to say,
in one word *Propriety;* . . . belongeth in all kinds of Common-wealth
to the Soveraign Power', *Leviathan*, 1904, 176, compare 240.

any part of them at pleasure. This is not much to be fear'd
in Governments where the *Legislative* consists, wholly or
in part, in Assemblies which are variable, whose Members
upon the Dissolution of the Assembly, are Subjects under
the common Laws of their Country, equally with the rest.
But in Governments, where the *Legislative* is in one lasting
Assembly always in being, or in one Man, as in Absolute
Monarchies, there is danger still, that they will think
themselves to have a distinct interest, from the rest of the
Community; and so will be apt to increase their own
Riches and Power, by taking, what they think fit, from the
People. For a Man's *Property* is not at all secure, though
there be good and equitable Laws to set the bounds of it,
between him and his Fellow Subjects, if he who commands
those Subjects, have Power to take from any private Man,
what part he pleases of his *Property*, and use and dispose
of it as he thinks good.

139.   But *Government* into whatsoever hands it is put,
being as I have before shew'd, intrusted with this condition,
and *for this end*, that Men might have and secure *their*
Properties, the Prince or Senate, however it may have
power to make Laws for the regulating of *Property* between
the Subjects one amongst another, yet can never have a
Power to take to themselves the whole or any part of the
Subjects *Property*, without their own consent. For this
would be in effect to leave them no *Property* at all. And to
let us see, that even *absolute Power*, where it is necessary,
is *not Arbitrary* by being absolute, but is still limited by
that reason, and confined to those ends, which required it
in some Cases to be absolute, we need look no farther than
the common practice of Martial Discipline. For the
Preservation of the Army, and in it of the whole Commonwealth, requires an *absolute Obedience* to the Command
of every Superior Officer, and it is justly Death to disobey
or dispute the most dangerous or unreasonable of them:
but yet we see, that neither the Serjeant, that could command a Souldier to march up to the mouth of a Cannon,
or stand in a Breach, where he is almost sure to perish,
can command that Soldier to give him one penny of his
Money; nor the *General*, that can condemn him to Death

§ **138** 19–23 The government of England is obviously meant; compare II, § 143.
    24–8 Compare II, §§ 143, 6–16; 163, 15–19; 164, 17–18.

for deserting his Post, or for not obeying the most des-
25 perate Orders, can yet with all his absolute Power of Life
and Death, dispose of one Farthing of that Soldiers
Estate, or seize one jot of his Goods; whom yet he can
command any thing, and hang for the least Disobedience.
Because such a blind Obedience is necessary to that end
30 for which the Commander has his Power, *viz.* the preservation of the rest; but the disposing of his Goods has nothing
to do with it.

140. 'Tis true, Governments cannot be supported without great Charge, and 'tis fit every one who enjoys his
share of the Protection, should pay out of his Estate his
proportion for the maintenance of it. But still it must be
5 with his own Consent, *i.e.* the Consent of the Majority,
giving it either by themselves, or their Representatives
chosen by them. For if any one shall claim a *Power to
lay* and levy *Taxes* on the People, by his own Authority,
and without such consent of the People, he thereby invades
10 the *Fundamental Law of Property*, and subverts the end
of Government. For what property have I in that which
another may by right take, when he pleases to himself?

141. *Fourthly*, The *Legislative cannot transfer the
Power of Making Laws* to any other hands. For it being
but a delegated Power from the People, they, who have it,
cannot pass it over to others. The People alone can appoint
5 the Form of the Commonwealth, which is by Constituting
the Legislative, and appointing in whose hands that shall
be. And when the People have said, We will submit to
rules, and be govern'd by *Laws* made by such Men, and in
such Forms, no Body else can say other Men shall make
10 *Laws* for them; nor can the people be bound by any *Laws*
but such as are Enacted by those, whom they have Chosen,
and Authorised to make *Laws* for them. The power of

§ 140 3–7 Here Locke's individual doctrine of property and his assumption about majorities and representation are joined with traditional
English constitutionalism. Elrington, 1798, characteristically comments
that 'only part of the citizens' should have a right to taxation by consent, so that 'the property of individuals may be more secure'. Compare note on II, § 158, 5.
§ 141 12–18 Added in the 2nd printing, 1694, see Collation: Locke
altered words in the earlier part of the paragraph after 1698. Compare
I, §§ 25, 3–4; 85, 20–1: Pareyson, 1948, comments that Locke's view
recalls the medieval theory of *concessio*.

the *Legislative* being derived from the People by a positive voluntary Grant and Institution, can be no other, than what that positive Grant conveyed, which being only to 15 make *Laws*, and not to make *Legislators*, the *Legislative* can have no power to transfer their Authority of making Laws, and place it in other hands.

142.   These are the *Bounds* which the trust that is put in them by the Society, and the Law of God and Nature, have *set to the Legislative* Power of every Commonwealth, in all Forms of Government.

First, They are to govern by *promulgated establish'd* 5 *Laws*, not to be varied in particular Cases, but to have one Rule for Rich and Poor, for the Favourite at Court, and the Country Man at Plough.

Secondly, These *Laws* also ought to be designed *for* no other end ultimately but *the good of the People*.   10

Thirdly, they must *not raise Taxes* on the Property of the People, *without the Consent of the People*, given by themselves, or their Deputies. And this properly concerns only such Governments where the *Legislative* is always in being, or at least where the People have not reserv'd any 15 part of the Legislative to Deputies, to be from time to time chosen by themselves.

Fourthly, The *Legislative* neither must *nor can transfer the Power of making Laws* to any Body else, or place it any where but where the People have.   20

CHAP. XII.

Of the Legislative, Executive, and Federative Power of the Commonwealth.

143.   The *Legislative* Power is that which has a right *to direct* how *the Force of the Commonwealth* shall be im-

§ **143**   *Chapter* XII   Though, as in the case of chapter XI (see note on II, § 134) there is nothing in the text to date the composition of this chapter, it is probably best regarded as part of the original text, before 1681. The separation of powers is hinted at several times

ploy'd for preserving the Community and the Members
of it. But because those Laws which are constantly to be
5 Executed, and whose force is always to continue, may be
made in a little time; therefore there is no need, that the
Legislative should be always in being, not having always
business to do. And because it may be too great a temptation to humane frailty apt to grasp at Power, for the same
10 Persons who have the Power of making Laws, to have also
in their hands the power to execute them, whereby they
may exempt themselves from Obedience to the Laws they
make, and suit the Law, both in its making and execution,
to their own private advantage, and thereby come to have
15 a distinct interest from the rest of the Community, contrary
to the end of Society and Government: Therefore in well
order'd Commonwealths, where the good of the whole
is so considered, as it ought, the *Legislative* Power is put
into the hands of divers Persons who duly Assembled,
20 have by themselves, or jointly with others, a Power to make
Laws, which when they have done, being separated again,
they are themselves subject to the Laws, they have made;
which is a new and near tie upon them, to take care,
that they make them for the publick good.

144.   But because the Laws, that are at once, and in a
short time made, have a constant and lasting force, and
need a *perpetual Execution*, or an attendance thereunto:
Therefore 'tis necessary there should be a *Power always*
5 *in being*, which should see to the *Execution* of the Laws
that are made, and remain in force. And thus the *Legislative* and *Executive Power* come often to be separated.

145.   There is another *Power* in every Commonwealth,
which one may call *natural*, because it is that which
answers to the Power every Man naturally had before he
entred into Society. For though in a Commonwealth

---

elsewhere, in II, § 91, in II, § 107 where it is part of the anti-
patriarchal argument, and II, § 127: the logical position indicating the
existence of a Federative Power is established in II, § 14. There is no
indication of an insertion or revision in 1689, and so no textual grounds
for supposing that it is historically related to William III's constitutional
position in respect of foreign policy.
16–22 The constitutional arrangements of England are those of the
'well order'd Commonwealth' Locke has in mind; compare II, §§ 138,
19–23; 167; 213.
§ 144   4–6   Compare II, § 153, 3–5.

the Members of it are distinct Persons still in reference 5
to one another, and as such are governed by the Laws of
the Society; yet in reference to the rest of Mankind,
they make one Body, which is, as every Member of it before
was, still in the State of Nature with the rest of Mankind.
Hence it is, that the Controversies that happen between 10
any Man of the Society with those that are out of it, are
managed by the publick; and an injury done to a Member
of their Body, engages the whole in the reparation of it.
So that under this Consideration, the whole Community
is one Body in the State of Nature, in respect of all other 15
States or Persons out of its Community.

146. This therefore contains the Power of War and
Peace, Leagues and Alliances, and all the Transactions,
with all Persons and Communities without the Common-
wealth, and may be called *Federative*, if any one pleases.
So the thing be understood, I am indifferent as to the 5
Name.

147. These two Powers, *Executive* and *Federative*,
though they be really distinct in themselves, yet one
comprehending the *Execution* of the Municipal Laws of
the Society *within* its self, upon all that are parts of it; the
other the management of the *security and interest of the* 5
publick without, with all those that it may receive benefit or
damage from, yet they are always almost united. And though
this *federative Power* in the well or ill management of it be
of great moment to the commonwealth, yet it is much less
capable to be directed by antecedent, standing, positive 10
Laws, than the *Executive;* and so must necessarily be left
to the Prudence and Wisdom of those whose hands it is in,
to be managed for the publick good. For the *Laws* that
concern Subjects one amongst another, being to direct

§ 145 7–9 Compare II, § 14; § 183, 8–9.
§ 146 On the federative power, see Introduction, 132, note 37 and references. Lawson, *Politica Sacra* (1660), 1689, 63, recognizes something of
this nature and has been supposed to be Locke's source. But in general
his doctrine of the separation of powers is quite different from Locke's,
and rather more specific. He bases it on Scripture (*Examination of
Hobbes,* 1657, 56), and recognizes the three powers now regarded as
usual: legislative, judicial and executive; see 1689, 72, 93, 97, etc.;
1657, 8. He is interested, perhaps, more in the gradation and nature,
than the independence of these powers, though like Locke and everyone
else he insisted on the independence of the judiciary.

15 their actions, may well enough *precede* them. But what
is to be done in reference to *Foreigners,* depending much
upon their actions, and the variation of designs and
interests, must be *left* in great part *to* the *Prudence* of those
who have this Power committed to them, to be managed
20 by the best of their Skill, for the advantage of the Commonwealth.

148.   Though, as I said, the *Executive* and *Federative*
Power of every Community be really distinct in themselves,
yet they are hardly to be separated, and placed, at the
same time, in the hands of distinct Persons. For both of
5 them requiring the force of the Society for their exercise,
it is almost impracticable to place the Force of the Commonwealth in distinct, and not subordinate hands; or that
the *Executive* and *Federative Power* should be *placed*
in Persons that might act separately, whereby the Force of
10 the Publick would be under different Commands: which
would be apt sometime or other to cause disorder and
ruine.

CHAP. XIII.

Of the Subordination of the Powers of the Commonwealth.

149.   Though in a Constituted Commonwealth, standing
upon its own Basis, and acting according to its own Nature,
that is, acting for the preservation of the Community,
there can be but *one Supream Power,* which is *the Legis-*

§ 149   *Chapter* XIII   In the view of the editor, this chapter was part
of the first version, but belongs to 1680–1 rather than to 1679. It is
relevant to the Filmer controversy, but rather more to the political programme and activities of Shaftesbury. It is concerned with the election,
summoning, prorogation and dissolution of parliament and ends with
a plea for parliamentary reform, all subjects of great importance to
Shaftesbury and his Whigs, especially in 1680 and 1681; see notes on
§§ 156, 157. Some of the remarks may conceivably have been added in
1689 as a reference to James II, but in general it seems to be a call to
constitutional, even revolutionary change made in defiance of Charles II.

4–5   The supremacy of the legislative is a characteristic of Locke's
theory and so typical of the body of thought which he represented that
it seems unnecessary to look for a source of this concept in Lawson
(e.g. 1657, 30) as Maclean wishes to do (1947, 70).

lative, to which all the rest are and must be subordinate, 5
yet the Legislative being only a Fiduciary Power to act for
certain ends, there remains still *in the People a Supream
Power* to remove or *alter the Legislative,* when they find
the *Legislative* act contrary to the trust reposed in them.
For all *Power given with trust* for the attaining an *end,* 10
being limited by that end, whenever that *end* is manifestly
neglected, or opposed, the *trust* must necessarily be *forfeited,* and the Power devolve into the hands of those that
gave it, who may place it anew where they shall think best
for their safety and security. And thus the *Community* 15
perpetually *retains a Supream Power* of saving themselves
from the attempts and designs of any Body, even of their
Legislators, whenever they shall be so foolish, or so wicked,
as to lay and carry on designs against the Liberties and
Properties of the Subject. For no Man, or Society of Men, 20
having a Power to deliver up their *Preservation,* or consequently the means of it, to the Absolute Will and
arbitrary Dominion of another; whenever any one shall
go about to bring them into such a Slavish Condition, they
will always have a right to preserve what they have not 25
a Power to part with; and to rid themselves of those who
invade this Fundamental, Sacred, and unalterable Law of
Self-Preservation, for which they enter'd into Society.
And thus the *Community* may be said in this respect to be
always the Supream Power, but not as considered under 30
any Form of Government, because this Power of the
People can never take place till the Government be dissolved.

150. In all Cases, whilst the Government subsists, the
Legislative is the Supream Power. For what can give Laws
to another, must needs be superiour to him: and since the

6–9   These phrases, and the whole doctrine of the paragraph, provide
a sharp contrast with Hobbes, *Leviathan,* chapter 18, revealing a systematic difference. It is difficult to believe that Locke had Hobbes in
mind when he wrote it.

7–8   The apparent contradiction between the '*Supream Power*' here
and in line 4 is explained by Lamprecht, 1918, 145, saying that 'the
supremacy of the legislative is complete under one condition and dis-
appears entirely under another condition'.

25–8   Compare II, § 129, 4.

31–3   See chapter XIX (§§ 211–43); compare II, § 157, 29–30.

§ **150**   Compare II, § 132, 22–7, II, § 134; and on lines 1–2 compare
II, § 153, 1–2 (taken by Bastide, 1907, 236, as typical of Locke's verbal
inconsistencies).

Legislative is no otherwise Legislative of the Society, but
5 by the right it has to make Laws for all the parts and for
every Member of the Society, prescribing Rules to their
actions, and giving power of Execution, where they are
transgressed, the *Legislative* must needs be the *Supream*,
and all other Powers in any Members or parts of the
10 Society, derived from and subordinate to it.

151. In some Commonwealths where the *Legislative*
is not always in being, and the *Executive* is vested in a
single Person, who has also a share in the Legislative; there
that single Person in a very tolerable sense may also be
5 called *Supream*, not that he has in himself all the Supream
Power, which is that of Law-making: But because he has
in him the *Supream Execution*, from whom all inferiour
Magistrates derive all their several subordinate Powers,
or at least the greatest part of them: having also no
10 Legislative superiour to him, there being no Law to be
made without his consent, which cannot be expected should
ever subject him to the other part of the Legislative, *he is*
properly enough in this sense *Supream*. But yet it is to be
observed, that though *Oaths of Allegiance* and Fealty are
15 taken to him, 'tis not to him as Supream Legislator, but
as *Supream Executor* of the Law, made by a joint Power
of him with others; *Allegiance* being nothing but an
Obedience according to Law, which when he violates, he
has no right to Obedience, nor can claim it otherwise than
20 as the publick Person vested with the Power of the Law,
and so is to be consider'd as the Image, Phantom, or
Representative of the Commonwealth, acted by the will of
the Society, declared in its Laws; and thus he has no Will,
no Power, but that of the Law. But when he quits this
25 Representation, this publick Will, and acts by his own
private Will, he degrades himself, and is but a single private
Person without Power, and without Will, that has any Right
to *Obedience;* the Members owing no *Obedience* but to the
publick Will of the Society.

152. The *Executive Power* placed any where but in a
Person, that has also a share in the Legislative, is visibly

§ **151** 22, 25 'Representative' and 'Representation' are used in the
technical, Hobbesian sense here—see Gierke, 1934, 82–3, though to
antithetical purposes, which is typical of the relationship between the
two men.

subordinate and accountable to it, and may be at pleasure
changed and displaced; so that it is not the *supream
Executive Power* that is exempt from *Subordination*, but 5
the *Supream Executive Power* vested in one, who having
a share in the Legislative, has no distinct superiour Legislative to be subordinate and accountable to, farther than
he himself shall joyn and consent: so that he is no more
subordinate than he himself shall think fit, which one may 10
certainly conclude will be but very little. Of other *Ministerial* and *subordinate Powers* in a Commonwealth, we
need not speak, they being so multiply'd with infinite
variety, in the different Customs and Constitutions of
distinct Commonwealths, that it is impossible to give a 15
particular account of them all. Only thus much, which
is necessary to our present purpose, we may take notice of
concerning them, that they have no manner of Authority
any of them, beyond what is, by positive Grant, and
Commission, delegated to them, and are all of them 20
accountable to some other Power in the Commonwealth.

153. It is not necessary, no nor so much as convenient, that the *Legislative* should be *always in being*.
But absolutely necessary that the *Executive Power* should,
because there is not always need of new Laws to be made,
but always need of Execution of the Laws that are made. 5
When the *Legislative* hath put the *Execution* of the Laws,
they make, into other hands, they have a power still to
resume it out of those hands, when they find cause, and to
punish for any mall-administration against the Laws. The
same holds also in regard of the *Federative* Power, that 10
and the Executive being both *Ministerial and subordinate
to the Legislative,* which as has been shew'd in a Constituted
Commonwealth, is the Supream. The *Legislative* also in this
Case being suppos'd to consist of several Persons (for if
it be a single Person, it cannot but be always in being, and 15
so will as Supream, naturally have the Supream Executive
Power, together with the Legislative) may *assemble and
exercise their Legislature,* at the times that either their
original Constitution, or their own Adjournment appoints,
or when they please; if neither of these hath appointed any 20

§ 153   1–3   Compare II, § 144, 3–5.
     18   'Legislature'—power of law-making: changed by Locke after
1698 from 'Legislative'; compare II, § 94, 27 and references.

time, or there be no other way prescribed to convoke them. For the supream Power being placed in them by the People, 'tis always in them, and they may exercise it when they please, unless by their original Constitution they are limited
25 to certain Seasons, or by an Act of their Supream Power they have Adjourned to a certain time, and when that time comes, they have a right to *Assemble* and *act* again.

154. If the *Legislative,* or any part of it be made up of Representatives chosen for that time by the People, which afterwards return into the ordinary state of Subjects, and have no share in the Legislature but upon a new choice,
5 this power of chusing must also be exercised by the People, either at certain appointed Seasons, or else when they are summon'd to it: and in this latter Case, the power of convoking the Legislative, is ordinarily placed in the Executive, and has one of those two limitations in respect of time:
10 That either the Original Constitution requires their *assembling* and *acting* at certain intervals, and then the Executive Power does nothing but Ministerially issue directions for their Electing and Assembling, according to due Forms: Or else it is left to his Prudence to call them
15 by new Elections, when the Occasions or Exigencies of the publick require the amendment of old, or making of new Laws, or the redress or prevention of any inconveniencies, that lie on, or threaten the People.

155. It may be demanded here, What if the Executive Power being possessed of the Force of the Commonwealth, shall make use of that force to hinder the *meeting* and *acting of the Legislative,* when the Original Constitution,
5 or the publick Exigencies require it? I say using Force upon the People without Authority, and contrary to the Trust put in him, that does so, is a state of War with the People, who have a right to *reinstate* their *Legislative in the Exerci*se of their Power. For having erected a
10 Legislative, with an intent they should exercise the Power

---

§ **155**   3–4   Compare II, § 215, 1, verbal parallel; see note on II, § 156 and references.
   4   'Original Constitution'—see II, § 154, 10; § 156, 35–6; § 218, 1; the only instances of the use of Constitution in our sense: elsewhere it means an overriding law.
   7, 18   '*state of War*'—see chapter III of *Second Treatise*.

of making Laws, either at certain set times, or when there is need of it; when they are hindr'd by any force from, what is so necessary to the Society, and wherein the Safety and preservation of the People consists, the People have a right to remove it by force. In all States and Conditions the 15 true remedy of *Force* without Authority, is to oppose *Force* to it. The use of *force* without Authority, always puts him that uses it into a *state of War,* as the Aggressor, and renders him liable to be treated accordingly.

156. The Power *of Assembling and dismissing the Legislative,* placed in the Executive, gives not the Executive a superiority over it, but is a Fiduciary Trust, placed in him, for the safety of the People, in a Case where the uncertainty, and variableness of humane affairs could not 5 bear a steady fixed rule. For it not being possible, that the first Framers of the Government should, by any foresight, be so much Masters of future Events, as to be able to prefix so just periods of return and duration to the *Assemblies of the Legislative,* in all times to come, 10 that might exactly answer all the Exigencies of the Commonwealth; the best remedy could be found for this defect, was to trust this to the prudence of one, who was always to be present, and whose business it was to watch over the publick good. Constant *frequent meetings of the* 15 *Legislative,* and long Continuations of their Assemblies, without necessary occasion, could not but be burthensome to the People, and must necessarily in time produce more dangerous inconveniences, and yet the quick turn of affairs might be sometimes such as to need their present help: Any 20 delay of their *Convening* might endanger the publick; and sometimes too their business might be so great, that the limited time of their sitting might be too short for their work, and rob the publick of that benefit, which could be had only from their mature deliberation. What then could 25 be done, in this Case, to prevent the Community, from being exposed sometime or other to eminent hazard, on one side, or the other, by fixed intervals and periods, set to

§ 156 §§ 154 and 155 deal with the election and dissolution, this paragraph with the summoning and proroguing, of English parliaments. Locke seems to have in mind the repeated postponements, cancellations, failures to summon characteristic of Charles II and the first object of Shaftesbury's activities in opposition, especially during the Exclusion Controversy—see notes on II, §§ 167, 213, and Introduction, 68.

the prudence of some, who being present, and acquainted
30 with the state of publick affairs, might make use of this
Prerogative for the publick good? And where else could this
be so well placed as in his hands, who was intrusted with
the Execution of the Laws, for the same end? Thus supposing the regulation of times for the *Assembling and*
35 *Sitting of the Legislative,* not settled by the original Constitution, it naturally fell into the hands of the Executive,
not as an Arbitrary Power depending on his good pleasure,
but with this trust always to have it exercised only for
the publick Weal, as the Occurrences of times and change
40 of affairs might require. Whether *settled periods of their
Convening,* or a *liberty* left to the Prince *for Convoking
the Legislative,* or perhaps a mixture of both, hath the least
inconvenience attending it, 'tis not my business here to
inquire, but only to shew, that though the Executive
45 Power may have the Prerogative of *Convoking* and
dissolving such *Conventions of the Legislative,* yet it is not
thereby superiour to it.

157. Things of this World are in so constant a Flux,
that nothing remains long in the same State. Thus People,
Riches, Trade, Power, change their Stations; flourishing
mighty Cities come to ruine, and prove in time neglected
5 desolate Corners, whilst other unfrequented places grow
into populous Countries, fill'd with Wealth and Inhabitants.
But things not always changing equally, and private interest
often keeping up Customs and Priviledges, when the
reasons of them are ceased, it often comes to pass, that
10 in Governments, where part of the Legislative consists of
Representatives chosen by the People, that in tract of
time this *Representation* becomes very *unequal* and disproportionate to the reasons it was at first establish'd upon.

§ 157 The reform of the franchise and electoral districts was a part
of the political programme of Shaftesbury and the Whigs under Charles
II, who introduced a Bill on the subject in the first parliament which
they controlled, that of March 1679; see Ogg, *Charles II,* 1955, II, 480–2.
The scheme of reform attributed to Shaftesbury (*Somers Tracts,* 1812)
included the disfranchisement of rotten boroughs like the one mentioned
in lines 14–21. This was presumably Old Sarum, near Salisbury, well-
known to Locke as the home of his friend David Thomas; see Introduction, 76. This paragraph, then, was most probably written as part of the
original in 1679, though it could have been added in 1681. Sir James
Fitzjames Stephen, 1892, 154–5, regards this as 'the oddest illustration
of the fanciful character of the results to which Locke's abstract principles led him in relation to civil government'.

To what gross absurdities the following of Custom, when
Reason has left it, may lead, we may be satisfied when 15
we see the bare Name of a Town, of which there remains
not so much as the ruines, where scarce so much Housing
as a Sheep-coat; or more inhabitants than a Shepherd is
to be found, sends *as many Representatives* to the grand
Assembly of Law-makers, as a whole County numerous in 20
People, and powerful in riches. This Strangers stand
amazed at, and every one must confess needs a remedy.
Though most think it hard to find one, because the Constitution of the Legislative being the original and supream
act of the Society, antecedent to all positive Laws in it, 25
and depending wholly on the People, no inferiour Power
can alter it. And therefore the *People*, when the *Legislative*
is once Constituted, *having* in such a Government as we
have been speaking of, *no Power* to act as long as the
Government stands; this inconvenience is thought incapable 30
of a remedy.

158. *Salus Populi Suprema Lex*, is certainly so just and
fundamental a Rule, that he, who sincerely follows it,
cannot dangerously err. If therefore the Executive, who
has the power of Convoking the Legislative, observing
rather the true proportion, than fashion of *Representation*, 5
regulates, not by old custom, but true reason, the *number
of Members*, in all places, that have a right to be distinctly
represented, which no part of the People however incorporated can pretend to, but in proportion to the assistance, which it affords to the publick, it cannot be 10
judg'd, to have set up a new Legislative, but to have
restored the old and true one, and to have rectified the
disorders, which succession of time had insensibly, as well
as inevitably introduced. For it being the interest, as well
as intention of the People, to have a fair and *equal* 15

§ **158** 1–14 Locke, in solving the difficulty about electoral reform in
accordance with that supreme law, the good of the people (§§ 157, 23–8;
158, 1), is dealing with a problem of his own making.

5 '*Representation*'—here used in its non-Hobbesian sense; compare
note on II, § 151, 22, 25. Elrington, 1798, comments that Locke 'had
no idea that he would be interpreted as attributing that power to the
multitude', that Locke would have excluded from the suffrage those
without property, that his remarks about proportioning representatives
to districts obviate universal suffrage. This sentence and § 140 are cited
by those who believe that Locke intended a definite restriction of the
franchise, e.g. Seliger, 1963 (i).

Representative; whoever brings it nearest to that, is an undoubted Friend, to, and Establisher of the Government, and cannot miss the Consent and Approbation of the Community. *Prerogative* being nothing, but a Power in
20 the hands of the Prince to provide for the publick good, in such Cases, which depending upon unforeseen and uncertain Occurrences, certain and unalterable Laws could not safely direct, whatsoever shall be done manifestly for the good of the People, and the establishing the Govern-
25 ment upon its true Foundations, is, and always will be just *Prerogative.* The Power of Erecting new Corporations, and therewith *new Representatives,* carries with it a supposition, that in time the *measures of representation* might vary, and those places have a just right to be represented
30 which before had none; and by the same reason, those cease to have a right, and be too inconsiderable for such a Priviledge, which before had it. 'Tis not a change from the present State, which perhaps Corruption, or decay has introduced, that makes an Inroad upon the Government,
35 but the tendency of it to injure or oppress the People, and to set up one part, or Party, with a distinction from, and an unequal subjection of the rest. Whatsoever cannot but be acknowledged to be of advantage to the Society, and People in general, upon just and lasting measures, will
40 always, when done, justifie it self; and whenever the People shall chuse their *Representatives upon* just and undeniably *equal measures* suitable to the original Frame of the Government, it cannot be doubted to be the will and act of the Society, whoever permitted, or caused
45 them so to do.

19–20 Compare chapter XIV.

Of PREROGATIVE.

159.   Where the Legislative and Executive Power are in distinct hands, (as they are in all moderated Monarchies, and well-framed Governments) there the good of the Society requires, that several things should be left to the discretion of him, that has the Executive Power. For the Legislators not being able to foresee, and provide, by Laws, for all, that may be useful to the Community, the Executor of the Laws, having the power in his hands, has by the common Law of Nature, a right to make use of it, for the good of the Society, in many Cases, where the municipal Law has given no direction, till the Legislative can conveniently be Assembled to provide for it. Many things there are, which the Law can by no means provide for, and those must necessarily be left to the discretion of him, that has the Executive Power in his hands, to be ordered by him, as the publick good and advantage shall require: nay, 'tis fit that the Laws themselves should in some Cases give way to the Executive Power, or rather to this Fundamental Law of Nature and Government, *viz.* That as much as may be, *all* the Members of the Society are to be *preserved.* For since many accidents may happen, wherein a strict and rigid observation of the Laws may do harm; (as not to pull down an innocent Man's House to stop the Fire, when the next to it is burning) and a Man may come sometimes within the reach of the Law, which makes no distinction of Persons, by an action, that may deserve reward and pardon; 'tis fit, the Ruler should have a Power, in many Cases, to mitigate the severity of the Law, and pardon some Offenders: For the *end of Government* being the *preservation of all,* as much as may be, even the guilty are to be spared, where it can prove no prejudice to the innocent.

§ 159   *Chapter* XIV   In the editor's judgment this chapter belongs to Locke's original composition of 1679; compare note on II, ℃ 149, chapter XIII. It may have been touched up in places in 1689, especially in the final paragraph, § 168, but Prof. K. M. D. Haley comments that Locke could hardly have written as he did of the discretionary power in § 161 after the controversy over James II's dispensations. This and the hints of Shaftesbury's quarrel with Charles II about the summoning of Parliament (see § 167) seem sufficient grounds for this dating.

160. This Power to act according to discretion, for the publick good, without the prescription of the Law, and sometimes even against it, *is* that which is called *Prerogative*. For since in some Governments the Law-making Power is not always in being, and is usually too numerous, and so too slow, for the dispatch requisite to Execution: and because also it is impossible to foresee, and so by laws to provide for, all Accidents and Necessities, that may concern the publick; or to make such Laws, as will do no harm, if they are Executed with an inflexible rigour, on all occasions, and upon all Persons, that may come in their way, therefore there is a latitude left to the Executive power, to do many things of choice, which the Laws do not prescribe.

161. This power whilst imployed for the benefit of the Community, and suitably to the trust and ends of the Government, *is undoubted Prerogative*, and never is questioned. For the People are very seldom, or never scrupulous, or nice in the point: they are far from examining *Prerogative*, whilst it is in any tolerable degree imploy'd for the use it was meant; that is, for the good of the People, and not manifestly against it. But if there comes to be a *question* between the Executive Power and the People, *about* a thing claimed as a *Prerogative;* the tendency of the exercise of such *Prerogative* to the good or hurt of the People, will easily decide that Question.

162. It is easie to conceive, that in the Infancy of Governments, when Commonwealths differed little from Families in number of People, they differ'd from them too but little in number of Laws: And the Governours, being as the Fathers of them, watching over them for their good, the Government was almost all *Prerogative*. A few establish'd Laws served the turn, and the discretion and care of the Ruler supply'd the rest. But when mistake, or flattery prevailed with weak Princes to make use of this Power, for private ends of their own, and not for the publick good, the People were fain by express Laws to get Prerogative determin'd, in those points, wherein they

§ 162   1–5   Compare references in note on II, § 74, 16–41, Locke's concessions to patriarchalism. Pareyson compares Locke's discussion of prerogative with Filmer's (Laslett's edition, 105–6).

found disadvantage from it: And thus declared *limitations
of Prerogative* were by the People found necessary in
Cases, which they and their Ancestors had left, in the 15
utmost latitude, to the Wisdom of those Princes, who
made no other but a right use of it, that is, for the good
of their People.

163. And therefore they have a very wrong Notion
of Government, who say, that the People have *incroach'd
upon the Prerogative,* when they have got any part of it
to be defined by positive Laws. For in so doing, they have
not pulled from the Prince any thing, that of right belong'd 5
to him, but only declared, that that Power which they
indefinitely left in his, or his Ancestors, hands, to be
exercised for their good, was not a thing, which they
intended him, when he used it otherwise. For the end of
government being the good of the Community, whatsoever 10
alterations are made in it, tending to that end, cannot be an
incroachment upon any body: since no body in Government can have a right tending to any other end. And those
only are *incroachments* which prejudice or hinder the
publick good. Those who say otherwise, speak as if the 15
Prince had a distinct and separate Interest from the good
of the Community, and was not made for it, the Root
and Source, from which spring almost all those Evils, and
Disorders, which happen in Kingly Governments. And
indeed if that be so, the People under his Government are 20
not a Society of Rational Creatures entred into a Community for their mutual good; they are not such as have
set Rulers over themselves, to guard, and promote that
good; but are to be looked on as an Herd of inferiour
Creatures, under the Dominion of a Master, who keeps 25
them, and works them for his own Pleasure or Profit. If
men were so void of Reason, and brutish, as to enter into
Society upon such Terms, *Prerogative* might indeed be, what
some Men would have it, an Arbitrary Power to do things
hurtful to the People.   30

164. But since a Rational Creature cannot be supposed
when free, to put himself into Subjection to another, for
his own harm: (Though where he finds a good and wise
Ruler, he may not perhaps think it either necessary, or

§ **163** 22–6 Compare I, § 156 note and references.

5 useful to set precise Bounds to his Power in all things)
Prerogative can be nothing, but the Peoples permitting
their Rulers, to do several things of their own free choice,
where the Law was silent, and sometimes too against the
direct Letter of the Law, for the publick good; and their
10 acquiescing in it when so done. For as a good Prince,
who is mindful of the trust put into his hands, and careful
of the good of his People, cannot have too much *Prerogative*, that is, Power to do good: So a weak and ill Prince,
who would claim that Power, which his Predecessors
15 exercised without the direction of the Law, as a Prerogative
belonging to him by Right of his Office, which he may
exercise at his pleasure, to make or promote an Interest
distinct from that of the publick, gives the People an occasion, to claim their Right, and limit that Power, which,
20 whilst it was exercised for their good, they were content
should be tacitly allowed.

165. And therefore he, that will look into the *History
of England*, will find, that Prerogative was always *largest*
in the hands of our wisest and best Princes: because the
People observing the whole tendency of their Actions to
5 be the publick good, contested not what was done without
Law to that end; or if any humane frailty or mistake (for
Princes are but Men, made as others) appear'd in some
small declinations from that end; yet 'twas visible, the
main of their Conduct tended to nothing but the care of
10 the publick. The People therefore finding reason to be
satisfied with these Princes, whenever they acted without
or contrary to the Letter of the Law, acquiesced in what
they did, and, without the least complaint, let them inlarge
their *Prerogative* as they pleased, judging rightly, that they
15 did nothing herein to the prejudice of their Laws, since
they acted conformable to the Foundation and End of all
Laws, the publick good.

166. Such God-like Princes indeed had some Title to
Arbitrary Power, by that Argument, that would prove
Absolute Monarchy the best Government, as that which
God himself governs the Universe by: because such Kings
5 partake of his Wisdom and Goodness. Upon this is founded
that saying, That the Reigns of good Princes have been

§ 166   1   Compare note on II, § 42, 24–32.

always most dangerous to the Liberties of their People. For when their Successors, managing the Government with different Thoughts, would draw the Actions of those good Rulers into Precedent, and make them the Standard 10 of their *Prerogative,* as if what had been done only for the good of the People, was a right in them to do, for the harm of the People, if they so pleased; it has often occasioned Contest, and sometimes publick Disorders, before the People could recover their original Right, and get that 15 to be declared not to be *Prerogative,* which truly was never so: Since it is impossible, that any body in the Society should ever have a right to do the People harm; though it be very possible, and reasonable, that the People should not go about to set any Bounds to the *Prerogative* of those 20 Kings or Rulers, who themselves transgressed not the Bounds of the publick good. For *Prerogative is nothing but the Power of doing publick good without a Rule.*

167. The Power of *calling Parliaments* in *England,* as to precise time, place, and duration, is certainly a *Prerogative* of the King, but still with this trust, that it shall be made use of for the good of the Nation, as the Exigencies of the Times, and variety of Occasions shall require. 5 For it being impossible to foresee, which should always be the fittest place for them to assemble in, and what the best Season; the choice of these was left with the Executive Power, as might be most subservient to the publick good, and best suit the ends of Parliaments. 10

168. The old Question will be asked in this matter of *Prerogative,* But *who shall be Judge* when this Power is made a right use of? I Answer: Between an Executive Power in being, with such a Prerogative, and a Legislative

§ **167** This overt mention of the constitution of England, clearly in Locke's mind throughout (compare II, § 143, 16–22, note and references), especially in reference to the summoning of Parliament (see note on II, § 149, chapter XIII), conceivably refers to the situation of late 1680–early 1681. Charles II then exercised his prerogative right to call parliament where he wished (see line 1) and summoned it at Oxford as a move against Shaftesbury and his Exclusionists: on Locke and the Oxford Parliament, see Introduction, 44.
§ **168** 1–2 'The old Question . . . *who shall be Judge?*'—a question fundamental to the *Second Treatise;* see §§ 13, 19, 20, 89, 93, 123, 131, 136, 181, 240, 241, and compare the references to Jephthah in note on II, § 21, 20. The question is raised in a very similar form in the *Epistola de Tolerantia:* if the magistrate and the subjects disagree

5 that depends upon his will for their convening, there can be
no *Judge on Earth:* As there can be none, between the
Legislative, and the People, should either the Executive,
or the Legislative, when they have got the Power in their
hands, design, or go about to enslave, or destroy them.
10 The People have no other remedy in this, as in all other
cases where they have no Judge on Earth, but to *appeal
to Heaven.* For the Rulers, in such attempts, exercising a
Power the People never put into their hands (who can
never be supposed to consent, that any body should rule
15 over them for their harm) do that, which they have not a
right to do. And where the Body of the People, or any
single Man, is deprived of their Right, or is under the Exercise of a power without right, and have no Appeal on
Earth, there they have a liberty to appeal to Heaven,
20 whenever they judge the Cause of sufficient moment. And
therefore, tho' the *People* cannot be *Judge,* so as to have
by the Constitution of that Society any Superiour power,
to determine and give effective Sentence in the case; yet
they have, by a Law antecedent and paramount to all
25 positive Laws of men, reserv'd that ultimate Determination
to themselves, which belongs to all Mankind, where there
lies no Appeal on Earth, *viz.* to judge whether they have
just Cause to make their Appeal to Heaven. And this

'quis erit inter eos judex? Resp. solus Deus: qui inter legislatorem et
populum nullus in terris est judex' (1765, 22: in the translation
'legislatorem' becomes 'supreme magistrate').

McIlwain, 1935, suggests that Locke was recalling here the doctrine
of Hunton's *Treatise of Monarchie,* 1643, for he also asks again and
again 'Who shall be the judge of the excesses of the sovereign lord in
monarchies of this composure?'. His conclusion is: 'There can be no
judge legal and constituted within that frame of government . . . an
Appeale must be made *ad conscientiam generis humani.* . . . The
fundamentall Lawes of that Monarchy must judge and pronounce
sentence in every man's conscience.' Hunton, it will be seen, was
talking of a particular form of government, a mixed monarchy, whereas
Locke seems to be talking of all possible forms of government.
Hunton's appeal is to everyone's conscience, which Filmer triumphantly
pronounced as plain anarchy, whilst Locke's final appeal is to God,
though he does occasionally talk of conscience in this connection
(see II, § 21, 26). He possessed Hunton's book, though it is not
mentioned over the crucial years, and he may have been influenced
by him. It seems much more likely, however, that it was Filmer's
criticism of Hunton (see, for example, 294–5) which was in question
and shows that the paragraph belongs to 1679. Locke contradicts
what is said in line 6 in II, § 240; see Polin, 1960, 225.

16–17 'any single Man'—Locke at his most anarchistic; see Kendall,
1941, 89, and Strauss, 1953, 237.

Judgment they cannot part with, it being out of a Man's power so to submit himself to another, as to give him 30 a liberty to destroy him; God and Nature never allowing a Man so to abandon himself, as to neglect his own preservation: And since he cannot take away his own Life, neither can he give another power to take it. Nor let any one think, this lays a perpetual foundation for Disorder: 35 for this operates not, till the Inconvenience is so great, that the Majority feel it, and are weary of it, and find a necessity to have it amended. But this the Executive Power, or wise Princes, never need come in the danger of: And 'tis the thing of all others, they have most need to avoid, 40 as of all others the most perilous.

CHAP. XV.

Of Paternal, Political, and Despotical Power,
considered together.

169. Though I have had occasion to speak of these separately before, yet the great mistakes of late about Government, having, as I suppose, arisen from confounding these distinct Powers one with another, it may not, perhaps, be amiss, to consider them here together. 5

170. *First* then, *Paternal* or *Parental Power* is nothing but that, which Parents have over their Children, to gov-

§ 169 *Chapter* XV This chapter is very similar to chapter IX; see note on II, § 123. It is repetitive and recapitulatory, it uses the general argument to reflect upon James II (see note on II, § 172, 10–22), it recalls II, §§ 2, 3, the introductory paragraphs clearly written in 1689 (see for instance, § 169 and § 171, 1–6). It has every indication of having been written in 1689 and it is interesting to see Locke, especially in § 174, linking his controversy with Filmer and his theory of property, with the political situation immediately after the Revolution.
§ 170 This paragraph was corrected in detail by Locke in the Christ's copy, see Collation: In rewriting lines 17–19 he omits a statement about 'the perfect use of Reason' and the attainment of manhood.
1 See II, § 69, 1, note and references, and on this paragraph as a whole compare chapter VI of the *Second Treatise* (§§ 52–76).

ern them for the Childrens good, till they come to the
use of Reason, or a state of Knowledge, wherein they
5 may be supposed capable to understand that Rule, whether
it be the Law of Nature, or the municipal Law of their
Country they are to govern themselves by: Capable, I say,
to know it, as well as several others, who live, as Free-men,
under that Law. The Affection and Tenderness, which
10 God hath planted in the Breasts of Parents, towards their
Children, makes it evident, that this is not intended to be
a severe Arbitrary Government, but only for the Help,
Instruction, and Preservation of their Off-spring. But happen it as it will, there is, as I have proved, no reason,
15 why it should be thought, to extend to Life and Death, at
any time, over their Children, more than over any body
else, neither can there be any pretence why this parental
power should keep the Child, when grown to a Man, in
subjection to the Will of his Parents any farther, than the
20 having received Life and Education from his Parents,
obliges him to respect, Honour, Gratitude, Assistance, and
Support all his Life to both Father and Mother. And thus,
'tis true, the *Paternal* is a natural *Government,* but not at
all extending it self to the Ends, and Jurisdictions of that
25 which is Political. The *Power of the Father doth not reach*
at all to the *Property* of the Child, which is only in his
own disposing.

171. *Secondly, Political Power* is that Power which
every Man, having in the state of Nature, has given up into
the hands of the Society, and therein to the Governours,
whom the Society hath set over it self, with this express or
5 tacit Trust, That it shall be imployed for their good, and
the preservation of their Property: Now this *Power,* which
every Man has *in the state of Nature,* and which he parts
with to the Society, in all such cases, where the Society
can secure him, is, to use such means for the preserving
10 of his own Property, as he thinks good, and Nature allows
him; and to punish the Breach of the Law of Nature in
others so, as (according to the best of his Reason) may
most conduce to the preservation of himself, and the rest
of Mankind. So that the *end and measure of this Power,*

20 'Education', etc—see note on II, § 58.
26 '*Property* of the Child'—see note on II, § 65, 20–7.
§ 171 1–6 Compare II, § 3, note and references.

when in every Man's hands in the state of Nature, being 15
the preservation of all of his Society, that is, all Mankind
in general, it can have no other *end or measure,* when
in the hands of the Magistrate, but to preserve the Members of that Society in their Lives, Liberties, and Possessions; and so cannot be an Absolute, Arbitrary Power 20
over their Lives and Fortunes, which are as much as possible
to be preserved; but a *Power to make Laws,* and annex such
Penalties to them, as may tend to the preservation of the
whole, but cutting off those Parts, and those only, which
are so corrupt, that they threaten the sound and healthy, 25
without which no severity is lawful. And this *Power
has its Original only from Compact* and Agreement, and
the mutual Consent of those who make up the Community.

172.   *Thirdly, Despotical Power* is an Absolute, Arbitrary Power one Man has over another, to take away his
Life, whenever he pleases. This is a Power, which neither
Nature gives, for it has made no such distinction between
one Man and another; nor Compact can convey, for Man 5
not having such an Arbitrary Power over his own Life,
cannot give another Man such a Power over it; but it is
the effect only of Forfeiture, which the Aggressor makes
of his own Life, when he puts himself into the state of War
with another. For having quitted Reason, which God hath 10
given to be the Rule betwixt Man and Man, and the

19–20   Compare II, § 87, 5–6, note and references, and II, §§ 87–9 on
the whole paragraph.
§ 172   11–22   This passage was rewritten and extended in the margin
of the Christ's copy, see Collation for the original version, printed
in the editions of Locke's lifetime. The effect is to give greater emphasis and to strengthen the implication that a despot, a king for
instance who uses force against his people, is a 'wild beast, or noxious
brute': compare the ferocious quotation from Livy added to the title
page in the Christ's copy at the time these corrections were made.
   Even in the original version, this seems to be a clear reference to
James II and his activities, in very hostile, even spiteful terms, which
is one of the indications that this paragraph and the whole chapter
were an insertion of 1689; see note on II, § 169, chapter XV. There
are many similar statements throughout the *Second Treatise:* compare
§ 10, 2–6; § 11, 24–30 (verbal parallel); § 16, 4–9 (verbal parallel);
§ 181, 20–2 (verbal parallel); § 182, 23; § 230, 39–41; and it is possible
that some of these were likewise put in or touched up in 1689. But
the sentiment is very close to the description of the subjects of absolute
monarchies as herds of animals (see I, § 156, note and references)
and both arise quite naturally from Locke's general theory; see Introduction, 109. Taken together they seem to express Locke's way of
describing despotism, emphasized and sharpened in 1689, and again
here in the later 1690's.

common bond whereby humane kind is united into one
fellowship and societie; and having renounced the way of
peace, which that teaches, and made use of the Force of
15 War to compasse his unjust ends upon an other, where he
has no right, and so revolting from his own kind to that of
Beasts by making Force which is theirs, to be his rule of
right, he renders himself liable to be destroied by the
injur'd person and the rest of mankind, that will joyn with
20 him in the execution of Justice, as any other wild beast, or
noxious brute † with whom Mankind can have neither
Society nor Security†. And thus *Captives,* taken in a just
and lawful War, and such only, are *subject to a Despotical
Power,* which as it arises not from Compact, so neither
25 is it capable of any, but is the state of War continued. For
what Compact can be made with a Man that is not Master
of his own Life? What Condition can he perform? And if
he be once allowed to be Master of his own Life, the
Despotical, Arbitrary Power of his Master ceases. He that
30 is Master of himself, and his own Life, has a right too
to the means of preserving it, so that *as soon as Compact
enters, Slavery ceases,* and he so far quits his Absolute
Power, and puts an end to the state of War, who enters
into Conditions with his Captive.

173. *Nature gives* the first of these, *viz. Paternal Power
to Parents* for the Benefit of their Children during their
Minority, to supply their want of Ability, and understanding
how to manage their Property. (By *Property* I must be
5 understood here, as in other places, to mean that Property
which Men have in their Persons as well as Goods.)
Voluntary Agreement gives the second, *viz. Political
Power to Governours* for the Benefit of their Subjects, to
secure them in the Possession and Use of their Properties.
10 And *Forfeiture gives* the third, *Despotical power to Lords*
for their own Benefit, over those who are stripp'd of all
property.

† that is destructive to their being.†

18 *Alternative Reading.* For its authenticity and status, see Collation: it was apparently an afterthought of Locke's, who seems to
have decided to revert to the original reading, and is critical to the
relationship of the two master copies and the texts which follow them;
see Editorial Note.

§ 173 4–6 Compare II, § 87, 5–6 note and references.

6 Compare II, § 27, 2–3.

10–12 Compare II, § 138 and Cicero, *ejus* (sc. of society) *autem
vinculum est ratio et oratio.*

174. He, that shall consider the distinct rise and extent, and the different ends of these several powers, will plainly see, that *paternal Power* comes as far short of that of the *Magistrate*, as *Despotical* exceeds it; and that *Absolute Dominion*, however placed, is so far from being one kind of Civil Society, that it is as inconsistent with it, as Slavery is with Property. *Paternal Power* is only where Minority makes the Child incapable to manage his property; *Political* where Men have Property in their own disposal; and *Despotical* over such as have no property at all.

CHAP. XVI.

Of CONQUEST.

175. Though Governments can originally have no other Rise than that before mentioned, nor *Polities* be *founded* on any thing but *the Consent of the People;* yet such has been the Disorders Ambition has fill'd the World with, that in the noise of War, which makes so great a part of the History of Mankind, this *Consent* is little taken notice of: And therefore many have mistaken the force of Arms, for the consent of the People; and reckon Conquest as one of the Originals of Government. But *Conquest* is as far from setting up any Government, as demolishing an House is from building a new one in the place. Indeed it often makes way of a new Frame of a Common-wealth, by destroying the former; but, without the Consent of the people, can never erect a new one.

§ 175 *Chapter* XVI This chapter cannot be dated with any certainty, nevertheless in the editor's opinion it belongs to the early stages of composition and was probably written in 1681 or 1682. Though it is connected with the rest of the text (see the cross-reference in II, § 112, 9–19) the relationship is with the assumed 1681 addition (§§ 100–23; see note on § 100 and on § 95, chapter VIII). Like chapters IX and XV it is recapitulatory, and like them it leads to a reflection on the origin, rights and powers of a monarchy which can only be English. It may then be pronounced an insertion, but there are cogent reasons for maintaining that it cannot be an insertion of 1689. An argument about conquest would have been irrelevant then. But in 1681 and 1682 there was a controversy over the Norman Con-

176. That the *Aggressor*, who puts himself into the state of War with another, and *unjustly invades* another Man's right, *can*, by such an unjust War, *never* come to *have a right over the Conquered*, will be easily agreed by
5 all Men, who will not think, that Robbers and Pyrates have a Right of Empire over whomsoever they have Force enough to master; or that Men are bound by promises, which unlawful Force extorts from them. Should a Robber break into my House, and with a Dagger at my Throat,
10 make me seal Deeds to convey my Estate to him, would this give him any Title? Just such a Title by his Sword, has an *unjust Conquerour*, who forces me into Submission. The Injury and the Crime is equal, whether committed by the wearer of a Crown, or some petty Villain. The Title
15 of the Offender, and the Number of his Followers make no difference in the Offence, unless it be to aggravate it. The only difference is, Great Robbers punish little ones, to keep

---

quest and its relevance to English government, a perennial issue but one which arose in an acute form between Brady, Petit, Atwood and others; see Pocock, 1957, chapter VII, 'The Brady Controversy'. This chapter, then, may be regarded as Locke's comment on this conquest controversy in terms of his political theory, which adds significance to his denial that conquest could never reach the ownership of land, nor the rights and institutions attached to such ownership, over a whole country; see, for example, II, § 184 and note on 26–32.

7–9 It is not quite clear who were the many who reckoned 'Conquest as one of the Originals of Government'. As Pocock has pointed out (1957, see especially 53–4, 148–50; compare Zagorin, 1954, 67–70), the English populist writers of the seventeenth century, including Milton, Locke and Sidney, all write as if the defenders of kingship and absolutism had argued from conquest, but in fact they did not. Filmer never used the argument, in anything like the form in which Locke attacked it, though his defender against Sidney, Edmund Bohun, finally approved of the justification of William III as a conqueror in 1688 as a way of settling Tory doubts (Bohun, *Diary*, 1853, 67, 101–13). Grotius is the only one of the great natural lawyers who even approached the position which Locke demolishes (*De Jure Belli*, III, viii, 8). There remains Hobbes, who assimilates patriarchal and despotic government as both based on force and presumably in some cases conquest as Locke discusses it, and sets it up as an alternative to his 'Commonwealth by Institution' (*Leviathan*, chapters 19, 20): he also talks of William I as a conqueror and of his successors exercising his right by conquest, in his *Dialogue of the Common Laws* and *Behemoth*. It seems likely that Locke had none of these writers specifically in mind, but was simply writing in the tradition which dictated that the conquest argument had to be refuted.

§ 176 8–11 Compare II, § 186, 23–5, where the dagger becomes a 'Pistol at my breast'. Molyneux, 1698, in paraphrasing this passage seems to have conflated the two contexts (1720, 16). Hobbes believed that 'Covenants extorted by feare are valide' (1904, 94), but here and in this chapter Locke may be re-echoing Pufendorf (see especially 1672, VII, vii, 3), who in turn comments on Grotius, 1625, II, 3, 4.

them in their Obedience, but the great ones are rewarded
with Laurels and Triumphs, because they are too big for
the weak hands of Justice in this World, and have the 20
power in their own possession, which should punish Offenders. What is my Remedy against a Robber, that so
broke into my House? *Appeal* to the Law for Justice. But
perhaps Justice is denied, or I am crippled and cannot stir,
robbed and have not the means to do it. If God has taken 25
away all means of seeking remedy, there is nothing left
but patience. But my Son, when able, may seek the Relief of the Law, which I am denied: He or his Son may
renew his *Appeal*, till he recover his Right. But the Conquered, or their Children, have no Court, no Arbitrator 30
on Earth to appeal to. Then they may *appeal*, as *Jephtha*
did, *to Heaven*, and repeat their *Appeal*, till they have recovered the native Right of their Ancestors, which was to
have such a Legislative over them, as the Majority should
approve, and freely acquiesce in. If it be objected, this 35
would cause endless trouble; I answer, No more than Justice does, where she lies open to all that appeal to her.
He that troubles his Neighbour without a Cause, is punished for it by the Justice of the Court he appeals to. And
he that *appeals to Heaven*, must be sure he has Right on 40
his side; and a Right too that is worth the Trouble and
Cost of the Appeal, as he will answer at a Tribunal, that
cannot be deceived, and will be sure to retribute to every
one according to the Mischiefs he hath created to his
Fellow-Subjects; that is, any part of Mankind. From 45
whence 'tis plain, that he that *Conquers in an unjust War,
can* thereby *have no Title to the Subjection and Obedience
of the Conquered.*

177. But supposing Victory favours the right side, let
us consider a *Conquerour in a lawful War,* and see what
power he gets, and over whom.

First, 'Tis plain he *gets no Power* by his Conquest *over
those that Conquered with him.* They that fought on his 5
side cannot suffer by the Conquest, but must at least be

---

31 'Jephtha'—see note on II, § 21, 20 and references.
§ 177 Molyneux, 1698, summarizes this paragraph: he quotes verbatim from lines 4–7, and uses phrases from lines 25–9; 1720, 16.
1–12 Compare Tyrrell, 1681, 85: 'Though some Governments have
begun by Conquest', yet those who fought with the conquerors 'had
no obligation to serve them, but from their own agreements which
included a share of the conquests'.

as much Freemen as they were before. And most commonly they serve upon Terms, and on Condition to share
with their Leader, and enjoy a part of the Spoil, and other
10 Advantages that attend the Conquering Sword: or at least
have a part of the subdued Country bestowed upon them.
And *the Conquering People are not,* I hope, to be *Slaves
by Conquest,* and wear their Laurels only to shew they
are Sacrifices to their Leaders Triumph. They that found
15 Absolute Monarchy upon the Title of the Sword, make
their Heroes, who are the Founders of such Monarchies,
arrant *Draw-can-Sirs,* and forget they had any Officers and
Soldiers that fought on their side in the Battles they won,
or assisted them in the subduing, or shared in possessing
20 the Countries they Master'd. We are told by some, that the
English Monarchy is founded in the *Norman* Conquest,
and that our Princes have thereby a Title to absolute Dominion: Which if it were true, (as by the History it appears
otherwise) and that *William* had a right to make War on
25 this Island; yet his Dominion by Conquest could reach
no farther, than to the *Saxons* and *Britains* that were then
Inhabitants of this Country. The *Normans* that came with
him, and helped to Conquer, and all descended from them
are Freemen and no Subjects by Conquest; let that give
30 what Dominion it will. And if I, or any Body else, shall
claim freedom, as derived from them, it will be very hard
to prove the contrary: And 'tis plain, the Law that has
made no distinction between the one and the other, intends
not there should be any difference in their Freedom or
35 Priviledges.

178.   But supposing, which seldom happens, that the
Conquerers and Conquered never incorporate into one
People, under the same Laws and Freedom. Let us see next
what Power a lawful Conquerer has over the Subdued;
5 and that I say is purely Despotical. He has an Absolute
Power over the Lives of those, who by an Unjust War have
forfeited them; but not over the Lives or Fortunes of those,

17 '*Draw-can-Sirs*'—chracters who kill off everybody on all sides,
a proverbial phrase from the Duke of Buckingham's play *The Rehearsal,* composed 1663/4, performed 1671 and often afterwards.
21–7 This is the only mention of the Norman Conquest—see note
on II, § 175 (chapter XVI): the 'some' who made it the foundation
of the English monarchy we discussed in the note to II, § 175, 7–9.
§ 178 5–7 Compare II, §23, 10–15, and note on II, § 24, 1–9—Locke
on slavery. Molyneux, 1698, paraphrases the two passages; 1720, 18.

who ingaged not in the War, nor over the Possessions even of those, who were actually engaged in it.

179. *Secondly*, I say then the *Conquerour* gets no Power but only over those, who have actually assisted, concurr'd, or consented to that unjust force, that is used against him. For the People having given to their Governours no Power to do an unjust thing, such as is to make 5 an unjust War, (for they never had such a Power in themselves:) They ought not to be charged, as guilty of the Violence and Unjustice that is committed in an Unjust War, any farther, than they actually abet it; no more, than they are to be thought guilty of any Violence or Oppression 10 their Governours should use upon the People themselves, or any part of their Fellow Subjects, they having impowered them no more to the one, than to the other. Conquerours, 'tis true, seldom trouble themselves to make the distinction, but they willingly permit the confusion of War 15 to sweep altogether; but yet this alters not the Right: For the Conquerours Power over the Lives of the Conquered, being only because they have used force to do, or maintain an Injustice, he can have that power only over those, who have concurred in that force, all the rest are innocent; and 20 he has no more Title over the People of that Country, who have done him no Injury, and so have made no forfeiture of their Lives, than he has over any other, who, without any injuries or provocations, have lived upon fair terms with him. 25

180. *Thirdly*, The *power a Conquerour gets* over those he overcomes *in a Just War, is perfectly Despotical*: he has an absolute power over the Lives of those, who by putting themselves in a State of War, have forfeited them; but he has not thereby a Right and Title to their Possessions. This 5 I doubt not, but at first sight will seem a strange Doctrine, it being so quite contrary to the practice of the World; There being nothing more familiar in speaking of the Dominion of Countries, than to say, such an one Conquer'd it. As if Conquest, without any more ado, convey'd a right 10 of Possession. But when we consider, that the practice of the strong and powerful, how universal soever it may be, is seldom the rule of Right, however it be one part of the subjection of the Conquered, not to argue against the Conditions, cut out to them by the Conquering Sword. 15

181. Though in all War there be usually a complication of force and damage, and the Aggressor seldom fails to harm the Estate, when he uses force against the Persons of those he makes War upon; yet 'tis the use of Force only, 5 that puts a Man into the State of War. For whether by force he begins the injury, or else having quietly, and by fraud, done the injury, he refuses to make reparation, and by force maintains it, (which is the same thing as at first to have done it by force) 'tis the unjust use of force that 10 makes the War. For he that breaks open my House, and violently turns me out of Doors; or having peaceably got in, by force keeps me out, does in effect the same thing; supposing we are in such a state, that we have no common Judge on Earth, whom I may appeal to, and to whom we 15 are both obliged to submit: For of such I am now speaking. 'Tis the *unjust use of force* then, that *puts a Man into the state of War* with another, and thereby he, that is guilty of it, makes a forfeiture of his Life. For quitting reason, which is the rule given between Man and Man, and using 20 force the way of Beasts, he becomes liable to be destroyed by him he uses force against, as any savage ravenous Beast, that is dangerous to his being.

182. But because the miscarriages of the Father are no faults of the Children, and they may be rational and peaceable, notwithstanding the brutishness and injustice of the Father; the Father, by his miscarriages and violence, 5 can forfeit but his own Life, but involves not his Children in his guilt or destruction. His goods, which Nature, that willeth the preservation of all Mankind as much as is possible, hath made to belong to the Children to keep them from perishing, do still continue to belong to his Children. 10 For supposing them not to have joyn'd in the War, either

§ **181** The French version (1691, etc., see Introduction, 24–5) differs more widely from the English in this paragraph than elsewhere, though the variations, which may have had Locke's approval, do not alter the sense.

13–14 'no common Judge on Earth'—compare note on II, § 168, 1–2 and references.

18–22 See note on II, § 172, 11–22 and references. Molyneux, 1698, after copying a phrase from II, § 178, 5–6, paraphrases this paragraph to this point, then reproduces these final phrases almost exactly; 1720, 18–19.

§ **182** 1–9 See I, § 89 on, and II, § 72 on, for Locke's general account of children's rights in the property of their fathers and compare Molyneux (1698), 1720, 19 and 21.

through Infancy, absence, or choice, they have done nothing to forfeit them: *nor has the Conqueror any right* to take them away, by the bare title of having subdued him, that by force attempted his destruction; though perhaps he may have some right to them, to repair the damages he has sustained by the War, and the defence of his own right, which how far it reaches to the possessions of the Conquered, we shall see by and by. So that he that *by Conquest has a right over a Man's Person* to destroy him if he pleases, has *not* thereby a right *over his Estate* to possess and enjoy it. For it is the brutal force the Aggressor has used, that gives his Adversary a right to take away his Life, and destroy him if he pleases, as a noxious Creature; but 'tis damage sustain'd that alone gives him Title to another Mans Goods: For though I may kill a Thief that sets on me in the Highway, yet I may not (which seems less) take away his Money and let him go; this would be Robbery on my side. His force, and the state of War he put himself in, made him forfeit his Life, but gave me no Title to his Goods. The *right* then *of Conquest extends only to the Lives* of those who joyn'd in the War, *not to their Estates,* but only in order to make reparation for the damages received, and the Charges of the War, and that too with reservation of the right of the innocent Wife and Children.

183. Let the *Conqueror* have as much Justice on his side, as could be supposed, he *has* no *right* to seize more than the vanquished could forfeit; his Life is at the Victors Mercy, and his Service and Goods he may appropriate to make himself reparation; but he cannot take the Goods of his Wife and Children; they too had a Title to the Goods he enjoy'd, and their shares in the Estate he possessed. For Example, I in the state of Nature (and all Commonwealths are in the state of Nature one with another) have injured another Man, and refusing to give satisfaction, it comes to a state of War, wherein my defending by force, what I had gotten unjustly, makes me the Aggressor. I am Conquered: My Life, 'tis true, as forfeit, is at mercy, but not my Wives and Childrens. They made not the War, nor assisted in it. I could not forfeit their Lives, they were not mine to forfeit. My wife had a share in my Estate,

that neither could I forfeit. And my Children also, being
born of me, had a right to be maintained out of my labour
or Substance. Here then is the Case; The Conqueror has
20 a Title to Reparation for Damages received, and the Children have a Title to their Father's Estate for their Subsistence. For as to the Wife's share, whether her own
Labour or Compact gave her a Title to it, 'tis plain, Her
Husband could not forfeit what was hers. What must be
25 done in the case? I answer; The Fundamental Law of Nature being, that all, as much as may be, should be preserved, it follows, that if there be not enough fully to
satisfy both, *viz.* for the *Conqueror's Losses,* and Childrens
Maintenance, he that hath, and to spare, must remit some-
30 thing of his full Satisfaction, and give way to the pressing
and preferable Title of those, who are in danger to perish
without it.

184. But supposing the *Charge* and *Damages of the
War* are to be made up to the Conqueror, to the utmost
Farthing, and that the Children of the vanquished, spoiled
of all their Father's Goods, are to be left to starve and
5 perish: yet the satisfying of what shall on this score, be
due to the Conqueror, will scarce give him a *Title to any
Countrey he shall Conquer.* For the Damages of War can
scarce amount to the value of any considerable *Tract of
Land,* in any part of the World, where all the Land is pos-
10 sessed, and none lies waste. And if I have not taken away
the Conqueror's Land, which, being vanquished, it is impossible I should; scarce any other spoil I have done him,
can amount to the value of mine, supposing it equally cultivated and of an extent any way coming near, what I had
15 over run of his. The destruction of a Years Product or
two, (for it seldom reaches four or five) is the utmost spoil,
that usually can be done. For as to Money, and such
Riches and Treasure taken away, these are none of Natures
Goods, they have but a Phantastical imaginary value: Na-
20 ture has put no such upon them: They are of no more
account by her standard, than the Wampompeke of the
Americans to an *European* Prince, or the Silver Money of
Europe would have been formerly to an *American.* And

§ **184**   17–19   Compare II, § 46, 6–8, note and references.
   21   'Wampompeke'—wampum; vocal equivalent of 'wampumpeag',
bead money of the Algonkin Indians.

five years Product is not worth the perpetual Inheritance
of *Land,* where all is possessed, and none remains waste 25
to be taken up by him, that is disseiz'd: Which will be
easily granted, if one do but take away the imaginary value
of Money, the disproportion being more, than between
five and five hundred. Though, at the same time, half a
years product is more worth than the Inheritance, where 30
there being more *Land,* than the Inhabitants possess, and
make use of, any one has liberty to make use of the waste:
But there Conquerers take little care to possess themselves
of the *Lands of the Vanquished.* No damage therefore,
that Men in the state of Nature (as all Princes and Gov- 35
ernments are in reference to one another) suffer from one
another, can give a Conqueror Power, to dispossess the
Posterity of the Vanquished, and turn them out of their
Inheritance, which ought to be the Possession of them and
their Descendants to all Generations. The Conquerour in- 40
deed will be apt to think himself Master: And 'tis the very
condition of the subdued not to be able to dispute their
Right. But if that be all, it gives no other Title than what
bare Force gives to the stronger over the weaker. And, by
this reason, he that is strongest will have a right to what- 45
ever he pleases to seize on.

185.   Over those then, that joined with him in the War,
and over those of the subdued Countrey that opposed him
not, and the Posterity even of those that did, the Conqueror, even in a just War, hath, *by* his *Conquest, no right
of Dominion:* They are free from any subjection to him, 5
and if their former Government be dissolved, they are at
liberty to begin and erect another to themselves.

186.   The Conquerour, 'tis true, usually, by the Force
he has over them, compels them, with a Sword at their
Breasts, to stoop to his Conditions, and submit to such a
Government as he pleases to afford them; but the enquiry
is, What right he has to do so? If it be said, they submit 5

29 'five hundred'—'five thousand' in the 1st edition. The disproportion is between the value of five years product and the value
of the land in perpetuity. Compare chapter V, especially § 40 on, and
note on § 45, 22–4.

35–6   Compare II, § 183, 8–9; 14, 3–9 and note.

§ 186 Molyneaux, 1698, reproduces this paragraph almost in full: he
follows Locke's exact words in lines 2–9, 14–16, 19–22. See II, § 176,
8–11 and references.

by their own consent; then this allows their own *consent* to be *necessary to give the Conquerour a Title to rule* over them. It remains only to be considered, whether *Promises, extorted by Force,* without Right, can be thought
10 Consent, and *how far they bind.* To which I shall say, they *bind not at all;* because whatsoever another gets from me by force, I still retain the Right of, and he is obliged presently to restore. He that forces my Horse from me, ought presently to restore him, and I have still a right to
15 retake him. By the same reason, he that *forced a Promise* from me, ought presently to restore it, *i.e.* quit me of the Obligation of it; or I may resume it my self, *i.e.* chuse whether I will perform it. For the Law of Nature laying an Obligation on me, only by the Rules she prescribes, can-
20 not oblige me by the violation of her Rules: Such is the extorting any thing from me by force. Nor does it at all alter the case, to say I *gave my Promise,* no more than it excuses the force, and passes the Right, when I put my Hand in my Pocket, and deliver my Purse my self to a
25 Thief, who demands it with a Pistol at my Breast.

187.   From all which it follows, that the *Government of a Conquerour,* imposed, by force, on the Subdued, against whom he had no right of War, or who joyned not in the War against him, where he had right, *has no Obli-*
5 *gation* upon them.

188.   But let us suppose that all the Men of that Community being all Members of the same Body Politick, may be taken to have joyn'd in that unjust War, wherein they are subdued, and so their Lives are at the Mercy of the
5 Conquerour.

189.   I say, this concerns not their Children, who are in their Minority. For since a Father hath not, in himself, a Power over the Life or Liberty of his Child; no act of his can possibly forfeit it: So that the Children, whatever
5 may have happened to the Fathers, are Free-men, and the Absolute Power of the *Conquerour* reaches no farther than the Persons of the Men, that were subdued by him, and dies

§§ **189, 190, 191** Here Locke returns to first principles; see I, § 88 on for inheritance, II, § 4 for natural freedom, now coupled with inheritance, and II, §§ 72, 73 and 116 for natural freedom from subjection to any government.

with them; and should he Govern them as Slaves, subjected
to his Absolute, Arbitrary Power, he *has no* such *Right
of Dominion over their Children*. He can have no Power 10
over them, but by their own consent, whatever he may
drive them to say, or do; and he has no lawful Authority,
whilst Force, and not Choice, compels them to submission.

190. Every Man is born with a double Right: *First, A
Right of Freedom to his Person*, which no other Man has
a Power over, but the free Disposal of it lies in himself.
Secondly, A Right, before any other Man, to *inherit*, with
his Brethren, his Fathers Goods. 5

191. By the first of these, a Man is *naturally free* from
subjection to any Government, though he be born in a
place under its Jurisdiction. But if he disclaim the lawful
Government of the Country he was born in, he must also
quit the Right that belong'd to him by the Laws of it, and 5
the Possessions there descending to him from his Ancestors,
if it were a Government made by their consent.

192. By the second, the *Inhabitants* of any Countrey,
who are descended, and derive a Title to their Estates from
those, who are subdued, and had a Government forced
upon them against their free consents, *retain a Right to
the Possession of their Ancestors*, though they consent not 5
freely to the Government, whose hard Conditions were by
force imposed on the Possessors of that Country. For the
first *Conqueror never* having *had a Title to the Land* of
that Country, the People who are the Descendants of, or
claim under those, who were forced to submit to the Yoke 10
of a Government by constraint, have always a Right to
shake it off, and free themselves from the Usurpation, or
Tyranny, which the Sword hath brought in upon them,
till their Rulers put them under such a Frame of Government, as they willingly, and of choice consent to. Who 15
doubts but the Grecian Christians descendants of the ancient possessors of that Country may justly cast off the
Turkish yoke which they have so long groaned under when
ever they have a power to do it? For no Government can

---

§ **192** 15–21 Locke modified this paragraph in the Christ's copy,
inserting here the passage on the Grecian Christians which in the
printed editions had come at the end; see Collation.

20 have a right to obedience from a people who have not
freely consented to it: which they can never be supposed
to do, till either they are put in a full state of Liberty to
chuse their Government and Governors, or at least till they
have such standing Laws, to which they have by themselves
25 or their Representatives, given their free consent, and also
till they are allowed their due property, which is so to be
Proprietors of what they have, that no body can take away
any part of it without their own consent, without which,
Men under any Government are not in the state of Free-
30 men, but are direct Slaves under the Force of War.

193.   But granting that the *Conqueror* in a just War has
a Right to the Estates, as well as Power over the Persons
of the Conquered; which, 'tis plain, he *hath* not: Nothing
of *Absolute Power* will follow from hence, in the continu-
5 ance of the Government. Because the Descendants of these
being all Free-men, if he grants them Estates and Possessions to inhabit his Country (without which it would be
worth nothing) whatsoever he grants them, they have, so
far as it is granted, *property* in. The nature whereof is,
10 that *without a Man's own consent* it *cannot be taken from
him.*

194.   Their *Persons* are *free* by a Native Right, and
their *properties,* be they more or less, are *their own, and
at their own dispose,* and not at his; or else it is no property. Supposing the Conqueror gives to one Man a Thou-
5 sand Acres, to him and his Heirs for ever; to another he
lets a Thousand Acres for his Life, under the Rent of
50 *l.* or 500. *l. per Ann.* Has not the one of these a Right
to his Thousand Acres for ever, and the other, during his
Life, paying the said Rent? And hath not the Tenant for
10 Life a *property* in all that he gets over and above his Rent,
by his Labour and Industry during the said term, supposing it be double the Rent? Can any one say, The King, or
Conqueror, after his Grant, may by his Power of Conqueror, take away all, or part of the Land from the Heirs

§ 194   In this paragraph Locke is, typically, using the land-law of his
time and country to illustrate what was, to him, a universal principle.
He is still slightly ambiguous on the point of an individual having
to consent as an individual to each act of alienation, cf. II, § 139, 3–8.

of one, or from the other, during his Life, he paying the 15
Rent? Or can he take away from either, the Goods or Money
they have got upon the said Land, at his pleasure? If he
can, then all free and voluntary *Contracts* cease, and are
void, in the World; there needs nothing to dissolve them
at any time but Power enough: And all the *Grants* and 20
Promises *of Men in power,* are but Mockery and Collu-
sion. For can there be any thing more ridiculous than to
say, I give you and yours this for ever; and that in the
surest and most solemn way of conveyance can be devised:
And yet it is to be understood, that I have Right, if I please, 25
to take it away from you again to Morrow?

195. I will not dispute now whether Princes are exempt from the Laws of their Countrey; but this I am sure,
they owe subjection to the Laws of God and Nature. No
Body, no Power can exempt them from the Obligations of
that Eternal Law. Those are so great, and so strong, in the 5
case of *Promises,* that Omnipotency it self can be tyed
by them. *Grants, Promises* and *Oaths* are Bonds that *hold
the Almighty:* Whatever some Flatterers say to Princes of
the World who all together, with all their People joined to
them, are in comparison of the great God, but as a Drop 10
of the Bucket, or a Dust on the Balance, inconsiderable
nothing!

196. The short of the *Case in Conquest* is this. The
Conqueror, if he have a just Cause, has a Despotical Right
over the Persons of all, that actually aided, and concurred
in the War against him, and a Right to make up his Damage and Cost out of their Labour and Estates, so he injure 5
not the Right of any other. Over the rest of the People,
if there were any that consented not to the War, and over
the Children of the Captives themselves, or the Possessions
of either he has no Power; and so can have, *by Virtue
of Conquest, no lawful Title* himself *to Dominion* over 10
them, or derive it to his Posterity; but is an Aggressor, if
he attempts upon their properties, and thereby puts him-

§ **195** 7–8 Compare I, § 6, 7: Hobbes (1904, 93) denied that a
covenant could be made with God 'without speciall Revelation',
though it was Filmer and his followers whom Locke thought of as
flatterers of Princes; see, for example, I, § 3.

self in a state of War against them; and has no better a
Right of Principality, he, nor any of his Successors, than
15 *Hingar*, or *Hubba* the *Danes* had here in *England;* or *Spar-*
tacus, had he Conquered *Italy* would have had; which is to
have their Yoke cast off, as soon as God shall give those
under their subjection Courage and Opportunity to do it.
Thus, notwithstanding whatever Title the Kings of *Assyria*
20 had over *Judah,* by the Sword, God assisted *Hezekiah* to
throw off the Dominion of that Conquering Empire. *And*
the Lord was with Hezekiah, and he prospered; wherefore
he went forth, and he rebelled *against the King of Assyria,*
and served him not, 2. Kings XVIII. vij. Whence it is plain,
25 that shaking off a Power, which Force, and not Right hath
set over any one, though it hath the Name of *Rebellion,*
yet is no Offence before God, but is that, which he allows
and countenances, though even Promises and Covenants,
when obtain'd by force, have intervened. For 'tis very
30 probable to any one that reads the Story of *Ahaz,* and
Hezekiah attentively, that the *Assyrians* subdued *Ahaz,*
and deposed him, and made *Hezekiah* King in his Father's
Life time; and that *Hezekiah* by agreement had done him
Homage, and paid him Tribute all this time.

§ 196   15 'Hingar' and 'Hubba'—presumably the Ingware and Ubba
named as the original Danish leaders of the first invasion (as distinct
from raids) of England in the 860's by the Anglo-Saxon Chronicle;
see Stenton, *Anglo-Saxon England*, 1943, 244.

15–16 'Spartacus'—the escaped gladiator who nearly conquered Italy
in the eighth decade B.C.

19–34 On Ahaz, Hezekiah and the Assyrians, see II Kings xvi,
xviii, xix, I Chron. xxviii, xxix, xxxii: Locke's alternative reading does
not seem to be accepted by modern biblical historians.

Of USURPATION.

197. As Conquest may be called a Foreign Usurpation, so *Usurpation* is a kind of Domestick Conquest, with this difference, that an Usurper can never have Right on his side, it being no *Usurpation* but where one *is* got into *the Possession of what another has Right to*. This, so far as it is *Usurpation*, is a change only of Persons, but not of the Forms and Rules of the Government: For if the Usurper extend his Power beyond, what of Right belonged to the lawful Princes, or Governours of the Common-wealth, 'tis *Tyranny* added to Usurpation. 10

198. In all lawful Governments the designation of the Persons, who are to bear Rule, is as natural and necessary a part, as the Form of the Government it self, and is that which had its Establishment originally from the People. Hence all Common wealths with the Form of Government 5 established, have Rules also of appointing those, who are to have any share in the publick Authority; and settled methods of conveying the right to them. For the anarchy is much alike to have no forme of government at all; or to agree that it shall be monarchical, but to appoint no way 10 to know or designe the person that shall have the power and be the monarch. Whoever gets into the exercise of any part of the Power, by other ways, than what the Laws of the Community have prescribed, hath no Right to be obeyed, though the Form of the Commonwealth be still 15

§ 197 *Chapter* XVII This chapter is obviously an addendum to chapter XVI and its probable date therefore is 1681 or 1682—see note on II, § 175. It is recapitulatory and parallels to its statements can be found in the *First Treatise*, §§ 71, 72, 78, 111, 119, 121, 122, but it does not seem to be the examination of Filmer's 'Title of Usurpers' promised in I, § 121, 11; see note there.
§ 198 5–12 This passage is difficult to interpret: 'For the anarchy' in line 8 seems not to fit what comes before, though it does make sense with what follows. It may all be due to a printer's confusion not properly put right by Locke. Unfortunately in the Christ's copy he failed to complete his correction. Having decided to move the passage printed here in lines 7–12 from an earlier position, he failed to delete it, with the result that the texts of the 4th, 5th, 6th and Collected editions give it in both positions, making the paragraph pretty well unintelligible—see Collation.

preserved; since he is not the Person the Laws have appointed, and consequently not the Person the People have
consented to. Nor can such an *Usurper,* or any deriving
from him, ever have a Title, till the People are both at
20 liberty to consent, and have actually consented to allow,
and confirm in him, the Power he hath till then Usurped.

CHAP. XVIII.

Of TYRANNY.

199. As Usurpation is the exercise of Power, which another hath a Right to; so *Tyranny* is *the exercise of Power
beyond Right,* which no Body can have a Right to. And
this is making use of the Power any one has in his hands;
5 not for the good of those, who are under it, but for his
own private separate Advantage. When the Governour,
however intituled, makes not the Law, but his Will, the
Rule; and his Commands and Actions are not directed to
the preservation of the Properties of his People, but the
10 satisfaction of his own Ambition, Revenge, Covetousness,
or any other irregular Passion.

§ 199 *Chapter* XVIII Up to the end of § 202 this chapter clearly
belongs to the series from chapter XVI, and was presumably written
in 1681 or perhaps 1682 (see notes on § 197, chapter XVII and § 175,
chapter XVI), which is confirmed by the reference to 'King James' in
§ 200, 3–4. But after § 202 the subject of tyranny is left behind, and
Locke discusses the related but much more interesting topic of resistance: this whole passage to § 210 may well be a later insertion. In
the editor's view it is most unlikely to have been an insertion of 1689,
for it all reads as if it were intended to apply to resistance under
contemplation, not to resistance which had taken place. Moreover its
statements are often quite inappropriate to the actions of James II:
the references to religion, for example, in § 209, 7 and § 210, 10–11—
see Introduction, 67–8. But they do describe the actions of Charles II, at
least as they were interpreted by Shaftesbury and the Exclusion Whigs.
There are sentences, and perhaps longer passages, which may have
been added in 1689, and § 205, 7–12 is an obvious example, but in
general it would seem that this part of the text was written before
Locke's departure for Holland in 1683, and may well be directly
connected with the Whig plans for overt resistance to Charles II in
those years.

6 The point that a government must never have its 'own private
separate Advantage' is made repeatedly; see II, § 138, 27; § 143,
15; § 163, 16 ('distinct and separate Interest'); § 164, 17–18.

200. If one can doubt this to be Truth, or Reason, because it comes from the obscure hand of a Subject, I hope the Authority of a King will make it pass with him. King *James* the first in his Speech to the Parliament, 1603. tells them thus; *I will ever prefer the Weal of the Publick, and* 5 *of the whole Commonwealth, in making of good Laws and Constitutions to any particular and private Ends of mine. Thinking ever the Wealth and Weal of the Commonwealth, to be my greatest Weal, and wordly Felicity; a Point wherein a lawful King doth directly differ from a Tyrant.* 10 *For I do acknowledge, that the special and greatest point of Difference that is between a rightful King, and an usurping Tyrant, is this, That whereas the proud and ambitious Tyrant doth think, his Kingdom and People are only ordained for satisfaction of his Desires and unreasonable* 15 *Appetites; the righteous and just King doth by the contrary acknowledge himself to be ordained for the procuring of the Wealth and Property of his People.* And again in his Speech to the Parliament, 1609. he hath these Words: *The KING binds himself by a double Oath, to the observation* 20 *of the Fundamental Laws of his Kingdom. Tacitly, as by being a King, and so bound to protect as well the People as the Laws of his Kingdom, and expressly by his Oath at his Coronation; so as every just King, in a setled Kingdom is bound to observe that Paction made to his People* 25 *by his Laws in framing his Government agreeable thereunto, according to that Paction which God made with* Noah, *after the Deluge. Hereafter, Seed-time and Harvest, and Cold and Heat, and Summer and Winter, and Day and Night shall not cease while the Earth remaineth. And* 30

§ 200 3-4 'King *James* the First'—'the First' added in errata to 3rd edition, 1698, and inserted in the Christ's copy: compare II, § 133, 12, and see note and references there.

5-38 See McIlwain, 1918 (an exact reproduction of King James's *Works*, 1616), 277, 278, 309-10, fairly exactly quoted, but with variations in spelling and punctuation and one interesting alteration: '*Property*' in line 18 reads 'prosperitie' in the original. Filmer quotes King James extensively, mostly from his *Trew Law of Free Monarchies*, and in *Patriarcha*, section 21, 103, he also uses the phrase about the tyrant and the law in lines 31-2. Locke does not appear to have owned any work of James I, but these speeches of 1603 and 1609 were used by others in the controversy of the early 1680's, see, for example, *Vox Regis, or the difference betwixt a King ruling by Law and Tyrant by his own will . . . in two speeches of King James to the parliaments in 1603 . . . 1609 . . . an Appendix to Vox Populi*, London, 1681. This paragraph was obviously written 1679-81, see note on II, § 199, chapter XVIII; compare Polin, 1960, 216.

*therefore a King governing in a setled Kingdom, leaves
to be a King, and degenerates into a Tyrant as soon as he
leaves off to rule according to his Laws. And a little after:
Therefore all Kings that are not Tyrants, or Perjured, will*
35 *be glad to bound themselves within the Limits of their
Laws. And they that perswade them the contrary, are
Vipers, and Pests both against them and the Commonwealth.* Thus that Learned King who well understood the
Notions of things, makes the difference betwixt a *King* and
40 a *Tyrant* to consist only in this, That one makes the Laws
the Bounds of his Power, and the Good of the Publick,
the end of his Government; the other makes all give way
to his own Will and Appetite.

201. 'Tis a Mistake to think this Fault is proper only
to Monarchies; other Forms of Government are liable to
it, as well as that. For where-ever the Power that is put in
any hands for the Government of the People, and the
5 Preservation of their Properties, is applied to other ends,
and made use of to impoverish, harass, or subdue them
to the Arbitrary and Irregular Commands of those that
have it: There it presently becomes *Tyranny*, whether
those that thus use it are one or many. Thus we read of the
10 Thirty Tyrants at *Athens*, as well as one at *Syracuse;* and
the intolerable Dominion of the *Decemviri* at *Rome* was
nothing better.

202. *Where-ever Law ends Tyranny begins,* if the
Law be transgressed to another's harm. And whosoever in
Authority exceeds the Power given him by the Law, and
makes use of the Force he has under his Command, to
5 compass that upon the Subject, which the Law allows not,
ceases in that to be a Magistrate, and acting wtihout Authority, may be opposed, as any other Man, who by force
invades the Right of another. This is acknowledged in subordinate Magistrates. He that hath Authority to seize my
10 Person in the Street, may be opposed as a Thief and a
Robber, if he indeavours to break into my House to Execute a Writ, notwithstanding that I know he has such a
Warrant, and such a Legal Authority as will impower him

§ 201   8–11   The Thirty Tyrants ruled in Athens 404–403 B.C., and the
tyrants of Syracuse were advised by Plato himself: the *Decemviri* were
a board of ten who were forced from the rulership of the Roman
Republic in 449 B.C. for tyrannical behaviour.

to Arrest me abroad. And why this should not hold in the highest, as well as in the most Inferiour Magistrate, I would gladly be informed. Is it reasonable that the Eldest Brother, because he has the greatest part of his Father's Estate, should thereby have a Right to take away any of his younger Brothers Portions? Or that a Rich Man, who possessed a whole Country, should from thence have a Right to seize, when he pleased, the Cottage and Garden of his poor Neighbour? The being rightfully possessed of great Power and Riches exceedingly beyond the greatest part of the Sons of *Adam,* is so far from being an excuse, much less a reason, for Rapine, and Oppression, which the endamaging another without Authority is, that it is a great Aggravation of it. For the exceeding the Bounds of Authority is no more a Right in a great, than a petty Officer; no more justifiable in a King, than a Constable. But is so much the worse in him, in that he has more trust put in him, has already a much greater share than the rest of his brethren, and is supposed from the advantages of Education, imployment and Counsellors to be more knowing in the measures of right or wrong.

203. May the *Commands* then *of a Prince be opposed?* May he be resisted as often as any one shall find himself aggrieved, and but imagine he has not Right done him? This will unhinge and overturn all Polities, and instead of Government and Order leave nothing but Anarchy and Confusion.

204. To this I Answer: That *Force* is to be *opposed* to nothing, but to unjust and unlawful *Force;* whoever makes any opposition in any other Case, draws on himself a just Condemnation both from God and Man; and so no such Danger or Confusion will follow, as is often suggested. For,

§ 202 16–19 The greater rights of the eldest brother are discussed at length in the *First Treatise;* see, for example, §§ 114, 115.

19–22 Compare I, § 42, for the limitations on the powers of the rich man. The example given here, of the wealthy landowner and the cottager with his garden, comes straight out of the rural England of Locke's day.

29–34 This point is made again in II, § 231.

32–4 Locke rephrased this; see Collation.

§ 203 It is possible that the text from this point to the end of the chapter is an addition to the original, perhaps of 1681–2, perhaps even of 1689: see note to § 199 (chapter XVIII), where it is argued that it was written before 1683.

205. *First,* As in some Countries, the Person of the Prince by the Law is Sacred; and so whatever he commands, or does, his Person is still free from all Question or Violence, not liable to Force, or any Judicial Censure or
5 Condemnation. But yet opposition may be made to the illegal Acts of any inferiour Officer, or other commissioned by him; unless he will by actually putting himself into a State of War with his People, dissolve the Government, and leave them to that defence, which belongs to every one in
10 the State of Nature. For of such things who can tell what the end will be? And a Neighbour Kingdom has shewed the World an odd Example. In all other Cases the *Sacredness* of the person *exempts him from all Inconveniences* whereby he is secure, whilst the Government stands, from
15 all violence and harm whatsoever; Than which there cannot be a wiser Constitution. For the harm he can do in his own Person, not being likely to happen often, nor to extend it self far; nor being able by his single strength to subvert the Laws, nor oppress the Body of the People,
20 should any Prince have so much Weakness and ill Nature as to be willing to do it, the Inconveniency of some particular mischiefs, that may happen sometimes, when a heady Prince comes to the Throne, are well recompenced, by the peace of the Publick, and security of the Govern-
25 ment, in the Person of the Chief Magistrate, thus set out of the reach of danger: It being safer for the Body, that some few private Men should be sometimes in danger to suffer, than that the head of the Republick should be easily, and upon slight occasions exposed.

206. *Secondly,* But this Priviledge, belonging only to the King's Person, hinders not, but they may be questioned, opposed, and resisted, who use unjust force, though they pretend a Commission from him, which the Law authorizes
5 not. As is plain in the Case of him, that has the King's Writ to Arrest a Man, which is a full Commission from the King; and yet he that has it cannot break open a Man's House to do it, nor execute this Command of the King

§ **205** 1 'Some Countries'—England is meant here; compare I, § 90, 32–4.
7–12 This passage seems to be an insertion of 1689 and a direct reference to James II, here accused of having put himself into a state of war with his people and dissolved the government. The 'Neighbour Kingdom' of line 11 is England again, an even more indirect reference but typical of Locke: compare above note and see Introduction, 91. The King

upon certain Days, nor in certain Places, though this Commission have no such exception in it, but they are the Limi- 10
tations of the Law, which if any one transgress, the King's
Commission excuses him not. For the King's Authority
being given him only by the Law, he cannot impower any
one to act against the Law, or justifie him, by his Commission in so doing. The *Commission,* or *Command of any* 15
Magistrate, where he has no Authority, being as *void* and
insignificant, as that of any private Man. The difference
between the one and the other, being that the Magistrate
has some Authority so far, and to such ends, and the private
Man has none at all. For 'tis not the *Commission,* but the 20
Authority, that gives the Right of acting; and *against the*
Laws there can be no Authority. But, notwithstanding such
Resistance, the King's Person and Authority are still both
secured, and so *no danger to Governor or Government.*

207. *Thirdly,* Supposing a Government wherein the
Person of the Chief Magistrate is not thus Sacred; yet this
Doctrine of the lawfulness of *resisting* all unlawful exercises of his Power, *will not* upon every slight occasion in-
danger him, or *imbroil the Government.* For where the 5
injured Party may be relieved, and his damages repaired
by Appeal to the Law, there can be no pretence for Force,
which is only to be used, where a Man is intercepted from
appealing to the Law. For nothing is to be accounted Hostile Force, but where it leaves not the remedy of such an 10
Appeal. And 'tis such *Force* alone, that *puts* him that uses
it *into a state of War,* and makes it lawful to resist him.
A Man with a Sword in his Hand demands my Purse in
the High-way, when perhaps I have not 12 *d.* in my Pocket;
This Man I may lawfully kill. To another I deliver 100 *l.* 15
to hold only whilst I alight, which he refuses to restore
me, when I am got up again, but draws his Sword to defend the possession of it by force, if I endeavour to retake
it. The mischief this Man does me, is a hundred, or possibly a thousand times more, than the other perhaps in- 20
tended me, (whom I killed before he really did me any)
and yet I might lawfully kill the one, and cannot so much
as hurt the other lawfully. The Reason whereof is plain;
because the one using *force,* which threatned my Life, I
could not have *time to appeal* to the Law to secure it: And 25

§ 207   13–14   Compare II, § 18.

when it was gone, 'twas too late to appeal. The Law could
not restore Life to my dead Carcass: The Loss was irreparable; which to prevent, the Law of Nature gave me a
Right to *destroy* him, who had put himself into a state of
30 War with me, and threatned my destruction. But in the
other case, my Life not being in danger, I may have the
benefit of appealing to the Law, and have Reparation for
my 100 *l.* that way.

208. *Fourthly,* But if the unlawful acts done by the
Magistrate, be maintained (by the Power he has got) and
the remedy which is due by Law, be by the same Power
obstructed; yet the *Right of resisting,* even in such manifest
5 Acts of Tyranny, *will not* suddenly, or on slight occasions,
disturb the Government. For if it reach no farther than
some private Mens Cases, though they have a right to defend themselves, and to recover by force, what by unlawful force is taken from them; yet the Right to do so, will
10 not easily ingage them in a Contest, wherein they are sure
to perish; it being as impossible for one or a few oppressed
Men to *disturb the Government,* where the Body of the
People do not think themselves concerned in it, as for a
raving mad Man, or heady Male-content to overturn a
15 well-settled State; the People being as little apt to follow
the one, as the other.

209. But if either these illegal Acts have extended to
the Majority of the People; or if the Mischief and Oppression has light only on some few, but in such Cases, as the
Precedent, and Consequences seem to threaten all, and they
5 are perswaded in their Consciences, that their Laws, and
with them their Estates, Liberties, and Lives are in danger,
and perhaps their Religion too, how they will be hindered
from resisting illegal force, used against them, I cannot

§ 208 Compare II, § 230, 1–11, and see Seliger, 1963 (ii), talking of
raison d'état.
  6–7 Elrington (1798) comments here that there are cases in which
redress is impossible, where it would injure innocent people, and
that no one 'has a right to overturn the peace of the Society he lives
in and reduce his fellow-citizens to a State of Nature, for the mere
purpose of obtaining redress'.
§ 209 The statements of this paragraph and § 210 are often taken to
refer directly to James II, and they seem more specific than the rest
of the passage from § 203; see note there. In the note on § 199 (chapter
XVIII) and in the Introduction, 67–8 it is argued that they are in fact
more appropriate to the situation of the early 1680's than of 1688–9.

tell. This is an *Inconvenience,* I confess, that *attends all Governments* whatsoever, when the Governours have 10
brought it to this pass, to be generally suspected of their
People; the most dangerous state which they can possibly
put themselves in: wherein they are the less to be pitied,
because it is so easie to be avoided; It being as impossible
for a Governor, if he really means the good of his People, 15
and the preservation of them and their Laws together, not
to make them see and feel it; as it is for the Father of a
Family, not to let his Children see he loves, and takes care
of them.

210. But if all the World shall observe Pretences of
one kind, and Actions of another; Arts used to elude the
Law, and the Trust of Prerogative (which is an Arbitrary
Power in some things left in the Prince's hand to do good,
not harm to the People) employed contrary to the end, 5
for which it was given: if the People shall find the Ministers, and subordinate Magistrates chosen suitable to such
ends, and favoured, or laid by proportionably, as they promote, or oppose them: If they see several Experiments
made of Arbitrary Power, and that Religion underhand 10
favoured (though publickly proclaimed against) which is
readiest to introduce it, and the Operators in it supported,
as much as may be; and when that cannot be done, yet
approved still, and liked the better: if a *long Train of Act-
ings shew the Councils* all tending that way, how can a 15
Man any more hinder himself from being perswaded in his
own Mind, which way things are going; or from casting
about how to save himself, than he could from believing
the Captain of the Ship he was in, was carrying him, and
the rest of the Company to *Algiers,* when he found him 20
always steering that Course, though cross Winds, Leaks in
his Ship, and want of Men and Provisions did often force
him to turn his Course another way for some time, which
he steadily returned to again, as soon as the Wind, Weather,
and other Circumstances would let him? 25

§ 210   3–5 'the Trust of Prerogative'—compare chapter XIV, especially §§ 163, 168; the definition of prerogative assumed here is the
same, but the phrase is new. Compare II, § 94, 1–10 on the sentiments
of the first part of this paragraph.
     14–15   'Long Train of Actings . . .'—see note on II, § 225, 6.
     20   'Algiers'—the slave market for Christians captured by Moorish
pirates.

Of the Dissolution of Government.

211. He that will with any clearness speak of the *Dissolution of Government*, ought, in the first place to distinguish between the *Dissolution of the Society*, and the *Dissolution of the Government*. That which makes the Community,
5 and brings Men out of the loose State of Nature, into *one Politick Society*, is the Agreement which every one has with the rest to incorporate, and act as one Body, and so be one distinct Commonwealth. The usual, and almost only way whereby *this Union is dissolved*, is the Inroad of For-
10 eign Force making a Conquest upon them. For in that Case, (not being able to maintain and support themselves, as *one intire* and *independent Body*) the Union belonging to that Body which consisted therein, must necessarily cease, and so every one return to the state he was in before, with
15 a liberty to shift for himself, and provide for his own

§ 211 *Chapter* XIX This chapter contains those statements of Locke's which associate his book most closely with the events of 1688–9. It is lacking in structure and obviously the result of successive correction and addition, but it seems to have belonged to Locke's original text, though perhaps not written before 1681 or 1682. The first part of the chapter, up to § 218, seems clearly to have been written well before 1688, especially § 218 itself which seems too hypothetical for a whig comment on the Revolution, even for Locke. Then come two paragraphs which were added in 1689 (§§ 219, 220), followed by a passage mainly belonging to the original text. The prolonged criticism of Barclay (§§ 232–9) seems to have been written in 1681 or 1682, certainly after he had added his material from Hooker. The final paragraphs seem to belong to the original, but were obviously modified and extended after the Revolution.

1–4 On the dissolution of government as opposed to the dissolution of society, and the community which survives the breakdown of government, see Introduction, 128. Maclean, 1947, points out an interesting parallel with the views of George Lawson here: compare *Politica Sacra* (1660), 1689, 24, 27, 59, 95, 217, etc., and his *Examination of Hobbes*, 1657, 15, etc. As in the case of the separation of powers (see note on II, § 146), Lawson is far more specific and rather different in his conceptions. He laid it down that when the government was dissolved, the countries maintained the community of England.

8–16 Compare II, § 175, 9–14, II, § 185 and Hobbes's *Leviathan*, chapter 29: 'When in a warre (forraign or intestine,) the enemies get a final Victory; so as . . . there is no farther protection of Subjects in their loyalty; then is the Common-wealth DISSOLVED, and every man at liberty to protect himselfe by such courses as his own discretion shall suggest to him' (1904, 242). In II, § 218, 14–15, Locke equates rebellion with foreign conquest in a similar way.

Safety as he thinks fit in some other Society. Whenever
the *Society is dissolved*, 'tis certain the Government of that
Society cannot remain. Thus Conquerours Swords often
cut up Governments by the Roots, and mangle Societies
to pieces, separating the subdued or scattered Multitude 20
from the Protection of, and Dependence on that Society
which ought to have preserved them from violence. The
World is too well instructed in, and too forward to allow
of this way of dissolving of Governments to need any more
to be said of it: and there wants not much Argument to 25
prove, that where the *Society is dissolved*, the Government
cannot remain; that being as impossible, as for the Frame
of an House to subsist when the Materials of it are scattered, and dissipated by a Whirl-wind, or jumbled into a
confused heap by an Earthquake. 30

212. Besides this over-turning from without, *Governments are dissolved from within.*

First, When the *Legislative* is *altered.* Civil Society being
a State of Peace, amongst those who are of it, from whom
the State of War is excluded by the Umpirage, which they 5
have provided in their Legislative, for the ending all Differences, that may arise amongst any of them, 'tis in their
Legislative, that the Members of a Commonwealth are
united, and combined together into one coherent living
Body. This *is the Soul that gives Form, Life, and Unity* 10
to the Commonwealth: From hence the several Members
have their mutual Influence, Sympathy, and Connexion:
And therefore when the *Legislative* is broken, or *dissolved,*
Dissolution and Death follows. For the *Essence and Union
of the Society* consisting in having one Will, the Legisla- 15
tive, when once established by the Majority, has the declaring, and as it were keeping of that Will. The *Constitution of the Legislative* is the first and fundamental Act of
Society, whereby provision is made for the *Continuation*

§ 212 10–14 Compare Hobbes, *Leviathan,* chapter 29, continuation
of passage quoted in footnote to § 211: 'For the Sovereign is the
publique Soule, giving Life and Motion to the Common-wealth', and
when it departs death follows. Locke seems to be deliberately putting
his legislative in the place of the sovereign, and though there are
very similar passages to this one in *Leviathan* about sovereignty and
the soul of a political society in Grotius (1625, II, ix, 1; 1712, 322)
and Pufendorf (1672, VII, iv, 1, 906) it may be that Locke had the
words of Hobbes specifically in mind here.
17–19 Compare II, § 134, 4–6 and note, and chapter XI generally.

20 *of their Union,* under the Direction of Persons, and Bonds
of Laws made by persons authorized thereunto, by the
Consent and Appointment of the People, without which
no one Man, or number of Men, amongst them, can have
Authority of making Laws, that shall be binding to the rest.
25 When any one, or more, shall take upon them to make
Laws, whom the People have not appointed so to do, they
make Laws without Authority, which the People are not
therefore bound to obey; by which means they come again
to be out of subjection, and may constitute to themselves
30 a *new Legislative,* as they think best, being in full liberty
to resist the force of those, who without Authority would
impose any thing upon them. Every one is at the disposure
of his own Will, when those who had by the delegation of
the Society, the declaring of the publick Will, are excluded
35 from it, and others usurp the place who have no such Authority or Delegation.

213. This being usually brought about by such in the
Commonwealth who misuse the Power they have: It is hard
to consider it aright, and know at whose door to lay it,
without knowing the Form of Government in which it
5 happens. Let us suppose then the Legislative placed in the
Concurrence of three distinct Persons.

1. A single hereditary Person having the constant, supream, executive Power, and with it the Power of Convoking and Dissolving the other two within certain Periods
10 of Time.

2. An Assembly of Hereditary Nobility.

3. An Assembly of Representatives chosen *pro tem-
pore,* by the People: Such a Form of Government supposed, it is evident.

214. *First,* That when such a single Person or Prince
sets up his own Arbitrary Will in place of the Laws, which
are the Will of the Society, declared by the Legislative,
then the *Legislative is changed.* For that being in effect

§ 213   5–13   It is obviously the constitutional arrangements for the
English legislature that are being described; compare II, § 167, note
and references, and II, § 223.
9–10   'within certain Periods of Time'—Locke changes his ground
here from the earlier discussion of the summoning of parliament,
which had left it at the discretion of the executive—see, for example,
§ 156, especially 33–5; this may mark this paragraph as having been
written later.

the Legislative whose Rules and Laws are put in execu-   5
tion, and required to be obeyed; when other Laws are set
up, and other Rules pretended, and inforced, then what the
Legislative, constituted by the Society, have enacted, 'tis
plain, that the *Legislative is changed*. Whoever introduces
new Laws, not being thereunto authorized by the funda-   10
mental Appointment of the Society, or subverts the old,
disowns and overturns the Power by which they were made,
and so sets up a *new Legislative*.

215. *Secondly,* When the Prince hinders the Legislative
from assembling in its due time, or from acting freely,
pursuant to those ends, for which it was Constituted, the
Legislative is altered. For 'tis not a certain number of Men,
no, nor their meeting, unless they have also Freedom of   5
debating, and Leisure of perfecting, what is for the good
of the Society wherein the Legislative consists: when these
are taken away or altered, so as to deprive the Society of
the due exercise of their Power, the *Legislative* is truly
altered. For it is not Names, that Constitute Governments,   10
but the use and exercise of those Powers that were intended
to accompany them; so that he who takes away the
Freedom, or hinders the acting of the Legislative in its
due seasons, in effect *takes away the Legislative,* and *puts
an end to the Government*.   15

216. *Thirdly,* When by the Arbitrary Power of the
Prince, the Electors, or ways of Election are altered, without the Consent, and contrary to the common Interest of
the People, there also the *Legislative is altered*. For if
others, than those whom the Society has authorized there-   5
unto, do chuse, or in another way, than what the Society
hath prescribed, those chosen are not the Legislative
appointed by the People.

§ 215   1–4   Compare II, § 155, 3–4.
§ 216   This paragraph seems to refer to the attempt of both Charles II
and James II to alter the parliamentary franchise by remodelling the
charters of boroughs; see Thomson, *Constitutional History,* 1938,
452–3. Although the Bill of Rights of 1689 declared that James II
had 'violated the freedom of election of members' and claimed that
'Election of Members of Parliament ought to be free', Locke's words
and meaning here do not seem to be as close to that document as
is so often assumed.

217. *Fourthly*, The delivery also of the People into the subjection of a Foreign Power, either by the Prince, or by the Legislative, is certainly a *change of the Legislative*, and so a *Dissolution of the Government*. For the end
5 why People entered into Society, being to be preserved one intire, free, independent Society, to be governed by its own Laws; this is lost, whenever they are given up into the Power of another.

218. Why in such a Constitution as this, the *Dissolution of the Government* in these Cases is to be imputed to the Prince, is evident: because he having the Force, Treasure, and Offices of the State to imploy, and often
5 perswading himself, or being flattered by others, that as Supream Magistrate he is uncapable of controul; he alone is in a Condition to make great Advances toward such Changes, under pretence of lawful Authority, and has it in his hands to terrifie or suppress Opposers, as Factious,
10 Seditious, and Enemies to the Government: Whereas no other part of the Legislative, or People is capable by themselves to attempt any alteration of the Legislative, without open and visible Rebellion, apt enough to be taken notice of; which when it prevails, produces Effects very
15 little different from Foreign Conquest. Besides the Prince in such a Form of Government, having the Power of dissolving the other parts of the Legislative, and thereby rendering them private Persons, they can never in opposition to him, or without his Concurrence, alter the Legislative
20 by a Law, his Consent being necessary to give any of their Decrees that Sanction. But yet so far as the other parts of the Legislative any way contribute to any attempt upon

§ 217 Compare II, § 239, 31–42 (added in 1694) and note 3, Introduction, p. 59: Locke may have had in mind here the possibility of a Catholic king submitting his country to the Pope, which was provided against by the Bill of Rights. But there is no close parallel and it seems more likely that he was contemplating the sort of action condemned in a King even by William Barclay; see II, § 238.
§ 218 It seems quite unlikely that even the cautious and devious Locke can have written this paragraph after the events of 1688-9—see note on II, § 211, chapter XIX.
  1 'such a Constitution as this'—that is, the English Constitution; see note on II, § 213, 5–13, and for the use of the word 'constitution' in our sense, II, § 155, 4.
  10–15 See II, § 211, 8–16 and note.
  18 Compare II, § 154, 3.

the Government, and do either promote, or not, what
lies in them, hinder such designs, they are guilty, and
partake in this, which is certainly the greatest Crime Men 25
can be guilty of one towards another.

219.   There is one way more whereby such a Government may be dissolved, and that is, when he who has the
Supream Executive Power, neglects and abandons that
charge, so that the Laws already made can no longer be
put in execution. This is demonstratively to reduce all to 5
Anarchy, and so effectually to *dissolve the Government.*
For Laws not being made for themselves, but to be by
their execution the Bonds of the Society, to keep every
part of the Body Politick in its due place and function,
when that totally ceases, the *Government* visibly *ceases,* 10
and the People become a confused Multitude, without
Order or Connexion. Where there is no longer the administration of Justice, for the securing of Mens Rights, nor
any remaining Power within the Community to direct the
Force, or provide for the Necessities of the publick, there 15
certainly is *no Government left.* Where the Laws cannot
be executed, it is all one as if there were no Laws, and a
Government without Laws is, I suppose, a Mystery in
Politicks, unconceivable to humane Capacity, and inconsistent with humane Society.   20

220.   In these and the like Cases, *when the Government
is dissolved,* the People are at liberty to provide for themselves, by erecting a new Legislative, differing from the
other, by the change of Persons, or Form, or both as
they shall find it most for their safety and good. For the 5
Society can never, by the fault of another, lose the Native
and Original Right it has to preserve it self, which can
only be done by a settled Legislative, and a fair and
impartial execution of the Laws made by it. But the state
of Mankind is not so miserable that they are not capable 10
of using this Remedy, till it be too late to look for any.

§ 219   This paragraph, and probably § 220, must have been written in
1689 to refer to James II having 'abdicated the government . . . and
withdrawn himself out of the kingdom' so 'that the throne is thereby
vacant', which were the words used in the Parliamentary resolutions:
compare note 3, Introduction, p. 59. The fact that these statements are
difficult to reconcile with what Locke says elsewhere about the dissolution of government as opposed to the dissolution of society (see Introduction, 129) may mark the passage as a subsequent insertion.

To tell *People* they *may provide for themselves,* by erecting
a new Legislative, when by Oppression, Artifice, or being
delivered over to a Foreign Power, their old one is gone, is
15 only to tell them they may expect Relief, when it is too
late, and the evil is past Cure. This is in effect no more
than to bid them first be Slaves, and then to take care of
their Liberty; and when their Chains are on, tell them,
they may act like Freemen. This, if barely so, is rather
20 Mockery than Relief; and Men can never be secure from
Tyranny, if there be no means to escape it, till they are
perfectly under it: And therefore it is, that they have not
only a Right to get out of it, but to prevent it.

221.   There is therefore, secondly, another way whereby
Governments are dissolved, and that is; when the Legisla-
tive, or the Prince, either of them act contrary to their
Trust.
5   *First,* The *Legislative acts against the Trust* reposed in
them, when they endeavour to invade the Property of the
Subject, and to make themselves, or any part of the
Community, Masters, or Arbitrary Disposers of the Lives,
Liberties, or Fortunes of the People.

222.   The Reason why Men enter into Society, is the
preservation of their Property; and the end why they chuse
and authorize a Legislative, is, that there may be Laws
made, and Rules set as Guards and Fences to the Prop-
5 erties of all the Members of the Society, to limit the Power,
and moderate the Dominion of every Part and Member
of the Society. For since it can never be supposed to be
the Will of the Society, that the Legislative should have a
Power to destroy that, which every one designs to secure,
10 by entering into Society, and for which the People submitted themselves to the Legislators of their own making;
whenever the *Legislators endeavour to take away, and
destroy the Property of the People,* or to reduce them to
Slavery under Arbitrary Power, they put themselves into
15 a state of War with the People, who are thereupon absolved from any farther Obedience, and are left to the

§ 221 1 'secondly'—presumably follows on to the '*First*' in § 212,
line 3, but the confusing numerations here may indicate successive re-
corrections to this whole area of the text: there is, e.g., no 'secondly'
to the '*First*' of line 4 of this paragraph.
§ 222 1–18 Compare II, § 135.
   1–2 Compare II, § 138, 3–4.

common Refuge, which God hath provided for all Men, against Force and Violence. Whensoever therefore the *Legislative* shall transgress this fundamental Rule of Society; and either by Ambition, Fear, Folly or Corruption, *en-* 20 *deavour to grasp* themselves, *or put into the hands of any other an Absolute Power* over the Lives, Liberties, and Estates of the People; By this breach of Trust they *forfeit the Power,* the People had put into their hands, for quite contrary ends, and it devolves to the People, who have a 25 Right to resume their original Liberty, and, by the Establishment of a new Legislative (such as they shall think fit) provide for their own Safety and Security, which is the end for which they are in Society. What I have said here, concerning the Legislative, in general, holds true also con- 30 cerning the *supreame Executor,* who having a double trust put in him, both to have a part in the Legislative, and the supreme Execution of the Law, Acts against both, when he goes about to set up his own Arbitrary Will, as the Law of the Society. He *acts* also *contrary to his Trust,* when he 35 either imploys the Force, Treasure, and Offices of the Society, to corrupt the *Representatives,* and gain them to his purposes: or openly pre-ingages the *Electors,* and prescribes to their choice, such, whom he has by Sollicitations, Threats, Promises, or otherwise won to his designs; 40 and imploys them to bring in such, who have promised before-hand, what to Vote, and what to Enact. Thus to regulate Candidates and *Electors,* and new model the ways of *Election,* what is it but to cut up the Government by the Roots, and poison the very Fountain of publick Se- 45 curity? For the People having reserved to themselves the Choice of their *Representatives,* as the Fence to their Properties, could do it for no other end, but that they might always be freely chosen, and so chosen, freely act and advise, as the necessity of the Commonwealth, and 50 the publick Good should, upon examination, and mature debate, be judged to require. This, those who give their

22–3   Compare II, § 87, 5–6, note and references.
23–5   Compare Lawson, *Politica Sacra* (1660), 1689, 62 (sovereignty may 'in some cases' be forfeit 'to the community'), and on trust generally (79, 217, etc.). See Maclean, 1947.
29–70   Probably an addition, or successive additions. Here Locke seems to have James II's attempts to control the elctorate specifically in mind (compare note on II, § 216); see Burnet, 1724, I, 719. The final lines can only refer to James II, and it seems likely that the whole passage was added in 1689, making the paragraph the longest in the book.

Votes before they hear the Debate, and have weighed the
Reasons on all sides, are not capable of doing. To prepare
55 such an Assembly as this, and endeavour to set up the
declared Abettors of his own Will, for the true *Representatives* of the People, and the Law-makers of the Society, is
certainly as great a *breach of trust,* and as perfect a Declaration of a design to subvert the Government, as is pos-
60 sible to be met with. To which, if one shall add Rewards
and Punishments visibly imploy'd to the same end, and
all the Arts of perverted Law made use of, to take off and
destroy all that stand in the way of such a design, and will
not comply and consent to betray the Liberties of their
65 Country, 'twill be past doubt what is doing. What Power
they ought to have in the Society, who thus imploy it
contrary to the trust went along with it in its first Institution, is easie to determine; and one cannot but see, that
he, who has once attempted any such thing as this, cannot
70 any longer be trusted.

223. To this perhaps it will be said, that the People
being ignorant, and always discontented, to lay the Foundation of Government in the unsteady Opinion, and uncertain Humour of the People, is to expose it to certain ruine;
5 And *no Government will be able long to subsist,* if the
People may set up a new Legislative, whenever they take
offence at the old one. To this, I Answer: Quite the
contrary. People are not so easily got out of their old
Forms, as some are apt to suggest. They are hardly to be
10 prevailed with to amend the acknowledg'd Faults, in the
Frame they have been accustom'd to. And if there by any
Original defects, or adventitious ones introduced by time,
or corruption; 'tis not an easie thing to get them changed,
even when all the World sees there is an opportunity for
15 it. This slowness and aversion in the People to quit their
old Constitutions, has, in the many Revolutions which have
been seen in this Kingdom, in this and former Ages, still

§ 223 5-7 Elrington, 1798, objects here that the right of changing
government depends not on the will of the people, but on their reason
dictating the necessity of it.

10-11 'in the Frame they have been accustom'd to'—there is a parallel phrase, perhaps accidental, in the *American Declaration of Independence,* ed. Becker, 1922, 10, 'the forms to which they are accustomed'.

17 'in this Kingdom'—here Locke again openly refers to England
and her Constitution; see II, § 213, 5-13, note and references.

kept us to, or, after some interval of fruitless attempts, still brought us back again to our old Legislative of King, Lords and Commons: And whatever provocations have 20 made the Crown be taken from some of our Princes Heads, they never carried the People so far, as to place it in another Line.

224. But 'twill be said, this *Hypothesis* lays a *ferment* for frequent *Rebellion*. To which I Answer,

First, No more than any other *Hypothesis*. For when the *People* are made *miserable*, and find themselves *exposed to the ill usage of Arbitrary Power*, cry up their 5 Governours, as much as you will for Sons of *Jupiter*, let them be Sacred and Divine, descended or authoriz'd from Heaven; give them out for whom or what you please, the same will happen. *The People generally ill treated*, and contrary to right, will be ready upon any occasion to ease 10 themselves of a burden that sits heavy upon them. They will wish and seek for the opportunity, which, in the change, weakness, and accidents of humane affairs, seldom delays long to offer it self. He must have lived but a little while in the World, who has not seen Examples of this in 15 his time; and he must have read very little, who cannot produce Examples of it in all sorts of Governments in the World.

225. Secondly, I Answer, such *Revolutions happen* not upon every little mismanagement in publick affairs. *Great mistakes* in the ruling part, many wrong and inconvenient Laws, and all the *slips* of humane frailty will be *born by the People*, without mutiny or murmur. But if a long 5 train of Abuses, Prevarications, and Artifices, all tending the same way, make the design visible to the People, and they cannot but feel, what they lie under, and see, whither they are going; 'tis not to be wonder'd, that they should then rouze themselves, and endeavour to put the rule into 10

18–23   This may be a reference to the events of 1688–9, and therefore a late addition, but it could perhaps as well refer to 1640–60 and the dynastic operations of the fifteenth century.
§ 225   6   Compare II, § 210, 14–15 (verbal parallel), and II, § 230, 12–16. The American Declaration of Independence has: 'But when a long train of abuses and usurpations pursuing invariably the same object . . .' (ed. Becker, 1922, 10).

such hands, which may secure to them the ends for which
Government was at first erected; and without which, ancient Names, and specious Forms, are so far from being
better, that they are much worse, than the state of Nature,
15 or pure Anarchy; the inconveniencies being all as great
and as near, but the remedy farther off and more difficult.

226. Thirdly, I Answer, That *this Doctrine* of a Power
in the People of providing for their safety a-new by a new
Legislative, when their Legislators have acted contrary to
their trust, by invading their Property, is *the best fence
5 against Rebellion,* and the probablest means to hinder it.
For Rebellion being an Opposition, not to Persons, but
Authority, which is founded only in the Constitutions and
Laws of the Government; those, whoever they be, who by
force break through, and by force justifie their violation
10 of them, are truly and properly *Rebels.* For when Men
by entering into Society and Civil Government, have excluded force, and introduced Laws for the preservation of
Property, Peace, and Unity amongst themselves; those who
set up force again in opposition to the Laws, do *Rebellare,*
15 that is, bring back again the state of War, and are properly
Rebels: Which they who are in Power (by the pretence
they have to Authority, the temptation of force they have
in their hands, and the Flattery of those about them)
being likeliest to do; the properest way to prevent the
20 evil, is to shew them the danger and injustice of it, who
are under the greatest temptation to run into it.

227. In both the forementioned Cases, when either the
Legislative is changed, or the Legislators act contrary to
the end for which they were constituted; those who are
guilty are *guilty of Rebellion.* For if any one by force
5 takes away the establish'd Legislative of any Society, and
the Laws by them made pursuant to their trust, he thereby
takes away the Umpirage, which every one had consented
to, for a peaceable decision of all their Controversies, and
a bar to the state of War amongst them. They, who re-
10 move, or change the Legislative, take away this decisive
power, which no Body can have, but by the appointment
and consent of the People; and so destroying the Authority, which the People did, and no Body else can set up,

12–16 Compare II, § 137, 12–17.

and introducing a Power, which the People hath not authoriz'd, they actually *introduce a state of War*, which is 15
that of Force without Authority: And thus by removing
the Legislative establish'd by the Society (in whose decisions the People acquiesced and united, as to that of
their own will) they unty the Knot, and *expose the People
a new to the state of War*. And if those, who by force 20
take away the Legislative, are *Rebels*, the *Legislators* themselves, as has been shewn, can be no less esteemed so;
when they, who were set up for the protection, and preservation of the People, their Liberties and Properties, shall
by force invade, and indeavour to take them away; and 25
so they putting themselves into a state of War with those,
who made them the Protectors and Guardians of their
Peace, are properly, and with the greatest aggravation,
Rebellantes Rebels.

228. But if they, who say it *lays a foundation for Rebellion*, mean that it may occasion Civil Wars, or Intestine
Broils, to tell the People they are absolved from Obedience,
when illegal attempts are made upon their Liberties or
Properties, and may oppose the unlawful violence of those, 5
who were their Magistrates, when they invade their Properties contrary to the trust put in them; and that therefore
this Doctrine is not to be allow'd, being so destructive to
the Peace of the World. They may as well say upon the
same ground, that honest Men may not oppose Robbers 10
or Pirates, because this may occasion disorder or blood-
shed. If any *mischief* come in such Cases, it is not *to be
charged* upon him, who defends his own right, but *on
him*, that *invades* his Neighbours. If the innocent honest
Man must quietly quit all he has for Peace sake, to him 15
who will lay violent hands upon it, I desire it may be
consider'd, what a kind of Peace there will be in the World,
which consists only in Violence and Rapine; and which
is to be maintain'd only for the benefit of Robbers and
Oppressors. Who would not think it an admirable Peace 20
betwixt the Mighty and the Mean, when the Lamb, without resistance, yielded his Throat to be torn by the im-
perious Wolf? *Polyphemus*'s Den gives us a perfect Pattern
of such a Peace, and such a Government, where in *Ulysses*
and his Companions had nothing to do, but quietly to 25

§ **228**   23–32   See the *Odyssey*, Book IX.

suffer themselves to be devour'd. And no doubt *Ulysses*, who was a prudent Man, preach'd up *Passive Obedience*, and exhorted them to a quiet Submission, by representing to them of what concernment Peace was to Mankind; and
30 by shewing the inconveniencies might happen, if they should offer to resist *Polyphemus*, who had now the power over them.

229. The end of Government is the good of Mankind, and which is *best for Mankind*, that the People should be always expos'd to the boundless will of Tyranny, or that the Rulers should be sometimes liable to be oppos'd, when
5 they grow exorbitant in the use of their Power, and imploy it for the destruction, and not the preservation of the Properties of their People?

230. Nor let any one say, that mischief can arise from hence, as often as it shall please a busie head, or turbulent spirit, to desire the alteration of the Government. 'Tis true, such Men may stir, whenever they please, but it will
5 be only to their own just ruine and perdition. For till the mischief be grown general, and the ill designs of the Rulers become visible, or their attempts sensible to the greater part, the People, who are more disposed to suffer, than right themselves by Resistance, are not apt to stir.
10 The examples of particular Injustice, or Oppression of here and there an unfortunate Man, moves them not. But if they universally have a perswasion, grounded upon manifest evidence, that designs are carrying on against their Liberties, and the general course and tendency of
15 things cannot but give them strong suspicions of the evil intention of their Governors, who is to be blamed for it? Who can help it, if they, who might avoid it, bring themselves into this suspicion? Are the People to be blamed, if they have the sence of rational Creatures, and can think
20 of things no otherwise than as they find and feel them? And is it not rather *their fault*, who puts things in such a posture that they would not have them thought, to be as they are? I grant, that the Pride, Ambition, and Turbulency of private Men have sometimes caused great Disorders in
25 Commonwealths, and Factions have been fatal to States

§ **230** 1–11 Compare II, § 208.
8–9 Parallel in the *American Declaration of Independence*, ed. Becker, 1922, 10: 'mankind are more disposed to suffer, while evils are sufferable, than to right themselves'.

and Kingdoms. But whether the *mischief* hath *oftener* begun *in the Peoples Wantonness,* and a Desire to cast off the lawful Authority of their Rulers; or *in the Rulers Insolence,* and Endeavours to get, and exercise an Arbitrary Power over their People; whether Oppression, or Disobedience 30 gave the first rise to the Disorder, I leave it to impartial History to determine. This I am sure, whoever, either Ruler or Subject, by force goes about to invade the Rights of either Prince or People, and lays the foundation for *overturning* the Constitution and Frame of *any Just Gov-* 35 *ernment,* is guilty of the greatest Crime, I think, a Man is capable of, being to answer for all those mischiefs of Blood, Rapine, and Desolation, which the breaking to pieces of Governments bring on a Countrey. And he who does it, is justly to be esteemed the common Enemy and Pest of 40 Mankind; and is to be treated accordingly.

231. That *Subjects,* or *Foreigners* attempting by force on the Properties of any People, may be *resisted* with force, is agreed on all hands. But that *Magistrates* doing the same thing, may be *resisted,* hath of late been denied: As if those who had the greatest Priviledges and Ad- 5 vantages by the Law, had thereby a Power to break those Laws, by which alone they were set in a better place than their Brethren: Whereas their Offence is thereby the greater, both as being ungrateful for the greater share they have by the Law, and breaking also that Trust, which 10 is put into their hands by their Brethren.

232. Whosoever uses *force without Right,* as every one does in Society, who does it without Law, puts himself into a *state of War* with those, against whom he so uses it, and in that state all former Ties are cancelled, all other Rights cease, and every one has a *Right* to defend him- 5 self, and *to resist the Aggressor.* This is so evident, that *Barclay* himself, that great Assertor of the Power and

36 'is guilty of the greatest Crime'. The 4th edition, 1713, the 1st Collected edition, 1714, and the 6th edition, 1764, all have 'is highly guilty of the greatest Crime', perhaps the reading of the hypothetical second master-copy—see Editorial Note.
    40–1   See II, § 172, 11–22 note and references.
§ 231   8–11   Compare II, § 202, 29–34.
§ 232   6–8   On Locke's purpose in singling out Barclay for such detailed attention, see note on II, § 239, 18–19. He mentions Filmer's use of this author in I, § 4, 15–16 and § 67, 32 without comment, but he possessed William Barclay's two major works (*De Regno et Regali Po-*

Sacredness of Kings, is forced to confess, That it is lawful
for the people, in some Cases, to *resist* their King; and
10 that too in a Chapter, wherein he pretends to shew that
the Divine Law shuts up the people from all manner of
Rebellion. Whereby it is evident, even by his own Doctrine,
that, since they may in some Cases *resist*, all resisting of
Princes is not Rebellion. His Words are these. *Quod siquis*
15 *dicat, Ergone populus tyrannicæ crudelitati & furori*
jugulum semper præbebit? Ergone multitudo civitates suas
fame, ferro, & flammâ vastari, seque, conjuges, & liberos
fortunæ ludibrio & tyranni libidini exponi, inque omnia
vitæ pericula omnesque miserias & molestias à Rege
20 *deduci patientur? Num illis quod omni animantium generi*
est à naturâ tributum, denegari debet, ut sc. vim vi repellant,
seseq; ab injuriâ tueantur? Huic breviter responsum sit,
Populo universo non negari defensionem, quæ juris naturalis
est, neque ultionem quæ præter naturam est adversus
25 *Regem concedi debere. Quapropter si Rex non in singulares*
tantum personas aliquot privatum odium exerceat, sed
corpus etiam Reipublicæ, cujus ipse caput est, i.e. totum
populum, vel insignem aliquam ejus partem immani &
intolerandâ sævitiâ seu tyrannide divexet; populo, quidem
30 *hoc casu resistendi ac tuendi se ab injuriâ potestas competit,*
sed tuendi se tantum, non enim in principem invadendi: &
restituendæ injuriæ illatæ, non recedendi à debitâ reverentiâ
propter acceptam injuriam. Præsentem denique impetum
propulsandi non vim præteritam ulciscendi jus habet.
35 *Horum enim alterum à naturâ est, ut vitam scilicet cor-*
pusque tueamur. Alterum vero contra naturam, ut inferior
de superiori supplicium sumat. Quod itaque populus malum,
antequam factum sit, impedire potest, ne fiat, id postquam
factum est, in Regem authorem sceleris vindicare non
40 *potest: Populus igitur hoc ampliùs quam privatus quisquam*
habet: Quod huic, vel ipsis adversariis judicibus, excepto

---

testati adversus Buchananum, Brutum, Boucherium et reliquos Monar-
chomachos, 1600, and *De Potestatae Papae*, 1609, two of the most
important and influential absolutist works, the first being directed in
part against the *Vindiciae*) in an edition of 1612 in one volume, Appendix B, no. 11. It was on his shelves in 1681, and on 15 July 1680
he bought a copy for the Earl of Shaftesbury. He noted the book in
1680 (II, § 236, 14–15 and note) and it seems likely that the passage
from this paragraph down to 239 was written in 1681; see II, § 211,
chapter XIX.

14–45 Passage on p. 375 of Locke's 1612 edition, inaccurately transcribed by him, with corrections in the errata of the 3rd edition, 1698,
see Collation.

*Buchanano, nullum nisi in patientia remedium superest.
Cùm ille si intolerabilis tyrannis est (modicum enim ferre
omnino debet) resistere cum reverentiâ possit,* Barclay
contra Monarchom, l. 3. c. 8.

45

In *English* thus.

233. *But if any one should ask, Must the People then
always lay themselves open to the Cruelty and Rage of
Tyranny? Must they see their Cities pillaged, and laid in
ashes, their Wives and Children exposed to the Tyrant's
Lust and Fury, and themselves and Families reduced by* 5
*their King, to Ruine and all the Miseries of Want and
Oppression, and yet sit still? Must Men alone be debarred
the common Priviledge of opposing force with force, which
Nature allows so freely to all other Creatures for their
preservation from Injury? I Answer: Self-defence is a part* 10
*of the Law of Nature; nor can it be denied the Community,
even against the King himself: But to revenge themselves
upon him, must by no means be allowed them; it being not
agreeable to that Law. Wherefore if the King shall shew an
hatred, not only to some particular Persons, but sets him-* 15
*self against the Body of the Commonwealth, whereof he
is the Head, and shall, with intolerable ill usage, cruelly
tyrannize over the whole, or a considerable part of the
People; in this case the People have a right to resist and
defend themselves from injury: But it must be with this* 20
*Caution, that they only defend themselves, but do not attack
their Prince: They may repair the Damages received, but
must not for any provocation exceed the bounds of due
Reverence and Respect. They may repulse the present attempt, but must not revenge past violences. For it is* 25
*natural for us to defend Life and Limb, but that an In-
feriour should punish a Superiour, is against Nature. The
mischief which is designed them, the People may prevent
before it be done, but when it is done, they must not revenge it on the King, though Author of the Villany. This* 30
*therefore is the Priviledge of the People in general, above
what any private Person hath; That particular Men are allowed by our Adversaries themselves, (Buchanan only
excepted) to have no other Remedy but Patience; but the
Body of the People may with Respect resist intolerable* 35
*Tyranny; for when it is but moderate, they ought to endure
it.*

234. Thus far that great Advocate of Monarchical Power allows of *Resistance*.

235. 'Tis true he has annexed two Limitations to it, to no purpose:

First, He says, it must be with Reverence.

Secondly, It must be without Retribution, or Punishment; 5 and the Reason he gives, is, *Because an Inferiour cannot punish a Superiour.*

First, How to *resist Force without striking again*, or how to *strike with Reverence*, will need some Skill to make intelligible. He that shall oppose an Assault only with a Shield 10 to receive the Blows, or in any more Respectful Posture, without a Sword in his hand, to abate the Confidence and Force of the Assailant, will quickly be at an end of his *Resistance*, and will find such a defence serve only to draw on himself the worse usage. This is as ridiculous a way of 15 *resisting*, as *Juvenal* thought it of fighting; *ubi tu pulsas, ego vapulo tantum.* And the Success of the Combat will be unavoidably the same he there describes it:

> ——*Libertas pauperis hæc est:*
> *Pulsatus rogat, & pugnis concisus, adorat,*
> 20 *Ut liceat paucis cum dentibus inde reverti.*

This will always be the event of such an imaginary *Resistance*, where Men may not strike again. He therefore *who may resist, must be allowed to strike*. And then let our Author, or any Body else joyn a Knock on the Head, 25 or a Cut on the Face, with as much *Reverence* and *Respect* as he thinks fit. He that can Reconcile Blows and Reverence, may, for ought I know, deserve for his pains, a Civil Respectful Cudgeling where-ever he can meet with it.

Secondly, As to his Second, *An Inferiour cannot punish* 30 *a Superiour;* that's true, generally speaking, whilst he is his Superiour. But to resist Force with Force, being *the State of War* that *levels the Parties,* cancels all former relation of Reverence, Respect, and *Superiority:* And then the odds that remains, is, That he, who opposes the

---

§ **235**   14–20 Juvenal, *Satires*, III, 289–90, 299–301: 'I writhe with the blows you put upon me. . . . This is a poor man's freedom; the more he is beaten, the more he implores, and he prostrates himself as he goes down in the struggle, so that he may come back a little with his teeth.'

unjust Aggressor, has this *Superiority* over him, that he has 35
a Right, when he prevails, to punish the Offender, both
for the Breach of the Peace, and all the Evils that followed upon it. *Barclay* therefore, in another place, more
coherently to himself, denies it to be lawful to *resist* a
King in any Case. But he there assigns Two Cases, whereby 40
a King may Un-king himself. His Words are,

Quid ergo nulline casus incidere possunt quibus populo
sese erigere atque in Regem impotentius dominantem arma
capere & invadere jure suo suâque authoritate liceat?
Nulli certe quamdiu Rex manet. Semper enim ex divinis id 45
obstat, Regem honorificato; *& qui potestati resistit, Dei*
ordinationi resistit: Non aliàs igitur in eum populo potestas
est quam si id committat propter quod ipso jure rex esse
desinat. Tunc enim se ipse principatu exuit atque in privatis
constituit liber: Hoc modo populus & superior efficitur, 50
reverso ad eum sc. jure illo quod ante regem inauguratum
in interregno habuit. At sunt paucorum generum commissa
ejusmodi quæ hunc effectum pariunt. At ego cum plurima
animo perlustrem, duo tantum invenio, duos, inquam,
casus quibus rex ipso facto ex Rege non regem se facit & 55
omni honore & dignitate regali atque in subditos potestate
destituit; quorum etiam meminit Winzerus. *Horum unus*
est, Si regnum [& rempublicam evertere conetur, hoc est,
si id ei propositum, eaque intentio fuerit ut] *disperdat,*
quemadmodum de Nerone fertur, quod is nempe senatum 60
populumque Romanum, atque adeo urbem ipsam ferro
flammaque vastare, ac novas sibi sedes quærere decrevisset.
Et de Caligula, quod palam denunciarit se neque civem
neque principem senatui amplius fore, inque animo
habuerit, interempto utriusque ordinis Electissimo quoque 65
Alexandriam *commigrare, ac ut populum uno ictu in-*
terimeret, unam ei cervicem optavit. Talia cum rex aliquis
meditatur & molitur serio, omnem regnandi curam &
animum illico abjicit, ac proinde imperium in subditos
amittit, ut dominus servi pro derelicto habiti, dominium.   70

42–70 and § 236   Locke's 1612 edition, 440–1, badly transcribed and
also amended in errata to 3rd edition (see Collation): the words '&
rempublicam . . . fuerit' (58–9) omitted in the printed editions, though
translated by Locke.
57   'Winzerus'—miscopy for Winzetus, that is, Ninian Winzet, Win-
get or Wingate, Scottish controversialist, who wrote against Knox and
Buchanan. Locke had obviously never heard of him.

236.   *Alter casus est, Si rex in alicujus clientelam se*
contulit, ac regnum quod liberum à majoribus & populo
traditum accepit, alienæ ditioni mancipavit. Nam tunc
quamvis forte non eâ mente id agit populo plane ut incom-
5 *modet: Tamen quia quod præcipuum est régiæ dignitatis*
amisit, ut summus scilicet in regno secundum Deum sit, &
solo Deo inferior, atque populum etiam totum ignorantem
vel invitum, cujus libertatem sartam & tectam conservare
debuit, in alterius gentis ditionem & potestatem dedidit;
10 *hâc velut quadam regni ab alienatione effecit, ut nec quod*
ipse in regno imperium habuit retineat, nec in eum cui
collatum voluit, juris quicquam transferat; atque ita eo
facto liberum jam & suæ potestatis populum relinquit, cujus
rei exemplum unum annales Scotici suppeditant. Barclay
15 contra Monarchom. Lib. 3. c. 16.

Which in *English* runs thus.

237.   *What then, Can there no Case happen wherein*
the People may of right, and by their own Authority help
themselves, take Arms, and set upon their King, im-
periously domineering over them? None at all, whilst he
5 *remains a King.* Honour the King, *and* he that resists the
Power, resists the Ordinance of God; *are Divine Oracles*
that will never permit it. The People therefore can never
come by a Power over him, unless he does something that
makes him cease to be a King. For then he divests himself
10 *of his Crown and Dignity, and returns to the state of a*
private Man, and the People become free and superiour;
the Power which they had in the Interregnum, *before they*
Crown'd him King, devolving to them again. But there
are but few miscarriages which bring the matter to this
15 *state. After considering it well on all sides, I can find but*
two. Two Cases there are, I say, whereby a King, ipso
facto, *becomes no King; and loses all Power and Regal*
Authority over his People; which are also taken notice
of by Winzerus.
20   *The first is, If he endeavour to overturn the Government,*
that is, if he have a purpose and design to ruine the King-

§ 236   14–15   This reference to Barclay appears on p. 73 of Locke's
Tablet (MS. f. 28—see note on II, § 22, 9–10 and references) thus:

80
Liberty
Barclay 1 3 c 16

dom and Commonwealth, as it is recorded of Nero, *that he resolved to cut off the Senate and People of* Rome, *lay the City waste with Fire and Sword, and then remove to some other place. And of* Caligula, *that he openly declar'd, that* 25 *he would be no longer a Head to the People or Senate, and that he had it in his thoughts to cut off the worthiest Men of both Ranks, and then retire to* Alexandria: *And he wish'd that the People had but one Neck, that he might dispatch them all at a blow. Such designs as these, when* 30 *any King harbours in his thoughts and seriously promotes, he immediately gives up all care and thought of the Commonwealth; and consequently forfeits the Power of Governing his Subjects, as a Master does the Dominion over his Slaves whom he hath abandon'd.* 35

238.   *The other Case is, When a King makes himself the dependent of another, and subjects his Kingdom which his Ancestors left him, and the People put free into his hands, to the Dominion of another. For however perhaps it may not be in his intention to prejudice the People; yet* 5 *because he has hereby lost the principal part of Regal Dignity, viz. to be next and immediately under God, Supream in his Kingdom; and also because he betray'd or forced his People, whose liberty he ought to have carefully preserved, into the Power and Dominion of a Foreign* 10 *Nation. By this as it were alienation of his Kingdom, he himself loses the Power he had in it before, without transferring any the least right to those on whom he would have bestowed it; and so by this act sets the People free, and leaves them at their own disposal. One Example of this is* 15 *to be found in the* Scotch *Annals.*

239.   In these Cases *Barclay* the great Champion of Absolute Monarchy, is forced to allow, That a King may be *resisted*, and *ceases to be a King*. That is in short, not to multiply Cases: In whatsoever he has *no Authority*, there he is no *King*, and may be *resisted*: For *wheresoever* 5 *the Authority ceases, the King ceases too*, and becomes like other Men who have no Authority. And these two Cases he instances in, differ little from those above mention'd, to be destructive to Governments, only that he has omitted the Principle from which his Doctrine flows; and 10

§ **239** 8-9 'those above mention'd'—presumably in §§ 212-24, especially § 217.

that is, The breach of trust, in not preserving the Form of
Government agreed on, and in not intending the end of
Government it self, which is the publick good and preservation of Property. When a King has Dethron'd himself,
15 and put himself in a state of War with his People, what
shall hinder them from prosecuting him who is no King,
as they would any other Man, who has put himself into
a state of War with them; *Barclay,* and those of his Opinion,
would do well to tell us. This farther I desire may be
20 taken notice of out of *Barclay,* that he says, *The mischief
that is designed them, the People may prevent before it
be done,* whereby he allows *resistance* when Tyranny is
but in design. *Such Designs as these* (says he) *when any
King harbours in his thoughts and seriously promotes, he*
25 *immediately gives up all care and thought of the Commonwealth;* so that according to him the neglect of the publick
good is to be taken as an evidence of such a *design,* or at
least for a sufficient cause of *resistance.* And the reason of
all he gives in these words, *because he betray'd or forced his*
30 *People whose liberty he ought carefully to have preserved.*
What he adds *into the Power and Dominion of a Foreign
Nation,* signifies nothing, the fault and forfeiture lying in
the loss of their *Liberty* which he *ought to have preserved,*
and not in any distinction of the Persons to whose Dominion
35 they were subjected. The People's Right is equally invaded,
and their Liberty lost, whether they are made Slaves to
any of their own, or a *Foreign Nation;* and in this lies the
injury, and against this only have they the Right of Defence. And there are instances to be found in all Countries,
40 which shew that 'tis not the change of Nations in the

18–19 Those of Barclay's opinion include Bilson and perhaps even
Hooker (see below), and it is clear that Locke has picked out Barclay
as typical of the whole absolutist school, insisting on his concessions
to resistance. Grotius had done this as early as 1625 in his *De Jure
Belli,* where (I, iv, 11) he cites the passage quoted in full by Locke in
§ 232. Mr Salmon shows (1959) that the example was followed by a
considerable number of writers who insisted on Barclay's admissions
as justifying action against despots, such men as Samuel Rutherford,
William Prynne, John Canne, Richard Baxter, Pierre Jurieu and James
Tyrrell (*Bibliotheca Politica,* 1691–2, 1718 ed., 106, printing the identical
passage as in §233, but differently translated). It is clear, then, that
Locke was merely following a well-established convention, but he dealt
more thoroughly with Barclay than anyone else. Although he was
quoted in the political literature of 1689, Barclay's name is more typical
of the period of Filmer, both in the 1640's and the early 1680's.
19–42 Passage inserted in 1694 (see Collation) and typical of the
way Locke expanded his text, making it very difficult to distinguish
original and addition. Compare II, § 217.

Persons of their Governours, but the change of Government, that gives the Offence. *Bilson,* a Bishop of our Church, and a great Stickler for the Power and Prerogative of Princes, does, if I mistake not, in his Treatise of *Christian Subjection,* acknowledge, That *Princes may for-* 45 *feit their Power,* and their Title to the Obedience of their Subjects; and if there needed authority in a Case where reason is so plain, I could send my Reader to *Bracton, Fortescue,* and the Author of the *Mirrour,* and others; Writers, who cannot be suspected to be ignorant of our 50 Government, or Enemies to it. But I thought *Hooker* alone might be enough to satisfie those Men, who relying on him for their Ecclesiastical Polity, are by strange fate carried to deny those principles upon which he builds it. Whether they are herein made the Tools of Cunninger 55 Workmen, to pull down their own Fabrick, they were best look. This I am sure, their Civil Policy is so new, so dangerous, and so destructive to both Rulers and People, that as former Ages never could bear the broaching of it; so it may be hoped those to come, redeem'd from 60 the Impositions of those *Egyptian* Under-Taskmasters, will abhor the Memory of such servile Flatterers, who whilst

42–5 Thomas Bilson (1547–1616, Warden of Winchester College, bishop successively of Worcester and Winchester), *The True Difference between Christian Subiection and Unchristian Rebellion,* 1585. This book was often quoted by the opponents of absolutism, for exactly the same reason as Barclay was and frequently alongside of him (by Prynne, for example)—because though an absolutist he admitted resistance in crucial cases. Locke does not seem to have possessed Bilson's book, and the form of words here implies that he did not know it first-hand.

48–9 'Bracton'—the judge (d. 1268) and author of *De Legibus et Consuetudinibus Angliae.* 'Fortescue'—Sir John Fortescue (1394?–1476?), Lord Chief Justice and author of *De Laudibus Legum Angliae.* 'the Author of the Mirrour', perhaps Andrew Horne (d. 1328), author of a work very popular with constitutionalists in the seventeenth century, but a highly suspect source, *The Booke called The Mirrour of Justices,* printed in the 1640's. Compare note on II, § 13, 1–3. Locke recommended Bracton and the Mirror in his *Thoughts on Reading and Study,* 1703, and his letter to Rev. Richd. King, 170 (*Works,* 1801, III, 272; XI, 306): in his *Education* (*ibid.* IX, 177) he requires a gentleman to 'take a view of our English constitution, in the ancient books of the common law'. There is, however, no evidence that he ever possessed or read any one of these books, a fact which bears on his indifference to constitutional history and constitutional development; see Introduction, 90 and note.

51 'Hooker'—see note on II, § 5, 9–28: this sentence indicates that the paragraph was written when, or not long after, Locke had decided to add the quotations from Hooker, perhaps in 1681; see note on II, § 211, chapter XIX.

65 it seem'd to serve their turn, resolv'd all Government into absolute Tyranny, and would have all Men born to, what their mean Souls fitted them for, Slavery.

240. Here, 'tis like, the common Question will be made, *Who shall be Judge* whether the Prince or Legislative act contrary to their Trust? This, perhaps, ill affected and factious Men may spread amongst the People, when the Prince only makes use of his due Prerogative. To this 5 I reply, *The People shall be Judge;* for who shall be *Judge* whether his Trustee or Deputy acts well, and according to the Trust reposed in him, but he who deputes him, and must, by having deputed him have still a Power to discard him, when he fails in his Trust? If this be reasonable in 10 particular Cases of private Men, why should it be otherwise in that of the greatest moment; where the Welfare of Millions is concerned, and also where the evil, if not prevented, is greater, and the Redress very difficult, dear, and dangerous?

241. But farther, this Question, (*Who shall be Judge?*) cannot mean, that there is no Judge at all. For where there is no Judicature on Earth, to decide Controversies, amongst Men, *God* in Heaven is *Judge:* He alone, 'tis true, 5 is Judge of the Right. But *every Man* is *Judge* for himself, as in all other Cases, so in this, whether another hath put himself into a State of War with him, and whether he should appeal to the Supreme Judge, as *Jephtha* did.

242. If a Controversie arise betwixt a Prince and some of the People, in a matter where the Law is silent, or doubtful, and the thing be of great Consequence, I should think the proper *Umpire,* in such a Case, should be the 5 Body of the *People.* For in Cases where the Prince hath a Trust reposed in him, and is dispensed from the common ordinary Rules of the Law; there, if any Men find themselves aggrieved, and think the Prince acts contrary to, or beyond that Trust, who so proper to *Judge* as the Body

§ 240 2 '*Who shall be Judge*'—see II, § 168, 1–2, note and references. This question occupies Locke until the end of the book, and the passage seems to have been part of the original text, perhaps following on to § 231, but much modified and extended in 1689—see note on II, § 211, chapter XIX.
§ 241 8 '*Jephtha*'—see note on II, § 21, 20 and references.

of the *People*, (who, at first, lodg'd that Trust in him) 10
how far they meant it should extend? But if the Prince,
or whoever they be in the Administration, decline that way
of Determination, the Appeal then lies no where but to
Heaven. Force between either Persons, who have no known
Superiour on Earth, or which permits no Appeal to a 15
Judge on Earth, being properly a state of War, wherein the
Appeal lies only to Heaven, and in that State the *injured
Party must judge* for himself, when he will think fit to
make use of that Appeal, and put himself upon it.

243. To conclude, The *Power that every individual
gave the Society,* when he entered into it, can never revert
to the Individuals again, as long as the Society lasts, but
will always remain in the Community; because without
this, there can be no Community, no Common-wealth, 5
which is contrary to the original Agreement: So also
when the Society hath placed the Legislative in any Assembly of Men, to continue in them and their Successors,
with Direction and Authority for providing such Successors, *the Legislative can never revert to the People* 10
whilst that Government lasts: Because having provided a
Legislative with Power to continue for ever, they have
given up their Political Power to the Legislative, and
cannot resume it. But if they have set Limits to the Duration of their Legislative, and made this Supreme Power in 15
any Person, or Assembly, only temporary: Or else when by
the Miscarriages of those in Authority, it is forfeited; upon
the Forfeiture of their Rulers, or at the Determination of
the Time set, *it reverts to the Society,* and the People
have a Right to act as Supreme, and continue the Legis- 20
lative in themselves, or erect a new Form, or under the
old form place it in new hands, as they think good.

FINIS.

§ **243**   21–2   Modified slightly by Locke; see Collation. The reference
to 'new hands', and perhaps much or even all of §§ 242, 243, seem to
belong to 1689.

COLLATION
of
FIRST TREATISE

COLLATION
of
FIRST TREATISE

EXPLANATION OF COLLATION

The collation lists variations from the copy text. The copy text is that of the Christ's copy (see Editorial Note) and variants from it are treated as rejected readings, rejected for the most part by Locke.

Entries are given under paragraphs in the following pattern.

First the line number or numbers, then the word or words affected, or guide words to the passage affected, then a square bracket.

After the square bracket, where necessary, the symbol or symbols for the authority(ies) for the adopted reading, then a semi-colon.

After the semi-colon, the variant reading or readings, separated by semi-colons, and each followed by the symbol for its source or sources.

The symbols are as follows:

Lo   means the reading of an alteration in manuscript found in the Christ's copy.

Lo *inserts*   means an insertion in manuscript found in the Christ's copy.

1   means the reading of the 1st printing, 1689/90.

1er   means the reading of the errata slip to the 1st printing.

(*so in* Lo's 1)   means that the reading is found in the corrections made by Locke in his copy of the 1st printing.

2   means the reading of the 2nd printing, 1694.

2er   means the reading of the errata list in the 2nd printing.

3   means the reading of the 3rd printing, 1698.

3er   means the reading of the errata list in the 3rd printing.

1–3 means a reading common to 1, 2 and 3.

1, 2 means a reading common to 1 and 2.

2, 3 means a reading common to 2 and 3.

4 means the reading of the 4th printing, 1713.

4+ means the reading of the 4th printing and of the texts wholly or partly derived from it (i.e. Col 5, 6).

Col means the reading of the 1st Collected edition, 1714.

5 means the reading of the 5th edition, 1728.

6 means the reading of the 6th (Hollis) edition, 1764.

After the variant(s), and sometimes between them, explanatory notes will sometimes be found. These are placed within brackets and printed in italics. They are concerned for the most part with the manner in which the manuscript corrections were carried out in the Christ's copy, and with the evidence for a possible second master-copy, other than the Christ's copy (see Editorial Note for a discussion of this point).

Notes

(1) Where the variant is found in 1, 2, or 3 only, it is sometimes printed immediately after the bracket, the other symbols being understood.

(2) In other instances where no symbol succeeds the bracket the reading adopted is an editorial emendation with no documentary authority. These are few.

(3) In some entries line numbers only are given, with no guide words or bracket.

These are usually longer passages where misunderstanding is unlikely, and it is sometimes necessary to infer that the reading adopted is from 3 or 2 and 3.

(4) The roman figures after the paragraph numbers in the collation for the *Second Treatise* are the numbers in the French version, from which all foreign language editions were published until the 20th century.

The collating methods used here are an adaptation of those laid down by McKerrow, 1939, and adopted by Bowers, 1953. The wavy dash (∼) is taken from these authorities, and has been found most useful in dealing with the very large number of punctuation variations and corrections collated here.*

* There is perhaps a possibility of confusion between the semi-colon used to separate variants from each other, and a semi-colon which is itself a variant. It seemed better, however, to run this very slight risk, rather than adapt, or invent, a special sign for the purpose of separation.

The use of this wavy dish is probably self-evident, for it simply stands for a word or phrase which has been cited merely in order to mark a varying punctuation point or points, and which does not itself vary. It thus makes it unnecessary to print that word or phrase again in order to register the variation(s). It is sometimes used in presenting variants other than those in punctuation.

The caret below the line (∧) is also taken from McKerrow and Bowers. It serves to draw attention to the absence of punctuation at a point where one or other of the variants does have punctuation.

An example of the use of the wavy dash and the caret below the line follows. In line 14 of II, § 166, the 1st printing reads 'Disorders,', the 2nd and 3rd printings read 'Disorders' with no punctuation, and the Christ's copy 'Disorders,' restoring the comma. It is represented thus: **14.** Disorders,] Lo, 1; ∼ ∧ 2, 3

By the use of this Collation is is hoped that the reader will be enabled to follow the history of every passage which shows significant variation in the documents collated, and to see the authority on which the editor has adopted his reading. But an exhaustive history of every tiny detail has not been attempted. The following things are *not* included in the Collation, except where the editor felt that there would be some point in including them.

Italics. The very extensive italicization made in manuscript in the Christ's copy has of course been adopted, but attention is not normally drawn to the fact that italic passages are the result of this final correction, nor to variants in the use of italics between the printings.

Spelling. The spelling of the Christ's copy (type and manuscript) is printed, and variations between this spelling and that of earlier or later printings (or between such printings) are not normally recorded. Spelling here includes the use of capitals and abbreviations, conventional signs (such as 1° for 'first'), etc.

Punctuation. The heavily corrected punctuation of the Christ's copy is reproduced, and attention drawn to the variants brought about by this correction. But variations in punctuation between 1, 2 and 3 which are not affected by the correction in the Christ's copy are not normally recorded.

Errata. Where a printing shows a variant peculiar to itself, and that variant is corrected in the errata list to the reading found in all other sources, it is not normally recorded.

These omissions have made possible considerable savings of time and printing effort. It is difficult to imagine many cases where the absence of these minutiae will frustrate the student in the pursuit of the history of Locke's text and it is hoped that the value of the Collation will be only negligibly reduced by these savings. They do mean, however, that the spelling, italics and punctuation of the 1st printing, the nearest to Locke's original manuscript, cannot be recovered, except where correction was made to the passages concerned in the Christ's copy.

Two further points are taken as understood in the Collation:

(1) Where only one variant is recorded from documents earlier than 4, all the other documents read as in the text printed by the editor.

(2) Readings of 4 and later printings are only recorded to sanction, or contrast with, readings adopted by the editor which do not appear in the earlier documents. The absence of these symbols does not always mean that these later printings always agree with the reading printed here.

Preface

9. Christendom:] Lo; ~ ; 1-3   **14.** self∧] Lo; ~ , 1-3
44-9. *their Patriarch, whom they have followed, is, or ought to be; that so they may either recant what, upon so ill Grounds, they have vented, or justifie his Opinions. For I should not* 1, 2   **57.** *wrong;*] Lo; ~ , 1-3
57-63. *Publick wrong (there being scarce a greater mischief to Prince and People, than the propagating wrong Notions concerning Government) they would be as ready to redress it. And that all times might not* 1, 2   **59.** *be as ready to*] Lo *inserts*   **62.** *Government, that*] Lo, 1, 2; ~ . That 3
79. Edit. 1680] *om.* 1, 2

FIRST TREATISE

§ 1

5. Sr. Rt: Filmer's *Patriarcha*] Lo; it 1-3   **7.** so,] Lo; ~ ;
1-3   **11.** the Book] Lo; Sir *Robert's* Book 1-3   **13.** it]
Lo; the *Patriarcha* of Sir *R.Filmer* 1-3   **21.** in truth]
Lo *inserts*

§ 2

5. Sir] *om.* 1   **16.** And...this] 2, 3; *italics* 1

§ 3

1-2. In...who] Lo; Since there have been a Generation of Men sprung up in the world who 1-3   **12.** also unsettled]

3; also so unsettled 1, 2 ('so' *deleted in* Lo's 1, *and in* 2er)
17. to serve their present turn] Lo *inserts*

§ 4

2–3. and...Life] Lo; and there is no remedy for it, we must
continue so; Life 1–3   **5–7.** other...Divine] Lo; though
I do not find Scripture or Reason any where say so; however
these men would perswade us, that Divine 1–3   **14.** has]
2, 3; have 1

§ 5 (*Paragraph number omitted in* 1)

3. or] Lo *inserts*   **5.** recollect. My] 3; recollect my 1;
recollect; My 2   **5–6.** is only] Lo *inserts* 'is'
11–13. *Italicized by* Lo   **13.** *Government.*] Lo, 1, 2; ~ ;
3   **13–16.** *Italicized by editor*   **15.** *Consent.*] Lo, 1, 2;
~ ; 3

§ 6

10. Men∧] Lo, 1, 2; ~ , 3   **25.** Writings.] Lo, 1, 2; ~ ; 3
45. Ark] 3; Arch 1, 2   **46.** Sons,] 1, 2; ~ ∧ 3
58. purpose.] 1, 2; ~ , 3

§ 7

6. *the*] Lo, 1; *thee* 2, 3

§ 8

42. *at*] *om.* 2, 3 (*present in Filmer*)

§ 9

13. and] or 1

§ 10

6. have] 2er, 3; had 1, 2   **10–11.** them. Without this,
What] 3; ~ ∧ without ~ ; ~ 1, 2 (~ : without ~ ∧ ~ *in* Lo's
1); ~ . Without ~ ; ~ 2er   **16.** limited] Lo, 1, 2; unlimited 3   **17.** all,] Lo; ~ ∧ 1–3

§ 11

7. the Business] Lo, 1, 3er; of business 2, 3   **13.** Struc-
ture∧] Lo; ~ , 1–3   **14.** Foundation. For] Lo; Foundation;
for 1–3   **16.** should doe] Lo; does 1–3   **30.** That] Lo;
that 1–3

§ 12

13. Proof] Lo; Proofs 1–3   **15–16.** he concludes *the
Royal*] Lo; *And indeed* (he concludes) *the Royal* 1–3

§ 14

3. to] Col; To 1–3   **21.** Treatises; and they] Lo; Treatises, which 1–3

§ 15

4. Adam:] Lo; ~ ; 1–3   **11.** him.] Lo; ~ ; 1–3
18. God:] Lo; ~ ; 1–3

§ 16

7. *Posterity*:] Lo; ~ , 1–3   **8.** *Creation.*] 4 +; ~ , 1–3
52. *Posterity*:] Lo; ~ ; 1–3

§ 17

2. by] *by* 1–3   **4.** by] *by* 1–3   **9.** He] Lo; he 1–3
11. *Nature.*] Lo; ~ , 1–3   **16.** when…only] Lo; by which only 1–3

§ 18

2. *Act*:] Lo; ~ ; 1–3   **7.** it, it was] 2er, 3; Published, it was 1, 2   **16.** place.] Lo; ~ ; 1–3   **19.** *Nature.*] Lo; ~ ; 1–3

§ 19

6. has this] Lo (*so in* Lo's 1); this has 1–3   **6.** *Creation,*] (*so in* Lo's 1) ~ ∧ 1–3   **8.** *World?*] 2er, 3; ~ ; 1, 2
10. (Bracket absent in 1 but inserted by Lo in his copy)
12. Posterity. What] Lo; Posterity; I say what 1–3
14. *Government,*] (*so in* Lo's 1); ~ ; 1–3   **16.** see;] (*so in* Lo's 1); ~ . 1–3

§ 20

8. Senses,] Lo, 1; ~ ∧ 1–3   **18.** *Posterity?*] Lo; ~ . 1–3
28. other?] Lo; ~ ; 1–3   **40.** see,…Matter,] Lo; ~ ∧ …~ ∧ 1–3

§ 21

5. Sovereignty.] 4 + ; ~ ∧ 1; ~ , 2, 3   **12.** Obs:] Lo, 3er; Ob. 1; Ob; 2, 3   **20.** *shews*] (*so in Filmer*); shew 1–3

§ 22

6. *shews*] shew 1–3 (*see* § 21, 20)

§ 23

1. Argument.] Lo; ~ , 1–3   **6.** From] from 1–3
9. *World.* Whereby] Lo; World; whereby 1–3   **24.** more] 1er (*so in* Lo's 1); *om.* 1–3

§ 25

, in *Hebrew*] in the Hebrew 1   **9.** interpreter.] Lo; ~ , 1;
~ ; 2, 3   **11–12.** which, v. 24.] which *Ver.* 24th 1
8. brute] Lo, 1; bruit 2, 3   **35.** *moving,*] Lo, 1; ~ ∧ 2, 3
6. signify] Lo; signifies 3
N.B. *The Hebrew in this paragraph is correct in the 1st
dition only, and the editor has amended accordingly*)

§ 26

, viz.] *om.* 3   **4.** *Living…Earth*] not ital. 1–3
. Kingdoms,] 2er, 3 (*so in* Lo's 1); ~ ; 1, 2   **9.** Beasts:]
er, 3 (*so in* Lo's 1); ~ , 1, 2 (*Hebrew amended by editor*)
0. executes] exercises 4, Col +   **11.** Dominion,] 2er, 3
(*so in* Lo's 1); ~ ∧ 1, 2   **11.** mentions] 2 er (*so in* Lo's 1);
~ ; 1, 2; *mentions* 3   **13.** words,] (*so in* Lo's 1); ~ ∧ 1, 3
4. ver. 26] *O.* 26 1 (*O. deleted in* Lo's 1)   **25.** thing,]
Lo; ~ ∧ 1–3   **26.** giving to one] Lo; giving one 1–3

§ 27

. upon the] 3; on the 1, 2   **10.** another:] Lo; ~ , 1–3
8. the 26*th*] the *om.* 1, 2   **37.** (*semi-colons inserted by
ditor*)   **38.** Heirs,] Lo; ~ ∧ 1–3   **42.** might eat] Lo;
night have eat 1–3
N.B. *The Hebrew in this paragraph has been amended
editorially*)

§ 28

. *A*——,] ~ ∧ 1–3

§ 29

. Men:] Lo; ~ , 1; ~ ∧ 2, 3   **7.** to more] Lo; no more 3
0. *A.,*] ~ ∧ 1–3   **15.** subjected] Lo *inserts*

§ 30

2. our *Image*] 1, 2; *own Image* 3   **23.** Species:] Lo;
~ , 1, 2; ~ ; 3   **23–4.** Text. God] Lo; Text, for God 1–3
next: God 3er)   **25–6.** *Dominion.*] Lo; ~ ; 1–3
2. *Dominion.*] Lo; ~ , 1; ~ : 2, 3

§ 31

0. Mankind:] Lo; ~ , 1; ~ ; 2, 3   **12–13.** *Fatherhood.*]
Lo; ~ ; 1–3   **22.** *World.*] Lo; ~ , 1–3   **25.** by] *ital.*
–3   **25.** *Adam,*] ~ ∧ 1–3

§ 32

. him.] Lo; ~ , 1; ~ ; 2, 3   **31.** Grant,] Lo; ~ ∧ 1–3
2–3. (for…delivered) *brackets* Lo *inserts*   **34.** *Succes-*

sion:] Lo; ~ , 1–3   **35.** enjoy'd.] Lo; ~ , 1–3   **37.** reversion:] Lo; ~ ; 1–3   **41.** say,] Lo; ~ ∧ 1–3
41. event∧] Lo; ~ , 1–3   **43.** grant] 1er, (*so in* Lo's 1);
2er, 3 grants 1, 2   **48.** him.] Lo; ~ , 1–3

§ 33

4. all.] Lo; ~ , 1–3   **5.** Blessing.] Lo; ~ ; 1–3   **7.** all:]
Lo; ~ , 1–3   **14.** say,] ~ ∧ 3   **17.** great] Lo; only 1–3
18. that] Lo, 1; *om.* 2, 3   **18.** People:] Lo; ~ , 1–3
20. World.] Lo; ~ ; 1; ~ : 2, 3   **30.** History.] Lo; ~ ,
1–3

§ 34

2. expressed,] Lo; ~ ∧ 1–3   **2–4.** belong to.... *The fear*]
Lo; belong to *Noah's* Sons, not *with a Subordination* or in
Succession, but as far forth and equally as to *Noah* himself.
The fear 1–3
(*This passage is twice corrected in the Christ's copy, the
final version being printed here. The first correction is incomplete and seems to have been intended to read as it does in the
4th and Collected editions,* 'to belong equally to them all, as
much to Noah's Sons as to Noah, and not to his sons *with a
subordination* or in *succession'. Hollis in the 6th edition prints
this version, and not that in the Christ's copy. This evidence
may suggest that, though it was not Locke's final copy for
posthumous printing, the Christ's copy may have had additions
made later than those in the hypothetical second master-copy
[see Editorial Note], and shows up Hollis as an editor.*)

§ 35

10. 211] 2. 11 1–3

§ 36

4. Words.] Lo; ~ ; 1–3   **5.** *Abrogated*;] Lo; ~ , 1–3
6. (for] Lo, 1er (*so in* Lo's 1); ∧~ 1–3   **6.** proved)] 1er
(*so in* Lo's 1); ~ ∧ 1–3   **6.** (*Lo inserts a comma after
'ever', a slip corrected by editor*)

§ 37

3. *right?*] (*so in* Lo's 1); ~ ∧ 1; ~ : 2, 3   **10.** only] Lo,
1, 2, 3er; *om.* 3

§ 38

2. and,] Lo; ~ ∧ 1–3   **5–6.** He...as] 2, 3; He comes, 2°
to insinuate as 1   **15.** 211. So] Lo; ~ so 1–3

§ 39

12. a Rabbet] Lo, 1; a *om.* 2, 3   **28.** but] 1; *ital.* 2, 3
31. understood:] ~ . 1   **39.** them ∧] Lo; ~ ; 1–3
41. another.] Lo; ~ ; 1–3   **45, 58.** hunger,...World,]
Lo; ~ ∧...~ ∧ 1–3   **59.** Creatures ∧] Lo; ~ , 1–3
62. not.] Lo; ~ ; 1–3

§ 40

4. other] Lo; else 1–3 ('anything else' 3er)   **13.** *Property*]
Lo, 3er; Propriety 1–3

§ 41

4. Soveraignty?] ~ , 1; ~ ; 2   **5.** another?] ~ , 1, 2
8. Men?] ~ ; 1; ~ : 2   **22.** Men,] Lo; ~ ∧ 1–3

§ 42

2. please:] Lo; ~ , 1; ~ ; 2, 3   **6.** to] in 1, 2
12. Plenty. As] Plenty; For as 1, 2

§ 43

2. Hand;] Lo; ~ , 1–3   **11.** Compact.] Lo; ~ , 1–3
22. Sovereignty,] Lo; ~ ∧ 1–3   **22.** Property.] Lo; ~ ;
1–3.

§ 44

1. Builds] Build 1   **2.** 16] 26 1–3 (*wrong verse*)
9. let *Rule*] let but *Rule* 1   **11.** Establish'd.] Lo; ~ , 1–3
25. Authority,]   ~ ∧ 1–3   **26.** Monarchy:] Lo;   ~ ;
1–3   **27–8.** as well as a Partner in the Transgression] 1;
(*phrase omitted at this point in* 2, 3 *and inserted after*
'enough' *in line* 15 *of paragraph* 45)   **34.** Life;] Lo; ~ .
1–3

§ 45

7. be.] Lo; ~ , 1–3   **10.** its] from Lo, 1, 3er; his 2, 3
11. *Face thou shalt*] *Face, shalt thou* 1   **21.** 19. It] Lo;
19. this 1–3   **24.** Representative,] Lo; ~ ∧ 1–3

§ 46

3. Men,] Lo; ~ ∧ 1–3   **5.** Language∧] Lo; ~ , 1–3
5. them.] Lo; ~ , 1–3   **10.** maintain] Lo, 1, 3er; attain
2, 3   **11.** good.] Lo; ~ ; 1–3

§ 47

5. *Eve:*] Lo; ~ , 1; ~ ; 2, 3   **6.** as their] Lo; as a 1–3
13. is,]Lo; ~ ∧ 1–3   **15.** her:] Lo; ~ , 1–3   **23.** him:]
Lo; ~ , 1; ~ ; 2, 3   **31.** him?] Lo, 3er; ~ , 1–3

33. her?] Lo, 3er; ~ , 1; ~ . 2, 3   34. to Men] to *om.* 1
38. Nations‸] Lo; ~ , 1–3

§ 48

11. Husbands.] Lo; ~ : 1–3   12. Power,] Lo; ~ ‸ 1–3
16. before that of his wife]—Lo *inserts*   17. Concernment; but] Lo; Concernment before that of his Wife: but
1–3

§ 49

8. Government,] ~ ‸ 3   14. it.] Lo; ~ , 1–3
16. Prince, the] Lo; Prince, and the 1–3   17. changed,]
Lo, 1; ~ ; 2, 3   19. over] Lo *inserts*   22–3. down to
the end of the Chapter.] Lo; down to *Ch.* 1. 1; down *Ch.* 1.
2, 3   30. to *Adam*] Lo *inserts*   31. so all through,
would] so, although he would 1 (*altered to* 'althrough' *in*
Lo's 1)   35. Reason.] Lo; ~ , 1–3   41–2. it had...de-
sired] Lo; and desired 1–3   42. only] Lo. *inserts*
47. himself,] ~ ‸ 3   52. 245] 254 1–3

§ 50

4. Children,] ~ ‸ 3   5. so] *om.* 1 (*inserted* 1er)

§ 51

3. him,] Lo, 1; ~ ? 2, 3   8. nothing:] Lo; ~ , 1; ~ ; 2, 3
11. or] Lo, 1; and 2, 3   13–18. *voluntas,...* Slave's] Lo;
voluntas, may there be allowed: But 'tis but an ill way of
pleading for Absolute Monarchy, and Sir *Robert's* bare
Sayings will scarce Establish it, one Slave's 1–3   23. be
confident] Lo; be as confident 1–3   23–4. *That...*
Fathers] Lo; *not ital.* 1–3   24–5. as certainly] Lo *inserts*
25. Free;] Lo; ~ , 1–3

§ 52

15. *Life:*] Lo; ~ , 1–3   23. whole.] Lo; ~ ; 1–3
24. Voluptuary,] ~ ‸ 1–3   30. Preservation?] 1, 2, 3er;
~ . 3

§ 53

9. living] 1er (*so in* Lo's 1), 2er; live 1, 2   15. which]
Lo *inserts*   18. *that*] *om.* 1 (*inserted* 1er)
29. Parents;] ~ ‸ 3

§ 54

1–2. Children,] 1; ~ ‸ 2, 3   3. it.] Lo; ~ , 1; ~ ; 2, 3
7. Appetite?] Lo; ~ , 1–3   13. making,] Lo; ~ ‸ 1–3

§ 55

4. them.] Lo; ∼ ; 1–3   **28–9.** Revelations:] Lo; ∼ ; 1–3

§ 56

7. this:] Lo; ∼ ; 1–3   **9.** Off-spring:] Lo; ∼ ; 1–3
28. Natures.] Lo; ∼ ; 1–3

§ 57

1. Example∧] Col, 5, 6; Examples 1; Example, 2, 3

§ 58

2. a Brutality] Lo, 1, 3er; the ∼ 2, 3   **3.** Angels.] Lo, 1;
∼ ; 2, 3   **7.** his] the 1   **8.** by.] Lo; ∼ ; 1–3
12. followers:] Lo; ∼ ; 1–3   **16.** Nations of the] Lo
inserts   **17.** their Governments, Religions, and Manners]
Lo (*comma after* 'Government' *om. in Christ's copy*), the
Religion, Government and Manners 1; the Religions, Governments and Manners 2, 3.   **18.** amongst them] Lo *inserts*
20. in use and credit amongst Men] Lo; in Fashion amongst
Men 1; in use amongst Men 2, 3   **25–40.** If precedents...
of Idolatry] Lo *inserts*

§ 59

3. them;] Lo; ∼, 1–3   **5.** them:] Lo; ∼, 1–3
12. perfection,] Lo; ∼ ∧ 1–3

§ 60

6. *Terms*] 2er, 3; Term 1, 2   **7.** *Whereas*] 6; *whereas* 1–3
22. Defender∧] Lo; ∼, 1–3   **24.** occasion;] Lo; ∼, 1–3
30. lop] 1er (*so in* Lo's 1), 2, 3; top 1   **31.** Notions:]
Lo; ∼, 1–3

§ 61

7. Mother:] Lo; ∼ ; 1–3   **19.** 27] 28 1–3 (*wrong ref.*)
27. 45] 11 1–3 (*wrong ref.*)   **28.** 22.7] 28.2 1–3 (*wrong
ref.*)   **30.** *begat*] 1, 2; *beget* 3   **39.** more.] Lo; ∼, 1–3
43. *A.*,] Lo, 1; ∼ ∧ 2, 3   **44.** it.] Lo; ∼, 1; ∼ ; 2, 3

§ 62

5. Mother.] Lo; ∼ ; 1–3   **6.** Commandment] Lo; Commandments 1–3   **11.** Honour? Can] 3er; ∼ ; ∼ 1–3
13. The] Lo, 1; the 2, 3

§ 63

3. having∧] 3 ∼,   **5.** them:] Lo; ∼, 1; ∼ ; 2, 3

7. *Father* (let] Lo; ~ , ~ 1–3   **9.** asunder)] Lo; ~ , 1–3
18. Title:] Lo; ~ , 1–3

§ 64

4. Power:] Lo; ~ , 1–3   **7.** Commandment.] Lo; ~ ; 1–3
9–11. in him,. . . 'tis certain] 2, 3; in him, and by *Honour thy Father* be commanded, that Obedience which is due to the Sovereign, 'tis certain 1   **13–14.** cannot, it follows from hence that, *Honour*] Lo; cannot, 'tis evident, *Honour* 1–3
19. it:] Lo; ~ , 1–3   **20.** Society∧] Lo; ~ , 1–3

§ 65

12. them:] Lo; ~ ; 1–3   **14.** the Parents. So] Lo; them, so 1–3   **15.** *Mother*∧] Lo; ~ , 1–3   **16.** Obedience;] Lo; ~ , 1–3   **19.** civil] Lo, 3er; such 1–3
20. Societies;] Lo; ~ , 1–3   **24.** another:] Lo; ~ , 1–3
26. not.] Lo; ~ ; 1–3   **28.** Monarchy;] Lo; ~ . 1–3
29. by every] Lo, 1, 2; to ~ 3   **31.** Fathers:] Lo; ~ , 1–3
32. besides∧] Lo, 1, 2; ~ , 3

§ 66

3. p. 23] O. 254 1–3 (*wrong ref.*)   **4.** And] Lo, 1; and 2, 3   **6.** Mother.] Lo; ~ , 1–3   **8.** Testament∧] Lo; ~ , 1–3   **15.** Subjects:] Lo; ~ , 1–3   **15.** they,] Lo; ~ ∧ 1–3

§ 67

19. them:] Lo; ~ , 1–3   **39.** his own] 1er (*so in* Lo's 1), 2, 3; is ~ 1   **43.** upon∧] Lo; ~ , 1–3

§ 68

2. shew,] Lo; ~ ∧ 1–3   **3.** Doctrine.] Lo; Doctrines, 1–3
12. it.] Lo; ~ , 1–3   **18.** *Vassals*] *Subjects* 1
18. *Slaves*:] Lo; ~ ; 1–3   **18.** *the*] his 1   **20.** a part. . . : He] they have a part as Fathers; He 1
20. them:] Lo; ~ ; 2, 3   **30.** rest:] Lo; ~ ; 1–3
33. Children.] Lo; ~ ; 1–3   **35.** *Children*:] Lo; ~ ; 1–3
37. Title,] Lo; ~ ∧ 1–3   **44.** Scripture:] Lo; ~ , 1–3
44. affirm,] Lo; ~ ∧ 1–3

§ 69

5. *Parents*:] Lo; ~ , 1; ~ ; 2, 3   **8.** Children.] Lo; ~ : 1–3   **9.** owed,] Lo; ~ ∧ 1–3   **9.** other:] Lo; ~ , 1–3
12. *A*.,] 1; ~ ∧ 1–3   **14.** also:] Lo; ~ ; 1–3
17. theirs.] Lo; ~ , 1; ~ ; 2, 3   **20.** Sense.] Lo; ~ : 1–3
30. *Children*:] Lo; ~ , 1–3

§ 70

5. Truth:] Lo; ~ , 1–3   **6.** For] Lo; for 1–3
9. reach'd.] Lo; ~ : 1–3   **12.** *Fountain*] 1 (*so Filmer*);
Foundation 2, 3   **13.** *Subjection,*] 1; Subjection∧ 1–3
17. *A.*] Lo (*so in* Lo's 1); *A.*'s 1–3   **22.** also] Lo *inserts*
29. cannot be but] Lo; must 1–3

§ 71

5. Children.] Lo; ~ , 1; ~ ; 2, 3   **14.** them. This] Lo;
~ , this 1–3

§ 72

2. Authority,] Lo; ~ ∧ 1–3   **2.** This] *ital.* 1–3

§ 73

(Title to ch. VII *Property*] Lo, 3er; *Propriety* 1–3)   **4.** those
from which] Lo, 3er; those which 1–3   **10.** *Grounds*] Lo,
1; *Ground* 2, 3   **26.** Children.] Lo; ~ , 1–3   **29.** *Government:*] Lo; ~ , 1–3   **35.** *Power.*] Lo; ~ ; 1–3

§ 74

13. then] Lo, 1er (*so in* Lo's 1), 2; them 1, 3   **17.** But
...cannot] but that cannot 1   **19.** Person.] Lo; ~ ; 1–3
19. Property] Lo, 3er; Propriety 1–3   **21.** *Brackets om.* 1
22. has] 2er, 3; have 1, 2   **24.** it] Lo, 2er, 3er; *om.* 1–3

§ 75

1. i.e.] Lo *inserts*   **4.** Monarchy)] (*so in* Lo's 1) 3; ~ ∧
1, 2   **5.** *Dominion,*] 2er, 3; ~) 1, 2 (*so in* Lo's 1); ~ ∧
1er   **6–7.** belong'd...equally] Lo; belong'd equally 1–3
8. had∧] 1er (*so in* Lo's 1), 2er, 3; ~ , 1, 2   **8.** it, the]
Lo; it, immediately upon *Adam's* Decease, the 1–3
10. divided:] Lo; ~ , 1–3   **17.** Posterity.] Lo; ~ ; 1–3
19–21. Lo *inserts brackets.*   **25.** Persons.] Lo; ~ , 1; ~ ;
2, 3

§ 76

17. *Dominion.*] Lo; ~ , 1; ~ ; 2, 3   **18.** Dominion.] Lo;
~ , 1; ~ ; 2, 3

§ 77

3. *Father*] Col, 5, 6; ~ , 1–3   **16.** purpose.] Lo; ~ , 1–3
24. which] Lo; and which 1–3   **32.** grounded on Private
Dominion] *ital.* 1–3 (*corrected by comparison with Filmer*)

§ 78

4–5. derive...The] derive their Titles from him; The 1
12–13. Again he says] Lo *inserts*   **13.** *be reputed, the*]
~ , ~ ∧ ~ 1–3   **21–2.** In other places he tells us] Lo *inserts*
38. *Crowns.*] Lo; ~ , 1; ~ ; 2, 3

§ 79

10. *Island*:] Lo; ~ , 1–3   **11.** needs] Lo *inserts*
19. it:] Lo; ~ , 1; ~ ; 2, 3

§ 80

10. People.] Lo; ~ , 1; ~ ; 2, 3   **12–13.** Understanding:]
Lo; ~ ; 1–3   **20.** Principles;] Lo; ~ ∧ 1–3   **20–1.** derive...from] Lo; derive any lawful Title to any ones
obedience from 1–3

§ 81

6. though] *om.* 1   **14.** obey.] Lo; ~ ; 1–3   **17.** Obedience:] Lo; ~ , 1–3   **20.** other.] Lo; ~ ; 1–3   **37.** follow.] Lo; ~ ; 1–3

§ 82

3. said:] Lo; ~ , 1–3

§ 83

3. Governments] 1er (*so in* Lo's 1); Government 1–3
5. Politys] Polity's 1–3

§ 84

8. as has] 2er, 3; as had 1; has 2   **9.** *Fatherhood.*] Lo;
~ , 1–3

§ 85

6. *Begetting*:] Lo; ~ ∧ 1, 2; ~ ; 3   **9.** followeth] followed
1   **12.** all, let] all. Lat 3er   **15.** too.] Lo; ~ ; 1–3
23. *Adam*∧] 1er (*so in* Lo's 1); ~ , 1–3

§ 86

2. this.] ~ , 1; ~ ∧ 2, 3   **11.** World thus,] (*so in* Lo's 1)
2er, 3; ~ ~ ∧ 1; ~ , ~ 2   **13.** Instinct,] Lo; ~ ∧ 1–3
15–16. and...his] 2er, 3; and gave him the means of his
1, 2   **16.** *Preservation.*] Lo; ~ , 1–3   **18–19.** Lo *inserts
brackets*   **19.** and] Lo; or 1–3   **21.** God.] Lo; ~ , 1;
~ : 2, 3   **22.** having] have 3   **29.** thereunto.] Lo; ~ ,
1–3   **30.** things,] Lo; ~ ∧ 1–3

§ 87

1. of] Lo; *om.* 3   **3.** time:] Lo; ~ , 1–3   **7.** Beings, which] Lo; Beings. Which 1–3   **8.** them:] Lo; ~ , 1–3
12. Subsistence:] Lo; ~ , 1–3

§ 88

3. Decease. For] Lo; Decease, for 1–3   **9.** it but] Lo; ~ , ~ 1–3   **11.** given:] Lo; ~ , 1–3   **11.** hath] had 1
15. then,] Lo; ~ ∧ 1–3   **18–19.** preservation,...Creatures, for] Lo; Preservation, is the Foundation of a right to the Creatures for 1; preservation, is the Foundation of a right, that is Creatures for ('Creature' *in* 2)   **19.** the particular] 2er, 3; there ~ 1, 2   **24.** Possessions.] Lo; ~ , 1–3
30. Inheritance.] Lo; ~ : 1–3   **33.** That] And that 1

§ 89

7. it. Hence] Lo; ~ ; and hence 1–3

§ 90

6. Child.] Lo; ~ , 1; ~ ; 2, 3   **13.** Children; is] 5, 6; ~ (~ 1, 2er, 3; ~ , ~ 2.   **16.** Subsistence.] ~ , 1; ~ ; 2; ~ : 3   **20.** Money.] 4 +; ~ ;) 1, 3; ~ , 2   **20–1.** tho' ...children,] Lo *inserts*   **23.** Parents,] Lo; Father 1–3
24. it.] Lo; ~ ; 1; ~ : 2, 3   **35.** Issue.] Lo; ~ ; 1–3
39. Magistrate:] Lo; ~ , 1–3   **41.** them:] Lo; ~ , 1–3

§ 91

11. rest:] Lo; ~ ∧ 1–3   **14.** it∧ by] Lo; ~ , ~ 1–3
23. their] there 3

§ 92

6. requires:] Lo; ~ , 1; ~ ; 2, 3   **9.** Governed.] Lo; ~ ; 1–3

§ 93

7–9. Nature. His, and his Brethrens, being equally founded on that Right they had to maintenance 1   **10.** else.] Lo; ~ ; 1–3   **14.** their peculiar Function 1   **17.** Father] 2er, 3; Fathers 1, 2   **22.** Men.] Lo; ~ ; 1–3   **24.** Life:] Lo; ~ , 1; ~ ; 2, 3   **28.** *Dominion.*] Lo; ~ ; 2, 3
29. was] 'twas 3er

§ 94

2. claims,] 4 +; ~ ∧ 1–3   **5.** him.] Lo; ~ ; 1–3
7. conveyance.] Lo; ~ ; 1–3   **9.** Succession: in] Lo; ~ ;

and in 1–3   **13.** Succession. And] Lo; ~ ; and 1–3
13. Succession$_\wedge$ of] 1, 2, 4 + ; ~ , ~ 2, 3

§ 95

4. Succession.] Lo; ~ ; 1–3   **6.** Ruler; Children] 2er, 3;
Ruler, and hereto Children 1, 2   **7.** to this] 2er, 3; *om.*
1, 2   **8.** to it] 2er, 3; *om.* 1, 2

§ 96

3. Title.] Lo; ~ ; 1–3   **6.** them.] Lo; ~ , 1–3
6–7. them, but I shall have more to say on this by and by.
This 1   **8.** Government,] ~ $_\wedge$ 1–3

§ 97

9. themselves:] Lo; ~ , 1–3   **12.** end.] Lo; ~ , 1–3
15. fully.] Lo; ~ , 1–3   **19.** Brethren:] Lo; ~ , 1–3

§ 98

2. he] *om.* 1   **4.** had...Title] had all Title 1   **8.** Children.] Lo; ~ ; 1–3   **13.** Inherited. For] 1er (~ . for *in*
Lo's 1), 2, 3; ~ $_\wedge$ ~ 1   **14.** rising] arising 1
18. Children.] Lo; ~ , 1–3

§ 99

2. *Eve,*] 1er (*so in* Lo's 1), 3; ~ $_\wedge$ 1, 2   **2–3.** (suppose...
Seth)] 4 +; *brackets om.* 1–3   **3.** have had] had *om.* 1
4. Mother.] Lo; ~ ; 1–3   **5.** *Fatherhood*$_\wedge$] Lo; ~ , 1–3
6. Children,] Lo, 1, 2; ~ $_\wedge$ 1–3   **7.** nothing,] Lo; ~ $_\wedge$ 1–3
9. them:] Lo; ~ , 1–3   **10.** did,] Lo, 1; ~ $_\wedge$ 2, 3
11. *Adam*$_\wedge$] Lo; ~ , 1–3

§ 100

3. Inheritance.] Lo; ~ , 1; ~ ; 2, 3   **6.** it:] Lo; ~ , 1–3
7. some] Lo *inserts*   **7.** own.] Lo; ~ ; 1–3   **9.** to]
Lo, 1; *om.* 2, 3   **9.** him:] Lo; ~ ; 1–3   **11.** own.] Lo;
~ : 1–3   **13.** Foster-Father:] Lo; ~ , 1; ~ ; 2, 3
14. the Child] Lo; him 1–3   **15.** Father:] Lo; ~ , 1–3
18. another.] Lo; ~ , 1–3   **19.** neglected,...Child,] ~ $_\wedge$
...~ $_\wedge$ 1–3

§ 101

4. *inherited*:] Lo; ~ ; 1–3   **13.** too.] Lo; ~ , 1–3
19. them:] Lo; ~ $_\wedge$ 1; ~ ; 2, 3   **25.** all:] Lo; ~ , 1; ~ ;
2, 3   **25–6.** Eldest,...Nature,] Lo; ~ $_\wedge$...~ $_\wedge$ 1–3
30. I am] 1er (*so in* Lo's 1), 2, 3; Am 1

§ 102

9. them:] Lo; ~ , 1–3   **12.** one,] Lo; ~ ʌ 1–3
13. those,] Lo, 1; ~ ʌ 2, 3   **14.** Children?] ~ . 1–3

§ 103

13. Fathers:] Lo; ~ , 1–3   **22.** him.] Lo; ~ , 1–3
24. Monarchyʌ] Lo; ~ , 1–3   **28.** Inheritance.] Lo; ~ ;
1; ~ : 2, 3

§ 104

(Chap. X title] to *Monarchical Power of Adam* 1)   **8.** *Sub-ject*] 1; Subjects 2, 3   **12.** *Heir.*] Lo; ~ , 1; ~ ; 2, 3
17. Thrones] Titles 1   **20–1.** Reigning upon our *A.*s
grounds, as good as his own. If 1   **23.** must] Lo, 1; Must
2, 3   **35.** ought to] ('ought' *added in Christ's copy, but*
'to' *omitted; added* 4 +)

§ 105

8. Obedience:] Lo; ~ , 1–3   **17.** Subjects,] ~ ʌ 1–3
20–1. without it. If they have not, we are discharged of our
Obedience to them, for he that has no Right to command, I
am under no obligation to obey, and we are 1   **22.** Heir.]
Lo; ~ ; 1–3   **29.** Power.] Lo; ~ ; 1–3   **31.** *Adam.*]
Lo; ~ , 1–3   **32.** stand:] Lo; ~ ; 1–3   **33.** Kings. Take]
Lo; Kings, and take 1–3   **34.** Obedience:] Lo; ~ , 1–3

§ 106

4. been, Not] Lo, 2er; ~ , not 1–3   **6.** settling…being]
settling of this therefore being 1   **8–10.** a Reformer…,
and be] a Writer of Politicks, one would think, should take
great care in settling this point, and be 1   **11–12.** purpose
…dressing] purpose. And by dressing 1   **14.** it,…to
give] it, is only to give 1   **15–16.** Ambition,…Men] Am-bition, which of itself, is but too apt to be intemperate, and
to set Men 1   **14.** keen.] Lo; ~ , 2, 3

§ 107

1. This…*A*] This our *A* 1   **2.** ordinarily] 1; ordinary
2, 3   **2.** he,] 4 + ; ~ ʌ 1–3   **3.** *Power*ʌ] Lo; ~ , 1–3
5. Sacred:] Lo; ~ , 1–3   **5.** so that no Consideration] so
that no Power, no consideration 1   **9–10.** *Institution*…
whom] *Institution* and *Adams Heir,* he to whom 1   **10.** as
in] as we see in 1   **18.** Persons,] Lo; ~ ʌ 1–3
19. *Aaron*:] Lo; ~ , 1–3

§ 108

13. one.] Lo; ~ ; 1–3 **18.** *Parents*.] Lo; ~ ; 1–3

§ 109

4. Issue:] Lo; ~ , 1–3 **7.** *Power*.] Lo; ~ ; 1; ~ : 2, 3
9. it:] Lo; ~ , 1; ~ ; 2, 3 **12.** Child:] Lo; ~ , 1–3
13. Heir,] Lo; ~ ; 1–3 **20.** full.] Lo; ~, 1–3

§ 110

3. say:] Lo; ~ , 1–3 **3–4.** therefore,] Lo; ~ ∧ 1–3

§ 111

4. is.] Lo; ~ : 1–3 **6–7.** touches: though] Lo; touch,
though 1, 2; touches, ~ 2er, 3 **10.** body.] Lo; ~ ; 1–3
19. Power.] Lo; ~ , 1; ~ ; 2, 3 **21.** Mankind.] Lo; ~ ;
1–3 **24.** is:] Lo; ~ , 1–3 **40.** *Heir*:] Lo; ~ , 1–3
44. divers] diverse 1 **46.** shew'd.] Lo; ~ ; 1–3
49. proved.] Lo; ~ ; 1–3

§ 112

14. general.] Lo; ~ ; 1–3 **22.** Brethren.] Lo; ~ ; 1–3
24. peopled, had by] peopled by 1 **24.** time,] Lo, 1; ~ ∧
2, 3 **25.** Men,...these] Men, had more Sons, then these 1
25. two:] Lo; ~ , 1–3 **27.** Scarce,...Construction,] Lo;
~ ∧...~ ∧ 1–3

§ 113

4. *thee*.] Lo; ~ , 1–3 **6.** is.] Lo; ~ ; 1–3 **9.** it∧] Lo;
~ , 1–3 **12.** *right*.] Lo; ~ ; 1–3 **19.** Scripture.] Lo;
~ , 1–3 **29.** signifie] Lo; signifies 1–3 **32.** *right*:]
Lo; ~ , 1–3 **33.** he,] Lo; ~ ∧ 1–3 **34.** *Brethren*.]
Lo; ~ ; 1–3 **38.** *Esau*.] Lo; ~ , 1–3 **42.** *Blessing*:]
Lo; ~ , 1–3 **46.** *right*:] Lo; ~ , 1–3 **46.** Dominion,]
Lo; ~ ∧ 1–3

§ 114

6. *Son*:] Lo; ~ , 1–3 **13.** *lived*:] Lo; ~ ; 1–3
14. Sons,] Lo; ~ ∧ 1–3 **18–20.** why...sent] Lo; why
should *Sarah* desire to Rob him of one of his *Subjects*, his
Slaves, by desiring to have him sent 1–3

§ 115

6–7. Brethren....not] Brethren. Which if it be not 1
8. he...into] (*so in* Lo's 1), 2, 3; let them look into 1
8. 5. 1. 2.] 5. 12 1–3 (*wrong ref*.) **8.** may there read] and

there he may read 1   **14.** *Joseph's*: what] Lo; *Joseph's*, and what 1–3   **15.** 48] (*so in* Lo's 1), 3; 58 1, 2   **18.** *Bow*.] Lo; ~ , 1–3   **20.** and] 1er (*so in* Lo's 1), 2er, 3; *om.* 1, 2   **21.** right.] Lo; ~ ; 1–3   **23.** Dominion. One] Lo; Dominion; but one 1–3

§ 116

4. would.] Lo; ~ ; 1–3   **7.** unalterable.] Lo; ~ ; 1–3

§ 117

3. *Jacob*.] Lo; ~ ; 1–3   **7–9.** This Text...or the] The words if one consider *thy Brethren*, and *thy Mothers Sons in them*, can never be understood literally of Esau, or the 1   **10.** words...could] words, *Sons* and *Brethren* could 1   **18.** (as] 1er (*so in* Lo's 1); (nay as 1–3   **18.** are) Slaves∧] 1er (*so in* Lo's 1); ~ ∧ ~) 1–3   **21.** *Isaac*,] ~ ∧ 1–3

§ 118

4. Death:] Lo; ~ , 1–3   **9.** Peoples] People 1–3   **21–3.** *Jacob*:...Right] Lo; *Jacob;* they being both Predictions of what should long after happen to their Posterities, and not the declaring the Right 1–3   **24.** either.] Lo; ~ ; 1–3   **36.** *Brethren*:] Lo; ~ , 1; ~ ; 2, 3

§ 119

8. *infinitum*.] Lo; ~ ; 1; ~ : 2, 3   **12.** guess,] Lo; ~ ∧ 1–3   **13.** do not] dot 3   **16.** *Heir*.] Lo; ~ ; 1; ~ : 2, 3   **24.** Son. This] Lo; Son; But this 1; Son. But this 2, 3   **32.** him.] Lo; ~ ; 1; ~ : 2, 3   **37.** for the setling] to settle 1   **38.** determining] determin 1   **42.** *Jurisdiction*:] Lo; ~ ; 1–3

§ 120

6. me.] Lo; ~ ; 1; ~ : 2, 3   **8.** *specifically*] *specially* 2, 3

§ 121

5. King;] Lo; ~ , 1–3   **6.** good.] Lo; ~ ; 1–3   **14.** in] 2er, 3; into 1, 2

§ 122

1. To] Lo; For, I say, to 1–3   **5, 15.** him, ...not,] Lo; ~ ∧...~ ∧ 1–3   **15–17.** whether...provided] Lo, 2er; whether it be called *Paternal*, *Regal*, *Natural*, or *acquired* Supreme *Fatherhood*, or supreme *Brotherhood*, provided 1, 2;

whether it be called *Paternal,* or *Regal, Natural,* or *acquired;* whether *Supreme Fatherhood,* or *Supreme Brotherhood,* provided 3

§ 123

2. *Fatherhood,*] Lo; ~ ; 1–3   **17.** be,] Lo; ~ ∧ 1–3

§124

9. of.] Lo; ~ ; 1–3   **14–15.** his...would] his Heir, and so on: If I say, all these his suppositions were as much demonstrations, as they are the contrary, yet they would 1
22. this:] Lo; ~ ; 1–3   **22.** let this be] yet, if it be 1
30. Govern,] Lo, 1; ~ ? 2, 3   **31.** known,] Lo, 1; ~ ∧ 2, 3
31. all.] Lo; ~ ; 2, 3   **32–3.** be...much] 1er (*so in* Lo's 1) 2, 3; be, so much 2, 3   **34.** to be so] *om.* 1

§ 125

3–4. helps...determine] Lo; helps nothing to Establishing the Power of those that Govern, or determine 1–3
7–8. Obey. ...*Fatherhood*] Lo; Obey; And this *Fatherhood* 1–3   **7, 8.** is;...heir,] Lo; ~ ∧ ~ ∧ 1–3   **22.** *Adam;*] Lo; ~ , 1–3

§ 126

13. way:] Lo; ~ , 1–3   **16.** Right:] Lo; ~ , 1–3
29. else:] Lo; ~ ; 1–3   **32.** it.] Lo; ~ ; 1–3

§ 127

9. Assignments:] Lo; ~ , 1–3

§ 128

4. and useful] Lo, 1; an useful 2, 3   **6.** would to] Lo, 1; ~ be 2, 3   **8.** is:] Lo; ~ ; 1–3   **13–14.** *Nakedness:*] Lo; ~ ; 1–3   **16.** use:] Lo; ~ , 1–3   **19.** by.] Lo; ~ ; 1–3   **25.** otherwise.] Lo; ~ , 1–3   **29.** Brethren.] Lo; ~ , 1–3   **31.** *Isaac*] Lo; ~ ∧ 1; ~ , 2, 3   **32.** says∧ she,] 1er (*so in* Lo's 1), 2, 3; ~ , ~ ∧ 1   **37.** are. He] Lo; ~ , but he 1–3

§ 129

6. *as*] 1; *a* 2, 3   **18.** Authority:] Lo; ~ , 1, 2; ~ ; 3
23. all?] 1er (*so in* Lo's 1); ~ ∧ 1–3   **27.** is] *om.* 1
30. too: If] Lo; too, if 1–3   **31.** doing.] Lo; ~ , 1–3
41. living:] Lo; ~ , 1–3   **45.** descent...if] Lo; descent, I know not why every man may not; and if 1–3

§ 130

16. Money?] Lo, 3er; ~ ; 1–3   **29.** Family∧ is,] Lo; ~ , ~ ∧ 1–3   **30.** *Adam*:] 4 + ; ~ ∧ 1–3   **33.** over] our 3

§ 131

1–2. *Sovereignty*. Let] Lo; ~ ; let 1–3   **2.** Societies.] ~ ; 1, 2; ~ , 3   **4.** own,] Lo; ~ ∧ 1–3   **9.** him?] Lo; ~ ; 1–3   **11.** done.] Lo; ~ , 1; ~ : 2, 3   **12.** and] Lo, 4 + ('or' *not deleted in Christ's copy*); or 1–3   **22.** Parties,] Lo; ~ ∧ 1–3

§ 132

5. Supremacy:] Lo; ~ ; 1–3

§ 133

1. granting] Lo; grant 1–3   **6.** *Abraham*,] ~ ∧ 1–3   **6.** *of*] *to* 1   **7.** he.] Lo; ~ ; 1–3   **7.** say,] Lo; ~ ∧ 1–3

§ 134

10. *Common-wealth*:] Lo; ~ , 1–3   **12.** *a*] *om.* 1   **19.** Kings:] Lo; ~ , 1; ~ ; 2, 3   **22.** matter?] Lo, 3er; ~ , 1–3

§ 135

2. *Adam*.] Lo; ~ ; 1–3   **5.** Family:] Lo; ~ , 1–3   **14.** Son;] ~ , 1–3   **16.** Friends, he] Friends. He 1–3

§ 137

6. *Adam*.] ~ , 1–3   **13.** 400.] Lo; ~ : 1–3   **14.** Argument.] Lo; ~ : 1–3   **19.** *Brethren*.] Lo; ~ ; 1–3   **21.** *Adam*:] Lo; ~ ; 1–3   **23.** *right*:] Lo; ~ ; 1–3   **28.** *teneatis*?] Lo; ~ , 1–3   **29.** Arguing:] Lo; ~ ; 1–3   **30.** an hypothesis] Lo; Principles 1–3   **31.** things,] Lo; ~ ∧ 1–3   **32.** his principles could not be] Lo; nor could be 1–3

§ 138

8–9. Husbands:] Lo; ~ ; 1–3   **11.** viz.] Lo; and that is, 1–3   **14.** *enjoy*.] Lo; ~ ; 1–3   **17.** Bible:] Lo; ~ ; 1–3   **19.** those,] Lo; ~ ∧ 1–3

§ 139

1. says our] *ital.* 1–3   **6.** so that] Lo *inserts*   **7.** here, proves] Lo; here, therefore, proves 1–3   **27.** *Children*?] Lo, 3er; ~ , 1–3

§ 140

3. Institution; all] Lo; ~ , and all 1–3   **5.** doors; and the]
Lo; ~ . The 1–3   **7–9.** will. . . .For] Lo (*reading of 3 not
crossed out*); will be all Ordinances of Man and not *of God*,
as our *A.*—says, *O*. 254 For 1; will all be the Ordinances of
Man, and not *of God*, as our *A.* says, *O*. 254. For 2, 3

§ 141

12. Nations,] ~ ; 1–3   **14–15.** labour. . .Nephews of] Lo;
not ital. 1–3   **26–7.** Pharamond;. . .Names] 2, 3; *Pharamond,* nay *Jupiter* and *Saturn* be names 1

§ 142

1. To] Lo; And therefore to 1–3   **3.** lot] 4 + ; Lot 1–3
12. Heir:] 1–3; Heir,— Lo. cor.   **17.** if] If 1–3
21. *Adam*.] Lo; ~ ; 1–3   **26–8.** same Right, how *Cham*
or Japhet were Princes by Right descending to him, notwithstanding any Title of Heir in his Eldest 1   **32.** Family.]
Lo; ~ , 1; ~ ; 2, 3   **38.** Kingdoms,] Lo; ~ ∧ 1–3

§ 143

7. Principles.] Lo; ~ ; 1–3   **12.** impossible.] Lo; ~ , 1;
~ ; 2, 3   **14.** *Babel,* the] Lo; ~ : The 1–3

§ 144

14. Posterities:] Lo; ~ , 1–3   **16.** Government;] (*so in
Lo's* 1), 3; ~ : 1; ~ ∧ 2; ~ , 2er   **22.** together.] Lo; ~ , 1;
~ : 2, 3   **30.** *Nations*; therefore] 2, 3, Nations; that therefore 1

§ 145

8–9. silent. . .says] Lo; Silent: And therefore the same
Grounds has the rest that he says 1–3

§ 146

18. of. As] Lo; of. And as 1–3   **21.** Monarchy:] Lo; ~ ;
1–3   **22.** said.] Lo; ~ , 1; ~ ; 2, 3   **27.** Master:] Lo;
~ , 1–3   **27–9.** abroad, and for having a City once built,
fixed Habitations to settle their Bodies and Families 1 (*in* Lo's
1 *corrected to version in* 2, 3)   **28.** our] Lo; their 1–3
36. Dominion.] Lo; ~ , 1; ~ ; 2, 3   **38.** *Authority*?] Lo;
~ . 1–3

§ 147

12–14. they?. . .the true] they, when at the same time he takes

ay the true 1   **22.** Subjects? Would] Lo; ~ ? And would
3   **23.** Government,] ~ ∧ 1–3   **31.** imitate:] Lo;
; 1–3   **40–1.** himself says∧ ...and then] 1er, 2, 3; him-
lf says, they were a Commonwealth, and then (*so in* Lo's 1
ey were' *inserted over the line after* 'says', *as if further cor-
ction were contemplated but abandoned*)   **49.** know] 1, 2;
ows 3   **57.** themselves:] Lo; ~ ; 1–3   **61.** Subjects,
d] 1er (*so in* Lo's 1), 2, 3; Subject had 1   **64.** Lordship]
ordships 1–3   **67.** careful] 4 + ; capable 1–3
–2. many, at least∧] ~ ∧ ~ ~ , 1–3

§ 148

Families:] Lo; ~ , 1–3   **7.** *Babel*:] Lo; ~ , 1–3
–17. Off-spring.... very] 2, 3; Off-spring, and his Lords of
amilies, thus understood; he gives us a very 1 (*in* Lo's 1
ffspring;...understood,)   **18.** p. 16] *om.* 1

§ 149

Kings:] Lo; ~ ; 1–3   **12.** these:] Lo; ~ ; 1–3
–7. purpose:...Vertue] Lo; purpose, nor are any of the
stances he brings proofs of any Power they had by Title of
atherhood as Heirs of *Adam's* Paternal Authority, nor by
ertue 1–3   **33.** Posterity:] Lo; ~ ; 1–3   **34.** *Edom*...
ings] 1er (*so in* Lo's 1), 2, 3; *Edom,* of Abraham; and 9
ings 1   **35.** Neighbours;] Lo; ~ : 1–3   **50.** cause:]
o, 1, 2; ~ , 3

§ 150

Prince.] (*so in* Lo's 1), 2, 3; ~ , 1   **11.** all:] Lo; ~ , 1–3
4. *Fatherhood*;] Lo; ~ , 1–3   **15.** Heir.] Lo; ~ ; 1–3
8. Title] 3; Titles 1, 2

§ 151

is] Lo; was 1–3   **6.** Lo *inserts brackets*   **7.** *Power*;]
o; ~ , 1–3   **7.** Sovereignty,] Lo; ~ ∧ 1–3

§ 152

were,] (*so in* Lo's 1), 2er, 3; ~ ? 1, 2   **4.** *Jurisdiction*?]
o in* Lo's 1), 3; ~ , 1, 2; *Jurisdictions*? 2er   **13.** *A*.] ~ , 3
4. Lordship?] Lo; ~ , 1–3   **17–20.** *Babel*?...the exer-
ise] *Babel* of Esau, and the 12 Dukes of *Edom,* why are these
rought in as examples, of the exercise of true *Patriarchal*
overnment, and joyn'd with those of *Abraham* and *Judah*?
the exercise 1   **17–18.** *Ismael;* and the Dukes] Lo; *Is-*
ael in the 12 Dukes 2; *Ismael* and the Dukes 3

20. *Government,* if] Col, 5, 6; *Government?* If 1–3, 4
21. Heirs] Posterity 1   **22.** Power?] Lo, 3er; ~ . 1; ~ ; 2,
22–7. I fear...*Jacob*] *om.* 1   **25.** from that time down
wards] Lo; since that 2, 3

§ 153

3. *Adam;*] Lo; ~ , 1–3   **4.** *Jews*:] Lo; ~ , 1–3   **5.** Peo
ple:] Lo; ~ , 1; ~ ; 2, 3   **5–8.** People:...I expected
People, and no mention of their being Heirs to *Adam,* o
Kings by Paternal Authority when they had them; I expected
8. Authority.] Lo, 1; ~ ; 2, 3   **13.** Government:] Lo
~ , 1–3   **14.** proves,] Lo; ~ ∧ 1–3   **16.** it:] Lo; ~ ; 1–
17. Monarchs;] Lo; ~ , 1–3   **18.** Paternal;] Lo; ~ , 1–.

§ 154

10. Heathens, Philosopher∧] (*so in* Lo's 1), 2er, 3; Heather
Philosophers, 1, 2   **11, 12.** Politician,...turn,] Lo; ~ ∧..
~ ∧ 1–3   **12–19.** Lo. *inserts* (*In* 1–3 *paragraph ends a*
'turn'. *The passage to be added is found in the margin of th*
Christ's copy. The phrase in 14–15 'in Authors who (tis vis
ible) write not for truth' *is at the bottom of the page, and it*
position in the text is indicated by '(1)' *after* 'observe'. *Thi*
has been done in such a way as to make it seem most likely
that Coste was copying a correction, which had been adde.
to in this way, and is one of the indications that his was a han.
reproduction of another master-copy. The 4 + *printings show*
variations, inserting italics where they might be expected, an.
read 'designs' *for* 'design'. *Though they omit the bracket roun.*
'tis visible' *it seems possible that they are copying the version*
copied by Coste, but direct and not via the Christ's copy.)
26. imply,] ~ ∧ 3   **30.** another.] ~ : 1–3   **32.** con
trary,] 1; ~ ∧ 2, 3   **32.** was] 1, 2, 4 + ; were 3

§ 155

3. *Egypt*:] (*so in* Lo's 1), 2, 3; ~ , 1   **4.** mockery,] (*s.*
in Lo's 1), 2, 3; ~ : 1

§ 157

2–3. out to] Lo, 1; out p. 18 to 2, 3   **6–7.** either. The Per
sons chosen were, *Moses* of] either *Moses* of 1 (*in* Lo's .
Moses,)   **19.** could] 1, 2, 4 + ; would 3

§ 158

6, 7. confess,...Governours,] Lo; ~ ∧... ~ ∧ 1–3

§ 159

1. 159.] *om.* 2, 3   **1–3.** *Not ital. in* 1

§ 160

8. Government,] Lo; ~ ∧ 1–3   **8.** than] Lo; then 1–3
10. one.] Lo; ~ ; 1–3   **14.** *Succession*∧] Lo; ~ , 1–3
15. more,] Lo; ~ ∧ 1–3   **16.** Ancestors.] Lo; ~ ; 1–3
20. not:] Lo; ~ , 1–3   **23.** *Isaac,*] Lo; ~ ∧ 1–3
24. *Jacob*∧] Lo; ~ , 1–3

§ 161

3. he,] Lo; ~ ∧ 1–3   **5.** to.] Lo; ~ ; 1–3   **6.** Family?]
Lo; ~ , 1–3   **18.** *Athaliah...Reigned*] *Athaliah? who
Reigned* 1, 2
(*This paragraph extensively corrected as to punctuation be-
tween* 1 *and* 2, 2 *and* 3)

§ 162

6. out] our 3   **8.** Succession;] Lo; ~ , 1, 2; ~ : 3
12. *Heir,*] ~ . 3   **27.** man and] man in peculiar and—
Lo. cor.   **28.** belong in peculiar to] Lo; belong all to 1, 2;
belong to 3
(*This paragraph also extensively corrected in punctuation between* 1 *and* 2, 2 *and* 3)

§ 163

2. King, he] 4 + ; King, that he 1–3   **11.** *David's or Solomon's*] Lo, 3er; *David or Solomon* 1–3   **16.** them?] Lo;
~ , 1–3   **17.** another.] Lo; ~ ? 1–3   **29.** time,] ~ ∧ 1–3
33. *Israel.*] Lo; ~ ; 1–3

§ 164

11. *Israelites;*] Lo; ~ , 1–3   **14.** Thought] 4 + ; Thoughts
1–3

§ 165

3. *Jud.:*] Lo; ~ ∧ 1–3   **3.** finds,] Lo; ~ ∧ 1–3   **4.** Justice;] Lo; ~ , 1–3   **5, 6.** Congregation,...resolved,...oc-
casion,] Lo; ~ ∧...~ ∧...~ ∧ 1–3   **8.** People;] Lo; ~ ,1–3
9. preserved,] Lo; ~ ∧ 1–3   **16.** or] Lo; nor 1–3

§ 166

4. *thereof?*] Lo; ~ , 1–3   **12.** Warrant,] Lo; ~ ∧ 1–3

§ 167

5. too.] Lo; ~ , 1–3   **10.** which Lo. *inserts*   **11.** him,]
Lo; ~ ∧ 1–3   **19.** There] Lo; there 1–3   **23.** the same
too] Lo *inserts*   **23–4.** *A*.,... allow,] Lo; ~ ∧ ... ~ ∧ 1–3

§ 168

12–13. Bondage,] Lo; ~ : 1–3

§ 169

4. thence] Lo; whence 1–3   **8.** it.] Lo; ~ ; 1–3 1150 ed.
cor.; 1750 all printings.   **11.** Footstep] Lo; Footsteps 1–3
14, 15. derived, ... or,] Lo; ~ ∧ ... ~ ∧ 1–3

COLLATION
of
SECOND TREATISE

COLLATION
of
SECOND TREATISE

EXPLANATION OF COLLATION

The collation lists variations from the copy text. The copy text is that of the Christ's copy (see Editorial Note) and variants from it are treated as rejected readings, rejected for the most part by Locke.

Entries are given under paragraphs in the following pattern.

First the line number or numbers, then the word or words affected, or guide words to the passage affected, then a square bracket.

After the square bracket, where necessary, the symbol or symbols for the authority(ies) for the adopted reading, then a semi-colon.

After the semi-colon, the variant reading or readings, separated by semi-colons, and each followed by the symbol for its source or sources.

The symbols are as follows:

Lo   means the reading of an alteration in manuscript found in the Christ's copy.

Lo *inserts* means an insertion in manuscript found in the Christ's copy.

1   means the reading of the 1st printing, 1689/90.

1er   means the reading of the errata slip to the 1st printing.

(*so in* Lo's 1) means that the reading is found in the corrections made by Locke in his copy of the 1st printing.

2   means the reading of the 2nd printing, 1694.

2er   means the reading of the errata list in the 2nd printing.

3   means the reading of the 3rd printing, 1698.

3er   means the reading of the errata list in the 3rd printing.

1–3   means a reading common to 1, 2 and 3.

1, 2   means a reading common to 1 and 2.

2, 3   means a reading common to 2 and 3.

4   means the reading of the 4th printing, 1713.

4+   means the reading of the 4th printing and of the texts
        wholly or partly derived from it (i.e. Col 5, 6).

Col   means the reading of the 1st Collected edition, 1714.

5   means the reading of the 5th edition, 1728.

6   means the reading of the 6th (Hollis) edition, 1764.

After the variant(s), and sometimes between them, explanatory notes will sometimes be found. These are placed within brackets and printed in italics. They are concerned for the most part with the manner in which the manuscript corrections were carried out in the Christ's copy, and with the evidence for a possible second master-copy, other than the Christ's copy (see Editorial Note for a discussion of this point).

Notes

(1) Where the variant is found in 1, 2, or 3 only, it is sometimes printed immediately after the bracket, the other symbols being understood.

(2) In other instances where no symbol succeeds the bracket the reading adopted is an editorial emendation with no documentary authority. These are few.

(3) In some entries line numbers only are given, with no guide words or bracket.

These are usually longer passages where misunderstanding is unlikely, and it is sometimes necessary to infer that the reading adopted is from 3 or 2 and 3.

(4) The roman figures after the paragraph numbers in the collation for the *Second Treatise* are the numbers in the French version, from which all foreign language editions were published until the 20th century.

The collating methods used here are an adaptation of those laid down by McKerrow, 1939, and adopted by Bowers, 1953. The wavy dash (∼) is taken from these authorities, and has been found most useful in dealing with the very large number of punctuation variations and corrections collated here.*

---

* There is perhaps a possibility of confusion between the semi-color used to separate variants from each other, and a semi-colon which is itself a variant. It seemed better, however, to run this very slight risk, rather than adapt, or invent, a special sign for the purpose of separation.

The use of this wavy dash is probably self-evident, for it simply stands for a word or phrase which has been cited merely in order to mark a varying punctuation point or points, and which does not itself vary. It thus makes it unnecessary to print that word or phrase again in order to register the variation(s). It is sometimes used in presenting variants other than those in punctuation.

The caret below the line (∧) is also taken from McKerrow and Bowers. It serves to draw attention to the absence of punctuation at a point where one or other of the variants does have punctuation.

An example of the use of the wavy dash and the caret below the line follows. In line 14 of II, § 166, the 1st printing reads 'Disorders,', the 2nd and 3rd printings read 'Disorders' with no punctuation, and the Christ's copy 'Disorders,' restoring the comma. It is represented thus: **14.** Disorders,] Lo, 1; ∼ ∧ 2, 3

By the use of this Collation it is hoped that the reader will be enabled to follow the history of every passage which shows significant variation in the documents collated, and to see the authority on which the editor has adopted his reading. But an exhaustive history of every tiny detail has not been attempted. The following things are *not* included in the Collation, except where the editor felt that there would be some point in including them.

Italics. The very extensive italicization made in manuscript in the Christ's copy has of course been adopted, but attention is not normally drawn to the fact that italic passages are the result of this final correction, nor to variants in the use of italics between the printings.

Spelling. The spelling of the Christ's copy (type and manuscript) is printed, and variations between this spelling and that of earlier or later printings (or between such printings) are not normally recorded. Spelling here includes the use of capitals and abbreviations, conventional signs (such as 1° for 'first'), etc.

Punctuation. The heavily corrected punctuation of the Christ's copy is reproduced, and attention drawn to the variants brought about by this correction. But variations in punctuation between 1, 2 and 3 which are not affected by the correction in the Christ's copy are not normally recorded.

Errata. Where a printing shows a variant peculiar to itself, and that variant is corrected in the errata list to the reading found in all other sources, it is not normally recorded.

These omissions have made possible considerable savings of time and printing effort. It is difficult to imagine many cases where the absence of these minutiae will frustrate the student in the pursuit of the history of Locks's text and it is hoped that the value of the Collation will be only negligibly reduced by these savings. They do mean, however, that the spelling, italics and punctuation of the 1st printing, the nearest to Locke's original manuscript, cannot be recovered, except where correction was made to the passages concerned in the Christ's copy.

Two further points are taken as understood in the Collation:

(1) Where only one variant is recorded from documents earlier than 4, all the other documents read as in the text printed by the editor.

(2) Readings of 4 and later printings are only recorded to sanction, or contrast with, readings adopted by the editor which do not appear in the earlier documents. The absence of these symbols does not always mean that these later printings always agree with the reading printed here.

Title-page

(In the 1st edition 'Original' is spelt 'Oringinal', which Locke does not correct in his own copy, but he does insert a comma after it. The comma after 'Extent' is added in the 2nd Edition, and the black letter for 'Civil Government' first appears in the 3rd edition.)

§ 1

4. or] Lo, 3er; nor 1–3

§ 3

1. *Power*ₐ] Lo; ~ , 1–3

§ 4 (i, i)

1. right,] Lo; aright 1–3   **9–10.** another:] Lo; ~ , 1–3

§ 5 (i, ii)

16–17. *Men, being*] Lo; *Men weak, being* 1, 2; Men, we all being 1er (*so in* Lo's 1), 2er, 3

§ 6 (i, iii)

7. *Nature*ₐ] Lo; ~ , 1–3   **7.** it,] Lo, 1, 2; ~ ₐ 3   **8.** one: And] Lo; ~ , and 1–3   **9.** it, that] Lo; ~ ; That 1–3   **11.** Liberty,] Lo; ~ ₐ 1–3   **11.** Possessions.] Lo; ~ ; 1–3   **14.** business,] (*so in* Lo's 1), 2, 3; ~ . 1   **15.** are,] (*so in* Lo's 1) 2, 3; ~ ₐ 1   **21.** ours.] Lo; ~ , 1–3   **22.** wilfully;] ∼ , 1–3 (*Locke has crossed out the comma in the Christ's copy but put nothing in its place*)   **24.** he,... can,] Lo; ∼ ∧... ∼ ∧ 1–3   **25.** may] Lo *inserts*

§ 7 (i, iv)

8. would,] 1, 4 + ; ∼ ∧ 2, 3   **9.** World,] 1, 4 + ; ∼ ∧ 2, 3

§ 8 (i, v)

14. security:] Lo; ∼ , 1–3   **16.** him.] Lo; ∼ , 1–3

§ 9 (i, vi)

2. Men:] Lo; ∼ , 1–3   **6.** Sanction∧] ∼ , 1–3

§ 10 (i, vii)

2. Law] ('Laws' *in first state of* 1)   **5–6.** *injury* done to some Person or other, and some other] Lo; injury done, and some Person or other, some other 1–3

§ 11 (i, viii)

13. *remit*:] Lo; ∼ ; 1–3   **25.** Measure,] Lo; ∼ ∧ 1–3

§ 12 (i, ix)

2. Law.] Lo; ∼ ; 1–3   **3.** demanded,] ∼ ∧ 1–3   **7.** like.] Lo; ∼ : 1–3   **18–19.** so truly] (truly so *in first state of* 1)

§ 13 (i, x)

7. too] to 3   **11.** Men.] ∼ , 1   **14.** easily] (easily *in first state of* 1); easic (*in second state of* 1) 2, 3
26–7. least...those] Lo; least question or controle of those 1–3   **29–31.** Much...another:] Lo; Which Men in the State of Nature are not bound to do one to another. 1–3 (4 *and* Col *do not follow Locke's correction in the Christ's copy here*; 6 *does*)

§ 14 (i, xi)

6. ever] Lo; never 1–3   **9.** others:] Lo; ∼ ; 1–3   **10.** an] Lo, 1, 2; and 1, 3   **15–17.** between...*Swiss*.] ('between the two Men in Soldania, in or between a *Swiss*' *in first state of* 1)   **20.** another. For] ('another for' *in the first state of* 1)

§ 15 (i, xii)

5. *do*] to 3   **17.** so,] Lo; ∼ ∧ 1–3

§ 16 (ii, i)

3. a sedate] (a *om. in first state of* 1)   **8.** Quarrel:] Lo; ∼ , 1–3   **10.** Destruction.] Lo; ∼ ; 1–3   **14.** being,] Lo;

~ ∧ 1–3   **15.** *Wolf*] (*so* [*not Ital.*] *in first state of* 1), 3;
Woolf (*so in second state of* 1), 2, 4, Col (*one of the signs
that* 4 + *was based on* 2)   **16.** such Men] they 1
18. Beasts] a Beast 1

§ 17 (ii, ii)

1. is,] Lo; ~ ∧ 1–3   **8.** it:] Lo; ~ ; 1–3   **11.** force∧]
Lo; ~, 1–3   **12.** Preservation:] Lo; ~, 1–3   **14.** it:]
Lo; ~, 1–3   **17.** *Freedom,*] Lo; ~ ∧ 1–3

§ 18 (ii, iii)

5. him:] Lo; ~ ∧ 1–3

§ 19 (ii, iv)

3. distant,] Lo; ~ ∧ 1–3   **5.** Violence,] Lo; ~ ∧ 1–3
8–9. is *properly the State of Nature*] are *properly in the State
of Nature* 3er (*correction made thus in Christ's copy but deleted*)   **14.** *Thief,*] Lo; ~ ∧ 1–3   **16.** kill,] Lo; ~ ∧ 1–3
17. Coat:] Lo; ~, 1–3   **17.** Law,] Lo; ~ ∧ 1–3
24. Case,] Lo; ~ ∧ 1–3   **26.** *Nature*:] Lo; ~ ; 1–3
27. *War,*] Lo; ~ ∧ 1–3

§ 20 (ii, v)

5. harm:] Lo; ~ ; 1–3   **8.** *continues,*] Lo; ~ ∧ 1–3
12–13. future:] Lo; ~ ; 1–3   **18.** *War.*] Lo; ~ : 1–3

§ 21 (ii, vi)

7. Earth,] Lo; ~ ∧ 1–3   **22.** mean,] Lo; ~ ∧ 1–3

§ 22 (iii, i)

12. *Men*] Lo; *not ital.* 1–3   **14.** it;] Col; ~ . 1–3 (~ ., *in
Christ's copy*)   **16.** not;] Lo, 1; ~, 2, 3   **16.** and] Lo
inserts

§ 24 (iii, ii)

5. Obedience ∧] Lo; ~, 1–3   **5.** other,] Lo; ~ ; 1–3
16. Service:] Lo, 1; ~ ; 1–3

§ 25 (iv, i)

6. Sons,] Lo; ~ ; 1–3   **11.** thing:] Lo; ~ ; 1–3   **13.** that]
Lo; That 1–3   **16.** that] Lo; That 1–3

§ 26 (iv, ii)

11. a means] ('some means' *inserted in Christ's copy but
crossed through*)

§ 27 (iv, iii)

7. with,] Lo; ~ ∧ 1–3

§ 28 (iv, iv)

26. others,] Lo; ~ ∧ 1–3

§ 29 (iv, v)

3. common,] 1er (*so in* Lo's 1), 2er, 3; ~ . 1, 2
7. doubt,] Lo; ~ ∧ 1–3   **8.** Nature,] Lo; ~ ∧ 1–3

§ 30 (iv, vi)

2. *Indian's*] 4 + ; *Indians* 1–3   **19.** Nature,] Lo; ~ ∧ 1–3

§ 31 (iv, vii)

4–5. Nature,] Lo; ~ ∧ 1–3   **7.** 17. is] Col, 5, 6; 12. Is 1–3, 4
8. Inspiration.] ~ ? 1–3   **8.** us?] Lo; ~ , 1–3   **8.** *enjoy.*]
Lo; ~ ? 1–3   **16.** *bounds*] Lo, 1, 2; bonds 3

§ 32 (iv, viii)

10. it;] Lo; ~ , 1–3

§ 33 (iv, ix)

2. Man,] 1, 2; ~ ∧ 3

§ 34 (iv, x)

12. Pains,] Lo; ~ ∧ 1–3

§ 35 (iv, xi)

9. property] Lo; propriety 1–3   **12.** whole:] Lo; ~ ; 1–3
23. introduces] 5, 6; introduce 1–3, 4, Col

§ 36 (iv, xii)

1–2. the measure of Property, Nature has well set, by the] 3;
The Measure of Property, Nature well set by the 1 ('Nature
will set' *in* Lo's 1); The measure of property, Nature has well
set, the measure of Property by the 2 (*the first* 'The measure
of Property' *is deleted in* 2er. *This is a possible explanation
of why* 4 *and* Col *read* 'Nature has well set the *measure of
Property* by the', *and is one of the indications that they are
based on a corrected copy of* 2)   **3.** all:] Lo; ~ ; 1–3
9–10. appropriated. This *measure* did] Lo, 6; appropriated;
which measure did 1–3; appropriated. *Measure* did Col, 4, 5
12. Body∧] Lo; ~ , 1–3   **18.** were,] 1er (*so in* Lo's 1);
~ ∧ 1–3   **28.** which] *om.* 1–3

§ 37 (iv, xiii) (*The French version begins* § xiv *at line* 30)

2. Men] 1; Man 2, 3   **4.** or [Men] had *agreed*,] or had

agreed, 1–3   **10–22.** To which let me add...in common.]
Lo *inserts* (*passage added in the margin of the Christ's copy,
and copied in a slightly different version on to final fly, this
last version followed here. Hollis has written in the margin
'vid. the end of vol.'*)   **25–32.** I have here...well cultivated?] Lo *inserts* (*second passage added in the Christ's
copy to the first, evidently as an afterthought, but not this
time copied on final fly. This addition runs over to the bottom
margin of opposite page, and Hollis has written at the end
of it* 'This belongs to opposite page'*)   **37.** which] Lo *inserts*
38. in] *om.* 1

§ 38 (iv, xv)

29. *common;* that] Lo; common. That 1–3

§ 40 (iv, xvii)

1. strange,] Lo; ∼ ∧ 1–3   **8.** it,] Lo ; ∼ ; 1–3
16. $\frac{99}{100}$∧] ∼ , 1–3

§ 41 (*No § no. in French version*)

8. one hundredth] Lo; $\frac{1}{100}$ 1–3   **9.** enjoy:] Lo; ∼ . 1–3

§ 42 (iv, xviii)

16, 17. see,...things,] Lo; ∼ ∧...∼ ∧ 1–3   **19.** in,] Lo;
∼ ∧ 1–3   **20.** it;] Lo; ∼ : 1–3   **24–32.** This shews,...
in hand.] Lo *inserts* (*added in the margin of the Christ's
copy*)

§ 43 (iv, xix)

4–6. But yet...Penny] Lo; But yet the Benefit Mankind
receives from one in a Year is worth 5 l. and the other possibly not worth a penny 1–3   **10.** thing:] Lo; ∼ ; 1–3
11. Products:] Lo; ∼ ; 1–3   **21.** this] (*Corrected to* 'his'
in the Christ's copy, but correction erased)   **21–2.** from
its being seed to be sown] Lo; from its sowing 1–3

§ 44 (iv, xx)

1. (*An insertion has been started in the Christ's copy, but
not proceeded with and crossed out*)   **2.** common, yet
Man] Lo; common: Man 1–3

§ 45 (iv, xxi)

1. *Labour*,] 4 + ; ∼ ∧ 1–3   **6.** Necessities:] Lo; ∼ ; 1–3

7–8. World, (where...*Money*) had] Lo; ~ , ~...~ , ~ 1–3
13. which] Lo, 1; with 2, 3   **21.** Parts and parcels of the
Earth] Lo; Parts of the World 1–3   **22.** which∧] Lo, 1;
~ , 1–3   **23.** thereof∧] Lo; ~ , 1–3   **23.** Mankind, (*in
the Christ's copy a bracket has been inserted instead of the
comma, but erased*)   **24.** Money)] Lo; ~ , 1–3
27. Mankind,] Lo; ~ ∧ 1–3

§ 46 (iv, xxii)

4. *duration*;] Lo; ~ , 1–3   **6.** themselves:] Lo; ~ . 1–3
7. things,] Lo; ~ ∧ 1–3   **8.** Life.] Lo; ~ : 1–3
10. had] Lo, 3er; hath 1–3   **11.** that he] that Lo *inserts*
12. affect] Lo, 1er (*so in* Lo's 1), 3er; effect 1–3
15. them;] ~ , 1–3   **17.** spoiled;] ~ , 1–3

§ 48 (iv, xxiii—*para. 47 not numbered*)

25. Product?] Lo, 3er; ~ . 1–3   **27.** Nature,] Lo; ~ ∧ 1–3

§ 50 (iv, xxv)

4. part,] Lo; ~ ∧ 1–3   **4–18.** it is plain, that the consent
of Men have agreed to disproportionate and unequal Possession of the Earth, I mean out of the bounds of Society and
Compact; for in Governments the Laws regulate it, they
having by consent found out and agreed in a way how a Man
may rightfully, and without injury, possess more than he
himself can make use of by receiving Gold and Silver, which
may continue long in a Man's Possession, without decaying
for the overplus, and agreeing those metals should have a
value. 1–3 (*The correction in the Christ's copy seems to have
been made at various times by both Locke and Coste. As it
stands the version there up to line 10 is incoherent, since the
corrections are not adequately inserted, and the text adopted
here is the result of comparison between these corrections
and the text of the 4th edition and the 1st Collected edition.
These differ from the text adopted in the following points:* 5. a
disproportionate (*'a' is also found in* 1, 2), 7. consent,
8. land, 9. overplus. *Since it seems unlikely that a coherent
version could have been made from the Christ's copy, this
passage is one of the clearest indications of the possibility that
the 4th and Collected editions were based on another master-
copy, where presumably the correction was clear, or perhaps
resulted from a collation of two master-copies. The 'a' in line
6, found in the 2nd but not the 3rd printing, is another sign
that the hypothetical second master-copy was of the 2nd
printing.*)

§ 52 (v, i)

10. Title. This] Lo; Title; which 1; Title, which 2, 3
11. *Parental*] Lo, 1, 2, 3er; *Paternal* 3 (*'Parental' is written in the margin of the Christ's copy, though 'Paternal' is not erased in the text. The hand is Locke's, not Coste's.*)
11. *Power.*] Lo; ~ ? 1–3

§ 53 (v, ii)

3. mistakes,] Lo; ~ ∧ 1–3   **4.** made,] Lo; ~ ∧ 1–3
4. Parents:] Lo; ~ , 1–3   **7.** *Power*∧] Lo; ~ , 1–3
10. that] Lo *inserts*

§ 54 (v, iii)

1. above, Chap. II,] ~ ∧ ~ ~ ∧ Lo 3er; above (2) 1–3
2. *equal,*] Lo; ~ ; 1–3   **6.** others,] ~ ∧ 1–3
8. *Equality,*] Lo; ~ ∧ 1–3   **10.** I] Lo, 1, 2; *om.* 3
12. hath,] Lo; ~ ∧ 1–3

§ 55 (v, iv)

6. by,] 1; ~ ∧ 2, 3

§ 56 (v, v)

3. Instant] 2er, 3; Instance 1, 2   **6.** which] Lo *inserts*
11. were,] ~ ∧ 1–3   **12.** Nature,] Lo, 1; ~ ∧ 2, 3
13. *Children,*] Lo; ~ ∧ 1–3

§ 57 (v, vi)

6. *Law:*] Lo; ~ ; 1–3   **7.** Law, which is] Lo; Law that
is 1–3   **7.** him;] 1; ~ , 2, 3   **11.** born,] 1; ~ , 2, 3
12. Notion,] Lo; ~ ∧ 1–3   **17.** vanish;] 1; ~ , 2, 3
19. that,] Lo; ~ ∧ 1–3   **21.** *Freedom:*] Lo; ~ . 1; ~ ; 2, 3
22. *Law,*] Lo; ~ ∧ 1–3   **23.** *Freedom*. For] Lo; Freedom.
For, 1; Freedom; for 2, 3   **24.** be,] Lo; ~ ∧ 1–3
25. Law:] Lo; ~ , 1–3   **25.** But Freedom is] Lo; and is
1–3   **25.** not,] ~ ∧ 2, 3   **28.** dispose, and order, as he
lists,] Lo; dispose and order freely as he lists∧ 1–3
29. Property,] Lo; ~ ∧ 1–3

§ 58 (v, vii)

13. not] Lo; no 1–3

§ 59 (v, viii)

5. State of Maturity] Lo, 2er; an Estate 1 ('E' *of* Estate
erased in Lo's 1); A State and and [*sic*] Maturity 2 (*presumably a misread correction*); A State of Maturity 3 ('A'

is clearly erased in the Christ's copy, though printed in 4 +)
19. one and twenty years,] Lo (*final comma omitted*); Twenty
one, 1–3   **27.** it;] ~ , 1–3   **30.** that,] Lo; ~ ∧ 1–3
32. Nonage;] Lo; ~ , 1–3   **34.** Son,] Lo; ~ ∧ 1–3

§ 60 (v, ix)

3. Reason,] Lo; ~ ∧ 1–3   **6.** Will (because] Lo; ~ , ~ 1–3
7. Guide)] Lo; ~ ; 1–3   **19.** Duty,] Lo; ~ ∧ 1–3

§ 61 (v, x)

7. him,] Lo, 1; ~ ∧ 2, 3   **12–13.** miss this *difference*,]
miss of it 1   **13–14.** allow their consistency] cannot but
allow of it 1   **25.** own:] Lo, 1; ~ ; 2, 3

§ 63 (v, xii)

7. Nature,] 1; ~ ∧ 2, 3

§ 65 (v, xiv)

4. them,] Lo; ~ ∧ 1–3   **6.** it belongs] Lo; belongs 1–3
7. another:] Lo; ~ . 1–3   **9.** Issue, if] Lo; Issue: If 1;
Issue; If 2, 3   **10.** Father.] Lo; ~ : 1–3   **16.** Provision?
If] Lo; Provision? And if 1–3   **26.** Children? that] Lo;
~ ; ~ 1; ~ , ~ 2, 3   **24.** Lives? Or can she] 2er, 3; Lives,
and she 1, 2   **39.** Son,] Lo; ~ ∧ 1–3   **39.** Man:] Lo;
~ . 1–3

§ 66 (v, xv)

3. the father] Lo; he 1–3   **4.** each] Lo, 3er; both 1–3
7. Country:] Lo; ~ ; 1; ~ , 2, 3   **8.** ought,] 1; ~ ∧ 2, 3
18, 20. those,...those,] Lo; ~ ∧...~ ∧ 1–3   **22–3.** Freedom,] Lo, 1; ~ ∧ 2, 3   **25.** dispose∧] (~ , *in Christ's copy*)
25. please,] 4 + ; ~ ∧ 1–3 (*obviously intention of previous
correction*)

§ 67 (v, xvi)

3. Child:] Lo; ~ . 1; ~ ; 2, 3   **5.** compliance too, more∧]
compliance to more, 1   **6–7.** less. This] Lo; less. And this
1; less; and this 2, 3   **9.** powers; viz. that which] Lo;
powers which 1–3

§ 68 (v, xvii)

1. support,] 1er (*so in* Lo's 1), 2, 3; ~ ∧ 1   **2.** return∧] 1er
(*so in* Lo's 1), 2, 3; ~ ; 1   **18.** Boy?] ~ . 1–3

§ 69 (v, xviii)

23. right,] Lo; ~ ∧ 1–3

§ 70 (v, xix)

11. varied,] Lo; ~ ∧ 1–3   **12.** expence,] Lo, 1; ~ ∧ 2, 3
12. which] Lo *inserts*   **12.** Child,] Lo; ~ ∧ 1–3

§ 71 (v, xx)

4. Subjection,] Lo, 1; ~ ∧ 2, 3   **8.** it.] Lo; ~ ; 1; ~ : 2, 3
10. separate; are] Lo; ~ , and 1–3

§ 72 (v, xxi)

3. Parents,] 1; ~ ∧ 2, 3   **6.** Children:] Lo; ~ , 1–3
9. the Instances of it] 4 + ; in Instances of *it* 1 ('in' *deleted in* Lo's 1); the Instances of *it* 2, 3   **13.** those,] Lo; ~ ∧ 1–3

§ 73 (v, xxii)

1. on] Lo; to 1–3   **8.** and] Lo *inserts*   **8.** and the inheritance of an Estate] Lo *inserts*

§ 74 (v, xxiii)

7. [which]] *om.* 1–3   **9.** enacting] exacting 1
9. Children;] Lo; ~ . 1; ~ : 2, 3   **10.** all] Lo *inserts*
11. Son:] Lo; ~ ; 1–3   **13.** still,] Lo; ~ ∧ 1–3
18. Children:] Lo; ~ ; 1; ~ , 2, 3   **18.** and since without] Lo; and when they were grown up: Since without 1–3. (*in* Lo's 1 *a bracket is opened before* 'Since', *and closed after* 'together' *in line* 16)   **20–1.** when they were grown up,] Lo *inserts* (*comma not in Christ's copy, but in* 4 +) **22.** continue; when] Lo; continue: And when 2, 3   **23.** it,] Lo; ~ ∧ 1–3   **33–4.** Children:] Lo; ~ , 1–3   **34.** it] Lo *inserts*   **35.** one,] Lo; ~ ∧ 1–3   **40.** Authority,] Lo, 1; ~ ∧ 2, 3   **41.** him,] Lo; ~ ∧ 1–3   (*Editor has inserted* 'P.' *in Hooker quotation.*)

§ 75 (v, xxiv)

2. tacit,] Lo; ~ ∧ 1–3   **2.** scarce avoidable] Lo; almost natural 1–3   **6.** Men,] Lo; ~ ; 1–3   **10, 11, 12.** sustain'd, . . . wonder, . . . Minority,] Lo; ~ ∧ . . . ~ ∧ . . . ~ ∧ 1–3
12. Age;] Lo; ~ , 1–3   **18.** Liberties,] Lo; ~ ∧ 1–3

§ 76 (v, xxv)

3. too:] Lo; ~ ; 1–3   **3.** able,] Lo; ~ ∧ 1–3   **4.** otherwise;] Lo; ~ : 1–3   **5.** Hereditary, . . . Kingdoms,] Lo;

~ ∧ . . . ~ ∧ 1–3   **6.** Manners,] 4 + ; Manors 1, 2; Man-
nors 3   **14.** certain,] Lo; ~ ∧ 1–3

§ 77 (vi, i)

13. see,] Lo; ~ ∧ 1–3

§ 78 (vi, ii)

2. Woman:] Lo; ~ , 1–3   **5.** Assistance,] Lo; ~ ; 1–3

§ 79 (vi, iii)

3. Species, this] Lo; ~ . This 1; ~ : This 2, 3   **12.** Copulation:] Lo; ~ ; 1–3   **16.** longer:] Lo; ~ ; 1–3
20. living,] Lo, 1; ~ ∧ 2, 3   **20.** Grass,] Lo; ~ : 1; ~ ; 2, 3
26. feeding,] Lo, 1; ~ ∧ 2, 3   **28.** Mates,] Lo; ~ ∧ 1–3

§ 80 (vi, iv)

8. Parents:] Lo; ~ , 1–3   **14.** liberty,] Lo; ~ ; 1–3
18. foresight and] Lo *inserts*   **19.** as to] Lo *inserts*
20. *lasting,*] Lo; ~ ∧ 1–3

§ 81 (vi, v)

2. in Man] in a Man 1

§ 82 (vi, vi)

5. somewhere,] ~ ; 1–3   **8.** free] Lo; true 1–3; tree 3er
('true' *apparently a misreading of copy by compositor of* 1,
though uncorrected in Lo's 1)   **9–10.** and at least gives
the Husband no more power over her than she has over his
life 1   **12.** has] Lo; ~ ∧ 1–3

§ 83 (vi, vii)

3. Right,] Lo; ~ ∧ 1–3   **13–22.** Power in the Husband, it
was not at all necessary to it; the condition of Conjugal
Society put it not in him, but whatsoever might consist with
Procreation and Support of the Children, till they could shift
for themselves: mutual Assistance, Comfort and Maintenance
might be varied, and regulated, by that contract which first
united them in that society; nothing being 1   **19.** Contract,]
Lo, 1; ~ ∧ 2, 3

§ 85 (vi, ix)

8. greater,] Lo; ~ ∧ 2, 3

§ 86 (vi, x)

21. Men,] ~ ∧ 1–3   **21.** that,] Lo; ~ ∧ 1–3

§ 87 (vi, xi)

14. Society; there] Lo, 1; Society: There 2, 3
20–3. Umpire; and by understanding indifferent rules and men authorized by the community for their execution decides all the differences 1 ('standing' *for* 'understanding' *in* 1er, *so in* Lo's 1)   **20.** Rules,] Lo, 1; ~ ; 2, 3   **21.** Parties;] Lo, 1; ~ : 2, 3   **25.** right;] Lo; ~ , 1–3   **25.** Offences,] Lo; ~ ∧ 1–3   **26.** Society,] Lo; ~ ∧ 1–3   **27.** established: Whereby] Lo; established; whereby 1–3
32. another:] Lo; ~ ; 1–3

§ 88 (vi, xii)

2. down,] Lo; ~ ∧ 1–3   **3.** which] Lo *inserts*
9–12. every Man...his power] Lo; every Man enter'd into Society has quitted his power 1–3   **11.** Commonwealth,] ~ ∧ 1–3   **15.** Cases,] Lo; ~ ∧ 1–3   **16.** given] Lo; given up 1–3   **17.** force,] Lo; ~ ∧ 1–3   **18.** it;] Lo; ~ , 1–3   **23.** punished,] Lo; ~ ∧ 1–3   **24.** to determin,] Lo *inserts*

§ 89 (vi, xiii)

1–2. Men are so united] Men so unite 1   **16.** Injuries,] Lo; ~ ∧ 1–3

§ 90 (vi, xiv)

1. Hence] Lo; And Hence 1–3   **1.** *Monarchy*,] Lo; ~ ∧ 1–3   **2.** counted] Lo; counted for 1–3   **5.** avoid,] Lo; ~ ∧ 1–3   **12.** to, for the decision of any] to, to decide any 1

§ 91 (vi, xv)

3. one,] 1; ~ ∧ 2, 3   **5.** from whose decision] Lo; from whence 1–3   **6.** Inconveniency,] Lo; ~ ∧ 1–3   **7.** the Prince] Lo; him 1–3   **16.** Prince:] Lo; ~ ; 1, 2; ~ . 3
18. it; now] Lo; it: but 1–3

§ 92 (vi, xvi)

6. Throne;] Lo; ~ , 1–3   **7.** all,] Lo; ~ ∧ 1–3

§ 93 (vi, xvii)

10, 17, 18. more,....asked,...State,] Lo; ~ ∧...~ ∧...~ ∧ 1–3   **21–2.** Subject,...grant,] Lo; ~ ∧...~ ∧ 1–3
22. Judges,] Lo; ~ ∧ 1–3   **23.** Security:] Lo; ~ . 1–3
24. Circumstances:] Lo; ~ ; 1–3   **25.** Power] Lo; a Power 1–3   **36.** Safety,] ~ ∧ 1–3

§ 94 (vi, xviii)

2. it hinders not] 2er, 3; it never hinders 1; it hinders 2
2. feeling:] Lo; ~ ; 1–3   **3.** perceive,] Lo; ~ ∧ 1–3
4. which] Lo *inserts*   **4.** of;] Lo; ~ , 1–3   **7.** him,]
Lo; ~ ∧ 1–3   **9.** *Society,*] Lo 1; ~ 2, 3   **13.** Man,]
Lo; ~ ∧ 1–3   **19.** Wisdom:] Lo; ~ ; 1–3   **19.** time,]
Lo; ~ ∧ 1–3   **20.** (as] Lo; ∧~ 1–3   **20.** us)] Lo; ~ ,
1–3   **24.** Government,] Lo; ~ ∧ 1–3   **27.** Legislature]
Lo; Legislative 1–3   **27.** placed] 2er, 3; so placed 1, 2
28. please. By] Lo; please, by 1–3   **29.** subject,] Lo; ~ ∧
1–3   **30.** Men,] Lo, 1; ~ ∧ 2, 3   **31.** established:] Lo;
~ ; 1–3   **32.** Authority,] Lo; ~ ∧ 1–3   **35.** Dependants.] Lo; ~ : 1–3   **36.** do,] Lo; ~ ∧ 1–3   **40.** *Society:*]
Lo; ~ , 1–3

§ 95 (vii, i)

2. this] 1, 2, 4 + ; his 3   **4–6.** *Consent. The only…is by
agreeing*] Lo; Consent, which is done by agreeing 1–3

§ 96 (vii, ii)

1. have,] Lo; ~ ∧ 1–3   **2.** individual, made a] 4 + ; ~ ∧
~ ~ 1–3 (~ ~ , ~ *in Christ's copy*)   **6–7.** being necessary to that which is one body to move] Lo; being one Body
must move 1–3

§ 97 (vii, iii)

1, 7, 8. Man,…Compact,…ties,] Lo; ~ ∧…~ ∧…~ ∧ 1–3
11, 12–13. Society,…liberty,] Lo; ~ ∧…~ ∧ 1–3
14. hath] *om.* 1

§ 98 (vii, iv)

1–2, 2. reason,…received,] Lo; ~ ∧…~ ∧ 1–3
4–6. whole: But…the Infirmities] Lo; whole, which, considering the Infirmities 1–3   **9.** Assembly. To which if
we add the variety] Lo; Assembly; and the variety 1–3
10. Opinions∧…Interests,] Lo; ~ ,…~ ∧ 1–3
11–13. Men, the coming…again. Such] Men, 'tis next impossible ever to be had. And therefore if coming into Society
be upon such terms, it will be only like *Cato's* coming into
the Theatre, *tantum ut exiret.* Such 1–3   **14.** duration,]
Lo; ~ ∧ 1–3   **15.** Creatures;] Lo, 1; ~ , 1–3   **16.** in:]
Lo; ~ , 1–3   **16.** suppos'd,] Lo; ~ ∧ 1–3

§ 99 (vii, v)

3. power,] Lo; ~ ∧ 1–3   **8.** Individuals,…into,] Lo; ~ ∧

...~ ∧ 1–3   **9.** that,] Lo; ~ ∧ 1–3   **11. a**] 2er, 3; *om.*
1, 2   **12.** that,] Lo, 1; ~ ∧ 2, 3   **13.** only,] Lo; ~ ∧
1–3

§ 101 (vii, vii)

1. Answer.] Lo; ~ , 1–3   **2, 3, 4.** wonder'd,...Men,...
love,] Lo; ~ ∧...~ ∧...~ ∧ 1–3   **11, 14, 15.** them,...
has,...Ease,] Lo; ~ ∧...~ ∧...~ ∧ 1–3   **21.** their *Origi-*
nal] it 1   **21–2.** beholding,...it,] Lo; ~ ∧...~ ∧ 1–3
22, 23, 27. Records,...have,...beginning,] Lo; ~ ∧...~ ∧
...~ ∧ 1–3

§ 102 (vii, viii)

2. fact,] Lo; ~ ∧ 1–3

§ 103 (vii, ix)

2. *Justin l.* 3. *c.* 4 will] Lo; Justin 1. will 1–3   **12.** History,]
Lo; ~ ∧ 1–3   **14.** best] least 1 (*signs of proof correction*
in 2)   **15.** has] be of 1 (*signs of proof correction in* 2)

§ 104 (vii, x)

3. shewing,] Lo, 1, 3; ~ ∧ 3   **3.** World,] Lo, 1; ~ ∧ 2, 3
5. *People*;] Lo; ~ : 1–3   **7.** Opinion,] Lo, 1; ~ ∧ 2, 3
7. Mankind,] Lo; ~ ∧ 1–3

§ 105 (vii, xi)

11. fit,] Lo, 1; ~ ∧ 2, 3   **13.** Pupilage;] Lo, 1; ~ , 2, 3
15. Offender,] Lo; ~ ∧ 1–3   **17–18.** Law-maker,...all,]
Lo; ~ ∧...~ ∧ 1–3   **20.** Property,] Lo; ~ ∧ 1–3
21, 22. him,...him,] Lo; ~ ∧...~ ∧ 1–3   **22.** to any]
'to' Lo. *inserts*   **25.** Man,] Lo; ~ ∧ 1–3   **25.** Father;]
Lo; ~ , 1–3   **26.** Mind,] Lo; ~ ∧ 1–3   **27.** it?] Lo;
~ . 1–3   **29.** Qualities,] Lo; ~ ∧ 1–3   **29.** Rule:] Lo;
~ , 1–3   **30.** met,] Lo; ~ ∧ 1–3   **31–2.** freedom,...
him,...ablest,] Lo; ~ ∧...~ ∧...~ ∧ 1–3   **34.** (living]
Lo; ∧~ 1–3   **35.** Swords,] Lo; ~ ∧ 1–3   **36.** *Mexico*)]
Lo; ~ , 1–3   **39.** weak,] Lo; ~ ∧ 1–3

§ 106 (vii, xii)

4, 6, 7. that,...Individuals,...who,] Lo; ~ ∧...~ ∧...~ ∧
1–3   **9.** mistake,] Lo; ~ ∧ 1–3   **11.** consider,] Lo, 1;
~ ∧ 2, 3   **15.** place,] Lo; ~ ∧ 1–3   **15.** hand;] Lo;
~ : 1–3   **16.** plain,...reason,] Lo; ~ ∧...~ ∧ 1–3
17, 19. Regard,...Original,] Lo; ~ ∧...~ ∧ 1–3

§ 107 (vii, xiii)

6. to Men all] 3 (*so in* Lo's 1); Men (all 1, 2; to Men (all 2er   **7.** Society.] 3 (*so in* Lo's 1); ~ .) 1, 2
7, 16. wonder,...Power,] Lo; ~ ∧...~ ∧ 1–3
17–18. them, it] Lo; them. It 1–3   **20.** those,] Lo; ~ ∧ 1–3   **25.** living (which] Lo; ~ , ~ 1–3   **26.** Ambition)] Lo; ~ , 1–3   **27.** it:] Lo; ~ ; 1–3   **32–7.** Laws. The...Justice where] Lo; Laws, where there was but very little Property, and wanted not the variety of Rulers and abundance of Officers to direct and look after their Execution, where 1–3   **38.** then∧] Lo; ~ , 1–3   **43.** be,] Lo; ~ ∧ 1–3

§ 108 (vii, xiv)

1, 12. see,...self,] Lo; ~ ∧...~ ∧ 1–3   **12.** Plurality] 1er (*so in* Lo's 1), 2er, 3; Pluralities 1, 2

§ 109 (vii, xv)

2. seems] seem 3   **15.** *General,*] 1; ~ ∧ 2, 3

§ 110 (vii, xvi)

7. Prescription:] Lo, 1; ~ ; 2, 3   **9.** uniting] Lo; united 1–3   **10.** Society,] Lo; ~ ; 1–3   **13.** (such] Lo; ∧ ~ 1–3   **14.** World)] Lo; ~ , 1–3   **18–26.** Government required: ...weale, all] Lo; Government required. It was given them for the publick Good and Safety, and to those Ends in the Infancies of Commonwealths they commonly used it, and unless they had done so, young Societies could not have subsisted, without such nursing Fathers; without this care of the Governours, all 1–3   **27–8.** Infancy; and] 'and' Lo *inserts*

§ 111 (vii, xvii)

1. though the *Golden Age* (before] (*so in* Lo's 1), 2, 3; But the golden Age (tho' before 1   **2.** Concupiscence,] ~ ∧ 1–3
10. Government:] Lo; ~ . 1–3   **12.** Business,] Lo; ~ ∧ 1–3

§ 113 (vii, xix)

17, 18, 20. Men,...*born*,...us,] Lo; ~ ∧... ~ ∧... ~ ∧ 1–3

§ 115 (vii, xxi)

6. places;] Lo; ~ , 1–3   **8.** multiplyed,] Lo; ~ ∧ 1–3
16–17. Kingdoms;...but only] Lo; Kingdoms, but only 1–3
18–19. Families,] Lo; ~ ∧ 1–3   **19.** the] (*so in* Lo's 1), 1er, 2er, 3; their 1, 2   **19.** will,] Lo; ~ ∧ 1–3

§ 116 (vii, xxii)

17. has] Lo *inserts*   **22.** else:] Lo; ~ . 1–3   **23.** Land,] Lo; ~ ∧ 1–3

§ 117 (vii, xxiii)

1–2. to mistake] Lo (*so in* Lo's 1); to the mistake 1–3   **7.** Society:] Lo; ~ ; 1–3   **9.** Commonwealth] Commonweal 1   **10.** *Free-men*] 1; Freemen 2, 3

§ 118 (vii, xxiv)

8. For] Lo; for 1–3   **10.** pleases?] Lo; ~ . 1–3   **17.** Freeman] 1; Freeman 2, 3   **23.** Ancestors.] Lo; ~ : 1–3

§ 119 (vii, xxv)

3. Consent; it] Lo; Consent: It 1–3

§ 120 (vii, xxvi)

11–12. he himself…is a] 2er, 3; he himself, and the Property of the Land, is a 1, 2 ('and the Property of the Land' *deleted* in Lo's 1)   **19.** Inheritance, Purchase, Permission] (*so in* Lo's 1) 2, 3; Inheritance, purchases Permission 1

§ 121 (vii, xxvii)

9–10. Possession, he] Lo; Possession: He 1–3   **11.** to] Lo *inserts*   **12, 13.** World,…he,] Lo; ~ ∧…~ ∧ 1–3   **19.** dissolved] *the paragraph ends here in* 1

§ 122 (vii, xxviii)

1. Country,] Lo; ~ ; 1–3   **3.** *Society*: This is] 2er, 3; Society; 'tis 1, 2

§ 123 (viii, i)

2. Lord∧] ~ ; 3   **4–5.** Why will he give up this Empire] Why will he part with his Freedom, this Empire 1   **9.** others. For] Lo; others; for 1–3   **10.** is] 4 + ; his 3   **11.** Justice,] Lo; ~ ; 1–3   **13.** a] Lo; his 1–3

§ 124 (1–4 viii, ii; 5–12 iii)

11–12. as well as] Lo, 1, 2; were as 3

§ 125 (viii, iv)

7, 8. heat,…negligence,…remiss,] Lo; ~ ,…~ ∧…~ ∧ 1–3   **8.** to make] 'to' Lo *inserts*

§ 126 (viii, v)

5. Injustice:] Lo; ~ ; 1–3

§ 127 (viii, vi)

2–3. condition,] Lo; ~ ∧ 1–3   **14.** by them to] Lo; by them, to 1; by it to them, to 2, 3   **14–15.** purpose,] Lo; ~ ∧ 1–3

§ 128 (viii, vii)

5. *Nature*:] Lo; ~ ; 1–3   **7.** Creatures. And] Lo; ~ , and 1–3   **8.** corruption,] Lo; ~ ∧ 1–3   **9.** other;] Lo; ~ , 1–3   **11–12.** and by...associations] Lo; and associate into less Combinations 1–3

§ 130 (viii, ix)

7. Conveniencies,] Lo; ~ ∧ 1–3   **7, 11.** assistance,...prosperity,] Lo; ~ ∧...~ ∧ 1–3   **11–12.** require:] Lo; ~ ; 1–3   **12.** necessary,] Lo; ~ ∧ 1–3   **12.** just;] Lo; ~ , 1–3

§ 131 (viii, x)

9. *Legislative*∧] Lo; ~ , 1–3

§ 132 (ix, i)

14–15. the Community may] Lo *inserts*

§ 133 (ix, ii)

7. or Citty in *English*] Lo *inserts*   **8–10.** and City amongst ...Commonwealth: And] Lo; and City much less; and 1–3   **11.** sense,] Lo; ~ ; 1–3   **12.** by King *James the First*] by K. *James* himself 1   **12.** and I take it to] Lo; which I think to 1–3

§ 134 (x, i)

4. Society; the] Lo; ~ : The 1–3   **7.** Legislative it self, is] ~ : It self is 1   **15.** *Legislative*,] Lo; ~ ∧ 1–3   **16.** appointed.] Lo; ~ : 1–3   **17.** that,] Lo; ~ ∧ 1–3

§ 135 (x, ii)

10. gave up] Lo; gave it up 1–3   **23.** Power,] Lo; ~ ∧ 1–3   **27.** Subjects. The] Lo; ~ ; the 1–3   **33.** must,] Lo; ~ ∧ 1–3

§ 136 (x, iii)

10. not,] Lo; ~ ∧ 1–3   **10.** ought,] Lo, 1; ~ ∧ 2, 3   **16.** or to punish] 2er, 3; or punish 1, 2   **23.** which] Lo *inserts*   **27.** Property∧] Lo; ~ , 1–3   **27.** uncertainty,] Lo; ~ ∧ 1–3

§ 137 (x, iv)

9. do, to give to any] Lo; do, to give any 1, 2; do, to any 2er, 3
9. one,...more,] Lo; ~ ∧...~ ∧ 1–3   **19.** him,] Lo; ~ ∧
1–3   **21.** who] Lo; that 1–3   **22.** Man,] Lo; ~ ∧ 1–3
25. Men:] Lo; ~ , 1–3   **25, 30.** better,...condition,] Lo;
~ ∧...~ ∧ 1–3   **39.** Pleasure, so] Lo; ~ : so 1; ~ : So 2, 3
40. *Laws*:] Lo; ~ ; 1–3   **43.** tempted,...hands,] Lo; ~ ∧
...~ ∧ 1–3   **44.** such purposes] 'such' Lo *inserts*
44. measures,] Lo; ~ ∧ 1–3

§ 138 (x, v)

8. it, too] 2er, 3; it. Too 1, 2   **11–12.** take their substance,
or any part of it from] Lo, 3er; take them, or any part of
them from 1–3   **13, 14, 15.** this,...that,...me,] Lo; ~ ∧
...~ ∧...~ ∧ 1–3   **20–1.** consists,...part,] Lo; ~ ∧...
~ ∧ 1–3   **25.** Assembly∧] Lo; ~ , 1–3   **25.** Man,] 1;
~ ∧ 2, 3   **27.** interest,] Lo; ~ ∧ 1–3   **28.** Community;]
Lo; ~ , 1–3   **29.** Power,...taking,...fit,] Lo; ~ ∧...~ ∧
...~ ∧ 1–3   **31–33.** it,...Man,] Lo; ~ ∧...~ ∧ 1–3

§ 139 (x, vi)

3. *their*] there 3   **10.** necessary,] Lo; ~ ∧ 1–3   **12.** ends,]
Lo; ~ ∧ 1–3   **18.** them:] Lo; ~ ; 1–3   **19, 23.** Serjeant,...*General*,] Lo; ~ ∧...~ ∧ 1–3   **24.** for not] 'for'
Lo *inserts*   **25.** can] Lo; cannot 1–3   **31.** rest;] Lo; ~ ,
1–3

§ 140 (x, vii)

7. them. For] Lo; them; for 1–3   **12.** take,] Lo; ~ ∧ 1–3

§ 141 (x, viii)

2. hands. For] 1; hands, for 2, 3   **3.** they,...it,] Lo; ~ ∧
...~ ∧ 1–3   **7–8.** to rules,] Lo *inserts*   **10.** the people]
Lo; they 1–3   **11.** those,] Lo; ~ ∧ 1–3   **12–18.** The
power...hands.] *om.* 1   **14.** other,] Lo; ~ ∧ 2, 3

§ 142 (x, ix)

11. raise] rise 3   **18.** The *Legislative*] 2, 3; The *om.* 1
('the' *in* Lo's 1)

§ 143 (xi, i)

6. need,] Lo; ~ ∧ 1–3   **8–9.** a temptation] 'a' Lo *inserts*
9. frailty∧] Lo; ~ , 1–3   **16.** Government:] Lo; ~ . 1–3
18, 21. considered,...Laws,] Lo; ~ ∧...~ ∧ 1–3
22, 23. Laws,...them,...care,] Lo; ~ ∧...~ ∧...~ ∧ 1–3

§ 144 (xi, ii)

1. Laws,] Lo; ~ ∧ 1–3

§ 145 (xi, iii)

9. was,] Lo, 1; ~ ∧ 2, 3   **9–10.** Mankind. Hence it is, that] ~ : so that 1

§ 147 (xi, v)

18–20. interests,...Skill,] Lo; ~ ∧...~ ∧ 1–3

§ 149 (xii, i)

1. Commonwealth,] ~ ∧ 3

§ 150 (xii, ii)

3. him:] Lo; ~ ; 1–3   **6, 7.** Society,...Execution,] Lo; ~ ∧...~ ∧ 1–3

§ 151 (xii, iii)

9. them:] Lo; ~ ; 1–3   **27–8.** Will,...the Members] Will. The Members 1

§ 152 (xii, iv)

2. Person,] Lo; ~ ∧ 1–3   **9.** consent:] Lo; ~ ∧ 1–3
17, 19. purpose,...is,...Grant,] Lo; ~ ∧...~ ∧...~ ∧ 1–3

§ 153 (xii, v)

6, 7. Laws,...make,...hands,] Lo; ~ ∧...~ ∧...~ ∧ 1–3
14. Persons (for] 2er; ~ ; ~ 1, 2; ~ ; (~ 3   **17.** Legislative)] 2er; ~ , 1–3   **18.** *Legislature,*] Lo; Legislative 1–3
22. People,] ~ ∧ 3

§ 154 (xii, vi)

1. made up] Lo, 3er; *om.* 1–3   **7.** it:] Lo; ~ ; 1–3
17. inconveniencies,] Lo; ~ ∧ 1–3

§ 155 (xii, vii)

7, 10, 12. him,...Legislative,...from,] Lo; ~ ∧...~ ∧... ~ ∧ 1–3

§ 156 (xii, viii)

3, 4. Trust,...him,] Lo; ~ ∧...~ ∧ 1–3   **5, 7.** uncertainty,...should,] Lo; ~ ∧...~ ∧ 1–3   **8, 13.** foresight, ...one,] Lo; ~ ∧...~ ∧ 1–3   **21.** publick;] Lo; ~ , 1–3
24, 26. benefit,...Case,...Community,] Lo; ~ ∧...~ ∧... ~ ∧ 1–3   **27, 32.** hazard,...hands,] Lo; ~ ∧...~ ∧ 1–3
35. not] 1, 2, 3er; nor 3

§ 157 (xii, ix)

3. Stations;] 1; ~ , 2, 3   **8.** Priviledges,] Lo; ~ ∧ 1–3
9. pass,] Lo, 1; ~ ∧ 2, 3   **10.** Governments,] Lo, 1; ~ ∧
2, 3   **14.** Custom,....it,] Lo; ~ ∧...~ ∧ 1–3   **19.** sends]
2er, 3; send 1, 2   **20.** County] 1, 2, 3er; Country 3

§ 158 (xii, x)

2. he,...it,] Lo; ~ ∧...~ ∧ 1–3   **5, 6.** proportion,...
regulates,] Lo; ~ ∧...~ ∧ 1–3   **9.** to,] Lo; ~ ; 1–3
9–10. assistance,] Lo; ~ ∧ 1–3   **11, 13.** judg'd,...disor-
ders,] Lo; ~ ∧...~ ∧ 1–3   **13.** insensibly,] Lo; ~ ∧ 1–3
14. introduced. For] Lo; introduced; for 1–3   **14, 15.** interest,...People,] Lo; ~ ∧...~ ∧ 1–3   **19.** nothing,] Lo; ~ ∧
1–3   **23.** direct, whatsoever] Lo, 2er; direct. Whatsoever
1, 2; direct; whatsoever 3   **24.** the establishing] 'the' Lo
inserts   **29.** places] Lo, 3er; *om.* 1–3   **32, 33.** Priviledge,...State,...Corruption,] Lo; ~ ∧...~ ∧...~ ∧ 1–3
36. part, or Party,] Lo; ~ ∧ ~ ~ ∧ 1–3   **38, 40.** Society,
...always,] Lo; ~ ∧...~ ∧ 1–3   **44.** permitted,] Lo; ~ ∧
1–3   **44.** caused] Lo; proposed 1–3

§ (159 (xiii, i)

2. hands, (as] Lo; ~ , ~ 1–3   **2–3.** Monarchies, and] ~)
~ *in Christ's copy*   **3.** Governments)] 4 + ; ~ , 1–3 (*in the
Christ's copy; the parenthesis was obviously inserted in error
after* 'Monarchies' *in line* 3)   **4, 5.** requires,...him,] Lo;
~,...~ ∧ 1–3   **6.** foresee,] Lo; ~ ∧ 1–3   **6–7.** provide,
by Laws, for all,] Lo; ~ ∧ ~ ~ ∧ ~ ~ ∧ 1–3   **8, 9, 10.** Laws,
...Nature,...it,...Cases,] Lo; ~ ∧...~ ∧...~ ∧...~ ∧ 1–3
12. it. Many] Lo; it; nay, many 1–3   **13, 15.** are,...him,]
Lo; ~ ∧...~ ∧ 1–3   **17.** require:] Lo; ~ ; 1–3   **21.** happen,] Lo; ~ ∧ 1–3   **23.** harm; (as] Lo; ~ , ∧~ 1–3
24. burning)] Lo; ~ ; 1–3   **26.** Persons,...action,] Lo;
~ ∧...~ ∧ 1–3   **27.** pardon; 'tis] Lo; pardon. 'Tis 1, 2;
pardon; 'Tis, 2er, 3   **28.** Power,...Cases,] Lo; ~ ∧...
~ ∧ 1–3   **29.** Offenders: For] Lo; ~ , since 1–3
30, 31. *all,*...spared,] Lo; ~ ∧...~ ∧ 1–3

§ 160 (xiii, ii)

1. discretion,] Lo; ~ ∧ 1–3   **4.** *Prerogative.* For] Lo; ~ ;
for 1–3   **6.** slow,] Lo; ~ ∧ 1–3   **7.** Execution:] Lo;
~ ∧ 1–3   **8.** for,...Necessities,] Lo; ~ ∧...~ ∧ 1–3
9. publick;] Lo; ~ ∧ 1–3   **9.** Laws,] Lo; ~ ∧ 1–3
11. rigour,...Persons,] Lo; ~ ∧...~ ∧ 1–3   **13.** power,
...choice,] Lo; ~ ∧...~ ∧ 1–3

§ 161 (xiii, iii)

5. scrupulous,] Lo; ~ ∧ 1–3   **5.** point:] Lo; ~ ∧ 1; ~ ; 2, 3
5–6. they...*Prerogative*] or questioning of Prerogative 1
7. for the good] 'for' Lo *inserts*

§ 162 (xiii, iv)

1. conceive,] Lo, 1; ~ ∧ 2, 3   **4, 8, 10.** Governours,...
mistake,...Power,] Lo; ~ ∧...~ ∧...~ ∧ 1–3   **12.** determin'd,...points,] Lo; ~ ∧...~ ∧ 1–3   **13, 15.** it:...
which] Lo; it: And declared limitations of Prerogative in
those Cases which 1–3   **15, 16.** left,...latitude,...Princes,]
Lo; ~ ∧...~ ∧...~ ∧ 1–3

§ 163 (xiii, v)

4. defined] 1, 2, 3er; designed 3   **4, 5.** doing,...thing,]
Lo; ~ ∧...~ ∧ 1–3   **7.** in his] Lo; in him 1–3   **7.** Ancestors,] Lo; ~ ∧ 1–3   **8.** thing, which they] Lo; thing
they 1–3   **12.** body:] Lo; ~ ; 1; ~ , 2, 3   **17.** it, the]
it. The 1   **18, 19.** Source,...Evils,...Disorders,] Lo; ~ ∧
...~ ∧...~ ∧ 1–3   **22.** good; they are not such] good,
such 1   **23.** themselves, to guard,] Lo; ~ ∧ ~ ~ ∧ 1–3
27, 28. brutish,...be,] Lo; ~ ∧...~ ∧ 1–3

§ 164 (xiii, vi)

4, 6, 7. necessary,...nothing,...Rulers,] Lo; ~ ∧...~ ∧...
~ ∧ 1–3   **7.** choice,] Lo; ~ ∧ 1–3   **9.** good;] Lo; ~ ∧
1–3   **10.** Prince,] Lo; ~ ∧ 1–3   **14.** which] Lo *inserts*
18–19. occasion,] Lo; ~ ∧ 1–3   **19.** Right,] Lo, 1; ~ ∧
2, 3   **19.** which,] Lo, 1; ~ ∧ 2, 3

§ 165 (xiii, vii)

1, 2. he,...find,] Lo; ~ ∧...~ ∧ 1–3   **3.** Princes:] Lo, 1;
~ ; 2, 3   **5–6.** good,...or if] Lo; good; or if 1–3
7. Men,] Lo, 1; ~ ∧ 2, 3   **11.** Princes,] Lo, 1; ~ ∧ 2, 3
13, 14. and,...rightly,] Lo; ~ ∧...~ ∧ 1–3

§ 166 (xiii, viii)

2. Argument,] Lo; ~ ∧ 1–3   **4.** Universe by: because] Lo;
Universe, because 1; Universe by, because 2, 3   **8.** Successors,] Lo, 1; ~ ∧ 2, 3   **9.** Thoughts,] Lo, 1; ~ ∧ 2, 3
12. People, was] Lo, 1; ~ ∧ ~ 2, 3   **12.** do,] Lo; ~ ∧ 1–3
13. pleased; it] Lo; ~ : It 1–3   **14.** Disorders,] Lo, 1;
~ ∧ 2, 3   **17.** that] Lo *inserts*   **18.** harm;] Lo; ~ , 1–3

19, 21. possible,...reasonable,...Rulers,] Lo; ∼ ∧...∼ ∧...
∼ ∧ 1–3

§ 167 (xiii, ix)

5. Occasions] 2er, 3; Occasion 1, 2   **6.** foresee,] Lo; ∼ ∧
1–3   **8.** Season; the] Lo; Season: The 1–3   **9.** Power,]
Lo, 1; ∼ ∧ 2, 3   **9.** most] 2er, 3; best 1, 2

§ 168 (xiii, x)

4. Prerogative,] Lo, 1; ∼ ∧ 2, 3   **6.** none,] Lo; ∼ ∧ 1–3
7. Legislative,] Lo, 1; ∼ ∧ 2, 3   **9.** enslave,] Lo; ∼ ∧ 1–3
12. attempts,] Lo, 1; ∼ ∧ 2, 3   **13.** hands [who] Lo;
hands, who 1–3   **14.** consent,] Lo; ∼ ∧ 1–3   **15.** harm)
do] Lo; harm, to do 1–3   **17.** Man,] 1; ∼ ∧ 2, 3   **17.** is
deprived] Lo; are ∼ 1–3   **17–19.** Right, or...they] Lo;
Right, or are under the Exercise of a power without right,
having no Appeal on Earth, they 1–3   **19.** Heaven,] Lo;
∼ ∧ 1–3   **24–5.** by...Laws of men] Lo *inserts*
27. Earth, *viz.* to judge whether] Lo; Earth, by a Law antecedent and paramount to all positive Laws of Men, whether
1–3   **32–3.** preservation:] Lo; ∼ . 1–3   **35.** think,]
Lo; ∼ ∧ 1–3   **35.** Disorder:] Lo; ∼ ; 1–3   **36.** great,] Lo,
1; ∼ ∧ 2, 3   **38.** But] Lo; And 1–3   **38.** Power,]
Lo, 1; ∼ ∧ 2, 3   **39.** Princes,] Lo; ∼ ∧ 1–3   **39.** of:]
Lo; ∼ . 1–3

§ 170 (xiv, ii)

1. *Power*∧] Lo; ∼ , 1–3   **2.** that,...Children,] Lo; ∼ ∧
...∼ ∧ 1–3   **8.** live,] Lo; ∼ ∧ 1–3   **8.** Free-men] 1;
Freemen 2, 3   **9.** Tenderness,] Lo; ∼ ∧ 1–3   **9.** which]
Lo; *om.* 1–3   **10.** Parents,] Lo, 1; ∼ ∧ 1–3   **11.** evident,] Lo, 1; ∼ ∧ 1–3   **14–15.** reason,...thought,] Lo;
∼ ∧...∼ ∧ 1–3   **15.** Death,] Lo, 1; ∼ ∧ 2, 3   **16.** time,]
Lo, 1; ∼ ∧ 2, 3   **17–19.** else,...than] Lo; else, or keep the
Child in subjection to the Will of his Parents, when grown to
a Man, and the perfect use of Reason any farther than 1–3
19–20. the having] as having 1   **21.** Assistance,] Lo, 1;
∼ ∧ 2, 3   **24.** Ends,] Lo; ∼ ∧ 1–3

§ 171 (xiv, iii)

2. Man,] Lo, 1; ∼ ∧ 2, 3   **3.** Governours,] Lo, 1; ∼ ∧ 2, 3
6. *Power*,] Lo, 1; ∼ ∧ 2, 3   **8.** Society,] Lo, 1; ∼ ∧ 2, 3
8. cases,] Lo; ∼ ∧ 1–3   **10.** Property,] Lo, 1; ∼ ∧ 2, 3
12. so,] Lo; ∼ ; 1–3   **14.** Mankind.] Lo, 2er; ∼ ; 1, 2;

~ : 3   **17.** general,] Lo, 2er; ~ . 1, 2; ~ ; 3   **24.** only,]
Lo, 1; ~ ∧ 2, 3   **25.** corrupt,] Lo, 1; ~ ∧ 2, 3

§ 172 (xiv, iv)

3. Life,] Lo; ~ ∧ 1–3   **3.** pleases. This] Lo; pleases; and
this 1–3   **3.** Power,] Lo; ~ ∧ 1–3   **5.** another;] Lo; ~ ∧
1–3   **5.** convey, for] Lo; convey. For 1–3   **7.** it; but]
Lo; it, but 1–3   **11–22.** Man, and the common...Secu-
rity. And] Man, and the peaceable ways which that teaches,
and made use of Force to compass his unjust ends upon another, where he has no right, he renders himself liable to be
destroyed by his Adversary, whenever he can, as any other
noxious and brutish creature that is destructive to his Being.
And 1–3 (*Correction made in the margin of the Christ's copy.
The alternative form of the last phrase [see footnote on the
paragraph] comes about in the following way. At the end of
the marginal correction on p. 301 Coste has written, evidently
on a later occasion,* 'vid. the leaf at the end'. *On the final fly-
leaf, accordingly, these words appear:* '301 noxious brute *that
is destructive to their being.* C'est ainsi que Mr. L. a corrigé
cet endroit dans l'Exemplaire par lequel il souhaite que son
Livre soit imprimé apres sa mort.' *Except for the word* 'their',
*this is a reversion to the text of the early printed editions [see
above]. None of the later printed editions follow these final
directions, though in his 6th edition, Hollis prints this alternative final phrase in a footnote with the comment:* 'Another
copy corrected by Mr. Locke, has it thus.' *This footnote appears in the editions which follow the 6th, including the American edition of 1773, see Appendix A, List of Printings. The
text of the 6th edition follows the correction in the margin of
the Christ's copy with only one tiny punctuation variation.
That of 4 and Col also follow that version, but with some
variation in the use of capitals and in punctuation.*)
23. only,] Lo, 1, 2er; ~ ∧ 2, 3

§ 173 (xiv, v)

11. Benefit,] Lo; ~ ∧ 1–3

§ 174 (xiv, vi)

1, 3, 6. He,...see,...it,] Lo; ~ ∧...~ ∧...~ ∧ 1–3

§ 175 (xv, i)

7. Arms,] Lo; ~ ∧ 1–3   **8.** People;] Lo; ~ , 1–3

§ 176 (xv, ii)

5. think,] Lo; ~ ∧ 1–3   **7.** master;] Lo; ~ ∧ 1–3

12. *Conquerour,*] Lo, 1; ~ ∧ 2, 3   **17.** ones,] Lo; ~ ∧ 1–3
21, 22. possession,...Robber,] Lo; ~ ∧...~ ∧ 1–3
30. Children,] 1; ~ ∧ 2, 3 (*comma deleted in Christ's copy*)
32. did,] 1; ~ ∧ 2, 3

§ 177 (xv, iii)

12. *not,*] Lo; *not Ital*∧ 1–3   **12.** hope,] Lo; ~ ∧ 1–3
26, 30. farther,...else,] Lo; ~ ∧...~ ∧ 1–3

§ 178 (xv, iv)

3. People,] Lo, 1; ~ ∧ 2, 3   **4.** *Subdued;*] Lo; ~ ∧ 1–3
7, 9. those,...those,] Lo; ~ ∧...~ ∧ 1–3

§ 179 (xv, v)

2, 3, 7. those,...force,...charged,] Lo; ~ ∧...~ ∧...~ ∧
1–3   **9, 13, 18.** farther,...one,...do,] Lo; ~ ∧...~ ∧...
~ ∧ 1–3   **19, 23.** those,...who,] Lo; ~ ∧...~ ∧ 1–3
24. provocations,] Lo, 1; ~ ∧ 2, 3

§ 180 (xv, vi)

2. *Despotical;*] Lo; ~ ∧ 1–3   **7.** World;] Lo; ~ . 1–3
14, 15. Conquered,...Conditions,] Lo; ~ ∧...~ ∧ 1–3
15. Sword] 2er, 3; Swords 1, 2

§ 181 (xv, vii)

4. only,] Lo; ~ ∧ 1–3   **8.** (which] Lo; ∧ ~ 1–3
9. force] Lo; ~ ; 1–3   **16, 17, 18.** then,...he,...it,] Lo;
~...~ ∧...~ ∧ 1–3   **21.** Beast,] Lo; ~ ∧ 1–3

§ 182 (xv, viii)

6. goods,] Lo; ~ ∧ 1–3   **6.** Nature,] Lo, 1; ~ ∧ 2, 3
11. absence,] Lo. *inserts*   **12.** them:] Lo; ~ , 1–3
13. title] Lo; right 1–3   **13.** him,] Lo; ~ ∧ 1–3
14. destruction;] Lo; ~ , 1–3   **15.** them,] Lo; ~ ∧ 1–3
18. by. So] Lo; ~ ; ~ 1–3   **31.** War, *not*] Lo; War, but
not 1–3

§ 183 (xv, ix)

2. side,] Lo; ~ ∧ 1–3   **10–11.** it comes] Lo; it is come
1–3   **11.** force,] Lo; ~ ∧ 1–3   **12.** Aggressor.] Lo; ~ ;
1–3

§ 184 (xv, x)

5. perish:] Lo; ~ , 1; ~ ; 2, 3   **13–15.** supposing it of

an extent any way coming near what I had over-run of his,
and equally cultivated too. The destruction 1   **14.** near,] Lo,
1; ~ ∧ 2, 3   **16.** spoil,] Lo; ~ ∧ 1–3   **17.** Money,] ~ ;
3   **19.** value:] Lo; ~ , 1–3   **20.** them:] Lo; ~ . 1–3
26, 28. him,...more,] Lo; ~ ∧...~ ∧ 1–3   **29.** five and
five hundred] five, and five thousand 1   **31.** *Land,*...
possess,] Lo; ~ ∧...~ ∧ 1–3   **34, 37, 39.** therefore,...
Power,...Inheritance,] Lo; ~ ∧...~ ∧...~ ∧ 1–3
41. Master:] Lo; ~ . 1–3   **43.** Right.] Lo; ~ : 1–3

§ 185 (xv, xi)

1. then,] Lo; ~ ∧ 1–3   **5.** *Dominion*:] Lo; ~ . 1–3

§ 189 (xv, xv)

5. Free-men] 1; Freemen 2, 3   **12.** say,] Lo; ~ ∧ 1–3

§ 190 (xv, xvi)

4. *inherit,*] Lo, 1, 2; ~ ∧ 3

§ 192 (xv, xviii)

3, 12, 13. those,...Usurpation,...Tyranny,] Lo, ~ ∧...
~ ∧...~ ∧ 1–3   **13.** which] Lo *inserts*   **15–21.** consent
to. Who...which they can never] Lo; consent to (which
they can never 1–3 (*a passage is inserted here which in* 1–3
comes at the end of the paragraph)   **30.** War. (*In* 1–3
the paragraph continues thus: War.) And who doubts but the
Grecian Christians, Descendants of the ancient Possessors of
that Country, may justly cast off the *Turkish* Yoke they have
so long groaned under, whenever they have a Power to
do it?)

§ 193 (xv, xix)

7. (without] Lo; ∧ ~ 1–3   **8.** nothing)] Lo; ~ , 1–3
8. them,...have,] Lo; ~ ∧...~ ∧ 1–3

§ 194 (xv, xx)

10. Rent,] ~ ∧ 1–3   **19–20.** ...nothing by Power enough
to dissolve them at any time. And all 1

§ 195 (xv, xxi)

2. sure,] Lo; ~ ∧ 1–3

§ 196 (xv, xxii)

1. *Conquest*∧] Lo; ~ , 1–3   **1.** this.] Lo; ~ , 1–3
3. all,...aided,] Lo; ~ ∧...~ ∧ 1–3   **9.** Power;] Lo; ~ ,
1–3   **9.** have,] Lo, 1; ~ ∧ 2, 3   **10.** *Conquest,*] Lo; ~ ∧

1–3   **11–12.** Aggressor...puts] Lo; Aggressor, and puts 1–3
13. them;] Lo; ~ ∧ 1–3   **15.** *Hubba*∧] Lo; ~ , 1–3
15. *England*;] Lo; ~ , 1–3   **16.** would have had] Lo
inserts   **25.** Force,] Lo; ~ ∧ 1–3   **27.** is] Lo *inserts*
27. that,] Lo; ~ ∧ 1–3

§ 197 (xvi, i)

8, 9. beyond,...Princes,] Lo; ~ ∧...~ ∧ 1–3

§ 198 (xvi, ii)

2. Persons,] Lo, 1; ~ ∧ 2, 3   **2.** is] Lo; being 1–3
4. People.] ~ ; *in Christ's copy*   **4–5.** People. Hence all
Commonwealths] Lo; People. The Anarchy being much
alike, to have no Form of Government at all: or to agree
that it shall be Monarchical; but to appoint no way to design
the Person that shall have the Power, and be the Monarch.
All Commonwealths 1–3, 4+ (*with punctuation variants*)
(*This sentence is corrected where it stands in the Christ's
copy, and then written out again in the margin as part of
the addition printed below in lines* 7–12)   **5.** Common-
wealths] Lo; Commonwealths therefore, with 1–3
6. appointing those,] Lo; appointing and conveying the Right
to those∧ 1–3   **7–12.** Authority;...monarch. Whoever]
Lo; Authority. And whoever 1–3   **16.** preserved;] Lo;
1; ~ , 2, 3   **21.** him,] Lo; ~ ∧ 1–3

§ 199 (xvii, i)

5. those,] Lo; ~ ∧ 1–3

§ 200 (xvii, ii)

4. the first] Lo, 3er; *om.* 1–3   **37.** *and Pests*] '*and*' Lo.
inserts

§ 201 (xvii, iii)

3. that.] Lo; ~ : 1–3

§ 202 (xvii, iv)

5, 7. Subject,...not,...opposed,] Lo; ~ ∧...~ ∧...~ ∧ 1–3
19. Man,] Lo, 1; ~ ∧ 2, 3   **20.** Country,] Lo, 1; ~ ∧ 2, 3
21. seize,] Lo, 1; ~ ∧ 2, 3   **21.** pleased,] ~ ∧ 3
25. reason,] Lo; ~ ∧ 1–3   **26.** Authority∧] Lo; ~ , 1–3
28. great,] Lo, 1; ~ ∧ 2, 3   **29.** King,] Lo, 1; ~ ∧ 2, 3
29. is] Lo *inserts*   **30.** in that] Lo; as that 1–3
32–4. Education,...wrong.] Lo; Education, and Counsellors
to have better knowledge, and less reason to do it, having
already a greater share than the rest of his Brethren. 1–3

§ 204 (xvii, vi)

6. For.] Lo; ~ , 1–3

§ 205 (xvii, vii)

6. Officer,] Lo, 1; ~ ∧ 2, 3   **9.** defence,] Lo, 1; ~ ∧ 2, 3
14. secure,] Lo, 1; ~ ∧ 2, 3   **15.** whatsoever;] Lo; ~ . 1–3
21. it, the] 2er, 3; it. The 1, 2   **22.** mischiefs,] Lo; ~ ∧
1–3   **22.** sometimes,] Lo, 1; ~ ∧ 2, 3   **23.** recompenced,] Lo; ~ ∧ 1–3   **24.** Publick,] Lo, 1; ~ ∧ 2, 3
25. Magistrate,] Lo, 1; ~ ∧ 2, 3   **26.** danger:] Lo; ~ .
1–3

§ 206 (xvii, viii)

1, 2, 5. Priviledge,…not,…him,] Lo; ~ ∧…~ ∧…~ ∧
1–3   **17.** insignificant,] Lo; ~ ∧ 1–3

§ 207 (xvii, ix)

8. used,] Lo, 1; ~ ∧ 2, 3   **11.** alone,] Lo, 1; ~ ∧ 2, 3
18. force, if I] 2er, 3; force: I 1; force; I 2   **20.** more,]
Lo; ~ ∧ 1–3   **27.** Carcass:] Lo; ~ . 1–3   **29.** him,]
Lo, 1; ~ ∧ 1–3

§ 208 (xvii, x)

10. Contest,] Lo, 1; ~ ∧ 2, 3   **15.** State;] Lo, 1; ~ ∧ 2, 3
16. one,] Lo, 1; ~ ∧ 2, 3

§ 209 (xvii, xi)

2. People;] Lo, 1; ~ , 2, 3   **3–4.** Cases,…Precedent,]
Lo; ~ ∧…~ ∧ 1–3   **5.** Consciences,] Lo; ~ ∧ 1–3
7. too,] Lo; ~ ; 1–3   **12.** People;] Lo; ~ , 1–3
12. which] Lo *inserts*   **13.** in:] Lo; ~ , 1; ~ ; 2, 3
14. avoided;] Lo; ~ . 1–3   **18.** Family,] Lo; ~ ∧ 1–3
18. loves,] Lo, 1; ~ ∧ 2, 3

§ 210 (xvii, xii)

5. end,] Lo, 1; ~ ∧ 2, 3   **6.** given:] Lo; ~ ∧ 1–3
6–7. Ministers,] Lo, 1; ~ ∧ 2, 3   **8.** proportionably,] Lo;
~ ∧ 1–3   **11.** favoured (though] Lo; ~ , ~ 1–3
11. against)] Lo; ~ , 1–3   **12.** supported,] Lo; ~ ∧ 1–3
14. still,] Lo, 1; ~ ∧ 1–3   **14.** better: if] Lo; ~ , and 1–3
15. way, how] Lo; ~ : How 1–3   **19.** him,] Lo, 1; ~ ∧
2, 3

§ 211 (xviii, i)

7. incorporate,] Lo; ~ ∧ 1–3   **11.** themselves,] Lo, 1;

~ ∧ 2, 3   **25.** it:] Lo; ~ ; 1–3   **28–9.** scattered, and dissipated] Lo, 2er; ~ ∧ and displaced 1, 2; ~ ∧ and discipated 3

§ 212 (xviii, ii)

3. *altered.*] Lo; ~ , 1–3   **4.** Peace,] Lo; ~ ∧ 1–3
6–7. Differences,] Lo, 1; ~ ∧ 2, 3   **7.** them, 'tis] Lo; them. 'Tis 1–3   **9.** united,] Lo; ~ ∧ 1–3   **23.** Men,] Lo, 1; ~ ∧ 2, 3   **23.** them,] Lo, 1; ~ ∧ 2, 3   **24.** Laws,] Lo; ~ ∧ 1–3

§ 213 (xviii, iii)

7. 1.] *First,* 1   **11.** 2.] *Secondly,* 1   **12.** 3.]*Thirdly,* 1

§ 214 (xviii, iv)

6. obeyed;] Lo; ~ , 1–3   **7.** pretended,] Lo; ~ , 1–3
7. inforced,] Lo, 1; ~ ∧ 2, 3   **8.** Legislative,] Lo, 1; ~ ∧ 2, 3   **8.** Society,] Lo, 1; ~ ∧ 2, 3   **9.** plain,] Lo; ~ ∧ 1–3

§ 215 (xviii, v)

3, 6. ends,...perfecting,] Lo; ~ ∧...~ ∧ 1–3   **7.** consists:] Lo; ~ ∧ 1–3   **10.** Names,] Lo; ~ ∧ 1–3

§ 216 (xviii, vi)

5. others,] Lo, 1; ~ ∧ 2, 3   **5–6.** thereunto,] Lo, 1; ~ ∧ 2, 3   **6.** way,] Lo; ~ ∧ 1–3

§ 217 (xviii, vii)

7. lost,] Lo; ~ ∧ 1–3

§ 218 (xviii, viii)

3. evident:] Lo; ~ , 1–3   **24.** them,] Lo, 1; ~ ∧ 2, 3
24. guilty,] Lo, 1; ~ ∧ 2, 3

§ 219 (xviii, ix)

9. function,] 2er, 3; ~ . 1, 2   **13.** Justice,] Lo, 1; ~ ∧ 2, 3   **17.** executed,] Lo, 1; ~ ∧ 2, 3

§ 220 (xviii, x)

6. lose] 1; loose 2, 3   **13.** Legislative,] Lo; ~ ; 1–3
16. them,] Lo; 1; ~ ∧ 2, 3   **20.** Relief;] Lo; ~ , 1–3

§ 221 (xviii, xi)

1. therefore, secondly,] ~ ∧ Secondly∧ 1–3   **2.** is;] Lo; ~ ∧ 1–3   **3.** Prince,] ~ ∧ 1–3

§ 222 (xviii, xii)

1. Reason] 2er, 3; Reasons 1, 2   **5.** the Members of] *om.*
1   **9.** that,] Lo; ~ ∧ 1–3   **11.** the] *om.* 1, 2
23. People;] Lo; ~ : 1–3   **24.** hands,] Lo, 1; ~ ∧ 2, 3
25. People,] Lo; ~ ; 1–3   **36.** either] Lo *inserts*
38. or openly] Lo; When he openly 1–3   **42, 62.** before-
hand,...of,] Lo; ~ ∧...~ ∧ 1–3   **66, 69.** Society,...
he,] Lo; ~ ∧...~ ∧ 1–3

§ 223 (xviii, xiii)

2, 3. ignorant,...Opinion,] Lo; ~ ∧...~ ∧ 1–3
4. ruine;] Lo; ~ : 1–3   **6.** Legislative,] Lo; ~ ∧ 1–3
7. Answer. Quite] Lo; ~ ∧ quite 1–3   **9, 10.** Forms,...
Faults,] Lo; ~ ∧...~ ∧ 1–3   **12, 16.** time,...has,] Lo;
~ ∧...~ ∧ 1–3   **16.** which] Lo *inserts*   **18, 22.** or,...
far,] Lo; ~ ∧...~ ∧ 1–3

§ 224 (xviii, xiv)

5. *Power*,] Lo; ~ ; 1–3   **6.** Governours,] Lo; ~ ∧ 1–3
8. please,] 1; ~ ∧ 2, 3   **13.** weakness,...affairs,] Lo;
~ ∧...~ ∧ 1–3

§ 225 (xviii, xv)

6, 8. Prevarications,...feel,] Lo; ~ ∧...~ ∧ 1–3
9, 11. wonder'd,...hands,] Lo; ~ ∧...~ ∧ 1–3
13, 14. Names,...Worse,] Lo; ~ ∧...~ ∧ 1–3

§ 226 (xviii, xvi)

1. *Doctrine* of a] Lo *inserts*   **6, 13.** Persons,...Peace,]
Lo; ~ ∧...~ ∧ 1–3   **16.** Power (by] Lo; ~ , ~ 1–3
18. them)] Lo; ~ ∧ 1–3

§ 227 (xviii, xvii)

7, 9, 11. Umpirage,...They,...have,] Lo; ~ ∧...~ ∧...~ ∧
1–3   **12–13, 14.** Authority,...Power,] Lo; ~ ∧...~ ∧ 1–3
14–15. authoriz'd, they actually] Lo; ~ ; actually 1–3
17. Society (in] Lo; ~ , ~ 1–3   **19.** will)] Lo; ~ ; 1–3
22–3. they,...protection,] Lo; ~ ∧...~ ∧ 1–3
24–5. Properties,...invade,] Lo; ~ ∧...~ ∧ 1–3
26. those,] Lo; ~ ∧ 1–3

§ 228 (xviii, xviii)

1, 5, 6. they,...those,...Magistrates,] Lo; ~ ∧...~ ∧...~ ∧
1–3   **13, 14.** him,...*him*,] Lo; ~ ∧...~ ∧ 1–3

24. Peace, and such] Lo; Peace. Such 1–3   **24.** Government,] Lo; ~ ∧ 1–3   **26.** doubt∧] Lo; ~ , 1–3
26. *Ulysses,*] Lo; ~ ∧ 1–3

§ 230 (xviii, xx)

12, 21. perswasion,...*fault,*] Lo; ~ ∧...~ ∧ 1–3
22. thought, to be] Lo; thought as 1–3   **35–6.** *Government, is*] Lo; Government; he is 1–3

§ 231 (xviii, xxi)

1, 10. *Subjects,*...Trust,] Lo; ~ ∧...~ ∧ 1–3

§ 232 (xviii, xxii)

(*Note on paragraphs in French Version*: xviii–xxii covers paras. 232–3, xxiii covers paras. 234–8.)   **13.** that,] Lo; ~ ∧ 1–3   **40.** *quisquam*] 2, 3; *quispiam* 1 (*Barclay, ed. 1612,* 'quisquam'; *ed. 1617* 'quispiam')

§ 235 (xviii, xxiii)

11. hand,] Lo, 1; ~ ∧ 2, 3   **58–9.** [& rempublicam... fuerit] *om.* 1–3

§ 236 (xviii, xxiii)

15. Lib. 3. c. 16] Lo, 1; *om.* 2, 3
(*The phrase* 'which in English runs thus', *coming in 2 and 3 between paragraphs 236 and 237, follows in 1 straight on to the end of paragraph 236 and runs* 'which may thus be Englished')

§ 238 (xviii, xxiii)

15. *own*] one 3

§ 239 (xviii, xxiv)

19–42. This farther...the Offence.] *om.* 1   **41–2.** Government,] Lo; ~ ∧ 1–3   **65.** them for, Slavery] Lo; them, Slavery 1–3

§ 240 (xviii, xxv)

2. *shall*] Lo, 1; should 2, 3   **8.** him] ~ ; 3

§ 241 (xviii, xxvi)

4. *Judge:*] 3; ~ . 1, 2

§ 242 (xviii, xxvii)

1. Prince∧] Lo; ~ , 1–3   **3.** Consequence,] ~ ; 3
13. Determination,] ~ ; 3   **18.** himself,] ~ ∧ 3
19. put] puts 3

§ 243 (xviii, xxviii)

9–10. Successors,] ~ ; 3   **21–2.** themselves, or...think good] Lo; themselves, or place it in a new Form or new hands, as they think good 1–3

BIBLIOGRAPHY

BIBLIOGRAPHY

(All books published in London unless otherwise shown)

AARON, R. I. 1936. *An Early Draft of Locke's Essay, together with Excerpts from his Journals*. (With Gibb, J.) Oxford.

AARON, R. I. 1937. (2nd ed. 1955.) *John Locke*. Oxford.

ABRAMS, P. 1961. *John Locke as a Conservative: an Edition of Locke's First Writings on Political Obligation*. Unpublished Dissertation in the Cambridge University Library. (Pagination of original Latin and English text retained in this version.)

ACOSTA, JOSÉ DE, 1608 (1880). *The Naturall and Morall Historie of the East and West Indies* [tr. E. Grimstone]. (Ed. Markham, C. R., 2 vols. 1880.) (Appendix B, no. 1.)

AINSWORTH, HENRY, 1622 (1639). *Annotations upon the Five Books of Moses*. . . . (Appendix B, no. 3.)

ALLEN, J. W. 1928. Sir Robert Filmer. In: Hearnshaw, F. J. C., ed., *Social and Political Ideas of the Augustan Age*.

ALLEN, J. W. 1938. *English Political Thought 1603–1660*, vol. I, 1603–44.

AQUINAS, SAINT THOMAS, 1624. *Summa Theologiae*. Lyons.

BAGSHAW, EDWARD, junior, 1660. *The Great Question Concerning Things Indifferent in Religious Worship*.

BARBEYRAC, JEAN, 1734. *See* Pufendorf, Samuel von

BARCLAY, WILLIAM, 1600 (1612). *De Regno et Regali Potestate.* Hanover. (Appendix B, no. 11.)

BARCLAY, WILLIAM, 1609 (1612). *De Potestate Papae.* Hanover. (Appendix B, no. 11.)

BARKER, Sir ERNEST, 1934. *See* Gierke, O. von

BARKER, Sir ERNEST, 1948. *See* Appendix A, British Printing no. 39.

BASNAGE DE BEAUVAL, HENRI, 1691. Review of Du Gouvernement Civil (*Histoire des Ouvrages des Sçavans*, 457).

BASTIDE, CH. 1907. *John Locke, ses Théories Politiques et leur Influence en Angleterre.* Paris.

BAXTER, RICHARD, 1680. *The Second Part of the Nonconformist's Plea for Peace.*

BAYLE, PIERRE, 1725–7. *Œuvres Diverses*, 4 vols. The Hague.

BECKER, CARL, 1922. *The Declaration of Independence.* New York.

BILSON, THOMAS, 1585. *The True Difference betweene Christian Subjection and Unchristian Rebellion.*

[BLACKBURNE, FRANCIS] 1780. *Memoirs of Thomas Hollis, Esq.*

BODIN, JEAN, 1566 (1945). *Methodus ad Facilem Historiarum Cognitionem* [Method for the Easy Comprehension of History, tr. and ed. Reynolds, B.] New York.

BODIN, JEAN, 1576 (1606). *Les Six Livres de la République* [The Six Bookes of a Commonweale, tr. Knolles, Richard].

BOHUN, EDMUND, 1684. *A Defence of Sir Robert Filmer, against Algernon Sidney.*

BOHUN, EDMUND, 1685. Edition of *Patriarcha, see* Filmer.

BOHUN, EDMUND, 1853. *Diary and Autobiography.* Beccles.

BOWERS, FREDSON, 1953. *The Dramatic Works of Thomas Dekker*, vol. I. Cambridge.

BOWERS, FREDSON, 1954. With Gerritsen and Laslett, *see* Laslett, 1954 (ii).

BRACTON, 1569, 1640, etc. *De Legibus et Consuetudinibus Angliae.*

BROGAN, R. P. 1959. John Locke and Utilitarianism, *Ethics*, LXVIII, 1.

BROWN, L. F. 1933. *The First Earl of Shaftesbury.* New York.

BUCKINGHAM, GEORGE VILLIERS, 2nd Duke of, 1672. *The Rehearsal.*

BURNET, GILBERT, 1724, 1734. *History of His Own Time.* 2 vols.

CARDAN, JEROME, 1640 (1663). Encomium Neronis. In: *Opera*, Leyden. (Appendix B, no. 19.)

BIBLIOGRAPHY 547

CARY, JOHN, 1698. *A Vindication of the Parliament of England in Answer to W. Molyneux.*

CASINELLI, W. 1959. *The Consent of the Governed,* Western Political Quarterly.

CHAMBERLAYNE, EDWARD, 1700. *Anglia Notitia, or The Present State of England.* . . . 19th ed.

CHERNO, M. 1959. *Locke on Property,* Ethics.

CHRISTIE, W. D. 1871. *A Life of . . . [the] First Earl of Shaftesbury,* 2 vols.

CLARENDON, EDWARD HYDE, 1st Earl of, 1676. *A Briefe View . . . Mr Hobbes Book Entitled* Leviathan. Oxford.

CLEMENT, SIMON, 1698. *An Answer to Mr Molyneux, his Case of Ireland.*

COLIE, ROSALIE, 1955–6. Publication of Lady Masham's letter to Jean Le Clerc of 12 January 1705. *History of Ideas News Letter* (cyclostyled), vols. I and II, New York.

COSTA Y MARTINEZ, JOAQUIN, 1898. *Colectivismo Agrario en España.* Madrid.

COX, RICHARD H. 1960. *Locke on War and Peace,* Oxford.

CRANSTON, MAURICE, 1956. Men and ideas: John Locke. *Encounter,* no. 39.

CRANSTON, MAURICE, 1957. *John Locke, a Biography.*

CUMBERLAND, RICHARD, 1672. *De Legibus Naturae Disquisitio Philosophica.*

CZAJKOWSKI, C. J. 1941. *The Theory of Private Property in Locke's Political Philosophy.* Notre Dame, Ind., U.S.A.

DE MARCHI, E. 1953. Le origine dell'idea della.toleranza religiosa nel Locke. *Occidente,* IX, 6, Turin.

DE MARCHI, E. 1955. Locke's Atlantis. *Political Studies,* III, 2, June.

DE ROCHEFORT, CÉSAR, 1658. *Histoire Naturelle et Morale des Isles Antilles,* Rotterdam. (Also attributed to de Poincy, L. and du Tertre, J. B.)

DRIVER, C. H. 1928. John Locke. In Hearnshaw, F. J. C. ed., *Social and Political Ideas of the Augustan Age.*

ELRINGTON, THOMAS, 1798. Annotated edition of *Second Treatise; see* Appendix A, British Printing no. 23.

ESSAY, 1705. [Anon.] *An Essay upon Government, wherein the Republican Schemes Revived by Mr Locke, Dr Blackal etc are Fully Considered and Refuted.*

FILMER, Sir ROBERT
Advertisement
    1653 (1679, 1680). *An Advertisement to the Jurymen of England touching Witches.* (Appendix B, no. 32.)
Anarchy

1648 (1679, 1680, 1949). *The Anarchy of a Limited or Mixed Monarchy.* (Appendix B, no. 29.)

Directions

1652 (1679, 1680, 1949). *Directions for Obedience to Governors.*

Forms

1652 (1679, 1680, 1949). *Observations upon Aristotles Politiques touching Forms of Government.*

Freeholder

1648 (1679, 1680, 1949). *The Freeholders Grand Inquest* [see *Collected editions*].

Necessity

1648 (1680, 1949). *The Necessity of the Absolute Power of All Kings.*

Original

1652 (1679, 1680, 1949). *Observations Concerning the Original of Government upon Mr Hobs Leviathan, Mr Milton against Salmasius, H. Grotius De Jure Belli.* (Appendix B, no. 30.)

Patriarcha

1680. *Patriarcha, or the Natural Power of Kings.* (Appendix B, no. 33.)

1685 (1949). [Ed. Bohun, Edmund.]

Collected Editions

1679. *The Freeholders Grand Inquest.*

1680. *The Freeholders Grand Inquest.* (Appendix B, no. 33.)

1684. *The Freeholders Grand Inquest.*

1696. *Observations Concerning the Original and Various Forms of Government* [reissue of 1684 ed.].

1949. *See* Laslett, 1949.

(*See* Laslett, 1949, 47–8. Concise Bibliography of the Works of Sir Robert Filmer.)

FORTESCUE, Sir JOHN, 1616, etc. *De Laudibus Legum Angliae.*

FOWLER, THOMAS, 1880. *Locke* (English Men of Letters).

FOX BOURNE, H. R. 1876. *The Life of John Locke.* 2 vols.

FURLEY, O. W. 1957. The Whig Exclusionists: Pamphlet Literature . . . 1679–81. *Cambridge Historical Journal,* XIII, 1.

FURLY, BENJAMIN, 1714. *Bibliotheca Furleiana . . . catalogus librorum B. Furly.* Rotterdam.

GARCILASO DE LA VEGA, 1633. *Le Commentaire Royale, ou L'Histoire des Yncas, Roys du Peru . . .* traduitte sur la version espagnolle par I. Baudoin. Paris. (Appendix B, no. 88.)

GARCILASO DE LA VEGA, 1670. *Histoire de la Floride, ou Relation de ce qui s'est passé au Voyage de Ferdinand de Soto.* Paris. (See Appendix B, no. 88.)

GEE, EDWARD, 1658. *Divine Right and Original of the Civill Magistrate.*

GERRITSEN, JOHAN, 1954. See Laslett, 1954 (ii).

GIERKE, OTTO VON, 1934. *Natural Law and the Theory of Society,* tr. and ed. Barker, Sir Ernest. 2 vols. Cambridge.

GOUGH, J. W. 1950. *John Locke's Political Philosophy, Eight Studies.* Oxford.

GREEN, T. H. 1895 (1931). *Lectures on the Principles of Political Obligation.*

GROTIUS, HUGO, 1625 (1712). *De Jure Belli ac Pacis, Libri tres . . . Editio Novissima.* Amsterdam. (Appendix B, no. 38.)

HARRISON, JOHN, and LASLETT, PETER, 1965. *The Library of John Locke.* The Oxford Bibliographical Society (Oxford University Press).

HOBBES, THOMAS, 1651 (1904). *Leviathan.* (Appendix B, no. 42.) [Facsimile reprint, ed. Waller, A. R., Cambridge, 1904.]

HOBBES, THOMAS, 1647 (1841). *De Cive.* In Molesworth, W., *English Works,* vol. II.

HOLLIS, THOMAS, *see* Blackburne, Francis.

HOOKER, RICHARD, 1632. *Of the Lawes of Ecclesiasticall Politie.*

HOOKER, RICHARD, 1666, 1676. *The Works of Mr R. Hooker.* (For these two, see Appendix B, no. 45.)

HOOKER, RICHARD, 1836. A new edition by Keble, John. 3 vols. Oxford.

HUNTON, PHILIP, 1643. *A Treatise of Monarchie.*

JAMES I, *see* McIlwain, C. H.

JOHNSTON, Mrs C. M. (*née* Ware), 1954. A Note on an Early Draft of Locke's *Essay. Mind,* no. 250.

JOHNSTON, Mrs C. M. (*née* Ware), 1956. Unpublished thesis for a D.Phil., Bibliography of Locke's Philosophical Works, Bodleian Library, Oxford.

JURIEU, PIERRE, 1689. *Lettres Pastorales Adressées aux Fidèles de France qui Gémissent sous la Captivité de Babylone.* Amsterdam.

JUSTINUS, 1543. *Ex Trogi Pompeii historiis, libri* XXXIII. Paris. (See Appendix B, no. 47.)

KENDALL, WILLMOORE, 1941. John Locke and the doctrine of majority-rule. *Illinois Studies in the Social Sciences,* vol. XXVI, no. 2, Urbana, Ill., U.S.A.

KING, PETER (7th Lord King), 1829 (1830). *The Life of John Locke, with Extracts from his Correspondence, Journals and Commonplace Books,* 1830 ed., 2 vols.

KNOX, ROBERT, 1681. *An Historical Relation of the Island of Ceylon.* (Appendix B, no. 49.)

LAMPRECHT, S. P. 1918. *The Moral and Political Philosophy of John Locke* (Archives of Philosophy, no. 11). New York.

LARKIN, P. 1930. *Property in the 18th Century, with Special Reference to England and Locke.* Cork.

LASLETT, PETER, 1948 (i). The Gentry of Kent in 1640. *Cambridge Historical Journal,* ix, 2.

LASLETT, PETER, 1948 (ii). Sir Robert Filmer. *William and Mary Quarterly,* 3rd Ser. v, 4, October.

LASLETT, PETER, 1949. Patriarcha *and other Political Works of Sir Robert Filmer* (Blackwell's Political Texts). Oxford.

LASLETT, PETER, 1952 (i). Locke and the first Earl of Shaftesbury. *Mind,* no. 241, January.

LASLETT, PETER, 1952 (ii). Letter in *Times Literary Supplement,* July.

LASLETT, PETER, 1952 (iii). Lord Masham's Library at Otes. Letter in *Times Literary Supplement,* August.

LASLETT, PETER, 1952 (iv). The 1960 Edition of Locke's *Two Treatises of Government. Transactions of the Cambridge Bibliographical Society,* I, 4.

LASLETT, PETER, 1954 (i). Masham of Otes. In: Quennell, P. ed., *Diversions of History.*[1]

LASLETT, PETER, 1954 (ii). Further Observations on Locke's *Two Treatises of Government,* 1690. With Bowers, Fredson, and Gerritsen, Johan, *Transactions of the Cambridge Bibliographical Society,* II, 1.

LASLETT, PETER, 1956. The English Revolution and Locke's *Two Treatises of Government. Cambridge Historical Journal,* XII, 1.

LASLETT, PETER, 1957 (i). John Locke, the Great Recoinage and the Board of Trade, 1695–1698. *William and Mary Quarterly,* 3rd ser. XIV, 3 July.

LASLETT, PETER, 1957 (ii). The Library of John Locke. With Harrison, J. R. *Times Literary Supplement,* December.

LASLETT, PETER, 1964. Review of C. B. Macpherson, *The Politics of Possessive Individualism,* Historical Journal.

LASLETT, PETER, see Harrison, John.

LAWRENCE, WILLIAM, 1680, 1681. *Marriage by the Morall Law of God Vindicated.* [Published in two parts in these

[1] (Reprinted from *History Today,* III, 8, August, 1953.)

years (second entitled *The Right of Primogeniture in Succession to the Kingdoms of England and Scotland*), but one work.]

LAWSON, GEORGE, 1657. *An Examination of the Political Part of Mr Hobbs his* Leviathan. (See Appendix B, no. 50.)

LAWSON, GEORGE, 1660 (1689). *Politica Sacra et Civilis*. (See Appendix B, no. 50.)

LE CLERC, JEAN, 1686–. [Editor] *La Bibliothèque Universelle*, Amsterdam, Wolfgang.

LE CLERC, JEAN, 1705. Éloge du Feu Mr Locke. *Bibliothèque Choisie*, VI, v.

LERY, JEAN DE, 1578. *Histoire d'un Voyage fait en la Terre du Bresil*. La Rochelle. (Appendix B, no. 51.)

[LESLIE, CHARLES,] 1698. *Considerations of Importance to Mr Molyneux's late Book.*

LEWIS, H. D., 1940. Is there a Social Contract? *Philosophy*.

LOCKE, JOHN

    Collected Works

        1714. 3 vols., Fo.

        1801. 10 vols., 8vo.

        1720. *A Collection of Several Pieces of Mr John Locke*, published by Mr Desmaiseaux under the direction of Anthony Collins.

    Individual Works, separate Publications

        Essay (1690)

            1706. 5th edition, Fo.

            1894. (Ed. Fraser, A. C., 2 vols.) Oxford.

            1961. *Everyman* Edition, by Yolton, J. W.

        Two Treatises (1690) (See Appendix A)

        Education (1693)

            1912. *The Educational Writings of John Locke* (ed. Adamson, J. W.). Cambridge.

    All other published works cited from one of the Collected editions. (*See* Aaron, Rand, Von Leyden, for works published from manuscript.)

LONG, P. 1959. A Summary Catalogue of the Lovelace Collection of the Papers of John Locke in the Bodleian Library, *Oxford Bibliographical Society*, New Series, VIII.

LUTHER, MARTIN, 1520 (1888). Sermon von den guten Werken. In: *Werke*, VI. Weimar.

MABBOTT, J. D., 1948. *The State and the Citizen.*

MCILWAIN, C. H. 1918. *The Political Works of James I.* Cambridge, Mass., U.S.A.

MCILWAIN, C. H., 1935 (1939). A Forgotten Worthy: Philip Hanton. Reprinted in *Constitutionalism and the Changing World*. Cambridge.

McKerrow, R. B. 1939. Prolegomena for the *Oxford Shakespeare:* A Study in Editorial Method. Oxford.

Maclean, A. H. 1947 (i). Unpublished Ph.D. dissertation on Locke as a political writer, Cambridge University Library.

Maclean, A. H. 1947 (ii). George Lawson and John Locke. *Cambridge Historical Journal,* ix, 1.

Macpherson, C. B. 1951. Locke on Capitalist Appropriation. *Western Political Quarterly,* iv, 4. Salt Lake City, Utah, U.S.A.

Macpherson, C. B., 1954. *The Social Bearing of Locke's Political Theory, Western Political Quarterly,* vii, 1.

Macpherson, C. B. 1962. *The Political Theory of Possessive Individualism.* Oxford.

Manwaring (or Maynwaring), Roger, 1627. *Religion and Allegiance in Two Sermons.*

Marvell, Andrew, 1672. *The Rehearsal Transprosed.* (Appendix B, no. 56.)

Masham, Damaris, 1705 (1955–6). Letter to Jean le Clerc on Locke's life. University of Amsterdam MSS. J. 57a (*see* Colie, Rosalie, for publication).

Mirror, The, 1642. *Mirroir des Justices* [? by Horne, Andrew].

Molyneux, William, 1698 (1720). *The Case of Ireland's being Bound by Acts of Parliament in England.* Dublin (1720 ed. London).

Monson, C. H. 1958. *Locke and his Interpreters,* Political Studies, vi, 2.

Moulds, H. 1961. *John Locke's Four Freedoms,* Ethics, lxxi, 2.

More, Sir Thomas, 1663. *Utopiae Libri Duo.* Oxford.

Moyle, Walter, 1698 (1727). An Essay on the Lacedæmonian Government Addressed to Anthony Hammond, Esq. In: *The Whole Works of Walter Moyle, Esq.* [edited by] Anthony Hammond, Esq., 1727.

Ogg, David, 1934 (2nd ed. 1955). *England in the Reign of Charles II.* 2 vols. Oxford.

Osler, Sir William, 1914. [Editor of letter of Locke to Thomas Herbert, 8th Earle of Pembroke, with note on Locke's cure of the 1st Earl of Shaftesbury. *Oxford Magazine,* 1914, March.]

Oxford University, Judgment of, 1683 (1812). The Judgment of the University of Oxford . . . against Certain Pernicious Books and Damnable Doctrines. In: *Somers Tracts,* 2nd edition by Walter Scott, viii.

Pareyson, L. 1948. [Critical edition of *Two Treatises* in Italian; *see* Appendix A, Italian printing no. 4.]

PARKER, SAMUEL, 1670. *A Discourse of Ecclesiastical Politie.*

PARRY, CLIVE, 1954. British Nationality Law and the History of Naturalization. Milan. *Communicazione e Studi* of the Institute of International Law in the University of Milan.

PEMBROKE, THOMAS HERBERT, 8th Earl of, 1683. Letter to Locke of 3 December 1683. *See* Osler, Sir William.

PETTY, Sir WILLIAM, 1662. *A Treatise of Taxes and Contributions.*

PLAMENATZ, J. P. 1936. *Consent, Freedom and Political Obligation.* Oxford.

POCOCK, J. G. A. 1957. *The Ancient Constitution and the Feudal Law.* Cambridge.

POLIN, RAYMOND, 1960. *La Politique Morale de John Locke.* Paris.

POLLOCK, Sir FREDERICK, 1890, etc. *Introduction to the History of the Science of Politics.*

POLLOCK, Sir FREDERICK, 1904. Locke's Theory of the State. *Proceedings of the British Academy,* i, 1903–4.

PRIDEAUX, HUMPHREY, 1875. *Letters . . . to John Ellis,* ed. Thompson, E. M. (Camden Society).

PUFENDORF, SAMUEL VON, 1660 (1672). *Elementa, Elementorum Juris-prudentiae Universalis Libri Duo.* (1672 editio novissima, Cambridge.) (Appendix B, no. 66.)

PUFENDORF, SAMUEL VON, 1672. *De Jure Naturae et Gentium Libri Octo.* Lund. (Appendix B, no. 65.)

PUFENDORF, SAMUEL VON, 1706 (1734). *Le Droit de la Nature et des Gens . . .,* par le baron de Pufendorf, traduit du Latin avec des notes par Jean Barbeyrac (5th ed. 2 vols. Amsterdam).

RAND, BENJAMIN, 1927. *The Correspondence of John Locke and Edward Clarke.* Oxford.

RAND, BENJAMIN, 1931. *An Essay Concerning the Understanding, Knowledge, Opinion and Assent.* Cambridge, Mass., U.S.A. (Draft B of Locke's Essay.)

ROBBINS, CAROLINE, 1950. Thomas Hollis. *The William and Mary Quarterly,* 3rd ser. VII, 3, July.

SADLER, JOHN, 1649 (1682). *Rights of the Kingdom.*

SAGARD, GABRIEL, 1636. *Histoire du Canada.* Paris. (Appendix B, no. 72.)

SAGARD, GABRIEL, 1632. *Le Grand Voyage du Pays des Hurons.* Paris. (Appendix B, no. 72.)

SALMON, J. H. M. 1959. *The French Religious Wars in English Political Thought.* Oxford.

SANDERSON, ROBERT, 1660 (1686). *De Obligatione Conscientiae Praelectiones Decem.*

SCHLATTER, R. B. 1951. *Private Property: the History of an Idea.*

SCHLATTER, R. B. 1957. *Richard Baxter and Puritan Politics.* New Brunswick, N.J., U.S.A.

SELDEN, JOHN, 1635 (1652). *Mare Clausum, Seu de Dominio Maris Libri Duo* (tr. Nedham, Marchamont, 1652).

SELIGER, M. 1963 (i). Locke's Theory of Revolutionary Action, *Western Political Quarterly.*

SELIGER, M. 1963 (ii). Locke's Natural Law, *Journal of the History of Ideas.*

SHAFTESBURY PAPERS, Public Record Office: old class-number, GD 24, present class-number, P.R.O. 30. (References are made P.R.O. 30, bundle number in roman figures, item number in arabic figures.)

SHAFTESBURY, ANTHONY ASHLEY COOPER, 1st Earl of, 1689 (1812). Some Observations Concerning the Regulating of Elections for Parliament, found among the Earl of Shaftesbury's papers. In: *Somers Tracts,* 2nd ed. by Walter Scott, 396–402. (No indication of Shaftesbury's authorship.)

SHAFTESBURY, ANTHONY ASHLEY COOPER, 3rd Earl of, 1705 (1851). Letter of February 1705, to Jean Le Clerc. *Notes and Queries,* 1st ser. 1851, 1.

SIBTHORPE (or SYBTHORPE), ROBERT, 1627. *Apostolike Obedience: Shewing the Duty of Subjects . . . Sermon.*

SIDNEY, ALGERNON, 1698 (1772). *Discourses Concerning Government.* In: *The Works of Algernon Sydney, a New Edition* [ed. by Joseph Robertson, pub. by Thomas Hollis], 1772.

SIMON, W. M. 1951. John Locke, philosophy and political theory. *American Political Science Review,* XLV, 2, June.

SMITH, JOHN, 1616. *A Description of New England* (Appendix B, no. 76.)

SMYRNIADES, L. 1921. *Les Doctrines de Hobbes, Locke et Kant sur le Droit de l'Insurrection.* Paris.

SOMERS, JOHN (Lord Somers), 1701. *Jura Populi Anglicani, or The Subject's Right of Petitioning.*

SPELMAN, Sir HENRY, 1626, 1664 (1687). *Glossarium Archaiologicum, Editio Tertia Auctior.*

STATE TRACTS, 1692. *State Tracts, being a Farther Collection of Several Choice Treatises Relating to the Government 1660–1689.*

STEPHEN, Sir JAMES FITZJAMES, 1892. *Horae Sabbaticae,* 2nd ser. (Reprint of articles from *The Saturday Review.*)

STEPHEN, Sir LESLIE, 1876 (1902). *History of English*

Thought in the Eighteenth Century. 2 vols. (3rd ed. 1902.)

STILLINGFLEET, EDWARD, 1681. *The Unreasonableness of Separation.*

STRAUSS, LEO, 1953. *Natural Right and History.* Chicago. (202–51 on Locke.)

STUBBE, HENRY, 1659. *An Essay in Defence of the Good Old Cause.* (Appendix B, no. 81.)

STUBBE, HENRY, 1659. *A Light Shining Out of Darkness.* (Appendix B, no. 80.)

TEMPLE, Sir WILLIAM, 1680 (1757). *An Essay upon the Original and Nature of Government.* (Published in *Miscellanea*, 1680: in vol. I of *Works* (4 vols.), 1757.)

TENISON, THOMAS, 1670. *The Creed of Mr Hobbes Examined.*

TERRY, EDWARD, 1655. *A Voyage to East-India.* (Appendix B, no. 82.)

THOMSON, M. A. 1938. *Constitutional History of England, 1642–1801.*

TUCKER, JOSIAH, 1781. *A Treatise Concerning Civil Government.*

TYNDALE, WILLIAM, 1528 (1848). The obedience of a Christian man. (In: *Doctrinal Treatises*, Parker Society, Cambridge.)

TYRRELL, JAMES, 1681. *Patriarcha non Monarcha.* (Anon., Appendix B, no. 84.)

TYRRELL, JAMES, 1691/2 (1718). *Bibliotheca Politica.*

TYRRELL, JAMES, 1692. *A Brief Disquisition of the Law of Nature, According to the Principle and Method laid down in Dr Cumberland . . . as also his confutation of Mr Hobs principles put into another method.*

VAUGHAN, C. E. 1925. *Studies in the History of Political Philosophy before and after Rousseau.* 2 vols. Manchester. I, 130–204: *The Social Contract*, Locke.)

VIANO, C. A., 1960. *John Locke, dal Razionalismo all' Illuminismo.* Turin.

Vindiciae contra Tyrannos (by Brutus, pseud.), 1579. Edinburgh [Basel]. (Appendix B, no. 16.)

VON LEYDEN, WOLFGANG, 1954. *John Locke, Essays on the Law of Nature.* Oxford.

VON LEYDEN, WOLFGANG, 1956. John Locke and Natural Law. *Philosophy*, XXXI, January.

VOX REGIS, 1681 (1808). [Anon.] *Vox Regis, or the Difference betwixt a King Ruling by Law and a Tyrant by His own Will . . . in Two Speeches of King James to the Parliaments in 1603 . . . 1609 . . . Appendix to Vox Populi.* (In Harleian Miscellany, vol. III.)

WALDMANN, M., 1959. A Note on John Locke's Theory of Consent, *Ethics*, LXVIII, 1.

WARRENDER, J. 1957. *The Political Philosophy of Hobbes: his Theory of Obligation*. Oxford.

WHITEHOUSE COLLECTION (papers of Locke in the possession of the late J. Howard Whitehouse, lately in care of Bembridge School, Isle of Wight, now in the Bodleian Library, Oxford).

WILLIS, RICHARD, 1697. [Anon.] *The Occasional Paper*, nos. 1–6.

WREN, MATTHEW, 1659. *Monarchy Asserted*. (Appendix B, no. 90.)

YOLTON, J. W. 1955. Locke and the Seventeenth Century Logic of Ideas. *Journal of the History of Ideas*, XVI, 4, October.

YOLTON, J. W. 1956. *John Locke and the Way of Ideas*. Oxford.

YOLTON, J. W. 1958. Locke on the Law of Nature, *Philosophical Review*, October.

YOLTON, J. W. 1961, *see* Locke, *Essay*.

ZAGORIN, P. 1954. *A History of Political Thought in the English Revolution*.

INDEX

INDEX

In this Index the roman numerals I *and* II *refer to the texts of the first and second* Treatises, *respectively, and the numerals following them refer to sections of the specified* Treatise. *Arabic numerals on their own refer to page-numbers in the Introduction.*

Aaron: I, 107, 157, 167

Abel: I, 76, 112, 118

Abimelech: I, 113; II, 109

Abraham: I, 114, 128, 130, 133, 135, 136, 137, 149, 152, 160, 162, 167, 169; II, 38

Absalom: I, 129

Absolute monarchy: 113; II, 13; and population, I, 33, 41; no form of government, II, 90, 137, 174; *see also* Absolute power

Absolute power, arbitrary power: I, 11–13, 23, 39, 106, 138, 146, 154; II, 8, 17, 23–4, 92, 107, 137, 149, 166, 171–2, 239; of Adam, I, 40, 50–72, 82, 151; II, 61; over animals, I, 40; II, 93; and property, I, 41–8; of father, I, 51, 63–74, 124, 152; II, 53, 64, 66; of eldest son, I, 117–18; of husband, II, 83; over slaves, II, 85; of conqueror, II, 178, 180, 188, 193; *see also* Absolute monarchy; Sovereignty

Acosta, Josephus: II, 102, 102 n.

Adam and Eve: I, 44, 47, 95; II, 56

Adam's authority, sovereignty: I, 3, 6, 8, 9–21, 23, 26–8, 35, 41–3 (and property), 48–9 (over Eve), 50, 67–9, 71, 78, 80–4, 98, 103–5, 122, 125, 130, 132–3, 139, 141–2, 144, 146, 152

Adam's children: I, 70; II, 36, 202; *see also* Abel; Cain; Seth

Adam's curse: I, 44–6

Adam's donation: I, 27, 29, 31, 85; II, 25

Adam's fatherhood: I, 110, 112, 122, 125, 146

Adam's heir: I, 105, 107, 110, 120, 135, 137, 140, 146–7, 157–8, 163; II, 61; Commonwealths as Adam's heirs, I, 132–3

Adam's kingship: I, 18–21, 29, 39, 125, 129

Adam's property: I, 21, 23–5, 29–31, 35–6, 39–41, 43, 75, 77, 85, 87, 91, 97, 103; II, 25

Adonibeseck: I, 149

Adoption of Children: I, 100; II, 65

Age: II, 54–6, 61

Agreement: and origin of government, I, 94; II, 102, 171, 173, 211, 243; and money, II, 36; and property, II, 45; *see also* Compact; Contract

Ahaz: II, 196

Ainsworth, Henry: I, 28, 28 n.

Algiers: II, 210

Aliens: punishment of, II, 9

Allegiance: II, 151 (oaths of)

Alliances, Leagues: II, 45, 156

America: 113; I, 45 (division of the world), 144 (tribes in), 144 n., 153; II, 14, 36, 37, 41, 43 (value of land), 45, 48, 49, 65, 92, 102 (no government in places), 105, 108, 184 (money of)

Ammonites: II, 21, 109

Animals: 109; I, 25–8, 56 (and their young), 58, 67, 84, 85, 86 (senses of); II, 79 and 81 (union of); man's dominion over, property in; I, 26–30, 38–41, 91, 92 (and definition of property), 96; II, 6; social habits and rules compared to men's, II, 1, 11, 16, 27, 62, 182; compared to subjects of absolute authority, II, 93, 163; despots as wild animals, II, 11, 172, 181, 182

Antiquaries: I, 141

Appeal, final appeal, appeal to heaven: II, 20, 21 (Jephthah), 87, 91, 93, 94, 168, 176, 207 (to law), 241–2

Apprentice, Apprenticeship: II, 69

Arbitrary power: II, 163, 170 (parental), 171–2, 201, 210 (and prerogative), 214, 216 (and elections), 221–3, 230

Arcana Imperii: I, 6

Aristotle: 15; I, 154; II, 74 n., 77 n.

Atheism: I, 154, 154 n.

Babel: I, 143, 145–8, 151

Bagshaw, Edward: 32 n., 84

Barbeyrac, Jean: 22 n.; II, 28 n.

Barclay, William: I, 4, 4 n., 67; II, 211 n., 217 n., 232, 232 n., 236 n., 239, 239 n.

Bastide, Charles: 61 n., 81 n.

Baxter, Richard: 115, 116 n.; II, 27 n., 239 n.

Bayle, Pierre: 17, 17 n.

Bellarmine, Cardinal: I, 6, 6 n., 12

Benjamin: I, 95, 155; Tribe of, I, 161, 164

Bilson, Thomas: II, 239, 239 n.

Birth-right: I, 112, 113, 115 (a double portion), 117, 119, 139

Blackwood, Adam: I, 4, 4 n., 67

Bodin, Jean: I, 8 n., 56 n., 129 n., 131 n.; II, 11 n.

Bohun, Edmund: II, 175 n.

Boston, Mass.: 26

Boyle, Robert: 31; I, 109 n.

Bracton: II, 239, 239 n.

Brama: I, 141

Brothers: relationship between, I, 74, 103, 113, 117, 119, 128–9, 139–40, 142

Burke, Edmund: 27; II, 73 n.

Caciques: II, 108 n.

Cade, Jack: I, 121, 121 n.

Cain: I, 68, 76, 99, 111–12, 118, 142

Canaan: I, 128, 147–8, 162, 167

Cannibalism: I, 57

Capitalism: 54–57

Carolina: 38 (Shaftesbury, Locke as Secretary of proprietors), 42 (*Constitutions of*), 42; I, 144, 144 n.; II,

12 n. (*Constitutions of*), 24 n. (ditto), 119 n.

Carpenter, W. S.: II, 20 n.

Cassiobury: 44, 44 n.

Cato: II, 98

Cervantes: I, 79 n.

Ceylon: *see* Knox

Charity: I, 42; II, 93

Children: I, 56–74, 87–93, 96–102, 109, 111; II, 2, 29, 39, 52–3, 55, 57–86, 101–2, 116–18, 170, 173, 176, 182–3, 189, 196, 209

Chinese, the: I, 141

Christ Church, Oxford: 30, 31, 33 (addresses at), 35 (Dr Fell), 37 (Locke's expulsion from), 52, 54, 69 (Locke's books at), 73, 77–9

Chronology: I, 150, 163, 165, 169

Churchill, the publisher: 19, 21, 22

City, cities: II, 38, 133 (word and meaning)

Civil, civilized: II, 30 (civilized part of mankind), 226 (civil government), 228 (civil war), 239 (civil policy)

Civil Society: *passim, see also* Society

Civitas: II, 133

Clarke, Edward: 18 n., 21, 54 n., 76–7

Commandment, the fifth: I, 62, 64, 65, 66, 67, 100

Commodities: I, 90; II, 43, 46, 48

Common sense: Preface: I, 137

Commoner, common land: II, 27–35, 46

Commons, House of: II, 223

Commonwealth: I, 71, 132–4, 146–7 (ancient constitution of mankind); II, 2, 3, 9, 17, 73, 86, 88, 98–103, 105–6, 110 (beginnings of), 116–18,

120–2, 124, 128, 131 (legislative and), 132 (defined), 134, 137 and 141 (form of), 142–3, 145–9, 151–2, 162, 175, 183, 197, 211–13, 222, 230, 243

Communism, community of property: 114; I, 24, 29, 30, 40 n., 88, 90; II, 6, 25–6 (God gave world in common), 27, 28 (labour and), 29–30, 32, 34, 38, 39–40, 44–6, 48, 83

Community: I, 90; II, 3 (force of), 6 (of nature), 14 (independent), 44, 87, 95, 97 (consent and), 116, 120, 127, 128 (mankind as a), 130, 131–2 (power of), 133 (not by itself a commonwealth), 134 and 136 (and legislative), 138 (law of, and property), 143, 145–6, 148–9, 156, 158–9, 163 (good of, and government), 171, 188, 198, 211, 219, 221, 243

Compact: 127; I, 43, 113, 126; II, 14 (and the state of nature), 23–4 (and slavery), 25 and 28 (and property), 35 (commons and), 45, 73, 78 and 81 (marriage), 97, 99, 116 and 118 (and descendants), 122, 171–2, 183

Concubine: I, 123 (and a wife)

Conquest, conqueror, conquered: 89; II, 112 (as beginning government), 176–7 (rights of conqueror), 178, 179 (limits of conqueror's power), 180–4 (conquest and property), 185 (and posterity), 186–9, 192 (and land), 193, 196 (summary), 197 (usurpation and), 211 (foreign conquest and dissolution of society), 218 (ditto and rebellion)

Conscience: 32, 97; I, 105, 110, 119 (settling of), 120 and 122 (obedience and), 125–6; II, 8 (reason and), 209

Consent, government by consent: 97 (not defined), 124–25; Preface (royal title in); I, 10, 43, 54 (fathers and procreation), 67, 94 (established government), 96, 126, 131, 148 (of people); II, 15 (and membership of society), 17, 22 (legislative power and), 23 (and slavery), 27 (and property), 32, 35 (and enclosure), 36 (and money), 38, 41, 46, 50 (and value), 74, 81 (and marriage), 94–9, 102 (and equality), 104–6 (universal origin of government), 112, 117, 119, 121, 122, 138 (alienation of property and), 139 (taxation and), 151, 158, 171

Constable: II, 202

Constitution: 89–91 (Locke and the 'ancient'); I, 51 (of government), 137 (God's order), 168 (of the Jews); II, 50, 76, 86 (of family and of commonwealth), 98, 116, 141 (as form of commonwealth), 152, 153–8 (the original), 168, 175 (frame of the commonwealth), 192 (frame of government), 205, 212, 218 (British), 220 (form of legislative), 223, 226, 230 (overturning of)

Contract: 127; I, 47 (marriage), 96 (and political power), 98 (and husband's power); II, 81, 82 (wife's rights by), 83, 194

Conveniencies of life: I, 41, 96; II, 26, 34, 36–7, 41, 44, 48, 130 (of political state)

Corporations: II, 158 (and representatives)

Coste, Pierre: 22, 22 n., 23, 23 n., 52 n.

Creation: of Adam, I, 15, 16, 19, 20, 36, 50 (not created supreme); over woman, I, 55, 67; of the beasts, I, 25, 26, 27

Cromwell: 30, 32; I, 79, 79 n., 121, 121 n.

Curse, the: I, 44, 45, 47, 47 n.

Custom, customs: I, 58, II, 157; II, 94 (sanctity of), 152 (and constitutions), 158 (and true reason)

David: I, 28, 30, 95, 161, 162, 163, 167, 169; II, 25

Death penalty: I, 128; II, 3 (definition of political power), 65, 74 (within family), 83, 86–7, 139 (in the army), 170

Declaration of Independence, American: 68; II, 210 n., 223 n., 225 n., 230 n.

Democracy: 83; I, 72; II, 132 (defined in terms of majority's functions)

Desmaisezaux, Pierre: 22 n., 42 n.

Despot, despotical, despotism: II, 172 (defined), 173 (and property), 174 (and paternal power), 196; see also Absolute power

Devonshire: II, 37

Dissolution: of government, 128, 129; II, 149 (precedes popular sovereignty), 150, 211 (distinct from dissolution of society), 212 (and legislative), 217, 218 (fault of monarch), 219, 220 (results), 221; of society, 114–15; II, 211, 218

Divine law: I, 111 and 115 (of Moses), 119, 128; II, 52, 142 (and legislative trust), 195 (God tied by), 232 (and rebellion)

Divine right: I, 3, 51, 81, 120, 126, 127, 140 (and heirs); II, 112

Division of powers, see Separation

Divorce and Separation: I, 62; II, 80–3

Don Quixote: I, 79

Draw Can Sir: II, 177

Earth, the: I, 37–9, 45 and 67 (Adam and), 84, 91; II, 27 (common to all), 32 (and property), 35, 38, 43, 45; see also Land

Economics: 41, 51, 99, 99 n.

Education: 41, 51, 98, 98 n., 99; I, 90 (natural right of), 93; II, 16 n., 56 (obligation of law of nature), 58, 58 n. (Locke and Tyrrell on), 61, 64 n., 67–9, 78, 81, 170, 202

Edwards, John: 17, 86

Egypt, Egyptian Bondage: I, 152, 155, 156, 163, 168; II, 239

Elder and younger: I, 48, 101, 105, 116, 118, 119, 120, 122, 142, 148, 161; II, 1, 110, 202

Election: I, 80 (of kings), 148 (by fathers); II, 106 (monarchies by), 132 (elective monarchy defined), 154 (parliamentary), 216 (alteration in methods of), 222

Elrington, Thomas: 27, 83 n., 134; 3 n., 10 n., 12 n., 20 n., 22 n., 23 n., 58 n., 73 n., 81 n., 82 n., 88 n., 94 n., 105 n., 129 n., 138 n., 140 n., 158 n., 208 n., 223 n.

Enclosure: II, 26 (wild Indians and), 28 n., 32 (and labour), 33, 35 (and consent), 35 n., 36 (effect on yield), 37, 38, 42 n., 48

England: 90; I, 37; II, 9, 41, 59 (law of), 165 (history of), 167 (Parliaments in), 196

English, the: Preface (the people of England); I, 144 (in Carolina)

Equality: 108; I, 50, 118 (of brethren), 139 (of all men); II, 4 (in the state of nature), 5 (by nature), 6–7, 54 (qualifications of), 55 (children and), 100, 102, 123, 131

Esau: I, 49, 113, 115, 117–19, 138, 149; II, 38

Essex, Earl of: 44, 45 n.

Estate, see Property

Ethics: 95, 96 n., 97

Eve: I, 29, 30, 44–5 (curse of), 47, 49, 67, 73, 99; II, 56

Executive, executive power: 110 (executive power of law of nature), 122; II, 13 (all have in state of nature), 74, 87 (origin of in governments), 91, 127, 130–1, 134 (and laws), 147, 148 (distinct from federal power), 150–6 (place in constitution, etc.), 158 (and summoning of legislative), 159, 161, 167, 168, 213, 219, 222

Family: I, 37, 59–, 91, 108 (Filmer's), 118 (distinct families), 130 (size of), 134 (servants in), 142–3 (division of earth between), 148, 156, 160–1; II, 1 (of the world), 36, 48, 69, 72 (private), 74 (consent to power over), 75, 77 (not political), 79 (animals), 85–6 (rule, slaves, in), 102, 105–12 (as origin of state), 115, 122, 162 (early, political), 209

Father, power of fatherhood: *passim;* I, 52 (power from begetting), 54 (joint power with mother), 62 (fifth commandment), 66 (natural and other), 142 (nations governed by); 158, etc. (as origin of government); II, 52 (paternal and parental), 59 and 61 (children and), 64 (fathers and mothers), 66 (power arises from education), 67–76 (nature of power, not political, alienable, from consent of children, and nonage, etc.), 86 (limits on power), 92 (fathers of countries), 110 (good kings as nursing fathers), 117–18 (and nationality), 182 (and conquest, property)

Federative, f-derative power: II, 45 (existence hinted at), 146 (defined), 147–8 (relation with executive), 153 (under legislative)

Filmer, Edward: I, 5 n.

Filmer, Sir Robert: 33 n. (Locke's early reading of), 45, 46 (early note on), 46, 46 n., 48, 57, 61, 64, 65, 67, 70–3 (editions of used by Locke), 77, 80–90 (and the constitution), 104, 106, 114 (and property), 117; I, 1 n., 5 n., 6 n., 7 n., 8 n., 11 n., 14 n., 16 n., 18 n., 23 n., 44 n., 56 n., 60 n., 64 n., 67 n., 76 n., 78 n., 105 n., 109 n., 121 n., 123 n., 126 n., 130 n., 136 n., 146 n., 148 n.; II, 1 n., 25 n., 28 n., 38 n., 39 n., 52 n., 57 n., 61 n., 73 n., 74 n., 77 n., 92 n., 93 n., 95 n., 99 n., 101 n., 102 n., 103 n., 105 n., 112 n., 113 n., 114 n., 116 n., 123 n., 132 n., 137 n., 162 n., 168 n., 169 n., 195 n., 197 n., 200 n., 232 n.; by name, Preface, I, 110, II, 1, 21 n., 22, 61; as 'our Author', 'our A. etc.', I, text, *passim;* his method of arguing, style, Preface, I, 12–13, 15, 18, 20, 23, 31–2, 44, 49, 60, 68, 77, 110, 137, 152

Force of a commonwealth: II, 96, 107 (foreign), 130 (as protection), 131, 132 (and majority), 136 (and property), 137, 143 (directed by legislative), 148 (and executive, federative), 155 (and executive), 218

Force (and Government): 130–4; II, 1, 17, 18, 19, 20

Force (violence): II, 172 (despot and), 175, 179, 182, 184 (title by), 186 (conqueror), 189, 192, 196, 202, 204 (to be countered by force), 205, 207 (appeal to), 208, 222 (excluded by government), 227 (and state of war), 228, 231–2, 235

Forests, *see* Woods and Forests

Forfeit, forfeiture: II, 172–3, 182–3, 188, 222 (of power on breach of trust), 239

Form of government: II, 106–7, 116 (set forms), 132 (democracy, oligarchy, etc.), 137 (form of commonwealth), 141 (people appoint), 142, 149, 201 (monarchy, etc.), 213 and 218 (the British), 223 (people attached to old ones); *see also* Government

Fortescue: II, 239, 239 n.

Fowler, Thomas: 60 n.

Fox, Bourne, H. R.: 60 n.

France: 27, 42, 43, 48, 51; II, 9, 73, 118

Freedom: 108; natural, I, 11, 13–15, 19, 50, 67; II, 4 (perfect in the state of nature), 61 and 87 (born free), 73 (of children), 95 (and natural equality), 105, 112 (of a people), 118, 123, 190, 191 (men naturally free of government), 194; 17 (right of), 23, 57–9 (and law), 61–3 (and reason), 66 (and duty to parents), 74 (free man's powers), 104, 192 (and property), 215 (freedom of debate in legislature); national self determination, I, 154; II, 102–3, 178, 217

Freeman, free-men: II, 60 (and reason), 74 (executing natural law), 85 (as servant), 99 (consenting to government), 103, 170 (children and), 176, 189 (children of conquered), 192 (property and)

French: I, 5, 5 n. (French language), 143 (French in Carolina)

Furly, Benjamin: 64 n., 69 n.

Generals: I, 158; II, 105–10 (as original political leaders), 139 (powers of)

Generation: I, 50, 52–5, 67 (power by right of), 71, 73–4, 85, 88, 96, 98–9, 101, 103; II, 52, 65, 79, 81, 83

God's will about government: I, 107, 126–7, 137, 140, 160 (positive command); II, 13

Gold: II, 37, 50; *see also* Money

Golden Age: II, 110, 111, 128

Goods: I, 91, 93 (defined), 96, 154 (persons as); II, 11 (forfeiture), 30, 173, 182 (of father), 183 (of conquered), 190

Government: *passim* and Preface (wrong notions of), II, 13 (God's object in appointing), 101 (antecedent to records), 163 (wrong notions of), 215 (names and); *see also* Forms of government, Dissolution of government, etc.

Government, object of: I, 92 (preserving rights and property), 93 (benefit of governed), 106 (peace); II, 42 (increase of land), 137–8 (preservation of property), 161 (trust and ends of), 167 (good of community), 225, 229 (good of mankind), 239 (public good and property)

Greece: I, 149, 153; II, 192 (Grecian Christians)

Green, T. H.: 60 n.; I, 129 n.

Grotius, Hugo: 34, 88, 100; I, 18, 50, 50 n., 51, 51 n., 52 n., 76, 76 n., 100 n., 123 n., 126 n.; II, 24 n., 25 n., 28 n., 45 n., 52 n., 58 n., 65 n., 66 n., 96 n., 175 n., 176 n., 239

Hannibal: I, 144

Harrington, James: 33; II, 27 n.

Hebrew: I, 25, 27, 31

Heir, heirs: I, 37 (of world), 74–5, 85 (not above other children), 96, 99, 103 (brother as), 106–, 15 (no dominion over brothers), 116 (of eldest son), 118–20, 124–7, 128 (rule of recognition), 129–30, 136–8, 140, 142, 146–9, 152, 154, 162–3, 166; II, 1, 76, 105, 114–15, 132 (in oligarchy, etc.), 194

Herbert, Thomas, Earl of Pembroke: 54 (letter to)

Hercules: I, 141

Heylyn, Peter: 46, I, 1 n.

Hingar: II, 196

History: I, 57, 113 (scriptural), 118, 127–8 (scriptural), 143 (of Babel), 168; II, 36 and 74 (first ages), 99 (instances in story), 101, 104 (government by consent in), 105, 106, 109 (Jephthah), 112, 165 (of England), 175 (of mankind), 230

Hobbes, Thomas: 29, 33, 46 (Filmer on), 48 (and Filmer), 61 n., 79, 81, 104 (problem of Locke's acquaintance with), 105; I, 129 n.; II, 1 n., 4 n., 5 n., 19 n. (Hobbesists), 21 n., 23 n., 25 n., 27 n. (property), 52 n., 57 n., 58 n., 93 n., 97 n., 99 n., 123 n., 125 n., 132 n., 137 n., 138 n., 149 n., 175 n., 195 n.; see also Leviathan

Holland: 28, 37 (Locke's departure for), 51, 62, 67, 77; II, 9

Hollis, Thomas: 23, 23 n.

Homer: I, 153, 154

Hooker, Richard: 15, 70 (Locke's use of), 74, 78, 98, 100, 123; II, 4 n., 5, 5 n. (note on Locke's quotations from), 15 (the judicious), 15 n., 60, 60 n., 61, 61 n., 74 n. (marginal quotations from), 90 n., 91 n., 94 n., 111 n., 134 n., 135 n., 239 (Locke's statement on), 239 n.

Hubba: II, 196

Human nature: I, 10 (principles of); II, 67 (principles of), 92 (absolute power and)

Hunton, Philip: 46 n.; I, 7, 7 n., 16 n.; II, 168 n.

Husbands: I, 47–9 (power of), 67, 98, 103; II, 2 (power of), 65 (parting from wives), 83; see also Wives

Imagination: I, 58 (as faculty of man)

Incest: I, 128

Incorporation: II, 38

Indians, American: I, 130 (planters in West Indies and); II, 9 (European law and), 26, 30, 43

Individual(s): II, 96 and 98 (consent of), 99 (compact between), 106, 243 (power of)

Industry, see Labour

Inheritance: I, 79–81, 84, 88, 89 (natural right of), 90, 91 (by natural law), 93–103, 118–20, 124, 129, 131, 161; II, 72–3, 184; see also Heir

Interest: II, 138, 143 and 163–4 (distinct interest from rest of country)

Ireland: I, 137

Isaac: I, 113, 114, 115, 117, 118, 128, 135, 146, 152, 160

Ishmael: I, 114, 115, 128

Italy: II, 196

Jacob: I, 48, 111, 113, 115, 116, 117, 118, 119, 137, 149, 150, 152, 155, 160, 161

James—King James I: 54; II, 133, 133 n., 200, 200 n.

James—King James II: 31, 45, 49, 54–5, 65, 95, 114; II, 17 n., 131 n., 133 n., 149 n., 169 n., 172 n., 200 n., 209 n., 219 n.

Jefferies, Judge: 59 n., 62; I, 129

Jephthah: I, 163; II, 21 (and a judge), 21 n., 109, 176 (appeal to heaven), 221 (appeal to supreme judge)

Jeroboam: I, 161, 162

Jews, the: I, 62, 107, 152 (history), 168; II, 24 (slavery among), 67 (Israelites), 101

Joshua: I, 149, 157, 163

Judah: I, 115, 118, 129, 155, 161; II, 196

Judge, judges: I, 158 (as leaders in Bible), 158 n., 163 (Jephthah), 167; II, 13 (in own cases), 18 (common judge), 20, 21, 89 (and institution of society), 91 and 93 (in absolute monarchy), 125 (as general), 125, 131, 168 (who shall be?), 181, 240, 241

Judicature: II, 87, 241

Jupiter: I, 141; II, 224

Jurieu, Pierre: II, 21 n., 239 n.

Justice: 97; I, 11; II, 5 (Hooker's maxims), 20 (perverting of), 136, 176, 219

Justin: II, 103

Juvenal: II, 235

Kindred: I, 90, 102, 108, 128

King, kings, princes: I, 8–10, 94, 104–7, 115, 119, 121, 132, 135, 137, 142, 146 (of mankind), 146–9, 151–3, 156–7, 161 (Saul), 162, 163 (God's choice of), 164–5, 167–8; II, 41 (of an American kingdom), 42 and 42 n. (wise and godlike), 71, 76, 92 (fathers of countries), 108 (of Indies), 109, 123 (in state of nature), 139, 151 (English), 162 (weak ones), 163–6 (prerogative, godlike princes), 168, 184, 194–6, 200 (and tyrants), 205 (persons sacred), 206 (and law), 210, 214, 215 (dissolving government), 216 (altering elections), 217 (foreign power and), 218, 221, 223, 232, 235, 239 (resistance to), 240 (people judge of), 242

King, Peter, First Lord: 15 n., 42 n.

King, Richard: 15 n.; II, 239 n.

Kingship, power of kings, monarchy: I, 53 (God's not from fatherhood), 71 (elective), 79, 81, 82, 113 (natural), 120 (abstract notions of), 134, 140; II, 53 (parental not regal power), 61, 86 (family as monarchy)

Knox, Robert: 68; II, 92 n.

Labour, industry: I, 42, 42 n. (right to product of), 45 (Adam's curse); II, 27 (labour and property), 28 (fixes property in things), 29–32 (labour and property), 35 (command to), 36–8 (and limits of property), 39, 40 (and value), 41–2 (and land), 43, 44 (ownership of), 45–8, 51, 83, 194, 196

Land: II, 32 (as property), 33 (appropriation), 36 (common), 37, 38 (measures governing possession), 40, 41 (in America), 42–3 (and labour), 44 (and money), 45, 48, 50 (possession and the laws), 192 and 194 (and conquest); and submission to government, II, 73, 116 (continuity of), 119 (and consent to), 120, 121 (jurisdiction of government over)

Language: I, 23, 23 n., 108, 147; II, 52, 215, 225

Law, laws: II, 11, 19, 20, 38 (and property), 45 (property and agreement), 57 (and freedom), 59, 60, 69, 70, 87, 88 (power of making defined), 93, 124 (none in the state of nature), 125, 129–30, 132, 134 (first law creates legislative), 136 (promulgated, standing), 137–8, 139 (of taxation, consent), 141–4 (legislative and), 147 (controlling executive), 150, 153, 154 (and people's needs), 157–60, 162 (as few laws as possible), 164, 168 (antecedent law of appeal to heaven), 171, 176, 178, 191–2, 195, 198, 199–202 (and tyranny), 205, 206 (and authority), 207–10, 212, 214 (will of society), 219 (bonds of society), 220, 222 (fence to property), 225 (wrong ones), 226, 227 (and trust), 228, 232, 242; *see also* Divine law, Municipal law, Law of nations, Natural law, Positive law

Law, the common law: 90, 91; I, 8, 37, 88, 91 n., 102; II, 138

Law of nations: I, 47

Lawrence, William: I, 123 n., 124 n.

Lawson, George: II, 96 n., 146 n., 211 n., 222 n.

Leclerc, Jean: 25

Legislative: II, 9 (will of), 88 (powers given to), 89, 91 (in absolute monarchy), 94 (in parliaments), 127 (origin), 134 (establishment fundamental), 136, 138, 141–2 (limits to), 143 (and executive), 149 (fiduciary), 150, 151–2 (and executive), 153 (not always in being), 154 (representative), 155, 156 (summoned by executive), 157–8, 168 (no judge of), 212 (alteration dissolves government), 213–23, 225 (people and a new one), 227 (and rebellion), 240 (people judge of), 243 (must not be changed)

Legislative power: II, 22 (and consent), 65 (of mother), 86 (in family), 131 (supreme), 132 (and constitution), 135

Legislator, legislators: II, 135 (person or assembly), 140, 143 (subject to laws), 154 (become subjects again), 159, 226 (trust and), 227 (rebellion of); *see also* Legislative

Letter from a Person of Quality: 42

Levellers, the: 34

Leviathan: 84 n., 85–8, 104, 109; II, 6 n., 9 n., 82 n., 89 n., 95 n., 98 (the mighty), 133 n., 211 n., 212 n.; *see also* Hobbes, Thomas

Liberty, liberties: 32, 50; II, 6 (not licence), 22 (natural, defined), 42, 57 (defined), 59 (and law), 63, 65, 87 (as part of property), 95, 121, 123, 129, 131; 149 (liberties of subject), 166, 189, 192, 212 (to resist), 221–2 (people's), 227, 228, 229, 234; *see also* Freedom

Lords, House of: II, 223

Luther, Martin: I, 64 n.

Machiavelli, Niccolo: 35, 91, 100–1

Magistrate, magistrates: (*Civil Magistrate,* Locke's early writing on), 33; I, 64–7, 90, 92; II, 2 (power over subject), 11 (reprieve and), 83, 89, 162, 202, 206, 207 (King as chief), 208 (unlawful acts of), 210 (subordinate), 218, 228, 231

Majority, majorities: II, 95 (include whole body politic), 96 (and greater force), 98 (consent of), 99 and 132 (power of), 139 (taxation and), 166, 176 (approval of legislative), 209 (and resistance), 212

Male and Female: II, 79–80 (longer association in mankind)

Man (as species): I, 30 (superiority of), 40, 56, 58, 86 (features shared with animals), 105, 145, 146 (division of), 156; II, 43; see also Mankind

Mankind: I, 89, 111, 139, 142 and 145 (unity and dispersal), 148; II, 6 (preservation of), 7, 8, 25 (given earth in common), 26, 27 consent of and property), 30 (civilized part of), 32, 35–7, 42, 45, 92, 93, 128 (by natural law, all one community), 129, 135, 137, 168, 171, 172, 182, 220, 229 (good of, end of government), 230 (enemy of)

Manor, Lord of: I, 73

Manwering, Manwaring: I, 5, 5 n.

Marriage: I, 47 (a contract), 59; II, 80–3; powers in, I, 48, 98, 103; II, 77–83

Massaniello (Aniello), I, 79, 79 n.

Master (of servants): II, 1, 23, 24, 29, 77, 85, 86

Maternal power: I, 60–7 (shares with father in power); II, 52 (equal title), 65 (widow's powers)

Mazel, David: 24, 25

Medicine, medical science: I, 7, 7 n., 52 (anatomists), 81 (change of doctors), 81 (Adam as doctor), 125

Mexico: II, 105

Milton, John: 46; II, 175 n.

Minority, see Nonage

Mirror, the: II, 13 n., 239, 239 n.

Molyneux, William: 17, 18 n., 26; II, 4 n., 5 n., 134 n., 176 n., 177 n., 178 n., 181 n., 182 n., 186 n.

Monarchy, see King

Money: I, 90 (commodities valued by), 130 (servants bought with); II, 18, 35, 36 (effects of its invention), 45 (increase of), 46, 47 (and consent), 48 (and inequality), 49 (enlarges possessions), 82, 84 (imaginary in value)

Montesquieu: 25, 27, 133; I, 56 n., 94 n.

Mordaunt, Lord and Lady: 58, 66, 103 n.

More, Saint Thomas: I, 147 n.

Moses: I, 111 (law of), 115, 157, 163

Mother, mothers: I, 6, 11, 55; II, 27 (nature as), 64, 65 (widow), 69–70, 82

Municipal law: I, 91, 123; II, 12, 67 (cf. natural law), 72, 147 (and executive), 170, 195; common law of England (law of the land), I, 8, 37, 88, 90 (of some countries), 102; II, 35, 138

Nation, nations: Pref. (salvation of); I, 143 (as families), 145; II, 41 (in America), 106, 239

Natural law: 31 (in Locke's early writings), 34 (Locke as theorist of), 47–8, 49 (note on, 1676), 73, 79, 92, 93–5 (in the Essay), 95 (Locke's theory of), 96, 100–1, 108 (and reason), 111, 111 n., 119; I, 16–17, 51, 86, 86 n., 91 (inheritance), 92–3, 101 (law of reason),

102, 113, 124 (succession), 126, 166; II, 1, 4 and 6 (in state of nature), 8 (everyone executes in state of nature), 11 (in the heart), 12 (particulars not to be given), 13, 16 (preservation), 22 (and liberty), 30–1 (and beginning of property), 37, 56 (parents and), 58, 59 (being free of it), 62 (reason and), 67, 74, 87, 88 (offences against), 96, 105, 124 (plain and intelligible), 125, 128 (makes mankind one society), 129–30, 134 (preservation), 135 (obliges in society), 136 (unwritten, found in heart), 142, 159, 170–1, 183, 186, 195, 207

Nature, natural: I, 47, 56, 58–9, 67 (equality in), 89 (God in), 96, 105 (right in), 111 (and primogeniture), 119; II, 4, 5 (equality by), 6, 12–15, 26 (hand of), 27, 29, 36 (sets bounds of property), 37 (things of), 40 (and value), 41–6 (her gifts), 51, 52 (obligations from), 62, 67 (bias of), 73, 83, 87, 94 (natural authority), 95 (force and liberty), 96, 106, 113, 114 (obligation), 115 (right), 118, 119 (freedom), 136 (power), 168; 171, 172; 182 (wills preservation), 184 (money not of), 186, 191; *see also* State of nature

Newton, Sir Isaac: 29, 54, 123 n.; I, 136 n.

Noah, Noah's sons: I, 6, 19, 25, 32–5, 37–8 (lived communally), 39 (the blessing), 46, 71; II, 25, 36 (peopling world), 137, 139–40 (division of earth), 140–2 (origin of nations), 146–7

Nonage, minority: II, 65, 67 (right of tuition in), 69, 74–5, 117 (and citizenship), 118 (choice of nationality), 173

Normans, Norman Conquest: II, 177

Oaths: II, 62 (of submission), 151 (of allegiance)

Obedience: I, 81, 104–5, 109–11, 120–2 (and conscience), 124–6, 147; II, 24, 32, 52 and 67 (to parents), 115, 134 (to legislative), 176, 192 (and consent), 222 (people's absolution from), 230

Ogyges: I, 141

Old Sarum: II, 157 n.

Oligarchy: II, 132 (defined)

Oxford: 17 (Bodleian Library), 28–37 (Locke at), 35–6 (disputations), 37 (burning of books at), 44 (Parliament at), 46, 55, 56, 57, 76, 93

Parental power: I, 50–1, 67–70, 96; II, 52–3, 55 (temporary), 58 (basis, education), 60–7 (not absolute), 71 (in society), 170 (defined); 173; *see also* Paternal power, Parents, etc.

Parents: I, 62–5, 71–2, 73–85 (and property), 89–90, 108–9, 120, 142, 148; II, 56 (duties of), 60–7, 72, 74, 77 (society with children), 80, 83; *see also* Father, Mother, Parental power, etc.

Pareyson, L.: I, 25 n., 28 n., 30 n.

Parliament: 58 (Convention Parliament), 68 (Locke on Stuart treatment of); II, 94, 138–9, 142, 143 (dissolution, etc.), 154 (summoning), 157, 160, 167 (summoning in England), 200 (James I and), 213, 213 n., 241

Party: II, 20, 42, 158

Passive obedience: II, 228

Patriarch, patriarchs: Preface; I, 8, 113, 128, 130, 136, 138, 154

Patriarchal power: 48 (*jus paternum*), 47 and 82–3 (Locke's patriarchalism of 1676); I, 148, 151–3; II, 74, 105–12 (Locke's concessions to)

Peace: I, 106 (as end of society); II, 7 (and natural law), 74, 131 (peace of people), 137, 172 (renouncing way of), 226 (and property), 228, 235

People, the: 32 (Locke's early view of); I, 77, 83, 156, 167; II, 89, 103, 111 (and distinct interest of monarch), 112 (naturally free), 137, 141 (appoint form of government); 142 (good of), 154, 155 (chose legislative), 156–8 (trust for safety of), 161, 162 (numbers of), 164, 165, 168 (no judge of), 178 (conquest), 198–9, 205, 209 (majority of), 213 (choice by), 217 (and foreign power), 218, 219 (when a confused multitude), 221–3, 224 (rebellion of), 225, 228, 230 (long-suffering), 239, 243

People, God's chosen: I, 157, 164, 167–8; *see also* the Jews, Israelites

People (a nation, nations): I, 141, 144, 146 (a free), 147, 148, 153; II, 89

People, consent of: 47 (*consensus populi*); Preface; I, 96 (government founded by), 148; II, 104, 216 (and change of legislative), 227

People, power of: I, 72; II, 149 (supreme power over legislative), 163 (and prerogative), 179, 219 and 225 (new legislative)

Person (i.e. personality): II, 6 (right to dispose of), 27, 44 and 173 (property in)

Peru: I, 57; II, 105

Petty, William: II, 27 n.

Petyt, William: 73, 90 n., 92

Pharamond: I, 141

Philosophers: I, 34, 52, 109 (philosopher's stone), 154

Pirates: I, 81; II, 176, 182

Planters: I, 130–1 (in West Indies), 130 n.

Plots, Popish and Other: 31, 31 n. (Monmouth's), 32 (Ryehouse, etc.), 36

Poets: I, 134, 154

Political power: 97; I, 48–9, 65–7, 106, 132; II, 1 (origin), 2 (defined), 4 (derivation), 71, 95, 171 (as trust), 174

Political society: I, 49, 131; II, 15, 77, 86–7, 89, 95, 102, 106, 211

Politics, politician: I, 70 (Filmer's), 71–7, 78, 80, 106 (reformer of), 109, 121, 154 (Christian politician)

Pollock, Sir Frederick: 60 n., 81 n.

Population: I, 33 (under Turks), 41, 106; II, 42 (numbers of), 74 (original sparseness)

Positive law: II, 30 (to determine property), 59, 81 (and marriage), 96, 119 (laws of a government), 122 (of a country), 125, 127, 134, 163 (and prerogative)

Power, powers, *see also* Force

(and government), Separation of powers, Patriarchal power, etc.

Prerogative: II, 111 (in golden age), 156 (of summoning parliament), 158 (defined), 159–68, 210 (trust of), 239, 240

Preservation: II, 6 (self), 11, 16 (fundamental law of nature), 17, 19, 23, 25 (natural reason and), 60 (offspring), 123, 128–9, 134, 137, 149, 159, 168, 170, 182, 209, 220, 227, 229

Pretenders: I, 119

Priests, priesthood: I, 107, 125, 157, 167 (Aaron, etc.); II, 76 (fathers as)

Primogeniture: I, 90–7, 111–12, 119

Prince, princes, see Kings

Profit: II, 43

Property, propriety, estate: 15, 47, 85, 96, 97, 97 n., 106–7, 113–20; I, 9, 16, 20–1, 23–5 (Adam's private dominion), 29 (in animals), 31 (fatherhood and the earth), 36–42 (Adam's and Noah's), 41–3 (gives no power over men), 48–9 (husband's, no power arising), 73 (and monarchy), 73 n., 74 (descent of), 75–7, 76 n., 85, 86 (in creatures), 86 n., 87 (Adam's, etc. in creatures), 88–92 (and children), 92 (defined in terms of dominion over animals), 92 n., 93, 97, 102, 128, 155 (power over substance); II, 3 (political power and), 6 (men as God's), 25 (and communism), 26 (property in person), 28–31, 32 (land), 35–9, 40 (labour and land), 44–6, 57, 59 (disposing of), 65 (parents and children),

69, 72 (discretion of father), 73 (inheritance of and allegiance), 74–5, 82, 85 (slaves and property), 87 and 87 n. (extensive definition of), 91, 105 (family), 107, 116, 120, 135, 136 (state of nature), 137, 170–1, 173 (children and), 174 (slavery and), 178–9 (conqueror and), 180, 182–3 (conquest), 191–6 (conquest and inheritance), 199 (tyrant and), 202, 209, 221 (and trust), 226, 228–9, 231

Property and Government, 116–20; I, 75–7, 84 (as foundation of sovereignty); II, 50 (law regulates property), 94 (end of government), 95, 119–22 (and nationality), 124, 124 n. (chief end of joining commonwealth), 127, 131 (legislative and), 134, 138–9 (government and consent), 140 and 142 (taxation and consent), 149, 172 (despots and propertyless), 200 n., 201, 222, 226, 239

Property and Labour, 74 n. (Locke Tyrrell and), 113–17; I, 40 n., 86 n.; II, 26–35, 36 (labour measures property), 37, 40 (labour and land), 44 (person and labour), 45 (labour and law), 46, 51

Public, the: Preface (public wrong); II, 148 (force of), 151 (public person, public will), 156, 158, 160, 164–6 (public good), 200, 205 (peace of), 212, 219, 225 (public affairs), 239 (public good)

Pufendorf, Samuel: 28, 34, 88 and notes, 100; I, 52 n., 126 n.; II, 14 n., 25 n., 26 n., 28 n., 45 n., 58 n., 65 n., 66 n.,

69 n., 74 n., 105 n., 176 n., 212 n.

Punishment: II, 8, 9 (aliens), 11–12, 87–8, 105, 128, 130, 151, 235 (of kings)

Queen, Queens: 66 n.; I, 11, 47, 47 n. (Mary and Elizabeth Tudor), 123

Reason; 107–9; I, 56 (dictates of), 58 (a faculty), 60, 86 (voice of God), 111 (and primogeniture), 112 (and scripture); II, 6 (natural law), 8 (and conscience), 10, 11 (the common rule), 12–13, 16 (common law of), 25 (natural), 26, 30, 31 (and inspiration, property), 32, 34, 52, 55 (age and), 56–7 (Adam and), 58–60 (and non-age), 61 (and freedom), 62, 91, 96 (and majorities), 98, 104 (and natural freedom), 158, 163–4 (natural creatures), 170–2, 181, 230, 239

Rebekah: I, 113, 118

Rebellion: II, 1, 93, 196, 218, 224, 226–8 (rebellare), 232

Rent: II, 194

Representation, Representative: 32; II, 88, 139 (and taxation), 151 (king as), 157–8, 192 (and consent to laws), 213 (assembly), 216, 222

Republic: II, 205 (prince as head of)

Resistance: II, 203–7, 208 (right of), 209 (the people), 212, 230 (people slow to), 232, 235, 239

Revelation: 82, 101, 107 n.; I, 16, 55–6, 60, 65; II, 25, 52

Revolutions: II, 223, 225

Romans, the: I, 169 (and the Jews); II, 102 (early history), 201 (decem viri)

Rousseau, J. J.: 25, 27, 91; I, 57 n.

Royal Africa Company: 56; II, 24 n.

Russia: II, 91

Sagard, Gabriel: II, 58 n., 106 n.

Saul: I, 95 (his family), 16 n. (the first King), 167, 168, 169; II, 109

Scotland: I, 124, 144 (Scots in Carolina)

Scripture: 107; I, 31–2, 34, 36 (parallel places), 38 (word of God), 60–2, 112 (and reason), 128, 138, 141, 145–6 (and forms of government), 150, 152, 153–4 (history), 168

Seir, Mount: I, 117; II, 38

Selden, John: I, 21, 21 n., 23, 23 n., 32, 165 n.; II, 38 n.

Self-preservation: I, 86, 88

Senate: II, 94, 139

Separation of Powers: 131–3; II, 91, 107 (balancing power), 127, 143 (temptation to tyranny without), 144 (legislative and executive), 146–8 (executive and federative), 151 (legislative and executive), 153, 159 (legislative and executive)

Septuagint: I, 25

Servant, Servants: I, 135; II, 2 (power over), 24 (and slaves), 77 (society with masters), 85–6

Seth: I, 68, 75–6, 99

Shaftesbury, Anthony Ashley Cooper, First Earl of: 28, 37–49 (intimacy with Locke), 40 (his heir), 44 (exile, death of), 45 (reading on politics with Locke), 49–50,

53, 54, 56, 58, 64, 68–9, 72
(his books, etc.), 75–8 (conjecture about *De Morbo
Gallico*), 100; I, 123 n.; II,
12 n., 149 n., 156 n., 157 n.,
159 n., 167 n., 199 n., 232 n.

Ships, Masters of: I, 131; II,
210

Sibthorpe, Robert: I, 5, 5 n.

Sidney, Algernon: 45 (and
plots), 61 (*Discourses*), 64,
77–8, 83, 84, 92; I, 5 n.,
56 n., 60 n., 65 n., 105 n.,
119 n., 123 n., 136 n., 165 n.;
II, 175 n.

Slaves, Slavery: Preface; I, 1–4,
9–10, 27, 42, 51 (equality
of), 66–9, 114, 117, 118,
130–1 (bought for money),
139 (sons as), 147 (people
not), 154; II, 2 (power
over), 17, 23–4 (defined),
24 n., 83 (and servants), 86,
91, 149, 168, 172 (and compact), 174 (and property),
176 (conquest), 192, 220,
222, 239

Society, Societies: 32 (civil);
human, I, 106 (peace end
of), 156; II, 14, 77 and 80
(conjugal), 83–4 and 86 (of
family), 93, 101 (want of),
110, 117, 118 (consent and),
122, 123, 127, 128 (all mankind), 163 (rational creatures), 172 (reason bond
of), 211 (dissolution of);
political, I, 83, 90, 92–3 (law
of), 131 (war and peace in),
144 (little, independent); II,
17 (state of), 19 (war in),
21, 22 (liberty in), 28 (laws
settle property in), 50, 71
(parents in), 73 (children's
choice), 85 (slaves outside),
87–8 (and property), 89, 90
and 92 (absolute monarchy
not one), 94–5, 97, 99, 102,

106, 107, 120, 129–32, 134
(property end of), 135, (law
of nature), 136, 137 (arbitrary power and), 142, 145,
147, 148 (force of), 149–51,
157–9, 166–8, 171 (preservation), 174 (absolute power
and civil), 211 (dissolution
of), 212 (legislative fundamental), 214 (laws will of),
216 (representation), 219,
220, 221, 222, 227, 232 (war
in), 243

Solomon: I, 61, 95, 161–3

Somers, John, Lord: 17, 17 n.,
28, 50–7 (and the 'College');
II, 139 n.

Somerset: 30, 40, 44 n., 55

Soto, Ferdinando: I, 153, 153 n.

Sovereignty: I, 64, 68 (unlimited), 75–6, 128 (life and
death), 130 (war and peace);
II, 11, 11 n., 88, 88 n.; *see
also* Absolute power

Spain: II, 36 (unappropriated
land in), 36 n.

Spinoza, B. de: 28, 87

State, States: 47 (form of the);
II, 45 (leagues between), 66,
208, 218 (officers of), 230

State of Nature: 82, 111–13;
I, 90 (intestacy), 130–1
(planters and patriarchs in);
II, 4 (men free in), 7 (law
in), 8 (men's power in), 11
(men's right to animals in),
17, 19 (defined), 20 (no appeal in), 21 (ending of),
27–30 (property and com-
munism in), 71 (parents in),
82–3, 88, 90 (inconveniences
of), 91 (absolute monarchs
still in), 93–5, 97, 99, 101,
103, 116 (liberty of), 124
(property insecure in),
125–8 (privileges, etc., of),
131, 135–7 (man's condition
in), 145 (states in), 171, 181,

183–4 (states in), 205 (prince when in with people), 211, 225 (pure anarchy); *see also* Nature

State of War: 20, 112; I, 131 (defined); II, 16–17 (defined), 18 (aggression in), 19 (compare state of nature), 20–1 (ending of), 24 (slavery and), 122, 155 (with people), 172 (despotism as), 176, 180–3, 196, 205 (prince in with people), 207, 212, 222, 226 (rebellion), 227, 232 (use of force without right), 235, 239 (king when in), 241; *see also* War

Station (in Life): II, 6 (men not to quit it wilfully)

Statute law, *see* Positive law

Stephen: Sir Leslie, 60 n., 96 n.; II, 24 n., 111 n., 118 n.; Sir James Fitzjames, 47 n., 82 n.; II, 157 n.

Strange Doctrine: 110, 110 n.; II, 9, 13, 180

Subjection: political subjection, I, 47, 65, 81, 105; II, 176, 179, 191; natural subjection, I, 69; II, 4, 102, 114; of women, I, 47–9, 62; of children, I, 50, 73, 100; II, 55, 61, 170

Subordination: II, 4, 6, 149 and 152–3 (of powers of commonwealth)

Succession: I, 94, 96, 106, 107 (of priesthood), 110, 119, 123–5 (complicated questions), 160–4; II, 110

Suffrage: II, 158 n.

Suicide: II, 23, 23 n., 135

Swiss: 112; II, 14

Sydenham, Thomas: 41, 76

Tamberlain: I, 141

Taxation: II, 139, 142

Tenant: II, 194

Thief, Thievery, etc.: II, 18–19 (when lawful to kill), 27 (and property), 176 (and conquest), 182, 186, 202, 207 (highwaymen), 228

Thomas, David: 40 n., 44 n., 76–7

Titius, C. G.: II, 28 n.

Toleration: 41, 64, 66, 73 (Locke, Tyrrell and), 99 (not mentioned), 102; I, 6 n.; II, 3 n., 9 n., 82 n., 108 n., 134 n., 135 n., 168 n.

Tories: 55, 64, 74; I, 137, 137 n.

Tractatus de Morbo Gallico: 75–8

Trade: II, 35, 157

Trade, Board of: 52, 56; II, 42 n., 64 n.

Tribe, Tribes: I, 144

Troy: I, 149, 154

Trust: 126–30 (concept of); II, 22 (of legislative), 59 (of father), 110–11, 134, 136, 139, 142 (of political power), 149 (of legislative), 155 (breach of), 156 (and ends of Government), 164 (prince and), 171 (express or tacit), 210 (of prerogative), 221–2 (dissolution of government and), 226–7 (laws and), 231, 239, 240 (people judge of), 242

Turks: I, 33; II, 91, 192

Tyndale, Wm.: I, 64 n.

Tyranny: I, 72, 148; II, 192, 197, 198, 200 (James I's distinctions), 210 (defined), 202 (and law), 208, 220, 229, 239 (resistance to)

Tyrrell, James: 17, 17 n., 18, 65, 69–71 (and Locke's books), 73–4 (relationship with Locke), 76, 77, 81 n., 82, 83–4, 92, 93–5; I, 16 n., 56 n., 60 n., 65 n., 100 n.,

119 n., 123 n., 124 n.; II,
16 n., 24 n., 27 n. (parallel
with Locke on property),
32 n., 58 n., 64 n., 65 n.,
66 n., 74 n., 77 n., 78 n.,
94 n. (property and government), 105 n., 108 n., 177 n.,
239 n.

Umpire, Umpirage: II, 75
(father as), 87 (community
as), 212 (legislative as), 227,
242
Understanding: II, 56–8 (and
will), 59 (minority), 60, 61,
77, 82 (marriage and), 94,
173
Usher, James: I, 136 n., 150 n.,
163 n., 165 n.
Usurpation, Usurpers: Preface;
I, 71–2, 79–80, 121, 134, 148;
II, 192, 197
Utopia: I, 147

Value: II, 40, 42 (labour and),
43–4 (and land)
Vaughan, C. E.: 81 n.
Vega, Garcilaso de la: 67; I,
57, 57 n.; II, 14, 14 n.
Venice: II, 102
Viner, Jacob: 116 n; I, 90 n;
II, 124 n.
Voltaire: 25, 35

Wages: II, 85
Wampompeke: II, 184
War: II, 16, 175 (most of history), 178–9 (and conquest),
181 (damage), 183–8, 192–3,
196, 228 (civil)
War and Peace, Power of: I,
130–2; II, 88 (defined), 145
(the federative)
Welsh, the: I, 144 (in Carolina)
West Indies: I, 130–1 (planters in), 153 (little kings in)
Whigs: 45, 53, 64–5, 90 (writers); II, 149 n., 199 n.

Whitehouse Collection: 17 n.,
18 n.
Will: I, 8, 41, 54 (father's),
58 (as a faculty), 63, 119,
140; II, 4 (independence of
in state of nature), 8, 9 (of
the legislative), 13, 22–3, 54,
57–8 (liberty and), 59 (property and), 61 (children under
others), 66, 69, 82 (hus-
bands and wives), 91, 135
(of God is natural law), 137
(of majority), 149, 151 (of
the society, public will), 158,
170, 199 (tyrants'), 212 (society's one will), 214, 222,
229
William the Conqueror: II, 177
William, King William III: 40,
45, 46, 49, 53 n.; I, 95 n.; II,
42 n., 143 n.
Winzerus, Winzetus, Ninian:
II, 235, 235 n., 237
Wives: I, 41, 48–9, 67, 98, 123
(difference from concubines);
II, 2 (power of husbands
over), 65 (parting from husbands), 77–8, 82, 86, 183
(goods of); see also Hus-
bands
Woods and Forests: I, 58; II,
28 (apples from), 37 and 92
(of America), 116
Workmanship: 107; I, 30, 52–4
(man as God's), 86; II, 6, 56,
79, 151, 153
World: I, 122, 124, 126, 136,
138, 139–42 (division of),
156; II, 26 (given to men in
common), 36 (first ages), 38
(parts of), 39, 49 (originally
America), 74, 106, 116
Wren, Matthew: II, 46 n. (and
money)

Xerxes: II, 101

Young, younger, see Elder and
younger